GREEK LYRI

Greek Lyric Poetry

A Commentary on
Selected Larger Pieces

Alcman, Stesichorus, Sappho, Alcaeus, Ibycus, Anacreon
Simonides, Bacchylides, Pindar, Sophocles, Euripides

G. O. HUTCHINSON

OXFORD
UNIVERSITY PRESS

OXFORD
UNIVERSITY PRESS

Great Clarendon Street, Oxford OX2 6DP

Oxford University Press is a department of the University of Oxford.
It furthers the University's objective of excellence in research, scholarship,
and education by publishing worldwide in

Oxford New York

Auckland Cape Town Dar es Salaam Hong Kong Karachi
Kuala Lumpur Madrid Melbourne Mexico City Nairobi
New Delhi Shanghai Taipei Toronto

With offices in

Argentina Austria Brazil Chile Czech Republic France Greece
Guatemala Hungary Italy Japan Poland Portugal Singapore
South Korea Switzerland Thailand Turkey Ukraine Vietnam

Oxford is a registered trade mark of Oxford University Press
in the UK and in certain other countries

Published in the United States
by Oxford University Press Inc., New York

British Library Cataloguing in Publication Data

Data available

Library of Congress Cataloging in Publication Data

Data available

ISBN 978-0-19-926582-4

3 5 7 9 10 8 6 4 2

Typeset by John Was, Oxford
Printed in Great Britain
on acid-free paper by
Antony Rowe Ltd, Chippenham, Wiltshire

To the memory of R. C. Hutchinson

Preface

BOOKS (in my experience) know the form they want to assume, and guide their fumbling authors until they find it. The curious evolution of this one may perhaps help readers to see its character and point.

My first intention was to write a commentary on all Pindar's epinicians. I hoped to devote more of my attention to literary matters than had most twentieth-century commentaries on Pindar, and to produce a handy set of volumes. I abandoned this enterprise, with a pang, partly because the progress of the Mondadori edition seemed to be meeting the need for handiness, and partly because I was becoming more and more absorbed by the whole genre and its development.

My next plan was to write a general book on ancient lyric poetry. But as I experimented, the genre of the commentary seemed best suited for the detailed and sustained literary exploration which the poetry appeared to be demanding. For these purposes, the most promising idea was a relatively ample but principally literary commentary, for scholars and graduates in the first instance, on a limited number of particularly substantial fragments, and specimen pieces from Bacchylides, Pindar, and drama. (Corinna, whom I take to be later, was excluded.)

I wrote the commentary mainly in the academic year 1997/8, when I enjoyed the blissful luxury of leave. Further modifications to my plan accrued: I had wanted to include some non-epinician Pindar, some Old Comedy, and some Latin lyric; but space, shape, and cohesion intervened.

When I had finished a first version of the commentary, I realized, topsy-turvily, that the book required much more extensive work on the papyri. I had worked mostly from published photographs, as my purpose had not been to offer any new collations of the sources. Engagement with the problems of the fragments impelled me onwards. This was not, and is not, intended as a definitive edition of the texts; but I did what was possible in the time remaining before my deadline, a period filled, not to say crammed, with teaching and administrative duties. I have collated from the original fifteen of the twenty-two papyri used for the text, with a microscope where one was available, with other magnifying apparatus where it was not; those in Oxford I have scrutinized repeatedly. The other seven papyri (four of which are slight) I have collated from photographs; I have deployed new or unpublished photographs of most. In the case of medieval manuscripts, I have simply made use of what lay to hand, whether original, microfilm, or facsimile; only nine of the manuscripts reported at length have been collated by me in any form. The final change of plan worth mentioning was (on advice) to write the apparatus and other such matter in Latin. The book was handed to the Press in January 2000.

The work is partial and provisional; yet in many respects this belongs to the conception. The book does not attempt to offer a final or decisive account but aspires to advance in some measure, by a personal, selective, but detailed treatment, the understanding and literary interpretation of this poetry. This seems to me a not inappropriate way to exploit the form of the commentary, at this time and with these poems.

Various particular features of the work should now be stated, unexciting as the statement will be. Although the text of the papyrus fragments rests on my own endeavours to read them, the book does not at all offer a proper papyrological re-edition. Dating, hands, and so forth are not discussed. Uncertain traces are sometimes discussed when important; but a great deal of palaeographical argument and material has been left, again on advice, in the margins of my copies. For the poetic text, not usually for commentaries or marginalia, any lectional signs in the papyrus are given explicitly in the main apparatus (save for letterless accents, etc., already in the text). The apparatus does not reproduce the actual vertical and horizontal ordering in more elaborate cases, and sometimes adjusts the horizontal placing. The reports of signs have been set in parentheses to enable the reader to separate them quickly. Outside these parentheses, papyrus readings are usually presented with accents, breathings, and apostrophes, to give the sense.

Partly to make the text and apparatus accessible, and partly because texts from medieval manuscripts are also being offered, 'pc' and 'ac' are normally employed to signal corrections in papyri and the readings they indicate; signs like ⟦ ⟧ and ˋ ˊ are kept to a minimum. It may be assumed that where the later reading has lost a letter from the earlier, that letter has been deleted; that where it has gained a letter or where one letter has been substituted for another, the new letter has been written above the line in the appropriate place. The apparatus states explicitly anything more complicated, such as the deletion of a replaced letter, the addition of dots around a letter to be substituted, or the correction of one letter into another.

Though I have admittedly suggested supplements to papyri in the past (and once had a risky suggestion confirmed by later evidence), for these texts at this point it seemed more important to nurture prudence. Consequently I have abstained from offering supplements of my own, save occasionally where argument calls for one. I have been less chary over mentioning conjectures of my own where the text is preserved with some completeness: here activity should perhaps be encouraged (if this is encouragement). Earlier supplements are often presented approximately, with a 'fere', in particular when the proponent read the papyrus differently from me; this is again for clarity. Remarks on the spacing of supplements rest on tracing and my approach to it. According to me, to trace μενοc one should not simply trace a μ, ε, ν, ο, and c but should if possible trace from the papyrus the collocations με, εν, νο, οc, since the interval between letters is vital. If one notes too variations in letters and intervals, and allows for differences in regularity between papyri, experiment can confirm the method to be fairly reliable (though time-consuming).

Medieval manuscripts are listed individually, not grouped with symbols; such symbols are not worth the nuisance of grasping for short texts or extracts.

The text itself follows in dialect the general convention of presenting for the most part a modified version of the papyrus tradition. This makes for simplicity in displaying the evidence, though it is not necessarily the practice I would have chosen for a full-scale edition of a given poet.

In the rest of the book, the emphasis falls on the commentaries. The introductions on each author try and offer some useful preliminaries to the close reading of particular works. Concrete points and context receive most attention; but critical preliminaries can be needed too. Archaeological matter is often included. Any ambitious interpretation of that matter is avoided here; the hope is merely to

incite readers of the poems towards fuller acquaintance with the
visual art and material culture of the poets' societies.

Brief introductions to each poem prompt the reader to consider
overall interpretation of it from the first. The metre is treated at
some little length: it is important for the reader of the book to
possess a sensibility to metrical form and its remarkable variety
in this literature. When there are concluding notes to chapters or
poems, these are not epitomes of the comments; they merely give
some thoughts best considered after the reading of the comments,
or else help the reader to draw together in mind some aspects of
comments and poem.

And so to the commentaries themselves. For many of the texts,
these commentaries are the most elaborate hitherto; but the em-
phasis intended for the book means that they sometimes omit or
treat lightly practical questions and scholarly controversies of no
great importance for interpretation, and (what I confess to more
nostalgia for) exploration of linguistic features found in the poems.

My attempts to interpret the poems are substantially affected by
my reading in various regions of critical theory, and by my reading
of modern literature. Some readers may find it helpful if I mention
that the word 'narrator' is very frequently used to denote the outer
speaker in each poem, the speaker whose words are not set, as it
were, in inverted commas. Where it is necessary to make the situ-
ation plainer, 'the chorus' is used sometimes instead (especially in
the commentary on Alcman) and the author's name occasionally.
(Some of the most forward-looking criticism, e.g. Docherty (1996),
chs. 5 and 6, is actually less anxious in this respect.) There are
two reasons for the prominence of the term 'narrator'. The first is
to keep it before the reader that the speaker, even when explicitly
connected to the author, is always a literary creation. The second
is that the interconnections, and differences, between the various
types of lyric are seen much more plainly if one compares narrators
rather than viewing 'the chorus', 'Anacreon', and so on as unre-
lated entities. Little obscurity should be caused by my extension of
'perfective' and 'imperfective' from linguistic phenomena to events
and situations in literary works; but some further explanation of the
area will be found in Hutchinson (1999). Otherwise, it is hoped that
the language employed will be clear to all kinds of reader.

A reasonably ample selection of bibliography is offered for each
poem. This is mainly of work from more recent times. Standard

commentaries and other books which cover most of the range here (such as Campbell (1982)) are not usually mentioned explicitly. The reader who follows up the references will have no difficulty in discovering more bibliography. And Gerber (1993, 1994) will afford an invaluable resource. Various kinds of discussion are mentioned. It is perhaps worth stressing that I believe strongly in the importance of both the textual and the literary traditions of scholarship which this book attempts to draw together.

The texts, the commentaries, and the introductions all together should give the reader a feeling for the particular art of each poet, for the diversity and scope of this literature, and for its changes with the course of time. The pleasure and excitement of studying it should, with luck, emerge too.

Exeter College, Oxford   G.O.H.
April 2000

Acknowledgements

MY first thanks must go to three papyrologists in the Ashmolean Museum, Oxford. Dr R. A. Coles, Dr G. Nisbet, and Dr D. Obbink have been endlessly willing to bring out from their incomparable treasury yet another awkwardly placed papyrus; they have been wonderfully generous with technical expertise and handy information. Dr B. Barker-Benfield, Dr M. Kaufmann, and Ms S. Pugh of the Bodleian Library, Oxford, have helped me to see papyri and manuscripts, and have arranged for me to use a microscope on the papyri. Mr N. G. Wilson has given me the great benefit of his palaeographical knowledge on a knotty point or two.

In Paris, M. A. Blanchard of the Institut de Papyrologie at the Sorbonne, and Mme M.-F. Aubert, M. M. Étienne, and Mme M. France at the Département des Antiquités Égyptiennes of the Louvre enabled me to study the papyrus of Alcman fr. 1 (and to find my way through an underworld). I am grateful to Exeter College and to the Faculty of Literae Humaniores for financing this trip.

Dr G. Waller of the Cambridge University Library and Dr S. McKendrick of the British Library have helped me to examine papyri in their collections. I am much indebted to the following for photographs, microfilms, and related assistance: Dr W. Brashear (Ägyptisches Museum und Papyrussammlung, Berlin); Professor R. Pintaudi (Biblioteca Laurenziana, Florence); Dr C. Römer (Institut für Altertumskunde, Cologne University); Dr M. C. Howatson, Professor P. J. Parsons, Dr D. Yatromanolakis. Dr I. C. Rutherford kindly let me see in advance of publication his highly important book on Pindar's *Paeans*. For sundry advice relating to the text I must thank Professor J. Diggle, Professor A. R. Dyck, and Professor D. Kovacs. Other kinds of advice have been given by Dr D. Feeney, Ms J. Johnson, Ms M. Stewart, and two readers for the Press; the guidance and encouragement of the latter were of the greatest value to me. I am extremely grateful to the Press for undertaking to publish this tricky and bulky book, and to Dr J. Waś for his copy-editing and typesetting.

Dr E. J. Beverley looked after my pupils with marvellous care and competence during a year of leave, and so made it possible for me to concentrate selfishly on writing. My wife has helped me with an English and an Italian quotation, my daughter has told me about horses; both have supported my enterprise without a word of complaint and with the sweetest enthusiasm. My debt to them is the deepest of all. I dedicate the book, however, to the memory of my grandfather, a novelist now little known. He lived from 1907 to 1975. His fastidious toil over his sentences still chastens, the large sympathy of his vision still inspires, the less heroic efforts of the epigone.

Contents

Abbreviations etc.

Periodicals are referred to more or less as in *L'Année philologique*. Ancient authors are referred to either as in, or more fully than in, Liddell and Scott⁹ (LSJ) and its *Revised Supplement* of 1996 (LSJ *Suppl.*), and *The Oxford Latin Dictionary*. Collections of papyri, inscriptions, and literary texts are usually referred to by the abbreviations used in those works. A few abbreviations remain:

ABV   J. D. Beazley, *Attic Black-figure Vase-painters* (Oxford, 1956)

ARV²   J. D. Beazley, *Attic Red-figure Vase-painters²* (Oxford, 1963)

CAH   *Cambridge Ancient History²⁻³* (Cambridge, 1970–)

LCS   A. D. Trendall, *The Red-figured Vases of Lucania, Campania, and Sicily* (2 vols.; Oxford, 1967), with supplements 1–3, *BICS* suppl. 26 (1970), 31 (1973), 41 (1983) (London)

LGPN   P. M. Fraser and E. Matthews, *A Lexicon of Greek Personal Names* (Oxford, 1987–)

LIMC   *Lexicon Iconographicum Mythologiae Classicae* (8 vols. in 16; Zurich, Munich, and Düsseldorf, 1981–97)

LSAM   F. Sokolowski, *Lois sacrées de l'Asie Mineure* (Paris, 1955)

ML   R. Meiggs and D. Lewis, *A Selection of Greek Historical Inscriptions to the End of the Fifth Century B.C.²* (Oxford, 1988)

OCD³   S. Hornblower and A. Spawforth (eds.), *The Oxford Classical Dictionary³* (Oxford, 1996)

Para.   J. D. Beazley, *Paralipomena: Additions to* Attic Black-figure Vase-painters *and to* Attic Red-figure Vase-painters² (Oxford, 1971)

PMGF   M. Davies, *Poetarum Melicorum Graecorum Fragmenta* (1 vol. to date; Oxford, 1991–)

RE   *Real-Encyclopädie der classischen Altertumswissenschaft* (Stuttgart, 1893–)

The edition used for citing fragments is mentioned explicitly, save with lyric fragments of the lyric poets themselves (not the dramatists). These fragments are referred to without 'fr.' ('Alcm. 1' etc.), save in the case of Bacchylides and Pindar; for them the numeration of the editions by Snell and Maehler is employed (for Pindar's *Paeans*, Rutherford's designation is added in brackets). For Alcman, Stesichorus, and Ibycus the numeration is that of Davies, *Poetarum Melicorum Graecorum Fragmenta* ('TA', 'TB' refer to his testimonia). For Sappho and Alcaeus it is that of Voigt, *Sappho et Alcaeus: Fragmenta* ('T' is sometimes used to denote a fragment that is more a testimonium); but an 'S' before a fragment of these poets refers to Page, *Supplementum Lyricis Graecis*). For other lyric poets the numeration is that of Page, *Poetae Melici Graeci* and *Supplementum Lyricis Graecis*. When a poem referred to is included in this book, its number in the text is added in bold between square brackets ('Alcm. 3 [2]' etc.).

TEXTS

^{ac}, a.c.	ante correctionem
^{pc}, p.c.	post correctionem
^c	post correctionem, si prior lectio legi non potest
^{il}, i.l.	in linea
^{sl}, s.l.	supra lineam
^{sscr}, sscr.	suprascriptum, suprascripsit
^{gl}	in codice lectio tamquam glossema scripta est
^{γρ}	in codice lectioni praepositum est γράφεται, sim.
^v	verso
^r	recto
acc.	accentus
codd.	codices
coni.	coniecit
corr.	correxit, correcto, etc.
del.	deleuit, deleto, etc.
e.p.	editor primus
recc.	recentiores
rell.	reliqui
[α]	α deest in omnibus testibus
⌊α⌋	α deest in uno teste, non omnibus
{α̇}	α̇ contra testes delendum est
⟦α⟧	α in Π deletum est
ʻαʼ	α addidit Π supra lineam

De auctoribus eorum supplementorum quae in textu leguntur tum in apparatu tacetur cum qui suppleuit is papyrum primus edidit.

ALCMAN

1: *PMGF* 1 (fr. 3 Calame)

papyrus: P. Louvre E. 3320/R56 (s. p. C. i). imagines: lithographica, Egger (1865), tab. L; photographicae, Blass (1879), tab. 1, et Turner (1987), 44–5 (col. ii depingit, partemque maximam col. iii). ipsam contuli papyrum; scholia tamen eius, quae et ante et post ex imaginibus contuli, tum conferre non potui: tam tenacibus uinculis me retinuit tertia columna. praeterea alia quoque scholia conseruat P. Oxy. 2389 (s. p. C. i) in frr. 6–8. imago: P. Oxy. xxiv (1957), tab. v. papyrum ipsam contuli. testimonia: u. 2 Σ Pind. *Ol.* 11. 15 a (solum in A=Ambrosiano C 222 inf. (s. xiii ex.), quem in pellicula hoc loco inspexi); 6 *Epimer. Hom.* ε 154 (ii. p. 314 Dyck) (codicem, Oxoniensem Coll. Novi 298 (s. xiv ex.), hoc loco (185ʳ) inspexi); 49 *Et. Magn.* 783. 20–6 Gaisford (*Et. Sym.* in adn.), cf. *Et. Gen.*: Marcovigi (1970), 25 et Calame (1970), 45; 61 Herodian. π. μον. λέξ. 2. 36 (ii. 942 Lentz) (φᾶρος); 64–5 Aristoph. Byz. fr. 33 Slater (61 Nauck); 71 *Et. Gen.* a 1116 Lasserre–Livadaras (cum *Et. Magn.* atque *Et. Sym.*), u. etiam Marcovigi (1970), 26 (ἀραιτασιειδήc); 81 Hesych. θ 1025 (θωcτήρια); 88 Hesych. γ 141 (γανδάνειν); de 1–35 cf. etiam Σ Clem. *Protr.* 36. 2 p. 200 Marcovich.

col. i

         ] Πͅωλυδεύκης.
    οὐκ ἐγῳν Λύκαιcον ἐν καμοῦcιν ἀλέγω
    Ἐνα]ρcφόρον τε καὶ Cέβρον ποδώκη
    ]ν τε τὸν βιατὰν
5   ]ͅ τε τὸν κορυcτάν
    Εὐτείχͅη τε Ϝάνακτά τ' Ἀρήϊον
    ]ά τ' ἔξοχον ἡμιcίων
   ——]

1. 1–35 cf. Σ Clem. (uide supra) Ἱπποκοωντιδῶν· Ἱπποκόων τις ἐγένετο ... (Herculem dicit bello cum Hippocoontidis conflato manu uulneratum esse, id quod Sosibium dixit affirmare Clemens). μέμνηται καὶ Ἀλκμάν ἐν ᾱ. μέμνηται καὶ Εὐφορίων ἐν Θραικὶ (fr. 29 Powell) τῶν Ἱπποκώοντος παίδων, ὡς (Kroll: τῶν codd.; cf. Σ Nicand. *Ther.* 3) ἀντιμνηστήρων τῶν Διοσκούρων   1 (πὼ i.e. accentum scribit Π))   2 Σ Pind. ἀλέγων· ὑμνῶν. καὶ Ἀλκμάν (Ἀλκαῖος Α)· οὐκ ἐγὼ Λύκον ἐν Μούcαις ἀλέγω (λύκ) (μόυ) (ἀλέ) 3 init. ἀλλ' Bergk (φόρ) (κή) 4 (ἀτὰν) 5].: ν potius quam η (κόρυcτὰν) 6 *Epimer.* Διογένης Διογενής, Πολυνείκης πολυνεικής ... · οὐ ... πάντως τὰ μὲν κύρια ἀεὶ βαρύνεται, τὰ δὲ ἐπιθετικὰ ὀξύνεται, ἀλλὰ εἴ που βαρύνεται τὸ κύριον, τὸ ἐπιθετικὸν ὀξύνεται. εἰ οὖν ἐcτιν Εὐτείχης ὄνομα κύριον παρ' Ἀλκμᾶνι, Εὐτείχη τ' ἄνακτ' ἀρήϊον, καὶ ὤφειλεν εἶναι τούτωι τῶι λόγωι εὐτειχέα (εὐτείχεα cod.)]η Π (Ϝάνακτά) Ἀρήϊτον coni. ΣΑ (ἠΐ) 7 (έξ) (cί)

]ν τὸν ἀγρόταν

] μέγαν Εὔρυτόν τε

10   ]πώρω κλόνον

]ᾳ τε τὼς ἀρίϲτωϲ

] παρήϲομεϲ

]ᾳρ Αἶϲα παντῶν

] γεραιτάτοι

15   ]έδιλοϲ ἀλκά.

ἀν]θρώπων ἐϲ ὠρανὸν ποτήϲθω

μηδὲ πη]ρήτω γαμῆν τὰν Ἀφροδίταν

F]άναϲϲαν ἤ τιν᾽

] ἢ παίδα . . . κω

20   Χά]ριτεϲ δὲ Διὸϲ δόμον

]ϲιν ἐρογλεφάροι

———]

]τάτοι

]τα δαίμων

]ι φίλοιϲ

25   ]ωκε δῶρα

].γαρέον

]ώλεϲ᾽ ἤβα

]ρονον

μ]αταίαϲ

30   ]έβα. τῶν δ᾽ ἄλλοϲ ἰῶι

] μαρμάρωι μυλάκρωι

].εν Ἄιδαϲ

8 ἀγρέταν Ahrens   9 (ἐν)   10 (πώρωκλό)   11]ᾳ potius quam]ε;
Ἀλκωνά] τε Bergk   (ἀτετὼ)   (ὡϲ)   12 οὐ] Ahrens   (ρή)   13 γ]ὰρ ten
Brink; τῶν θιῶν γ]ὰρ Snell   (ἀ(?)ραιϲαπαντῶν)   14 καὶ Πόροϲ] Blass, cl. ΣΑ
(αἰτά)   15 -π]έδιλοϲ Ahrens:]εδειλοϲ (ἐδ) Π: ἀπ]έδιλοϲ Blass   λύθη δ᾽ ἀπ]έδιλοϲ
Penwill: Διὸϲ uel θιῶν δ᾽ ἀπ. West   (κᾱ)   16 ἀν]θρώπων fere Blass; init. μῆτιϲ
Blass: μή ποκ᾽ coni. Page (μήποτ᾽ iam Sitzler)   (ἡϲ)   17 μηδὲ πη]ρήτω fere
Blass:]ρητωι Πᵃᶜ   (γᾱ)   (δῑ)   18 (ἀν)   ἤ Πᵖᶜ: ηι Πᵃᶜ   (ἡ[ι])   τιν᾽ Diels: τινα Π
19 (πάι)   Πόρκω legunt, cl. Hesych. ν 416 Νηρεύϲ· θαλάϲϲιοϲ δαίμων. Ἀλκμὰν καὶ
Πόρκον ὀνομάζει; de hac lectione tamen, praecipue de ρ, dubitandum est   (᾿.κὼ)
21 ἰερογλεφάροι Ahrens (cum αὖψα παρ]ῆν)   (ἀροὶ)   22 (τά)   24 (φί)
25 ἐδ]ωκε Ahrens   δ᾽ ὥρα Hinz   26].: uestigium, ut uidetur, summo γ
adaequatum; ὡϲ πα]γὰ ῥέον Sitzler (malim μ]έγα ῥέον, sed nec ε nec α omnino satis
facit)   (ρέ)   27 (ὠλεϲῆ)   29 μ]αταίαϲ fere Sitzler   (τάιᾱϲ)   30 (ἐβατῶ)
(ὦι)   31 (λά)   32].: c non ueri simile   Ἄιδαϲ Pamphilus (u. ΣΑ; cf. Pind.
Pyth. 4. 44): Ἀΐδαϲ Aristophanes (cf. 2)   (ἀΐδᾱϲ)

] αυτοι
']πον. ἄλαϲτα δὲ
col. ii   35   Ϝέργα πάϲον κακὰ μηϲαμένοι.

ἔϲτι τιϲ ϲιῶν τίϲιϲ·
ὁ δ᾽ ὄλβιοϲ ὅϲτιϲ εὔφρων
ἀμέραν [δι]απλέκει
ἄκλαυϲτοϲ. ἐγὼν δ᾽ ἀείδω
40   Ἀγιδῶϲ τὸ φῶϲ· ὁρῶ
Ϝ᾽ ὥτ᾽ ἄλιον, ὅνπερ ἇμιν
Ἀγιδὼ μαρτύρεται
φαίνην. ἐμὲ δ᾽ οὔτ᾽ ἐπαινῆν
οὔτε μωμήϲθαι νιν ἁ κλεννὰ χοραγόϲ
45   οὐδ᾽ ἁμῶϲ ἐῆι. δοκεῖ γὰρ ἤμεν αὐτά
ἐκπρεπὴϲ τὼϲ ὥπερ αἴ τιϲ
ἐν βοτοῖϲ ϲτάϲειεν ἵππον
παγὸν ἀεθλοφόρον καναχάποδα
†τῶν ὑποπετριδίων ὀνείρων†.

50   ἦ οὐχ ὁρῆιϲ; ὁ μὲν κέληϲ
Ἐνητικόϲ; ἁ δὲ χαίτα
τᾶϲ ἐμᾶϲ ἀνεψιᾶϲ
Ἀγηϲιχόραϲ ἐπανθεῖ
χρυϲὸϲ ὡϲ ἀκήρατοϲ.
55   τό τ᾽ ἀργύριον πρόϲωπον,

34 (ον·ἄλ)   35 Ϝέργα ten Brink: ἔργα Π (ερ)   (πά)   (μῇϲὰμέ)   36 (τίτιϲϲιῶντί̈)
37 (ὁ(ὅ?)δ᾽ὅλβὶ)   38 [δι]απλέκει fere Bergk; fortasse uestigium ex ι restat
39 ἄκλαυτοϲ Sitzler   (ἀκ)   (οϲ·)   (ἐι)   40–1 (ἀγ)   (φῶϲορῶ)   Ϝ᾽ Wilamowitz:
ε Π (ε᾽); τὸ φῶϲ ὁρῶ·|ϲ᾽ legit et intellexit Puelma, sed hoc ϲ non scripsit Π   ὥτ᾽ Π^pc
(ὥτ): ὥιτ᾽ Π^ac   (ἀλ)   ὅν περ᾽ West   (ἅμ)   42 (ἀγὶ)   (τύ)   post 42 paragraphum
inserit Π   43 φαίνην Schubert: -εν Π   (φάινεν·)   ἐπαινῆν Farnell: -εν Π   (αἰνὲν)
44 μωμήϲθαι Bergk: -έϲθαι Π   (μῶμέ)   (νᾶ)   (νᾱ)   45 (δ᾽ἁμῶϲἐῆι·)   δοκεῖ
Canini: -έει Π   ἤμεν Π^pc (·η· sscr.): εἴμεν Π^ac   (ἐί)   46 ἐκπρεπὴϲ: ἐμ- Bergk   (τὼϲ)
ὥπερ Schubert: ὥιπερ Π (ὥι)   (ἁι)   47 (τόιϲϲτᾱ)   48 (πᾱ)   (φόρονκἀνὰ)
49 *Et. Magn.*, *Sym.* ὑποπετριδίων (ὑποπτέρων ὀνείρων *Magn.*)·... ἐχρῆν οὖν εἰπεῖν
καὶ τῶν ὑποπτέρων ὀνείρων τῶν ὑποπετριδίων, ⟨καὶ⟩ ὑπερθέϲει τῶν ὑποπετριδίων. οὔτωϲ
Ἡρωδιανὸϲ ἐν τῶι περὶ παθῶν (ii. 237–8 Lentz)   uersum grauiter esse corruptum
putauit Hutchinson (iam θάϲϲον᾽ pro τῶν coniecerat Headlam)   (τῶ)   (δίωνονέι)
50 (ῆ)   ὁρῆιϲ Ahrens: -ῆϲ Π   (κέ)   51 Ἐνητικόϲ Diels: Ἐνε- Π: Ϝενη- coni.
Page   (ἐνέτικόϲ·ἁ̈)   52 (τᾶϲεμᾶϲ)   (ᾶϲ)   53 (χό)   (ἐι)   54 ω: de
spatio cf. 65   (ώ̈]τ᾽ Diels   (κή)   55 (πρό)

διαφάδαν τί τοι λέγω;
Ἀγησιχόρα μὲν αὖτα·
ἁ δὲ δευτέρα πεδ' Ἀγιδὼ τὸ Ϝεῖδος
ἵππος Ἰβηνῶι Κολαξαῖος δραμήται.
60 ταὶ Πεληάδες γὰρ ἇμιν
Ὀρθρίαι φᾶρος φεροίcαις
νύκτα δι' ἀμβροcίαν ἅτε Cήριον
ἄcτρον ἀυηρομέναι μάχονται.

———

οὔτε γάρ τι πορφύρας
65 τόccoc κόρος ὥcτ' ἀμύναι,
οὔτε ποικίλος δράκων
παγχρύcιος, οὐδὲ μίτρα
Λυδία, νεανίδων
col. iii   ἰανογ[λ]εφάρων ἄγαλμα,
70 οὐδὲ ταὶ Ναννῶc κόμαι,
ἀλλ' οὐδ' Ἀρέτα cιειδήc,
οὐδὲ Cυλακίc τε καὶ Κλεηcιcήρα.
οὐδ' ἐc Αἰνηcιμβρ[ό]τας ἐνθοῖcα φαcεῖc
"Ἀcταφίc τέ μοι γένοιτο,
75 καὶ ποτιγλέποι Φίλυλλα

56 διαφάδαν Π^{pc}: -φράδαν Π^{ac} (φά) 57 (χό) αὖτα (ἄυ): αὐτὰ van Groningen 58 (ἁ) (πὲ) Ἀγιδὼ Π^{pc}: -ωι Π^{ac}: -ὼν Ahrens (ἀγιδὼ) Ϝεῖδος Hiller: εἶδος Π 59 Ἰβηνῶι Smyth: Εἰ- Π (βή) (ἀι) δραμήται Ahrens: -εῖται Π (ἐι) post 59 paragraphum inserit Π 60 Πεληάδες Sitzler: Πελει- Π (άδ) (ἁμ) 61 *Herodian.*: φάρος . . . καὶ οὐδέτερον ὁπότε cημαντικὸν τοῦ ἱματίου ἢ καὶ τοῦ ἀρότρου, ὡc καὶ παρ' Ἀλκμᾶνι Ὀρθρίαι: ὀρθρίαι saepe editur: Ὀρθίαι Aristophanes (Ϝορθίαι Garzya) (ἰαιφᾶροcφέρόι) aliquid super ιc scriptum est 62 Cήριον Bergk: Cιρ- Π^{ac}, tum ι del. (ει uoluit): Cιρ- ΣB fr. 6 ii. 18 63 ἀυηρομέναι Page (ἀϜη- Bechtel): ἀυει- Π (μέ) 64–5 Aristoph. φηcι γὰρ ὁ γραμματικὸc Ἀριcτοφάνηc οὐ μόνον cημαίνειν τὸ κακῶc παθόντα ἀντιδιατιθέναι ἀλλὰ τεθεῖcθαι καὶ ἀντὶ ψιλοῦ τοῦ ἀμείψαcθαι ὀτιοῦν. καὶ φέρει χρῆcιν ἔκ τε Ἀλκμάνοc τὸ "οὐ γὰρ πορφ.–ἀμύναcθαι" οὔτε Π^{pc}: οὔτι Π^{ac} (φύρᾱc) (ὥcτ'αμύ) 66 (κί) 67 πανχρύcιος Π (χρύ) (ρᾱ) 68 (δίᾱνεανί) 69 ἰανο[γ]λεφάρων fere Blass 70 (νῶcκό) 71 *Et. Gen., Magn., Sym.* ἀρετacιειδήc (ἀραι- codd.)· ἀρετacιοειδὴc καὶ κατὰ cυγκοπὴν ἀρετacιειδὴc ὡc cιοειδὴc cιειδήc . . . οὕτωc Ἡρωδιανὸc περὶ παθῶν (ὡc–παθ. om. *Gen. B, Sym.*, οὕτωc–παθ. om. *Magn.*) (ρέτᾱcιει) 72 (cὑλακίc) (κλεἠcιcή) 73 (δ'ἐc) Αἰνηcιμβρ[ό]τας Blass (ἀὶ) (βρ') (θὁιcαφὰcειc) 74 (ἀcτἀφιcτέ) 75 (φίλυλλἄ)

Δαμαρέτα τ' ἐρατά [τ]ε Ϝιανθεμίς"·
ἀλλ' Ἁγησιχόρα με τείρει.

⟨——⟩

οὐ γὰρ ἁ καλλίσφυρος
Ἁγησιχ[ό]ρ[α] πάρ' αὐτεῖ·
80   Ἁγιδοῖ δὲ παρμένει
θωςτήριά [τ'] ἄμ' ἐπαινεῖ.
ἀλλὰ τᾶν . . . . . . (.)ιοι
δέξαςθε· ςιῶν γὰρ ἄνα
καὶ τέλος. . . . . ςτατις
85   Ϝείποιμί κ', ἐγὼν μὲν αὐτά
παρςένος μάταν ἀπ . ράνω λέλακα
γλαύξ· ἐγὼν δὲ τᾶι μὲν Ἀώτι μάλιστα
Ϝανδάνην ἐρῶ, πόνων γὰρ
ἇμιν ἰάτωρ ἔγεντο·
90   ἐξ Ἁγησιχόρας δὲ νεάνιδες
ἰρ]άνας ἐρατᾶς ἐπέβαν.

⟨——⟩

τῶ]ι τε γὰρ ςηραφόρωι
ạ[ὐ]τῶς ἐδ . . . . '
τῶι κυβερνάται δὲ χρή
95   κῆν νᾶϊ μα . . . .
ἁ δὲ τᾶν Ϲηρηνίδων

---

76 (δᾱ)   (ατᾱ́)   Ϝιανθεμίς Hiller: 'Ι- Π, ΣΑ   (ϊανθεμίς)   77 (χό)   τείρει Π, non τηρεῖ, id quod legerunt e.p. (Egger), Blass; τείρει ΣΒ fr. 7 i (b) quoque. multi autem τηρεῖ etiam ut coniecturae fauent   78 (ᾱ̈)   79 Ἁγηςιχ[ο]ρ[α] fere ten Brink   (ἀγ)   (πάρ'αὐτεῖ)   80 (ἀγὶδόι)   δὲ παρμένει· δὲ ἴκταρ μένει legit Blass, sed κ non scriptum est; ob iuncturam uero in media columna hoc spatio litterae collocantur, cf. 79 (eandem iuncturam per totam columnam meminisse oportet) (μέ)   81 Hesych. θ 1025 θωςτήρια· εὐωχητήρια καὶ ὄνομα ⟨ἑορτῆς⟩   θωςτήρια· uestigia ex α incertissima   (θὼςτήρια[.]ᾱ̣μεπαὶνεῖ)   82 (τᾶν)   [εὐχ]ᾲς Blass, sed hoc scriptum non est. λιτᾳς (λὶτας) etiam arridet, postea ςιοι (ςὶοὶ) legi possit (cf. ΣΒ fr. 8?); sed tum difficultatem opponat spatium quod post ας relinquatur   83 (θε·) ἄνα intellexit Schubert   (ᾱνᾱ)   84 (ος·)   χοροςτάτις mea sententia non legendum est; quarta enim littera imprimis repugnat. ne χοροιςτάτις quidem legere potui   (.ςτά)   85 Ϝείποιμί Page: εἴπ- Π   (μί κ')   (αὐτᾱ́)   86 (μάτᾱν) ἀπὸ θράνω legit Blass; ọ placet, θ non multum   (ρᾱ̈)   λέλακα Πᵖᶜ: βέβακα Πᵃᶜ   87 (γλαύξ·)   (τᾱ̣μενᾱωτῑ)   μάλιστα Πᵖᶜ: -ται Πᵃᶜ   88 Hesych. γανδάνειν (i.e. Ϝανδ-)· ἀρέςκειν   Ϝανδάνειν Page: ἀνδ- Π   (ἀνδᾱ́)   (ὠ·)   89 (ᾱ̣μινὶά)   90 (ἀν) 91 ἰρ]άνας Hutchinson (εἰρ]ήνας iam Blass, ἰρ]ήνας Page), cf. *SEG* 26. 461. 2:]ηνας Π   (τᾱ̀)   92 τῶ]ι Blass   (.ιτε)   (φό)   93 ạ[ὐ]τῶς fere Blass   (τῶ) ἐδάμεν legit Mariotti   95 (νᾱ̀ι)   μάλιςτ' ἀκούην (μαλιςτακόνεν) non legendum est   96 (ἀδετᾶν)

8   *Alcman*

ἀοιδοτέρα με.....
ϲιαὶ γάρ, ἀντὶ δ' ἔν̣δ̣εκ̣α̣
παίδων δεκ........ει
100   φθέγγεται δ... ἐπὶ Ξάνθω ῥοαῖϲι
κύκνοϲ. ἁ δ' ἐπιμέρωι ξανθᾶι κομίϲκαι

col. iv   [
           [
           [
105   [

scholia etc.: (1) **ΣA**, in P. Louvre E. 3320 scripta. eadem manu plerumque conscripta sunt atque carmen (quam ipsam ob causam magno sunt usui). saepe tamen uix possunt legi.

ad u. 2:   ὅτι τοιαύτη ἡ
διάν(οια)· τὸν Λυκαι-
ον οὐ ϲυνκατα-
ριθμ(ῶ).......
[..]...[..]τιδαιϲ
ου μ[
του[
.ε̣ια.[..]...[.]
εϲται οὐ μόνον
τὸν Λύκαιο(ν) ἀλλὰ
καὶ τοὺϲ λοιποὺϲ
Δηριτίδαϲ οὓϲ ἐπ' ὀ-
νόματος λ.γ..

6 (man. 2):   Φερεκύ(δηϲ) ἕνα
τ(ῶν) Ἱπποκωντιδ(ῶν)
Ἀρήϊτον. μήπο-
τ' οὖν κ(αὶ)... ϲὺν τῶι τ
δεῖ γρ(άφειν) ἢ τ(ὸν) Ἀρήϊτον
ὁ Ἀλκμ(ὰν) Ἀρήϊον.

14:    ὅτι τὸν Πόρον εἴρηκε τὸν αὐτὸν
τῶ(ι) ὑπὸ τοῦ Ἡϲιόδο(υ) μεμυθολογη-

97 (ρᾶ) μ[ὲν αὐδά von der Mühll: μ[ὲν οὐδέν Page   98 (αἰγαρ·) ἀντὶ δ' ἔνδεκα: cf. ΣA; in textu αντ........ Π, ubi ιδεν uestigiis apta sint   δεκ Blass (ita Π ipsam legere credebat): αεκ Π, ut uidetur   δεκὰϲ οἵ (ἅδ' Wilamowitz, ὡϲ Puelma) ἀείδει legit Blass; ante ει tamen δ improbabile est   (ει·)   100 δ' ἄρ' ὦτ'(δ...ωιτ lecto) Blass; sed ω non arridet   (ξά)   101 (νοϲ·ἁ̄) ἐπιμέρωι fere Blass: ἐπειμ- Π (θᾱικὸ)   105 coronis   ΣA 2 οὓϲ ⟨οὐκ⟩ Pavese

μένωι Χάει.

32:     Ἀριϲτο(φάνηϲ) Ἀΐδαϲ (fr. 384 A Slater)· Πάμφιλο(ϲ)
    Ἄιδαϲ.

37:     ..... Ἀγιδοῦϲ ......

38:     Ἀρί(ϲταρ)χ(οϲ) ὅ[

43 (man. 2):   ὅτι .....[..] τηϲ.η.(.).ᵖ.
    πα..[..].....

48 (man. 2):   ....
    ... α .... αγηϲ ...

49:     ὅτι τὰ θαυμα-
    ϲτὰ καὶ τερατώδη οἱ
    ποιηταὶ εἰώθα(ϲι) τοῖϲ
    ὀνείροιϲ προϲάπτειν καὶ
    παρομοιοῦν διὰ τὸ φαίνεϲθαι
    κατὰ τὸν ὄνειρον τοιαῦτα.
    ὑποπετρίδι(α) εἴρηκε ὡϲ
    ὑπὸ π[έ]τρα⟨ι⟩ οἰκοῦντα
    ἐν α .[.]ι τόπω⟨ι⟩. παραγρά(φει)
    δὲ Ὁμ(ηρι)κ(ά), ὡϲ ἐν τῆ⟨ι⟩ Ὀδυϲϲείαι (24. 11–12)·
    "πὰρ δ' ἴϲαν Ὠκεανοῖο ῥοὰϲ
        καὶ Λευκά-
    δα πέτρην, ἠδὲ παρ' ἠελίοιο πύλαϲ καὶ δῆμο(ν) ὀνείρων".

59:                       ο[
    τα γένη ἐϲτὶν [   ]ικῶν ἵππων [.].[
                   E[ἰ]βην-
    ....[.]....
        ...εια.[...]...
           την

61–2:   super φᾶροϲ: αροτο, fortasse deletum. sub col. ii:
    Ἀριϲτο(φάνηϲ)
    Ὀρθίαι φᾶροϲ· Ϲωϲιφάνηϲ ἄροτρον. ὅτι
    τὴν [Ἀγι]δὼ καὶ Ἀγηϲιχόραν περιϲτεραῖϲ εἰκάζουϲι.

49 θαυμαϲρὰ Π, ut uidetur   Ὁμ(ηρι)κ(ά): etsi ομ⁷ uel sim. legitur, Ὁμηρικά (coni.
Hutchinson) debet intellegi potius quam Ὅμηρον (Blass, Diels); cf. e.g. Σ Ap. Rhod.
1. 1026, 3. 53–4b, 876   59 E[ἰ]βηνο(ϲ) Blass   61–2 Ὀρθίαι. φᾶροϲ Ϲωϲιφάνηϲ
(ita fere Campbell) uerborum in papyro compositio minus probabilem reddit. ὅτι
nouam adnotationem incipit (unde signum iuxta 62 positum)   [Ἀγι]δὼ fere
Blass:]ζὼ Π (ζω), ut uidetur   εἰκάζουϲι ten Brink: ἰ- Π

70–6, super col. iii: *tres uersus in quibus paene nihil legi potest, tum haec*:
　　　　　　．．．．διδασκαλ．．．．．．．．．．．．[
　　　　　　．．．．．．κ.τά．．．．．．．．．．．．．．．．． ουδετ.ιν..[
　　　　　　．．．．．．．．．．．．．．．．．α Ϲυλακίϲ τ(ε) κ(αὶ) Κλεηϲιϲήρ[α
　　　　　　.κ(αὶ) Ἀϲταφὶϲ．．．．．．κ(αὶ) Φίλυλλα．．．．．．．．．．．
　　　　　　　　　　　　　　　　　κ(αὶ) Ἰανθεμ[ίϲ

79 (man. 2 uel 3):   ἀν(τὶ τοῦ) αὐτοῦ

80 (man. 2 uel 3):   ... Ϲταϲικλ...

81:      θωϲτήρια· ἑορτ[ή.

83:      ὅτι τὸ ἄνα ἄνυϲιϲ.

89:      ἀρέϲκειν ἐπιθυμῶ.

95:      ναῖ· ναι Ἄρι...[

98–9: (in margine incipit, pergit sub col. iii):   ειδ....

　　　　　　．．．．．．．．．．．．．．．．．
　　　　　　　　　　ἀλλὰ διὰ
　　　　　　　　　　τὸ τὸν
　　　χορὸν ὅτε μὲν ἐ[κ] ῑᾳ παρθένων ὅτε δὲ ἐκ ῑ. φη(ϲιν) οὖν
　　　τὴν χορηγὸν．．．．．．．ἀντὶ ῑα ἄ⟨ι⟩δειν ῑ. ἐξῆν γὰρ `[
　　　ἀριθμὸν εἰπεῖν．．．．εἴπερ οὐκ ἐβούλετο τὸν ἀριθ[.]..
　　　παρθένων．．．．．．．．．．．．．．．．．．．．．．．[.].
　　　．．.αι..υ．．．．．．．．．．．．．．．．．．．．．．[.]..
　　　ῑθ ἐξῆν....

signa critica: × 49, 59, 61, 83, 98; Ϲ 62; < 77; signum parum lucidum 87

(2) **ΣΒ**, in P. Oxy. 2389 scripta
frr. 6 + 7:
(fr. 6) col. i   ].ϲ ἵππος Κολαξαῖος
　　　　　　　　　] οὕτωϲ ἡ Ἀγιδὼ προ
　　　　　　　　　δευ]τέρα κατὰ τὸ εἶδος
　　　　　　] ἵππος Κολ[αξαῖος　　]ϲ Ἰβηνὸν
　　　5　　Κολ]αξαίου δε[　　　].[.]....
　　　　　　Ἰβ]ηνοῦ· πε[ρὶ δὲ　　　　]υϲ τῶν
　　　　　　]ν Ἀρίϲταρχος ο[　　　　]..· ἀμ-
　　　φότερ]α ταῦτα γένη ἵπ[πων　　　]καλε

70–6 in primo et secundo exscriptorum uersuum plus quam dedi credo legi posse
οὐδὲ ταὶ Ναυ[νῶϲ κόμαι (Blass) legunt　　　super Ϲ, Θ sscr.　　　Ἰανθεμ[ίϲ fere Blass
ante κ(αὶ) Ἰ., κ(αὶ) Δαμαρέτα legunt　　81 ἑορτ[ή Blass　　98–9 u. 9 αι Ὀλυμπι
legunt　　**ΣΒ** (fr. 6) col. i. 4 πρὸ]ϲ ueri simile; et ob hoc supplementum et ob
fibras, uersus duorum fragmentorum columnae ita collocandi sunt　　5]..: ωι
sscr.

```
        ] δὲ ἀμφοτέρω[ν            ]. ὄντων
  10    ]ερειν τὸν Ἰβην[ον        ] τοὺϲ
        Ἰβην]ρύϲ φηϲιν τῆϲ Λ[υδίαϲ   ]ναι
        ]ρυτου δὲ βούλετ[αι        ] Λυ-
   δ    ]. ο Ἀλκμαν· cω[            ]. ν
        ]ν ἔθνοϲ ἀποφ[              ]. ρι·
  15    ]κεῖϲθαι προϲα[            ].. ω
        μ]άρτυν. περὶ δὲ τῶ[ν        ]ων
        ]coκν[. . .]oc δι.[          ]νεα.[
        ]. . . ωϲ γρ[          ]δε.[
        ]ονποντοντουτο[
                    desunt v uu.
  25                            ]..
                                ]. ε
                                ]. ια
                                ]ια
```

col. ii
```
        ἇμιν ὀ.ρθρίαι φᾶροϲ φεροίcαιϲ νύκτα δι'
        ἀμβροϲιά.ν ἅτε Cίριον ἄcτρον ἀνειρομέναι
        μάχονται
        εἰρημέν[
   5    τὴν Ἀγιδῶ [
        αυταιϲ ὀρ[θρίαϲ
        δὲ τοῦτο λ.[
    /   νάκιϲ εἰϲα[              Ἁ-
        _____
        ταρνίδεϲ.[
  10    [
        αδ.....[
        χονται ταϲ[
        ϲιν καθάπερ [καὶ Πίνδαροϲ (Nem. 2. 11)  ].‘ὀρει-
        ᾶν γε Πελει.άδων μὴ τηλόθεν Ὠαρίωνα
  15    νεῖϲθαι." ἐὰν [
        οὕτωϲ ἀκουϲα[              Ἀγηϲιχό-
        ρα καὶ ἡ Ἀγιδὼ .[
        ουϲαι τὸ τοῦ Cιρ[ίου ἄcτρον
        μαχόμεναι πε[
  20    Πλειάδων τὸ α[
```

13 Cω[cίβιοϲ δὲ aut Cω[ϲιφάνηϲ δὲ e.p. (Lobel)   15 ω: ο sscr.   17 Εὔδοξο]ϲ ὁ Κν[ίδι]οϲ coni. e.p.   19 ante] littera, ut uidetur, e textu qui sub nostro iacet ποντον Π^{pc} ([[το]]πον´τον´): τοπον Π^{ac}   26 super ε η sscr., del.   col. ii. 11 nec αδιαμ nec, puto, αδιομ; fieri potest ut spatio unius litterae pausa indicetur

γάρ· ὡc Πελει[άδεc
ρουcιν πα.[
....[.]αδια[
..].. ναιμ..[.].[
25   πειν τι· εἶναι γὰρ [ἀμβρο-
     cίαν ἀντιcτροφο[κανα-
     χάποδα ὥcτε ηλ[
     λείπειν· τιμων[
     .]ν ἄcτρον ἄτε C[ίριον
30   λόγον τοιοῦτον [
     ἡμᾶc περὶ τῆc [
     .]..νου ἀcτρ[
     ..]ᾳπο[

(fr. 7) col. iii?

(a)

                              ].[
                         ] Φίλυλλα Δαμαρέ-
          τα   ].· καθ' ὑπόθεcιν ταύ-
          τ-   ]ηc Αἰνηcιμβρό-
5   τ-   ]βου[
                              . .

(b)

                              ].[
                         ].α βλέπηι .[
                     λ]οιπὰc παρθ[ένουc   ˌἈγη-
                     cιχό,ρα με ˌτˌείρˌει
5   ].ἀλλ' Ἀγηcιχˌόρα με τείρει. οὐ

          γὰρˌ ἁ καλλίcφυροc Ἀγηˌcιχόρα παρ' αὐτεῖ·
          ο]ὐχ ὡc νῦν μὴ παρο.[
          ]τηc Ἀγηcιχόραc αλλᾳ[
          ].αι ὅτι ἐαν ει[.].τη[

21 · potius quam initium litterae ω   23–4 νύκ[τ]α δι' ἁ[μβροcίαν ἄτε Cίριον
ἄcτρον ἀνει-|ρο]μέναι μ[άχ]ο[νται e.p., probabiliter, nisi quod prima littera u. 23 inicit
scrupulum   25 aliquid super πε scriptum deletum est   26 ἀντιcτροφο[
Π^{pc}: ἀντὶ τούτω[ν (αντιτουτω) Π^{ac}   27 (χάποδα)   28 τιμων: ἡμῶν ponderauit
e.p. (ut lectionem papyri); sed uix placet   col. iii?: fr. 7 (a) et (b) praebere coll.
iii et iv credidit e.p., uersum columnae 'iii' (a) 2 uersui 25 fr. 6 col. ii adaequari
(a) 4–5 initia supplere fr. 13 (.. | τα) suspicatus est e.p   (b) 7 παρού[cηc e.p.,
probabiliter   9 nec εἰc τῆ[c nec εἰ[c]ω τῆ[c scriptum est (Αἰcνηcιμβότᾱc | ἐλ]θῆιc
pergunt Page, Barrett)

]. ηις οὐδεμίαν [
]. ειν πα[ρθ]ενο[
]ε τείρ[ει

col. iv?

(*c*)

] κα.[
] τετ[
] με[
] εκ[

.   .

(*a*)

ειςκ[
_____
ταδο.[
.[
.

fortasse etiam fr. 8 ad uersus carminis 82–3 attinet:

.   .
]μεν..[
]ω θεοι δε[
.   .   .

2: *PMGF* 3 (fr. 26 Calame)

papyrus: P. Oxy. 2387 (s. a. C. i ex. uel p. C. i in.), frr. 1–3. imagines: P. Oxy. xxiv
(1957), tabb. 1–11; Calame (1983), iuxta p. 80; Turner (1987), 42–3 (desunt uu. 6–10).
papyrum ipsam contuli. u. '99' ut uidetur explicat cod. Cyrilli P (Coisl. 394, s. x),
u. Reitzenstein (1890–1), 6 (Alcm. 142), cf. Hesych. ο 579.

10]: θ non omnino placet   col. iv?: (*c*) hac columna stetisse monstrare fibras
asseuerauit e.p.   (*a*) 2 ταδο non modo paragraphus sed etiam metrum suadet
ne partem putemus esse uersuum carminis 103–5

fr. 1

Ὀλ]υμπιάδες περί με φρένας
]ς ἀοιδας
]ωδ' ἀκούσαι
]ας ὀπός
5   ] ͅαρα καλὸν ὑμνιοιͅςᾶν μέλος
]ͅοι
ὕπνον ἀ]πὸ γλεφάρων ςκεδͅαςεῖ γλυκύν
]ͅς δέ μ' ἄγει πεδ' ἀγῶνͅ' ἴμεν
]ͅιςτα κόμ[αν ξ]ανθὰν τινάξω.
——]
10   ]ͅςχ[ἀπ]ͅαλοὶ πόδͅες
.   .   .   .   .   .

fr. 2

.   .
]αν[
] [
]ͅνιͅ· [
.   .

fr. 3

col. 1   ]
                                    ]ͅος·
                                    ]
[κ]ͅιρυερά͵

2. inter fr. 1 et fr. 3 nescimus quantum intercesserit; sin fragmenti 1 primam colum-
nam fragmenti 3 prima columna subsequitur, tum intercesserunt uu. aut 20 aut 29
(aut 38). fr. 3 col. ii enim uidemus a tribus ultimis strophae uersibus incepisse, in
ultimo desiisse. fr. 2 autem, quod finem uersus continet, e.p. (Lobel) iudicauit eidem
columnae atque fr. 1 pertinere. uu. '109–18' denique (nam numeros consuetos reti-
neo) separatim reperiuntur, in fragmento scilicet quod demonstrant fibrae hoc loco
constitisse   post ternos uersus Π paragraphum ponit, coronidem post strophas;
pro hac paragraphum substituimus, paragraphos omittimus ceteros   1 Μῶςαι
initio Giannini   (ῥί)   3 ἱμείρ]ω coni. e.p.   (κού)   4 παρςενηῖ]ας Barrett
Fοπός coni. Hutchinson   5 (κᾱλονϋμ)   (cᾶν)   6]ͅ: fort. ς, ε; uix μ
7 ςκεδαςεῖ: ςκέδαςεν Barrett   (ςεί)   8 (γωνϋμ)   9 ἄχι τά]χιςτα Barrett: ἄχι
μά]λιςτα Page; ἔνθα μά]λιςτα (e.p.) et ὄφρα τά]χιςτα (Peek) longiora sint spatio, modo
ὕπνον ἀ]πὸ in 7 recte se habet   (ξω·)   10]ͅ: ε, ο, ς (fr. 2 u. 3 ι·)   '32']ͅ:
λ, α   (oς·)

'35'   ]α
                                        .].αϲ·

——]   ]

.   .   .

ueri simile est deesse aut xxiii uu. aut xxxii

col. iii   λυϲιμελεῖ τε πόϲωι, τακερώτερα
            δ᾽ ὕπνω καὶ ϲανάτω ποτιδέρκεται·
            οὐδέ τι μαψιδίωϲ γλυκῆα κήνα.

——

        ϝα[ϲ]τυμέλοιϲα δέ μ᾽ οὐδὲν ἀμείβεται
'65'   ἀ̣[λλὰ τὸ]ν πυλεών᾽ ἔχοιϲα
        ὤ τ̣ι[ϲ] α̣ἰγλάε̣ντοϲ ἀϲτήρ
        ὠρανῶ διαιπετήϲ
        ἢ χρύϲιον ἔρνοϲ ἢ ἀπαλὸ̣[.....]ον
        ̂.]ν
'70'   ]. διέβα ταναοῖϲ πο[ϲι
        ]ομοϲ νοτία Κινύρα χαριϲ
        π]αρϲενικᾶν χαίταιϲιν ἴϲδει.

——]

        ϝα]ϲτυμέλοιϲα κατὰ ϲτρατὸν
        ] μέλημα δάμωι
'75'   ]μαν ἐλοῖϲα
        ]λέγω.
        ]εναβαλ᾽ α̣ι̣ γὰρ ἄργυριν
].(.)[.]ία

'36' (ᾱϲ·)   '61' (πό)   '62' (δ᾽)   ϲανάτω e.p.: ϲανάτωι Π^pc ('ϲ· s.l.): θανάτωι
Π^ac   (ται·)   '63' negauit e.p. se aut γλυκῆα aut κήνα legere posse; quae tamen re
uera scripta esse microscopio clare reperiuntur. ακη enim satis plana sunt; ante quae
aut η aut ν aut π cum accentu, potius ˆquam ᵕ   (κῆακήνᾱ)   '64' ϝα[ϲ]τυμέλοιϲα
Giannini: Α[ϲ]τυ- Π   (ἀ[.]τυμέ)   (δέμ᾽)   '65' ἀλλὰ τὸ]ν Page (ἀλλὰ e.p.): ἀ
δὲ τὸ]ν Giannini, breuiora spatio   πυλιῶν᾽ coni. Page   (ὦν᾽)   '66' ὤ fere
Barrett, e.p. (ὤ] illi): ὤ̣ι̣ Π, ut fere legit Barrett (ὤ]ι̣)   '67' (διᾶι)   '68' (χρῡ)
(η̣)   ἀπαλὸ[ν ψίλ]ον e.p., breuiora spatio, ut uidetur: ἀπαλὸ[ν πτερ]όν coni. Hutchinson
'70' (ἐβὰ)   (οἷϲ)   '71' καλλίκ]ομοϲ coni. Page: νυμφοκ]όμοϲ Guerrini   (ἰᾱκινύρᾱ)
'72' ἐπὶ π]αρϲενικᾶν e.p., initio ἄ τ᾽ Bowra, ἤν (eiacul.) Page, οὐκ Guerrini (cf. ad '71');
παρϲενικᾶϲ Page   (κᾶν)   (ἴϲδει·)   '73' ϝα]ϲτυμέλοιϲα Giannini: Α]ϲτυ- e.p., ut
paene certo Π   (μέ)   '74' (δᾱ́)   '75' (λοῖ)   '76' (γω·)   '77' (ά
(ut uidetur))   (βάλ᾽ἀιγαράρ)   '78' (ἰᾱ)

16   *Alcman*

　　　　　]α Ϝίδοιμ' αἴ πως με.... φίλοι
'80'　　　].[".]ιc ἀπαλᾶc χηρὸc λάβοι·
　　　　　] ετιc κήναc γενοίμαν.
——]
　　　　　]δα παίδα βα[.]ύφρονα
　　　　　]μ' ἔχοιcαν
　　　　　]εν ἁ παίc
'85'　　　] χάριν.
　　　　　.　　.　　.　　.　　.

　　　　ueri simile est deesse aut v aut xiv uu.

col. iii　η[
　　　　　o[
　　　　　μ[
　　　　　μ[
'95'　　　εί.[
　　　　　ου.[
　　　　　cυ.[

'79' Ϝίδοιμ' Giannini: ἰδ- Π　(ἰδοιμ'άι)　με....: μεcιο bene legatur, littera ultima
conturbatis fibris difficillima est. nec ν nec ι satis faciat; με, cιοὶ φίλοι, (coni. Page)
ut emendatio placeat (cf. Σ). φιλοῖ quoque considerauit Page, Φιλοῖ Barrett　(φί)
'80-4' propter fibras adiunxit e.p. hoc fragmentum:

　　　　　..]cο.[
　　　　　αἶψα κ[
　　　　——
　　　　　νῦν δ' [
　　　　　παιδι.[
　　　　　...]. ε[

(νῦνδ',].'ε[; paragraphum scripsit Π, ignoratur num coronidem addiderit). αἶψά κ(ε)
intellexit ille. tum ἀc]cον [ἰο]ῖc' Peek, Barrett (quamquam ι[aliquanto melius legatur
quam ν[); αἶψά κ' [ἐγὼν ἶ]κέτιc (ἶ]κ. iam e.p.) Page. sine causa tamen e.p. fragmentum
adiunxisse suspicatus est Hutchinson, id quod confirmatum est opera R. A. Coles
et G. Nisbet　　'80' ἰο]ῖc', ita ut '81' ἶ]κέτιc, etiam fragmento illo remoto allicit
([".]ἴcαπαλᾶc)　(λάβοι')　　'81'].: κ, χ, υ; certe non π (ἐ]πέτιc coni. Calame)
(νᾶc)　(μαν')　　'82' (παι)　βα[c]ύφρονα fere e.p. (θ ille): βα[ρ]υ- Page; et hoc et
illud spatio sit aptum (cf. fr. 11. 3)　'84' (ἀπαὶc)　'85' (ιν')　'95' (εἰ)
'96' (ὀυ)　'97' [: λ, χ, α; Cυλ[ακι(-) propter ῡ (cῡ Π) Hutchinson; cf. 1 [1]. 72 et
fortasse 3 fr. 4. 5 |]ὐτὶ (τί Π^ac) cυ. (λ, μ, α)[

ὀλκ[
οccαι̣[

'100' ἀλλα . [
       εcδε . [
       βᾶμε . [
       . .]κεc . [
       .] . . εc[
'105' [
       [
       [
       [
       ——]
       . [
'110'   δ[
       . [
       c[
       ε[
       κ . [
'115' ἴcτε̣[
       οιδε[
       ευδε[
       ————
       ] . . τ

scholia in Π scripta; conscripserunt complures manus

super fr. 1 col. i:

                                    ]
       ]τα[   ]
       π]α̣ρενγρά(φεται) ἐν̣ [το]ῖc ἀντιγρά(φοιc) αὕτη
       ] πέμπτωι .   κα̣ὶ̣ ἐν ἐκείνω̣ι̣
       ] Ἀρ(ιcτο)νί(κου) περιεγέγρα(πτο) ἐν δὲ τῶι Πτολ(εμαίου)

'98' ὀλκ[α- e.p.; Cyrill. P ὀλκάc˙ . . . καὶ παρὰ Ἀλκμᾶνι αειδῶν (ἀηδών Edmonds, cf.
ἀηδών Hesych.; tum καὶ εἰρήνη (εἰρήνη Hesych.), unde Latte ἀοιδὰ Cειρήνων)   (ὀλ)
'99' (cάι)   '100' (ἀλ)   '102' (βᾶ)   '113' (έ)   '115' (ἴc)   '116' (ὀι)
Σ: super fr. 1 col. i 4 ἐν̣ . . τῶι] e.p.

18   *Alcman*

5   ἀπερ[ἰ]γρα(πτος) ἦν.
           ]

ad u. 3: aliquid obscuri (non μ° π, non enim ο sscr. sed ε; π̆ᵉ̩ ̣?); ad u.
tertium fr. 1 col. ii, marg. sin.: ω[; '34' [κ]ρυερά· ψυχρά; '35' ἀπάρχε(ται)
πε( ); '72' uestigia tantum; '79' μ°π, ut uidetur: μό(νον, -ως) Π(τολεμαῖος)
coni. e.p.; '82' ῥᵘπ: ὀμ(οίως) Π coni. e.p., quamquam de μ nimium dubitauit,
puto

STESICHORUS

3: *PMGF* 222 (b)

papyrus: P. Lille 76 a+73+111 c+76 c+76 b (s. a. C. iii). perspexit Lloyd-Jones
rectum fragmentorum ordinem. imagines: Meillier, Ancher, Auger (1976), pp. 356–
8 (111 c, 76); Turner (1980), tabb. i–ii (76a+73); Boyaval et Meillier (1984), tabb.
iii–iv; Bremer (1987), tabb. 7–8, ante p. 41; Turner (1987), 125 (76 a+73 tantum);
ineditas quoque imagines uarias liberalitate larga mihi commodauit P. J. Parsons. e
quibus omnibus contuli papyrum.

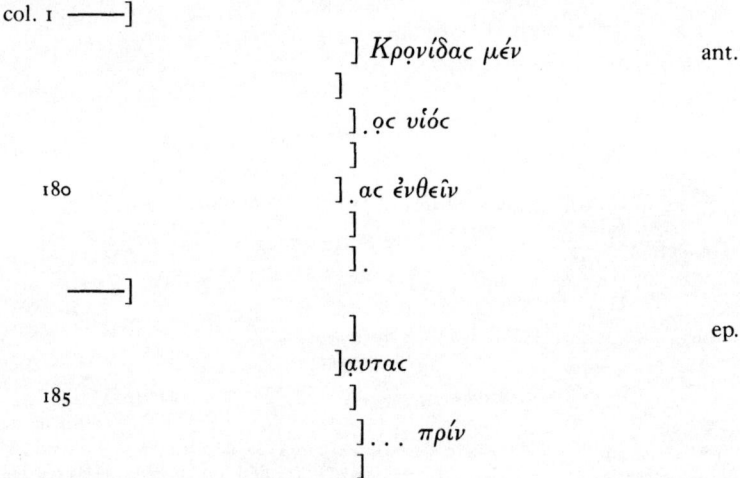

col. 1 ——]

           ] Κρονίδας μέν   ant.
           ]
           ]̣ος υἱός
           ]
180   ]̣ας ἐνθεῖν
           ]
           ].
                                              ep.
           ]
           ]αυτας
185   ]
           ]... πρίν
           ]

3. col. i uersu 166 incepit; ante u. 176 fortasse uestigia pauca litterarum exstant
singularum   178 non ϛϲ

μ]έγα νεῖκος
]

==]

190   ] . . εν εἴcω   str.

] . . .

] παῖδας

]

]

195   ]

] . [.]

──]

] . ος ἔγειρεν   ant.

]

] . . . . .

200   ]

col. ii   ἐπ' ἄλγεςι μὴ χαλεπὰς ποίει μερίμνας,
μηδέ μοι ἐξοπίcω
πρόφαινε ἐλπίδας βαρείας.

───

οὔτε γὰρ αἰὲν ὁμῶς   ep.
205   θεοὶ θέcαν ἀθάνατοι κατ' αἶαν ἱράν
νεῖκος ἔμπεδον βροτοῖςιν,
οὐδέ γα μὰν φιλότατ'· ἐπὶ δ' αμε . α . νόον ἀνδρῶν
θεοὶ τιθεῖcι.
μαντοcύνας δὲ τεὰς ἄναξ ἑκάεργος Ἀπόλλων
210   μὴ πάcας τελέccαι.

══

αἰ δέ με παῖδας ἰδέcθαι ὑπ' ἀλλάλοιcι δαμέντας   str.
μόρcιμόν ἐcτιν, ἐπέκλωcαν δὲ Μοίρα[ι],
αὐτίκα μοι θανάτου τέλος cτυγερο[ῖο] γέν[οιτο
πρίν ποκα ταῦτ' ἐcιδεῖν

188 μ]έγα Parsons   197] . : aut γ aut τ   ἄλ]γος?   εγειρεν imperf. aut infin.
199 fortasse alia scribebat manus   π]ερὶ ἥβας Massimilla   207 ἀμέρα⟨ι ἐ⟩ν
Parsons: ἀλλοῖ' ἀν legit Meillier: ἀμέρ⟨ιο⟩ν Pavese   ἀνδρῶν legit Bremer   211 ἀλ-
λάλοιcι: fortasse -οις Π   coronide Π, ita ut P. Oxy. 841, 3876, finem triadis solet
indicare   213 cτυγερο[ῖο] multi   γέν[οιτο Meillier, Pavese   214 πρίν ποκα
West: πρὶν τόκα Π (sine accentibus, ut semper)

215   †ἄλγεϲι† πολύϲτονα δακρυόεντα [
      παῖδαϲ ἐνὶ μεγάροιϲ
      θανόνταϲ ἢ πόλιν ἁλοίϲαν.
      _____

      ἀλλ᾽ ἄγε, παῖδεϲ, ἐμοῖϲ μύθοιϲ, φίλα [ant.
      τᾶιδε γὰρ ὑμὶν ἐγὼν τέλοϲ προφα[
220   τὸν μὲν ἔχοντα δόμουϲ ναίειν π.[
      τὸν δ᾽ ἀπίμεν κτεάνη
      καὶ χρυϲὸν ἔχοντα φίλου ϲύμπαντα [
      κλαροπαληδὸν ὃϲ ἂν
      πρᾶτοϲ λάχηι ἕκατι Μοιρᾶν.
      _____

225   τοῦτο γὰρ ἄν, δοκέω,   ep.
      λυτήριον ὔμμι κακοῦ γένοιτο πότμο[υ
      μάντιοϲ φραδαῖϲι θείου,
      †αἴτε νέον† Κρονίδαϲ γένοϲ τε καὶ ἄϲτυ [
      Κάδμου ἄνακτοϲ,
230   ἀμβάλλων κακότατα πολὺν χρόνον [   ].
      πέπρωται γεν.[.].αι."
      ═══════

      ὡϲ φάτ[ο] δῖα γυνά, μύθοιϲ ἀγ[α]νοῖϲ ἐνέποιϲα,   str.
      νείκεοϲ ἐν μεγάροιϲ.[...]ιϲα παῖδαϲ,
      ϲὺν δ᾽ ἅμα Τειρ[ε]ϲίαϲ.[.....]λοϲ. οἱ δ...θ.[

col. iii   α.[   ]

215 ἄλγεϲι: ἄλγεϲ⟨ϲ⟩ι e.p.: ἀλγιϲτ⟨α⟩ uel αὐγαῖϲι coni. Hutchinson; fortasse etiam post
δακρυόεντα transferri possit uox illa quaecumque   δακρυόεντα metitus est Gallavotti,
δακρύοϵντα Barrett: δακρύεντα coni. Ruijgh   -εντά [τ᾽ Meillier: -εντ᾽ ἀ[λάϲτοιϲ Barrett:
-εντ᾽ ἀ[γεῖϲαν Slings: -εντ(α) [ἔπ᾽ ἄλγη Page   216 μμεγάροιϲ Π   218 [τέκνα (hoc
Maltomini), πίθεϲθε West: [νῦν φρονέοιτε Barigazzi   219 ὔμ⟨μ⟩ιν e.p.   προ[φαίνω
multi   220 τὸμ μὲν Π   .[: a potius quam ε, o, etc.   πᾳ[ρὰ νάμαϲι Δίρκαϲ Barrett:
πᾳ[τρίαιϲ ἐνὶ Θήβαιϲ Diggle   222 [πατρόϲ multi   228 αἴτε νέον (τ potius quam
γ): αἴ γ᾽ ἐτεὸν Lloyd-Jones, Barrett: αἴ γε νοεῖ e.g. Hutchinson (cum infinitiuo, in fine
uersus locato)   [ϲαώϲει Barrett, Lloyd-Jones, West   230 [αἴτ(ε) Parsons olim,
Ancher: [ἃ βαϲιλείαι (cum γεν⟨έ[θ]λαι) Lloyd-Jones: [ἃ περὶ Θήβα]ϲ (cum γεν[έ]ϲθαι)
Bremer   ].: uestigium ante π 265, quae littera dextrorsum demota est, debet
esse ipsum pars litterae; fortasse ϲ   231 aut γεν.[.].αι aut γεν...αι; γεν⟨έ[θ]λαι
Lloyd-Jones, Barrett: γενά[ρ]χαι West, Parsons; γενέϲθαι non excludendum uidetur
esse   232 φάτ[ο] Parsons   ἀγ[α]νοῖϲ Barrett   233 ἐμ μεγάροιϲ Π   π[αύο]ιϲα
Barrett   super .[id stat quod habent pro littera; ut u. l. ἐ[ργ(οιϲα) intellexit Barrett.
equidem hoc esse putauerim aliquid fortuiti; cf. 201, 226, 285   234 Τειρ[ε]ϲίαϲ
Meillier   τ[εραϲπό]λοϲ Barrett, quod spatio fortasse non sit aptissimum   οἱ δ᾽
ἐπίθο[ντο fere Barrett   235 .[: ν (aut μ) potius quam υ

236   το.[   ] Θηβαν
       γαῖα[   ]
       κατ.[   ]α

       τον.[χρ]υϲόν τ᾽ ἐρίτιμον ἔχοντα   ant.
240   παμ[   ].ϲθενηϲαν
       ηδοϲ.[κ]λυτὰ μᾶλα νέμοντο
       ...[   ].
       .[.].μ[   ]ειραϲ ἵππουϲ
       .[..].[   ]
245   .[

       .[ep.
       .[   ].μουϲ ἀϲάμουϲ
                   ]
                   ἐ]νὶ ϲτήθεϲϲι φίλοιϲι
250   ]
                   ]εοϲ ἂν δ᾽ ἔθορ᾽ αὐτόϲ
                   ]

                   μ]ῦθον ἔειπε   str.
                   ].λωϲ
255   ].ατε βουλάν
                   ]
                   ]ιϲ πιθήϲαϲ
                   ]
                   ]

———]
260   ]ε πολλαχα.υ...   ant.
                   ].α
                   ]

236 .[: ν aut μ   τὸν [μὲν Meillier   237 γαῖα[ν Meillier   238 κατ potius
quam και (de spatio cf. πρατ 224, φατ 232)   239 τὸν δ᾽ [ἀπίμεν κτεάνη fere
Parsons (cl. 221)   240 παμ[potius quam παλλ[πρ]όϲθεν ἦϲαν Lloyd-Jones:
ε]ὐϲθένηϲαν coni. Parsons; ἔνηϲαν Instone   241 ἠδ᾽ ὅϲα Parsons   μῆλα West
243 εὐέθ]ειραϲ West   247 χρη]ϲμοὺϲ Meillier   255 ατ, non αδ   φίλ]τατε
Bremer   257 μύθο]ιϲ Parsons   260 πολλὰ γὰρ ὑμῖν legere noluit Parsons,
uoluit Bremer (πολλὰ γὰρ υἱῶν legit Massimilla): πολλά γα θυμόν legit Parsons; ante υ
ego potius ρ quam θ dixerim stare   262 fortasse restat aliquid

                                    ]
                                    ]cac
265   πολλα[   ]
       θεοὶ δόμεν[   ]
       ⎯⎯⎯
       τῶν ταμ[   ]   ep.
       ἀγεν ταδ[   ]. αιc
       πολλὰ δ[
col. iv . [   ]υcιν θέντεc μεγάλαιc ε. [
271   . [   ]γοc
       . [   ]. εν ἕλικαc βόαc ἠδὲ καὶ ἵπ[πουc
       . [   ]. αιcαν
       ═══
       c. [   ]. οιτο μόρcιμόν ἐcτι γεν[str.
275   ... [   ]μον Ἀδράcτοι᾽ ἄνακτοc
       . [   ]νοc δώcει περικαλλέα κο[ύραν
       . [   ]α
       . [   ]. τον δωcοῦντι δᾶμοc
       .. [   ]ου
280   ⎯]   ]οι᾽ ἄνακτοc

                                    ]. ω διαμπερέωc Ἐτεο[κλ-   ant.
                                    ]. εν cτήθεccιν αἰνω[
       θ. [   ]. νεχεν Πολυνείκεοc [
       ω. [   ].
285   τευξ[   ]ταν πόλει τε πάcαι
       μα. [   ]αν
       ἀει π. [   ]ε πένθοc
       ⎯⎯⎯

268] : ζ, ξ?   270 ἄν]υcιν ... ἐπ[ὶ λύπαιc Parsons   271 Ἄρ]γοc e.g. Parsons
272] : γ, τ, etc.   273 κα]τ᾽ αἶcαν Haslam, Parsons, West   274 γεν[έcθαι
Lloyd-Jones, Pavese   275 δό]μον Haslam, Parsons   276 ὅc δέ cε δεξάμε]νοc
West   κο[ύραν Merkelbach, Pavese, Schwartz   280 Ἀδράcτ]οι᾽ Barigazzi,
Pavese   281 super o partem litterae uident; hic quoque ego aliquid uiderim
fortuiti   Ἐτεο[κλέουc Barigazzi   282 αἰνῶ[c Barrett, Schwartz   285 τεύξ[ηι
Page   286 ματ[ρί τ᾽ Page

	του[	]ον　　　　ep.
	θεω[	].ςηι μάλιϲτα παντῶν
290	..[	]τοιϲιν."
	ὣϲ φάτ[ο	ὀ]νυμάκλυτοϲ· αἶψα δ' α[
	δόμω.[	]
	ὤιχετ[	].το φίλωι Πολυνείκεϊ π[
	Θηβαι.[	]

295	...ομ..[	].ν ϲτειχεν μέγα τεῖχ[οϲ　str.
	.....[	].... αὐτῶι
	.....[	].ιπποιϲ τιϲανακρο.[
	ανδρε.[	]
	πομπ.[	].δ' ἵκοντο Ἰϲθμόν
300	ποντιο.[	]
	κραι..[	].υχαιϲ

	αυτα[	] ἄϲτεα καλὰ Κορίνθου　ant.
	ῥίμφα δ[	] Κλεωνὰϲ ἦνθον

in margine papyri: iuxta u. 300 γ̄; 302 ×.

288–90 τοῦ[το ῥύοιτο κακ]όν, | θεῶ[ν ὅτιϲ εὖνο]ος ἦι μάλιϲτα παντῶν | το[ῖϲ ὀϊζυροῖϲ βρο]τοῖϲιν (hoc βρ. Haslam et West) exempli causa Parsons　288].: ο potius quam ω　291–2 φάτ[ο Τειρεϲίαϲ ὀ]νυμάκλυτοϲ Parsons, West　ἀ[ναϲτὰϲ Parsons; ἄ[ποικοϲ | δόμων [ὅ γ' ἥρωϲ Page (etiam sic fere suppleri possit: ἀ[πήνθε | δόμων· [ὁ δ')　293–4 ϲὺν δ' ἄρ'ἔπο]ντο... τ[αγοί | Θηβαίω[ν ἄριϲτοι Page; sed 293 π[potius quam τ[　296 ἅμ' αὐτῶι posse legi arbitratus est Parsons　297 ut τ' ἵϲαν interpretatus est Barrett　ἄκρο[- Meillier, Schwartz　299 πομ potius quam πεμ　πομπα[ῖϲι θεῶν Barrett　300 ποντίου ['Εννοϲίδα West: πόντιον [ἀμφίαλον e.g. Parsons　301 ν.[potius quam π.[　]ευχαῖϲ legi possit　302 αὐτὰ[ρ West　303 δ' [εὔκτιμέναϲ] Barrett, West

SAPPHO

4: fr. 1 Voigt (et Lobel–Page)

papyrus: P. Oxy. 2288 (s. p. C. ii), quae uersuum 1–21 partes exhibet. imago: P. Oxy. xxi (1951), tab. i; Turner (1973), tabb. 4–5 (unde Tzamali (1996), 73); exempla eiusdem manus in Turner (1987), exx. 18 et 19. papyrum ipsam contuli. totos uersus, totum uero carmen praebet Dion. Hal. *Comp.* 23. 11 (173–9) et *Epit.* 114–16. hi codices commemorabuntur libri ipsius *De compositione*: P (Parisinus gr. 1741, s. x med.) et F (Laurentianus 59. 15, s. xi in.); hi commemorabuntur codices epitomes: D (Darmstadiensis 2773, s. xiv in.), L (Laurentianus 60. 25, s. xiv), M (Monacensis gr. 327, s. xiv in.), Ma (Marcianus gr. 444, s. xiv med.), Va (Vaticanus gr. 102, s. xiv). in PF Aujac–Lebel (1981), Usener–Radermacher (1904–29, cf. etiam ii, pp. xii–xiii), alios sequor; in libris singulis autem epitomes Piccolomini (1892) et Usener–Radermacher sequor, qui tamen non narrant quid legat Parisinus gr. 2918 (s. xiv in.). auctores alii: u. 1 Hephaest. 14. 1 [I = Parisinus gr. 2676, s. xv] (bis; cf. Choerob. *In Hephaest.* 14, p. 249 Consbruch [K = Marcianus gr. 483, s. xiv, U = Vaticanus gr. 14, s. xiii–xiv]), ΣA 14 (Ἄφρ.); 1 (bis), 2, 3 Choerob. 14, pp. 249–50; 3 ΣA Hephaest. 11, p. 146 Consbruch (μή-όν.), Choerob. 80, p. 244; 4 Choerob. 14, p. 253 (bis); 5 Hephaest. 14. 1, Choerob. 14, p. 251, Hesych. κ 1683 (κάτ.), Prisc. 1. 37; 6 Apoll. Dysc. *Adv.* p. 197 Schneider (*Gramm. Gr.* ii/1. 1)?, Prisc. 1. 37?; 9–10 Herod. π. μον. λέξ. 2. 42 (ii. 948 Lentz) (κάλ.–στρ.), Hesych. ω 112 (ὤκ. στρ.), cf. Athen. 9, 391 F; 19–20 *Et. Gen.* AB cit. 90 Calame (Calame (1970), 31), *Et. Magn.* p. 485. 42 (ὦ-άδ.), *Et. Gud.* col. 294. 39 Sturz (ὦ-άδ.), cf. *Anecd. Par.* Cramer iv. 63. 3–4; Herod. π. μον. λέξ. 2. 43 (ii. 949 Lentz).

> πο͵ικιλόθρο͵ν' ἀθανάτ' Ἀφρόδιτα,
> π͵αῖ Δ͵ί͵ος δολ͵όπλοκε, λίccομαί cε,
> μή͵ μ' ἄcαιcι ͵μηδ' ὀνίαιcι δάμνα,
> π͵ότνια, θῦμ͵ον·
> ——]
> 5 ἀλ͵λὰ τυίδ' ἔλ͵θ', αἴ ποτα κἀτέρωτα,
> τ͵ὰc ἔμαc αὔ͵δαc ἀΐοιcα πήλοι,

4. Dion. (eadem uerba *Epitome*): θήcω δὲ καὶ ταύτης παραδείγματα τῆς ἁρμονίας (sc. τῆς γλαφυρᾶς), ποιητῶν μὲν προχειρισάμενος Cαπφώ . . . ἄρξομαι δὲ ἀπὸ τῆς μελοποιοῦ· ποικιλόθρον'-έcco. (23. 13 μικροῦ δεῖν δι' ὅλης τῆς ᾠδῆς, 14 ὅλην τὴν ᾠδὴν ἀνασκοπούμενος) 1 θρο[Π (non φρο) ποικιλόθρον' fere Π, PF, LMa, Hephaest.: -οφρον fere DMVa, Choerob. Ἀφρόδιτα: accentum testantur Choerob., Σ Hephaest.: -αν P 2] .δ[·] .ςδολ[Π 3] .αcαιc͵[Π ἀνίαιcι *Epit.*, Choerobosci K 4] ΄τ͵ιαθυμ͵[Π (θύ) 5] .ατυιδελ[Π (τυίδέλ) τυίδ' fere Π, Hephaest., Choerob. (testatur ipse pp. 251–2), Prisc.: τύδ' fere PF, *Epit.* αἴ ποτα Hephaest. (praeter I), Choerobosci U: αἴποτε Choerobosci K, αιποτι fere Prisc.: -ε ποκα P, *Epit.*: -ε ποτὲ F κἀτέρωτα fere PF, Hephaest., Choerob., Hesych.: τ' ἔρ. *Epit.*: cατερωτα fere Prisc. 6] .cεμαcαν[Π (ἐμαcάν) αὔδαc *Epit.*: -ωc P: -εc F πήλοι fere F, Apoll. ipse: πολυ fere P, *Epit.*

ἔκλυες, πάτροις δὲ δόμον λίποισα
χρύσιον, ἦλθες,
—]

ἄρμ᾽ ὐπασδεύξαισα. κάλοι δέ ς᾽ ἆγον
10 ὤκεες στροῦθοι περὶ γᾶς μελαίνας,
πύκνα δίννεντες πτέρ᾽, ἀπ᾽ ὠράνω αἴθε-
ρος διὰ μέσσω·
—]

αἶψα δ᾽ ἐξίκοντο. cὺ δ᾽, ὦ μάκαιρα,
μειδιαίσαις᾽ ἀθανάτωι προσώπωι,
15 ἤρε᾽ ὄττι δηῦτε πέπονθα, κὤττι
δηὖτε κάλημμι,
—]

κὤττι μοι μάλιστα θέλω γένεσθαι
μαινόλαι θύμωι. "τίνα δηὖτε †πείθω
.ιψ c᾽ ἄγην†, ἐς cὰν φιλότητα; τίς c᾽, ὦ
20 Ψάπφ᾽, ἀδικήει;
—]

καὶ γὰρ αἰ φεύγει, ταχέως διώξει·
αἰ δὲ δῶρα μὴ δέκετ᾽, ἀλλὰ δώσει·

7]λυεςπατρο[Π (εc·)   8]ρυcιονηλθ[Π (ον·)   χρύcιον fere Π: -ειον PF, *Epit.*
9 αcδ Π   ὐπαcδεύξαιcα fere Π, F: ὑποζεύξαca P, *Epit.*   καλοῖc F   αγον F, *Epit.*,
Herod.: -ων P   10 εccτρου[Π (ὀυ)   γᾶc P, *Epit.*: τᾶc F   11].κναδιν[Π (δὶν)
δίννεντεc Ahrens: δίν[ν Π: δινν͜ην τεc F: δινήντεc P: δινεῦντεc *Epit.*   ἀπ᾽ ὠ. fere P, *Epit.*:
-α πτω. F   12 μεccω[Π   μέccω Π: μέcω fere F, *Epit.*: -μέcπω P   13]ψαδεξικο[
(ἴκ) Π   αἴψ᾽ ἄλλ᾽ P   cὺ F: τὺ fere P, *Epit.*   ὦ: ἀ Lobel   14]ειδιαιc[Π (ante ε
reperitur uestigium quod illi textui pertinet qui sub nostro iacet)   μειδιαίcaιc᾽ fere
Π, F: μειδιάcαc᾽ P, *Epit.*   15]ρεοττιδ[Π   δηὖτε Hermann: δ᾽ ἦν τὸ fere P, *Epit.*:
om. F   16] .υτεκ[Π (reliqua inferiori pertinent textui)   δηὖτε fere Π, P: δεῦρο
F, *Epit.*   17]ωττι[Π; non]ο (τί)   κώττι μοι fere Π: κωττ᾽ ἐμῶι fere PF: κώτι γ᾽
ἐμῶι fere *Epit.*   γένεcθαι PF, LMaVa: -έcθω DM   18–19]αιν̣᾽λαι[Π   μαινόλαι
fere Π, P, *Epit.*: λαι F   δηὖτε fere F, *Epit.*: δ᾽ ἐντε- P   πείθω: Πείθω fere Rapicius
]ψcαγην̣[Π, ut uid.;]αιc legere noluit Turner (c .ἄ)   .ψ c᾽:]ψc Π: μαῖc᾽ Pᵖᶜ: βαῖc᾽
Pᵃᶜ: καὶ c- F, *Epit.*: ἄψ c᾽ (cum ϝὰν (Edmonds)) coni. Lobel: β]αῖc᾽suppl. Parca: μαῖc
Bergk: μαῖc᾽ Bücheler: μάψ Blomfield: παῖδ᾽ Amato   πείθεις | ἄψ {c} Hutchinson
(πείθωμ᾽ | ἄψ {c} iam Di Benedetto): Πείθων | φᾶc Slings: πείθωμαί c᾽ Blass   c᾽ ὦ
fere P: ὦ fere F, *Epit.*   20 Ψάπφ᾽ fere PF, ψαφ᾽ *Et.* Gen., ψατ etc. *Et. Magn.*,
Gud.: Caπφὼ *Epit.*:]πφ[Π   ἀδικήει *Et. Gen.*, et grammatici ipsi, ut uid. (-ήη etc. *Et.
Magn.*, *Gud.*): -η fere P, *Epit.*: -ηc F: -ηcι Meillet   21]ιγ[Π   αἰ Rapicius: εἰ P,
Epit.: ἢ F   φεύγει: -οι *Epit.*   22 δέκετ᾽ P: δὲ καὶ (sic) τ᾽ fere F, *Epit.*   δώcε F

αἰ δὲ μὴ φίλει, ταχέως φιλήσει
κωὐκ ἐθέλοισα."

———]

25 ἔλθε μοι καὶ νῦν, χαλέπαν δὲ λῦcον
ἐκ μερίμναν, ὄccα δέ μοι τέλεccαι
θῦμοc ἱμέρρει τέλεcον, cὺ δ' αὔτα
cύμμαχοc ἔccο.

———]

5: fr. 16 Voigt

papyri: Π¹ = P. Oxy. 1231 = Bodl. MS Gr. Class. c. 76/1 (P) (s. p. C. ii) (uu. 1–30, 32; 28–30 fragmentum sunt priuum); Π² = PSI 123 (s. p. C. ii–iii) (uu. 31–2). imagines: P. Oxy. x (1914) tab. II (postea aliqua fragmenta sunt addita), Turner (1987), 46–7; PSI ii (1913), in fine libri. P. Oxy. 1231 ipsam contuli, PSI 123 ex imagine. uu. 3–4 (ἔγω–ἔρ.) adfert Apoll. Dysc. *Synt*. 3. 172 [A = Parisinus gr. 2548, s. xi].

col. i   ο]ἰ μὲν ἰππήων cτρότον, οἰ δὲ πέcδων,
οἰ δὲ νάων φαῖc' ἐπὶ γᾶν μέλαι[ν]αν
ἔμμεναι κάλλιcτον, ἔγω δὲ κῆν' ὄτ-
τω τιc ἔραται.

———]

5   πά]γχυ δ' εὔμαρεc cύνετον πόηcαι
π]άντι τ[ο]ῦτ'· ἀ γὰρ πόλυ περcκέθοιcα
κάλλοc [ἀνθ]ρώπων Ἐλένα, [τὸ]ν ἄνδρα
τὸν [. . . . .] . cτον

———]

23 om. F   φιλήcει *Epit*.: φιλεῖ P   24 κωὐκ ἐθέλοιcα Bergk: κωϋ κεθέλουcα F: κ' ὠν κ' ἐθέλοιc P: κῶ εἰ καὶ θέλειc fere *Epit*.: κωὐκὶ θέλοιcα idem Bergk: κωϋ κε θέλοιcα Lobel: κωὐκ ἐθέλοιcαν Schäfer: κωϋ cε θέλοιcαν Knox   25 χαλέπαν: ἐπᾶν F 26 ὄccα fere F, LMa: ὄ cα P, DMVa   τελέccαι Carteromachus: -έcαι P, *Epit*.: -εccε F   27 ἱμέρρει Tollius: ἱμέρει fere P, *Epit*.: ιμαρερερει F   τέλεcον *Epit*.: -ccον PF 28 ἔccο D: ἔco F, LMMaVa: ἔcτω P   **5.** 2 (φᾶιc) μέλαι[ν]αν: μελαί[ν]αν (cum γᾶc uel γᾶι) editori primo (Hunt) in mentem uenit   3–4 Apoll.: καὶ δεόντωc ἡ Cαπφὼ ἐπιτεταμένωι μᾶλλον ὀνόματι (sc. quam φιλεῖν) ἐχρήcατο· ἐγὼ–ἔραται κῆν'fere Π¹, A²ᶜ: καὶ ἡ v- fere codd. rell. Apollonii   (ον·) (κην'ότ)   5 (εύμ) (cύν) 6 τ[ο]ῦτ': nec spatium nec v omnino placet   ἀ: α postea corr. aut retractatum est (τ'ἀ) περcκέθοιcα plene satis facit   (cκέ)   7 καλοc Π¹ᵃᶜ, λ sscr.   8] . : α, η, ι?   μέγ' ἄρ]ιcτον Gallavotti, [πανάρ]ιcτον Page

καλλ[ίποι]ς', ἔβα 'ς Τροΐαν πλέοι[ςα.

10   κωΰδ[. .] . ῖδος οὐδὲ φίλων το[κ]ήων
πά[μπαν] ἐμνάςθη, ἀλλὰ παράγαγ' αὖταν
`   ]ςαν

——]

]αμπτον γὰρ [
] . . . ν κούφως τ[   ]οη . [.] .

15   . .]με νῦν Ἀνακτορία[ς] ἀνέμναι-
ς' οὐ] παρεοίςας·

——]

τὰ]ς κε βολλοίμαν ἔρατόν τε βᾶμα [
κἀμάρυχμα λάμπρον ἴδην προςώπω
ἢ τὰ Λύδων ἄρματα κἀν ὄπλοιςι

20   . . . . .]μάχεντας.

——]

] . μεν οὐ δύνατον γένεςθαι
] . ν ἀνθρωπ[. . π]εδέχην δ' ἄραςθαι

col. ii   desunt v uel ix uersus

?προς[

——]

ὠςδ[

30   . .] . [?
.] . [.]ωλ . [
τ' ἐξ ἀιδοκή[

——]

9 καλλ[ίποι]ς' Lobel   (ας'τροϊαν)   [ςα: uestigium ex α fortasse cerni potest
10] . : α, ε; de α cf. 20. 4 λαι   κωΰδ[ὲ πα]ῖδος iam e.p., Edmonds   (κῶνδ[. .]ῖ)
11 suppl. Theander (etiam ante πα repertum)   (μνᾶςθ'α)   (ἄγαγ')   12 Κύπρις
huius u. initio e.p., proximi Theander   13 εὔκ]αμπτον Wilamowitz: ἄγν]αμπτον
Schubart: γν]άμπτον Sitzler   14 Ἔρος κ. fere Theander, id quod uestigia ex-
cludunt   ]οη . : ς potius quam ω (cf. 18. 3)   ν]όης[ι]ν Theander: ππ]όης[ι]ν Schubart
15 κἄ]με Lobel: ἄ] με Fraccaroli, spatio breuius;]μ potius quam]ς   ]α potius quam
]ο; ὀν- exspectatum esset (sed cf. 44. 11)   μναι Π¹ in marg.: μνα in textu   16 ς'
οὐ] Agar   (ςας·)   κε e.p.: τε Π¹   17 (ερᾱ)   18 (κᾱμάρ)   19 κἀν
ὄπλοιςι: καὶ πανόπλοις Page   20]μάχεντας Π¹ᵖᶜ:-ες Π¹ᵃᶜ: πεςδο] fere et Rackham
et Vogliano, spatio conuenientius quam ἱππο] quidem (Wilamowitz)   fieri potest
ut carmen hoc uersu terminatum sit   21] . : ν (cf. u. 17 ἔρατον et 18. 1) melius
quam ρ aut ι; non ς; ὄλβιο]ν fere Milne: ἀλλ' ἄρα]ν (cum παῖς]αν ἀνθρώπ[ωι) fere Sitzler
22]α?   (δ'ἄρᾱ)   32 α[Π¹   ἀδοκή[τω uel -ων suppl. e.p. Π² (Vitelli)

28 Sappho

6: fr. 31 Voigt

textum praestat totum [Long.] *Subl.* 10. 2 (1–3); cuius nullus liber auctoritate fruitur nisi P (Parisinus gr. 2036, s. x). quae autem hoc loco scripsit, ea transcribunt plenissime Jahn–Vahlen (1967), 23–4; uide porro Mazzucchi (1992), 28–9. papyrus: P. Flor. apud Manfredi (1965) (s. p. C. iii), operis soluta oratione scripti, quod uu. 11–14 (ἄγρ.) uertit, uu. 14 (χλωρ.)–16 exscribit; imago: Manfredi tab. 1 (2), ex qua contuli papyrum. testes alii: uu. 1–16 cf. Catull. 51. 1–12; 1–2 Apoll. Dysc. *Pron.* 75a, cf. Apoll. Dysc. *Pron.* 106a in marg. (uide infra); 7–16 cf. Plut. *Mor.* 763 A, *Demetr.* 38. 4; 7 Plut. *Mor.* 763 A (ὥc); 9–10 Plut. *Mor.* 81 D (cum *Anecd. Par.* Cramer i. 399); 13 *Epimer. Hom.* ι 14 (ii. 377 Dyck) (codicem hoc loco inspexi (195ʳ)).

φαίνεταί μοι κῆνος ἴcος θέοιcιν
ἔμμεν' ὤνηρ ὄττιc ἐνάντιόc τοι
ἰcδάνει καὶ πλάcιον ἆδυ φωνεί-
cαc ὑπακούει

⟨——⟩

5 καὶ γελαίcαc ἰμέροεν· τό μ' ἦ μάν
καρδίαν ἐν cτήθεcιν ἐπτόαιcεν.
ὡc γὰρ ⟨ἔc⟩ c' ἴδω βρόχε', ὥc με φώνηc·
οὐδὲν ἔτ' εἴκει·

⟨——⟩

ἀλλὰ κὰμ μὲν γλῶccα †ἔαγε†, λέπτον
10 δ' αὔτικα χροῒ πῦρ ὑπαδεδρόμακεν,

6. [Long.]: (ἡ Cαπφὼ) τὰ ἄκρα αὐτῶν (h.e. τῶν cυμβαινόντων ταῖc ἐρωτικαῖc μανίαιc παθημάτων) καὶ ὑπερτεταμένα δεινὴ καὶ ἐκλέξαι καὶ εἰc ἄλληλα cυνδῆcαι· φαίνεται—πένητα. οὐ θαυμάζειc...; κτλ.   1–2 Apoll.: Αἰολεῖc κῆνοc· φαίν.–ὤνηρ Cαπφώ   1 μοι: Fοι Ahrens, ex Apoll. Dysc. *Pron.* 106a (οἱ Αἰολεῖc cὺν τῶι F· φαίνεταί Fοι κῆνοc Cαπφώ, ubi A (A¹, ut uid.) in marg. φαίνεταί μοι κῆνοc; Lobel autem et Page, et Voigt, φ. F. κ. pro fragmento habent nouo (165)   θεοιc Apoll.   2 τοι Portus: τὸ P: τε | τ' coni. Page   3 φωνείcαc Neue: -φων· cαῖc P   5 γελαίcαc Buttmann: γελᾶιc Pᵃᶜ, γελᾶc Pᵖᶜ   τό μ' ἦ μάν Lobel: τὸ μὴ ἐμάν P: τὸ δή μοι Privitera (δῆμοι maluit Hutchinson): τὸ δὴ ἔμαν Ahrens: τό μοι μὰν amicus Döderleinii   6 cτήθεcιν Portus: -εccιν P ἐπτόαιcεν Hunt: -αcεν P   7 ⟨ἔc⟩ c' ἴδω fere Ahrens: ⟨εἰ⟩cίδω Beattie   φώνηc· Lobel: φωνὰc P: φώναιc' Danielsson   8 ἔτ' εἴκει: ἔτ' ἴκει Toup: ἔπηκεν Gallavotti   9–10 Plut. *Mor.* 81 D: νέωι δὲ ἀνδρὶ γευcαμένωι προκοπῆc ἀληθοῦc ἐν φιλοcοφίαι τὰ Cαπφικὰ ταυτὶ παρέπεται, κατὰ–ὑπ., ἀθόρυβον δὲ κτλ.   9 κὰμ fere Portus: κᾶν P (ἀλλ' ἄκαν fere Boivin): κατὰ Plut.   γλῶccα ἔαγε P: γλῶccά γε Plutarchi codd.: γλῶccαν γε Anecd. (cf. praeterea Cat. 51. 9 *lingua sed torpet*): γλῶccα πέπαγε fere Barnes: γλῶccά μ' ἔαγε Sitzler: γλῶcc' ἀπέαγε Beattie: γλῶcca cέcαγε coni. Gallavotti: γλ. γέγακε (cum ἄκαν) coni. Page   λέπτον: λοπ⟨ ⟩ Anecd.   10 δ' om. Plut. χροῒ Blomfield: χρῶι fere P, Plut.   ὑπαδεδρόμακεν fere P: ὑποδεδρόμαικε Plutarchi codd.: -δρομεν Anecd.: ὑπαδεδρόμηκεν Wilamowitz

ὀππάτεϲϲι δ' οὐδὲν ὄρημμ', ἐπιρρόμ-
βειϲι δ' ἄκουαι,

⟨——⟩

†έκαδε μ' ἴδρωϲ ψῦχροϲ κακχέεται†, τρόμοϲ δέ
παῖϲαν ἄγρει,, χλωροτέ‚ρα δὲ π‚οίαϲ
15 ἔμμι, τεθ‚νάκην δ' ὀ‚λίγω 'πιδε‚ύηϲ
φα‚ίνομ' ἔμ' αὔτ‚αι.

⟨——⟩

ἀλλὰ πὰν τόλματον, ἐπεὶ †καὶ πένητα† ...

Π col. ii. 1–5:

με ὁ βόνβοϲ ὁ ἰλ[
ὤτων καὶ ὁ τρόμ[οϲ
τοῦ ϲώματοϲ κα[
καὶ μετὰ ταῦτα τ[
5 φηϲιν· χλωροτέ[ρα δὲ κτλ.

7: fr. 96 Voigt

papyrus (seu potius codex ex membrana factus): P. Berol. 9722 (s. p. C. vii). imagines: Schubart (1902), tab. 1 (uu. 1–20 tantum); Vogliano (1942), 114; nouas imagines et uu. 1–35 et reliqui codicis beneuole ad me miserunt W. Brashear et D. Yatromanolakis. imagines tamen et nouas et ueteres, ut difficile sine dubio fuit facere, ita difficile est saepe legere; quam ob rem qui ipsum uiderunt codicem, eos in obscuris quibusdam tamquam duces sequi cogor.

11–12 ὀππάτεϲϲι Voss: -εϲι P   ὄρημμ' Hoffmann: ὀρῆ μὴ P   ἐπιρρόμβειϲι: ἐπιβρόμειϲι Bergk; cf. Π col. ii. 1 (u. infra)   ἄκουαι fere Robortello: ἄκουε P   13 Epimer.: ἴδρώϲ· τοῦτο παρ' Αἰολεῦϲιν θηλυκῶϲ λέγεται. ἀναδέχεται κλίϲιν ἀκόλουθον θηλυκῶι γένει· ἀδ.–χέ.   ἔκαδε μ' ἴδρωϲ ψυχρὸϲ κ'ακχέεται P (cf. [Long.] 10. 3 καθ' ὑπεναντιώϲειϲ ἅμα ψύχεται καίεται κτλ.): ἀδέμ' ἴδρώϲ κακὸϲ χέεται Epimer.: κὰδ δέ μ' ἴδρωϲ κακχέεται Schneidewin: κὰδ δέ μ' ἴδρωϲ ψῦχροϲ ἔχει Page (ἐκ δέ κτλ. Privitera): ψύχροϲ ἴδρωϲ κάκχέεται Stark: ἐκ δέ μ' ἴδρωϲ ψῦχροϲ P   τε[,]ο‚ιαϲ Π   15]λιγω Π   'πιδεύηϲ Hermann: ἐπιδε[Πᵖᶜ: δ' ἐπιδε[Πᵃᶜ: πιδεύϲην P: 'πιδεύην Ahrens   16]‚ιν, τ[Π   φα]ινομ' ἔμ' αὔτ[αι Π (suppl. e.p. (Manfredi)): φαίνομαι P   17 ἐπεὶ [| καὶ πένητα Vahlen: ἐπεί κεν εἴη {τα} Mazzucchi

30   *Sappho*

. . . . .

              ] Ϲαρδ .[. .]
         πόλ]λακι τυίδε [ν]ῶν ἔχοιϲα
[―――]
    ὠϲπ .[. . .] .ὠομεν· .[. . .] . .χ[. .]
    ϲε θέα〈ι〉ϲ' ἰκέλαν, Ἀρί-
5   γνωτα, ϲᾶι δὲ μάλιϲτ' ἔχαιρε μόλπαι.

    νῦν δὲ Λύδαιϲιν ἐμπρέπεται γυναί-
    κεϲϲιν, ὠϲ ποτ' ἀελίω
    δύγτοϲ ἀ βροδοδάκτυλοϲ Ϲελάννα,
    〈―――〉
    πάντα περ〈ρ〉έχοιϲ' ἄϲτρα. φάοϲ δ' ἐπί-
10 ϲχει θάλαϲϲαν ἐπ' ἀλμύραν
    ἴϲωϲ καὶ πολυανθέμοιϲ ἀρούραιϲ.

    ἀ δ' 〈ἐ〉έρϲα κάλα κέχυται, τεθά-
    λαιϲι δὲ βρόδα κἄπαλ' ἄν-
    θρυϲκα καὶ μελίλωτοϲ ἀνθεμώδηϲ.
    〈―――〉
15 πόλλα δὲ ζαφοίταιϲ', ἀγάναϲ ἐπι-
    μνάϲθειϲ' Ἄτθιδοϲ, ἱμέρω〈ι〉
    λέπταν ποι φρένα κ[.]ρ. . .βόρηται.
    〈―――〉

---

7. 2 πόλ]λακι Gomperz, Fraccaroli   (τυΐ)   ]ων ἔχοιϲα: illa pars codicis quae haec
continebat hodie, ut D. Yatromanolakis benigne asseuerauit, reperiri non potest.
iusto tamen eam loco stetisse praeclare demonstrant imagines ueteres   3 π . : o
potius quam ε?   ] .ω: ζ parum probabile (ὠϲ πο[τ' ἐ]ζώομεν Blass)   (μεν·)   4–
5 -ϲε Lobel: ϲὲ e.p.   θέα〈ι〉ϲ' Wilamowitz: θέαϲ (non θέαι) Π: θέοιϲ' Maas   (ϊκ)
Ἀρίγνωτα ut nomen proprium Wilamowitz: ἀριγνώταϲ Zuntz: ἀριγνώτα〈ι〉 (cum θέαι
ϲ') Lobel (-α〈ι〉 iam Edmonds)   ϲᾶι Fraccaroli: ϲε Π   (ιϲτ')   6 ἐμπρέπεται: ενπρ-
Π: ἒ]ν πρ. Voigt   7 ὠϲ ὄτ' coni. West   (ποτ')   8 ϲελάννα e.p. (Schubart):
μήνα Π   9 περρέχοιϲ' e.p.: περέχ- Π   11 (ϊϲ)   12 ἀ: κὰδ coni. Page
ἐέρϲα e.p.: ἔρϲα Π   16 ἱμέρω〈ι〉 e.p.   (ϊμ)   17 ποι: Ϝοι Calame   ]ραϲα fere
legit e.p.:]ρ . .ω? Lobel et Page

κῆθι δ' ἔλθην ἀμμ.[..]..ισα τόδ' οὐ
νωντα[..]υστονυμ[..(.)] πόλυς
20 γαρύει [..(.)]αλο.π[.....(.)].ο μέссον.

ε]ὔμαρ[ες μ]ὲν οὐ.α.μι θέαιсι μόρ-
φαν ἐπή[ρατ]ον ἐξίcω-
сθαι cυ[..]ρος ἔχηιcθ' ἀ[..(.)].νιδηον

```
[                    ]το[...(.)]ρατι
25  μαλ[              ].ερος
    καὶ δ[.]μ[         ]ος Ἀφροδίτα
⟨——⟩
    καμ[              ] νέκταρ ἔχευ' ἀπὺ
    χρυсίας [          ].αν
    ...(.)]απουρ[      ] χέρсι Πείθω
[——]
30  [            ]θ[..]ηсενη
    [              ]ακιс
    [              ]εδα...αι
[——]
    [              ]ες τὸ Γεραίстιον
    [              ]. φίλαι
35  [              ]υστον οὐδενο[
[——]
    [              ]ερον ἰξο[μ
         .   .   .
```

18 κῆθι Wilamowitz: κηθυ Π   το potius quam τα   ἀμμ' ἔλπις ἴсα West, breuiora
spatio (τοδ')   19 νῶντ' e.p.: νῶ⟨ι⟩ν Wilamowitz   ἅ[π]υστον e.p.: ἅ[κο]υστον
Theander ὔμ[ην] West   20 αλος aut αλον ὸν] τὸ fere Lobel hoc uersu carmen
finiri nonnulli putant; recte opinor, quamquam non scripta est coronis. pauca igitur
dicentur de eis difficillimis quae sequuntur supplendis et legendis   21 ε]ὔμαρ[ες
Diehl, μ]ὲν Vogliano οὐκ legit Lobel, οὖν Vogliano ἄμμι θέαιсι Page (Lobel et Page
tamen de spatio dubitant): αἰμιθέαιсι Diehl   22 ἐπή[ρατ]ον Lobel   23 (χηсθ')
27 (χευ'?)   36 (ἰξ)

ALCAEUS

8: fr. 129 Voigt (et Lobel–Page)

papyri: P. Oxy. 2165 (s. p. C. ii) fr. 1 col. i. 1–32 =Π¹; 2166 (*c*) (1360) (s. p. C. ii) =
Π². haec in bibliotheca Bodleiana asseruatur (MS Gr. Class. a. 16 (P)), illa in Museo
Ashmoleiano. imago Π¹: P. Oxy. xviii (1941), tab. vi. papyros ipsas contuli. cancellis
dimidiatis (ˌ) ea includuntur quae in una tantum exstant papyro (in Π¹, nisi u. 9
(γ), 11 (δ)). ad u. 21 φύcγων uidentur esse referenda Diog. Laert. 1. 81, *Sud.* c 118,
Hesych. φ 1059. cf. praeterea P. Oxy. 3711 col. ii. 1–30.

>] . ρατα τόδε Λέcβιοˌι
> . .] . . . . ς εὔˌδεˌιˌλον τέμενοˌc μέγα
> ξῦˌνον κάτˌ, ccαˌν· ἐν δὲ βώˌμοιc
> ἀθαˌνάτων, μακάˌρων ἔθηˌκαν.
>
> 5 κἀˌπωνύˌμαccαˌν ἀντίˌαον ˌΔˌία,
> cὲ δ' Αˌἰολήιαν, κυδαˌλίμαˌν θˌέον,
> πάˌνˌτων γενέθλαν· τὸν δὲˌ τέρˌτοˌν
> τονδεκεμήλιονˌ, ὠˌνˌύμαˌccˌ[α]ν
> ⟨——⟩
> Ζόννυccον ὠμήcˌταν. ἄˌχˌ[ˌι]ˌτ', εὔνοοˌν
> 10 θῦμον cκέθοντεˌc ἀμμετˌέρᾳ[c] ἄραc

---

8. 1 Ἥρα, τᾶ⟨ι⟩ fere Gallavotti; ηρα uestigiis conueniat   (ἀτἀτόδελέc Π¹)   2 (ἐν
Π¹)   τέμενος Π¹ᵖᶜ: -ονc Π¹ᵃᶜ   3 ξυ Π²   (ξῦ Π¹)   ἐccαν Π¹:]ˌcca[Π² (]ˌ : ε, η, ι;
de spatio cf. e.g. 66. 8 ιc, 73. 12 ιc, 76. 9 ηc)   (cαν· Π¹)   (βώ Π¹)   4 ˌτων Π¹
μακα- Π¹ᵖᶜ, μακα[Π²: μανα- Π¹ᵃᶜ   κᾳν Π²   ἔθηκαν: uar. lect. in Σ?   (ἔθηκαν· Π¹)
Π² paragraphum post hunc uersum inserit (neque alibi marginem seruat sinistrum);
Π¹ paragraphos inserit nullos   5 κἀπωννύμαccαν Π¹ᵖᶜ, etiam Π², ut distantia ab
initio uersus uidetur indicare: -ωννμ- Π¹ᵃᶜ   (κἀ(?)πωνν'ν'ύ Π¹)   μαc Π²   ]ˌα Π²
(ἰαονδία· Π¹, ἀον[ˌ]ια· Π²)   6 cε Π²   (cὲ Π¹)   Αἰολήαν West   (λήι Π¹)   κυ
Π¹   ]ᵧθ[Π²   κυδαλίμαν Π¹ᵖᶜ (ι inserto i.l.): -αλμαν Π¹ᵃᶜ   (ἱμανθέ Π¹)   7]ᵧ[Π²
(πάν Π¹)   (αν· Π¹, Π²)   ]ˌτερ[.]ˌν Π²   (τόνδετέ Π¹, τέ Π²)   8 τονδεκεμηλιον:
τόνδε κεμήλιον Π¹ (τόνδεκὲμήλιον; cf. Σ in Π²): τὸν δεκεμήλιον noluit e.p. (Lobel), τὸν
δὲ κεμήλιον considerauit: τὸν Ϲεμελήιον Beattie   μαccˌ[Π¹, μαˌ[. . .]ᵧ Π²   (ωνύ Π¹)
9 (ζόν Π¹)   (μήcταν· Π¹,]ταν· Π²)   αˌ[. .]ˌτ Π¹, αγ[Π²   (ἀγ Π²)   (ἐνύ Π¹)   10 (θῦ
Π¹)   cκέθοντεc Π¹ᵖᶜ: cχέθ- Π¹ᵃᶜ   (ἄ(?)ρᾶc Π¹)

ἀκούσατ᾽, ἐκ δὲ τῶ₁ν₁δ₁ε μόχθων
₁ἀργαλέας τε φύγας ς[
⟨——⟩
τὸν Ὕρραον δὲ παῖδα₁ πεδελθε̣έτω
κήνων Ἐρ[ίνν]υς, ὤς πο₁τ᾽ ἀπώμ̣νυ̣μεν,
15   τόμοντες ἄ.φ[᾽.]ν..ν̣
₁μηδάμα μηδένα τὼν ἑταίρων,
⟨——⟩
ἀλλ᾽ ἢ θάνοντες γᾶν ἐπιέμμε̣νοι
κείςεςθ᾽ ὐπ᾽ ἄνδρων οἳ τότ᾽ ἐπικ.᾽ην,
ἤπειτα κακκτάνοντες αὔτοις
20   δᾶμον ὐπὲξ ἀχέων ῥύεςθαι.
⟨——⟩
κήνων ὁ φύςγων οὐ διελέξατο
πρὸς θῦμον, ἀλλὰ βραϊδίως πόςιν
ἔ]μβαις ἐπ᾽ ὀρκίοιςι δάπτει
₁τὰν πόλιν ἄμμι δέδ[.]..[.]ε̣ίπαις
⟨——⟩
25   οὐ κὰν νόμον [..]..ε̣.[   ].᾽[ ]
γλαύκας α[.]..[.]..[

11 (τ᾽ἐκδετῶ Π¹)   υ[.]εμ̣οχθ̣ Π¹,]υδεμο[Π²; super o, fortasse ᾽τ᾽ Π¹   12 (λέ
Π¹)   (φύ Π¹)   ς[Π¹ᵖᶜ (aut ᾽ς[aut ᾽ε[s.l.): ρ[Π¹ᵃᶜ: ς[ἀωτε suppl. e.p. ut uariam
lectionem, ρ̣[ύεςθε i.l.; hoc accepit in textum   13 (ὕρρ Π¹)   πεδελθέτω Π¹ (paene
nihil restat ex τ)   14 (κή Π¹)   (ὤς Π¹)   (τ᾽ Π²)   μ̣[..]μεν Π²; -εν Π¹ᶜ⁽ᵐᵃⁿ·²⁾,
Π²ᶜ⁽ᵐᵃⁿ·²⁾   (ὤμ Π¹)   15 (τόμ Π¹)   αμφ? e.p.; et spatium et φ placent   (ά..[
Π¹)   υ | et Π¹ (cf. 130 a. 11) et Π² hic deficit Π²   16 (δά)   (δένατὼν)
17 (αλλ᾽ἠθά)   (γᾶ)   (έμμ)   18 (κείςεςθ᾽υπάν)   (οι,τοτ᾽έ)   ante ην, fortasse υ;
Lobel et Page adducunt P. Oxy. 2166 (c) (1360 = Π²) fr. 26, quod ex hoc loco fortasse sit
profectum:
                         ]α[
                         ].μ[
                         ].ικα[

(u. 3 .ι potius quam υ; πι legi possit). in Π¹ tamen a post κ haud bene legatur
19 (ήπ)   (κάκκτά)   (αύ)   20 (δᾶ)   (ὐπὲξαχέ)   ῥύεςθαι Π¹ᵃᶜ (᾽ρ᾽ s.l.): λύεςθαι
Π¹ᵃᶜ   (ύεςθαι᾽)   21 Diog. φύςκωνα δὲ (sc. Πιττακὸν Ἀλκαῖος ἀποκαλεῖ) καὶ γάςτρωνα
ὅτι παχὺς ἦν   φύςγων: φύςκ- fere Diog., Suda, Hesych. (cf. 130 b [9]. 2 = 17, 6 = 21?)
(κήνων,ο,φύ)   (λέξ)   22 (θῦμον᾽αλλα,βραῖδίωςπό)   23 ἔ]μβαις:]ν- Π¹   (νβ)
(κί)   (δά)   24 (άμ)   (δέδ)   ειπαις (εἴπᾱις᾽) Π¹ᵖᶜ: ειπαι (εἴπᾱι) Π¹ᵃᶜ. ε probabile;
π potius quam τ, ut spatium monstrat; ς (et ᾽) manus altera i.l. addidit. π[ολ]ίταις
igitur (Gallavotti) excludi potest; δό[λοι]ς π̣[ρο]ε̣ίπαις Kamerbeek, ubi δόλοις falsum
est, προ- spatio non bene conuenit, participium autem εἴπαις, ut se animo obuiam
profert, ita secum ducit difficultates   25 κὰν νόμον Π¹ᵖᶜ: κανο- Π¹ᵃᶜ (ου,κὰν᾽ν᾽ό)
]ον, fortasse; aliquid super ᾽o᾽ scriptum est   26 (γλάν)   Ἀ[θ]αν[ά]ας fere Diehl,
quod optime cum uestigiis congruere uidetur

34   *Alcaeus*

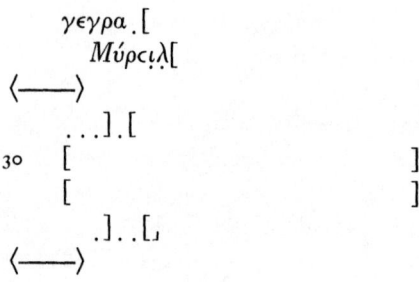

γεγρα.[
Μύρcιλ[
⟨——⟩
...].[
30   [   ]
       [   ]
     .].. [.
⟨——⟩

scholia scripta in margine papyrorum: Π¹ u. 4 . εθηκα (κᾱ (?)); Π² u. 5]ιον
ἰκέcιον, u. 7 ἀν(τὶ τοῦ) τρίτον, u. 8]κεμηλιον

9: fr. 130 b Voigt (130. 16–39 Lobel–Page)

papyri: P. Oxy. 2165 (s. p. C. ii) fr. 1 col. ii. 9–32 (cum fr. 2 col. ii. 1)=Π¹; Π²=P.
Oxy. 3711 (s. p. C. ii), docti cuiusdam operis liber, commentarii fortasse in Alcaeum,
quod opus in fr. 1 ii. 31–7 uersus 9–11 =24–6 (ὡc–πόλεμον) ideo exhibet ut enucleet.
imagines: Π¹, P. Oxy. xviii (1941), tab. vi; Π², P. Oxy. liii (1986), tab. x. papyros
ipsas contuli. cancellis dimidiatis (ˌ ˌ) saepiuntur ea quae in una sola papyro exstant
(in Π¹, nisi in u. 11 (γων)). testimonia: u. 6 (τωνδέων) *Epimer. Hom.* κ 155 (ii. 454
Dyck) (codicem ipsum hoc loco (205ʳ) inspexi); u. 10 (λυκαιχμίαιc) Hesych. λ 1369
(H (=Marc. gr. 622, s. xv) cum r (Vat. gr. 23, antistoecharii ex Hesychio aucti codice,
s. x)).

     ˌἄγνοc τοὶ̣c βιότοιc . . (ˌ)ιc ὀ τάλαιc ἔγω
     ζώω μοῖραν ἔχων ἀγροϊωτίκαν,
     ἰμέρρων ἀγόραc ἄκουcαι
     καρυ̣[ζ]ο̣μέναc, ὦ Ἀγεcιλαΐδα,
     ⟨——⟩

27 π[? (γρᾰ?)   28 (μύ)   32 coronis   **9.** numeros uersuum
hunc ad modum scribimus: 1 [Voigt] = 16 [Lobel–Page]. 130 a enim ab hoc carmine
segregauit Gallavotti, rectissime uero, ut metrum comprobat; non tamen scripta est
coronis. ultimos autem uersus illius exscribemus carminis: περ .[.]...[. .].ενκ.υθυ
καταccάτω· | αυτο.[....]ε καππέτων | ἐχέπ[. .].[.]α τεῖχοc βαcιλήϊον (Σ: τὸ τῆc "Ηραc)
1 = 16 ἄγνοc Π¹ᵖᶜ: ἀγνοιc Π¹ᵃᶜ; super α, λί(?) sscr.   τοὶc legit Burzacchini   ἄλγεινον
βίοτον νῦν coni. Rösler   (βιό)   post βιότοιc τ uel π, ut uidetur; ante ι, aliquid s.l.,
e.g. ˈˈ; παῖc legit Gallavotti; ne τλᾶιc quidem debet excludi   (τάλᾱᾱιcέ)   2 =
17 (ζώ)   ἀγροϊωτίκαν e.p.: ἀκροΐκω- Π¹   (ἀκροϊκωτίκᾰν (post ν macula; ν· legit e.p.))
3 = 18 (ὀρᾱcᾰ)   4 = 19 (κᾱ)   (μέναcὼ'γ)   (ἰδᾱ)

5=20   καὶ β[ό]λλας. τὰ πάτηρ καὶ πάτερος πάτηρ
       καγγεγήρας' ἔχοντες πεδὰ τωνδέων
       τὼν ἀλλαλοκάκων πολίταν,
       ἔγω[γ'] ἀπὺ τούτων ἀπελήλαμαι
       〈——〉
       φεύγων ἐσχατίαις'.」 ὡς δ' Ὀνυμακλέης
10=25 Ὠθάναος ἐοίκησα λυκαιχμίαις,
       φεύγων」 τ¡ὸν」 πό¡λ¡εμον. ¡στάσιν γάρ
       πρὸς κρ.[....]ς †οὐκ ἄμεινον† ὀννέλην.
       〈——〉
       .].[...]τ[..]. μακάρων ἐς τέμ[ε]νος θέων
       ἐοίκης[α] μελαίνας ἐπίβαις χθόνος
15=30 .λι.[.].[.].[.]. συνόδοισί μ' αὔταις
       οἴκημ⟨μ⟩ι κάκων ἔκτος ἔχων πόδας·
       〈——〉
       ὄππαι Λε[σβί]αδες κριννόμεναι φύαν
       πώλεντ' ἐλκεσίπεπλοι. περὶ δὲ βρέμει
       ἄχω θεσπεσία γυναίκων
20=35 ἴρα[ς ὀ]λολύγας ἐνιαυσίας
       〈——〉

5=20 (ασ·τᾱπά)   (πά)   (πά)   6=21 Epimer.: . . . Ἀλκαῖος φησι "τῶνδεων",
ὅπερ τινὲς ἀγνοίαι τἀκριβοῦς ἀνέγνωσαν "τῶνδε⟨ν⟩ων", ἵν' ἦι τῶν δείν⟨ων⟩   καγγέγηρας'
e.p.: κακ- Π¹   (ἀσέ)   (ἐδατὼν,δέων)   7=22 (ἀλλοκά) πολίταν Π¹ᵖᶜ (ε deleto;
τ uetere in ι mutato, τ nouo inserto?): πολεταν Π¹ᵃᶜ (πολῖτᾱν)   8=23 ἔγω[γ']
fere Page (cf. γω in 129 [8]. 21)   (έγ)   (τόντωνἀπελή)   9=24 ἐσχατίαις',
quod in Π¹ esset, e.p. (ἴαις·, ut uid., re uera Π¹)   ὡςδ Π²   φεύγων. ἐσχατίαις δ'
ὡς Hutchinson   (ως,δὀνὐμακλέ Π¹)   10=25 Hesych. λυκαιχμίας· ὁ λυκόβροτος
Ὠθάναος: ωθαναιος Π¹ (legit e.p. Π² (Haslam); ἔνθα[δ'] οἷος legerant Lobel et Page):
ωθαναος Π² (ὠθᾱ Π¹)   εοικησα Π², εοικησα Π¹   (ἐόι Π¹)   λυκαιχμίαις: λυκαιχμιαις
Π¹ᵖᶜ, Π²: -αιμιαις Π¹ᵃᶜ: -αιχμίας Hesych. in r, -αιχλίας Hesychii H   (λὐκἀίχμἴᾱις Π¹)
11=26 φευ[...]τονπολεμον Π¹: φευγωντ[..] | πο[.]εμον Π²; φεύγων coniecerat Diehl
(στά Π¹)   12=27 κ potius quam χ   κρέ[εσονα]ς recte reiecit e.p., propter
et tertiam litteram et spatium   οὐκ ἄμεινον· οὐ κέρδιον coni. e.p.: οὐ κάλλιον Page
ὀννέλην; Hutchinson   (ἀμεινονὀννέλην·)   13=28 (τέ θέ)   14=29 ἐοί[κησα
noluit Page; e κης parua tantum uestigia   ἐπίβαις Π¹ᵖᶜ (ι inserto i.l.): αεπιβας Π¹ᵃᶜ
(ἀινᾱς[[α]]επίβαισχθό)   15=30 aut κλ aut χλ   (λῐ) ante συ, η potius quam ν
(σὐνό)   μ' αὔταις Π¹ᵖᶜ(ᵐᵃⁿ·ᵃˡⁱᵃ) (τ del., μ sscr.): ταύταις Π¹ᵃᶜ; -ν pro μ' coni. Page   (ἀυτ)
16=31 οἴκημ⟨μ⟩ι e.p.: -ημι Π¹   (όι)   (κάκωνέ)   ἔχων Π¹ᵖᶜ(ᵐᵃⁿ·ᵃˡⁱᵃ): ἔων (έων) Π¹ᵃᶜ
(δας·)   17=32 (ὄππᾱι) (ἀδ)   κριννόμεναι Π¹ᵖᶜ (ὀ): -αμεναι Π¹ᵃᶜ   (φὐᾱν)   18=
33 (πώ·)   (σί)   (οι·πέ)   (βρέ)   19=34 ἄχω e.p.: αλχω (ἀλχω) Π¹   (σίᾱγυναίκ)
20=35 (ῖρ)   (ὔγ)   (σίας)

].[.'].[.]ν ἄπυ πόλλων πότα δὴ θέοι
].[']ϲκ...ν....πιοι;
          ].....
.να[   ]...μεν

schol. uel sim. in uu. 9–11 (Π²):

          Αἶνοϲ Θραίκηϲ πόλιϲ .
Αἴνου τοῦ Γερωι.[ ].....[
δὲ τὴν Αἶνον Ἀλωπεκον[νήϲιοι
η[..].ουντο δ' ὑπὸ Θραικῶ[ν ..].ε

in marg. u. 10 Π² ζ(ήτει)

10: fr. 298 Voigt (*SLG* 262)

papyri: P. Colon. 2021 (P. Köln 59) (s. p. C. i) = Π¹; P. Oxy. 2303 (s. p. C. i) fr. 1 = Π²,
uu. 15–28 tantum. imagines: Π¹, Merkelbach (1967), tab. i (post p. 161), et van Erp
Taalman Kip (1987), tab. 6 (post p. 40), et http://www.rrz.uni-koeln.de/phil-fak/ifa/
NRWAkademie/Papyrologie/Abbildungen/II 59/PK2021r (mense August. a. 1999
uisebam); Π², P. Oxy. xxi (1951), pl. xi, et van Erp Taalman Kip (1987), tab. 5. Π¹ ex
imaginibus contuli; Π² contuli ipsam. cancellis dimidiatis (ʟ ⌟) ea quae una tantum
praebet papyrus includimus. hoc carmen tangit etiam 306 A h, ex opere de lyricis:
P. Oxy. 2506 (s. p. C. ii), frr. 108 + 84 (quae coniunxit Lloyd-Jones). papyrum ipsam
contuli.

col. i (Π¹)   ⌞]ϲαντας αἰϲχυν[...]τα τὰ μῆνδικα
          ]ην δὲ περβάλοντ' [ἀ]νάγκα
          ].ενι λαβολίωι πα[..]αν.
——]
          .....]. Ἀχαίοιϲ' ἦϲ πόλυ βέλτερον
5   ].ηντ. κατέκτανον

21 = 36 (ἀ(?)πυπόλλων)   πότα: π, non τ   (πότ)   (θέ)   22 = 37 'Ολύμπιοι legit
e.p.   (οι·)   24 = 39 μεν Π¹ᵖᶜ ⁽ᵐᵃⁿ·ᵃˡⁱᵃ⁾: μεϲ Π¹ᵃᶜ   coronis   10. 1 αἰϲχύν[νον]τα τὰ
Lobel: αἰϲχύν[θεν]τα τὰ Page   (ϲχῠ)   μῆνδικα Σ: μημδ- Π¹ᵖᶜ: μηδ- Π¹ᵃᶜ   (τᾰμη͜ν͜δῐκᾱ)
2 (βᾰ)   [ἀν]άγκα (de [ἀν] cf. Σ): [ὀν]άγκαν Luppe, coll. Σ: [ἀν]άγκαι e.p.   (κᾱ)
3 τώμ]φενι Gallavotti, ἄμ]φενι Liberman: αὔ]χενι e.p. (sed χ parum, φ satis probabile)
(ἐνὶ)   λαβολίωι pro adiectiuo habuit Hutchinson; cf. ad Σ   (λᾱ)   πά[χη]αν
Treu: 'πα[λοί]αν Lloyd-Jones, spatio longius   (πᾰ(?)[.]αν·)   [ἀν]άγκα⟨ν⟩ | ἄμ]φενι
λαβολίωι πά[χη]αν ualde arridet   4 καὶ γάρ] κ' Gallavotti: ἦ μάν] κ' Kassel
(αἴοιϲῆϲπολυβἔλτερόν)   5 αἱ φῶτα θεοϲ]ύληντα Treu   (ηντ.)   (κτᾰ)

]....εοντες Αἴγαις

]. ἔτυχον θαλάccαc.

——]

]εν ναύωι Πριάμω πάϊς
Ἀ]θανάας πολυλάϊδος

10] ἐπαππένα γενήω.

δυςμέ]νεες δὲ πόλιν ἔπηπον

——]

]..[..].ας Δαΐφοβόν τ' ἄμα
]ον οἰμώγα δ' ἀ[π]ὺ τείχεος
]ι παίδων ἀΰτα

15]ον, πέδιον κάτ,η,χε.

——]

λ]ύ,cc,αν ἦλθ' ὀλόα,ν, ἔχων
].,.[.].,νας Πάλλαδος, ἃ θέω,ν
].. cι θε,οcύλαιcι πάντων
]ατα μακάρων, πέφυκε.

——]

20].ι δ' ἄμφο,ιν παρθενίκαν ἔλων
]. παρεcτάκο,ιcαν ἀγάλματι

6 πλέοντες probabile; οὕτω κε π]αρπλέοντες Lloyd-Jones (γαῖς) 7].: c potius quam κ ῥαϊτέρα]ς Page (cā) (c·) 8 ἀλλ' ἀ μέν] Page (ναύω) (αἰς) 9]θ̣: cf. e.g. 16, ον 15 (ᾱ̆ςπολυλᾱϊδ) 10 ἐπαππένα Page: ἀπαππένα Π¹ᵖᶜ (ε in a corr.), cf. Σ: ἀπε- Π¹ᵃᶜ: ἐπαμμένα Lobel (ἀππενᾱ) γενήω e.p.: -είω Π¹ 11 (νέες) πόλιν: πόλιν⟨δ'⟩ Lobel: πόλιν ⟨τ'⟩ Page: πόλη' Lloyd-Jones (ἐπῆπὸν) 12 (ᾱc·(?)δᾱϊ) (μᾱ̆) 13 ἔπεφν]ον e.p. ἀ[π]ὺ Lobel, Page 14 ἴκοιcα κα]ὶ Barrett (ἴκανε κα]ὶ malim): ὄρωρε κα]ὶ Page: ἔλαμψε κα]ὶ Lloyd-Jones: ἔνωρτο κα]ὶ Gallavotti (ᾱ̆ΰτᾱ) 15 Δαρδάνι]ον Page, Treu; de spatio u. comm. ad 20].....κατ[.]χε Π² (ex πεδιον (?) nihil exstat nisi pedes litterarum; qui tamen in πεδιον, sim., haud facillime coguntur) (διὸνκᾱτῆ(pro ἦ)χε· Π¹) 16 Αἴας δὲ λ] e.p. Π¹]υccαν Π¹;]υ[..]ανηλ Π² (ad cc spatium sufficit: sinister enim ramulus, ut ita dicam, papyri dextero trunco hic propius admotus est) (cᾱνῆ Π¹) (οᾱ[.]ε Π² (οᾱν Π¹; ἐχ Π²) 17 .[.].νας Π¹ (primum uestigium, quod alte stat, pars accentus potest esse; uix pars ν, a):].. [. .'].ας Π²; εἰς ἰρ]ον [ἄ]γναις fere Gallavotti: ἐς ναύ]ον [ἄ]γναις fere Page, Kassel; ον[α]γν tamen hiatui in Π² male accommodentur (νᾱc Π¹) παλλα[.]οcαθεω[Π² (ᾱδὸcᾱ Π¹; ἄλλα[.]οc·ᾱ Π²) 18 ἄνδρ]εccι fere e.p., θνάτ]οιcι fere Page]οcυ Π¹ (οcυλᾱι Π¹; cύ Π²) ϙαντων Π² (πᾱ Π²) 19]ατα μακαρων πεφυκε Π²:].ατα πεφυκε Π¹, quae μακάρων non omisit, fortasse transtulit; δεινο]τᾱτα μ. π. Gallavotti; αἰνο]τᾱτα Page (τᾱ πεφυκε Π¹; κά, κε. Π²) 20 χέρρες]cι Page, Treu: ἐν χέρ[cι West (δ'α Π²)]ιν Π¹ (ἰν? Π¹) εν Π² (ᾱνελὼν Π¹; ἱκᾱ Π²) 21]ιcαν Π¹ᵖᶜ (ι, a sscr.):]αcιν Π¹ᵃᶜ (τᾱκοι Π²) (ἀλ Π²)

] ὀ Λόκρος οὐδ' ἔδ,ειϲε
] . οϲ πολέμω δοτέ⟨ρ⟩,ραν
——]

]δε δεῖνον ὐπ' [ὄ],φρυϲι

col. ii (Π¹)   cμ,[   ]ι. δνώθειϲα κατ' οἴνοπα
26   .. [.] .,[   ]ι.. ἐκ δ' ἀφάντοι[ϲ
ἐξαπ,[   ]ι.. ἐκύκα θυέλλαιϲ.

αιδη .,[   ],φ[
ἴραιϲ .[
30   Αἴαϲ αχ .[
ἀνδροϲ[

.. μ .[
... ρ .[
ἔβαϲκε[
35   παννυχια[

22 ἔρυϲϲ'] e.p. Π¹, Kassel: ἔξηλκ'] West (ἤλκηϲ' malim): ὔβριϲϲ'] Page   ἔδειϲε Π²:]ειϲε
Π¹   (οὐδ'ἐ Π²; ` ......]ἐὶ Π¹)   23 παῖδα Δ]ίοϲ Page: τὰν βάρ]εοϲ West, sed
propter interuallum ante 'o' angustum ε (uel ρ) minus bene legatur   δοτέ⟨ρ⟩,ραν e.p.
Π² (Lobel): δοτε, αν Π²:] ,αν Π¹   (ἐμωδό Π²; ἄν Π¹)   24–36: 25–31 in Π¹ ut
adulterini obelis notantur; uersui 24 autem sinister deficit margo. nisi obeli potius
indicant uersus locum alienum occupare, quod ueri minus simile est, sumendum
est aut 24–31 in ambabus papyris eodem loco stetisse aut 25–32 in Π² esse omissos.
sin 25–32 sunt omissi, ut Fowler opinabatur olim, tum 33–6 initia supplent eis iv
uersibus qui in Π² ultimi exstant, hunc in modum: κατ' οἴνοπα | ἔβαϲκε [πόντο]ν, ἐκ δ'
ἀφάντοι[ϲ | παννυχίοιϲ ἐκύκα θυέλλαιϲ. | πρωτοι .[... .]φ. sed hoc potius putandum est,
Π¹ initia, Π² fines uersuum 24–7 praebere; 24–31 suspicor re uera esse adulterinos.
Rösler tamen 25–31 aliquo ante ι transtulit   24–6 fragmentum ex Π² accedit
aliud ((b)),]να[| .] . . [|] . .[; quod primo ((a)) posse adiungi sinistra perspexit e.p.
24]ν· ἀ δέ, (b) modo addito, considerauit e.p. (ν·ᾱ Π² (b))   υπ[.]φρυϲιν Π²:]φρυϲι
Π¹   (ρὺ Π¹)   25 cμ[Π¹,] . . δ κτλ. Π²   cμ[έρδνα Tarditi: cμ[έρδνον e.p. Π¹: cμ[οίωϲ
Lloyd-Jones   π[ε]λ[ι]δνώθειϲα e.p. Π². Π², (b) addito; sed ante δ uestigium quod, nisi
quid fortuiti est, ε tribui possit, ι non possit; λ nimis alte iacere uideatur (φ possit
esse?)   in (b) ante 'π' fortasse ς potius quam ą aut ν   (τ'όι Π²)   26 .. [.] .
(fortasse ą .[) Π¹,] ,εκ κτλ. Π²   ą̈ξ[ε e.p. Π¹   πό]ν̣τ̣[ον] e.p., addito (b)   ,εκ:
punctum tantum, quod ν possit esse; κ planum, paene aeque planum ε   ἐκ: e.g. cὺν
coni. Hutchinson (εκ ε 27?)   ἀφάντω Barner, illicito hiatu   (δ'αφά Π²)   27 εξαπ[
Π¹,] ,εκυ κτλ. Π²   ἐξαπ[ίν]ąϲ e.p. Π¹   (ὑκαθύ(?)έλλαιϲ· Π²)   28 αιδη .[Π¹,]φ[
κτλ. Π²   (αἰδή Π¹)   hoc uersu cessat Π²   29 (ῑραῖ)   30 (ἀιᾱϲ·(?))   Ἀχą[ι
e.p.   31 (ρὸ .[`.`]; accentuum autem secundus reapse super .[positus est; post
interuallum acc., uel sim., tertius)   34 (βᾰ)   35 ą[potius quam ọ[

πρῶτοι.[

δεινα..[

ἄϊξε πόν[

ὦρϲε βια[

___

40   ....ιϲε[

πανταπε[

...].ονο.[

δ[.]..ροϲενο[

___

.υ..δεκαμ[

45 ζώει μενω.[

αταν βροτ.[

ὦ υρραδον.[

⟨——⟩

ἐπε. κελητο[

.....ωπ[

.

scholia: in Π¹, supra col. i,]πόλεμοϲ |].ντι (quae ad priorem columnam potius referenda sunt); u. 1 μήνδικα τὰ μὴ ἔ[νδικα, τ]ὰ μὴ ἔ[ν δίκη⟨ι⟩ κε[ί]μενα; 2 τὴν ἀγχόνην· | οὕτωϲ εἴρη|κε δεϲμὸν τὴν ἀνάγκ|ην; 3 λε[υ]ϲ.ω⟨ι⟩ (λε[υ]ϲμῶ⟨ι⟩ e.p.; sed λε[υ]ϲτῶ⟨ι⟩ quoque legi possit, ut uidetur); 5 θεοϲύλη(ν) ὄντα; 10 ἀφημμένη; infra col. i haec:

]μέλοντο δὲ ἕνεκεν [..]ν

].ι τὴν πόλιν και[

].ουα.ορ° ἐπιλεγομεν[

].χάριν ἀνδρὸϲ οϲ[

in Π², u. 25 (aut 26) litterae paucae ex scholio trium (aut quattuor) uersuum

37 fortasse κ[38 (ᾱϊξε)   41 (τᾱ)   42].: τ, π   43 (οϲ.) 44 init. ο potius quam δ?   post υ δ, λ   οὐδ' ὧδε legit Snell   (ᾱ (?))   45 μὲν ὦν[ηρ e.p.   46 (ἄτᾱν)   47 Ὑρράδ⟨ι⟩ον Lloyd-Jones: Ὕρραδ' interpretatus est Gallavotti   (ὑρρᾰ)   48 κέλητο[ϲ e.p.   49 finis uersus scholii locum initii uersus carminis, ut uidetur, usurpat   Σ: emendauit e.p. Π¹ (u. 5 tamen ita Kassel); ὅροϲ interpretatus est Lloyd-Jones

fr. 306 A h:

```
            . .
          ]πι[
          ]νο[
          ]εποι . [
        ] . . . αι . . [
   5    ]λλα καὶ τ . . ὑπὸ τῶν[
        Αἴ]αντα κατη⟨ι⟩τιαμένο[ν
        ]α [ἐ]πὶ τῆι Κασσάνδρα[ι
        ]καὶ γὰ[ρ] αὐτ[. . .] . γαλ . [
        ]αιπραιτ[
  10    ]ροτετ[
        ]αρελθω[
        ]ης Ἀθην[
        ] . ρινακ . ατ[
        ]σποιηται[
  15    ]ναι τὸν ἐρω[
            .   .   .
```

IBYCUS

11: *PMGF* S151

papyrus: P. Oxy. 1790 frr. 1–3, 10, 12 (s. a. C. i; frr. 10 et 12 inseruit Cockle); imagines: P. Oxy. xv (1922) tab. iii (uu. 41–8 tantum); Barron (1969), tabb. v et vi; Turner (1987), 48–9 (uu. 41–8 tantum). papyrum ipsam contuli.

col. i   . . .]αι Δαρδανίδα Πριάμοιο μέ-   ant.
            γ' ἄς]τυ περικλεὲς ὄλβιον ἠνάρον
          . . .]οθεν ὀρνυμένοι
         . .] . ος μεγάλοιο βουλαῖς

     ⟨——⟩

fr. 306 A h. 6–8 suppleuit emendauitque Lloyd-Jones   8 αὐτ[ὴν τῶι] ἀγάλμ[ατι fere Lloyd-Jones; ηντωι tamen spatio sunt longiora, μ non scriptum est   9 aliquid simile ϲ super τ scriptum est (uersus difficilis est; πραιοτ[?)   **11.** Π nullos paragraphos scripsit nisi carminis fine   1 (μέ)   2 (νάρ)   3 Ἄργ]οθεν e.p. (Hunt)   4 Ζη]νὸς e.p.; de ν tamen dubitari potest

5   ξα]νθᾶς Ἑλένας περὶ εἴδει   ep.
    δῆ]ριν πολύυμνον ἔχ[ο]ντες
    πό]λεμον κατὰ δακρ[υό]εντα.
    Πέρ]γαμον δ' ἀνέ[β]α ταλαπείριο[ν ἄ]τα
    χρυ]σοέθειραν δ[ι]ὰ Κύπριδα.
    ⟨═══⟩

10 ..]. δέ μοι οὔτε ξειναπάταν Π[άρι]ν   str.
    ..] ἐπιθύμιον οὔτε τανίσφυρ[ον
    ὑμ]νῆν Κασσάνδραν
    Πρι]άμοιό τε παῖδας ἄλλου[ς
    ⟨───⟩

    Τρο]ίας θ' ὑψιπύλοιο ἀλώσι[μο]ν   ant.
15 ἄμ]αρ ἀνώνυμον· οὐδεπ[
    ἠρ]ώων ἀρετὰν
    ὑπ]εράφανον οὕς τε κοίλα[ι
    ⟨───⟩

    ...] πολυγόμφοι ἐλεύσα[ν   ep.
    Τροί]αι κακόν, ἤρωας ἐσθ[λούς.
20 τῶν] μὲν κρείων Ἀγαμέ[μνων
col. ii [ἆ]ρχε Πλεισθε[νί]δας βασιλ[εὺ]ς ἀγὸς ἀνδρῶν
    Ἀτρέος ἐσθ[λο.] πάις ἔκγ[ο]νος.
    ⟨═══⟩

    καὶ τὰ μὲν ἂ[ν] Μοίσαι σεσοφι[σ]μέναι   str.
    εὖ Ἑλικωνίδε[ς] †ἐμβαίεν λόγω[ι·
25 θνατὸς δ' οὔ κ[ε]ν ἀνὴρ
    διερ.[......].† τὰ ἔκαστα εἴποι,
    ⟨───⟩

    ναῶν ο[.... ἀρι]θμὸς ἀπ' Αὐλίδος   ant.
    Αἰγαῖον διὰ [πό]ντον ἀπ' Ἄργεος

5 (θᾶς) (ἐιδεῖ)   9 (δα·)   10 νῦ]ν e.p.   (όυ)   (πάτ)   11 ἧς] Wilamowitz,
id quod spatio est multo aptius quam ἔcτ'] (Maas)   12 (νῆν)   14 ἀλώσι[μο]ν
Maas   15 ἄμ]αρ Wilamowitz: οὔκ] ἄρ' e.p.   (ώνυμον·)   οὐδ' ἐπ[ελεύσομαι
Wilamowitz   17 (ὄυστεκοί)   18 νᾶες] e.p., procul dubio ut poeta uoluit;
spatio tamen uerbum non conuenit   (γόμφοιελεύ)   19 (ᾶι)   21 (˘ super [α]
exstat)   22 ἐσθ[λὸς] Barron, quod spatio paulo melius conuenit quam -ού e.p.)
(ἀΐς, ut uid. (cf. 24))   ἔκγ[ο]νος Barron (νός·)   23 (μοί)   (μέναι)   24 λόγω[ι:
πόδα Murray   (εὐέλικωνίδε[.]εμβαίεν)   25 θνατὸς: αὐτὸς West   26 (δῖ?)
27 (ὢν)   ὄ[σσος] Barron   ἐπ' Αὐλίδος Woodbury   (λί)   28 (γαῖ)   ἀπ' Ἄργεος
e u. 36 illatum esse coni. Hutchinson

30

ἠλύθο[ν ἐc Τροία]ν
ἱπποτρόφο[ν, ἐν δ]ὲ φῶτεc
⟨——⟩
χ]αλκάcπι[δεc, υἶ]ες Ἀχα[ι]ῶν.   ep.
τ]ῶν μὲν πρ[οφ]ερέcτατος α[ἰ]χμᾶι
....]. πόδ[αc ὠ]κὺc Ἀχιλλεύc
καὶ μέ]γαc Τ[ελαμ]ώνιοc ἄλκιμ[ο]ς̣ [

35   ....]...[.....]λο[.]πυροc.
⟨══⟩
.............]cτοc ἀπ' Ἄργεοc   str.
.... Κυάνι]ππ[ο]c ἐc Ἴλιον
]
].. [.]..ς
⟨——⟩

40   ....]ạ χρυcόcτροφ[οc   ant.
col. iii   Ὕλλιc ἐγήνατο. τῶι δ' [ἄ]ρα Τρωῖλον
ὡcεὶ χρυcὸν ὀρει-
χάλκωι τρὶc ἄπεφθο[ν] ἤδη
⟨——⟩

Τρῶεc Δ[α]ναοί τ' ἐρό[ε]ccαν   ep.
45   μορφὰν μάλ' ἐΐcκọν ὅμοιον.
τοῖc μὲν πεδὰ κάλλεοc αἰέν
καὶ cύ, Πο⟨υ⟩λύκρατεc, κλέοc ἄφθιτον ἑξεῖc,
ὡc κατ' ἀοιδὰν καὶ ἐμὸν κλέοc.
══

schol. ad 37–9:

]ιμαχοc ἐν τῶι περὶ ....ρου φηcί· τὸν [......]ν
]ν τοῦ Κυανίππου· οὕτω λέγε⟨ι⟩ τὸν .[......]ςχα

29 (λύθ) ọ[crederes, potius quam ς[30 ἐν δ]ὲ Barron   31 (ὦν·)
33 ἤνθε]ν̣ (seu ἤλθε]ν) Hutchinson   34 [Αἴαc e.p.   35 (ροc·)   36 κάλλι]cτọc
Barron   37 Κυάνι]ππ[ο]c Barron (cf. Σ)   (ἰλ)   39 καὶ Ζεύξιππος, ὃν] ἁ̣ Barron:
Φοίβωι κυcαμέν]α postea idem Barron, quae breuiora sunt spatio   40 χρυcόcτροφοc
(có) Πᵃᶜ: χρυcεό- Πᵖᶜ, ᵐᵃⁿ·¹; etiam ρ alterum e o uel c corr.   41 (γήν)   42 (ὡc)
ὡcαὶ coni. West   43 (χάλ) (ἄπε) (ἤδ)   44 (ὁιτ'ερό)   45 (μάλεῖc)
(οιον·)   46 τοῖc Πᶜ (aliqua re dum scribitur in ιc correcta)   (πέδ)   (αἰεν·)
47 Πο⟨υ⟩λυ- e.p.   (λύκ)   (ξεῖc)   48 (κλεόc·)   coronis   Σ 1 (ci/)
1–2 [Ἄδραcτο]ν | [πάππο]ν Barron   2 (πουˑ)   λέγε⟨ι⟩ Barron

] . του τὴν γένεϲιν ταύτην ἀναπεπλ[ακέν]αι ὡϲ
]ϲι Αἰγιαλέα τοῦ Ἀδρά[ϲ]του γενόμε[. . . . . .]εϲτρα
5]τοιϲελ[.] . . . . α

ANACREON

12: *PMG* 347 fr. 1 (frr. 71–2 Gentili)

papyrus: P. Oxy. 2322 fr. 1 (s. p. C. ii uel iii in.). imago: P. Oxy. xxii (1954), tab. i.
papyrum ipsam contuli.

καὶ κ[ό]μ[η]ϲ, ἥ τοι κατ᾽ ἁβρόν
ἐϲκία[ζ]εν αὐχένα.

νῦν δὲ δὴ ϲὺ μὲν ϲτολοκρόϲ·
ἡ δ᾽ ἐϲ αὐχμηρὰϲ πεϲοῦϲα
5 χεῖραϲ ἀθρόῃ μέλαιναν
ἐϲ κόνιν κατερρύη,

τλῆμον . ϲ τομῇι ϲιδήρου
περιπεϲοῦϲ᾽. ἐγὼ δ᾽ ἄϲῃιϲι
τείρομαι· τί γάρ τιϲ ἔρξῃι
10 μηδ᾽ ὑπὲρ Θρῄικηϲ τυχών;

οἰκτρὰ δὴ φρονεῖν ἀκου[
τὴν ἀρίγνωτον γυναῖκ[α,

3 ἀναπεπλ[ακέν]αι Handley   4 Ἀδρά[ϲ]του K. F. W. Schmidt   **12.** 1 κ[ό]μ[η]ϲ:
e μ restat, ut uidetur, uestigium pedis sinistri infimi   2 (να.)   3 (λὀκρόϲ)
4 ἐϲ Π^{pc}: ἐϲ τ᾽ Π^{ac}   5 ἀθρόῃ Π^{pc} (ι et fortasse a del., η sscr. inter a et ι): ἀθρόαι Π^{ac}
(νᾶν (?))   7 τλήμον[ο]ϲ, τλημόν[ω]ϲ e.p. (Lobel)   (μῆι)   9 ἔρξηι e.p.: -η Π
10 ὑπὲρ Θρῄικηϲ e.p.: ὑπὲρ Θρηικίηϲ Π^{ac} (ϲ ex ι correctum est): ὑπερθήκηϲ, ut uid., Π^{pc}
(ρ, ι, ι del.; ρ potius deletum quam retractatum est)   11 nouum carmen hoc
loco inceptum noluit e.p.; etsi scripta esset coronis, illam non uideremus   ἀκού[ω
e.p.

πολλάκιc δὲ δὴ τόδ' εἰπ[εῖν
δαίμον' αἰτιωμένͅ[ην·
——]
15   "ὤ]c ἂν εὖ πάθοιμι, μῆτερ,
    ε]ἴ μ' ἀμείλιχον φέρουcα
    π]όντον ἐcβάλοιc θυΐοντα [
    π]ορφυ[ρ]έοιcι κύμαcι[
  ——]
    ].[   ]..[.].. [
     .   .   .

in margine papyri: iuxta u. 2×; 3×

13: *PMG* 358 (fr. 13 Gentili)

textum totum praestat Athen. 599 c–d; u. 3 adfert etiam *Et. Gud.* s.u. μήτι (col.
392. 11–15 Sturz, cf. Gaisford (1848), 448. 29. 'Et. Sorb.' quod uocant codex est *Et.
Gudiani* Paris. suppl. gr. 172; de quo codice uide Cellerini (1988), 14, 25).

cφαίρηι δηὖτέ με πορφυρέηι
βάλλων χρυcοκόμηc Ἔρωc
νήνι ποικιλοcαμβάλωι
cυμπαίζειν προκαλεῖται.
⟨——⟩
5   ἡ δ', ἐcτὶν γὰρ ἀπ' εὐκτίτου
  Λέcβου, τὴν μὲν ἐμὴν κόμην,
  λευκὴ γάρ, καταμέμφεται,
  πρὸc δ' ἄλλην τινὰ χάcκει.
⟨——⟩

15 μῆτερ Π^{pc} (η altero del., ϵ sscr.): μήτηρ Π^{ac}   16 (μ')   17 (θυΐ)   **13** Athen.
Χαμαιλέων δ' [fr. 26 Wehrli] ἐν τῶι περὶ Cαπφοῦc καὶ λέγειν τινάc φηcιν εἰc αὐτὴν πε-
ποιῆcθαι ὑπὸ Ἀνακρέοντοc τάδε· cφαίρηι–χάcκει. καὶ τὴν Cαπφὼ δὲ πρὸc αὐτὸν ταῦτά φηcιν
εἰπεῖν [250, *PMG* 953]· κεῖνον κτλ.   1 δηὖτέ Seidler: δεῦτέ Athen.   πορφυρέηι
Barnes (cf. 347 fr. 1 [**12**]. 18): πορφυρενι Athen.   3 *Et. Gud.* . . . . ἐκεῖθεν νήνιοc
νήνιϊ, καὶ κατὰ κρᾶcιν τῶν δύο ῑῑ εἰc ἓν μακρὸν νήνι, οἷον· νήνι κτλ.   ποικιλοcαμβάλωι
Seidler: ποικίλουc ἀμβάλω *Et. Gud.*: ποικίλοc λαμβάνω Athen.   5 ἀπ' εὐκτίτου
Barnes: ἀπευκτικοῦ Athen.

14: *PMG* 417 (fr. 78 Gentili)

textum exhibet totum Heracl. *Hom. Prob.* 5. 10. praeter O (Oxoniensem bibl. Collegii Noui 298, s. xiv ex.) omnes testes huius partis Heracliti ex M descendunt (Mediolanensi Ambrosiano B-99-sup., s. xiii), qui hodie finem tantum Heraclitei praebet operis. O, quem contuli (144ᵛ), omnino parum sed non nihil ualet (cf. 5. 4 ὀρθόν); in libris reliquis, errores singulorum uix sunt mentione digni. 1–3 τί–φεύγειc praebet excerptio quoque grammatica, in Vat. gr. 12 fol. 99ʳ (uide Bühler (1968), 238); 10 κοῦφα cκιρτ. utitur Himer. 9. 19.

> πῶλε Θρηικίη, τί δή με
> λοξὸν ὄμμαcι βλέπουcα
> νηλέωc φεύγειc, δοκεῖc δέ
> μ᾽ οὐδὲν εἰδέναι cοφόν;
> ⟨——⟩
> 5   ἴcθι τοι, καλῶc μὲν ἄν τοι
> τὸν χαλινὸν ἐμβάλοιμι,
> ἡνίαc δ᾽ ἔχων cτρέφοιμί
> ⟨c᾽⟩ ἀμφὶ τέρματα δρόμου.
> ⟨——⟩
> νῦν δὲ λειμῶνάc τε βόcκεαι
> 10 κοῦφά τε cκιρτῶcα παίζειc,
> δεξιὸν γὰρ ἱπποπείρην
> οὐκ ἔχειc ἐπεμβάτην.
> ⟨——⟩

14. Heraclit. καὶ μὴν ὁ Τήιος Ἀνακρέων, ἑταιρικὸν φρόνημα καὶ cοβαρᾶc γυναικὸc ὑπερηφανίαν ὀνειδίζων, τὸν ἐν αὐτῆι cκιρτῶντα νοῦν ὡc ἵππον ἠλληγόρηcεν [-κεν O], οὕτω λέγων· πῶλε–ἐπεμβάτην   1–3 exc. gramm. ἰcτέον ὅτι ἐπὶ τῶν οὐδετέρων τῶν ἐπιθέτων cυμβαίνει, ὅταν μὲν αὐτὰ χωρὶc ἄρθρου ἦι, ἀντὶ ἐπιρρημάτων λαμβάνεcθαι, ὡc τὸ τί–φεύγειc, ἀντὶ τοῦ λοξῶc   1 Θρηικία O   3 νηλέωc Bechtel: -εῶc codd. δοκεῖc Bergk: δοκέειc codd.   7–8 cτρέφοιμί c᾽ Bergk: cτρέφοιμ᾽ M: cτρέφοι δ᾽? O (assentitur N. G. Wilson): cτρέφοιμ᾽ ἄν idem Bergk   12 οὐκ ἔχειc H. Stephanus: οὐχ ἕξειc codd. (ἕζειc A = Vat. gr. 871)   ἐπαμβάτην Silk

SIMONIDES

15: *PMG* 542

exhibet atque excutit Plat. *Prot.* 338 A 6–347 B 3. cuius libros hos commemorabimus: P. Oxy. 1624 (s. p. C. iii, Dublinii asseruatur; carminis uu. 38–9 tantum praestat; imagines in Mus. Ashm. seruant, quibus sum usus); B (Bodl. MS E. D. Clarke 39, a. 895 p. C.; imagines: Allen (1898–9), ii, foll. 350ʳ–351ᵛ, 359*ʳ–359*ᵛ, 360ʳ–361ʳ; librum ipsum a 338 A 6 usque ad 347 B 3 contuli); W (Vind. supp. gr. 7, s. xi; in hoc libro e Burnet aliisque pendeo); T (Ven. app. cl. 4. 1, c. a. 950 p. C. (uid. Boter (1989), 55–6); hic e Burnet pendeo). auctores alii (non omnes): uu. 1–3 Arist. *EN* 1100ᵇ21–2 (ἀγ., τετρ.–ψ.), *Rhet.* 3, 1411ᵇ26–7 (ἄνδρ. ἀγ., τετρ.), Diog. Laert. 1. 76 (ἄνδρ'–χαλ., sine μέν), Sopat. ap. Stob. 4. 5. 51 (τετρ.), Iulian. *Conviv.* 333 B (τετρ.–τετυγ.), Damasc. *Vit. Isid.* fr. 332 Zintzen (τετρ.–'τεταγ.'), *Sud.* π 1658 (ἄνδρ. ἀγ. ἀλαθέα γεν. χαλ.), cf. Basil. Achrid. *Laud. Iren.*, Regel (1982), 312 (ἄνευ ψ. τετρ.); 11–13: Polyb. 29. 26 (χαλ. ἐcθλ. ἔμμ.), Diog. (τὸ Πιττ., χαλ. ἐcθλ. ἔμμ.), *Sud.* π 1658 (item), *Anecd. Nov.* Boiss. 210 (Johann. Chumn. *Epist.* 4) (χαλ. ἐcθλ. εἶναι); 14 Arist. *Metaph.* 982ᵇ30–1 (θεὸc–γέρ.) [Aᵇ = Laur. 87. 12, s. xi, E = Par. gr. 1853, s. x], Asclep. ad loc. (*Comm. Arist. Gr.* vi/2) (liberius); 24: Plut. *Mor.* 470 D, 485 C, 743 F, 1061 B εὐρ.–χθον.; 29–30 ἀνάγκ.–μάχ. (saepe sine δ'): Aristid. 54 (*Lept.*). 104, Diog. 1. 76, Stob. 1. 4. 2ᶜ [F = Farn., bibl. mus. nat. III D 15, s. xiv], Synes. *Ep.* 103, *Patr. Gr.* 66, 1476 D, Zenob. uulg. 1. 85, Greg. Cypr. Mosq. 1. 50, Apost. 3. 6, Σ Plat. *Leg.* 818 B, *Sud.* α 1826, 1828, c 440, Anna Comn. *Alex.* 12. 3. 3, al. (cf. etiam Plat. *Leg.* 818 B, Procl. ad Plat. *Crat.* 157, Liv. 9. 4. 16).

ἄνδρ' ἀγαθὸν μὲν ἀλαθέωc γενέcθαι
χαλεπὸν χερcίν τε καὶ ποcὶ καὶ νόωι
τετράγωνον ἄνευ ψόγου τετυγμένον

vi (uel xv) uu. desunt

⟨———⟩

οὐδέ μοι ἐμμελέωc τὸ Πιττάκειον
νέμεται, καίτοι cοφοῦ παρὰ φωτὸc εἰ-
ρημένον· χαλεπὸν φάτ' ἐcθλὸν ἔμμεναι.

15. cum dicitur 'vi uu. desunt', etc., tum numeri hanc quam uides strophae dispositionem sequuntur; numeri autem in margine scripti morem sequuntur B uersus Simonidis, ut aliorum, nota > designat in margine; 14 ἄνδρα–18 tamen praeterit   1–3 Plat. 339 A–B 4 λέγει γάρ που Cιμωνίδηc πρὸc Cκόπαν τὸν Κρέοντοc υἱὸν τοῦ Θετταλοῦ ὅτι ἄνδρα–τετυγμένον. τοῦτο ἐπίcταcαι τὸ ἄιcμα . . .;, cf. 344 A 2–4 etc. (343 C 7 τὸ πρῶτον τοῦ ἄιcματοc)   1 ἄνδρ': ἄνδρα codd. (de scriptione plena posthac tacebitur)   2 χερcί codd. (339 B, 344 A)   11–13 Plat. 339 C 2–5 προϊόντοc τοῦ ἄιcματοc λέγει που· οὐδέ . . . ἔμμεναι, cf. D 3–7 (. . . ὀλίγον δὲ τοῦ ποιήματοc εἰc τὸ πρόcθεν προελθὼν ἐπελάθετο . . ., cf. 344 B 6), etc.   11 οὐδ' ἐμοί coni. Hutchinson   Πιττάκειον W: -ιον B (cf. e.g. 341 E 7, 344 C 2) T

θεὸς ἂν μόνος τοῦτ' ἔχοι γέρας· ἄνδρα δ' οὐκ
15 ἔστι μὴ οὐ κακὸν ἔμμεναι
ὃν {ἂν} ἀμάχανος συμφορὰ καθέληι.
πράξαις {μὲν} γὰρ εὖ πᾶς ἀνὴρ ἀγαθός,
κακὸς δ' εἰ κακῶς 〈   〉

uersus deest

〈———〉
τοὔνεκεν οὔ ποτ' ἐγὼ τὸ μὴ γενέσθαι
δυνατὸν διζήμενος κενεὰν ἐς ἄ-
πρακτον ἐλπίδα μοῖραν αἰῶνος βαλέω,
πανάμωμον ἄνθρωπον, εὐρυεδέος ὅσοι
25 καρπὸν αἰνύμεθα χθονός·
ἐπὶ δ' ὕμμιν εὑρὼν ἀπαγγελέω.
πάντας δ' ἐπαίνημι καὶ φιλέω,
ἑκὼν ὅστις ἔρδηι μηδὲν αἰσχρόν· ἀνάγ-
30 και δ' οὐδὲ θεοὶ μάχονται.
〈———〉

iii (uel xii) uu. desunt

〈   〉 ἄγαν ἀπάλαμνος, εἰ-
35 δώς τ' ὀνησίπολιν δίκαν,

14–16 Plat. 341 D 9–E 3 . . . εὐθὺς τὸ μετὰ τοῦτο ῥῆμα· λέγει γὰρ ὅτι θεὸς-γέρας, 344 C
2–5 ἀδύνατον καὶ οὐκ ἀνθρώπειον, ἀλλὰ θεὸς-καθέληι   14 ἔχοι γέρας Plat., Arist. Aᵇ:
ἔχοι τὸ γ. Arist. E   15 ἔστιν B (W?)   16 ἂν del. Bergk   ἀμάχανος Boeckh:
ἀμήχ- codd.   17–18 Plat. 344 E 5–8 . . . ἔμμεναι δὲ ἀδύνατον· πράξας . . . κακῶς,
cf. 345 A 4 κακὸς δὲ [δ' εἰ Ast] κακῶς   17 πράξαις Boeckh: -ας codd.   μὲν del.
Hermann   18–20 e Plat. 345 C 3 ἐπὶ πλεῖστον δὲ καὶ ἄριστοί εἰςιν οὓς ἂν οἱ θεοὶ
φιλοῦσι uersus fingunt (e.g. καὶ τοὐπὶ πλεῖστον ἄριστοι τούς κε θεοὶ φιλέωσι Hermann)
21–30 Plat. 345 C 4–D 5 . . . τὰ ἐπιόντα γε τοῦ ἄισματος ἔτι μᾶλλον δηλοῖ. φησι γάρ·
τοὔνεκεν-ἀπαγγελέω, φησίν . . . πάντας δ'-μάχονται, cf. 346 D 3–E 4   22 διζήμενος
κενέαν W, -ος (?) κενεαν T, -ός κεν ἐὰν B   24 εὑρεδέος Wilamowitz: -εδοῦς fere codd.
Plat., Plut. *Mor.* 743 F, 1061 B, cf. *SLG* 395 (b). 2: -οδοῦς Plut. codd. plerique 470 D,
485 C   26 ἐπὶ δ' Bergk: ἔπειθ' BT (W, ut uid.) (345 C, 346 D)   ὕμμιν Hermann:
ὑμῖν BT (W, ut uid.) (345 C, 346 D)   in εὑρὼν ὢ Bᶜ⁽ʔ⁾ 346 D 5   27 πάντα Tᵃᶜ
ἐπαίνημι B 346 D 8, E 2, Bᵖᶜ, ⁿᵉᶜ ¹ ⁿᵉᶜ ² 345 D 3: -ιν Bᵃᶜ 345 D 3 T (W, ut uid.)   28 ἔρδηι:
ἔρδηι B et 345 D 4 et 346 E 3   29 ἀνάγκαι Aristid., Diog., Stobaei F, Synes.:
-ηι codd. Plat., etc.   34–40 Plat. 346 B 8–C 8 . . . λέγει ὅτι ἐγώ, ὦ Πιττάκε, οὐ
διὰ ταῦτά σε ψέγω, ὅτι εἰμὶ φιλόψογος, ἐπεὶ ἔμοιγ' ἐξαρκεῖ ὃς ἂν μὴ κακὸς ἦι μηδ' ἄγαν-
μωμήςομαι, οὐ γάρ εἰμι φιλόμωμος, τῶν-γενέθλα, ὥςτ' . . .· πάντα-μέμεικται   ex οὐ–ἦι
et οὐ–φιλόμ. (cf. etiam 346 D 6–7) uersiculos faciunt quos μηδ' ἄγαν excipiat, e.g. οὐκ
εἴμ' ἐγὼ φιλόμωμος· ἐξαρκεῖ γ' ἐμοί | ὃς ἂν ἦι κακὸς (horum alius aliud)   35 τ'
ὀνησίπολιν Hermann (ὀνασι- ille): γε ὀνήσει πόλιν (tum δικαν B, cf. e.g. 345 C 7, E 3,
346 B 2)

ὑγιὴς ἀνήρ. ⟨　　　⟩ οὔ νιν ἐγώ
μωμήςομαι· τῶν γὰρ ἀλιθίων
ἀπείρων γενέθλα. πάντα τοι καλὰ τοῖc-
40　　ίν τ' αἰcχρὰ μὴ μέμεικται.
⟨———⟩

16: PMG 543

textum totum praebet Dion. Hal. *Comp.* 26. 14–15 (221–3). nulli certe alii libri auctoritate praediti sunt quam P (Parisinus gr. 1741, s. x med.) et M (Marcianus gr. 508, hac parte c. a. 1330 p. C.). etiam hic tamen illius est apographon (uide Aujac (1974), 40–1), nec tum commemoratur cum idem legit atque P. quas autem lectiones proprias adfert, ne his quidem facili animo tribuenda est auctoritas. nam etsi alibi in eum lectiones confluxerunt ex F (Laurentiano 59. 15, s. xi in.), qui hic deficit, multa tamen M ipse peccat, multa conicit. (quod ad F ut fontem attinet, uide e.g. Usener et Radermacher (1904–29) ii/1. 39 ad u. 6, 104 ad uu. 1, 5.) quaedam recte coniciunt W quoque (Parisinus gr. 1798, s. xvi) et G (Guelferbytanus gr. 14, s. xv?). P exscribit Davison (1968a), 259; praeterea utor Aujac et Lebel (1981), Usener et Radermacher (1904–29), aliis. 7–9 praebet etiam Athen. 396 E.

　　... ὅτε λάρνακι
ἐν δαιδαλέαι
ἄνεμός τε †μην† πνέων
κινηθεῖcά τε λίμνα δείματι
5　ἔρειπεν· οὐδ' ἀδιάντοιcι παρει-

36 οὔ νιν fere Schleiermacher (μιν ille): οὐ μὴν codd. lacuna uarie collocari potest; οὔ μιν ὦ φίλ' ἐγώ Maas　　37 ἀλιθίων Schneidewin: ἠλιθίων codd. Plat.: τ[......| θιων [tantum P. Oxy. 1624 fr. 12　　38 solum νεθλ[P. Oxy.　　39 τοίcίν Page: -ί T?W?: -ι B　　40 μέμικται B quidem　　Plat. 344 B 2–5 ... ἀλλὰ τὸν τύπον αὐτοῦ τὸν ὅλον διεξέλθωμεν καὶ τὴν βούλησιν, ὅτι ... ἔλεγχός ἐcτιν τοῦ Πιττακείου ῥήματος διὰ πάντος τοῦ ἄιcματος: quae uidentur indicare hac strophe carmen ad finem esse perductum　　16. Dion. ἐκ δὲ τῆς μελικῆς τὰ Cιμωνίδεια ταῦτα. γέγραπται δὲ κατὰ διαcτολὰς οὐχ ὧν Ἀριcτοφάνης ἢ ἄλλος τις κατεcκεύαcε κώλων ἀλλ' ὧν ὁ πεζὸς λόγος ἀπαιτεῖ. πρόcεχε δὴ τῶι μέλει καὶ ἀναγίνωcκε κατὰ διαcτολάς, καὶ εὖ ἴcθ' ὅτι λήcεταί cε ὁ ῥυθμὸς τῆς ὠιδῆς καὶ οὐχ ἕξει cυμβαλεῖν οὔτε cτροφὴν οὔτ' ἀντίcτροφον οὔτ' ἐπωιδόν, ἀλλὰ φανήcεταί cοι λόγος εἰc εἰρόμενος. ἐcτὶ δὲ ἡ διὰ πελάγους φερομένη Δανάη τὰς ἑαυτῆς ἀποδυρομένη τύχας. ὅτε–μοι　1 ὅτι M　　2 δαιδαλέαι W: -λαίαι P　　3 τε μὴν P: τέ μιν Schneidewin (νιν melius fuisset): τε, νιν post ὅτε translato, coni. Hutchinson　　4 τε Brunck: δὲ P　　δείματι W: δεῖ ματι P: δείμα M　　5 ἔρειπεν M: ἔριπεν P　　οὐδ' Brunck: οὐτ' P (οὔτ' M): οὐκ Thiersch　　ἀδίαν τοῖcι P: ἀδειαντῆcι (-οῖcι ᵃᶜ?) M

αἷς ἀμφί τε Περσέϊ βάλλε φίλαν χέρα
εἶπέν τ', "ὦ τέκος, οἷον ἔχω πόνον.
10   σὺ δ' ἀωτεῖς, γαλαθηνῶι δ' ἤτορι
κνώσσεις, ἐν ἀτερπέϊ δούρατι χαλκεογόμφωι
†δενυκτιλαμπει† κυανέωι {τε} δνόφωι †ταδεις†·
    ἄλμαν δ', ὕπερθε τεᾶν κομᾶν
15 βαθεῖαν παριόντος κύματος, οὐκ ἀλέγεις,
οὐδ' ἀνέμου φθόγγον, πορφυρέαι
κείμενος ἐν χλανίδι, πρόσωπον καλὸν ⟨   ⟩.
    εἰ δέ τοι δεινὸν τό γε δεινὸν ἦν,
καί κεν ἐμῶν ῥημάτων
20 λεπτὸν ὑπεῖχες οὖας.
    κέλομαι ⟨δ'⟩, εὗδε, βρέφος· εὑδέτω δὲ πόν-
τος, εὑδέτω ⟨δ'⟩ ἄμετρον κακόν·
    μεταβουλία δέ τις φανεί-
η, Ζεῦ πάτερ, ἐκ σέο·
25 εἰ δέ τι θαρσαλέον ἔπος εὔχομαι
ἢ νόσφι δίκας, σύγγνωθί μοι . . ."

6 βάλε M   7–9 Athen. Cιμωνίδης δ' ἐπὶ τοῦ Περσέως τὴν Δανάην ποιεῖ λέγουσαν· ὤ-
κνώσσεις   7 τέκος Athen.: τέκνον P   8 cὺ δ' Athen.: οὐδ' P   ἀωτεῖς Casaubon:
αὖτε εἷς Athen.: αυταις P (αὐταῖς M)   γαλαθηνῶι δ' ἤτορι Athen.: ἐγαλαθηνωδει θει P:
ἀγαλαθηνώδει vac. M (ἀγαμ- ᵃᶜ): γ. ἤθεϊ Bergk   9 κνώσσεις Athen.: κνοώσσεις P:
om. M   10 ἀτερπέῖ P   δούρατι G: δούνατι P   -γόμφωι P   11 δε νυκτὶ
λαμπεῖ P: νυκτί τ' ἀλαμπεῖ Bergk (ἀλαμπεῖ iam Ilgen): δὲ νυκτὶ λάμπεις Nietzsche:
⟨τῶι⟩δε νυκτιλαμπεῖ Page (νυκτιλαμπεῖ iam Ursinus): ⟨ὦ⟩τε νυκτὸς ἀλαμπέϊ (uel -έος)
Hutchinson (δίχα νυκτὸς iam Usener)   τε del. Blass   12 δνόφωι M: δνόφων
P (δν°φ⌢)   ταδ' εἰς P: ταθείς Schneidewin: cταλείς Bergk: ἀλείς coni. West: e.g.
καλ⟨υφθ⟩είς Hutchinson: τ' ἀδεής Headlam   13 ἄλμαν Bergk: αὐλέαν P (-αίαν M):
ἄχναν Page   ὕπερθεν P   τεᾶν κομᾶν Ahrens: τεαν κόμαν P   14 βαθειᾶν
Ahrens: -εῖαν P   16 πορφυρέαι M: πυρφ. P   17 ἐν χλανίδι M: ἐχλανιδι P
πρόσωπον καλὸν M: πρόσωπον κ. πρόσωπον P   προφαίνων suppl. Ahrens   18 δέ τι
M   ἦν Sylburg: ἦι P (ἢ M)   19 καὶ M: κε P   20 λεπτὸν Stephanus: -ῶν P
21 δ' add. Bergk   22 δ' add. Thiersch   23 μεταβουλία G: μαιταβουλία P
25 εἰ δέ τι Hutchinson (εἴ τι iam Schaefer): ὅτι δὴ P: ὅττι δὲ Mehlhorn   26 ἢ
νόσφι δ. Victorius: ηνοφι δ. P (ἢν οφειδίας M)

BACCHYLIDES

17: carmen 3

papyrus: P. Lond. inv. 733 (A), s. ii ex.–iii p. C., in uolumine priore; textum correxit in primis A³, qui aliud usurpauit exemplar (cf. 18. 55–7). imagines: Scott (1897) (aliquot fragmenta in fine libri sunt reperienda, inter quae 21a, 21b; aliquot absunt). papyrum ipsam contuli. fragmenta commentarii: P. Oxy. 2367, s. p. C. ii, frr. 1–4. imago: P. Oxy. xxiii (1956), tab. viii. papyrum ipsam contuli.

col. vi   Ἀριστο[κ]άρπου Cικελίας κρέουσαν   str. 1
           Δάματρα ἰοστέφανόν τε κούραν
           ὕμνει, γλυκύδωρε Κλεοῖ, θοάς τ᾽
           Ὀ[λυ]μπιοδρόμους Ἱέρωνος ἵππ[ο]υς.

        ——]
  5   .....]το γὰρ cὺν ὑπερόχωι τε νίκαι   ant. 1
           cὺν ἀγ]λαΐαι τε παρ᾽ εὐρυδίναν
           Ἀλφεόν ....] Δεινομένεος ἔθη-
           καν [ὄ]λβιον τ[.........]ν κυρῆcαι.

           θρόηcε δὲ λ[αὸς   ep. 1
  10   ἃ τρὶc εὐδαίμ[ων
col. vii   ὅc, παρὰ Ζηνὸc λαχὼν
           πλείcταρχον Ἑλλάνων γέρας,
           οἶδε πυργωθέντα πλοῦτον μὴ μελαμ-
           φαρέϊ κρύπτειν cκότωι.

17. inscr. (in marg.) Ἱέρωνι Cυρακοcίωι ἵπποιc [Ὀλύ]μπια   1 (κάρ)   2 (ἰο-
cτέφανόν)   3 (κύ)   Κλεοῖ Blass: Κλειοῖ A   (ἆc)   4 Ὀ-: prima syllaba
uersus quarti strophae antistrophaeque in papyro semper tertium potius uersum
terminat (δρό)   (ἴε)   5 cεύον]το e.p. (Kenyon), φέρον]το Platt, al., ἴεν]το
Edmonds, quorum uerborum nullum spatio bene conuenit   (ὀχ, acc. tum deleto,
ut uid.)   (κᾶι)   Νίκαι scribunt   6 Ἀγ]λαΐαι scribunt   (ἴαι)   (δίν)   7 τόθι]
Palmer   (μέν)   8 τ[έκοc Edmonds, cτεφάνω]ν e.p.   (cαι·)   9 [ἀπείρων |
Blass   10 (ἀ)   [ἀνήρ | e.p.   11 (ὁ)   12 (πλεί)   γέρας A¹ᵖᶜ (corr.
i.l.): γένοc A¹ᵃᶜ   13 μελαμ- A¹²ᵖᶜ (λη in αμ corr.): μελλη A¹ᵃᶜ   14 φαρέϊ e.p.,
tamquam lectionem Aᵖᶜ: φαρθι A²²ᵖᶜ: φαρθιν A¹ᵃᶜ   (τωι·)

15 βρύει μὲν ἱερὰ βουθύτοις ἑορταῖς,   str. 2
   βρύουσι φιλοξενίας ἀγυιαί·
   λάμπει δ᾽ ὑπὸ μαρμαρυγαῖς ὁ χρυ-
   cόc, ὑψιδαιδάλτων τριπόδων cταθέντων
   ⟨——⟩

   πάροιθε ναοῦ, τόθι μέγι[c]τον ἄλcοc   ant. 2
20 Φοίβου παρὰ Καcταλίας [ῥ]εέθροιc
   Δελφοὶ διέπουcι. θεόν, θε[ό]ν
   τις ἀγλαϊζέτω· ὁ γὰρ ἄριcτοc [ὄ]λβων.
   ⟨——⟩

   ἐπεί ποτε καὶ δαμασίπ[π]ου   ep. 2
   Λυδίας ἀρχαγέταν,
25 εὖτε τὰν πεπ[
   Ζηνὸς τελε[.........]cιν
   Cάρδιες Πέρcα̣[ν ....cτρ]ατῶι
   Κροῖcον ὁ χρυcạ[

   ═══

   φύλαξ᾽ Ἀπόλλων. [ὁ δ᾽, ἐc] ἄελπτον ἆμαρ   str. 3
30 μολὼν πολυδ[άκρυο]ν̣, οὐκ ἔμελλε
   μίμνειν ἔτι δ[ουλοcύ]ναν· πυρὰν
   δὲ χαλκοτειχέοc .[.....].θεν αὐ[λᾶc

   ────

   ναῆcατ᾽, ἔνθα cυ[......] τε κεδ[ant. 3
   cὺν εὐπλοκάμοι[c τ᾽] ἐπέβαιν᾽ ἄλα̣[
35 θ]υγατράcι δυρομέναιc. χέρας δ᾽
   [ἐc αἴ]πὺν αἰθέρα c[φ]ετέρας ἀείραc
   ──]

15 ἱερὰ Α³ʾ (ἳ s.l.): ερα Α¹   (θύ)   ἑορταῖς: ρ ε τ correctum est   16 -ξενίαις
Richards, alii (αι·)   17 (δʾ)   18 (δάλ) (πόδ)   19 (ναόν)   20 (έθρ)
21 θε[ό]ν: θ[εό]ν suppl. Palmer   22 (αγλαϊζέθωγαρ) ἄριcτοc [ὄ]λβων Α³ (ν, ο
del.; c, ω sscr.): -ον -ον Α¹   (ων·)   23 (πεï (?))   κοτε fortasse Α³ʾ, si quidem
π in κ mutauit; cf. 72   (cιπ)   24 (δï)   (γέ)   25 πε[πρωμέναν Palmer
26 τελέ[ccαντοc Wackernagel, κρί]cιν Weil, alii, quae coniuncta spatium excedant
27 (Cά)   ἁλίcκοντο post]ν Wackernagel   cτρ]ατῶι Palmer   28 χρυcά̣[ορος
Palmer: -ά̣[ρματοc e.p.   29 (αξʾ)   (ἀμ)   30 (fortasse λών, acc. deleto)
31 δ[ουλοcύ]ναν Jebb (ναν·)   32 (χέ)   π[ροπάροι]θεν e.p., longius spatio; adde
quod ι non conueniunt relicta ante θ uestigia   33 (ήcατ᾽έ)   cὺ[ν ἀλόχωι] e.p.,
spatio longius, ut uidetur   κεδ[ναι e.p.   34 εὐπλοκάμοι[c τ᾽] Platt   (αιν᾽άλ)
35 (ρά)   (μέναιc·)   χε ueri similius quam κε   36 (εί)

.]...νεν· "ὑπέρ[βι]ε δαῖμον,   ep. 3
πο]ῦ θεῶν ἐστι[ν] χάρις;
πο]ῦ δὲ Λατοίδ[α]ς ἄναξ;
40   ......]ιν Ἀλυά[τ]τα δόμοι
] μυρίων
]ν

════]
]ν ἄςτυ   str. 4
]δίνας
col. viii   Πακτωλός· ἀ[ε]ικελίως γυνα[ῖ-
46   κες ἐξ ἐϋκτίτων μεγάρων ἄγονται.

⟨———⟩

τὰ πρόςθεν {δ᾿} [ἐχ]θρὰ φίλα· θανεῖν γλύκιστον."   ant. 4
τός᾿ εἶπε, καὶ ἀβ[ρο]βάταν κέ[λε]υςεν
ἅπτειν ξύλινον δόμον. ἔκ[λα]γον
50   δὲ παρθένοι, φίλας τ᾿ ἀνὰ ματρὶ χεῖρας

ἔβαλλον· ὁ γὰρ προφανὴς θνα-   ep. 4
τοῖςιν ἔχθιςτος φόνων.
ἀλλ᾿ ἐπεὶ δεινο[ῦ π]υρὸς
λαμπρὸν διάϊ[ςςεν μέ]νος,
55   Ζεὺς ἐπιςτάςας [........]θες νέφος
ςβέννυεν ξανθὰ[ν φλόγα.

═════

ἄπιςτον οὐδὲν ὅτι θ[εῶν μέ]ριμνα   str. 5
τεύχει· τότε Δαλογενὴ[ς Ἀπό]λλων

37 γέ]γ[ω]νεν e.p.; exstant tamen uestigia quae inferius iacent quam ut cum ω con-
gruant   (νεν·)   ὑπέρ[βι]ε Blass   (πέρ)   38 (ριc·)   39 (τοῖ)   (αξ·)
40 ἔρρους]ιν Frick   (νά)   41 ante μυρ, c del. A³²   42 (ν·)   44 ἐρεύθεται
αἵματι χρυςο]δίνας e.p. (φοινίςςεται Blass)   (δίν)   45 (λός·)   γυνα[ῖ-: forsitan ex
ι uestigium possit dispici   46 (κτῖ, ut uid.)   (ται·)   47 δ᾿ del. Fraccaroli
[ἐχ]θρὰ Palmer   supra αφιλ, νῦν (νυν) scripsit A³ (cf. app. ad Pind. *Ol.* 6 [18]. 18)
(γλύκιστον·)   48 (τοc᾿)   ἀβ[ρο]βάταν A¹ᵖᶜ (βά): -βαώταν A¹ᵃᶜ: ἀκρότατον Hutchin-
son   pro uersu toto τόθ᾿ ἀβροβάταν ⟨ἐπέταν⟩ κέλευςεν Housman   49 (ἁπτ) (μον·)
50 (νοι·)   51 ἔβαλλον A¹ᵖᶜ (ε in ο corr.): -εν A¹ᵃᶜ   (ον·)   θνα- A¹ᵖᶜ (ι del., ν sscr.):
θια- A¹ᵃᶜ   52 (ἐχθ)   (φονων·)   53 (αλλ᾿)   54 (διαϊ)   55 [μελαγκευ]θὲς
e.p.   (cτά)   56 (cβέ)   φλόγα Palmer   58 (τεύχει·τοτεδᾶ)

φέρων ἐς Ὑπερβορέο[υς γ]έρον-
60   τα ςὺν τανιςφύροις κατ[έν]αςςε κούραις

δι' εὐςέβειαν, ὅτι μέ[γιςτα] θνατῶν   ant. 5
ἐς ἀγαθέαν ⟨ἀπ⟩έπεμψε Π[υθ]ώ.
ὅςο[ι] ⟨γε⟩ μὲν Ἑλλάδ' ἔχουςιν, [ο]ὔ-
τι[ς], ὦ μεγαίνητε Ἱέρων, θελήςει

65   φάμ]εν ςέο πλείονα χρυςὸν   ep. 5
Λοξί]αι πέμψαι βροτῶν.
εὖ λέ]γειν πάρεςτιν, ὅς-
τις μ]ὴ φθόνωι πιαίνεται
. . . . .]λη φίλιππον ἄνδρ' ἀ[ρ]ήϊον
70   . . . .]ίου ςκᾶπτρ[ο]ν Διό[ς
====]
. . . .'] κων τε μέρο[ς . . . .]α Μουςᾶν.   str. 6
. . . .]μαλέαι ποτ[. . . . . . .'] ιων
. . . .] . ος ἐφάμερον α . [
    [ ]·[. . . .]α ςκόπει βραχ[
——]
75   πτερό]εςςα δ' ἐλπὶς ὑπ[νόημα   ant. 6
. . .]ερίων· ὁ δ' ἄναξ [Ἀπόλλων
. . . .'] . ος εἶπε Φέρη[τος υἱ-
col. ix   ι,] "θνατὸν ἐῦντα χρὴ διδύμους ἀέξειν
⟨——⟩

59–60 (ορέ) (έροντα·) (ςφύ) κατ[έν]αςςε: suppl. Palmer   61 (αν·)   62 (θέ) ⟨ἀπ⟩έπεμψε Hutchinson: ⟨ἀν⟩- Blass, alii: ⟨ἐπ⟩- e.p.   (θω·)   63 γε inseruerunt Blass, alii   (αδ')   (']υ)   paragraphum sub hoc u., non 64, collocauit A   64 (άιν) μεγαίνητ' ὦ Wilamowitz: μεγαίνητος coni. Hutchinson   (ϊε)   65 φάμ]εν Blass; apicis φ uestigia fortasse possunt uideri   (πλεί)   66 Λοξί]αι Blass, alii   (]ᾱι) 67 εὖ λέ]γειν, quod suppleuerant Blass, alii, confirmat Σ fr. 2. 5   (ός)   68 -τις μ]ὴ Palmer   πιαίνεται A³, cf. Σ fr. 2. 6, 8: ἰαίνεται A¹ (ϊαι)   70 (ςκα: supra α macula est tamquam acc. deleto)   71 ἰοπλό]κων Blass   ἔχοντ]α Blass   (ςᾶν·) 72 (έαι)   ποτ[A¹: κοτ[A³?? (plenius π in κ quam u. 23 correctum esset)   73]ʋ, αι possis   (ἄμ)   74 ςκόπει coni. Lobel, cl. Σ fr. 3. 4: ςκοπεῖς A. post ςκοπεῖς nota tantum deletionis, deleta, quoad uideri potest, littera nulla; forsitan is qui notam scripsit ς alterum deletum uoluerit   καίρι]α Jebb, cl. Σ fr. 3. 4   βραχ[ύς ἐςτιν αἰών e.p.   75 .'] εςςα A, πτε in Σ fr. 3. 6: πτερόεςςα iam suppleuerat Fränkel   (δ') ὑπ[ολύει Snell; cf. Σ fr. 3. 7   ]ορημα Σ fr. 3. 8   76 ἐφάμ]ερίων Blass, sed spatio non optime conuenit; ex imaginibus ρ in β correctum esse credas, sed falso   (ων·οδ') 77–8 ante ος, λ uel δ   υῖ suppl. Platt, alii   ἐῦντα A²? (ευ'ν'τα[ν]): εῦτ' ἂν A¹   (έξ)

γνώμας, ὅτι τ' αὔριον ὄψεαι   ep. 6
80   μοῦνον ἁλίου φάος,
χὤτι πεντήκοντ' ἔτεα
ζωὰν βαθύπλουτον τελεῖς.
ὅcια δρῶν εὔφραινε θυμόν· τοῦτο γὰρ
κερδέων ὑπέρτατον."
⟨══⟩
85   φρονέοντι cυνετὰ γαρύω. βαθὺς μέν   str. 7
αἰθὴρ ἀμίαντος· ὕδωρ δὲ πόντου
οὐ cάπεται· εὐφροcύνα δ' ὁ χρυ-
cός. ἀνδρὶ δ' οὐ θέμις πολιὸν π[. .]εντα
⟨──⟩
γῆρας θάλ[εια]ν αὖτις ἀγκομίc⟨c⟩αι   ant. 7
90   ἥβαν. ἀρετᾶ[c γε μ]ὲν οὐ μινύθει
βροτῶν ἅμα c[ώμ]ατι φέγγος, ἀλ-
λὰ Μοῦcά νιν τρ[έφει.] Ἱέρων, cὺ δ' ὄλβου

κάλλιcτ' ἐπεδ[είξ]αο θνατοῖc   ep. 7
ἄνθεα. πράξα[ντι] δ' εὖ
95   οὐ φέρει κόcμ[ον cι]ω-
πά· cὺν δ' ἀλαθ[είαι] †καλῶν†
καὶ μελιγλώccου τις ὑμνήcει χάριν
Κηΐac ἀηδόνος.
══

commentarii fragmenta:

fr. 1 (cf. carminis uu. 63–5):

·
]ελλ[
]cκα[
χρ]υcον[

79 (τ')   80 (λἴ)   81 (οντ'έτ)   82 (θύ)   (εἰc·)   83 (ὅc)   (εὔ)
(μον·)   84 (έων)   (τον·)   85 (ύω·)   86 (τοc·ϋ)   87 (cάπεται·)
(δ')   88 (coc· (?))   (δ')   post ον, π uel γ   π[αρ]έντα Jebb: π[ρο]έντα coni. e.p.
89 (θά)   ἀγκομίc⟨c⟩αι e.p.   90 (βαν·)   (νύ)   91 (ά)   c[ώμ]ατι Ingram
(γοc·)   92 (ϊέ)   93 (ιcτ')   94 (άνθ)   (δ')   96 (πα·cυνδ')
καλῶν: κ aut χ; καλά Hutchinson: κλέων Fränkel: λακών Housman   97 (γλώ)
98 (ἴαc)   ἀηδόνος Aᴵᴾᶜ (o in δ corr.): αηοονοc Aᴵᵃᶜ

        μ]εγαλω[
5   ]ηνουτος[
     πλ]ειοναχ[ρυcον
     .   .   .   .

fr. 2 (cf. uu. 67–8):

                    .   .
                ].. [
                ]. κ[
                ]. ει. [
                ]. νǫ.. [.]. . [
5   ]. θρω⁰ευλεˣ[
                φθον]ωιπιε [
                ]. φθǫ[ν
                ]. ια. [
                    .   .

fr. 3 (cf. uu. 73–6):

                    .   .
                ]. [
                ]αφε[. . . . . .].
                εφ]ημερο . [. . .]εc
                ]. αταερευνα   [
5   ]οτιολιγοχρο   [
                ]ςηπτε . [
                ]ạφθειρειτο[
                ]ǫημαελπιζον[
                ]ανθρωπο[.]πλ[.]υ [
10   ]καιεπιτυχεịν [
                ]. τω. [. . .]. [
                ]. ων. [
                ]νται. [
                    .   .

fr. 4 (cf. uu. 83–6):

                ]ρα[.]. εcου[
                γ]αρπαντος[
                ]εcτ[.]ν

Σ **fr. 2.** 1–2, 3–8 in fragmentis stant separatis, quae coniunxit e.p. (Lobel)   5 αν]
θρω⁰ Snell   ˣ: cf. fr. 11. 4, Σ Alcm. 3 [2] super fr. 1 col. i, u. 2   6 πιε, i.e. πιαί-
(e.p.)   8]πιαị[uestigiis consonet   **fr. 3.** 2 ε: aut θ   3 -οị [ὄντ]εc e.p.
4 δυ]νατὰ Lloyd-Jones   6–8 πτε | ρόεccα δ' ἐλπὶc δι]αφθείρει τὸ | τῶν ἀνθρώπων
ν]όημα e.p.   9 πο[ι] aptius spatio quam πο[ν] quidem   **fr. 4.** 1 εὐφ]ρα[ι]νε
e.p.

5]ạεαυ
   ]νтιαλε
   ]μαιβα
   ]τονδυ
   ]φῆᾱνε
   ]. τουδωρ
10]αρμε
   ]. θη
   ]ν
   ].

PINDARUS

18: carmen Olympicum 6

ii libri medii aeui quos semper adducimus (uox 'rell.' includit hos tantum): A (Ambrosianus C 222 inf., s. xiii ex.); B (Vaticanus gr. 1312, s. xii ex.), L (Vaticanus gr. 902, s. xiii ex.), E (Laurentianus 32. 37, c. 1300 p. C.), G (Gottingensis philol. 29, s. xiii med.), H (Vat. gr. 41, s. xiv in.); C (Parisinus gr. 2774, c. 1300 p. C.), N (Ambrosianus E 103 sup., s. xiii ex.), O (Leid. Voss. gr. Q 4 B, c. 1300 p. C.; non adducitur nisi in uu. 76–105), Ø (Vaticanus gr. 915, c. 1300 p. C.). sparsim adducuntur etiam D (Laur. 32. 52, s. xiii ex.), F (Laur. 32. 33, s. xiii ex.), M (Perus. B 43, s. xv), P (Pal. gr. 40, s. xiv in.), Q (Laur. 32. 35, s. xiii ex.), X (Par. gr. 2709, s. xv), Xw=q (Vind. phil. gr. 198, c. 1320 p. C.), Zn=Δ (Neap. II. F. 5, 1310–20 p. C.), m (Bod. Auct. F. 3. 25, s. xiv), Γ (Par. gr. 2465, s. xiv), Ω (Mosqu. Syn. gr. 501, s. xv). A e deminutis imaginibus contuli quas mihi M. C. Howatson liberaliter commodauit, B ex imaginibus quas Irigoin (1974) uulgauit; m autem ipsum contuli. in reliquis praecipue e Mommsen (1864a) et Turyn (1948) pendeo, quorum hunc etiam melius quam illum legere in AB reperii. papyri: P. Oxy. 1614, Cantabrigiensis Add. 6366 (s. v uel vi p. C.), col. iii (pag. 2').110–50 (uu. 71–95)=Π¹; PSI 1277 (s. p. C. ii), 1–5 (uu. 103–5), edita a Pieraccioni (1948)=Π². neutrius uulgata est imago; illius imaginem Oxonienses in Mus. Ashm. locarunt. Π¹ ipsam Cantabrigiae contuli, Π² contuli ex imagine quam R. Pintaudi benigne fieri iussit. cum praesto sunt et papyrus et posteriores libri, tum in apparatu critico dicitur quo modo papyrus et A et B uersus carminis disposuerint; hoc enim non nullius momenti est ad traditionem textus intellegendam. (A uersus carminis tres fere uno uersu suo, hoc est eadem linea, scribit, interuallo separatos.) testimonia (selecta): uu. 1–2 *Anecd.*

5 φρονέο]ντι e.p., ἅ λέ|γω] Hutchinson   7 post υ, δ uel λ suspensum et deletum   **18.** inscr. Ἁγηcίαι Cυρακουcίωι ἀπήνηι fere ACN: υἱῶι Cωcτράτου ante ἀπ. B, post LEGH (inscr. om. Ø); ὡc μὲν ἔνιοι, Cυρακουcίωι, ὡc δὲ ἔνιοι, Cτυμφηλίωι ΣBCEQ, sim. ΣA

18: carmen Olympicum 6　　57

Oxon. Cramer ii. 423 (χρυс. κίον.), cf. 486, *Etym. Gen.* AB cit. num. 170 Calame, Greg. Naz. *Epist.* 9. 1 (χρυс. ὑπόcτηcον εὐτ. θαλάμωι κίον.) [M = Mutinensis Estensis 229, s. xi; P = Parisinus gr. 506, s. x; Π = Patmiacus 57, s. x], *Orat.* 43. 20 (ὑποcτ. εὐτ. θαλάμωι χρυс. κίον.) [Q = Patmiacus 43–44, s. x; S = Mosquensis Syn. gr. 57, s. ix; C = Parisinus Coisl. 51, s. x], Georg. Lacap. *Epist.* 4 p. 29. 12–14 Lindstam (χρυс. ὑποcτ. εὐτ. θαλάμωι κίον.) (in *Etym. Magn.* 514. 56–7 V solus χρυсᾶc ὑφιcτᾶν κίον. τῶι θαλάμωι introducit); 3–4 Plut. *Mor.* 804 D (ἀρχ.–τηλ.), Luc. *Hipp.* (3). 7 (ἀρχομένου ἔργ.–τηλ.) [B = Vindobonensis 123, s. x; Γ = Vaticanus gr. 90, s. x; Ω = Marcianus 840, s. x/xi], Σ Theocr. 1 init. b (ἀρχ.–τηλ.), cf. [Dion. Hal.] *Art. Rhet.* 2, Iul. *Orat.* 3, 116 A, Elian *In Porph. Isag.* 16 p. 40 Busse, David *In Porph. Isag.* 1 p. 96 Busse (*CMAG* xviii/1 et 2), Eust. *Il.* 312. 13, etc.; 22 Heraclid. Miles. fr. 19 Cohn (Φίντ.); 25–6 Lexic. *Vindob.* η 293 (ἐκεῖναι γὰρ ἐξ ἄλλων ὁδ. ἥγ. ἐπ.); 41 Ion *FGrHist* 392 F 6 (*Epid.* 8. 20–1 von Blumenthal) (χρυс.)?; 58 Cornut. 22?; 84 Poll. 3. 17 (μητρομ.); 89–90 Plut. *Mor.* 995 E (γνῶν. τ' ἐπ. ⟨　⟩), Gal. *Protr.* 7. 5 Barigazzi (*CMG* v. 1. 1. 126; i. 15 Kühn) (εἰ–ῦν), Σ Lycophr. 433 (πρὸс τὸν χοροδιδάcκαλον Αἰνέαν ἔφη . . . εἰ–ῦν); (99 loci Iul. *Epist.* 4, 428 B, atque etiam Lib. *Epist.* 149. 1, etc. (cf. 1329. 2), Agath. *Hist.* 1 *praef.* 12, potius ad *Ol.* 7. 1 fortasse referendi); 100–1 cf. Eust. *Il.* 1078. 1–2 (add. in Laur. 59. 3).

ₗΧρυcέαc ὑποcτάcαντεc εὐτει-　　　　　　　str. 1
χεῖ προθύρωι θαλάμου
κίοναc ὡc ὅτε θαητὸν μέγαρον
πάξομεν. ἀρχομένου δ' ἔργου πρόcωπον
χρὴ θέμεν τηλαυγέc. εἰ δ' εἴ-
η μὲν Ὀλυμπιονίκαc,
5　βωμῶι τε μαντείωι ταμίαc Διὸc ἐν Πίcαι,
cυνοικίcτηρ τε τᾶν κλεινᾶν Cυρακοc-
cᾶν, τίνα κεν φύγοι ὕμνον
κεῖνοc ἀνὴρ ἐπικύρcαιc
ἀφθόνων ἀcτῶν ἐν ἱμερταῖc ἀοιδαῖc;

⟨———⟩

ἴcτω γὰρ ἐν τούτωι πεδίλωι　　　　　　ant. 1
δαιμόνιον πόδ' ἔχων
Cωcτράτου υἱόc. ἀκίνδυνοι δ' ἀρεταί
10　οὔτε παρ' ἀνδράcιν οὔτ' ἐν ναυcὶ κοίλαιc
τίμιαι· πολλοὶ δὲ μέμναν-

1 εὐτειχεῖ: -τυχεῖ C, Greg. *Epist.* ΜΡΠ, *Orat.* QᵃᶜSC, Georg.: -τοιχεῖ M (-οχεῖ *m*ᵃᶜ): -τοίχου Hecker　　θαλάμου: θαλάμωι M, Georg., V *Etym. Magni*, cf. Greg.: θαλάμων Hutchinson　　2 ὡс ὅτε: ὡсτε CØ　　3 ἀρχομένου codd. Pindari, Luciani B, Σ Theocr., Plut.: -ουc Luciani ΓΩ (cf. Iul.)　　5 βωμοῦ AˢˡNˢˡ, cf. Σ 7 a　　μαντείου Nˢˡ　　6 Cυρακοссᾶν B, ita fere EGHCØ: -ουсᾶν AL, sim. N: -ουсс- Π¹ in u. 92, cf. A in Bacch. 5. 184–5　　κεν: κε B quidem: καὶ ΑΗ　　φύγη(ι) GH　　7 ἐπικύρcαιc CØ: -ac rell.　　8 τὠυτῶι Bergk　　10 οὔτε παρ' ἀνδρ.: οὔτ' ἐν ἀνδρ. A: οὔτ' ἐπὶ δούραcιν Stadtmueller　　οὔτε ναυcὶ EGC

ται καλὸν εἴ τι ποναθῇι.

Ἀγηςία, τὶν δ᾽ αἶνος ἑτοῖμος ὃν ἐνδίκου
ἀπὸ γλώςςας Ἄδραστος μάντιν Οἰκλεί-
δαν ποτ᾽ ἐς Ἀμφιάρηον
φθέγξατ᾽, ἐπεὶ κατὰ γαῖ᾽ αὐ-
τόν τέ νιν καὶ φαιδίμας ἵππους ἔμαρψεν.

⟨——⟩

15   ἑπτὰ δ᾽ ἔπειτα †πυρᾶν νεκ-   ep. 1
     ρῶν τελεσθέντων† Ταλαϊονίδας
     εἶπεν ἐν Θήβαισι τοιοῦ-
     τόν τι ἔπος· "ποθέω ςτρατιᾶς ὀφθαλμὸν ἐμᾶς,
     ἀμφότερον μάντιν τ᾽ ἀγαθὸν καὶ
     δουρὶ μάρναςθαι." τὸ καί
     ἀνδρὶ κώμου δεσπόται πάρεςτι Cυρακοςίωι.
     οὔτε δύςηρις ἐὼν οὔτ᾽ ὢν φιλόνικος ἄγαν,
20   καὶ μέγαν ὅρκον ὀμόςςαις τοῦτό γέ οἱ ςαφέως
     μαρτυρήςω· μελίφθογ-
     γοι δ᾽ ἐπιτρέψοντι Μοῖςαι.

⟨===⟩

ὦ Φίντις, ἀλλὰ ζεῦξον ἤδη   str. 2
μοι ςθένος ἡμιόνων
ᾇ τάχος, ὄφρα κελεύθωι τ᾽ ἐν καθαρᾶι
βάςομεν ὄκχον, ἵκωμαί τε πρὸς ἀνδρῶν
25   καὶ γένος. κεῖναι γὰρ ἐξ ἀλ-
     λᾶν ὁδὸν ἁγεμονεῦςαι
     ταύταν ἐπίςτανται, ςτεφάνους ἐν Ὀλυμπίαι
     ἐπεὶ δέξαντο. χρὴ τοίνυν πύλας ὕμ-
     νων ἀναπιτνάμεν αὐταῖς.

---

12 Ἀγηςία Schroeder: Ἀγ- codd.   ἐνδίκου Herwerden: ἐν δίκαι codd.: ἐνδίκας Snell
13 γλώςςας A: -ης rell.   Ἀμφιάραον AG²CØ   14 ἐφθέγξατ᾽ A   φαιδίμους L¹¹EN
15 πυρᾶν: πυρᾶι Bernhardy   νεκρῶν: νεκροῖς coni. Wilamowitz   τελεσθέντων: τελε-
ςθειςᾶν Pauw: τ᾽ ἐδεςθέντων Bergk: τε δαιςθέντων Herwerden   πυραὶ νεκρῶν τέλεςθεν.
τὸν Robertson   Ταλαονίδας ABᵃᶜE?   16 Θήβαισι LCNØ: -ηςι A: -αις BEGH
τοιοῦτό τι B   17 τ᾽ om. A   δορί A   18 πάρεςτι: νῦν πάρεςτι fere recc. multi,
cf. app. ad Bacch. 3 [17]. 47   Cυρακοςίωι BGH, sim. N²Ø: -ουςίωι ALEC, sim. N¹
19 δύςηρις Ω: δύςερις AB rell.   φιλόνικος Cobet: -νεικος codd.   20 ὀμόςςαις fere
L²C¹¹Ø:-ας rell.   21 ἐπιτρέψοντι: -τέρψ- A   23 ᾇ Δ, sim. CᵖᶜHN, cf. BʸᵖEʸᵖ:
αἷ AEØ, sim. rell.: αἴ εἰς B   24 ἀνδρός Hartung   25 ἀλλᾶν G: ἄλλαν AB
rell. (ἅλαν C)   26 Ὀλυμπίαι: Ὀλυμ B¹   27 ἀναπεπτάμεν᾽ A

πρὸς Πιτάναν δὲ παρ' Εὐρώ-
τα πόρον δεῖ σάμερον ἐλθεῖν ἐν ὥραι.

⟨——⟩

ἅ τοι Ποσειδάωνι μιχθεῖ-   ant. 2
ca Κρονίωι λέγεται

30   παῖδα ἰόπλοκον Εὐάδναν τεκέμεν.
κρύψε δὲ παρθενίαν ὠδῖνα κόλποις·
κυρίωι δ' ἐν μηνὶ πέμποις'
ἀμφιπόλους ἐκέλευσεν
ἥρωϊ πορσαίνειν δόμεν Εἰλατίδαι βρέφος,
ὃς ἀνδρῶν Ἀρκάδων ἄνασσε Φαισά-
ναι, λάχε τ' Ἀλφεὸν οἰκεῖν.

35   ἔνθα τραφεὶς ὑπ' Ἀπόλλω-
νι γλυκείας πρῶτον ἔψαυς' Ἀφροδίτας.

⟨——⟩

οὐδ' ἔλαθ' Αἴπυτον ἐν παν-   ep. 2
τὶ χρόνωι κλέπτοισα θεοῖο γόνον·
ἀλλ' ὁ μὲν Πυθῶνάδ', ἐν θυ-
μῶι πιέσαις χόλον οὐ φατὸν ὀξείαι μελέται,
ὤιχετ' ἰὼν μαντευσόμενος ταύ-
τας περ' ἀτλάτου πάθας·
ἁ δέ, φοινικόκροκον ζώναν καταθηκαμένα

40   κάλπιδά τ' ἀργυρέαν, λόχμας ὑπὸ κυανέας
τίκτε θεόφρονα κοῦρον. τᾶι μὲν ὁ χρυσοκόμας
πραΰμητίν τ' Ἐλείθυι-
αν παρέστασέν τε Μοίρας·

⟨===⟩

ἦλθεν δ' ὑπὸ σπλάγχνων ὑπ' ὠδῖ-   str. 3
νός τ' ἐρατᾶς Ἴαμος

28 σάμερόν μ' Boeckh   29 Ποσειδάονι LCNØ   Κρονίωνι A^pcE   30 παῖδα ἰόπλοκον Bergk: παῖδ' ἰοπλόκαμον codd. (παῖδ' ἰοβόστρυχον recc. multi)   τεκέμεν: -εσθαι A^il   31 κρύψε: κρύψαι A^ilL^ilCN^ilØ: ἔκρυψε N^sl   32 ἐσκέλευεν A   33 Ἐλατίδαι B^pc   34 λάχε ACNØ: ἔλαχέ B, ita fere LEGH   37 πιέσαις Ø^il, sim. C^il: πιέσας A, πιέσσας B, rell. ita ut hi   μελέτηι B   38 ταύτης A   περ': περ AECN^1Ø   πάθας: -ης ALN: -ους B   39 καταθηκαμένα: κατακαμένα A^ac: καταθηκομένα Ø   40 λόχμαις ὑπὸ κυανέαις A   42 Ἐλείθυιαν PQ: Εἰλ- AB rell.   παρέστασέν fere PQm: παρέστασέ A (η s.l.) B rell.: παρέστας' ἔν Peek   43 ἦλθεν Fm: ἦλθε AB rell.   ὠδῖνός τ' ἐρατᾶς: τ' om. A: ὠδίνεσς' ἐραταῖς Wilamowitz: ὠδῖνός τ' ἐρατὸν Bergk σπλάγχ. φυγὼν ὠδῖν' ἐρατὸν Schulze

ἐς φάος αὐτίκα. τὸν μὲν κνιζομένα

45   λεῖπε χάμαι· δύο δὲ γλαυκῶπες αὐτόν
      δαιμόνων βουλαῖςιν ἐθρέ-
      ψαντο δράκοντες ἀμεμφεῖ
      ἰῶι μελιссᾶν καδόμενοι. βαςιλεὺς δ' ἐπεί
      πετραέссας ἐλαύνων ἵκετ' ἐκ Πυ-
      θῶνος, ἅπαντας ἐν οἴκωι
      εἴρετο παῖδα τὸν Εὐάδ-
      να τέκοι. Φοίβου γὰρ αὐτὸν φᾶ γεγάκειν

⟨——⟩

50   πατρός, περὶ θνατῶν δ' ἔςεσθαι   ant. 3
      μάντιν ἐπιχθονίοις
      ἔξοχον· οὐδέ ποτ' ἐκλείψειν γενεάν.
      ὣς ἄρα μάννε· τοὶ δ' οὔτ' ὦν ἀκοῦσαι
      οὔτ' ἰδεῖν εὔχοντο, πεμπταῖ-
      ον γεγενημένον. ἀλλ' ἔν
      κέκρυπτο γὰρ σχοίνωι βατιᾶι τ' ἐν ἀπειρίτωι,

55   ἴων ξανθαῖςι καὶ παμπορφύροις ἀκ-
      τῖςι βεβρεγμένος ἁβρόν
      cῶμα. τὸ καὶ κατεφάμι-
      ξεν καλεῖσθαί νιν χρόνωι ςύμπαντι μάτηρ

⟨——⟩

      τοῦτ' ὄνυμ' ἀθάνατον. τερ-   ep. 3
      πνᾶς δ' ἐπεὶ χρυσοστεφάνοιο λάβεν
      καρπὸν Ἥβας, Ἀλφεῶι μές-
      ςωι καταβαὶς ἐκάλεσσε Ποσειδᾶν' εὐρυβίαν,
      ὃν πρόγονον, καὶ τοξοφόρον Δά-
      λου θεοδμάτας σκοπόν,

---

44 κνυζομένα EᵖᶜC¹Ø   45 δύο ABCNØ: δύω LEGH   48 πετραέσσης A
50 πατρός γε A   ἔσσεσθαι A   51 οὐδέπω τέκεν λείψειν A   53–4 γεγενημένον
Ahrens: γεγεναμένον BLEGHCNØ: γεγεννναμένον A   ἀλλ' ἔν | κέκρυπτο fere Boeckh:
ἀλλ' ἐγ | κέκρυπτο B, ita fere LECNØ: ἀλλ' ἐγκρύπτετο GH: ἀλλ' ἐκρύπτετο A: ἀλλὰ |
κέκρυπτο Hermann   σχίνωι B   βατιᾶι Wilamowitz: βατίαι Xm: βατείαι AB rell.
ἀπειρίτωι Heyne: ἀπειράντωι codd. (-άτωι Em, cf. Günther (1998), 132–3): ἀκηράτωι
Heinrichs   55 ξανθαῖςί τε καὶ A   βεβρεγμένος: βεβραγμένος H, Thom. Mag.: Σ 92 b
Ζηνόδοτος γράφει ἀντὶ τοῦ βεβρεγμένος ⟨   ⟩   56 κατεφάμιξεν A (η s.l.) m: -ξε B
rell., ut uid.   νιν ACNØ: μιν rell.   57 τερπνὸν . . . λάχεν Heyne   58 καταβαὶς
Turyn: -βὰς codd.   ἐκάλεσσε BE alii: -εσε ACN alii   Ποσειδᾶν' BLGHCNØ: -ῶν'
A, sim. E   59 θεοδμάτου AN

60 αἰτέων λαοτρόφον τιμάν τιν' ἑᾶι κεφαλᾶι,
νυκτὸς ὑπαίθριος. ἀντεφθέγξατο δ' ἀρτιεπής·
πατρία ὄσσα μεταυδασέν τε νιν· "ὄρςο, τέκος,
δεῦρο, πάγκοινον ἐς χώ-
ραν ἴμεν φάμας ὄπισθεν."

⟨═══⟩

ἵκοντο δ' ὑψηλοῖο πέτραν   str. 4
ἀλίβατον Κρονίου
65 ἔνθα οἱ ὤπασε θησαυρὸν δίδυμον
μαντοσύνας, τόκα μὲν φωνὰν ἀκούειν
ψευδέων ἄγνωστον· εὖτ' ἂν
δὲ θρασυμάχανος ἐλθών
Ἡρακλέης, σεμνὸν θάλος Ἀλκαϊδᾶν, πατρί
ἑορτάν τε κτίςηι πλειστόμβροτον τεθ-
μόν τε μέγιστον ἀέθλων,
70 Ζηνὸς ἐπ' ἀκροτάτωι βω-
μῶι τότ' αὖ χρηστήριον θέςθαι κέλευςεν.⌋

⟨═══⟩

ἐξ οὗ πολύκλειτον καθ' Ἕλλα-   ant. 4
νας⌋ γένος Ἰαμιδᾶν·
ὄλβος ἅμ' ἔσπετο. τιμῶντες δ' ἀρετάς
ἐς φανερὰν ὁδὸν ἔρχονται· τεκμαίρει
χρῆμ' ἕκαστον. μῶμος ἐξ ἄλ-
λων κρέμαται φθονεόντων
75 τοῖς οἷς ποτε πρώτοις περὶ δωδέκατον δρόμον

60 λαότροφον Σ 102 c (A), cf. 102 a, d, f, 103   62 μεταύδασέν Bergk: μετάλλασε B, ita fere LEGHCΘ: μετάλλασσε ALᴾᶜ: μετάλασσε LᵃᶜN: μετάνςτασέν quoque Bergk   μεταλλάσσαντί ἰν Hermann   νιν A: μιν rell.   τέκος Σ 107 g (τὸ δὲ ἑξῆς λεγόμενον· ἐφθέγξατο "ὄρςο, τέκος", ubi τέκος BEL, τέκνον Q): τέκνον codd., Σ 107 a, b   63 χώραν ALⁱˡ: χῶρον rell.   67 ἄγνωτον AL   θραςυμήχανος BAᵃˡG²   68 πατρί Hermann: πατρί δ' A: πατρί θ' rell. (hic nec A nec B nec, ut puto, ceteri uersum terminant)   69 κτίςηι: -ει B, -οι E   πλειστόβροτον B   70 αὖ A: αὐτῶι rell.   κέλευςε: κέλευςέ νιν A   71 Ἕλ | B, νας | Π¹ (tamquam γένος | A, sed nihil nisi uersum suum finit; cf. 88, 93)   δᾶν | Π¹AB   72 ὄλβος ΠᶦᵃᶜΘm: ὄλβος δ' rell., Σ 122 a (A) lemm. εςπε[Π¹   το | A   τάς | Π¹AB   73 μαι | Π¹, ρει | AB   74 (χρημ' Π¹)   ἐξ | Π¹B   ε[Π¹   των | Π¹AB   75 τοῖς οἷς: τοίςίν Bothe   πρώτοις Π¹ALⁱˡEGHCᵖᶜN²: πρῶτον BLˢˡCᵃᶜN¹Ø   περὶ[Π¹   κατον | Π¹AB

ἐλαυνόντεccιν αˌιˈδοία ποτιˌcτά-
ξηι Χάρις εὐκλέα μορφˌάν.
εἰ δ᾽ ἐτύμως ὑπὸ Κυλλά-
νας ὄροֿ, Ἀγηcία, μάτρωεc ἄνδρεc
⟨—⟩
ναιετάοντεc ἐδώρη-   ep. 4
cαν θεῶν κάρυκα λιταῖc θυcίαιc
πολλὰ δὴ πολλαῖcιν Ἑρμᾶν
εὐcεβέˌωc,ˌ ὃc ἀγῶναc ἔχει μοῖράν τ᾽ ἀέθλων,
80   Ἀρκαδίαν τ᾽ εὐάνορα τιμᾶι,
κεῖνοc, ὦ παῖ Cωcτράτου,
cὺν βαρυγδούπωι πατρὶ κραίνει cέθεν εὐτυχίαν.
δόξαν ἔχω †τιν᾽ ἐπὶ γλώccαι ἀκονᾶc λιγυρᾶc†,
ἅ μ᾽ ἐθέλονˌτˌα προcέλκει καλλιρόαιˌcιˌ πνοαῖc.
ματρομάτωρ ἐμὰ Cτυμ-
φαλίc, εὐανθὴc Μεˌτώπα,
⟨═⟩
85   πλάξιππον ἇˌΘήβαˌν ἔτικτεν·   str. 5
τᾶc ἐρατˌεινὸˌν ὕδωρ
πίομαι ἀνδρˌάcιν,ˌ αἰχμˌαταˌῖˌcι πλέκων
ποικίλον ὕμˌνον. ὄˌτρυˌνˌον νῦν ἑτˌαίρουc,
Αἰνέα, πρῶˌτον μˌˌὲν Ἥραν

76 ποτι | Π¹ΑΒ   ποτιcτάξηι fere Π¹ (]cτάξη) L, Σ 127 a D lemm.: -ξει GHCO²: -ζει
ABENO¹Ø   τι | Π¹ΑΒ   εὐκλεᾶ ΑΒ alii   μορφάν: μορφήν ACNOᴾᶜØ: μοῖραν Hecker
φά(ή)ν | Π¹ΑΒ   77 (δ᾽ Π¹)   ὄροc Π¹, Γᵃᶜ?: ὄροιc ΑΒ, ita fere rell.   οc (οιc) | Π¹ΑΒ
ρεc Π¹   ρεc | Π¹ΑΒ   78 ἐδώρηcαν Π¹ΑΒ²m, recc. alii: δώρηcαν Β¹ rell.: ἐδωρήcαντο
Hermann   ὦν | Π¹ΑΒ   λειταῖc Π¹ᵃᶜ   αιc | Π¹ΑΒ   79 μαν Π¹   εˌ[Π¹ (uestigia
tenuissima)   ωc | Π¹ΑΒ   χει | Π¹ΑΒ   (τ᾽ Π¹)   80 ίαν | Π¹ΑΒ   (τ᾽ Π¹)   τιμὰν
Α   (μᾶϊ Π¹; μᾶιˑ legit e.p. (Grenfell))   τι | Π¹Β, μὰν | Α   κῖνοc Π¹ᵃᶜ (postea ι in ει
corr.)   του | Π¹ΑΒ   81 βρυ- Π¹ᵃᶜ   τρὶ | Π¹ΑΒ   εὐτυχείαν Π¹ᵃᶜ   αν | Π¹ΑΒ
82–3 καὶ δόξαν NᵃᶜO   ἔχων N   (τιν᾽ Π¹)   πὶ | Π¹ΑΒ   (γλωccαϊ Π¹ (γλωccᾶιˑ legit
e.p.); γλώccη,. Α; γλώccαι, Β, sim. H)   λιγ Π¹   ρᾶc | Π¹ΑΒ   (ἅ μ᾽ Π¹)   ονˌ[ ]ᾳ
Π¹   τιν᾽ κτλ.: τιν᾽ ἐπὶ γλώccαc (iam Bergk) ἀκόναι λιγυρᾶc· | ἀλλ᾽ (tum προcέλκει . . .
πνοαῖc ματρ.) Beattie: τιν᾽ ἐπὶ γλώccαc ἀκόναν λιγυρᾶc (tum προcέλκει . . . πνοαῖc, ματρ.)
Dover: τοι (nisi τὶν) ἐπὶ γλώccαc ἀκόναι λιγυρᾶι Hutchinson: τιν᾽ ἐπὶ γλώccαι λιγυρᾶc
ἀκόναc Bergk: τιν᾽ ἐπὶ γλώccαι δόνακοc λιγυροῦ MacDiarmid   προcέλκει GᵞᵖHᵞᵖTricl.:
προcέλκοι Eᵞᵖ: προc[έρ]πει Π¹, προcέρπει rell.   πει | Π¹ΑΒ   καλλιρόαιcι Grenfell:
-ρόαι[cι]ν Π¹: -ρόοιcι codd.   πνοιαῖc Π¹CNOØ   84 τρο | Β, μά | Π¹Α   τˌωρ Π¹
cτυμφαλιc Π¹   θὴc | Α   πα | Π¹Β   85 (ἵππονά Π¹)   ἔτικτεν G, alii: ἔτικεν Π¹:
ἔτικτε ΑΒ, alii   ἔτι | Π¹Β   τᾶc: τεc Π¹ᵃᶜ   δωρ | Π¹ΑΒ   86 ανδρˌ[. . . .]ᾳιχμˌ[. . .]ιˌ[
Π¹   κων | Π¹ΑΒ   87 ετˌ[Π¹   ρουc | Π¹ΑΒ   88 (νεα· Π¹) tamquam
νέα | Α   ενη Π¹   Ἥ | Π¹Β, ραν | Α

Παρθενίαιν κελαδῆϲαι,

γνῶναί τ' ἔπειτ' ἀρχαῖοιν ὄινειδοϲ ἀλαθέϲιν

90 λόγοιϲ ιεἰι φεύγομεν, Βοιιωτίαν ὗν.

ἐϲϲὶ γὰρ ἄγγελοϲ ὀιρθόϲ,

ἠϋκόμων ϲκυτιάλα Μοι-

ϲᾶν, γλυκὺϲ κρατὴρ ἀγαφθέγκτων ἀοιδᾶν.

⟨——⟩

εἶπον δὲ μεμνᾶιϲθαι Ϲυραικοϲ- ant. 5

ϲᾶν ιτει κιαὶ Ὀρτυγίαϲ.

τὰν Ἱέριων καθαρῶι ϲκάπτωι διέπων,

ἄρτια μιηδόμενοϲ, φοινικόπεζαν

95 ἀμφέπιει Δάματρα λευκίπ-

που τε θυγατρὸϲ ἑορτάν

ικαὶ Ζηνὸϲ Αἰτναίου κράτοϲ· ἀδύλογοι δέ νιν

λύραι μολπαί τε γινώϲκοντι. μὴ θράϲ-

ϲοι χρόνοϲ ὄλβον ἐφέρπων,

ϲὺν δὲ φιλοφροϲύναιϲ εὐ-

ηράτοιϲ Ἁγηϲία δέξαιτο κῶμον

⟨——⟩

οἴκοθεν οἴκαδ' ἀπὸ Ϲτυμ- ep. 5

φαλίων τειχέων ποτινιϲόμενον,

100 ματέρ' εὐμήλοιο λείποντ'

Ἀρκαδίαϲ. ἀγαθαὶ δὲ πέλοντ' ἐν χειμερίαι

Παρθενίαι B ιαˏ[...]αδ Π¹ ϲαι | Π¹AB 89 τεπειˏ[Π¹ (τ᾽ε)]νοˏ[.]ειˏ[Π¹ δοϲ |
Π¹ λα | B ἀλαθέϲιν EN𝑚 quidem: -ϲι Π¹AB alii θέϲι | A 90 γοιϲ | Π¹ αν |
B, ὗν | Π¹A ἔϲϲι: εεϲι Π¹ᶜ: εε ˏι Π¹ᵃᶜ: ἔϲτι (tum ὀρθόϲ | ἠϋκ.) Wilamowitz θόϲ | Π¹AB
91 ηϋ Π¹ κὺϲ | AB ἀγαφθέγκτων fere BLEGHCNOΘ: ἀφθόγγων A: ἀγαφθόγγων
Mommsen δᾶν | Π¹AB 92 εἶπον (imper.; εἰπόν Stephanus) pro indicat. habuit
Wilamowitz μεμνῆϲθαι CNOΘ Ϲυρακοϲϲᾶν B, ita fere LᵃᶜEGHCΘ: -κουϲϲᾶν Π¹,
-κουϲᾶν A, ita fere ut hi LᴾᶜNO ρα | Π¹B]κˏ[Π¹ ίαϲ | Π¹AB 93 Ἱέρων Aᶜ
(ἴερ Π¹) tamquam ρῶι | A ϲκάπτωι Π¹AEGHCNOΘ: ϲκάπτρωι BL πων | Π¹AB
94 ζαν | Π¹AB 95 (αμφˏ Π¹) επˏ[Π¹; post hunc uersum suum finit columnam.
ceteros autem uersus omisit, ut uidetur Δάματρα etiam B, credo: Δάμητρα A (Δήμ.
Aˢˡ): Δάματραν NL² ἑορτάϲ A 96 νιν ACNOΘ: μιν rell. 97 μολπαί: πολλαί
CΘ θράϲϲοι Boeckh (cf. Σ 163 b (A) μὴ ταράϲϲοι): ˏραύϲοι A (ψ potius dicas quam θ,
cf. 22, 67): θραύϲοι rell.: θραύϲαι Hermann 98 εὐηράτοιϲ AʸᴾBLEGHCN²O²Θ:
εὐκράτοιϲ AN¹O¹ 100 μήτερ' ANO λείποντ' Xwm: λιπόντ' AB rell. εὐμηλόν
τε λείποντ' Ἀρκαδίαν Hartung πέλοντ' ἐν BGHNOΘ: -ονται γ' ἐν A: -ονται τ' ἐν C:
-ονται Lⁱˡ (-οντι ἐν s.l.) E

νυκτὶ θοᾶς ἐκ ναὸς ἀπεσκίμ-
φθαι δύ' ἄγκυραι· θεός
τῶνδε κείνων τε κλυτὰν αἶαν παρέχοι φιλέων·ˌ
δέcπˌοτα ποντˌόμεδοῦ, εὐθὺˌν δὲ πλόον κˌαμάτων
ἐκτὸˌc ἐόντα δίδοˌι, χρυcαλακˌάτοιο πόcιˌc
105   Ἀμφιτρίταc· ἐˌμῶν δ' ὑμ-
νˌων ἄεξ' εὐτερπὲc ἄνθοc.

⟨═══⟩

SOPHOCLES

19: *Aiacis* uu. 1185–1222

libri: L (Laurentianus 32. 9, s. x med.); G (Laurentianus, conv. soppr. 152, a. 1282
p. C.), R (Vaticanus gr. 2291, s. xv), Q (Parisinus, suppl. gr. 109, s. xvi); A (Parisinus
gr. 2712, c. 1300 p. C.), D (Neapolitanus II. F. 9, s. xiv in.), Xr (Vindobonensis
phil. gr. 161, a. 1412 p. C.), Xs (Vindobonensis suppl. gr. 71, s. xiv partis post.), Zr
(Marcianus gr. 616, s. xv); C (Parisinus gr. 2735, s. xiii partis post.), F (Laurentianus
28. 25, s. xiii uel xiv), H (Laurentianus 32. 40, s. xiii uel xiv), N (Matritensis gr. 4677,
s. xiii partis post.), P (Heidelbergensis Palat. gr. 40, s. xiii uel xiv), V (Marcianus
gr. 468, s. xiii uel xiv); T (Parisinus gr. 2711, s. xiv), Ta (Marcianus gr. 470, s. xv).
L solum contuli, ex imaginibus a Thompson Jebbque editis (1885); in ceteris usus
sum in primis Dawe (1973–8), ii. 43–4, (1996); Lloyd-Jones et Wilson (1990a). uu.
1188–90 apparent *Sud.* δ 1401 (δορυccόντων μόχθων, cf. Eust. *Il.* 1292. 20), 1193–
6 ω 268 (ὤφελε-Ἄρη), 1202 ο 747 (οὔτε-ὄτοβον) [A=Parisinus gr. 2626, s. xii, S=
Vaticanus 1296, a. 1205 p. C., G=Parisinus gr. 2623, s. xv, M=Marcianus gr. 448, s.
xiii]; 1219–20 Eust. *Il.* 649. 54.

1185   Χο. τίc ἄρα νέατοc, ἐc πότε λή-   str. 1
        ξει πολυπλάγκτων ἐτέων ἀριθμόc,

101 ἀπεcκίμφθαι ΒΕΗCNᵖᶜØᶜ?, Eust., ita fere LG: -ῆφθαι Α: -άφθαι Νᵃᶜ: -έφθαι Ο
102 τῶνδε κείνων Ρ: τῶν δ' ἐκείνων ΑΒ rell.: τῶν τε κείνων Heyne   παρέχει GCⁱˡNⁱˡOⁱˡ
103] οˌταπο.τοˌ[(pro ν putaris η esse scriptum) Π²   ποντομέδων Boeckh   δον |
Π²Β, Α? (interuallum quoddam)   εὔθυνε πλόον καμάτων δ' Α   κˌ[Π²   των |
Π²ΑΒ   104 χρυ | Π²ΑΒ   cιc | A   105 φι | Π² (ueri sim.), τρί | Β   δ' om.
Α   ]μωνδυμνˌ[Π²   ἄεξ': δέξ̇: δέξ' ALNOᶜ: δὲ δέξ' Bergk   εὐπρεπὲc EG   θοc | Π²ΑΒ
19. paragraphis papyri scaenicorum strophas non uidentur discernere; nam alios in
usus eos reseruant   1186 πολυπλάκτων GRQOD

τὰν ἄπαυστον αἰὲν ἐμοὶ δορυccοή-
τῶν μόχθων ἄταν ἐπάγων
1190 †ἀνὰ τὰν εὐρώδη Τροίαν†,
δύcτανον ὄνειδοc Ἑλλάνων;

ὄφελε πρότερον αἰθέρα δῦ-   ant. 1
ναι μέγαν ἢ τὸν πολύκοινον Ἀιδαν
1195 κεῖνοc ἀνὴρ ὃc cτυγερῶν ἔδειξεν ὅπ-
λων Ἑλλαcιν κοινὸν Ἄρη.
ὢ πόνοι πρόγονοι πόνων·
κεῖνοc γὰρ ἔπερcεν ἀνθρώπουc.

ἐκεῖνοc οὔτε cτεφάνων   str. 2
1200 οὔτε βαθειᾶν κυλίκων
νεῖμεν ἐμοὶ τέρψιν ὁμιλεῖν,
οὔτε γλυκὺν αὐλῶν ὄτοβον,
δύcμοροc, οὔτ' ἐννυχίαν τέρψιν ἰαύειν.
1205 ἐρώτων δ', ἐρώτων ἀπέπαυcεν, ὤμοι.
κεῖμαι δ' ἀμέριμνοc οὔτωc,
ἀεὶ πυκιναῖc δρόcοιc
τεγγόμενοc κόμαc,
1210 λυγρᾶc μνήματα Τροίαc.

καὶ πρὶν μὲν αἰὲν νυχίου   ant. 2
δείματοc ἦν μοι προβολὰ
καὶ βελέων θούριοc Αἴαc.
νῦν δ' οὗτοc ἀνεῖται cτυγερῶι

1187–8 ἄπαυτ- West in Aeschylo   δορυccοήτων L: -όντων fere rell., *Sud.*   1190 ἀνὰ
τὰν: om. Hᵃᶜ, add. H¹: ἂν τὰν Ahrens: τάνδ' ἀν' Lobeck   εὐρώδη (εὐ- DXsHO): εὐρυεδῆ
Musgrave   Τροίαν: Τροίαν Dindorf: χθόνα Pearson   1192 ὄφελε PTTa: ὤφελε
fere rell., *Sud.*   1195 cτυγερῶν: -ὸν *Sud.*   1196 ἀνήρ: ἀνὴρ codd., *Sud.*
ὃc: ὃ Lᵃᶜ   Ἑλλαcιν LFTTa: -cι rell., *Sud.*   Ἄρη LADXrXs, Sudae A: Ἄρην rell.,
ita fere Sudae SGM   1197 ὢ: ὦ TTa: ἰὼ rell.   1199 κεῖνοc XsᵖᶜFHT
quidem   οὔτε: οὐ Hermann   1200 βαθειᾶν LAˢ¹ZrPTTa: βαθεῖαν fere rell.
1202 ὄτοβον Lⁱ¹GRQCᵃᶜFᵃᶜNᵃᶜVᵃᶜTTa, *Sud.*: ὅττοβον Lˢ¹ rell.   1203 δυcμόρωι
Blaydes   1205 ἐρ. δ' ἐρ. GRQ: ἐρ. ἐρ. δ' fere rell.   ἀπέπαυcεν: ἀπέcπαcεν Zr:
ἀπέcπαcέ μ' N: ἀπέπαυcέ μ' Blaydes   1207 πυκναῖc GRQHNOP   1210 λυγρᾶc
Brunck: -ᾶc codd.   1211 καὶ: om. TTa: ἦ Dawe   αἰὲν νυχίου G. Wolff: ἐννυχίου
codd. (οὖν ἐνν. TTa)   1214 ἀνεῖται ADXrXsZrTTa, ΣL in marg. sin.: α . . . . ται
L (a prius L¹, fortasse -κειται a.c.; ἔγκειται K): ἔγκειται fere rell.   cτυγερῶc Lᵃᶜ

1215 δαίμονι. τίς μοι, τίς ἔτ᾽ οὖν τέρψις ἐπέσται;
γενοίμαν ἵν᾽ ὑλᾶεν ἔπεστι πόντωι
πρόβλημ᾽ ἁλίκλυστον, ἄκραν
1220 ὑπὸ πλάκα Coυνίου,
τὰς ἱερὰς ὅπως
προσείποιμεν Ἀθάνας.

EURIPIDES

20: Medeae uu. 627–662

libri: L (Laurentianus 32. 2, s. xiv in.; Tr = Triclinii correctiones in L), P (Palatinus gr. 287, s. xiv in.); B (Parisinus gr. 2713, s. xi), O (Laurentianus 31. 10, c. 1175 p. C.), C (Vaticanus gr. 910, s. xiv), D (Laurentianus 31. 15, s. xiv), E (Athous, Μονὴ Ἰβήρων 209 (olim 161), s. xiv in.), A (Parisinus gr. 2712, s. xiii ex.), V (Vaticanus gr. 909, c. 1250–80 p. C.). gV = gnomologia in Vatopediano 36 (s. xii). LPB ex iis imaginibus contuli quas uulgauit Spranger (1920, 1939–46, 1938); in ceteris praecipue Diggle (1981–94) et van Looy (1992) secutus sum. praeterea J. Diggle dubitationes quasdam meas de L amice resoluit. 633–5 adfert Eust. Il. 568. 25–6 (μήποτ᾽–ὀϊστόν).

Χο. ἔρωτες ὑπὲρ μὲν ἄγαν ἐλ-   str. 1
θόντες οὐκ εὐδοξίαν
οὐδ᾽ ἀρετὰν παρέδωκαν
630 ἀνδράσιν· εἰ δ᾽ ἅλις ἔλθοι
Κύπρις, οὐκ ἄλλα θεὸς εὔχαρις οὕτω.
μήποτ᾽, ὦ δέσποιν᾽, ἐπ᾽ ἐμοὶ χρυσέων τόξ-
ων ἀφείης, ἱμέρωι χρί-
635 cας᾽, ἄφυκτον οἰστόν.

cτέργοι δέ με Cωφροcύνα, δώ-   ant. 1
ρημα κάλλιστον θεῶν.

1216 ἐπέσται: ἔτ᾽ ἔcται Blaydes   1217 ὑλῶεν fere GRQFᵖᶜNOPTTa   1218 πόν-
τωι Morstadt: -ου codd.   1219 ἄκραν: ἱερὴν Eust.   1220 ὑποπλάκα fere L,
Eust.   20. 631 οὕτω L: [C]: οὕτως rell.   633 μήποτ᾽ BOCV A in ras.: μὴ
δέ ποτ᾽ fere L(P)DE ΣB   634 ἀφείης Naber: ἐφείης BODEAP ΣB: ἐφίης L (-εις
Tr) V, Eust.: [C]   636 cτέργει EP: [C]

μηδέ ποτ' ἀμφιλόγους ὀρ-
γὰς ἀκόρεστά τε νείκη,
640 θυμὸν ἐκπλήξας' ἑτέροις ἐπὶ λέκτροις,
προσβάλοι δεινὰ Κύπρις· ἀπτολέμους δ' εὐ-
νὰς σεβίζους' ὀξύφρων κρί-
νοι λέχη γυναικῶν.

645 ὦ πάτρις, ὦ δώματα, μὴ   str. 2
δῆτ' ἄπολις γενοίμαν
τὸν ἀμηχανίας ἔχουσα δυσπέρατον αἰῶ
οἰκτροτάτων ἀχέων.
650 θανάτωι, θανάτωι πάρος δαμείην
ἀμέραν τάνδ' ἐξανύσα-
σα. μόχθων δ' οὐκ ἄλλος ὕπερ-
θεν ἢ γᾶς πατρίας στέρεσθαι.

εἴδομεν, οὐκ ἐξ ἑτέρων   ant. 2
655 μῦθον ἔχω φράσασθαι·
σὲ γὰρ οὐ πόλις, οὐ φίλων τις ὤικτισεν παθοῦσαν
δεινότατον παθέων.
ἀχάριστος ὄλοιθ' ὅτωι πάρεστιν
660 μὴ φίλους τιμᾶν καθαρᾶν
ἀνοίξαντα κλῆιδα φρενῶν·
ἐμοὶ μὲν φίλος οὔποτ' ἔσται.

---

638 ἀμφὶ λόγους fere BᵃᶜCV¹P   642 προσβάλοι BODEV: -βάλλοι L: -βάλοιμι AP
(-βάλλοιμ' ὦ Tr): [C]   643–4 ἀπτολέμους L(P)BODEAV³: ἀπολ- CV, Tr   δ'
om. L(P)OC   κρίνοι etiam Tr ΣB: κρίνει L, Pˢˡ (postea deletum est)   σεβίζοιμ'
ὀξ. κρῖναι (κρ. Scaliger) Badham: σέβουσα ξυμφρόνων κρίνω Weil   645 δώματα
Nauck: δώμα** L (δῶμά τ' ἐμόν Tr): δῶμα rell.   647 τὸν ἀμηχανίας: ἐν ἀμηχανίαις
Reiske   648 δυσπέρατον: -αστον B ΣB: -αντον OC?   αἰῶ Stinton: αἰὼν' fere
codd. (αἰῶ | ν' B quidem)   649 οἰκτροτάτων: -οτάτων τ' Hutchinson: -ότατον
Musgrave: -ότατόν γ' Willink   650 θαν., θαν. P quoque: θαν. L   651 ἀμ. τάνδ'
TrP quoque: τάνδ' ἀμ. L: πρὶν ἀμ. τάνδ' E, cf. Vᵍˡ: [C]   ἐξανύσαι EV²   652 δ'
om. B   655 μῦθον Nauck: μύθων codd.   656 οὐ φίλ. τις ante οὐ πόλ.
L(P)   657 ὤικτισεν Musgrave: ὤικτειρεν fere codd.: οἰκτιρεῖ (-ερ-) Wieseler
658 δεινότατον Tr: δεινότατα rell. (quod ad P attinet, cf. P e.g. in *Alc.* 159, *IA* 317)
659 πάρεστι: παρέσται Tr: παρέστη Badham   660 καθαρᾶν Badham: -ὰν codd.,
gV   661 ἀνοίξαντα etiam gV: -αντι L(P)B²   662 οὔποτ': οὐκ Tr, non L

COMMENTARY

ALCMAN

Introduction

THE history of lyric begins for us with some extraordinary and enigmatic fragments from the Spartan poet Alcman. Both this historical position and the Spartan environment can subtly mislead approaches to the poetry; a rapid survey of some of the context may prove helpful. The commentaries on the two largest fragments will argue that they present particularly elaborate and sophisticated art. The brief survey of the Spartan context will not show that the environment makes such poetry a positive probability (even for Augustan Rome such a line of argument would be dubious); but it should make it clear that the environment poses no obstacle to this understanding.

Alcman's date would give little ground to endow his poetry with a patina of mysterious antiquity. He mentions Leotychidas I (Alcm. TA10a = Alcm. 5 fr. 2 col. ii. 13–22), whom the earliest sequence of kings (Herodotus') would place in the last quarter of the seventh century. Whatever his exact date, he should belong in the seventh century. He is thus contemporary with (or later than) various elegiac and iambic poets of whom we can form a reasonable notion, such as Archilochus and Tyrtaeus. If he is writing late in the seventh century, the view with the most to support it, he will be little earlier than Alcaeus. In literary terms, Alcman is not particularly lonely.[1]

Our knowledge of Sparta in the seventh century is not great; but in some ways we have more firsthand evidence than for the fifth:

---

[1] Date of Alcman: West (1965); Harvey, (1967); Schneider (1985). King-lists: Hdt. 7. 204, 8. 131. 2; discussion and setting out of lists: Forrest (1980), 19–23 (cf. (1969), 106–10); Cartledge (1979), 341–6, (1987), 101. Rhianus, a rather unencouraging source, associated Leotychidas with the 'Second Messenian War' (*FGrHist* 265 F 43), and Schneider (1985) consequently supposes that Alcman and Tyrtaeus were contemporaries (despite Pausanias' claims about Tyrtaeus). Schneider's learned article certainly reminds one that all archaic chronologies rest on a rather fragile basis. If the Homeric poems also belong in the seventh century, as they might perfectly well, the literary context for Alcman becomes still richer. Cf. for this view Burkert (1976); West (1995), esp. 209 (warfare). But Alcman is likely to be writing after the *Iliad* at least (cf. esp. Alcm. 77).

for evidence from outside Sparta is always prone to generality and distortion (often idealizing distortion). The material evidence is the most arresting. However, there is some danger of bunching all the seventh- and sixth-century evidence together with the object of producing an antithesis to the standard views of classical Sparta. The great developments in Spartan art occur in the sixth century. Even the well-known terracotta grotesque masks may not begin before 600; the more ambitious style of vase-painting, Laconian III, probably does not begin until around 580. Work in bronze and stone really flowers in the sixth century. None the less, work in ivory had begun in the middle of the seventh century, not to mention figures in lead. Laconian II is not without its attractions (see the fish cups, Lane (1933–4), pl. 30), and substantial exports of pottery were beginning. Spartan and probably Spartan bronze hydriae belong around the very start of the sixth century. Excavation of the Old Menelaion shows monumental building in the late seventh or early sixth century, even apart from the first temple of Artemis Orthia (*c.*700) and its all-stone successor (570–60). The society is evidently growing in creativity; it is also growing in prosperity and even luxury, doubtless through the Spartans' possession of Messenia.[2]

One or two points about art are also suggestive, even if one is necessarily thinking of sixth-century art in particular. An interest is shown then, but at other times too, in amusing figures. This is not, and could hardly be, the same kind of humour as that to be found in Alcman's fragments (e.g. 17 on Alcman's own tastes in food); but it shows susceptibilities that the later evidence might not have encouraged us to look for. (Yet did all fifth-century Spartans always keep straight faces?) Notable too in Laconian III, where mythological figures begin to be depicted, is an interest in Greek myth

---

[2] On the archaeological evidence, see Cavanagh, Crouwel, Catling, and Shipley (1996); Stibbe (1996). Dawkins (1929) presents the crucial excavations from the temple of Artemis Orthia; for the excavation at the Menelaion see Catling (1977); for earlier material, Tod and Wace (1906) is still of use. Stibbe (1972) is the standard work on the figured 6th-cent. pottery; cf. Boardman (1998), 108, 185–8. For the hydriae, cf. Diehl (1964), 7–11 (the Grächwil jar is now thought to have at least some relation to Sparta). Fitzhardinge (1980) offers a splendidly illustrated synthesis of the art. The archaeology is put in a larger context by, among others, Cartledge (1979), chs. 8 and 9; Osborne (1996), 177–85. The chronology of the pottery (and so of the other art) adopted by Lane (1933–4) was revised downwards by Boardman (1963); this revision is generally accepted, cf. e.g. Stibbe (1972), 8–9. On trade in pottery see Nafissi's chapter in Stibbe (1989). For monumental building note also the mid-6th-cent. Doric capital, which attests by chance another sizable temple (Cavanagh, Crouwel, Catling, and Shipley (1996), 207–8).

in general, not only the figures of special importance in Sparta. This should prevent precipitate inference from the emphasis on local myths and figures in the fragments of Alcman. In Pindar's poetry too the myths and figures of the victor's or chorus's city play a prominent role. We should not deduce from Alcman that the Spartans at this time were unusually insular.[3]

The much-disputed political and social changes of the seventh century cannot be considered properly here. Tyrtaeus' Εὐνομία (the name is significant, whoever conferred it) shows concern with the structure of Spartan society, as established in their 'constitution'. Tyrtaeus' words (fr. 4 West, cf. fr. 2) and the constitution itself (Plut. *Lyc.* 6. 2) show together a mixture of hierarchy, popular power, and interest in the divine; the constitution shows precise arrangements and elaborate organization of the citizen body.

Alcman's maidens are obviously joined in some form of lifestyle which involves or includes singing and dancing, under the guidance of an admired leader; the same, it must be stressed, is also true of the boys (10 (*b*); they are 'beardless'). Spartan choruses, of boys and of girls, were famous later too. The institution seems to encourage the girls, at least in the fiction of the poetry or the convention of the society, to nurse an amorous devotion to their leader. One may here be seeing a formal structuring of the girls' lives into homosexual attachments; or the poetry may be exploiting informal expectations about the behaviour of girls. It might well be that the Spartans had already instituted that formidable system of military training which makes the direst inventions of public schools look tame. It is very probable that the society was much concerned with war. However, Callinus' elegies of martial exhortation show that Tyrtaeus' were nothing unique; and the pattern of life for the girls appears to have something in common with that of contemporary Lesbos. Whether the boys might perhaps have joked with each other we do not know. The maiden songs suggest that the lifestyle and feelings of the girls are to charm and amuse the audience, not simply to be nodded at in grim approbation.[4]

---

[3] Standard myths appear in Alcman too (68, 69, 70 (*b*), 77, 80, etc.), as in Tyrt. fr. 12. 1–8 West. The humorous element in Spartan art is well brought out by Fitzhardinge (1980), 46, 55, 95.

[4] Even Tyrtaeus' depiction of youth is intriguing (fr. 10. 27–30 West). 'Xenophon's' later picture of the deportment of adolescents (*Lac.* 3. 4–5) is painted with the obvious intent of rescuing the Spartan system from the common accusations of sexual impropriety (cf. 2. 14). On laughter cf. some of the material of David

Spartan religion at this period is an obscure subject. Some promi-
nent recipients of cult appear in the likeness of gods widely wor-
shipped in Greece, such as Apollo and Artemis (Orthia); others
have a place in Greek culture, but as figures of myth associated
with Sparta, such as Menelaus and Helen; the Dioscuri come in be-
tween. We have fairly little basis beyond the fragments of Alcman
for extrapolating the kind of religious ritual behind the poems; ela-
borate constructions designed to house the poems are unlikely to
find the reality. More can perhaps be learnt from what the poems
actually emphasize. What we can note, in general, is the attention
given to display and artistry in the context of religion: the building
of temples, and especially the choral performances. Alcm. 1 [**1**] and
3 [**2**] bring out, subtly but centrally, the visible and audible beauty
of their own dazzling occasions.[5]

The liveliness of seventh- and sixth-century Sparta can hardly
be questioned. There remains a temptation, it appears, to treat
Alcman's poetry as unsophisticated. The maiden songs have even
been described as, for their original audience, 'surely a very simple
entertainment'. While their 'gaiety' is assumed (without sufficient
argument), it seems to be felt that the spirit and attractiveness of
the songs result automatically from their being about girls. The
commentaries that follow will attempt to show that they are more
complex and refined works of art than is generally supposed. Noth-
ing we know about the society makes this unlikely.[6]

A little can be said about the poet himself and his activity. An-
cient scholars disputed whether he came from Lydia, probably on

(1989). Important later evidence on Spartan choruses is Sosibius *FGrHist* 595 F 5,
Polycrates *FGrHist* 588 F 1 (cf. Boring (1979), 42–3). Cf. also Alcm. 11, with Parker
(1989), 144. For inference from the girls' way of life to the boys' cf. Osborne (1996),
182–3. Alcm. 98 appears to refer to Spartans' common meals. Sallares (1991), 170–1,
might seem to underrate female structures in the public consciousness of the society,
male as well as female. Cf. also Thommen (1999), esp. 135.

[5] On Spartan religion see Wide (1893); Ziehen (1929); Hooker (1980), ch. 3; Parker
(1989). There is no space to discuss the valuable material collected by Calame (1977)
around these poems as occasions. However, the evidence does not in my opinion suf-
fice to link these poems to rites of initiation (this does not exclude the relevance of
structural ideas). Cf. Stehle (1997), 87–8. Stehle's own interesting notion of Alcm.
1 [**1**] as matrimonial advertisement for the singers does not, I think, gain sufficient
support from Plut. *Lyc.* 15. 1: the justification of Sparta's seemingly improper
education of girls is a familiar intellectual construction, rather than evidence for the
meaning of ritual in the 7th cent.

[6] 'Surely a very simple entertainment' (Page (1951*a*), v); Barrett's echo ((1961),
683) sounds less crude.

the basis of his poems alone, or one part of one poem (16, with which cf. 5. 2 col. ii. 9–10). There is certainly nothing in his name to indicate a Lydian paternity, so far as one can tell from names extant on Lydian inscriptions; it looks simply like a Doric version of the name Alcmaeon (cf. Pind. *Pyth.* 8. 46; Hes. fr. 193. 1 Merkelbach–West). It is more interesting that he, and probably he only, has been assigned the job of producing poetry to be sung at festivals involving choruses of youths and maidens. The Spartans are sufficiently interested in the excellence of these performances to assign him this professional role. No doubt he did more for the performances than simply write the words; but the precise nature of his relation to the young performers is unclear. Alcm. 26, addressed to girls and declaring that the narrator's limbs can no longer bear him up, is most naturally referred, as by the author who quotes it, to the old poet's life of toil with choruses. Certainly other fragments refer to the poet by name, and show that, in some types of poem at least, he could bring in the idea of himself. Poem 39, which says that Alcman invented 'these words and this song', might appear to introduce him into a relatively formal poem sung by others. Poem 58 might suggest a symposiastic context; he is said to have composed for weddings (TA6). It is possible, if a conjecture suggested on 3 [2]. '97' should be right, that we might see the same girl as part of the chorus in at least two different poems, with different chorus-leaders (unless there are two girls of the same name). The implications of this for the girls and for Alcman's activity might be of interest.[7]

The poems make some use of local dialect. This forms a striking contrast with the epic and elegiac tradition, where for the most part a form of Ionic is used regardless of the author or audience. (So in Tyrtaeus.) It is notable that this type of poetry, in the case of Alcman at least, should be thought to have sufficient connections with the locale for local dialect to have some impact on its language. How much is unclear. Ancient editors have imported some dialect features which are too late for Alcman's time, notably ϲ for θ. Other features, however, are guaranteed by metre, notably the use of ϝ, employed in a proper name (1 [1]. 76 ϝιανθεμίϲ), as well as in words where the metrical effect of a ϝ might in theory derive from epic. The poems display numerous alternative forms, attested

---

[7] Disputes on Alcman's origin: see TA1a–9. For the names on Lydian inscriptions see Gusmani (1964), 232–4, (1980–6), 142–6.

by metre, and so cannot simply be written in a local dialect. Their un-Laconian feminine participles in -οιϲα are standard too in Stesichorus and Pindar. Provided these are genuine, it is very tempting to infer, not a mysterious connection with Cyrene, but what became or was already a common feature of language for this branch of lyric, a feature probably derived from Aeolic.[8]

Alcman's metres seem characterized by striking forms, easily grasped: runs of dactyls, including types with (probably) no pause; single-short forms like lekythia or iambic dimeters, or the series of cretics in 58; straightforward aeolic forms like glyconics and pherecrateans; more elaborate aeolo-choriambic entities, sometimes with considerable 'dactylic' repetition. These forms would not necessarily seem simple in Alcman's time; but in any case the largest fragments show him combining such units into ambitious and elegant designs.

1: *PMGF* 1 (fr. 3 Calame)[9]

We do not know how long the poem was, i.e. how many columns preceded the final three columns and four lines represented by the papyrus. In our evidence comes first a series of mostly incomplete lines which deal with myth (1–35). Then 66 mostly complete lines take us almost to the end of the poem, marked by a coronis; they deal principally with the festival at which the poem is being per-

[8] Risch (1954) argues for a connection with Cyrene; his view is accepted e.g. by Schmitt (1977), 55. Distribution: Nöthiger (1971), 90–2. On 'c' < θ, see Colvin (1999), 169–71. The material on initial ϝ in Alcman is admittedly very limited; Hinge's examples of its neglect (1997) do not seem compelling. For internal ϝ see 1 [1]. 71 n. The meagre epigraphic material in *IG* v/1 and *SEG* 11 (1950–4) is supplemented particularly in *SEG* 26 (for 1976–7), notably by no. 461, published by Peek (1974) (cf. Gschitzner (1978), Meiggs and Lewis (1988), 312); note also Shipley in Cavanagh, Crouwel, Catling, and Shipley (1996), 214. Tyrtaeus' Ionic is not wholly 'pure': note χαίταϲ ὑπὲρ κ. at Tyrt. fr. 20. 14 West, etc. (cf. Nöthiger (1971), 103). See further for Alcman's dialect the introduction to the commentary on Stesichorus.

[9] On 1 [1] see especially, besides the commentaries of Garzya (1954), Calame (1983), Pavese (1992), the following: Blass (1879, 1885); Diels (1896); Wilamowitz (1935); Schwenn (1937); Davison (1968b); Page (1951a); Taillardat (1953); von der Mühll (1976a); Nicastri (1962–3); Marzullo (1964); Garvie (1965); Pavese (1967); West (1965), 194–202, (1967), 7–14; Cataudella (1972); Halporn (1972); Rodríguez Adrados (1973); Calame (1977); Giangrande (1977); Puelma (1977); Hooker (1979); Segal (1998c); Campbell (1987); Most (1987), 13–14; Eisenberger (1991); Hinz (1993); Robbins (1994); Stehle (1997), 30–9, 73–88; Mariotti (1997); Too (1997).

formed. The chorus speak of themselves and of two women, Agido and Hagesichora, who have a different role in the festival from themselves; Hagesichora is none the less the leader of the chorus.

The nature of the occasion as a whole is not made particularly clear by the poem; evidence from outside it is too distant to help. The poem itself is not directly a hymn or prayer to a deity. The extant portion does allude to a ritual action by the chorus, who are carrying a robe to a goddess of the dawn (61), and to religious actions by Agido and Hagesichora, who are praying, it seems, to the gods (78–83). Agido also calls to the sun to shine (41–3); the choral narrator speaks of her desire to please the Lady of the Dawn (87–8). In the extant portion the chorus are not hymning this deity; they are commenting on their own actions in performing the dance, and in particular they are commenting on the actions, and praising the persons, of the two women. The narrator's words are meta-ritual, as it were. Alcm. 3 [2] indicates that this handling of the song is conventional.

Various elements come into question. The praise of the women is clearly fundamental to the passage; given that Agido as well as the chorus's leader is praised, the praise will not be solely the poet's depiction of the chorus's world and mind. It seems plausible that one point of the poem is to enhance the glory of specific individuals; doubtless such glory was, for the individuals and their families, an important aspect of the ritual itself. The poem also offers, however, a more self-contained image of the girls' world and nature. In part, the words bring out the seen beauty of the performers; but there is more to the poem than that. It evokes the maidens' minds and concerns in a way that delights and amuses for itself. One must stress again that the ethos of the poetry is not produced simply by dealing with girls; the poetry constructs it through its art. The creation of a vivid but generalized character for a chorus, which concerns Pindar's maiden songs too, connects the poem with Athenian drama: choruses of old men, or girls, are obvious examples.

One feature of what happens is particularly important; its importance is emphasized by its probable recurrence in 3 [2]. That is the surprising separation of chorus from chorus-leader on the day of the performance, through the separate function required of the leader. This is a fixed feature of the occasion, no doubt; how far it has a religious or social meaning, how far the exploitation of it is due to the poet, we cannot say. Certainly the response of the chorus appears to be presented, not as a ritualistic deprivation, but as feeling which exists outside the ritual, and indeed makes the chorus anxious about their performance within it. A kind of little drama, so to speak, is staged on the edge of the ritual; part of the charm of the poem, apparent in a different way in 3 [**2**], is an interplay between 'official' sentiment and 'private' thought.

Not that they are here in conflict. The poem is striking both for its range and mobility, and for the hierarchical outlook that runs all through it. Everything is shaped into structures of superior and inferior, and the different structures interrelate. The whole poem is densely interwoven, not only in imagery but in many other aspects of poetic art. As will be seen, this is a poem richly connected, and yet exuberantly diverse.

Metre

1. – ∪ – × – ∪ –
2. × – ∪ ∪ ∪ – –
3. – ∪ – × – ∪ –
4. × – ∪ ∪ – ∪ – –
5. – ∪ – × – ∪ –
6. × – ∪ ∪ – ∪ – –
7. ᷉ ∪ – × – ∪ –
8. × – ∪ ∪ – ∪ – –
9. – ∪ – × – ∪ – × – ∪ ˗ –
10. – ∪ – × – ∪ – × – ∪ – –
11. – ∪ – × – ∪ – ×
12. – ∪ – × – ∪ – –
13. – ᷉ – ∪ ∪ – ∪ ∪ – ∪ ∪
14. – ᷉ – ∪ ∪ – ∪ ᷉ –

The stanza takes strongly marked forms, and combines them into a large and effective structure (Bacch. 17 str., for example, is larger). The first eight lines form a metrical entity, not regularly divided off in sense: a trochaic line (lek) alternates with an aeolic (hag). It is misleading to call the stanza triadic: the divisions are not notably emphatic, and the listener will scarcely segregate the first two couplets from the second two as strophe and antistrophe. The hiatus at the end of 57 shows that there is pause between the two halves of the stanza, as one would expect after a pendant form. Cf. Hinz (1993). Indeed, there is pause after both lek and hag (hiatus at 38, 39, 56, 65, 69, 70, 79, 81; on 41 see n.). For the juxtaposition of different types of metrical unit cf. e.g. Alcm. 4 fr. 1. 4–6, 38 (lek pher)).

After this alternation, the next four lines all expand the trochaic movement: two periods of 3 tr (hiatus 45, 72), and two pairs of lek without pause (elision 18). The poet exploits this pattern at individual moments. For series of matching single-short lines or units cf. Alcm. 19, 20, 59 (*a*), 60. The movement then changes strikingly to double-short (cf. Parker (1997), 49): dactyls, followed by an entity that is in its varying forms either dactylic or aeolic with double-short first half. Two shorts can be replaced by a long. The former of the 'lines' is separated by word-end but not pause, which enhances its running effect; it might be thought that this is enhanced by the existence of the more dactylic variant for the latter. For runs of dactyls cf. Alcm. 17, 27 (allegedly the whole stanza consisted of these dactyls, but Hephaestion might be dividing like the papyrus of 3 [2]; cf. also Parker (1997), 48–9, 265). The freedom at the end of the strophe is particularly remarkable: closes are commonly the strictest point in metre. (Some rather uncompelling justification in Cole (1988), 133–4, 225–6.) In view of the lucid form of the rest, artistic audacity seems at least as likely an explanation as primitive imprecision.

1–35. The poem begins by telling of the fate of the sons of Hippocoon. (Cf. Davison (1968*b*), 441–4; Page (1951*a*), 30–3; Robbins (1994), 11–14.) In the account of later writers, the Hippocoontidae were destroyed by Heracles (e.g. Diod. 4. 33. 5–6; Paus. 3. 15. 3–5: see Davison, and add Σ Pind. *Ol.* 10. 78 a and b). Σ Clem. *Protr.* 36. 2, p. 200 Marcovich, need not attest this version for Alcman: μέμνηται, despite the insertion of τῶν Ἱπποκόωντος παίδων in the second clause only, can and probably should be taken to refer to the Hippocoontidae, not the story. (Cf. e.g. Σ Arist. *Knights* 762 a (I), Σ Nicand. *Ther.* 460 d, on the other side Σ Ap. Rhod. 1. 996–7; καὶ Ἀλκμάν probably relates to Sosibius on either view.) Sosibius involved Heracles, as Clement like Arnobius attests (*Protr.* 36. 2, p. 54 Marcovich; *FGrHist* 595 F 13); Sosibius might well, but need not, have derived his story from this poem of Alcman. The participation of Heracles, then, is not certain.

This poem would seem to have involved the Dioscuri in the conflict. The mention of Polydeuces in 1 is unlikely to be incidental; this is confirmed by Σ Clem., who ascribes to Euphorion (fr. 29 Powell) the story that the Hippocoontidae were rival suitors to the Dioscuri. One must find improbable a gross confusion in the scholiast of Hippocoontidae with Apharetidae, the Dioscuri's famous rival suitors. (So Wilamowitz in Schubart and Wilamowitz (1907), 60 n. 1, and Jacoby (1923–), III b Noten 376 n. 154.) Some reasonable learning lies behind this and other notes (cf. the use of

Euphorion fr. 32 Powell on p. 189 Marcovich). We do not at all
know that the cause of the conflict was the same in Euphorion and
Alcman; in view of line 16 here, no firm argument can be based on
line 17. A novel, and an amorous, version would not be unlike Eu-
phorion. If the cause of the conflict was the same in both poets, the
scholion has been slightly remiss (but no more) in not attributing it
to Alcman too. More definitely, rivalry in love would be less at home
in a version where both Heracles and the Dioscuri took part. Since
Heracles' battle led to the restoration of Tyndareus, such a version
is easy to imagine; the Sosibius makes it a notable possibility for
this poem. In short, then, the Dioscuri clearly participated here;
Heracles might well have done. If he did so, the romantic motiva-
tion, already entirely uncertain for this poem, becomes positively
unlikely. We would assuredly be unwise to regard it as probable.

The narrative preceding line 1 could have been mannerist rather
than lengthy; but in either case the catalogue of names is both
imposing and significant. It evokes the epic accumulation of names
of the dead (examples at *Il.* 16. 415–17, 694–6, 21. 209–10); the
encounter has been made into a huge conflict, with a populous cast.
The epic examples are rhetorical, and show the power of the slayer
(note *Il.* 16. 418, 692, 21. 211). The point here is similar, but the
catalogue is more ostentatious, and the point is theological; it will
be elaborated at length. Relevant here is the forceful series of names
in the final lament of Aeschylus' *Persae*.

1. The resounding name of the Spartan deity ends the clause. It
is probably opposed with some effect to the name of the scorned
Lycaethus.

2. The emphatic first person, and the contemptuous dismissal,
create an air of authority in the narrator. Cf. Tyrt. fr. 12. 1 West.
The sphere of the pronouncement is far removed from that of girls.
The abruptness of the asyndeton, if genuine, gives an arresting
energy to the moment.

ἀλέγω: different senses of the verb combine. It seems to have the
meaning 'count among', cf. Pind. *Ol.* 2. 78; but the line does not
mean that Lycaethus is not thought dead. The idiom here conveys
that he is reckoned of no account: cf. Eur. fr. 519 Nauck, and for the
gesture Aesch. *Ch.* 989 (cf. also Hdt. 3. 95. 2). The normal sense
of ἀλέγω, 'regard', thus colours the passage too. The reason for this

contempt is likely to be that Lycaethus was not a son of Hippocoon (so ΣA, cf. Paus. 7. 18. 5 for Derites; otherwise Apollod. 3. 10. 5). **καμοῦϲιν**: already so used in Homer (*Il.* 23. 72 etc.).

3. The name is guaranteed by Pausanias (3. 15. 1) and Apollodorus (3. 10. 5). ἀλλ' is the most suitable supplement: otherwise one would expect to see οὔτε or some negative in the following lines. It also seems unlikely that all these Hippocoontidae, one of them here ἔξοχον ἡμιϲίων, should be dismissed as unworthy of the list. If their formidable qualities are acknowledged, a much sharper point emerges.

ΣA, however, appears to suggest that the names after Lycaethus' too are those of sons of Derites; but this conflicts with both Pausanias and Apollodorus, not to mention Pherecydes for 6 (not under *FGrHist* 3). Pavese's insertion of a negative ((1967), 114 n. 2, (1992), 12–13) seems a satisfactory solution.

ποδώκη: the word comes in epic (e.g. Hom. *Il.* 2. 764, 860, Hes. fr. 72. 3 Merkelbach–West), but also in prose (e.g. Simon *Eq.* 11, Thuc. 3. 98. 2, Xen. *Cyn.* 4. 2); so one cannot be sure that its flavour is peculiarly epic. Contrast Ibyc. S151 [**11**]. 33; that whole catalogue is much more intimately connected with Homer.

4. **τὸν βιατάν**: nouns in -τηϲ with the article come too at the end of the second half of the period (identical in metre) and of the single-short first line in the following stanza (8). The obtrusive patterning cannot be accidental. The idea of describing the fallen probably derives from Homer, but the form is un-Homeric. The word βιατήϲ itself, common in Pindar (e.g. *Pyth.* 6. 28), is absent from epic. In general, the phrases, by enhancing the might of the slain, enforce the moral.

5. **κορυϲτάν**: δύω Αἴαντε κορυϲτά Hom. *Il.* 18. 163, *al.*; χαλκοκορυϲτήϲ as epithet *Il.* 16. 536 etc.

7. **ἔξοχον ἡμιϲίων**: probably epic in flavour (*Il.* 18. 54, 437 ἔξοχον ἡρώων, of Achilles; cf. *Od.* 18. 205); certainly heroic in content. ἡμίθεοϲ comes only once in Homer, *Il.* 12. 23; cf. Hes. *WD* 160, fr. 204. 100 Merkelbach–West, Alc. 42. 13, etc. As the close to the strophe, the phrase is resonant and pointed.

8. **ἀγρόταν**: 'hunter', cf. Hom. *Od.* 16. 218, does not seem impossible; presumably it is implied that he was outstanding or famous, and the hunt can display heroism (as with the boar of Calydon).

10. κλόνον: the stem is found in later lyric as well as in epic (e.g. Sapph. 43. 5, Bacch. 13. 118, Pind. *Dith.* fr. 70 b. 14).

11. The first letter must be a short vowel; not ιου, and ε would come closer to τ.

12. παρήϲομεϲ: after τὼϲ ἀρίϲτωϲ the word cannot be scornful. Whether positive (cf. Soph. *Trach.* 499–500 καὶ τὰ μὲν θεῶν παρέβαν) or negative (cf. Virg. *Aen.* 10. 185–6 'non ego te . . . transierim'), it gives the narrator a role like a poet's: it draws attention to the organization as resulting from the narrator's will.

13–14. *Αἶϲα* appears as a divinity in epic (Hom. *Il.* 20. 127–8). *Πόρος* (cf. ΣΑ) is not found elsewhere in archaic or classical poetry, save at Alcm. 5 fr. 2 col. iii, where again he is old, and probably primeval. This recurring feature suggests some degree of poetic creation in Alcman's figure, not only (if at all) local cult. The poetry is certainly moving outside the epic cosmos. Whatever the proposition of the sentence, it also moves us forcefully from the heroic past to the most ancient divinities. Cf. on these lines West (1967), 7–9; Most (1987), 13–14.

15. If ἀπ]έδιλοϲ is right, the phrase involves a striking metonymy, whatever its sense. The most likely view is that it is separate from 16, and denotes the precipitate haste of sinners (the phrase seems to suit less well the prompt aid of gods). Cf. West (1967), 9, and his examples (but not his view of this passage) at (1978a), 243, especially [Aesch.] *PV* 135 (add Pind. *Nem* 1. 50, Eur. *Hec.* 933–4). The first two syllables of the line will have denoted vanity or failure.

16–17. With grim authority, the narrator presents her wisdom paratactically. In 17 the status of the narrator makes this talk of 'marriage' striking: her status does not here confine her. (Cf. Stehle (1997), 32.) The imperatives show that the discourse has moved from the past to a universal time which includes the present and future.

The sense of hierarchy so important to the poem is embodied in drastic images. Perhaps Bellerophon is in mind at 16 (cf. Pind. *Isth.* 7. 44–7); but the phrasing makes the idea sound pointedly contrary to nature. Pind. *Pyth.* 10. 27 uses the less colourful ἀμβατός. Aphrodite is not the most hopeless, but the most desirable, of goddesses to envisage 'marrying' (compare Anchises and contrast, say,

Tityus); the fantasy is given colour of a different kind. Other goddesses may have been mentioned in what follows. The one point in the stanza where consecutive periods are identical is exploited here with pithy neatness.

19. The usual reading Πορκώ is not impossible, but unattractive as an account of the first three letters; the ρ seems very dubious.

20–1. δέ suggests that a clause begins with Χά]ριτες; the verb in 21 is most likely present indicative. The point is no doubt connected with the divine place, inaccessible to mortals (cf. 16); it may well be connected with the special attractiveness of these goddesses, who cannot be attained by mortals. For the Graces' loveliness and connection with loveliness cf. e.g. Hes. *Theog.* 910–11, fr. 70. 38 Merkelbach–West, Hom. *Il.* 17. 51, Ibyc. 288. 1; they can be married to gods (Hom. *Il.* 14. 267–8, Hes. *Theog.* 945–6). The image of the goddesses at the house of Zeus at the end of this stanza will form a significant contrast with the fate of the ἡμίθεος at the end of the preceding stanza, and with the whole account of the killings.

ἐρογλεφάροι suits the context and the Graces; but it is a most unusual formation. There are no compounds ἐρωτο- or ἐρο- in classical poetry (ἐρατο- first Limen. 26 ἐρατογ[). One would have to compare ἰμεράμπυξ, ἰμερόγυιος, ἰμερόφωνος (Bacch. 17. 9, 13. 137, Sapph. 136). Ahrens's ἱερο- remains of interest; cf. Alcm. 26. 1.

25. For the rest of the stanza the verbs appear to be aorist.

26. The required – ◡ – at the end of the line makes the rest a puzzle. A faint possibility might be μ]έγα ῥέον, to agree with a neuter noun; μέγα would be predicative (in a comparison, perhaps, for the destructive ἥβα). But one would expect to see some of the cross-stroke of ε: note the ligature in 2, 39, 56, 87, 100. There seems to be a slight trace to the left of γ, level with its top.

27. The ω is not very satisfactory, especially at the bottom. If ωλες', the form must be transitive. ἥβα might denote the assailants by metonymy; if so, the Dioscuri (and Heracles) would be more suitable than the gods in many of the proposed alternative myths. It would be more contrived to make the victims' own ἥβα destroy them; ἥβη on its own is not sufficiently negative or dynamic (cf. Hom. *Il.* 6. 407, 16. 753), and even if a word for 'own' and an adjective could be accommodated, the phrasing would still seem somewhat strained.

It cannot be known whether a new myth is introduced in this stanza; but the most natural supposition is that the myth of the Hippocoontidae is resumed (Robbins (1994), 15).

29. μ]ạταίαc: α suits the traces better than ε, and the accent makes the supplement virtually inevitable. Moralizing continues.

30–1. Detail, and series, now return to the narrative; but now the victims are not named. The detail and colour now attach to the means of destruction, which are made to end the two identical consecutive lines. The rhetoric supports the conclusion of the stanza. The different weapons make it implausible that Heracles alone is involved.

μαρμάρωι μυλάκρωι: subject and expression, taken together, make use of the *Iliad* seem plausible, cf. 12. 161 μυλάκεccι, 16. 734–5 πέτρον | μάρμαρον. But even so the combination is different, and a different form is used; it is not attested elsewhere, but must be the basis for μυλακρίc (Hippon. fr. 162 West, etc.).

34–5. The formulation is pointed, but not epigrammatic; it presents the sequence of theological cause and effect as if it were (and should have been) self-evident.

ἄλαcτα: the word comes in Homer and elsewhere (*Il.* 24. 105 etc.). Cf. (if rightly read) Stes. S13. 3 ἄλ[αc]τạ πạθοῖcα.

κακὰ μηcαμένοι: cf. Hom. *Od.* [24]. 199 κακὰ μήcατο ἔργα etc.

36. The moral is drawn together at the start of the new stanza in a generalizing conclusion of potent brevity, enhanced by the asyndeton; this also serves as a point of contrast from which the poem moves to other things. The universal statement in the generalizing present forms a transition from treatment of the past to treatment of the immediate present. The abstract noun as subject, the emphatic ἔcτι (there exists), and the dry τιc (there exists *some*), give the formulation telling detachment and wisdom. Cf. the more emotional Hom. *Od.* [24]. 351 ἦ ῥα ἔτ᾽ ἐcτὲ θεοὶ κτλ., Eur. *HF* 772–3 θεοὶ θεοὶ | τῶν ἀδίκων μέλουcι, *Antiope* xlviii. 57–8 Kambitsis (223 Kannicht). For τίcιc cf. Hom. *Od.* 13. 144; Sol. fr. 13. 25 West, etc. τιc is not being used as e.g. in Eur. fr. 21. 4 Nauck ἀλλ᾽ ἔcτι τιc cύγκραcιc.

37. Continuing in tones of authoritative wisdom, the narrator turns to happiness, but with the gloomy suggestion that continuous happiness is rare (all sin produces unhappiness, but not all unhappiness is produced by sin). Cf. Bacch. 5. 50–5.

38. The imagery may seem faint, but the striking ἀμέραν probably leads into the imagery of light and sun that follow. The abruptness of the transition in 39 compels the language into contact as the mind explores the two sentences for connections. Even if they had no relation in content (and the hint of deliverance, and the talk of the blessed man, suggest they have), the link of the metaphor would still form part of the rhetoric. It is effective that the image is much more forceful in 40.

ἄκλαυςτος makes it unlikely that ἀμέραν refers only to a single day (cf. Pavese (1967), 120–1); contrast Sem. fr. 7. 99–100 West and cf. Bacch. fr. 11. 1–3. [δι]απλέκει makes it unlikely too; cf. Pind. *Nem.* 7. 98–100, Hdt. 5. 92 ζ 1. For ἀμέραν cf. e.g. Eur. *Ion* 720.

39. ἀείδω: the first person again has the ring as of a poet (the verb is transitive, see 40–1 n.); cf. also Pind. *Nem.* 1. 33–4, *Isth.* 1. 14–16. It indicates too, however, a return to the narrator's more immediate sphere, that of the ceremony. The first person singular here denotes the whole choir in the act of singing; in 60 the first person plural denotes the choir in the act of carrying the ritual object. As in tragedy, the singular or plural can be used to denote the chorus, though sometimes the first person singular will emphasize the feeling of each member as an individual. (Cf. Hooker (1979), 221–2.) The first person singular predominates in this poem, and justifies use of 'the narrator'.

The writing now moves into a series of assertions about present states: essentially about Agido and Hagesichora's beauty, seen now, rather than about actions in progress. The actions of Agido in carrying out the ritual, and of the chorus in singing, form a kind of background to these assertions.

40–9. φῶς: the syntax gives tremendous force to the image: contrast Hom. *Od.* 17. 41 ἦλθες Τηλέμαχε, γλυκερὸν φάος. The name is also forcefully positioned. φῶς suggests deliverance, through the ceremony; it suggests too the perspective of the girls, and how they link cosmic and social hierarchy, the public ceremony, and the values of maidens.

ὁρῶ | ϝ᾽ ὦτ᾽ ἄλιον: Puelma's ὁρῶς᾽ ((1977), 7–15) might seem at first to suit the papyrus. But the low-lying letter with its bottom stroke tucked to rise upward to the right looks much more like ε than ϲ in this hand; cf. the ε at the start of 46, 47, 51. The papyrus generally omits digammas, and ε᾽ is an intelligible way of representing the elided pronoun. The line-end is more likely to show pause lightly infringed by an elided post-positive monosyllable than an anomalous absence of pause between lek and hag: cf. on Sapph. 31 [6]. 9–12. The reading adopted gives a bolder, more dramatic text in both 39–40 and 40–1.

ὁρῶ ὡc is not a normal way of saying 'I regard, envisage someone as'; the verb stresses the present moment and spectacle. (Cf. Sol. fr. 34. 5 West.) The 'I' is moving to the special perspective of the girls.

The daring metaphor of φῶc is now spelt out, with explanatory asyndeton. The image of the sun perhaps suggests that Agido is alone and incomparable.

ὅνπερ κτλ.: the relative clause draws the ceremony into the image; but despite the ἇμιν the syntax presents the ceremony as secondary to the girls' interest in Agido herself. The repetition of the name, at the same point in the line, probably stresses the significant person.

μαρτύρεται: is likely to have some connection with ritual. Why should Agido call the sun to witness simply as a rhetorical point, why should the chorus not do so for themselves? The ceremony concerns a goddess with the title Aotis (87), and probably takes place at the end of the night (62–3); 80–3 indicate that she is participating in a rite, together with Hagesichora. It may not unreasonably be conjectured that Agido's activity has some connection with the break of day. That could perhaps be figured in her calling the sun to shine in witness; but more likely the word means simply 'call to'. Cf. ἐπιμαρτύρομαι Hdt. 5. 92 η 5, Thuc. 6. 29. 2, and note also Aesch. *Eum.* 643.

ἐμέ: the highly emphatic pronoun stresses that the relationship of the chorus to their leader is what compels this position. (Cf. Pind. *Parth.* 2. 33, where the pronoun marks a contrast of the maidens' level with the gods' knowledge.) How could *they* fail to dwell on their leader Hagesichora? Hence the narrator refers to Hagesichora by her function, and not, as commonly, her name, even if the designation plays on it (cf. and contr. 10 (*b*). 10–12). (It is theoretically conceivable that the audience did not know it yet; but the point would remain.) The run of thought in 43–54 (and 43–57) makes it seem clear that Hagesichora is the χοραγόc; note ὁ . . . κέληc in 50 taking up 47. Lines 78–91, and 90–9, reinforce the likelihood.

οὔτ' ἐπαινῆν κτλ.: the expression shows the girls' devotion, and tact. The structure in this and the next stanza elegantly combines an uncompetitive balance of praise with a fuller attention to the one more important to the girls. In this instance, the poem, so intensely hierarchical, refuses to rank. That itself is not an unhierarchical feature, just as mortals should decline to rank gods, and not only for prudential reasons (cf. Call. fr. 194. 72 Pfeiffer).

χοραγόc: the word appears first in Alcman (cf. 4 fr. 6. 2 (plural?), 10 (*b*). 11, 15–16 (plural)). The stem is used in lyric at Pind. *Pae.* fr. 60 (b) (G4) col. ii. 13; Soph. *Ant.* 1147, Eur. *Hel.* 1454 (neither of humans), Arist. *Lys.* 1314–15 (of Helen, with εὐπρεπής). It is also, of course, in ordinary usage at Athens and in Attica from the fifth century on (cf. e.g. *IG* i³. 966. 2, *SEG* 40 (for 1990). 128).

ἐκπρεπής: cf. Hom. *Il.* 2. 483 (in a passage perhaps used here), with ἐν.

τὼc κτλ.: the βοτά may be conceived of as the girls themselves (less plausibly as all those women here present). The tenor would then become more immediate and visual, and the chorus would be displaying the extravagant modesty seen in 85–7. αὐτά implies the paradoxical assertion for Hagesichora of a supremacy parallel to but separate from Agido's. The special concern of the chorus with Hagesichora is expressed with this more extended sentence, and its more elaborate handling of imagery. The comparison offers the dense world of a simile (commentators note Hom. *Il.* 2. 480–1), but the means of comparing has here a more dynamic form. (Cf., not in an image, *Il.* 2. 123–30.) In the midst of the cattle the horse is suddenly 'placed'.

The word-order of 47 enhances the hierarchical contrast of animals (Hom. *Il.* 2. 480–1 make a contrast within the species). (Cf. Osborne (1998), 27, on horses.) The horse itself is then glorified in a string of unconnected adjectives, splendidly set in the most dactylic part of the stanza. The onomatopoeic speed, and the epic resonance of the language, plunge us into the world of the image. For the rhythm cf. e.g. Ibyc. 287. 6–7; Virg. *Aen.* 8. 596. Girls are indeed often compared to fillies (cf. Calame (1977), i. 411–12, etc.); but the development of the image may suggest a man's sphere. Note ἀεθλοφόρον and cf. Tyrt. fr. 20. 9–11 West.

Since in epic πηγός is added to the standard ἀ(ε)θλοφόρος for horses only at Hom. *Il.* 9. 124=266, it may be that there is a connection with that specific passage. If so, the reduction of twelve horses to one may underline the crucial singularity of Hagesichora; the epithets are expanded still further. καναχήπουϲ is used of horses at *Certamen* A 45 (B 100), so might, but need not, have existed in hexameter poetry before Alcman. ὠκύπουϲ is common of horses in epic (Hom. *Il*. 2. 383 etc.); in lyric cf. Pindar's ἀκαμαντοπόδων, *Ol*. 3. 3.

†τῶν ὑποπετριδίων ὀνείρων†: ὑποπετριδίων itself is a puzzle. It cannot be turned into ὑποπτεριδίων. ΣA's ingenious attempt to provide a rock is no more convincing than shady siestas (West (1965), 195). The application of the word to ὀνείρων on the latter view requires a use of adjectives quite unlike the style of Alcman or the period. But it is not only a word that puzzles: the genitive too is extremely curious. It can scarcely be ablative; and in 'a horse of dreams' (of the kind one sees in dreams) the genitive comes all the more strangely after the intervening epithets. Nor can the article be accounted for naturally. These are a good many problems for three words. One is driven to the conclusion that they are corrupt.

50–4. ἦ οὐχ ὁρῆιϲ; The long sentence is succeeded by a curt question, the immersion in the world of the image by direct demonstration of the present. The chorus bring the listener in with challenging assurance; they aim (with whatever success) to remove any thought of subjectivity. The separate sentence οὐχ ὁρᾶιϲ or ὁρᾶτε is most readily paralleled from exchanges in drama (Ar. *Knights* 419, *Wasps* 420, *Lys*. 1032; Eur. *IT* 267, *Or*. 760); the opening particle gives it extra edge. Although the image is carried through syntactically (ὁ μὲν κέληϲ), the position at the start of the new stanza gives this moment special impetus; cf. 'Weißt du's *noch* nicht?' at the start of a new paragraph in Rilke, *Duineser Elegien* 1. 23 (cf. 5. 59–60).

ὁ μὲν κέληϲ κτλ.: the elaborate syntax of the comparison (45–9) turns into abrupt parataxis. The copious description of the horse is answered by an abrupt identification; similarly, perhaps, the leader is named and related to the chorus. The names both begin the line.

κέληϲ comes already in epic, with ἵπποϲ (Hom. *Od*. 5. 371, cf. *Il*. 15. 679). It is also an ordinary word (with the form κελὲξ in the Laconian *IG* v/1. 213. 37 etc. (*c*.450–31?)). The sort of race it implies (cf. 48, 59) does not appear in the main narrative world of epic.

Ἐνητικόϲ: the place-name presumably gives a pithy suggestion of modern luxury, and connoisseurship. The use of remote names was popular with Alcman: Alexander Polyhistor περὶ τῶν παρ' Ἀλκμᾶνι τοπικῶς εἰρημένων (*FGrHist* 273 F 95, 96, 100? cf. Aristid. 28. 54). **ἁ δὲ χαίτα κτλ.**: the description of Hagesichora luxuriates after the brevity of what precedes; it takes up the appeal to sight from ἦ οὐχ ὀρῆις; over the intervening clause. The horse itself was the subject in 50–1, but here the subject is Hagesichora's hair: the indirectness of this assertion of supremacy adds to its expressiveness. The language conjoins the ideas of the horse (χαίτα, cf. Silk (1974), 136–7), of natural blossoming, and of gold. The last idea is elaborated: it evokes luxury and supremacy. (Eur. *IT* 1236 χρυσοκόμαν, for example, is much plainer.)

τᾶς ἐμᾶς ἀνεψιᾶς: the relationship to the narrator is emphasized, as it is not with Agido. No doubt the closeness is more important than the exact kinship, as in many uses of such words, in various cultures and periods. Cf. West (1965), 196. Hesych. κ 971 may well be relevant.

ἀκήρατος: already in Homer (*Il.* 24. 303); its usage of gold (already Archil. fr. 93a. 6–7 West) was presumably familiar in ordinary language, cf. Hdt. 7. 10 α 1 and especially Plat. *Polit.* 303 E 4.

55–6. A kind of chiastic structure is formed with 50–4, expressively cut short in the second half. Silver ingeniously takes up gold; the abrupt address to the listener on the pointlessness of words joins up with the opening challenge to the listener's sight in 50. For all the liveliness, the structure is intricate; it forms part of larger structures itself.

ἀργύριον: Hagesichora has not been bronzed by a gymnastic lifestyle. For the word used of whiteness cf. Sapph. 34. 5, and further ἀργυροδίνης of rivers in epic and later (e.g. Hom. *Il.* 21. 8).

διαφάδαν: also Sol. fr. 37. 1 West.

τί τοι λέγω; The obtrusive dismissal of utterance both stresses the present sight and dwells vivaciously on the narrator's role as narrator.

57. The utterance, and the dramatic gesture, attain an extreme of simplicity, as words are renounced; but the bare words load the name and the sight with significance.

58–9. The chorus turn to Agido and complete a large pattern: Agido has preceded Hagesichora in the earlier stanza (39–43), and now follows her in this. The lines on Agido are again relatively brief; the design gives a long continuous space to the treatment of Hagesichora. Agido is accorded equal honour, however; she is separated from comparison with Hagesichora even while the expression of her pre-eminence is highly competitive. The ranking of horses is knowing and expert (cf. on the names ΣB col. i). The comparison with horses must continue the imagery of 45–8, and 51. The point of comparison is still beauty, not speed (with Ϝεῖδοϲ cf. Tyrt. fr. 10. 9 West, Archil. fr. 196a. 7 West). Hence the running is part of the vehicle for expressing superiority, not the tenor: we should not be postulating foot races and confusing the sentence. ('The second in beauty will lose the race badly' is not an idea to import; nor is 'the second in beauty will be a much less handsome horse as she runs'.) With effective obliquity, the chorus are indicating that Agido's supremacy is so great that whoever comes next to her will still be a long way behind (cf. Virg. *Aen.* 5. 320, Hor. *Odes* 1. 12. 16–18). The dative in 59 will presumably transfer the construction of 'compete' etc. to the activity of which the competition consists: cf. Hom. *Od.* 8. 188 ἐδίϲκεον ἀλλήλοιϲι.

Puelma (1977), 29–32, makes ἁ δέ Hagesichora; he is followed by Robbins (1994), 8–9. But then μέν and probably ἁ δέ would seem less apt. Janni's defence ((1964), 60–1) does not seem sufficient. With the same person here before μέν and before δέ, and no sequence of actions, Homeric and Herodotean parallels for the ἁ δέ seem unsatisfying. The context would be going out of its way to mislead the listener into thinking a different person was in question.

60–3. The Πεληάδεϲ have been thought to be: the stars, a rival choir, Hagesichora and Agido.

The stars are likely to be relevant in some way, and ordinary doves are not (doves ΣA 61–2; stars ΣB col. ii). The ceremony appears to be taking place at the end of the night: it is at least in part for the lady of the dawn (87, cf. 61), the Peleiades are rising through the darkness of night (62–3), Agido is calling the sun to shine (41–3). The language used in 62–3, if not literal, must be borrowed from the stars as an object of comparison, elaborately carried through. The stars, then, must be involved. ταὶ Πεληάδεϲ will not be merely a poetic comparison like that with the owl in 87 or the horse in 59: the article makes that improbable. Consequently, if it referred to doves as well as stars, it would have to be also a title for the two women, 'the Doves', ingeniously applied to refer to the constellation too. This seems strained.

Even the now standard notion that the two women were known as 'the Pleiades' has the air of a desperate hypothesis. It is, furthermore, an odd title and comparison to use for them: there were notoriously seven Pleiades (Hes. fr. 169 Merkelbach–West; Simon. 555. 3–5). 'Fighting us' is a very strange description for the dazzling splendour of their beauty; it seems too a little odd that the chorus's beloved leader should be 'fighting' them, however metaphorically. The notion would probably not have been suggested but for ΣA; but it is apparent that the scholia had here no more evidence to go on than we do (for example of special titles or ceremonies).

The rival choir is an even more uncomfortable notion: why should our singers alone be encumbered with a robe (or plough), and why should they be carrying it to the goddess while conducting an unfair singing competition? And how can μάχονται mean 'compete'?

It is much more natural to suppose that these stars, at a suitable time of year, are rising just before the sun (Hes. *WD* 383–4, with West (1978*a*), 255–6). The heliacal rising of the constellation is so commonly used in indications of date (e.g. Hippocr. *Reg.* 3. 68. 2) that there is no difficulty in the choice of them here. The comparison with the bright and menacing Sirius is part of the poetic point (see below). The movements of the heavenly bodies are very frequently seen in terms of attack (e.g. Hes. *WD* 619–20, Stat. *Theb.* 12. 50 'tertius Aurorae pugnabat Lucifer'); it is not surprising if this is extended beyond these bodies themselves, as when Hesiod's snail delightfully 'flees the Pleiades', at the appropriate time of year (*WD* 572). It is particularly unsurprising when the maidens are engaged in bringing a robe to the goddess of dawn, Ὀρθρίαι. (A nominative plural adjective (same accent in Doric) would leave φᾶρος φεροίcαιc bare; the middle syllable of Ὀρθίαι should not be short.) The Pleiades are, in a fanciful conceit, impeding the rise of the sun and thus the festival. The two women are needed to ward them off: it is their beauty alone which will cause the festival to succeed by pleasing the gods or goddess, and it is the light of their shining beauty which will vanquish the heavenly maidens. The chorus is turning the earlier imagery of light and brightness, especially that of 39–43, into a fantastic and, from the author's perspective, a playful idea.

This passage does not require the creation of new titles or entities, and focuses attention on things that are dwelt on in the rest of the poem. The advantages of this line of approach seem considerable, however one understands γάρ in 60 and 64. One way would be roughly this. Whoever comes second to Agido in beauty comes a long way behind. One can see this because we have the Pleiades fighting against us as we carry the robe (Agido and Hagesichora do not participate, cf. 78–81). This point in turn is made clearer as the narrator explains why the Pleiades are fighting them: not the stars' motive, but why the fight is in progress and cannot be ended. The chorus are not beautiful enough to ward them off (aorist). The light of Agido (40) indicates already the contrast involved; the contrast is now developed at length. In some ways the chorus' point has been deflected by the end: they are showing that Hagesichora is more beautiful than any of themselves, and convey this by declaring that it is Hagesichora with whom they are in love (77). None the less, Hagesichora is distressing them both because they love her and because they want her aid. She is distressing them, as yet another γάρ explains (78), by not being with them; she is concerned with other things. That stanza presents in another aspect, audible rather than visual, their feeling of inadequacy to the demands of the ceremony without her. In both respects, their fears are of course misguided.

Since in the threat of the Pleiades we are dealing with an imaginative and light-hearted conceit, it would be exceedingly pedantic to object that Agido and Hagesichora's beauty ought to have repelled the Pleiades already, and that the threat must apply to them too. There is no difficulty in the successive γάρs: it is common enough for explanations to develop with one γάρ hanging on another: cf. e.g. Bacch. 11. 59–66, Soph. *OT* 473–82, Ar. *Birds* 253–7. A less satisfactory means of treating the γάρs on this general view of the Pleiades would be to suppose that we had two γάρs with the same point of reference (Denniston (1954), 64–5, with examples from prose and tragedy); but I have looked through Homer, Hesiod, and Pindar and found no fully satisfying parallel. Hes. *Theog.* 721–5 might seem the most promising (721 was deleted by Ruhnken).

Stehle (1997), 79–85, perhaps comes nearest to the view suggested here. She sees the Pleiades as bringing the start of the hot summer, and thus threatening the work of ploughing which the ceremony marks; dawn is a cool time, and suitable for such work, so the goddess of dawn is opposed to the summer. Agido and Hagesichora will protect the maidens through their beauty (she reads τηρεῖ). This particular kind of conflict between dawn and Pleiades seems awkward, especially in view of the ritual appeal to the Sun; the whole explanation appears too involved. But we find many of the same points plausible. The playfulness of the passage for the audience is seen further in the language of 62–3. The comparison of the Pleiades, a relatively dim though conspicuous cluster, to the bright and baneful Sirius in itself shows the maidens' exaggerated alarm. In the context of the time (note ἱρ]άνας 91), μάχονται probably contrasts with the real warfare faced by men, who are themselves urged to fight in Tyrtaeus (Tyrt. frr. 10. 13, 15, 11. 33 West). Homeric comparisons of actual warriors to Sirius may possibly contribute to the sense of play. (See especially *Il.* 22. 25–32, with Richardson (1993), 108–9.) Robbins (1994), though he adopts a different view of the passage, suggests a contrast between the 'fighting' here and the battle in the myth. In relation to what immediately precedes, the assertion of states is now succeeded by action in progress, of an animated but (for the listeners) figurative and entertaining kind.

Πεληάδες: for more on the name and the stars see Kidd (1997), 274–5.

νύκτα δι' ἀμβροσίαν: the portentousness is increased by the use of an epic phrase in this dactylic part of the stanza, as in 48. Cf. Hom. *Il.* [10.] 41, 142 (and *Od.* 4. 574).

64–77. Let us suppose, then, that the chorus are explaining why the Pleiades are still fighting them; they have not the resources of beauty to repel their attack. Are they (*a*) wearing the beautiful things they mention, are the beautiful women they mention part of their number, or are the chorus (*b*) mentioning things and women separate from themselves, who would be insufficient means of defence? Lines 64–5 seem to favour (*a*). Although the meaning of κόρος has to be extended, there is no ἆμιν, and the syntax is elliptical, it makes a better sequence to say 'the purple we have is not abundant enough to ward them off, nor is this gold snake or this bonnet sufficient' than to say 'there does not at all exist a sufficiently great abundance of purple to ward them off nor do we have for this purpose a gold snake or bonnet'. The description in 68–9 makes excellent sense with (*b*); with (*a*) νεανίδων might be self-referential (cf. perhaps 90), but a generalized description looks preferable, and acceptable (cf. e.g. Aesch. *Supp.* 21–2). In 71 the laudatory epithet might seem more likely with (*b*), but not impossible with (*a*).

In 73–7 we may take it that 77 is not part of what 'you' would say in the house of Aenesimbrota: the γάρ in 78 requires that this should be the chorus' utterance, justified by 78–9. With (*b*), 73–6 would lose the thread of argument and cohesive sequence. One is bound to see the names and negatives as connected with 64–72; but it would not be germane or justified to say of separate well-known beauties (note ϲιειδήϲ in 71), 'you will not ask that they should fall in love with you'. With (*a*), one possibility would be to imagine modesty from the girls; but this does not accord well with 71 or probably 70, or with the beautiful objects preceding. More plausible is a relative modesty: if you went to a place where all these women belonged, and Hagesichora too, the one you would long for would not be any but she. (Sappho would then be more relevant than witches; the mother of these four (Campbell (1983), 189) suits the rhetoric less well.) In this case, the line of thought would take a twist at 73, but a twist informed by the interval from Agido and Hagesichora that has been implicit from the start. From saying that their ornaments and singers, beautiful as they are, are not beautiful enough for this fanciful purpose, they pass to saying that the rank-and-file singers are not the ones you would fall in love with; from there they pass to their own longing for Hagesichora, which motivates this verdict. The case for (*a*) would seem to be the stronger.

On this understanding, then, some members of the chorus would be named. We find this as a convention in Aristophanes: we see there indeed conventional names, and play with the convention when a female chorus is disguised as men. (Cf. Ar. *Ach.* 608–14, *Wasps* 230–4, *Lys.* 254, 259 (321 more disputable), *Eccl.* 293; Soph. fr. 314. 183–96 Radt?) The chorus would also be drawing attention to, and so revivifying, the visual impact of their appearance. (Cf. Pind. *Parth.* 2. 6–12, and many passages in comedy and tragedy.)

64–9. The author might seem to revel in the luxury which has come to Sparta; it is amusing to compare with these lines the moralizing sequences in e.g. Cato, *Orig.* vii. 9 Chassignet. But the glamour and finery are also a vital part both of impressing the spectators and of pleasing the goddess. Cf. Eur. *El.* 167–97, Ar. *Lys.* 1189–93/4. The actual flaunting is elegantly conveyed through the narrator's confession of inadequacy.

The stanza begins from material objects, and moves gradually to people (note the incidental description in 68–9).

οὔτε: with the heap of negatives in the stanza it is interesting to compare Tyrt. fr. 12. 1–9 West (cf. fr. 11. 15–16). However, the present passage is on my view only indirectly a priamel. (Otherwise Race (1982), 54–5.)

τι and τόccoc κόροc, where κόροc probably keeps some flavour from its usual meaning, suit the characteristic lavishness of the chorus's expression.

ποικίλοc conflicts, as a description of the object, with παγχρύcιοc. The word is designed to suggest at first, with a touch of humour, a real snake; cf. West (1966a), 249–50, for such words of snakes (note Theogn. 602, and perhaps Hes. *Theog.* 300). Cf. Davies (1984), 16 n. 7; Sancassano (1996–7), 84–7. There is similar play at Pind. *Pyth.* 8. 46–7 (cf. Pfeijffer (1999), 534). The enjambement of παγχρύcιοc, Λυδία, and ἰανογ[λ]εφάρων may also perhaps throw some emphasis on luxury and beauty.

μίτρα | Λυδία: cf. Sapph. 98 a. 10–11, Pind. *Nem.* 8. 15, and the introduction to the commentary on Sappho below.

νεανίδων . . . ἄγαλμα: the descriptive ornamentation (cf. Alc. 140. 6–7) heightens the argument. νεανίδων would seem to show that the audience does not consist simply of girls.

ἰανογ[λ]εφάρων: probably connected with ἰοβλέφαροc (Bacch. 9. 3, etc.); cf. Taillardat (1953) (so Ϝιανο-?). ἰανόφρυν appears at *Suppl. Hell.* 906. 13 (ἰ Π?). Such compounds are more commonly used of goddesses: cf. ἑλικοβλέφαροc Hes. *Theog.* 16, *Hom. h.* 6. 19, Simon. 555. 2, ἀγανοβλέφαροc Ibyc. 288. 3–4, ἰοβλέφαροc Bacch. l.c., 19. 5, etc.

70. The phrasing forms a transition between things and people. The nominative of the hair and the genitive of the person perhaps suggest a significant contrast here with 51–3 ἁ δὲ χαίτα | τᾶc ἐμᾶc ἀνεψιᾶc | Ἁγηcιχόραc (cf. also 101).

The list of names may bring out the difference of world and voice from the mythological part of the poem, with its list of names in 3–11.

71. cιειδήc: the ornamental yet significant epithet, like ἐρατά in 76, again shows a different world from the similar epithets in 3 etc. Both are used of nymphs by Hesiod (*Theog.* 350, 353). The absence of internal digamma is notable (cf. Risch (1954), 28); contrast Ar. *Lys.* 1252 cιοείκελοι.

72. Cυλακίc: see on 3 [2]. '97–9'.

73. The (feminine) second person, though generalizing, gives vivacity to the syntax.

74. τε: the conjoining particles perhaps further, unrealistically, the rhetorical purposes of the list, rather than imitating a somewhat comprehensive desire in the speech or thought of the second person. Lines 74–5 place the names and verbs in the matching halves of the period so as to produce an elegant chiasmus.

77. The huge sequence encompassing the whole stanza ends plaintively with a short and simple utterance. This moves us, touchingly, to the narrator's real and present situation, from which we have been becoming increasingly remote. The beloved name comes with force.

τείρει: τηρεῖ would not be a violent conjecture; Alcman would probably have written TEPEI (not TEPE) for either. But it is not an attractive suggestion: it makes the point of the following negative clause (introduced with γάρ) less apparent, whereas it fits τείρει very neatly, and likewise 3 [2]. '61–70'. (Cf. Calame (1977), ii. 91.) Even if 78–9 were made a question the sequence 78–81 would be somewhat odd. (παρμένει would be a curious choice of verb, and the δέ would be unwelcome.) In τείρει language naturally used of love (Hes. fr. 298 Merkelbach–West, *al.*) is applied to the beloved; cf. e.g. Theogn. 1235 ὦ παῖ ἄκουcον ἐμεῦ δαμάcαc φρέναc (contr. 1388).

78–9. Earlier, the chorus had stressed Hagesichora's presence (50, 57); now they stress her absence. (On αὐτεῖ cf. Rodríguez Adrados (1973), 339–40.) That is to say, they can see her, but she is physically separated from them. Although the audience themselves can see the situation, and know the convention, there remains a forceful and effective shift from Ἁγηcιχόρα μὲν αὔτα, 57. (This shift may worry ΣB, col. iii? (b); cf. also 3 [2]. '70' n.) As the chorus probably imply at 98–9, and 85–7, and as one would expect, the χοραγόc would usually join in their singing and dancing (cf. Ar. *Lys.* 1314–15). But on this occasion she takes a separate part in the ceremony from the chorus. This separation is not a temporary accident, but a definite feature of the occasion, with which the poet makes much play. The same is evidently true in 3 [2], where the probable leader has her own ceremonial function, seemingly different from Hagesichora's here, and is again visible to but separated from the chorus ('61–4').

καλλίcφυροc: the epic compound lends dignity (cf. Hom. *Il.* 9.

557, Hes. *Theog.* 384, etc.); but the adjective also suits the narrator's longing.

81. θωcτήρια: only here in extant literature and inscriptions (glosses in ΣA and Hesychius). The θ has not been changed into c.

82–4. The reading in 82 is difficult. αc seems very promising, χ not possible. λίτας would suit traces and space nicely (' is attractive). But if cιοι follows, the space between αc and ι is larger than one would expect. It is just conceivable that a middle c was written and deleted between αc and c (there are possible traces of a deletion mark).

At all events, it seems likely that the chorus voice their own prayer to the gods, and that this prayer displays their subordination to the two women whose prayer they are merely supporting. For even from 81 it appears that Agido and Hagesichora are engaged in prayer to the gods (cf. 42). Yet the generalization in 83–4, which turns to the third-person cιῶν, briefly recalls the authority of the pronouncements in the preceding section of the poem (especially 36). Even this generalization drives home another hierarchical subordination, that of mortals to gods. (Cf. Tyrt. fr. 19. 10 West.)

ἄνα: ἄνη (with ἄ) only at Aesch. *Th.* 713, Call. *H.* 1. 90.

The end of 84 is problematic. The now standard reading χοροcτά-τις (cf. Blass (1885), 15–16) does not suit the traces, in particular of the letter before cτ (ω would seem more inviting). The reading does not seem an unmitigated loss. The accents are puzzling. χοροcτάτης, 'chorus-leader', first appears in Hellenistic inscriptions (*IG* xii/2. 527. 33, 645 a. 36 (319–17 BC), etc.); it does not come in literature until Celsus (ii AD) ap. Orig. *Cels.* 5. 33. χοροcτα- may very well have appeared in earlier literature, to judge from Hermes. fr. 7. 58 Powell, Call. *H.* 5. 66, *Hec.* fr. 85. 2 Hollis; but the extant early uses of χορὸν ἴcτημι, ἴcταcθαι do not justify us in assuming at this date the special sense of leading a chorus. (Clearly not at Pind. *Pae.* 2 (D2). 99; perhaps just 'dance', cf. χοροcτacία, but see Radt (1958), 78–9.) The address to the leader (nominative for vocative) would be the only one in this poem or 3 [2].

85–9. The chorus regard their singing without Hagesichora now (ten instead of eleven) as an ugly noise. The ἐγών in 85 is unlikely to denote each individual member as separate from all the others: the context emphasizes their separation from Hagesichora. For the singular pronoun used of their utterance note 39, and also 43. The leader was presumably especially able at singing; cf. Dem. 21. 60, with Macdowell (1990), 281.

The image of the owl is given great mordancy. The plain monosyllable γλαύξ is doubtless an ordinary Laconian word (cf. *GDI* 4510, Tod and Wace (1906), 85 no. 785). It stands out at the end of the clause and the beginning of the line (cf. the effect at Arat. 999). The contrast with παρcένοc makes the image a paradox, which the absence of an 'as' sharpens; the verb is vigorous; ἀπὸ θράνω, if correct, adds to the pungent satire. (For the absence of 'as' see Diggle (1997), 102–3, with literature.) The creature obviously lacks the dignity of the horse in 47–9. The present singing of the audience must refute this extreme modesty: so the self-deprecation will have a humorous quality. The judicious subjectivity of Ϝείποιμί κ' probably enhances the effect. This passage is the clearest example of distance in perspective between the narrator and the listener (and author).

It is likely to be significant that the owl is a bird of the night (there are other ill-sounding birds). The picture suggests they are the less likely to please the goddess of the dawn, as they name her in the same line. For the performance pleasing the goddess cf. Alcm. 45. For the owl's nocturnal noise cf. Ar. *Lys.* 760–1, Shakespeare, *Richard II* 1771 Wells–Taylor 'For nightowles shreeke where mounting larkes should sing.' This notion gives a forceful point to μάταν, which suits this context of seeking the gods' approval; μάταν itself could perhaps have been justified otherwise by reference to Pind. *Ol.* 2. 87 ἄκραντα, Virg. *Georg.* 1. 403.

θράνω would be a very suitable word, with no obvious alternative. θρᾶνοc denotes wooden objects of various kinds (in literature Soph. *Inach.* fr. 269a. 41 Radt, *al.*), and can refer to a beam high up (*IG* ii/iii². 463. 51 (307/6)).

In 87–9 the purpose of the festival comes to the fore again. The mention of the goddess's past aid transports the poetry swiftly to religious gravity and moving emotion.

ἰάτωρ is not found elsewhere, but is presupposed in ἰατορία (Bacch. 1. 149 ἰατο[, Soph. *Trach.* 1001). For the language cf. Pind. *Nem.* 4. 1–2.

90–1. δέ: the structure of 85–91 is paratactic but intricate. The δέ in 87 contrasts the chorus's wishes with their attainments (μέν 85). The μέν in 87 sets the goddess against Hagesichora, as hierarchically superior, though parallel. One expects the δέ clause in 90 to be governed by ἐγών too; but a fresh start is made. At the same time, ἐξ Ἁγηϲιχόραϲ δέ probably also forms a contrast with ἐγὼν μὲν αὐτά, so strong is the expectation created by those words.

ἱρ]άναϲ: peace from actual war must be denoted here (so Eisenberger (1991), 287). The word is particularly unlikely to denote victory in contests with rival choirs: 'peace' does not mean 'victory', and given the μέν and the δέ of 87 and 90 the connection with πόνων . . . ἰάτωρ should not be ignored. Nor can 'peace' be used at this period to denote tranquillity of mind. Even the examples in Plato show that metaphorical peace indicates an absence of metaphorical war, and needs a specified absence of conflict with, say, opponents or passions (cf. e.g. *Rep.* 329 c 4, *Theaet.* 172 D 5; even at *Smp.* 189 B 2 the point is the absence of conflict with Eryximachus, not at all mental ease). The ceremony has led to peace for the Spartans; it might no doubt have led to victory too, but it is 'lovely' peace that 'maidens' will dwell on. National events are seen from the chorus's perspective; the third-person νεανίδεϲ marks the perspective, with some distance in the expression.

The general point seems clear; exactly what action of Hagesichora is implied in 90–1 would have been clearer to the original audience than to us. The γάρ in 92 suggests that Hagesichora has brought peace by leading, or preparing, performances of the chorus which have pleased the goddess, or the gods, and so led to the divine granting of peace. In the context of 87–9 this does not seem impossibly hard to understand. If, however, the comparison in 92–3 suggests that they are referring to her actual participation, it is apparent from 98–9, and from her general role, that on other occasions she sings and dances with them. A reference to other occasions would perhaps also be more consistent with their claim (85–7) to ineffectiveness without Hagesichora, although they have become less modest by 100–1. In this case, their connection with the cult of this goddess might extend beyond the present festival.

The end of the stanza contrasts with the end of the preceding stanza, where Hagesichora is causing the chorus pain, and with the end of the stanza before, where the chorus are anxious about a fanciful 'fight' with stars. The song has spread in time, to convey the larger present of the political situation, and decisive help in the past.

92-5. The last stanza of the poem multiplies images. The first image continues the comparison with horses used of Hagesichora and Agido earlier; but the emphasis is now on their own obedience. Once again the poem stresses hierarchy; in this stanza Hagesichora is part of the same team and concern as the chorus, but in command. Cf. Hesych. c 339 ϲειραφόρον· ἡγεμονικόν. There are commonly two outer, unyoked horses in a team (cf. Eur. *IA* 221–4; Hdt. 3. 102. 3 (camels)); but the poet turns the idea into singularity.

ϲηραφόρωι: the word itself comes next at Aesch. *Ag.* 842, 1640; it was presumably in ordinary usage (cf. Hdt. loc. cit., Ar. *Clouds* 1300).

ạ[ὐ]τῶϲ fits the space (cf. αὐτά in 85); it would seem to make a comparison back. Cf. e.g. Hes. *Theog.* 600, where ὡϲ αὔτωϲ makes the return from a simile.

The nautical image brings in something new to at least this part of the poem.

These lines do not appear to form part of a priamel: 96–101 do not provide the expected parallel statement about the chorus's obedience to Hagesichora or the like. It seems probable that the train of thought was to some extent oblique and demanding, as in other parts of the poem.

96-101. ἁ in 101 must refer to Hagesichora; so the subject of φθέγγεται in 100 must be someone else, most likely the subject of the preceding clause. The subject of that clause is fairly plainly the chorus: the restoration of 98 is made very probable by ΣA. Giangrande (1977), 156–60, has Hagesichora in 98, set against a complete choir of eleven (of which she herself is usually part), form almost a match for that choir in terms of singing, that is of volume; this seems involved and unconvincing. Puelma takes a similar line ((1977), 46–8). Hagesichora does not seem to be singing now.

To make Hagesichora ἁ in 96, as is often done now, has awkward implications for the structure. At best the chorus would be commenting on the choir including its leader: she is not more tuneful than the Sirens, we are reduced in number, but we are singing well and she is beautiful. But it seems curious to speak about her singing in 96–7 and then pronounce her by implication absent from the singing. The comparison in 96–7, then, should be between the Sirens and the chorus (the plurality of the Sirens suits this well). In this context, a ἁ referring to the δέκαϲ in 99 would be unnatural. It may be less unattractive to make 96–7 say that the Sirens' voice (*vel sim.*) is more tuneful: the chorus are not even as a rule supremely melodious and now they are deprived of their leader, but none the less are singing splendidly. The surprise here for the listener is the change from modesty to pride. One might say that such a change is often found in the related case of poets speaking about their work, and that a movement to assertion particularly suits the end of a work. One might add that the earlier modesty was partly an expression of admiration for Hagesichora, which is not lost here; and that the pride is softened by the mild gestures of modesty that precede it (96–8), particularly by the description of themselves as mere παίδων. None the less, the chorus's change of tone is not to steal in unperceived. This is made clear by the striking correspondence between κύκνος in 101 and γλαύξ in 87. Both occur at exactly the same point in the stanza (and so the music); both are followed by a pause, describe the chorus's singing, and refer to birds. The earlier passage is deliberately reversed. The true merits of the performance are established; simultaneously, the maidens' unnecessary modesty and timidity are charmingly underlined and exposed.

Cηρηνίδων: cf. Pind. *Parth.* 2. 13. Whether the Muse is a Siren at Alcm. 30 is far from clear.

ἀοιδοτέρα: cf. ἀοιδότατος at Pind. fr. 70. 1, Eur. *Hel.* 1109, Theocr. 12. 7, etc.

cιαὶ γάρ: the chorus again stress hierarchy; compare the emphasis on ςιῶν at 83. Here the phrase has a curt simplicity, cf. Alc. 6. 10 πρόδηλον γάρ, 119. 11 κάλον γάρ, Anacr. 358 [**13**]. 7 λευκὴ γάρ.

The numbers in 98–9 have a deliberately prosaic and practical quality which suits the modest recognition.

παίδων: one should contrast cιαί at the same point in the preceding line, and also νεανίδες in 90.

The letter before ε at the end of the line is unlikely to be δ. ε is joined on the left, near the middle, by a horizontal stroke; this would be compatible with θ, c, τ, etc., but not with δ (contrast the rising ligatures from the bottom of δ at 51, 59, *al.*).

κύκνος: on the alleged tunefulness of swans note Ar. *Birds* 769–84 (with Dunbar (1995), 476), *Frogs* 207, Eur. *IT* 1104–5. The distant river gives romanticism to the image. Note the nightingale used to denote the poet at Bacch. 3 [**17**]. 98 (end of the ode).

Hagesichora's golden hair runs through this part of the poem

(51–4, cf. 70). ξανθᾶι is a desirable colour at this period (cf. Archil. fr. 196a. 52 West, Simon. fr. 22. 9 West; Alcm. 3 [2]. 9; cf. also Hom. *Il.* 1. 197, etc.); but the link with 51–4 makes it more than conventional here. That is confirmed by the play with the preceding line, where ΞΑΝΘ comes at exactly the same point in the same metrical form. The faraway place is set against the immediate sight, and the narrator against Hagesichora.

ἐπιμέρωι: ἐφίμερος of hair Anaxil. fr. 37 Kassel–Austin.

κομίσκαι: for the diminutive cf. 162 (incert. auct.) fr. 2 (*a*). 8 παρ]cενιcκ[αι, Ibyc. S257 (*a*) fr. 1. 11 παιδ]ίcκον. It probably expresses the chorus's affection.

The stylistic texture of the poem as one looks over it contrasts remarkably with that of the roughly contemporary Spartan Tyrtaeus. His sentences are ample, his movement for the most part is smooth and stately; the language is relatively homogeneous, and densely Homeric. There is little comparing. The difference is largely, though not entirely, connected with genre (for one may think of Solon's images, or the pungent opening of Callinus fr. 1 West). In Alcman's poem one sees an extraordinary range of sentence length, with many moments of forceful or affecting simplicity, diction ranging from the heroic to the conversational, bold surprises and twisting, challenging movements, abundance and yet continuity of imagery, and intensive exploitation of stanza and rhythm. A less remote comparison might be with Archil. fr. 196a West, amorous in its matter, and closer to lyric, if not actually lyric, in its form. There we find effectively brief sentences, some with a colloquial sound (e.g. 26, 31), some with an expressive simplicity (e.g. 19, 22, 24). Some evocative images are used, particularly the comparison with the fawn in 47, which conveys both the narrator's sympathy and his distance. But some of the imagery is euphemistic, some insulting, some proverbial, and the text does not make nearly so rich an impression as Alcman's. Nor, naturally enough, does it give the same sense of drawing in different worlds of thought or of constructing a hierarchical cosmos. No ranking of poems is intended here: we see rather the remarkable range of Greek literature at this period.

2: *PMGF* 3 (fr. 26 Calame)[10]

This poem presents a related situation to 1 [**1**], but handles it in a rather different manner. The ceremony resembles that of the other poem, but does not seem to be identical with it. Again it appears to take place at night or early dawn (7); there is again an individual to whom the chorus are devoted, but who is not with them, as she is taking a different part in the ritual. She is carrying (less probably had been carrying) a garland; if this was part of the ceremony at all in 1 [**1**], which seems unlikely, the poem would concern, and probably be sung at, a different point. (The garland is discussed by Calame (1977), i. 356–7, ii. 107–9, 127–8, and by Bruschi (1994), 46.) In Alcm. 60 the narrator herself is carrying a garland (compare the robe (?) carried by the chorus in 1 [**1**], and the branches carried by them in Pind. *Parth.* 2). It is tempting to suppose that the chorus have a relationship with Astymeloisa that extends beyond the ceremony, and that she, like Hagesichora, is usually or often their leader. It is notable that in 1 [**1**] Agido, who is not their leader, does not receive the amorous thought and discussion received by Astymeloisa here, and probably by Hagesichora there. At all events, '64' would seem to suggest that there is some idea of separation here. The language seems to treat it with something of the intensity elsewhere accorded to the passions of poets, or rather of first-person narrators who are formally identified with the author. And yet the poem creates for the listener an opposition or incongruity between the passion and its setting which suggests that at least the narrator's perspective is not the only one.

Metre

1. – ∪ ∪ – ∪ ∪ – ∪ ∪
2.   – [∪] – ∪ – ∪ – –
3. – ∪ – – – ∪ – –
4. – ∪ – ∪ – ∪ –
5. – – ∪ ∪ – ∪ – × – ∪ –
6. – [ ] ∪ (?) –

[10] For 3 [**2**] see especially, after the original publication (Lobel in Lobel *et al.* (1957)), Giannini (1959); Page (1959); Peek (1960); Barrett (1961); Treu (1965), 444–6; Sisti (1971–2); Renehan (1972); Calame (1977, 1983); Davies (1984, 1986*a*); Guerrini (1991); Bruschi (1994); Stehle (1997), 88–93.

7. – ∪ ∪ – ⊡ – ∪ ∪ – ∪ ∪
8. – ⊡ – ∪ ∪ – ⊡ – ∪ ∪
9. – ∪ ∪ – ∪ ∪ – × – ∪ – –

The form of the stanza is entirely different from that of 1 [**1**], but works with related units, and suggests a related interest in overall design. Π actually sets it out as if a triad, although 1–3 are quite different from 4–6. (For the coronis marking the end of a triad cf. Stes. 222 (b) [**3**] and Haslam in Haslam *et al.* (1990), 1; note also P. Oxy. 841 col. xxii.) The stanza opens with 3 da followed without pause by 2 tr (1–2 might less plausibly be seen as an aeolo-choriambic entity). Two single-short periods follow, 2 tr, tr cr (3–4). The stanza closes with a series of dactyls, ended by an aeolo-choriambic entity which passes from double-short to single-short (7–9). In between come an aeolo-choriambic line, where the single-short movement bulks largest, and a line largely unrepresented by the papyrus but much shorter (5–6). The double-short in 7–8 must recall that of 1, and in general 1–4 and 7–9 should be contrasted in the predominance of single-short or double-short within a pattern where double-short is succeeded by single-short. The aeolo-choriambic 9 is itself given a partner earlier in the stanza (5). The last part of the stanza resembles 13–14 in the stanza of 1 [**1**]; but its relation to the rest is organic, rather than a sudden change. The whole stanza, which is shorter than that of 1 [**1**], is more interconnected and less sequential. Both stanzas display an elaborate interest in metrical structure.

The scholion at the head of the poem demands consideration here, for its possible textual significance. The author of the note is later than, or contemporary with, Aristonicus and Ptolemy. The former is presumably the scholar of the Augustan period (cf. for the abbreviation P. Oxy. 3710. 35); the latter may be Epithetes (cf. Dihle (1959)).

The heading, at the top of a column, over what looks like the start of a poem, is plausibly referred to the poem as a whole, not to one strophe. Lines 2–5 seem a distinct entity, separated from line 1; 1–5 are placed high above the text. It does not seem a likely place for a comment on a single stanza; overflow, and anticipated lack of space, seem improbable. For αὕτη cf. Σ Pind. *Pyth.* 4 inscr. b 2 (no noun), *Ol.* 5 inscr., 7 *init.* (BCQ), *Pyth.* 5 inscr., 6 inscr., *Nem.* 11 inscr. a, *Isth.* 5 inscr. a, Σ Bacch. fr. 25. 9 (p. 128 Snell–Maehler). The movement of a strophe between books sounds curious (can this same metrical structure have been used twice?); the failure to mention the poem to which the new strophe was attached seems stranger. This strophe could hardly constitute an independent poem, like the triad of Pind. *Pae.* 6 (D6) in the theory of Rutherford (1997*b*) and D'Alessio (1997). (In considering discussion of a stanza no less probable than that of a poem, Lobel may be unduly influenced by implausible possibilities for the marginale on '79'.) Allegation of a misplaced poem is made the more likely by the mention of the fifth book. Poem 1 [1] most likely comes from the first book (Σ Clem.). The poems were arranged by type; we cannot be sure that there were only two books of maiden songs, but, given that there were six books of Alcman in all (*Suda*), and that he did not only write maiden songs (note e.g. 10 (*a*) 5, (*b*)), an evident maiden song in the fifth book surprises.

'The copies' usually denotes all the manuscripts known to the writer; since the supplement is very probable, all these manuscripts are accused of inserting what does not belong. They cannot be accused of mislocating a genuine poem in its proper place as well as in the fifth book; so we should not supplement 'in the first book and' before 'and the fifth'. Perhaps it is unlikely, further, that the line would begin so far to the left of the poem itself (cf. 9); the phrase is also unlikely to have been written before π]αρενγρ^α. These points would make too against supposing that a spurious poem has been interpolated in two places. If the point is only that the poem is spurious, why dwell on the book-number and insertion? παρεγγράφω would not be unnaturally used of what had been inserted where it did not belong, as a vigorous transference from the common 'interpolate'; cf. Didymus' cυνεῶϲθαι, Σ Pind. *Nem.* 11 inscr., and compare the ἐμβαλὼν οὓϲ οὐ προϲῆκε of a literal interpolation by Aristarchus (Athen. 181 c).

ἐκείνωι cannot mean 'this' copy or book; probably, in this context, it denotes the fifth book. The author of the note (or his source) disagrees with the placing of the poems in the manuscripts, including those 'of' Aristonicus and Ptolemy. Cf. Σ Eur. *Hec.* 13. The sentence seems to denote that Aristonicus' edition or manuscript expressed a critical view by a sign; the pluperfect, the imperfect, and ἀπερ[ί]γρα(πτοϲ) indicate something visible. (Nickau (1977), 10–12, needs modification.) καὶ ἐν ἐκείνωι, with the earlier [το]ῖϲ, prevents us from supposing a mere omission. It would be odd for Aristonicus to have the same poem transcribed in two books and then to mark it on its second appearance as misplaced. This confirms the earlier argument that in all copies the poem appeared only in the fifth book.

But what did Aristonicus' sign mean? Elsewhere this relatively unusual word refers to matter judged inauthentic, mostly more than one line, and sometimes substantial passages (one line Athen. 39 D, Σ Hom. *Od.* 4. 498, 11. 525). Yet later editors too can use signs that normally denote spuriousness to denote misplacement or other complications (e.g. Christ's Pindar, or Lachmann's Lucretius). One can see the proximity of operation in the use of the verb with Homeric lines thought inappropriately inserted from elsewhere (e.g. Σ Hom. *Od.* 18. 115–16). We can have no assurance, however, that Aristonicus was not marking the poem as spurious (whatever the author of this note took him to mean). It is not apparent why this poem should not be classified as a maiden song, as in the disagreements on placing and classification together (Σ Pind. *Nem.* 11 inscr. a (and *Pyth.* 2 inscr.), Σ Bacch. fr. 25). Its anomalous and late position might be the result of a dubious origin or reputation. If this were so, we would not be in a position to assert its authenticity with vehemence; however, nothing in the fragments of this fine work at all belies its close kinship with 1 [1]. It will be most prudent to write on the assumption that it is genuine.

1. The Muses form a standard beginning, in Alcman as elsewhere (cf. 5 fr. 2 ii. 22–3, 8. 9–11 (?), 14, 27, 28?, 30?); but the poem proceeds, immediately it would seem, into what is presented as if it were a dramatic situation: the narrator is inspired to go and join the singing and dancing. Contrast 8. 9–11, 14, 27. Hexameter poems (very notably the Delian Hymn to Apollo) and odes of Bacchylides and Pindar often start with contemplation of the poem proper, which is about to begin. The device is more striking with a choral narrator talking of a choral performance, for the performance has visibly begun and is acknowledged to have begun. It is conceivable that the chorus sang the opening as they entered. At any rate, there seems to be a close parallel to this presentation of the event as future in Pind. *Parth.* 2. 6–20 (despite 66–70), and also in *Pyth.* 10. 4–6. Related too are places where choral narrators tell of hearing sounds that have made them come (so Pind. *Pae.* 6 (D6). 7–18, [Aesch.] *PV* 127–35, Eur. *Hel.* 179–90; cf., even if not choral, Alcm. 10 (*a*). 6–10?). Here, however, the narrator might appear to be speaking as an individual member of the chorus who has heard others singing (cf. 5), and so come. The future in 7 remains obscure: it is not easily referred to the speaker (unless this is a relative clause of purpose or the like). Barrett's aorist ((1961), 685) is an interesting conjecture. In any case, narrative and the witnessed scene are arrestingly deployed.

'Ολ]υμπιάδες: the epithet is used with *Μοῦcαι* at Hom. *Il.* 2. 491, Sol. fr. 13. 51 West, etc. At Hes. *Theog.* 25, 52 *Μοῦcαι* comes first and starts the line.

5. καλόν would seem to bring out verbally the musical beauty of the occasion.

6. The first letter consists of the foot of an upright, with a small stroke rising diagonally to the right of it. This resembles the occasional serif seen e.g. in fr. 11. 2 π rather than presenting the more rounded bottom of c or ε, even as seen in fr. 14. 1.

7. For the expression cf. Hom. *Il.* 20. 341 ἀπ' ὀφθαλμῶν cκέδαc' ἀχλύν.

γλυκύν, though Homeric, is also pointed (cf. *Il.* 1. 610, *Od.* 15. 7, and also Sapph. 63. 2–3).

8. The verbs in this and the following line convey animated motion. The whole stanza has been taking particularly far the standard notion of the choral narrator as a single person.

ἀγῶν': the ritual is happening in a place of assembly, it would seem, not a sacred enclosure. The word is emphatically public.

9. ξ]ανθάν, probably like ἀπ]αλοί in 10, presents the performers' beauty as it were from a third-person perspective, with adorning epithets. Both adjectives are used with these nouns in epic and elsewhere: see 1 [**1**] 96–101 n., and for ἀπ]αλοὶ πόδες Hom. *Il.* 19. 92, Sapph. or Alc. 16. 1–2, *al.*

The shaking of the hair shows vigorous movement; hair seems not to have been bound up at this period. The words accentuate the beauty the audience see. Cf. Ar. *Lys.* 1311–12/13.

'61–2'. Even if we knew, what there is no reason to suppose, that there was no column between fr. 1 and fr. 3 col. i, we could still not pronounce a column of 39 lines unlikely (cf. Barrett (1961), 683 n. 2, cautiously put). Cf. e.g. P. Oxy. 2165 (Alc. 129 [**8**]–130 b [**9**]), let alone e.g. P. Oxy. 4502.

The language depicts a violent assault on the consciousness of the person in love (doubtless the narrator, cf. '64', '75–81'). This is highly characteristic of first-person love poetry: cf. e.g. Archil. fr. 196 West ἀλλά μ' ὁ λυcιμελὴς ὦταῖρε δάμναται πόθος, 193, Sappho

108   *Alcman*

31 [6], 47, 130 (λυcιμέλης, cf. Ibyc. S257 (*a*) fr. 1. 14 β]αρύνομαι δὲ γυῖα), Ibyc. 287 (2, τακέρ' ὄμμαcι δερκόμενος, of Eros, cf. Anacr. 459), Pind. fr. 123. 10–12 (τάκομαι). λυcιμέλης is also used of Eros or ἔρος at Hes. *Theog.* 121, [911], of sleep at Hom. *Od.* 20. 57. τακερός is not found in epic. The phrasing in the second clause is opulently hyperbolic, cανάτω forming an advance on its partner ὕπνω; it is also highly expressive.

The ethos contrasts strongly with the mood and concerns of the opening. The language need not imply that the desirable girl herself feels desire: cf. Ibyc. 287. 2 above.

'**63**'. The pronoun followed by the name should not make us think that Astymeloisa is not the subject of '61–2': the narrator uses the name of the admired freely (cf. esp. 1 [**1**]. 77 followed by 79). Another female would make the connection with '63' and '64' awkward; Eros might be a possibility.

μαψιδίως: γλυκῆᾳ is likely to denote attractiveness, hardly gentleness (Calame). Assuming a person to be in question, we may doubt the possible senses for μαψιδίως 'untruly', and 'without effect' (cf. Sisti (1971–2) for this second). For the former, we would need some word of saying. For the latter, we would need some connection with intent, or at the least some suggestion that her beauty brought her benefit: so the use of words for 'in vain' indicates. (Mart. 5. 25. 11 'o frustra locuples' would be a dubious counter-example.) On the other hand, it is well attested for μαψιδίως and words related in stem or meaning to denote immoral, disorderly, or wanton behaviour: Hom. *Il.* 2. 214, *Od.* 2. 58, Hes. fr. 10a. 85 Merkelbach–West μαψιδίῃ φιλότητι (Alcyone and Ceyx), Sol. fr. 34. 7 West μάτην, Aesch. *Supp.* 198 τὸ μὴ μάταιον (decorous behaviour for maidens), Eur. *El.* 1064 ματαίω (Clytemnestra and Helen). The narrator may, then, be commenting on the absolute propriety (note τι) of Astymeloisa's behaviour on this public occasion, for all the impact of her look. One may note the severity Dicaeopolis requires of his fair daughter as κανηφόρος (Ar. *Ach.* 253–4). This approach connects satisfactorily with the next line; we might say that we had parataxis there instead of γάρ.

'**64**'. Astymeloisa gives her full attention to the public ceremony: her performance of her part is described in much of the stanza. ἀμείβεται implies some attempt by the narrator to communicate, and may suggest some interplay with the present song, which Astymeloisa ignores.

'**65**'. **πυλεῶν**: οὕτως καλεῖται ὁ στέφανος ὃν τῆι "Ηραι περιτιθέαςιν Λάκωνες, ὥς φηςιν Πάμφιλος (Athen. 678 A; note ΣA Alcm. 1 [**1**]. 32). The phrasing and context might suggest that the appellation was thought peculiar to this cult, within Sparta; it might then bear on the cult for this poem, and for Alcm. 60. The word also appears strikingly at Call. fr. 80. 5 Pfeiffer.

'**66–7**'. The language now changes from extreme simplicity (64–5) to elaborate imagery and syntax. Unfortunately the details are obscure. Astymeloisa's public action is portrayed in language which seems to convey her loveliness, for the narrator and for the listener. The comparison with the shooting star draws in an exciting image, treating it with richly nominal language (not 'as when a star').

διαιπετής: Renehan (1972), objecting especially to the treatment of the οὐρανός as if it were the αἰθήρ, interestingly suggests that διαιπετής is Alcman's spelling of the epic δι(ε)ιπετής (it would be better actually to emend to διει-; the αι is unlikely in this epic word). That epithet was interpreted in various ways (cf. *Hom. h. Aphr.* 4, Emped. fr. 91. 9 Wright, Eur. *Bacch.* 1267, fr. 971 Nauck; Schulze (1892), 237–41). Yet the genitive remains unconvincing; the plural 'stars of heaven' (Aesch. *Th.* 401) are another matter. The genitive is more plausibly governed by διαι-; cf. for the formation Aesch. *Supp.* 782 ἀμπετής (πέτομαι), προπετής Pind. *Nem.* 6. 63 (πίπτω). A shooting star flying along rather than falling downwards might treat the οὐρανός less objectionably, in imaginative language; for the figurative flying cf. Aesch. *Supp.* 782, Virg. *Aen.* 5. 527–8, Ov. *Met.* 15. 847–50. Fleet movement through the heavens might suit διέβα (cf. '73'); possibly brightness and fleetness, both suggested here, were taken up in '69'.

αἰγλάεντος: αἰγλήεντος Ὀλύμπου Hom. *Il.* 1. 532, etc. In lyric Bacch. fr. 20 B. 14 (of the sea).

'**68**'. These objects could be further comparisons; they might be related to what follows. At any event, they can hardly be governed by ἔχοιсα, and be conjectured alternatives to the ritual garland (so Peek (1960), 173–4).

'**70**'. **διέβα**: an action occurring before the song, or just now accomplished? We seem to see action during the song in Pind. *Parth.* 2. 66–75.

τανᾱοῖc: the epithet has a quasi-epic function. It might itself be taken (so Calame) from epic τανᾱύπουc, an obscure epithet of sheep (Hom. *Od.* 9. 464, *al.*); but if so the original context would have to be forgotten.

'**71**'. The abundant and allusive ornamentation of the language is something seen frequently in subsequent lyric. The style here suits another luxurious foreign enhancement of beauty, and also elevates it. One may compare 1 [**1**]. 68–9 on the μίτρα *Λνδία*, where the object and origin are more plainly given, but a decorative phrase on maidens follows.

Κινύρα: one would have supposed a specific connection with myrrh; Myrrha (Smyrna) was Cinyras' daughter. Cf. Stat. *Silv.* 5. 1. 214 'Cinyreiaque germina'. The genitive remains surprising. Cinyras appears in Hom. *Il.* 11. 20–3, Tyrt. fr. 12. 6 West, Pind. *Pyth.* 2. 15–17, *Nem.* 8. 18, etc. Cf. Baurain (1980).

'**72**'. π]αρcενικᾶν: this might be a generalization, or it might, for example, make the (other) girls present a foil to the supremely acclaimed Astymeloisa (cf. '73', '74'). ἅ τ' (Bowra) would be possible for the space; it appears less unattractive than the exclamation ἤν. (Guerrini's supplements (1991) νυμφοκόμος and οὐκ ἐπὶ π] open interesting lines of thought; but his plural is not altogether satisfactory.)

'**73**'. The thought of the remaining lines would seem to be that Astymeloisa is now among the people; the narrator cannot therefore do what she wishes she could, obtain Astymeloisa's love, perhaps by giving her a silver cup. κατὰ cτρατόν should describe where Astymeloisa is rather than where she is famed. The words themselves are most naturally so taken; and it is inviting to connect what prevents the narrator from making addresses here with the ceremony that prevents Astymeloisa from responding to the narrator's love in '64'. Mere generalized expatiation on her longing in this and presumably the next stanza seems less plausible, especially in the light of 1 [**1**]. If this is so, the poem is exploiting the separation of chorus and leader in a dramatic opposition of public ceremony and private feeling. The remarkable treatment of the ritual will presumably have seemed charming to the audience; the narrator's perspective is different.

Ϝα]cτυμέλοιca: the name occurred in the first line of the preceding stanza too. Compare the appearance of Hagesichora's name near the end of two consecutive stanzas in 1 [1] (77, 90). The play on the name ('74') is saved for now.

cτρατόν: this ceremony at least, if the view above is correct, would seem to involve more than just women.

'74'. μέλημα δάμωι: presumably on this specific occasion, rather than a general celebrity (cf. Pind. *Pyth*. 9. 97–100). The word is also found at Sapph. 163; not otherwise before Pindar (also frr. 95. 4, 217), Aesch. *Ch*. 235.

'75'.]μαν: perhaps optative.

'77'. If the accent on α before βάλ' is actual (and it looks relatively clear), that would suggest that βάλ' is the exclamation, and begins a new clause or sentence. Cf. 26. 2, 111.

ἄργυριν: even in this hypothetical situation the present luxury is stressed. (Humbler love-gifts are normal.) The word is used at Pind. *Ol*. 9. 90 (a prize); cf. Pherecr. fr. 135 Kassel–Austin.

'79'. ϝίδοιμ' αἴ πωc: even when we allow for Homeric usage, the narrator is tentative.

The letter before φ was taken by Lobel to be ν, of which there appear at first sight to be the diagonal stroke and the right-hand vertical. The apparent diagonal, however, is on some displaced fibres, which ought, puzzlingly, to be horizontal. The removal of the separate fragment in '80–4' may ease the difficulties a little; but φιλοι remains enigmatic. φιλοῖ (optative) is an uninviting form, and does not explain the preceding letters; a nominative φίλοι can scarcely be accommodated. The με, ϛιοὶ φίλοι, mentioned by Page seems the only plausible way to create sense (it occurred to me too); the scholion implies textual variation on this passage. For the exclamation cf. Hom. *Od*. 24. 514, Ar. *Plut*. 854, Men. fr. 362 Körte, Com. Adesp. 1093. 97 Kassel–Austin. This would make the passage still more animated, and extravagant.

'80–4'. The placing of the fragment now in the apparatus appeared to me doubtful on physical and, especially, textual grounds. The colour of the scrap, for example, does not favour the idea. More decidedly problematic is the sense. The idea of the narrator's becoming the suppliant of Astymeloisa is much more naturally made parallel to the idea of seeing whether she would take the narrator's hand than an immediate result of her taking it. For both '79–80' and '81' express an attempt to gain love, perhaps with the help of a gift ('77'); Astymeloisa's taking of the hand would show that the love was given. There is no room for complicated imaginary narratives in which Astymeloisa makes the first move but supplication is needed, immediately, to induce her to proceed further. Because of my doubts, Dr R. A. Coles and Dr G. Nisbet very kindly inspected the fibres with me and moved the fragment about in a digitalized image; I am extremely grateful to them for their expert knowledge and advice. It can now safely be said that the grounds which led Lobel to suggest the placing were illusory, although he regarded it as 'guaranteed' and 'not in doubt'. This is not to say that the fragment could not have come where Lobel placed it, but that the horizontal fibres give no positive reason at all to think it did. In view of the difficulties, the fragment can reasonably be left out of account in considering these lines.

It is an obvious possibility that Ϝίδοιμ' and γενοίμαν are not only parallel but both optatives of wish (note the shortness of '78'). If so, then the narrator might be wishing rather than intending because she has no silver cup, or, more likely, because she is vainly wishing she could make an appeal to Astymeloisa now, while Astymeloisa is performing her public ritual action. This would fit in well with '61–70'.

'80'. ἀπαλᾶc: again, the epithet adorns and suggests the chorus' beauty as if from an external viewpoint. The word is not used of hands before this passage and Sapph. 81. 5 ἀπάλαιcι χέρcιν, Alc. 45. 6.

χηρὸc λάβοι: note now Simon. fr. 22. 10 West.

'82–5'. The adjective in 82 might seem effectively unexpected of a παίc (note '84'). For the word βαθύφρων cf. Sol. fr. 33. 1 West, Pind. *Nem.* 7. 1.

'91'. The same strophe, and so presumably the same poem, seems to continue in this column. η rather than ι (so Lobel): the cross-bar is plainly visible.

'97–9'. The c in '97' is fairly clear (οὖ would be unlikely). There seems no alternative to the supplement Ϲυλ[ακι(-). It is interesting that a nightingale appears in this vicinity (cf. 10 (*a*). 6?), or at any rate singing does; singing appears in that of 3 fr. 4. 5.

Both 1 [1] and 3 [2] turn the festival and the situation of the song itself into something visually and emotionally arresting, almost the-

atrical. The idea of separation may be part of the meaning of the
festival on some ritual level; but there is more to the poems than
ritual or religious propriety. (Religious wisdom and hierarchy are
clearly important in 1 [1].) In this poem, the public and fictively
private aspects of the situation are set to some degree against each
other, within the imaginative fancy of the poetry. The pains of the
maidens are probably not taken too gravely by the listeners; all
redounds to the praise of Astymeloisa. The passionate language
(notably in '77–81') is unlikely to have been seen from an iden-
tical perspective by the narrator and by the audience. None the
less, it retains a power which makes the poem an interesting and
absorbing experience for a listener and spectator. If we may as-
sume the poem to be genuine, to have this work as well as 1 [1]
enables us to see something of the poet's range within cognate and
recurring settings and themes. Such range within recurrence was
to prove an important part in the talent of various lyric poets, not
least Pindar.

STESICHORUS

Introduction

IN Stesichorus' work we see a radically different sort of poetry from
Alcman's. The relation of author, narrator, and listener is almost
as different from that in Alcman as it is from that in Sappho or
Alcaeus.

   Stesichorus is associated in tradition with the Greek west, and
earliest and most persistently with the city of Himera, on the north
coast of Sicily, a connection one should provisionally accept. One
should not, however, see the supposedly unusual features of his
work as produced by an unusual environment. For Sicilian cities in
the sixth century, including Himera, were by no means eccentric in
their culture; if anything, they were particularly keen to emphasize
their Greek qualities (but perhaps they were merely exuberantly
rich). Much the same holds of Magna Graecia, for all its differences

from Sicily. Pottery excavated at Himera certainly shows some connections in commerce with non-Greek peoples, but far more prominent are the large and varied connections with mainland (and east) Greece.

A small sign of cultural affinities is seen when in the sixth century a Himeraean makes a dedication, on an Attic pottery base, in standard and epicizing language (Manni Piraino (1974), 266, pl. 42.2; *CEG* i. 392). It is revealing for a sense of proud display when a maker of the temple of Apollo at Syracuse (*c*.600) proclaims in huge letters his καλὰ Ϝέργα (Dubois (1989), 90–2). Temple A at Himera was even earlier; temple B, from around 550, boasted striking terracotta metope sculptures. The sixth century seems, from the remains of buildings, to have been a very lively and prosperous time for the city. Its coinage, beginning perhaps 550–40, is one of the earliest in Sicily, and of those earliest much the most abundant. Stesichorus seems to have belonged in a cultivated and wealthy environment. We have little ground for saying how far, if at all, his career took him beyond Himera or Sicily.[1]

One way of exploring the relation between poet and place might be through the dialect of his poetry. The dialect of Himera is an obscure subject. It is said to have been, in accordance with the mixed origins of the city, a mixture of Doric and the dialect of Chalcis (Thuc. 6. 5. 1). The sixth- and fifth-century inscriptions are inconsistent with each other, some appearing Doric, some Ionic; they do not even agree over η < ᾱ. A recently discovered and unusually extensive inscription is basically Ionic, and contains a Euboean form;

---

[1] Ibyc. S166 is unlikely to be by Stesichorus (cf. Barron (1984), 20). We cannot make much of Stes. 216 in isolation (Agamemnon located in Sparta). Even if the origin of the idea were political, it would be rash to assume that Stesichorus was its originator (a common type of assumption), let alone that he was writing for Spartans. For a more promising, but still questionable, argument on Sparta, cf. Burkert (1987), 51 (the palinodes on Helen only possible there). The notion that the association with Himera derives from Stes. 270 (Davies (1991–), i. 141) does not appear inviting: it does not seem particularly plausible that such a deduction would be made. For Himera see Adriani *et al.* (1970–88); Bonacasa (1982); Kraay (1984); Allegro *et al.* (1991, 1993–4); Allegro and Vassallo (1992); Vassallo and others (1991); Vassallo (1993–4, 1996); R. J. A. Wilson (1996), 103–5. For Sicily more generally, see Gabba and Vallet (1980), esp. Voza (1980) and Arighetti (1980) (131–6 on Stesichorus); Holloway (1991), ch. 2; for Sicily and Magna Graecia, Carratelli (1996). The displays of temple sculpture, and of terracotta dedications, from Selinus in the Museo Archeologico at Palermo give special opportunities for encountering Sicilian art diachronically.

this, however, is shortly followed by apocope, a feature very rare in Ionic inscriptions.[2]

Stesichorus' dialect is basically Doric (a vague term). It cannot be assumed that even this primary choice was caused by his locale: the people of Himera seem not to have spoken Doric uniformly, Doric lyric existed elsewhere, and his form of Doric, used by some later lyric poets regardless of place, could already have been traditional or fashionable. His poetry certainly does not present either a quasi-Himeraean mixture of Ionic and Doric or, despite the occasional Euboean form, a sharply localized identity. There is a great range of widespread Doric elements which he shares with Alcman (e.g. ᾱ, ποταύδη, ἔχοντι, δωϲοῦντι, ἱαρόϲ, ἦνθον, τίν, ποκα, πεδά, αὐτεῖ; note -οιϲ and -αιϲ used freely). Alcman seems to employ less widespread, Laconian, features in his vowels (ω, η for secondary long *o*, *e*; -ιο for -εο); no parallel attempt can be seen in Stesichorus. But in Alcman himself ω, η are editorial interpretations of *o*, *e*; the ι of ϲιόϲ might, like the ϲ, be editorial interference (note also the unmetrical attempts to import a short infinitive at 1 [1]. 43). On the other hand, Stesichorus deploys more non-Doric features than Alcman does (so -οιο gen., οἱ nom., neglect of initial ϝ); in the first case, the source is certainly epic, and in view of the many epic features in his expression it is natural to see the same source elsewhere. So Stesichorus' dialect seems more affected by epic than Alcman's, and might be less localized; certainly the signs of localized dialect are rare. Place is not, as in the Lesbian poets, proclaimed by his very language.[3]

---

[2] Brugnone (1997), 268, ll. 5–6. For the other most notable inscriptions of Himera see Dubois (1989), 11, 13–14, nos. 7, 11, 14, and further Manni Piraino (1976); Arena (1994), 157–8. γέεϲ (l. 14) is another striking form from the inscription in Brugnone (1997). For apocope as un-Ionic see Thumb, Kieckers, and Scherer (1932–59), ii. 282–3.

[3] The participles in -οιϲα (Aeolic?) add to the complexities. The most striking item that appears local is the infinitive εἶν S15. i. 7 (correption seems excluded by the placing of the ν at the end of the line). This form is essentially attested only from Euboea, Oropus, Chios; it is not Stesichorus' fixed form even of this word (contrast εἴμειν S102. 5). κρέϲϲον (S11. 11), if original, could be viewed as an epic form, cf. West (1971), 304 n. 3, (1998–), i, p. xx. Poem 222 (b) [3], and P. Oxy. 3876, make unusual localized forms look the rarer. Stesichorus' language as known earlier is treated by Nöthiger (1971). Save with pronouns, long datives are (roughly) the usual Ionic forms and much preferred in Homer, short are the Doric forms (cf. Chantraine (1986–8), i. 193–7, 201–2); so Alcman's and Stesichorus' practice is both poetic and un-Homeric. S27. i. 2 φυγην subscr. ει looks an aberration (contrast e.g. 222 (b) [3]. 214), though interesting for the tradition. There appears to be

The apparent scarcity of topical reference in his work must always have made him difficult to date. The ancient assertions mostly place his activity mainly in the first half of the sixth century, but we can have little confidence that their testimony reposes on anything solid. An early anecdote (TA8) connects him with Phalaris, which probably fits that period; but the connection of Phalaris in this story with Himera, and of this story, in a different version, with another tyrant, does not inspire confidence. Stesichorus might seem more generally to have attracted the devisers of biographical stories from an early period; this makes chronological statements the more suspicious. Simon. 564.4 (TA1a) οὕτω γὰρ Ὅμηρος ἠδὲ Ϲτασίχορος ἄειϲε λαοῖϲ would suggest that he died before Simonides' time; Stes. 209 (*Nostoi?*) is likely to have been written after, not before, the *Odyssey*.[4]

How Stesichorus' poetry was performed we have virtually no direct evidence. Ϲτασίχορος ἄειϲε in Simon. 564. 4 might be poetic or might rest on ignorance. Grave doubts have been expressed at the idea of a chorus chanting enormous poems (the *Oresteia* had two books, the *Geryoneis* probably over 1,300 lines (S27. ii. 6, 10)). Yet it might be difficult to show that these doubts (which I feel myself) have a more absolute foundation than modern musical conventions. The supposed 'epic style' of Stesichorus is a less appealing argument: these poems are plainly transforming the epic genre in some sense, and one does not see why the mode of performance should not be different as well as the metrical design. Such is our ignorance that we cannot even definitely show that the narrator's first person singular was understood to denote the poet rather than a chorus: a necessary but not a sufficient condition for solo singing. If in his *Palinodes* Stesichorus narrated his temporary blinding for speaking ill of Helen, as is commonly imagined, then we might reasonably suppose a first-person narrator equated with the poet. However, the story might be a biographical invention that arose from the exis-

no evidence yet for Stesichorus' handling of the first-person plural active (-μεϲ in Alcman); nor for Alcman's version of γε (γα in Stesichorus).

[4] On the question of an allusion to the Hesiodic *Catalogue*, see West (1985), 134. For Aristotle's story of Stesichorus and Phalaris cf. Bianchetti (1987), 72–3. On Phalaris' date see Luraghi (1994), 21 n. 1. Comment on a contemporary eclipse (Stes. 271, cf. West (1971), 306) seems so unlike what we know of Stesichorus that one is tempted to imagine partial conflation with Pindar, also mentioned by the two sources; one can see this already in the Plutarch. At any rate, one should wait for more direct evidence before using this item in dating.

tence of the *Helen* and the two *Palinodes* (turned into one palinode to make the story work better?). If the poems referred explicitly to his own earlier work, that would help (cf. Hes. *WD* 11–12); but even this is uncertain (Stes. 192 need not show it). Even κλήϊζω in 274 (i) is far from assured in authenticity, and need not be spoken by a poet (cf. e.g. Alcm. 1 [1]. 39).[5]

These agnostic points all have a more positive side. At least in the body of the poem, we see little sign of a first-person speaker formally equated with either an author or a performer or performers, or with much suggestion of personality at all: rather, save in 192 (address to Helen), we appear to see an 'impersonal' narrator. Nor do we see signs of an audience with any specific identity, on any specific occasion, in any specific city. Despite attempts to find political significance in Stesichorus' myths, it is more notable what a range of already central Greek myths he tells fully: fall of Troy, homecomings, Thebes, Heracles, Calydon, etc. It may be that these appearances are delusive; but the prominence in Alcman of myths connected with a single place suggests here too a large difference between these poets' work.[6]

This brings us to the question of how Stesichorus is related to epic. The question has many levels. Thus there is the basic level of language. Stesichorus' dialect, though affected by epic, differentiates him firmly from it; but he borrows from epic many words and phrases, as the commentary illustrates. There is, again, a narratological level. The narrative is developed, like Homer's, with little reference to a specific context and is presented, as in Homer, by what is often called an 'impersonal' narrator. (In fact, Homer's narrator is full of ethos if we consider knowledge rather than emotion or morality, and Stesichorus' may have been too.) The close relation in language makes it reasonable to assume that Stesichorus' manner of narrative is influenced by Homer or the epic tradition. As Stes. 209 demonstrates, Stesichorus was interested in

---

[5] Cf. Dover (1968), 215. ἐμεῦ in 210. 1, if part of the quotation at all, need not be the poet, as Ar. *Pax* itself reminds us. As to Helen, it could be thought that Aristarchus and Aristodemus' account of Pindar's response to the Aeginetans in *Nem.* 7 rested on a related, if more prosaic, deduction (Σ *Nem.* 7. 70, 150 a, cf. 94 a). The tale that Stesichorus' name was a sobriquet (TA19) is very unlikely to depend on archaic evidence, and need imply no knowledge about performance. For the performance of Stesichorus see West (1971), 309, and (1992), 338–9; Haslam (1974), 33, (1978), 29 n. 1; Burkert (1987); Davies (1988a); D'Alfonso (1994) (51–2, 123–4 on 'subjective' assertions).

[6] On Stesichorus' broad approach to myth cf. Arighetti (1994).

the specific poems the *Iliad* and *Odyssey*, and the vision of each poem might be relevant on another level again, that of morality and meaning. This has often been disregarded for Stesichorus. Yet when, using passages apparently derived from the *Iliad*, he makes the monster Geryon a noble and tragic hero, we should see not simply a Homerizing realism but an Iliadic range and balance of sympathies.[7]

There is also the fundamental area of metre. Stesichorus' metre retains much of the double-short character of dactylic hexameters, so that together with the language, it can create, sometimes, a very epic resonance. On the other hand, his metres also distinguish themselves markedly from the sound of epic, by his incorporation in his stanzas of single-short elements or of anapaestic as well as dactylic openings to the period. It is doubtful whether we are in a position to assert that Stesichorus was the inventor of dactylo-epitrite or that the fragments show him gradually achieving this invention. More tangible is the stanzaic and triadic form. As we have seen, it is hardly satisfactory to call the stanza of Alcm. 1 [1] a triad in itself. In Stesichorus the combination of stanza-building with a larger design becomes visible to us for the first time. We shall see from the best-preserved example how the form can be used to enrich and intensify, so that phrases stand out, moods fill stanzas, stanzas are detached, contemplated, and compared. The form creates narrative of a different kind from the flowing movement of Homeric hexameters: a distinctively lyric mode of narrative.[8]

The detailed relation of Stesichorus to the *Iliad* and *Odyssey* can profitably be explored through specific examples. A short mention of one or two will prepare us for things we shall see more of in the Theban poem. A fragment presumably from the *Nostoi* (209) reworks a scene from the *Odyssey*, where Helen interprets an omen to Telemachus (15. 171–8). It looks as if Stesichorus omits some subtle human interaction before the speech (*Od.* 15. 167–71), and gives the opening of Helen's prophetic utterance a more portentous

---

[7] Carson is strongly aware of Stesichorus' sympathy for Geryon ((1999), 5–6); her own highly impressive poem concentrates on Geryon's perspective. See Carson (1999), 4–5, on Stesichorus and Homer, and further Fowler (1987a), 35–6, Parsons (1996a), 1442–3. Stesichorus' close use of the Homeric poems, especially in 209, enables us to sidestep questions about Homer's standing in the first half of the 6th cent. (cf. Snodgrass (1998)). On verbal borrowings from Homer in 222 (b) [3] see also Haslam (1978); Bremer (1987); Maingon (1989).

[8] On Stesichorus' metre cf. esp. Haslam (1974, 1978); also West (1969), 143–5, (1971), 311–13, (1982), 49–51; Parker (1997), 85–6.

and grandiose quality, in part precisely with Homeric language (2–3). The speech also amasses impressive elements from other speeches in the Homeric vicinity (with 10, 11 cf. *Od.* 15. 68, 127). The will of Athena is incorporated too, and appears to stand out sonorously in the verse (8, cf. S89. 7).

In the depiction of Geryon's killing (S15) the actions of Heracles and the arrow are separated by the end of the antistrophe from the reaction of Geryon, pathetically depicted in an Iliadic simile. The lyric form thus intensifies the change in perspective. The rich description of the arrow is also of interest. In particular the piling up of epithets at the start of the antistrophe, with the sentence running over, shows an imaginative fullness of language more like Old English epic than Greek: ὀλεϲάνοροϲ αἰολοδε[ίρ]ου | ὀδύναιϲιν Ὕδραϲ. Finally, Geryon's own reply, S11, to one who bids him flee (Menoetes? S11) is well known to recall Sarpedon's speech at *Il.* 12. 310–28. Yet, whatever exactly the situation here, and the complete wording, the two alternatives Geryon contemplates are set out with far more careful and precise correspondence than in Sarpedon's speech, or in the monologues considering options like *Il.* 21. 553–70, 22. 99–130 (even 9. 412–16 is different): αἰ μέν 8, αἰ δ᾽ 16; ἀγή[ραοϲ 9, γῆ]ραϲ 16–17; ἐν Ὀλύμπ[ωι 10, ἐν ἐ[ἀπάνευ]θε θ[ε]ῶν μακάρω[ν 18–19; κρέϲϲον 11, πολὺ κά[λλιον 20; ἐ]λέγχεα 11–12, ὀνείδε[22. The speech is organized with elaborate care, the phrases are to be compared.

These examples show Stesichorus' concern with dignity, intricate crafting, and an expressive and significant handling of the verse. All this will prove relevant to what is much the most substantial continuous fragment of Stesichorus.

3: *PMGF* 222 (b)[9]

In this fragment the mother of Oedipus' sons reacts with alarm to a prophecy by Teiresias, which speaks of them killing one another; she urges them to divide the legacy of Oedipus between them by lot, so that one rules and the other takes the possessions elsewhere. They do this; Teiresias makes a speech which (among other things) tells how Polynices will go to Argos and marry the daughter of the king. The fatal Argive expedition will of course follow.

Some of this story clearly existed already. The *Iliad* knows of war between Polynices and Eteocles, and probably knows of Adrastus' making both Tydeus and Polynices his sons-in-law (cf. 4. 365–410, 5. 800–7, 14. 113–25). Hesiod refers to a great war at Thebes over the flocks of Oedipus (*WD* 162–3), perhaps the inheritance. The division of the inheritance appears to be implied by the story that Amphiaraus' wife Eriphyle was bribed by Polynices with a Theban heirloom, the necklace of Harmonia. This story is alluded to in the *Odyssey* (15. 247). (The reference of the allusion is confirmed by art from the first half of the sixth century: a Late Corinthian vase, now lost (formerly Berlin F 1655, Payne (1931), no. 1471; Schefold (1993), 282), and the Chest of Cypselus (Paus. 5. 17. 7; cf. Payne (1931), 139–40)—not to mention Stesichorus' own *Eriphyle*.) The mutual fratricide too may well be attested before Stesichorus. It appeared in the *Thebaid* (cf. F3 Davies); an Etruscan bronze sheet from soon after 600 (Florence, Mus. Arch.) seems to show the duel of the brothers, watched by two females, probably their mother and Antigone. The brothers may also be depicted there as swearing an oath. (See Krauskopf (1974), 14–17, (1981), 696, 703; Schefold (1993), 287.) For the depiction of the mother one may compare how the mother (called Euryganeia at least by Pausanias) looked on in dismay at the duel in a later painting by Onasias (second quarter of fifth century; Paus. 9. 5. 10).

---

[9] On the fragment see esp. Meillier, Ancher, and Auger (1976), 287–351, 356–8; Meillier (1977, 1978–9); Parsons (1977) (fundamental), and (1984), 521–4; Ancher (1978); Gostoli (1978); Haslam (1978); West (1978*b*); Tosi (1978/9); Diggle (1979); Thalmann (1982); Maltomini (1985); Bremer (1987) (the principal commentary); March (1987), 126–33; Beck (1988); Burnett (1988); Jakob (1988); Massimilla (1988); Maingon (1989); Judet de la Combe (1996); Pavese (1997); Gentili (1999). Davies (1979), a very valuable commentary on the whole of Stesichorus, does not include this poem (or P. Oxy. 3876).

In some respects, Stesichorus' own story is unclear. Is the mother Oedipus' second wife, as (it appears) in the *Oedipodeia* (F2 Davies; cf. Σ Eur. *Phoen.* 1760 (*FGrHist* 16 F 10))? Or is she also the mother of Oedipus, who in the *Odyssey* kills herself on discovering the incest, but in Euripides lives on, as Oedipus lives painfully on and rules in the *Odyssey* itself (11. 275–81)? (March (1987), 126–33, urges the former case; Mastronarde (1994), 20–2, argues for agnosticism.)

We can, however, see at least one respect in which Stesichorus has either invented or chosen from different possibilities. The knowledge of the coming disaster is not based on a curse or prayer by Oedipus, as in the *Thebaid* (F3 χερcὶν ὑπ' ἀλλήλων καταβήμεναι Ἄϊδος εἴcω); it is probably not based on an oracle delivered to Laius. Stesichorus chooses to concentrate on Teiresias' prophecy now. He can thus create a refined and searching scene. The mother, who is assigned an important role (contrast e.g. Hellan. *FGrHist* 4 F 98), responds directly to the respected Teiresias, in anxiety, not antagonism. The relations between emotion, good sense, and the refusal of truth are subtly and lucidly explored.

What was the extent of this poem's story? (Designed connection with the *Eriphyle* may be set aside.) The papyrus displays the remains of seven triads; eight preceded it, if we can trust the line-number 300. We probably can: the number comes at the right point in the triad, and even the first hand at S27. ii. 10 made only a small mistake. If this pace of narration was exhibited earlier, the beginning of at least the main narrative cannot be far back in time. The length and fullness of other poems by Stesichorus, the absence of any signs in them of narrative mannerism, and the demand of the passage itself for fulfilment, make it appear very likely that the story reached at least the brothers' death (otherwise Burnett (1988), 110–13). This suggests that by using Teiresias' prophecy Stesichorus is creating large arches of narrative within his poem, rather than between his poem and the past. This fragment develops, in manifold ways, what we may call the poetry of 'before'.

Metre

str., ant.

1. – ⏑ ⏑ – ⏑ ⏑ – ⏖ – ⏕ – ⏑ ⏑ – –
2. – ⏑ ⏑ – ⏑ ⏑ – ⏒ – ⏑ – –
3. – ⏑ ⏑ – ⏑ ⏑ – ⏒ – ⏑ ⏑ – ⏑ ⏑ – –

4. – ∪ ∪ – ∪ ∪ –
5. ⩘ – ∪ ∪ – ∪ ∪ – ⩘ – ∪ – –
6. – ∪ ∪ – ∪ ∪ –
7. ⩘ – ∪ – ∪ – ∪ – –

ep.

1. – ∪ ∪ – ∪ ∪ –
2. ∪ – ∪ ∪ – ∪ ∪ – ∪ – ∪ – –
3. – ∪ – ∪ – ∪ – –
4. – ∪ ∪ – ∪ ∪ – ⩘ – ⩔ – ∪ ∪ – –
5. ⩘ – ∪ – –
6. – ⩔ – ∪ ∪ – ⩖ – ∪ ∪ – ∪ ∪ – –
7. – – – ∪ – –

The metre is a version of dactylo-epitrite. However, between D and D Stesichorus can use -- instead of the expected ×: str. 1 (211), ep. 4 (207, 291), 6 (230, 272, 293), not str. 3 or 4. This freedom is not directly visible in other Stesichorean dactylo-epitrite, though the *Iliou Persis* shows connected phenomena. No doubt the feature is connected to the origins of the metre; but one may note that   occurs only once in the strophe or antistrophe (211), despite far more opportunities. In the epode the prolonged double-short sequence stands in effective contrast with the isolated single-short lines 3, 5, 7. Another instance of   seems to occur in the strophe at 215, but this, suspiciously, is before e, and there are other problems here (and possible expedients). – – – ∪ ∪ – can also replace – ∪ ∪ – ∪ ∪ – (str. 1: 211, 217; ep. 4: 249, 6: 230).

The strophe is strongly differentiated from the epode. The strophe (in standard notation: 1 DxDx, 2 Dxex, 3 DxDx, 4 + 5 DxDxe, 6 + 7 DxEx) is elegantly designed in an ababb structure, with 4 + 5 and 6 + 7 expanding b in contrasted ways. All periods begin with D, and there are no periods of e only. In the epode (1 + 2 DxDxex, 3 Ex, 4 DxDx, 5 xex, 6 DxDx, 7 -- ex), there seem to be three periods of e only, which alternate with periods of D only; the first period mixes them, unlike the first period of the strophe. The epode and strophe end similarly, but the epode has a heavier form, which departs from the norms of the metre, and seems to produce a special weight (210, 231; cf. for the form S148 col. ii. 7, also closing the epode). Less weighty are the (double-short) blunt endings to strophe and epode in the dactylo-anapaestic *Geryoneis*. In general the metre of that poem seems markedly lighter, without either the retardation of epitrites or the solemnity of what look like full hexameters.

In terms of sense, the organization in our fragment of whole stanzas and frequently of individual lines appears significant and impressive. Later poets may 'develop' the dactylo-epitrite metre further (cf. Haslam (1978),

56–7); but we should not allow such retrospective vision to obscure the accomplished and purposeful artistry of Stesichorus.

186. πρίν: in this position is most likely an adverb.

188. μ]έγα νεῖκος: used by Homer in narrative and speech (*Il.* 13. 122, 17. 384, etc.); cf. also Hes. *Theog.* 87. The phrase here is at least as likely to come from speech, direct or reported, as from ordinary narrative. (Cf. Bremer (1987), 136.) It need not show that a quarrel has already begun. Line 233, however, makes it probable that some discord has arisen.

190. Is the mother here summoning her sons inside the palace, the woman's sphere (cf. P. Oxy. 3876 ('ined.' in *PMGF*) fr. 4. 7)? At any rate, the speech takes place, significantly, within its walls (233).

197. ἐγειρεν could be a short infinitive (268 looks a probable instance of this dialect feature); ἄλ]γος, say, would be a possible supplement, with the subject possibly Teiresias or his prophecy. It is likely that the speech or its introduction starts the stanza (the stanza need not start the speech). The awakening of the queen from a dream, for example, can hardly be narrated here.

201–31. The queen's long speech responds to a prophecy from Teiresias (probably in direct speech). As will be argued, that prophecy made the future, which is commonly unknown and undetermined, certain and fixed. This speech powerfully presents a human reaction to the unbearable prediction. The speaker attempts to escape its certainty, expresses her response to the events forecast, and seeks to create and determine the future for herself. The concentration on direct speech within a narrative generates both sympathetic insight and ironic detachment.

The queen's gender must affect the impact of her speech, especially as it is set between speeches by an old man and is addressed to young men. She is anything but a hysterical female: indeed, her control and balance contrast with the impulsiveness of her sons. She thinks about the city too (esp. 228–9), more broadly than one or both of them will (285–7). But distinctively female emotion is made to underlie and animate the speech, predominantly maternal feeling (cf. Geryon's mother in S13, and Danae in Simon. 543 [**16**]). The emotion is in itself anything but irrational, by contrast with the brothers' future hatred. It gives the speech a particular tonality and intensity.

The speech exploits the divisions of stanza very forcefully, with each stanza marking a new development, and ending strongly. In Geryon's speech (S11) the thought seems more to overflow the divisions of stanza: cf. 8, 16, 25; 22.

201–3. This part of the speech (until 218) is addressed to Teiresias, despite the presence of the sons. The device heightens the pathos and intensity of the mother's attempts to evade the prophecy; it also produces a more forceful connection between this and the utterance that it takes up. Compare the negative imperatives at the start of Geryon's reply S11. 5–7 μή μοι θα[| τα δεδίϲκ[| μηδεμελ[. This might be a reason for thinking that the speech did not begin before 198.

ἄλγεϲι might refer (*a*) to existing distress, or (*b*) to future woes, according to the role of ἐπί ('in addition to' or 'at'). If (*a*), ἄλγεϲι might denote either the queen's miserable past (so Bremer; cf. Stat. *Theb.* 7. 476) or, perhaps more likely, just the present quarrel. The position of ἐξοπίϲω rather supports (*a*): it suggests a differentiation between the pain of anxiety felt now (201) and the future events themselves which are the object of that anxiety. πρόφαινε supports this understanding of ἐλπίδαϲ. Identity of content between the two clauses seems in any case attractive. The balance of epithets and nouns in the clauses is none the less neat, and significant. The painfulness of emotion and event forms a basis for the mother's plea which is extremely reasonable on an ordinary level, but in the context of prophecies futile. μερίμναϲ and ἐλπίδαϲ both show a wish to make the outcome uncertain; the combination πρόφαινε ἐλπίδαϲ is suggestively awkward (prophetically revealed, but mere objects of expectation).

χαλεπάϲ: an epithet for μέριμναι (an un-Homeric word) in Hes. *WD* 178; but so plain an adjective need not have a particularly epic flavour (cf. Sapph. 1 [4]. 25 n.). This speech, save in the god's titles at 209, has few strikingly ornate epic adjectives; that suits its emotional character. One may contrast the later speech of Teiresias.

πρόφαινε: the word is often associated, in various senses, with prophecies and signs. Cf. e.g. Hom. *Od.* 12. 394, Hdt. 7. 37. 2.

ἐλπίδαϲ βαρείαϲ: the combination is not found elsewhere in literature of the eighth to fifth centuries. The epithet is again forcefully plain; but unlike χαλεπάϲ it defines ἐλπίδαϲ, and so gives a particularly emphatic close.

204–10. Most of the stanza suggests the authoritative wisdom of a lyric, elegiac, or iambic narrator more than the purposeful speeches of epic (cf. e.g. Archil. fr. 13. 5–9 West). Yet in this speech from a character the wisdom is ironically misguided. In Homer, the characters rarely generalize metaphysically at any length, especially as part of an argument. *Il.* 24. 524–33 (Achilles to Priam), *Od.* 18. 130–7 (Odysseus to Amphinomus) form unusual, and much more strongly marked, instances. Other examples are much shorter than ours (so *Il.* 4. 317), or more tightly connected to the context (*Il.* 17. 176–8 (16. 689–90 are probably spurious); *Od.* 14. 83–8). θεοὶ θέcαν (205) indeed comes several times in Homeric speeches (*Il.* 9. 637, *Od.* 11. 555, 23. 11, cf. *Il.* 1. 290); but it is not general there. Hes. *WD* 289 θεοὶ . . . ἔθηκαν, Archil. fr. 13. 5–6 West θεοὶ . . . ἔθεcαν are closer to the scope of this passage.

The universal present given here is meant to illuminate the future, or rather to make it more obscure. The lines sound, on one level, both neatly balanced and wise. The mother is not claiming that all human emotions are short-lived: the οὐ . . . αἰὲν ὁμῶc seems cautious and sensible. (Contrast the rather more sweeping Soph. *OC* 607–13, let alone the grandiose system of Empedocles: Martin and Primavesi (1998), 127–45.) By including the converse φιλότατ' and the broader generalization that follows, she presents a vision of more range than if she had merely spoken of conflict. ἱράν lends further weight to the utterance; it also emphasizes αἶαν, a word which perhaps strengthens the plausibility of resisting absolute assertions. θεοὶ τιθεῖcι must elegantly match, not accidentally repeat, θεοὶ θέcαν, as is indicated by the correspondence of βροτοῖcιν with ἀνδρῶν and probably of ἔμπεδον with ἐπὶ δ' αμε.α..

However, the extension to friendship suggests of itself a minor irony: the present arrangement may not last either. More importantly, the last two lines of the stanza (209–10) undermine what precedes. It is not an unknown future about which the mother is making a reasonable speculation: there is a prophecy. μὴ πάcαc at the start of the last period is in a way related to οὔτε . . . αἰέν at the start of the first; but the wish for an exception now sounds extremely unpromising, and unhopeful. (The placing of μὴ πάcαc in the sentence is expressive.) In such a poem and with such a prophet, the forecast is not likely to contain falsehoods.

The separation of Teiresias from Apollo in fact brings out the divine power behind the prophecy, and probably behind the coming event. The wish about Apollo sounds more forlorn than the request to Teiresias that ended the previous stanza. The divine was much stressed in 204–8, especially for the listener: θεοὶ τιθεῖcι stands in a period on its own, and θεοί immediately follows ἀνδρῶν. But now a more specific god appears, adorned with epic titles (Hom. *Il.* 15. 253 etc.), in a more specific situation. The effect is grim; the consecutive long syllables make it grimmer (cf. Haslam (1978), 38).

ἱράν: the word is unusual with the whole earth rather than one land; cf. Soph. *Phil.* 707 (Bremer). A standard epic epithet for earth is avoided.

νεῖκος κτλ.: for the antithesis of strife and friendship, and their possible impermanence, cf. Hom. *Il.* 7. 301–2. The opposition in the curse at *Thebais* F2. 9–10 Davies is related (Bremer); if earlier, it might enhance the irony here. The alternating impact of Empedocles' Νεῖκος and Φιλότηc, now illuminated by P. Strasb. 1665–6, is not of course a matter of human psychology. Φιλότηc at Hes. *Theog.* 224 is sexual love.

ἐπὶ κτλ.: after δ' α, με is to be preferred to λλο. The two λs would be too squashed together, the end of the first λ too high (contrast even 211). The bottom of the next letter comes low, and so favours ε against ο (contrast e.g. μο twice in 212). Parsons' ingenious emendation doubtless gives the right kind of sense (cf. Hom. *Od.* 18. 136, etc.; Fränkel (1960*b*)); but one would expect a dative to go with ἐν. It is more natural to supply one from the previous clause in Theogn. 429–30. Pavese does not in my opinion show that ἐπιτίθημι would be a suitable verb here ((1997), 264).

μαντοcύνας: the sense 'prophecy' could be thought unusual (cf. Bremer (1987), 143). But the concrete use of such nouns is entirely consonant with the epic language; cf. e.g. ἐφημοcύνη (Hom. *Il.* 17. 697), cυνημοcύνη (22. 261), ὑποθημοcύνη (*Od.* 16. 233), φραδμοcύνη (Hes. *Theog.* 626); note παιγμοcύναc Stes. 232. 2. Presumably μαντοcύναc denotes several predictions within Teiresias' one utterance; this seems the more plausible if he predicted disaster both to the sons and to the city. With πάcαc, μαντοcύναc can hardly be a poetic plural; cf. *Hom. h. Herm.* 472; Hes. fr. 240. 9 Merkelbach–West; Soph. *OC* 354. 'Not this one and so not all' would be a very strained understanding.

211. This stanza moves away to contemplate the terrible possibility that the prophecy comes true after all. It is swept aside with the practicality of the next stanza and the willed optimism of the stanza after that; but its position at the start of the triad may give it special force for the listener. In contemplating this future, which could be thought a fact, the queen is both displaying her subjective response to it and rescuing herself from direct contact with it: the idea of dying before she witnesses it forms a barrier between her and her imagined future perception of the event.

The notion of mutual slaughter has obviously occurred in Teiresas' prophecy. The appalling idea is effectively contained in a period of its own; two metrical licences make the period sound, strikingly, much more like a hexameter than a dactylo-epitrite line. It is, however, not the calamity in itself but her own experience of it which the queen is imagining.

Whatever the actual fate of the queen in the poem, there will be significant links from here to later in the narrative; 286 probably confirms this. In Euripides she kills herself after witnessing the fratricide (*Phoen.* 1455–9; cf. Krauskopf (1990), 685; Stat. *Theb.* 11. 634–47).

212. The idea of fate is also effectively given a period of its own. μόρcιμον at the start is taken up and reinforced by Μοίρᾳ[ι] at the end; the mother wishes to present in strong form the condition she hopes is false.

ἐπέκλωcαν δὲ Μοίρᾳ[ι: cf. Hom. *Il.* 24. 209–10 (*Μοῖρα* weaving), 525 (the gods), *Od.* 7. 196–8 (*Κλῶθεc*), Callin. fr. 1. 9. West (*Μοῖραι*). The present passage has no demonstrative or other reference back; it follows on closely from, and personifies, μόρcιμόν ἐcτιν. It is uncertain whether the Fates are acting with reference primarily to her or her sons; the accusative με rather than the usual dative allows the latter possibility, which seems more attractive, and smoothes the movement into what follows.

213–15. The shaping of the sentence gives αὐτίκα both weight and force; the wish itself occupies a whole line (213). αὐτίκα denotes the present, as it does not always in such contexts (contrast Hom. *Il.* 18. 98, cf. 96, 24. 226); but the timing is in part a powerful way of expressing feeling about the experience she would escape (note ποκα). The passionate idea is made more impressive by the contravention of logic. Instead of saying 'if they are fated to kill themselves, may I die before I see it', she includes the seeing in both halves. This is more striking than the technically illogical idea of dying before one's fated time.

cτυγερο[ῖο] is not only conventional (cf. Hom. *Od.* 24. 414, Stes. S15. ii. 1) but strengthens the paradox. θανάτοιο τέλος Hom. *Il.* 3. 309 etc.

215. A problematic line. Even with an epithet the dative ἄλγεϲ⟨ϲ⟩ι would hang too vaguely on to ἐϲιδεῖν. A feminine accusative at the end of the line for ἄλγεϲϲι to go with is not easily found, and the word-order would seem too elaborate for Stesichorus. (The plural is acceptable: cf. Aesch. *Ag.* 50; Eur. *Hel.* 202.) It is possible that the metrical problem is connected: if ἄλγεϲϲι or whatever were transposed to follow δακρύοεντα, one would avoid the unwelcome double short υο in place of an anceps between D and e (cf. Haslam (1978), 38–41). If ἄλγεϲι were to be emended, one could think along the lines of, say, ἄλγιϲτ⟨α⟩ (cf. 223. 4–5 for the trio) or even αὐγαῖϲι (for ὄϲϲοιϲι, cf. *Hom. h. Herm.* 361, etc.; the confusion of αι and ε appears already in the Timotheus papyrus, cf. Mayser and Schmoll (1970), 83, 85–6).

The synonymous epithets placed next to each other can be seen to carry a considerable charge of pathos; compare and contrast S14. 4–5, S15. ii. 5.

πολύϲτονα: the word comes in Homer (*Il.* 1. 445 etc.), and elsewhere (Archil. fr. 3. 3 West, Pind. *Pae.* 6 (D6). 99 etc.).

216–17. What has Teiresias told the queen? He surely has not said: '"*If* your sons both insist on reigning over Thebes, catastrophe is bound to ensue, and then it will be either mutual fratricide or the sack of the city"' (Bremer (1987), 158). The bold wish that Apollo would not fulfil a prophecy or a part of one would hardly be called for or make plausible sense if the prophecy were merely conditional. The present stanza itself seems rather overblown if the killing is merely a possible event which can be avoided. The abstract arguments addressed to Teiresias in 204–8 would also seem somewhat out of place if the queen were merely contending that the condition he has spoken of will not in fact be realized. And if she intended simply to act on his advice, why does she tell him not to reveal grim expectations about the future? Certainly 209–10, and probably the whole preceding passage, do not fit a mere conditional warning which can be readily heeded. Line 226 πότμο[υ seems inappropriate too. The implications of this view will be considerable.

More difficult is the question whether Teiresias has prophesied that either the sons will kill each other or the city will fall. If he has, the present sentence is oddly framed. There is strong emphasis on the condition that it is absolutely fated the queen's sons should die: if so, she wishes to die first. In such a context, it is strange for the fated event to become at the end of the sentence only an alternative possibility. This is not like the passionate illogicality over seeing: it produces curious sense and a weak anticlimax. On the other hand, we could imagine that Teiresias has prophesied various events that will ensue from the quarrel, including the destruction of the city (achieved later by the Epigoni); this could then be added as a disaster that the queen will also escape seeing by immediate death. The ἤ would appear rather than καί because of the implied negativity in the wish (may I die before, i.e. without, seeing this or this; cf. in this respect Soph. *Ant.* 1245). The participial clauses are governed by ἐcιδεῖν, with ταῦτ' introducing them, cf. e.g. Thuc. 3. 18. 3 (with Classen and Steup (1892–1922), iii. 34). Lines 228–31, when rightly understood, support this view: see on 229.

ἐνὶ μεγάροιc θανόντας: the formulation is varied and weakened from 211. The phrasing gains force from, and gives force to, the setting of the speech in the family's home (ἐν μεγάροιc 233); it heightens too the separation of family and city. One may doubt whether παῖδας ἐνὶ μεγάροιc in itself forms enough of a unit to count as an epic phrase (cf. Hom. *Il.* 24. 603 etc.; *CEG* i. 138. 2).

218–24. The queen now propounds a scheme of her own to cause the future; the irony is the sharper in that the scheme is immediately accepted and realized in the narrative (234–45).

218. ἀλλ' ἄγε: frequent in Homer, but not only Homer (*Il.* 1. 62 etc.; cf. e.g. Sapph. 43. 8 ἀλλ' ἄγιτ'; Alc. 38 a. 4 ἀλλ' ἄγι (to one person)). It is used at a less emphatic point of division (middle of the second line in a stanza) at Stes. S88. i. 7; cf. S10. 5.

παῖδες: the sons whose death was contemplated at the beginning and end of the previous stanza are now addressed with assured practicality (211, at the same point in the stanza and melody; 216). The sombre parenthesis in the thought is left behind.

219. τέλος: with ταῖδε not τόδε and with a verb like προφα[ίνω, τέλος seems to mean more than 'task' even on the surface. Whatever the range of τέλος at this period, the word has ironic connections with

the divine fulfilment of prophecy which the queen wants to avoid
(τελέccαι 210).

προφα[: the supplement προφα[ίνω is probable. There should
then be a connection with the appearance of the verb at 203, as
Bremer notes ((1987), 153). However, it would seem unlikely that
the queen, who will be supported by Teiresias, is here emphati-
cally overruling his pronouncement (cf. Bremer (1987), 156). The
connection is, rather, an ironic one for the listener. Both τέλοc and
προφα[ίνω through their resonances undo the queen's authoritative
stance.

220–2. The construction is subtle, and exploits the syntactic possi-
bilities of Greek, where a participial clause can be more emphasized
than a main clause. From the queen's point of view, the important
thing is that one son should stay in Thebes (ναίειν) and that one
should go away (ἀπίμεν). From the sons' point of view the impor-
tant thing is the division of the inheritance, and the parallel clauses
with ἔχοντα are given much weight. cύμπαντα is carefully inserted,
and the second participial clause made longer, to recommend the
less attractive option.

φίλου . . . [: with the likely supplement πατρόc cf. 209. 11, and
Hom. *Il.* 19. 422, *Od.* 17. 43, etc. It would most naturally be sup-
posed that Oedipus is no longer alive.

cύμπαντα: cύμπαc usually refers to a plurality of people; but cf.
Pind. *Ol.* 6 [**18**]. 56. The interweaving of nouns and adjectives in
the line is notable. The speech is rich in separations of epithet from
noun: 201, 205, 213, 226, 227. Our material is insufficient to say
how typical the present density is.

223. κλαροπαληδόν: a new word to us, but not particularly in-
ventive. Cf. κληροπαλήc Hom. *h. Herm.* 129; for the formation of
the adverb cf. ἐπικλοπάδαν S15. ii. 6–7 (Haslam (1978), 53), Risch
(1974), 365). The length and position of the word (before ὃc ἄν)
give it emphasis.

   The idea need not spring from events in Stesichorus' time (so
Bremer). The arrangement could be seen as an extension of the
Homeric casting of lots to apportion divisions of an inheritance
(*Od.* 14. 208–9, cf. *Il.* 15. 289–92). In a mortal context, the casting
of lots leaves one especially open to the will of the gods. The irony is
brought out here by ἔκατι Μοιρᾶν. This word ends the stanza, with
great emphasis. One can hardly fail to connect it with the mention

3: <i>PMGF</i> 222 (b)

of Moirai in 212; they have indeed willed the fratricide, and the present arrangement will only further their design. But it seems stylistically implausible that the queen should be seen to make the connection, purposefully. The subtlety lies rather with the author.

225. The stanza begins confidently. δοκέω is modestly authoritative rather than hesitant; but it emphasizes for the listener the queen's error. The first person of δοκέω is not used without a construction like this before the fifth century except at the unelevated Anian. fr. 5. 9 West; it would be ὀίω in Homer (*Il.* 8. 536–7, *Od.* 23. 261, etc.). Stesichorus is probably advancing, with a purpose, unusually close to colloquial expression.

226. λυτήριον: our view of the word affects our sense of the passage and Stesichorus' language. It is probably a noun. Neuter nouns in -τήριον (-ια), though theoretically derived from adjectives in -τήριος, appear long before them: first ποτήριον (ML 1. 1–2), θελκτήριον (Hom. *Il.*, *Od.*), θρεπτήρια (Hes. *WD* 188); in archaic hexameter ἀκρωτήρια, χρηστήρια, ψυκτήριον; in lyric one finds, besides ποτήριον and ἀκρωτήρια, θωστήρια (Alcm. 1 [1]. 81) and λυτήριον (Pind. *Pyth.* 5. 106 'means to pay back', stylistically much better than an adjective; also Ap. Rhod. 4. 704 'means to expiate', and probably Soph. fr. 758 Radt 'means to release from' (cf. LSJ *Supp.*)). An adjective in -τήριος seems first to appear in Heraclit. fr. 35 Marcovich (cωτήριος); in poetry they come first, and very productively, in tragedy. To judge from other such nouns, and the other uses of this one, it is unlikely to be a poetic invention; its use here is likely to convey an almost technical force and assurance, 'a means to release you'.

ὕμμι: she judiciously emphasizes their benefit rather than the whole family's (us).

κακοῦ . . . πότμο[υ: the combination is not found in literature of the eighth–sixth centuries. It is, like βαρείας in 203, an effectively plain but individual word.

227. We must consider the relation between the link here and later of Teiresias and deliverance and Teiresias' earlier prophecy of disaster. If Teiresias had made a purely conditional prophecy, then the present phrase would be easily explained. Not the precise instructions, but the warning would have come from Teiresias. Such a prophecy, however, was seen earlier to be incompatible with the text (216–17 n.). Even here, the queen regards the family or the city as doomed (230–1); this must be in accord with Teiresias' prophecy, which would not then be conditional. This passage, then, further supports what the earlier passage had established.

Little is to be gained by evolving a complicated compromise for this passage, whereby Teiresias had said that the doom on the house was certain, but that a delay might be obtained by avoiding the quarrel. For the city has also to be fitted in; the reference in 228 must point to the reference in Teiresias' prophecy (217). But we would land ourselves in hopelessly convoluted or strained conceptions if we made the prophecy assert that the destruction, either of one but not both of the house and the city, or of both together but at an interval in time, could be delayed by ceasing the quarrel. Such an approach would also mean that the end of the speech became a clumsy and obscure resumption of Teiresias' prophecy. If, on the other hand, the idea of delay is a sad improvisation by the queen, that will be highly effective.

How is it, then, that the queen can say Teiresias has prompted her plan, that Teiresias can join her in attempting to prevent the quarrel (234), that he can make a speech (ending 290) which is thought to urge the brothers to accept the plan? The first is not particularly strange: it is Teiresias' prophecy which has caused her to devise this scheme; she naturally emphasizes that she is learning from, not defying, what he has said. Teiresias' later speech is far from clear to us in tenor; to what extent it is simply supporting the scheme is scarcely to be determined. (Maingon (1989), 55, suggests it is essentially a revelation of disaster.) But the second point perhaps remains (234). Let us at any rate hypothesize that Teiresias is simply supporting the queen throughout. Why does he not sit back and accept that fate is ineluctable?

Greek literature can exploit the tensions between foreknowledge (or divine knowledge) and human (or anthropomorphic) action; it does not eliminate them in universal quietism. A couple of examples may illustrate the complications: at Soph. *Ant.* 1023–32 Teiresias advises Creon to retract, implying the situation can still be rescued (note 1032), but he later reveals that disaster will occur (1060, cf. *OC* 624; 1064–90); this is not unravelled for the audience. At Aesch. *Th.* 377–83, 568–91, Amphiaraus has been attempting to prevent the Argives from attacking; but he has, in accordance with legend, an unconditional foreknowledge of his own mode of death (587–9) and so, one infers, of the attack. A Euripidean woman, characteristically, makes such problems overt by asking Amphiaraus why he is sacrificing if he is doomed (*Hyps.* fr. 1. v. 20 Cockle); the chorus of the *Agamemnon* bring out a different problem with Cassandra's prescience (1296–8). In this passage things would be less problematic. Teiresias' support for the queen and his prophecy fit together in that both spring from his perceiving the gravity of the position. (Likewise in the *Antigone*, though things are made easier in Stesichorus by the sequence of speeches and the probable change in Teiresias' addressee.) His action does not seem unnatural, and is explicitly marked out by the poet (234). The remains of his subsequent speech are fragmentary; but it seems almost inevitable that, if it urges the plan, it derives pathos or irony from Teiresias' knowledge of what will happen in the end (note especially 275–80). The poet, then, would be gaining positive effect from the complexities.

φραδαῖϲι: often used with a genitive or the like of a divinity's advice, *CEG* i. 247, 321, Aesch. *Ch.* 441, Eur. *Phoen.* 667. Perhaps θείου carries more than its usual force (it is used, e.g., of a herald at Hom. *Il.* 4. 192); note Stes. 209. 1. The queen is being extremely polite to Teiresias, and also suggesting sacred support for her proposed plan of rescue. φραδή itself first seems to come, apart from this passage, at Alc. 113. 2; it is akin to the epic φραδμοϲύνη.

228. †αἶτε νέον† : τ is assuredly preferable to γ, as is shown by the trace to the left of the upright, and by the spacing of ιτ (contrast ιγ in 231 with ιτ in 239). νέον is unsatisfactory either as an adverb or as an adjective. The sense 'again' (once more) is not well supported by Hom. *Il.* 2. 88 αἰεὶ νέον ἐρχομενάων. As an adjective, if applied to γένοϲ only it would give an improbable position to τε; its application to ἄϲτυ would be peculiar. αἶτε is difficult to make into a satisfactory sentence. But ἐτεόν too would pose problems, for one would expect someone to have asserted that Zeus will rescue the city. On our argument about Teiresias' prophecy, that seems improbable; on other views it is unlikely too. Replacements for the corrupt words could pursue many paths (e.g. αἴ γε νοεῖ, with an infinitive, cf. Pind. *Nem.* 10. 86; the contraction is normal, cf. S15. i. 8, S88. ii. 10, 232. 2). One may even bear in mind that, as τ must be wrong, a Homeric κε with subjunctive could be considered (cf. Alc. 69. 3).

229. The isolated phrase effectively evokes the long past of doomed Thebes.

γένος . . . Κάδμου must denote the Thebans, who are normally called Καδμεῖοι or the like in poetry, including Pindar and tragedy. Before Stesichorus cf. Hom. *Il.* 4. 385–91 etc., *Od.* 11. 276, Hes. *Theog.* 326, fr. 193. 2 Merkelbach–West, etc., in Stesichorus P. Oxy. 3876 ('ined.' in *PMGF*) fr. 39. 15. For γένος note Aesch. *Th.* 302–3 πόλιν καὶ στρατὸν | Καδμογενῆ, Eur. *Phoen.* 808. No listener could understand the words to refer to Eteocles or Polynices; that would need a reference to Labdacus at least.

The queen hopes Zeus will rescue or show kindness to the city. If γενέ[θ]λαι is correct, he would do so by postponing the fate of the royal house; but in any case the form of the sentence connects help for house and city. Given the earlier reference to the sack of the city as part of Teiresias' prophecy (217), one would imagine that the destruction of house and city were linked in the prophecy, not seen as exclusive alternatives.

230–1. Two lines here begin with three long syllables, an effectively weighty conclusion.

Others have compared Hdt. 1. 91. 3, where Apollo says he has delayed Croesus' downfall three years beyond its destined time; gods delay fate conspicuously in the *Aeneid* (see Fordyce (1977), 121–2). Cf. Pind. *Pae.* 6 (D6). 81–98 (Apollo delays Troy's fall, but Zeus brings it about since it is destined).

πολὺν χρόνον brings out the pathos of the queen's attempt to turn inevitable bad into good. The phrase is hardly distinctive enough to have a strongly epic flavour; cf. e.g. Ar. *Birds* 200, Thuc. 1. 86. 4. The apparent vertical of the last letter in 230 is not real.

πέπρωται κτλ.: the last words of the epode, as in 210 effectively marked off as a period, highlight for the listener the grimness of the real position. For the listener stanza and sentence darken as they develop.

232–3. The narrator's emphasis is not on the irony of the eventual future but on the queen's immediate attempt, laudable, rhetorically apt, and, it seems for the moment, successful (234). Her words do not sound especially gentle, any more than Odysseus' in *Il.* 2. 189; it is rather that she is refraining from the tactless anger the occasion might have allowed.

Line 233 most naturally suggests that the quarrel is already in progress. ἐν μεγάροις is significant: they are quarrelling within the family home.

The resumption of the narrative is marked with heavily epicizing language: it recalls the epic ὣc φάτο, δῖα γυναίκων, μύθοιc' ἀγανοῖcι (Hom. *Od*. 15. 53).

234. Teiresias, unlike the queen and the sons, is named. This, thanks to the shape of the sentence, may mark out his intervention; cὺν δ' ἅμα certainly accentuates it (the combination does not appear elsewhere in archaic literature). He seems a more helpful sort here than in some tragedies; but here too his mood may change. The sons' compliance sets up various narrative structures, immediate and more distant.

τ[εραcπό]λοc is plausible in itself, if a little long. It would be found only here; it would match Homer's ὀνειροπόλοc and οἰωνοπόλοc (*Il*. 1. 63, 69).

239–45. The narrative in 236–43 refers to the two lots, Thebes (236–7) and the possessions (239–43); the latter clearly begin the new stanza. It is notable that the narrative is more copious than the speech both in detailing the possessions and in assigning them epithets (239, 241, 243).

239. χρ] υcόν τ' ἐρίτιμον: ἐριτίμοιο χρυcοῖο Hom. *Il*. 9. 126, 268.

242. κ]λυτὰ μᾶλα: Hom. *Od*. 9. 308.

243. εὐέθ]ειρας ἵππουc would be a lyric version of the epic ἐϋτριχαc . . . ἵππουc (Hom. *Il*. 23. 13, *al*.). The epithet is found at Anacr. 418, Simon. 519 fr. 84. 6; cf. further Ibyc. S151 [**11**]. 9 n., Pind. *Ol*. 2. 26.

246–52. Line 253 evidently introduces a speech (Teiresias'?). This passage seems to provide a reason for it. Instead of a continuation of placid obedience, we have '*x* himself leaped up' and the apparently derogatory 'obscure, unintelligible', perhaps accompanying 'prophecies'. 'Himself' suggests that the leaping expresses lively feeling rather than denoting the mounting of a horse; for the emotional connotations add to Parsons (1977), 29, examples of leaping up from a throne in great fear or anger (Hom. *Il*. 20. 62, Hdt. 7. 212. 1; Hdt. 3. 155. 1). cτήθεccι too might well have to do with emotion. The outcome of the sortition might be the reason for this rise in temperature. The poet would seem to have created a dramatic moment, which conveys the fragility of the accord. The prophecies did not seem at all obscure to the queen; if this supplement is correct, it shows a different and more scornful attempt to evade unwanted prediction.

247. ἀcάμουc: not epic; next extant Anacr. 403. 1, Aesch. *Dict.* fr. 46 a. 5 Radt, *Ag.* 1596 (of χρηcμοί [Aesch.] *PV* 662).

249. cτήθεcci φίλοιci: Hom. *Il.* 4. 313 etc.

253–91. After the introduction in 253, 254 must be part of a speech, and 255 and in the context 257 look as if they are. The reading in 260 is uncertain; 266 and the epode appear in the context like speech, and 273 should lead straight into 274. One suspects some sort of sequence of πολλάς (cf. 260, 265, 269). In short, the passage seems to be made up of speech, and most likely a single speech; if so, Teiresias'. The speaker becomes clear in 274–80, which predict the near future for Polynices. Lines 281–7 name Eteocles and Polynices. There is talk of disaster for a city, most likely Thebes; it is not clear whether Teiresias is admonishing or prophesying. Polynices' departure follows the speech, most likely at once. If Polynices was one of the inflamed parties, as seems probable from 274–80, he has evidently changed his attitude as a result of the speech. This need not mean that the speech was pacific (would one expect this after 251, and probably 247?). The end of the scene does not look particularly tranquil.

253–73. The content cannot be clearly recovered. In 255 φίλ]τατε (Bremer) is only one of many possibilities, and not an especially appealing one. At least some of the instances of πολλά (260, 265, 269) might well bear some relation to the talk of possessions and gifts in 272–80. The mention of the gods in 266 (cf. 289) is bound to create some connection with the queen's reflections on gods in 204–8. Lines 270–3 plainly speak of the sortition. The cattle receive an epithet (272), but the enumeration is evidently shorter than in 239–43.

253. μ]ῦθον ἔειπε: Hom. *Il.* 2. 156 etc.

260. The letter after γα appears too straight and upright for θ; one should rather choose ρ, though it would be big, and would require a drop in the line. The stroke before ν perhaps looks at an unlikely angle for ι.

272. ἕλικαc βόαc: Hom. *Il.* 9. 466 etc. ἠδὲ καὶ ἵππον is differently used at *Il.* 23. 609.

274–80. The assured prediction of the future reminds one of Teiresias in Pind. *Nem.* 1. 60–72; but in the doubtless full narrative of Stesichorus this anticipation will have a different structural function. Within the scene, Teiresias' knowledge emphasizes his authority, both for the listener and for the sons (who have perhaps complained about oracles, 247). He stands in a different relation to the future from the queen. The reference to what is μόρςιμον must connect with 212 (and 231), and suggest for the listener what else is fated. The anaphora of 'give' must itself produce some contrast with the further future, whether in warning, prediction, or something in between. The division of stanzas is clearly being exploited with force, and the words within the stanza are being arranged with rhetorical purpose. -οι' ἄνακτος at the end of the stanza and of an earlier line are much more likely to be a pointed repetition than a clumsy coincidence (cf. 205 and 208). The rhetorical shaping of the stanza is of course itself infused with ironies: Adrastus' gift of his daughter will have disastrous consequences, for Polynices, Thebes, and himself.

275. Ἀδράςτοι' ἄνακτος: the phrase and its echo in 280 nicely illustrate the complications of epic forms in lyric. An epic ending is combined with an un-epic elision (cf. later Simon. 519 fr. 35 (*b*) 3 (and fr. 20. 10 West!), Bacch. 5. 62, etc.); the elision itself imitates the epic neglect of digamma, in a word where epic (especially the *Odyssey*) much prefers to keep it.

276. περικαλλέα κο̣[ύραν: Hom. *Il.* 16. 85; περικαλλέ[α ν]ᾶςον Stes. S8. 2.

281–7. It is not certain that ετεο[is the name rather than ἐτεόν, but metre and 283 recommend it . If so, the two opposed names seem to come in forcefully: the queen has referred to them only as παῖδες, so far as we can tell. (-)εχεν looks likely to be an infinitive. But the passage is sadly obscure. In 285 various endings to τεύξ[are possible.

In 285–7 it is evidently Thebes rather than Argos that is in question: μα τ[looks plausible in 286. The disaster is being portrayed with vigorous rhetoric: note πάςαι (285, cf. S11. 22 καὶ παντὶ γέ[νει), and ἀεί (287). The reference to the queen looks back to her speech from a different perspective, especially to her depiction of her grief at the fratricide. Whatever the nature of this speech, there is a

sinister contrast between its language and the attempted optimism
of the queen.

One might infer from 285–6 that Oedipus is dead.

διαμπερέως: this form in epic first at Hes. fr. 280. 3 Merkelbach–
West.

288–90. Parsons restores 288–90 as a wish; but the emphasis on
μάλιστα παντῶν perhaps seems implausibly overdone.

291. ὀ]γυμάκλυτος: Hom. *Il*. 22. 51.
Page (Parsons (1977), 33) thinks that Polynices is the subject
from αἶψα on. If Polynices departs abruptly, without a word, that
would have interesting implications. Unfortunately, one could also
imagine Teiresias as the subject of e.g. αἶψα δ᾽ ἀ[πήνθε | δόμων,
with Polynices as subject of ὤιχετ᾽ (often simply 'went' in Homer).
In either case, the adverb seems to indicate some continuance of
strong emotion; it does not seem very plausible that it is showing
unquestioning compliance by Polynices (cf. Hom. *Il*. 2. 808).

295–303. The journey of Polynices and his entourage towards Ar-
gos obviously formed a contrast with the intense scene or scenes
before it. The account is brisk, and conveys the speed of the journey
(303); the narrative seems to concentrate on places passed through.
Epithets and ornamental descriptions appear to abound. At the
same time, the speech of Teiresias creates a grim momentum in
this rapid movement towards the city of Adrastus. In Stat. *Theb*.
1. 324–89, rightly compared by Parsons ((1997), 33–4), Polyn-
ices' choice of destination is accident or supernatural design, and
he travels alone. The solitude of the exile may well be an aspect
that Stesichorus has rejected in favour of dignity and pomp. Cf. a
Chalcidian skyphos-krater by (attributed to) the Phineus Painter
(Copenhagen VIII 496, *c*.530; Rumpf (1927), 15 no. 19, tabb. 37–
9) and the story e.g. in Eur. *Hyps*. fr. 8 etc. pp. 76–9 Cockle, *Pho*.
408–21.

295. μέγα τεῖχ[ος: Hom. *Il*. 7. 463 etc.

302. ἄστεα καλά: this combination is not found in literature of the
eighth–sixth centuries. The plural is unexpected.

This discussion has shown the sophistication and depth of Stesi-
chorus' writing. The stanzas and triads are essential to the pro-
duction of a narrative form more elaborate, ponderous, and osten-
tatiously turned in upon itself than the narrative of Homer. This

fragment takes these qualities still further than what we can see of the *Geryoneis*; it may be relevant that the *Geryoneis* seems a slightly less sombre poem (if more sombre than one might have expected). Irony, pathos, and the exploration of theology and psychology are realized in this fragment through the close exploitation of artistic form. We must give the lyric element in Stesichorus its full weight, and perceive that Stesichorus has fashioned out of the epic something of a quite different character. Only then can we start to do his poetry justice.

SAPPHO

Introduction

SAPPHO was from Mytilene. Her date is more problematic. Her reference to Lydian power at 16 [**5**]. 19–20 should predate the fall of Sardis (547–5). Herodotus (2. 134–5) says that her brother was involved with the courtesan Rhodopis at Naucratis, who, he says, flourished in Amasis' reign (570–26, alas); Rhodopis would seem to have retired from her profession *c*.540 or later. Sappho, however, called her brother's beloved Doricha (15 b. 11, cf. 7. 1; Posidipp. XVII Gow–Page; Athen. 596 c). There is no reason to accept Herodotus' identification, which is characteristic of fifth- and fourth-century chronological constructions; but plainly he was willing to think that Sappho lived in the reign of Amasis, presumably not only in the earlier part of his reign and presumably not only in the later part of her life (the brother sounds young). A later tradition, however, has her flourish around 612/609 (or 600/599), or go into exile around the turn of the century (Sapph. (T) 249, 251, 253). It would be very sanguine to assume that this tradition had access to any straightforward information on Sappho's date not available to Herodotus. However, it may be that both this later tradition and Herodotus are supposing Sappho and Alcaeus contemporaries, as on the red-figure kalathoid vase of the 470s Munich 2416 (see the introduction to the commentary on Alcaeus). The same may be true of Athenaeus, who locates Sappho in the time of Alyattes (*c*.610–560; if either of the poets mentioned Alyattes, Alcaeus is the more likely). The best ground for assigning the poets to the same time is Sappho's possible mention of Myrsilus (Κλεανακτιδα[, 98 b. 7); however, she may be referring to the family, which would fix the time much less firmly. If the poets are contemporaries, one can use Alcaeus' date, itself far from certain (see the introduction to the commentary on Alcaeus): Sappho may have been active in the period *c*.600–570.[1]

Mytilene was the most important of several substantial cities on Lesbos. It was very close to, but reassuringly separated from, the mainland of Asia Minor, dominated by the formidable power of Lydia. The Lydians, as excavations of Sardis have shown, were deeply influenced by Greek material culture, and so interested in its products and skills; with their gold, they were a prime source of wealth and luxury for Mytilene. Interaction between the peoples was considerable; it seems to have included intermarriage (see below). Mytilene clearly had interests in the coast, most notably in the Troad (Hdt. 5. 94–5); it was also concerned with Aenus in Thrace (Ephor. *FGrHist* 70 F 39; Alc. 43; P. Oxy. 3711. 33–6). It showed enterprise in trade: unlike the other Lesbian cities, it was formally involved in Naucratis (Hdt. 2. 178. 2–3; cf. also 3. 14. 5).[2]

[1] Sappho from Mytilene: see Hdt. 2. 135. 1, 6, Arist. *Rhet.* 2, 1398[b]13–14, etc. Sappho's own fragments offer sufficient confirmation, note 71. 3, 98 b. 7 (cf. Alc. 112. 23, T468), etc. (and possibly Sapph. T203, note P. Oxy. 3711 fr. 1. 4–5; Alc. 303 A a. 7 (but metre?)?). Dioscor. XVIII. 4 Gow–Page (iii BC?) and the *Suda* (T253) claim she comes from Eresus; see Jacoby (1923–) II D. 687, though his statement about 5th-cent. coins is mistaken, cf. Wroth (1894), lxx–lxxi. Against Herodotus' identification of Doricha with Rhodopis, cf., after Athen. 596 C, Wehrli (1969), ix. 80; Braun (1982), 43 (but believing the later evidence); otherwise but with whimsy Boardman (1994), 142. Herodotus' date for Rhodopis is probably confirmed by a base ascribed to her dedication at the end of her career, dated *c*.540 or later (Jeffery (1990), 102); Ael. *Var. hist.* 13. 33, which puts her earlier, does not inspire confidence (and the Pharaoh is not named at Strab. 17. 1. 33). There were Greeks in Naucratis by *c*.625 (Coulson and Leonard (1981), 7); but questions about Herodotus' views on Naucratis can be left aside here. For Sapph. 98 b. 7 cf. Alc. 112. 23, with Σ, 306 a. 13, T468, and also Sapph. 71. 3 Πενθιλήαν, with Alc. 75. 10, T472, etc.
[2] Lydia: commerce with Greeks and military power, Hanfmann (1983), 33, 85; on Lydia and money Howgego (1995), 1–4; Greek influence on culture: sculpture Hanfmann and Ramage (1978), 14, 17, terracotta Ramage (1978), 38–41; Winter (1993). (Greek deities too were of interest: note later *artimús ibśimsis*, to whom Croesus had made such a contribution.) Gold refinery: Hanfmann (1983), 37–41; cf. Pedley (1972), 84 (no. 303). Reputation for wealth and sophistication Archil. fr. 19. 1 West; Alcm. 16; Sapph. 39. 2–3, 132. 3; Alc. 69 (306 (1); P. Oxy. 3711 fr. 2. 6–9?; Anacr. 481). Lydian influence on Lesbos: note the resemblance between

Excavations at Mytilene have afforded relatively little archaic material. Antissa suggests, *a fortiori*, the probable wealth of Mytilene. Pottery at Mytilene shows the expected areas of import for the eastern Aegean; it also shows close contact with the facing coast, and production in Mytilene of Aeolic grey ware. One notes from the remains the artistry with which a feline head has been incised on a sherd; a large sculptured head (no photograph) is said to be of fine quality. In the slight remains of sixth-century architecture, there appears a mixture of Ionic, Doric, and Aeolic features. At the least, we see in the material remains both local tradition and the impact of the outside world.[3]

In such an environment, one would not expect a literature innocently separated from the outside world and its poetry; connections with epic, for example, in the Mytilenean poets are evident enough. A more difficult question is whether there was a local tradition. Shadowy predecessors and possible Aeolic archaisms form a fragile basis for the reconstruction of an Aeolic tradition of poetry. More promising are Sappho and Alcaeus' metres. One may abstain from invoking the uncertainties of Indo-European verse, and still note that both poets are working within a system distinguishable from that of other poets around this time. Single-short cola play very little part. They cultivate almost exclusively a type of metre used later by other poets as part of their repertoire. In this type, to simplify, a choriambic core is surrounded by single-short elements, and may itself be expanded in a double-short fashion. They avoid large strophes. Of strophes with more than one sort of colon, only a single type, the sapphic stanza, is clearly used by both poets; they use it frequently. Neither poet is likely to be deriving this whole metrical system solely from the other; there is evidently (cf. Sapph. 106) some poetic tradition.[4]

an early coin-type, most likely Mytilenean, and Croesus' coins (Bodenstedt (1981), 97). Note also Pind. fr. 125 (interesting for its conceptions rather than its story), and West (1997), 526–31, for argued Near Eastern influence on Sappho.

[3] For the archaeology of Lesbos see Spencer (1995*a*); Buchholz (1975) for Methymna; Schaus (1996) for Eresos. For Canadian excavations of Mytilene, Williams and Williams (1985, 1988, 1989, 1990, 1991), Williams (1995); imported pottery Schaus (1992); architecture Betancourt (1977), 87; Williams and Williams (1990), 190, (1991), 178, 181, Williams (1993). Female head: Williams and Williams (1990), 191; own ware: Williams and Williams (1991), 184; feline head: Williams and Williams (1991), pl. vi. 1. Antissa: Spencer (1995*b*). On the place of Mytilene within Lesbos note recently Mason (1993).

[4] Cf. also Kannicht (1997), 361, who remarks on the Lesbian avoidance of exces-

The relation between language and locale has been much considered. We may set aside a search for origins, and still note certain points. Sappho and Alcaeus' variant forms show that their resources must extend beyond their own current speech. Some forms in Sappho marked as unusual by the rest of the corpus are ἀδικήει (or even ἀδίκησι) 1 [4]. 20, φίλοιc dat. 44. 12, Περάμοιο 44. 16 (the first two at the ends of lines); note also the omission of augments (e.g. 94. 6), and 1 [4]. 26–7 n. Now in 44 as a whole, by comparison with say 1 [4], the number and nature of instances, though not extraodinary, does appear notable. Neither the use of a myth, nor the double-short element in the second book's metre, nor the length of the poem (over 34 lines, roughly 1½–2 columns), justifies one in seeing here a quite different type of work: a notion which might possibly be relevant to the hexametric fragments of epithalamia. Only the gap before 44 in P. Oxy. 1232 is intriguing. It seems natural to relate the expansion of language in 44 to Sappho's expansion of her poetry to appropriate a mythical scene. That in turn would confirm that Sappho's linguistic norms are not immovable and unconscious, and suggest that they play some role in her work which is related to content.[5]

For all the unusual forms in the Lesbians, Alcman seems notably freer. His handling of dative plurals, for example, shows much less tendency habitually to follow rules than the Lesbian poets' (even when we allow for the identity of a short dative from an *o* or *ā* stem with the Lesbian accusative). The language of the Lesbian poets, then, tends to be relatively restricted; but the usual acceptance of restrictions must be a matter of deliberate choice.

Important too is the distance from epic, and elegy and iambus. Any substantial sequence of lines in Sappho or Alcaeus will contain numerous dialect features which are alien to those genres (and indeed Stesichorean lyric); many are reinforced by later inscriptions (such as *SEG* 36 (for 1986), no. 752), and some confirmed

---

sively simple patterns. The 'aeolic base' at the start of many forms of colon would demand more elaborate treatment in a fuller account than the above.

[5] Bowie (1981) is a particularly rewarding treatment of the dialect; Hamm (1958) presents basic facts. Discussion starts effectively from Lobel (1925 and 1927: the former more cautious than the latter). See also esp. Morpurgo Davies (1976); Hooker (1977); on the inscriptions, see Hodot (1990), and on Aeolic inscriptions more widely Blümel (1982). The slight pieces of archaic writing found in the recent excavations might prove to have points of linguistic interest; see Williams and Williams (1989), 178, (1990), 191. On the meaning of the myth in 44 cf. Roberts (1997), 258, 263.

by metre. Their texts look much further removed from epic than Alcman's.

On a basic level, then, the Lesbians deliberately write in a language which seems particularly defined, and particularly distant from other poetry. Whatever the authors' intentions, or the role of tradition, in Alcaeus' work as a whole the character of the language supports effectively the appearance of immersion in a specific and local political world. (Theognis is much less specific and concrete.) In Sappho, the language supports the appearance of concentration on her own different but even more specific world, limited and personal. This appearance, or primary level, is important to the poets' impact; but as the language itself shows, once we ascend even as high as vocabulary, the totality of the poets' effect is much more complex.[6]

We may now come to what can be known about Sappho herself. Sappho's brother Charaxus was evidently wealthy, and involved with trade (cf. 252, 254, add Posidipp. XVII Gow–Page); her brother Larichus poured wine in the prytaneion, which she presented as a position of honour (203, 252). One would infer that her family was rich, and its position not undistinguished (note 71. 3). Larichus was evidently young, Charaxus was perhaps youthful, when Sappho wrote her poems about them; she may have been reasonably young then herself. Other poems speak of her daughter, evidently in the bloom of her beauty and dependent on her mother for ornaments (132; 98 b. 1–3, if genuine); 58 may speak of her own old age. It is striking for the structure of families and society that she could sing poems which did not show her brother in a good light (5, 15 b, 254 a).[7]

---

[6] On vocabulary note already Leumann (1959), 134–5; see Kazik-Zawadzka (1958), chs. 6 and 7; Bowie (1981), ch. 3; Broger (1996).

[7] On brothers cf. also 213 a, esp. b, d, h. The amount of money spent by Charaxus may be an inference rather than evidence from Sappho, but it sounds a reasonable one (cf. e.g. 5. 5 (note even Alc. 117 b. 26–7); not that Sappho would in any case have been precise). Herodotus' account does not fully explain Rhodopis' and Charaxus' actions after her liberation. Sappho's age: one may note that *puellae* at Hor. *Odes* 4. 9. 11 of Sappho probably alludes to Anacr. 358 [13], on the view mentioned by Chamaeleon, that Sappho is the girl from Lesbos; Anacreon shares the stanza. On Sappho and her 'world' see, among much else, Wilamowitz (1913), 17–78; Page (1955, philologically fundamental); Merkelbach (1957); Fränkel (1960a), 40–51, 93–4; (1962), 191–214; West (1970a); Saake (1972); Privitera (1974); Dover (1978), 173–9; Stehle (1981); Jenkyns (1982), ch. 1; Burnett (1983), pt. 3; Rissman (1983); Parker (1993); duBois (1995); Williamson (1995); the many important essays in Greene (1996); Tzamali (1996); West (1996), 12–18; L. H. Wilson (1996); Snyder

In considering the nature of Sappho's milieu, it will be most prudent to concentrate on material from her own poetry, and especially poetry randomly preserved and reasonably extensive. Four of the five best-preserved 'papyrus' poems throw light on Sappho's world. In 94, a woman leaves Sappho (named); Sappho says, 'Remember me, *for* you know how we looked after you, concerned ourselves with you.' She goes on to recall 'our' pleasant experiences, the counterpart of 'our' sufferings now (4, the woman): their luxurious parties, and 'our' attendance at festivals (24–7). The language implies some sort of group, most clearly at 8, and presumably at 11 and 26; the woman's participation in the group's enjoyments has been a benefit conferred on the woman. Sappho speaks not of her own love but of the group's activities; she might be thought in some sense to be speaking for it, perhaps even to organize it. The emphasis on the group in the speech, and the position of πὰρ ἔμοι, make it seem possibly more natural and elegant to take the phrase as 'at my house' rather than 'beside me'. It sounds as if the absence will be permanent.[8]

In 96 [7], another woman has left 'us' (3, cf. 18); she formerly rejoiced in the singing of one woman, and longs for another. She is now conspicuous among the Lydian women in Sardis. In 16 [5], the speaker longs for Anactoria, who is no longer present. Ancient readers evidently thought of the speaker in this and other poems about Anactoria as Sappho (219). This seems likely: it is a plausible assumption that the narrator of substantial fragments is as a rule to be formally associated with Sappho rather than with anyone else. The narrator is named as Sappho in 1 [1] as well as 94; cf. also 65, 133. Poem 2 describes a temple and a sacred grove; a banquet is evidently to take place there, at which Aphrodite is invoked to pour the nectar (cf. 96 [7]. 26–9).[9]

(1997); Stehle (1997) (esp. ch. 6); Rosenmeyer (1997*b*). The emphasis here is on more recent contributions. Many of the works cited include detailed discussion of the poems commented on later.

[8] For πεδήπομεν cf. Page (1955), 77, citing Hom. *Il.* [10.] 516 (LSJ *Supp.* concurs). Other poems and the nature of symposia make it unlikely that group activities are not in fact referred to in the poem. One could in theory take all the first-person plurals either as denoting the narrator and the woman only or as plurals for singulars (note 4; cf. Chantraine (1986–8), ii. 33, Pind. *Ol.* 11. 8, etc.); but that would only accentuate the role of Sappho at 8. Theogn. 627–8, 1041, 1241–2 do not support taking πὰρ ἔμοι as 'beside me'; the preposition there means 'in the presence of'.

[9] The last conception is remarkable, even if we allow for the honour associated with the task; but it may surely have more to do with the resources of the poetry

These fragments suggest a group which engages in song and parties. It appears different from male groups like Alcaeus' in that we see points of emphasis not evident with those groups: attendance at religious occasions, where some of the banqueting takes place; the limited part of their lives for which some women participate in the group; the notion (in 94) that the group as a whole are benefiting at least one of these members by allowing her to take part; the amorous feeling that is shown to bind a good many of the members. There seem some grounds for supposing that Sappho plays an especially important role in the group.

Why are the women leaving (if we may assume they are not all the same woman)? In the case of 96 [7] at least, it can hardly be to go into exile (cf. 98 b). The woman there also seems of marriage-able age (note γυναίκεςςιν 6–7, not παρθένοιςι). One might maintain that the women of 16 [5], 94, 96 [7] had been in Mytilene while their husbands were there on business, and had been given tempo-rary membership of the club; but the language in 96 [7] makes it sound as if the woman's pre-eminence among the Lydians is not the resumption of a previous state. The most promising hypothesis would appear to be that she is going to be married there. The failure of the poem to mention marriage explicitly does not seem much of an obstacle: no other cause is mentioned in the extant poem either, but some situation is evidently presupposed.

On the other hand, in 131 Atthis deserts Sappho, in some sense, for the enemy Andromeda, fairly plainly no member of the group (cf. also Mica in 71). There look here to be an informality and an independence which do not square altogether easily with a definite arrangement, such as is suggested in 94, or with the status of an unmarried girl, if some arrangement has been made by her parents. If there is anything in this divergence, it would be simplest to

than with the beliefs of the participants. Note also for a sanctuary of Aphrodite Alc. 41, 296 b. At Athens and elsewhere, women's festivals might include private symposia: cf. Pingiatoglou (1994), esp. 42–3, 49–50. Other speakers appear in extant poems, so with short fragments one cannot be sure that the speaker 'is' Sappho. But this will often be plausible even with short fragments, especially when names linked with her are mentioned; it might seem doubtful for 102, where the speaker seems to be a girl in the control of her mother. The question is interesting for 121. The geographical range of women's movement implied in 96 [7] receives additions from later reports. S216 A (see Gronewald (1974)) speaks of some of her 'pupils' as coming from Ionia; 219 (*Suda*) makes Anactoria (probably) come from Miletus, Gongyla from Colophon. This Ionian origin has perhaps a fair chance of deriving from the poems. Note the converse in Anacr. 358 [13].

conclude that Atthis (and Mica?) has a different pattern of life from
the women departing. The length of Sappho's acquaintance and
relationship with Atthis makes this an easy hypothesis (49. 1 and
Ter. Maur. 2154–5, even if 49. 2 comes from a different poem; note
further S476).[10]

If one supposes that some of the group are unmarried and leave
it when they marry, one can, incidentally, relate Sappho's poems
about weddings to her other work. This is an advantage when her
poetry otherwise seems so firmly connected to her own group and
herself, and when poems related to weddings bulk so large in her
output (beside the 'epithalamia' (see 103–17) note 27, 30, 43?, prob-
ably 44).

Love appears to be widely spread, within the group. In 16 [5],
96 [7], and probably 94, love is felt by or for the departing woman;
in 96 [7] that woman loves two others, one of them (Atthis) a woman
elsewhere loved, at some times, by Sappho (49, 131, etc.). There
is no sign of the lover's jealous exclusiveness evident in 'Theognis'
(e.g. 1268–70, 1311–17), and spectacularly displayed by Aristo-
geiton and Hipparchus (Thuc. 6. 54–9). Equally, there is no sign
here of the resentment felt when Sappho is spurned for others out-
side the group (131, cf. 71; note also 1 [4]. 20; on 31 [6] see ad loc.).
We have no means of determining the relation of the picture in these
poems to historical reality; but the possible importance of conven-
tion, both literary and social, is brought home by the partheneia
of Alcman (1 [1], 3 [2]), where the whole chorus professes love for
Astymeloisa and probably Hagesichora.

Sappho implies the immortality of her work (55, with test., cf. 65.
8–10, with Theogn. 237–54); she thus imagines audiences beyond
her group. One would imagine the same was true at least of the
poems on her brothers (at least she would want the brothers to read
them!). It is plausible to suppose, however, that the group, which
was concerned with song, would hear performances of Sappho's
songs, which were concerned with them; one might even think of
them as the first audience for most of the non-ritual poems. No
doubt some or all of the occasions were in a sense banquets (cf. 2,
with 96 [7]. 26–9; 81). The poem might appear, at least fictionally,

[10] The *Suda* separates Atthis from the 'pupils', including Anactoria (253). In 24 a
the speaker addresses a contemporary or contemporaries; we do not know that love
is being spoken of.

to presuppose the group's knowledge of individuals and situations (so 16 [**5**], 96 [**7**]. 16).[11]

Despite the historical importance of the group, various questions that have concerned us may take on, within the poems themselves, a more literary aspect too. Thus, whatever the actual role of Sappho in the group, the narrator in the poems can adopt through her very function an authoritative stance. That authority, and the whole part of the narrator, can become a focus of the poetry, and the object of questioning or complication. The scenes of parting and being apart, whatever the historical reality, are a notable part of the major papyrus fragments (not preserved to illustrate such scenes). This indicates that, from a literary point of view, Sappho's 'world' does not simply enwrap the poetry in itself. The 'world' of this corpus, no less than Virgil's bucolic 'world', is seen partially from the perspective of those losing it, and in relation to other spheres. Related contrasts might seem to be exploited in the wedding poetry (e.g. 107, 114).

An emphasis on the poems themselves may help us in considering how specifically female Sappho's poetry is. The question is made inevitable by the importance of the first example of women's writing; but here one can only draw attention to the complications of an answer, even within this period. If we attempt to range the subject-matter in this respect, we observe that the depiction of subjective experience in love, of pain rather than perception, produces least apparent difference from the general type of language used by male contemporaries, and least explicit proclamation of gender. (On the κῆνος . . . ὄττις of 31 [**6**]. 1–2 see ad loc.) Even description of the object of love, as in 16 [**5**] and 31 [**6**], is relatively undistinctive, since the object is a woman, and the aspects described would appear attractive to a Greek male too. The listener encounters something much more distinctively female within the poetry itself when Sappho recreates the social context of the emotion, the life of her group of women. Thus the atmosphere of 2 or 94 is strikingly female (note ἀ͵πάλαι δέραι in 94. 16), for all the kinship with male poetry of parties and nature. More important still is the presentation, especially in 16 [**5**], of an attitude to the place of love in life which is contrasted with an attitude indicated as male. Men too could actually speak of love as the only thing worth living for (so Mimn. fr. 1 West); but

[11] The view taken here on posthumous fame differs from that of Rösler (1980), 72–5, which in my opinion rather strains the evidence.

in 16 [5] an implicitly male concern with war is made the foil to the female narrator's approach. Now one might reasonably say that the listener's response to all Sappho's poems must inevitably have been shaped by the knowledge of her gender. But it remains notable that the poems pronounce gender most directly in their creation of a world and their embodiment of values.

The creation of a female world is important too in Alcman, however different the process and point. But comparison with Alcman brings out other aspects of Sappho's poetry too. One should avoid external and deterministic explanations of difference. Thus Sapph. 44 happens to provide a vivid illustration of Sappho's sense for a whole society, its hierarchies and its unity in a great occasion. But if we eschew speculation on remoter causes, we can still register the poetic differences and resemblances between the maiden songs, written for public occasions, and most of Sappho's poems on women, written for private gatherings. Alcm. 1 [1], with its elaborate sense of hierarchy, its metaphysical range and generalizations, its large stanzas and large structures, its multitude of styles, its interwoven and multiple imagery, naturally but significantly contrasts with most of Sappho's poems. In Sappho there is much less overt stress on formal hierarchies among humans (despite, or partly because of, Sappho's own position?). The poems are concerned not so much with the general relation of mortals and immortals as with the vividly known Aphrodite (even elegy is more interested in metaphysical generalization). They are intense and miniaturist in their handling of the small stanza, and less extreme, save with different speakers, in their stylistic movements within the poem. They prefer few images, or the single, intently extended, image. The antithesis must not be overdrawn. Sappho exploits accumulation no less than Alcman. Alcman's writing too is refined and subtle; Sappho's refinement must not obscure the vigour of her rhetoric, nor for that matter her force in argument or attack.

The element of humour in Alcman is not conspicuous in Sappho; but here we come to an interesting point. The humour in the partheneia springs largely from a sense of distance between the author and the narrator, from the narrator's unwittingly misplaced attitudes. There is an interval, however, between Alcm. 1 [1] and Alcm. 3 [2], with its more intense language of love. In Sappho's poems the author and narrator are formally identified; yet gaps can appear between the author and the person speaking, and the limited or partial perspective of the narrator can emerge. The effects and the extent vary. Sappho shows a considerable range in the narrator's engagement and in the handling of the narrator (1 [4] and 31 [6] provide a good illustration of range in handling). The poems of the two authors stand at a markedly different distance from their amorous content; but Sappho's poems do not offer a uniform measure of closeness to the content by contrast with a uniform measure of distance in Alcman. There are continuities as well as contrasts between the two poets. Thus in Alcman one sees the private within the public; in Sappho there is often a personal perspective marked out against more commonplace attitudes (so in 16 [5] and, in a different way, 31 [6]). No two authors better illustrate together the width of possibilities and the interconnectedness of Greek lyric art.[12]

4: fr. 1 Voigt (and Lobel–Page)[13]

The poem makes much use of traditions; yet it is as imaginative in its conception as it is surprising in its detail. The relation to Homer is commonly regarded as crucial. Sappho, it is often thought now, makes her prayer like a Homeric warrior, and is a kind of warrior herself (cf. 28). This approach concentrates too much on some parts of Homer, and on the prayer form itself, which even in extant literature is not confined to warriors. Other scenes in epic are no less pertinent: in particular, the appearance of Aphrodite to Helen (a figure of interest to Sappho) in Hom. *Il.* 3. 383–420 (cf. Rissman (1983), 4–7; Steinrück (1999), who brings in the *Cypria*). There Aphrodite's female beauty is emphasized, despite her disguise (*Il.* 3. 396–7; cf. *Hom. h. Aphr.* 84–90, 171–82, and further *Il.* 5. 338, *Cypria* fr. 4 Davies, *Hom. h. Aphr.* 61–7, *h.* 6. 5–17); it is remarkable that Sappho, though she describes Aphrodite's sparrows, does not describe the goddess's undisguised beauty, save obliquely (14;

---

[12] For degrees of distance from the material of love cf. Conte's metaphor of *lungimiranza* ((1991), 71).

[13] On 1 [4] see n. 7 and Cameron (1939, 1964); Koster (1968); Krischer (1968); Gentili (1972), 64–6; Bonanno (1973); Turner (1973), 21–7; Svenbro (1975); Stanley (1976); Carey (1978), 370–1; Bonelli (1980); Parca (1982); Höllein (1991); Slings (1991); Calame (1999), 25–6; Petropoulos (1993); Erbse (1997); Pulleyn (1997), 140–1; Steinrück (1999). The notes on this poem even more than others have to leave unnoticed many topics and ideas discussed in the scholarly literature.

contrast fr. 54). This is one instance of Sappho's avoiding the obvious.

Helen imagines trickery from Aphrodite, a perpetual characteristic of the goddess, and looks back to when she originally ensnared her for Paris (Hom. *Il.* 3. 399–412, cf. 5. 421–5; note the trickery in *Hom. h. Aphr.*); the danger of the goddess's power even to her favourite swiftly becomes apparent (413–17). In the forefront of this poem she emerges as benign, to Sappho, and towards Sappho her deceptiveness is perceived only in some light-hearted teasing; but the background within this poem itself, and the tradition, make us aware how notable this good will is. The goddess's mockery at Sappho for her passion reminds one of Athene's delighted railery at her favourite in Hom. *Od.* 13. 287–96, followed by her promise of help; at any rate, the passage brings out the extraordinary intimacy between goddess and mortal in this contemporary fiction. Whatever the familiarity in Sappho's language on Aphrodite elsewhere (and that too is poetry), the epic form and resonance of this encounter make the relationship to the goddess within the poem seem remarkable. They also make more visible things outside the narrator's perspective.

Metre

1. $-\cup-\text{x}-\cup\cup-\cup--$
2. $-\cup-\text{x}-\cup\cup-\cup--$
3. $-\cup-\text{x}-\cup\cup-\cup-\text{x}$
4. $-\cup\cup--$

This stanza might be thought to predate Sappho and Alcaeus, who both make extensive use of it, but rarely (if ever) share other stanzas. There are differences between their usage. In Sappho there is pause after lines 1 and 2 (cf. on 31 [6]. 9–10); but none at the end of 3, where there is often no word-end. In Sappho one can think of 3–4 as a repetition of the typical aeolic structure 1 and 2 (single-short round a choriambic core) which is then expanded with a choriambic addition, and a double-short heavy ending instead of single-short heavy ending. One may compare the expansion D in Stes. 222 (b) [3], the shape of the stanza in Sapph. 94, and the joining of aeolic cola in 96 [7]. In Alcaeus there is always word-end after the third line, with the partial exception of 362. 3–4 (κὰτ τὼ | cτήθεος ἄμμι). There is not much run-over between stanzas in Sappho (cf. esp. 1 [4]. 9, 16 [5]. 9, 22. 13, 31 [6]. 5); Alc. 42. 12 strikingly starts a new sentence with the fourth line. This small form is inventively exploited by Sappho in individual poems and stanzas, as will appear.

1. The poem begins in the present, in a situation which the narrator wishes to be resolved. The narrator's tone in the first stanza is intense. A potent atmosphere is created by the solemnity of the religious form, the sense of urgency in the narrator, and the direct contact of address (at this point such contact, as is usual in prayer, lies for certain only in the narrator's will). Poem 86, a prayer to Aphrodite, looks similar.

πο₁κιλόθρο₁ν': ποικίλοφρον is more weakly attested than its rival, which appears in the ancient book-text; and it is more likely to have been corrupted from -θρον' than the other way round. Cf. also the opening address in Bacch. 14 B. 1 'Εcτία χρυ₁cόθρο₁ν'. Aphrodite is depicted on thrones perhaps from the seventh century; the poem begins by emphasizing grandly her divine status. Cf. Delivorrias (1984), 88–90. The word is found only here; but compounds in -θρονοc are often used in epic and in Pindar and Bacchylides, essentially always of females (occasionally in Pindar and Bacchylides even of mortal females, as at Bacch. 17. 123–4). So Aphrodite's gender is also marked from the start in this all-female poem.

For the pair of epithets followed by the divine name cf. 53.

2. δολ₁όπλοκε at the end of this sequence of epithets is striking, despite Theogn. 1386 (it comes in the genitive at Lyr. Adesp. *PMG* 949 (Simonides, see Johnstone (1997); cf. also Ibyc. S199. 2)). Deceit is highly characteristic of Aphrodite (e.g. Hom. *Il.* 3. 405, 5. 349, *h. Aphr.* 7); cf. 188, μυθόπλοκοc of Eros. The address forcefully conveys the goddess's artful power, and suggests that the narrator wishes her to deceive. The metaphor in the compound was standard (cf. Theogn. 67, Aesch. *Ch.* 220, Eur. *Ion* 1410), and the compound itself may have been so already (note the derivative noun at Theogn. 226).

λίccομαί cε: not wheedling, but common and pressing language in a prayer (e.g. Pind. *Isth.* 6. 44–5).

3. The request itself comes in the largest of the three periods: the form of the stanza is effectively exploited.

The goddess appears, strikingly, as the source both of Sappho's pain and of her rescue (5). Her power to harm is made apparent.

ἄcαιcι: the stem is common in the Lesbian poets, not in epic or lyric; the word itself seems from Alc. 39 a. 11, Anacr. 347 [**12**]. 8, Hdt. 1. 136, 3. 41. 1 to be a strong one.

δάμνα: cf. Hom. *Il.* 14. 198–9, *h. Aphr.* 3, 251, where it is used of Aphrodite's might.

4. π‚ότνια strengthens both the religious dignity and the personal contact of the appeal. It has the same position in the stanza at 6. 10.

5. The change to the positive wish is marked by a new stanza. Sappho often asks goddesses to come 'here' (2. 1 (to Aphrodite), cf. 35; cf. also 17. 1–2 (Hera), 53 (Graces), 127 (Muses); Alc. S286. ii. 1 (34. 1)); cf. e.g. Ar. *Knights* 591 (Nike), *Thesm.* 1159 (Demeter and Kore). In this context, unlike 2. 1, the specification of place marks for listeners that the setting of the poem is separate from the present performance. 'Come' is a standard Greek prayer (see Ausfeld (1903), 516; Pulleyn (1997), 134–45, 219 (judicious on magic)). But the notion will be given a special force by what follows.

αἴ ποτα: the poem uses a common feature of prayers (cf. Pulleyn (1997), 65–6) to move back to a particular occasion in the past. Often those praying (or asking) will refer to past services by or past favours to themselves or their families; but in neither case, naturally, do the speakers elaborate (contrast Hom. *Il.* 1. 394–407 with 503–4 (Arist. *EN* 1124ᵇ15–16); cf. further e.g. Hom. *Il.* 1. 39, 15. 372–4, *Od.* 17. 240–2; *Od.* 3. 98–101, *h. Dem.* 63–4; (past favours) *Il.* 5. 116–17, Pind. *Isth.* 6. 42–3). Sappho's detailed account to Aphrodite of what Aphrodite did is marked as non-realistic by this background. There is related non-realism in epic, and in Sappho herself (e.g. Agamemnon's speech on Tydeus in Hom. *Il.* 4. 370–400; Sapph. 94. 9–10); but in this poem the evident artifice brings out for the listener that there is more to the poem than the perspective of the narrator.

Sapph. 86. 5–6 suggest the possibility of an intriguing parallel to this passage.

κάτέρωτα may suggest to the listener, at this point, a single occasion rather than numerous epiphanies. Cf. Hom. *Il.* 1. 503–4 and Soph. *OT* 164–5 εἴ ποτε καὶ προτέρας ὕπερ | ὀρνυμένας πόλει . . . (rightly referred to the Sphinx e.g. by Wunder (1856), 33). But the idea that this occasion is repeating even a single earlier occasion will come to acquire an ironic significance.

6. πήλοι builds up to the description of the journey, and accentuates the goddess's divinity.

7. ἔκ‚λυες: enjambment emphasizes the decisive action (aorist), by contrast with ἀΐοιcα. π‚αῖ Δ‚ί‚ος (2) is now taken up in more concrete form. **λίποιcα:** cf. 86. 6, 127, Alc. 34. 1; Nisbet and Hubbard (1970), 345.

8. χ‚ρύcιον: it is perhaps preferable, despite 16 [5]. 2 n., to take the word with δόμον, not ἄρμα: cf. 127 δεῦρο δηὗτε Μοῖcαι χρύcιον λίποιcαι . . . The papyrus's punctuation indicates the same interpretation. The other, more complicated, order would remove emphasis from the crucial ἦλθ‚ες at the end of the stanza (cf. ἔλ‚θ' at the beginning of this stanza, ἔλθε at the beginning of the last stanza). Cf. also Slings (1991), arguing from the treatment of stanza-end in the Lesbians. For the metal splendour of Zeus' house cf. Hom. *Od.* 4. 71–5; here it initiates the unexpected physicality with which the journey is described.

9–12. The stanza contrasts in atmosphere with the one that precedes. As at the start of the next stanza, a phrase flows over and blurs the actual point of division; but here, despite the syntax, it establishes for this stanza the theme of the chariot.

The stanza makes very clear to the listener the narrative perspective which the poem is including. The narrative is not simply one rhetorically and hopefully constructed by the narrator; it incorporates a more distanced vision too. The charm of the description contributes to the distance; and the contact with the addressee, though formally maintained (c' 9), seems only formal.

More generally, 7–12 dwell on places other than 'here' (where the narrator is); this enhances the goddess's action in coming, to an extent, but also marks a narrative element distinct from the urgency of prayer.

9. ἆγον: the imperfect is not showing how Aphrodite seemed to the narrator when she arrived (8). 'Over the black earth from the sky through the air in the middle' seems too general for that, especially περὶ γᾶc μελαίναc. Rather, an extended action is being viewed at the time of its occurrence, with an emphasis on description: cf. 44. 13–34 (αὖτικ' 13).

10. cτροῦ‚θοι is effectively delayed. Aphrodite is associated with doves and geese from the sixth century (dove: e.g. statue, Syracuse, Mus. Naz. *c.*560, West-Greek (no. 56 in Delivorrias (1984)), cf. Arnott (1996), 619; geese: e.g. statuette, Hanover, Kestner-Mus.

1899.67c, late sixth century (no. 63; Simon (1985), 245)). Connection with sparrows is merely conjectured at Ar. *Lys.* 723; we then come to late sources: Σ Hom. *Il.* 2. 308–19; Apul. *Met* . 6. 6. 3 (the chariot itself is drawn by doves). From the late sixth century, and probably earlier, Aphrodite appears riding geese, swans, and other creatures, but never sparrows (Delivorrias (1984), 95–101, e.g. goose: terracotta, Paris, Louvre CA 1747, early fifth century (no. 905); Erotes riding sparrows in a late source: Xen. Eph. 1. 8. 2). She can appear in a chariot, but in art it is rarely drawn by birds at all (by swans on a red-figure vase of *c.*400, Providence, Rhode Island School of Design 25.085 (no. 1212), *al.*); in Latin literature it is drawn by swans or doves (e.g. Ov. *Met.* 10. 708–9, 14. 597; cf. Alc. 307 c (Apollo)?). Sappho is at least likely to be making a noteworthy choice from among different possibilities, and to be making it with a view to pleasing and detaching effect.

The epithet is one usually employed of horses or eagles, not of other birds (note Pind. *Nem.* 3. 80). The whole description resembles some descriptions of eagles, notably Archil. fr. 181. 10–11 West ὠκέως δι᾽ αἰθέρος | λαιψηρὰ κυ̣κλώσας πτερά. The chariot and ς᾽ ἆγον make one think of e.g. Hom. *Il.* 16. 383 τὸν δ᾽ ἔκφερον ὠκέες ἵπποι. There may be some element of parody in the conception and expression.

The little birds are set by the shaping of the line against the vast distance they travel. The traditional epithet with γᾶς enhances this effect. It comes in the *Iliad* and *Odyssey* 7 times (not including κελ-); but it recurs often elsewhere (16 [5]. 2, 20. 6?, Alc. 38 a. 10, 130 b [9]. 14, Sapph. or Alc. 27. 1?; Archil. fr. 130. 2 West, Alcm. 89. 1, Semon. 1. 14, Sol. frr. 36. 5, 38. 5 West, Pind. *Ol.* 9. 50 (*Nem.* 11. 39)). So it need have no specifically epic resonance.

11. The busy movement of the sparrows' wings is set against their cosmic journey. Jenkyns (1982), 10, points out the liveliness of flocks of sparrows. On π̣ύκνα cf. Kidd (1997), 511–12.

13. αἶψα δ᾽ ἐξίκο̣ντο perhaps recalls Homer (*Il.* 5. 367 etc.), although αἶψα comes in Sappho elsewhere (60. 5). The overlapping phrase matches that which began the last stanza. It stresses how in this sentence the poetry has become separated from the addressee: we have 'they arrived', not 'you arrived', as one might have expected. σύ δ᾽ follows, in contrast, with a vocative phrase which intensifies the present address. Now it will become apparent that within the narrative the goddess's contact with the narrator was real and reciprocal.

14. μ‚ειδιαίϲ‚αιϲ᾽: the smile partly displays the radiant beauty of the goddess of love. Cf. *Hom. h.* 10. 2–3; Sil. 7. 466–7 (and note Hes. *Theog.* 205; for the dative Hom. *Il.* 7. 212). The deity of Aphrodite is strongly emphasized in the conventional ὦ μάκαιρα (cf. especially Pind. *Nem.* 7. 94, Soph. *Phil.* 400) and the unconventionally used ἀθανάτωι. As is soon apparent, the smile also conveys Aphrodite's amusement; such amusement suggests, as is soon confirmed, a friendly if superior attitude (cf. Athena amused by Odysseus, Hom. *Od.* 13. 287, and Zeus amused by his daugher, *Il.* 5. 421). The amusement of the goddess complicates the response of listeners; they see from the perspective not only of their fellow mortal but also of the authoritative deity.

15. The presentation of the goddess's speech begins with the 'long line' of the stanza. The indirect speech is notable, the more so as the passage moves into direct speech in 17. It is not usual for a speech to be reported indirectly in epic, and Sappho herself, unlike Alcaeus, uses direct speech freely, cf. 44. 11, 94. 3, 95. 8? (contrast Alc. 129 [8]. 5–9, 13–20; but cf. Alc. 122?). The device here marks, like the address, the connection with the present prayer; it highlights the double perspective in time, in voice, and in sides of the narrator, as she reports now Aphrodite's questions about herself then. The vivid evocation of the original speech heightens the effect.

The trick-weaving goddess's questions at first affect absolute ignorance of the narrator's plight, in a play on divine omniscience (cf. *Il.* 1. 365); but the developing speech makes clear the affectation, as does the heavy repetition of ὄττι δηὖτε, and the idea of recurrence itself. Aphrodite is well aware what is up. δηὖτε is often used by mortals falling in love once more (130. 1, Alcm. 59, Anacr. 11, 13, 49, 55, 68, 83); the second-person version must, with so much repetition, convey mockery (cf. the critical question in Archil. fr. 88 West; there is probably play or mockery in Sapph. 22. 11–16). The turn may also lightly make, at some level, metapoetic play with an opening device in love poems (Aphrodite's addressee is a poet). At any rate, the present occasion becomes, from the goddess's pretended viewpoint, not a miraculous moment but a tiresome rerun. And yet this implies for the listener a strikingly close relationship.

17–18. κ‚ὦττι κτλ. The phrase remains quite unexplicit, until the enjambment, where a mocking epithet is added to θύμωι (cf. 5. 1–2]οι θύμωι κε θέληι γένεϲθαι; 60. 5–6). This epithet refers to the same state of mind that causes the narrator such distress (note the echo at 26–7). But the language of madness in ancient literature is typically used in criticism from outside or at the edge of love (cf. e.g. Soph. *Ant.* 790, Prop. 3. 24. 17); it is here detached and affectionately bantering. For μαινόληϲ, -ιϲ cf. Archil. fr. 196a. 30 West; Aesch. *Supp.* 109 διάνοιαν; Bacch. fr. 20 A. 43.

18–19. τίνα κτλ. Direct speech now begins, and directness. Instead of the repeated ὄττι, we have a repeated τίϲ. Our text does not rise to the occasion, and corruption and loss prevent us from seeing the exact words used.

In the papyrus ψ looks the most plausible reading; some of the vertical looks visible lower down than the high trace. A tall α (cf. Turner (1973), 26) is not likely to be this tall, in the general environment (contrast 13 and Turner's example from the same scribe's Plato). Parca (1982), who favours β]αῖϲ', sees the high trace as part of a circumflex; but the rounding suggests that it is the top of a stroke. Turner rightly allows that there is not enough space for an ι after the supposed α. ϲ seems certain. The short mark and accent could be thought of as means to show that this is not ϲὰ or ἄγην (an apostrophe might be expected in this connection, but cf. e.g. 17. 9 δἴαντ, Alc. 179. 6 διάϲπιδοϲᾶν[; note also P. Oxy. 3695 fr. 12. 18, and ll. 3 and 12, with Haslam (1986), 5). The dot beside ϲ is not explained (the angle of the preceding stroke would not let us combine dot and stroke into δ). It might be random (cf. 11 after π,υκν), and is suspiciously low.

ἄ]ψ seems the most plausible account of the papyrus reading, though the space is somewhat large in relation to 20 (cf. 44. 25 for ψ itself); it is also the most promising text. The many attempts to make something of μαιϲ do not appeal; βαῖϲ' ('setting out to bring her to your love' (Parca)) is no more inviting. ϲ' is likely to be accusative: one would expect τοι for the unemphatic dative. With ϲε . . . Fὰν, the expression seems curious (to lead you back into her friendship): the beloved should not be the subject, and the eager narrator should not be the object, of ἄγην. The best subject would be Aphrodite (note 16 [5]. 11). The infinitive might be corrupt (τρόπην, aorist passive, whether or not possible, might suggest possibilities); one should prefer, though, to turn attention to words not preserved in the papyrus, and so less securely attested. Thus πείθω, though acceptable in itself (cf. Alc. 283. 8, and Ar. *Birds* 164 for the sense of the subjunctive), could conceivably be altered to πείθεις | ἄψ ἄγην: one can say to a god πιθοῦ (Aesch. *Supp.* 527, cf. Pind. *Pyth.* 1. 59), and the verb here may be both conative and tinged with irony. The corruption to the first person would be easy in this context.

20. Sappho is addressed by name in speeches elsewhere (65. 5, 94. 5, 133. 2). Here the name intensifies for the listener the coalescence of singer, narrator, and character. The use of the name is very unlike her use of Aphrodite's (1); but it suggests Aphrodite's friendliness, and her new directness. This question, unlike the teasing one before it (τίνα δηὖτε), implies sympathy with the narrator's viewpoint (ἀδικήει); like Pentheus' to Cadmus, it implies intention to help (Eur. *Bacch.* 1320–2). The next stanza shows that the movement is significant.

ἀδικήει, which ends the stanza strikingly, appears to suggest that relations between the mortals have changed: cf. Theogn. 1283 (note ἔτι); Plat. *Phaedr.* 252 c 5–6; and also Alc. 71; Sapph. 88 a. 17. This is relevant to ἄψ. There is nothing to indicate here a special contract for membership of the group; cf. Calame (1999), 26.

If the true reading were ἀδίκησι, the form would still be an unusual one (to end the stanza?). Contrast e.g. 31 [6]. 14 ἄγρει, Alc. 117 b. 29 ὀμίλλει. Cf. Hamm (1958), 161–2, 172.

The question 'who' is never answered, for the past or for the present. One point of this is to highlight deftly for the listener the irony of Aphrodite's τίνα δηὖτε. Even within the past situation the narrator had loved many a girl (or woman); the present involves, one naturally imagines, another girl again. Rather than make this point crudely with a string of names, the abstraction implies a sequence indefinitely repeatable. The irony is directed not at promiscuity but at susceptibility and the impermanence of each crisis.

21–4. One might expect the speech to be followed by a statement that Aphrodite had actually helped the narrator. The poem, again unexpectedly and artificially, replaces such a statement with the goddess's authoritative forecast of success. The move and the language enhance and generalize the goddess's might, and continue the abstraction: the stanza blocks any revelation of the beloved's identity. The leap that follows from the speech to the present (25) emphasizes that, for all the satisfaction granted then, and for all the talk of injustice and suffering, the narrator's emotions have changed and are transient.

The language has a solemn and incantatory character quite different from the teasing earlier; but it too has rhetorical vigour and force. Line 21 most likely suggests, not the normality of mutual gifts in such relationships, but the great passion Aphrodite will produce in this case, so that the girl's giving gifts is remarkable. The last instance of the three, in the 'long line', might seem at first to lack the neat extremity of the first two, merely repeating the verb; but it in fact produces the greatest extreme: the girl will love even though she does not want to. The power of Aphrodite is portrayed with vigorous paradox; the ending of the stanza and the narrative create a pause in which the listener can linger on the sinister implications of this power for the victim (cf. δολόπλοκε in 2). Such implications are saliently ignored by the narrator, who in what follows sees only her own emotions (note the contrast with 26–7 and 17).

There is no call to import the accusative participle, which spoils the rhetoric, and is too involved for this author.

25. Dramatic asyndeton returns us abruptly to the present situation, which still demands resolution. The language is intense.

χαλέπαν, emphatically placed, shows none of the detachment heard in Aphrodite's voice and suggested in the structures of endless recurrence. The combination with μέριμναι is found at Hes. *WD* 178; but the word has little specifically epic colouring, and is used of love-pains elsewhere (Archil. fr. 193. 2 West, Theogn. 1337, etc.). Note its appearance in a related context at Sapph. 86. 8. Cf. Stes. 222 (b) [3]. 201–3 n.

λῦcον: aorist for the decisive act, like τέλεcον (27). The narrator now casts her wish positively, not negatively as at the start (3–4).

26–7. The language recalls Aphrodite's (17–18), but there is no μ͜αινόλαι: the vehemence is put into the straightforward ἰμέρρει. θῦμος is passionately made the subject, and the more distanced μάλιcτα does not appear. The listener is forced to confront the two different presentations, the more so as the Aphrodite who spoke then is being appealed to now, and the link strengthens the rhetoric of prayer.

τέλεcον forcefully takes up τέλεccαι. The variation in form displays conspicuously the poet's actual liberty in language (cf. Bowie (1981), 130–1).

cὺ δ' aὔτα: personal engagement is demanded of the goddess (aὔτα is called for now by ἔϲϲο); the narrator's personal engagement in the address is strongly depicted. As at the start, we do not know that the contact is reciprocal; but the probability has increased.

28. cύμμαχοc: the metaphor need not be the basis of the poem. The word is often found in prayers (Archil. fr. 108. 1 West etc.; note further Eur. *Tro.* 469), earlier in extant poetry than the primary meaning 'ally' (Pind. *Isth.* 6. 28, Aesch. fr. 132. 9 Radt, etc.). Even literal cύμμαχοc means more than 'fighting with' (ML 17. 2–5); ἐπίκουροc too is used in prayers (Eur. *Or.* 1300, Timoth. 791. 204–5). How far the metaphor of fighting is activated depends on how important *Iliad* 5 is to the poem (cf. e.g. Winkler (1996), 92–4). But other prayers show the intensity of this moment (note Plutarch on the Archilochus); the narrator's image of Aphrodite is remote from the amused Aphrodite with which the epiphany began.

No summing-up can do justice to the poem; but an overall interpretation requires analysis of the detail. Scholars disagree with each other, and themselves, how seriously the poem is to be taken. This question can only reasonably be asked in respect of its impact, as seen after careful reading. To object that love must be taken seriously in Sappho, or in this earnest prayer, seems to press our evidence too hard, or to equate too straightforwardly the narrator with the author. Any adequate answer is likely to be complex. The figure of Aphrodite is a source of intensity in the poem, but also of humour and of charming fantasy. The form of the prayer is also a source of intensity; but the manner in which it is developed displays artifice and detachment in the author, and its rhetoric of re-enactment engenders ironies. However, the sequence of Aphrodite's speech shows earnestness prevailing over humour; and the form of the prayer encloses the poem with passion. One should, then, allow seriousness or weightiness to play the largest part in the poem; but the elements which go beyond or against the narrow perspective of the praying lover are too significant to be simply overwhelmed. Intimations of humorous and ironic angles on the narrator, of grimmer sides to Aphrodite, of wider and more distanced interests from the author, are vital both to the poem as it unfolds and to the total impression it makes. Its potent and emotive rhetorical structure is not destroyed, but its overall impact is crucially qualified and coloured, by conflicting and distancing elements. The fully attentive listener will not be simply stirred, or simply amused. Nor is the poem a chaotic congeries of irresolvable opposites; the numerous surprises and obliquities in its development make it clear to the listener that this is a sophisticated and organized creation. However, the impact of the work cannot be converted into a take-away meaning, which one could merely separate from the subtle, and thought-provoking, experience of hearing or reading the poem.

5: fr. 16 Voigt[14]

Helen is one of the three central figures in the poem, who are all female. It is sometimes suggested that Sappho is presenting in a radically new light a figure who was more conventionally made the object of execration, as in Alc. 42 and 283. In fact, Helen is always controversial: within the *Iliad* itself she is a figure whom different people regard differently (note 24. 774–5). Stesichorus' poems not only contained but advertised diverging approaches to her (two palinodes, 223); Euripides continues the antinomies, drawing on Stesichorus and Gorgias (and perhaps [Hesiod] and Herodotus). Alcaeus' poems themselves could easily be read as, in part, reaction (283 is especially intriguing). Sappho's poem, it will be argued, is more subtle than a simple commendation of Helen; in the Homeric poems, Helen acknowledges her error but is sympathetically handled, and the presentation in Sappho is not widely distant. This makes it difficult to see the poem as straightforwardly anti-Homeric. The poem, within its own drama, is not shy of controversy; but the treatment of Helen, like the thought and movement of the poem, is complex and sophisticated.

Metre

See on 1 [4].

1. This seems certain to be the start: the previous stanza in the papyrus is about Doricha, the love of Sappho's brother, and cannot be connected to this poem.

---

[14] On 16 [5] see n. 7 (including Rosenmeyer (1997*b*)) and Theander (1934), 63–79; Eisenberger (1959); Koniaris (1967); Bona (1978); des Bouvrie Thorsen (1978); Liebermann (1980); Most (1981); Meyerhoff (1984), 54–75; Martinelli Tempesta (1999).

The stanza has the form of a priamel; but this is a striking example in that weight is thrown not only onto the different things evaluated but onto the people who evaluate.

o]ἰ: the masculinity of the pronoun at first seems irrelevant. The ordering of words removes the emphasis from ϲτρότον, as if it were assumed an army were κάλλιϲτον, and the only question were the sort. (For the division cf. e.g. Pind. *Nem.* 9. 34.) This throws the narrator's quite different view into relief.

ἰππήων, πέϲδων are words used by Homer (e.g. *Il.* 11. 150–1); but here one can hardly be sure that he is alluded to, let alone that he is the target (for πεζοί plural cf. e.g. Aesch. *Pers.* 19, Arist. *Ach.* 662, Thuc. 6. 97. 1). The *Iliad* may be one element in the male militarism which the poem dismisses; but the structure of the stanza presents rather a crowd of contemporary men.

2. νάων: for ϲτρατόϲ used of ships too cf. e.g. Aesch. *Pers.* 728, Hdt. 3. 17.

μέλαι[ν]αν: better than μελαί[ν]αν, with νάων. When noun and adjective are separated by even one word other than a mere preposition in Sappho, the adjective as a rule comes first. In 1 [5]. 8 an exception was hesitantly allowed, with a single word between; but with verb, preposition, and different noun before the adjective the order becomes implausibly complicated for Sappho (an initial adjective makes one wait for the noun). Note the adjective put first in the substantial separations at 31 [6]. 9–10, 44. 5–7. Here, then, the adjective adds pomp to the false assertion rather than unwanted substance to the ships.

3. κάλλιϲτον would seem less remarkable to the Greeks than to us (but cf. Kant, *Kritik der Urteilskraft* §28, pp. 108–9 Vorländer). One may think of the all-important beauty of shining armour in the *Iliad* (for armies cf. 4. 431–2, 13. 340–1, 20. 156–7), or of ὄψεωϲ λαμπρότητι of the Sicilian Expedition, εὐπρεπεϲτάτη even in Thucydides (6. 31. 1, 6). None the less, the perspective of beauty comes as a surprise, and evokes a hyper-masculine world. The first two lines have given the armies no poetic help to support their claims.

Superlatives are rare in Sappho: only at 8 below (probably); 27. 9 ὅττι τάχιϲτα (cf. Alc. 6 a. 7, 58. 15, 367. 2); 104 b ἀϲτέρων πάντων ὁ κάλλιϲτοϲ (cf. Theogn. 1117; the status of 104 b as a fragment is uncertain); 105. 2 ἄκρον ἐπ' ἀκροτάτωι. In this context the word is given considerable weight.

ἔγω has an authoritative ring: the point cannot be merely a subjective preference of no greater validity than the enthusiasts' for navies, still less a statement valid only in relation to the speaker. The narrator's opinion as to what is most beautiful (1) is inconsistent with the opinions in what precedes (see 4 n.); (2) relates to the love of any person; (3) can be understood (i.e. grasped) by all; (4) leaves the specific allocation of what 'is most beautiful' to the subjectivity of the individual lover. Clearly, then, this is a view of general application; to suppose no special validity is claimed for it makes (1) and (4) a most peculiar mixture. Authority is conferred by the very gesture of independence (cf. e.g. Eur. *IT* 386–91), and, as often, an argument supports the gesture. None the less, it is interesting to compare the authoritative tones in Alcman (1 [1]. 2), in Pindar (e.g. *Ol.* 1. 36, 52–3), and in Greek intellectual prose (e.g. Hecat. *FGrHist* 1 F 19, Hdt. 4. 36. 2, Hipp. *Morb. Sacr.* 1. 10, 22 Grensemann, etc.). Cf. Sapph. 58. 25–6.

4–5. κῆν' ὄττω: part of the point is that there is no one thing to be declared most beautiful; it depends on the subject of the perception. Love, however, is the supreme source of such perceptions.

ἔραται: subjunctive. The word is placed with force at the end of the stanza. One cannot say that the word applies to the preceding instances too, so that Sappho is merely extending these instances into a generalization. In a poem where an antithesis is drawn between love and delight in armies (17–20), and an instance of love demonstrates the overruling of expected values (11–12), it would be inept to give ἔραται an extended sense. (Rissman (1983), 32–3, lists Homeric examples with war as object, but rather misses their sense of paradox.) Cf. des Bouvrie Thorsen (1978).

6–7. πά]γχυ, εὔμαρες, π]άντι: we hear the ringing confidence of a Greek intellectual, and the pressing tones of an argument (cf. Lys. 3. 28, 16. 7; Gorg. *Hel.* 8, Dem. 19. 83, etc.). The π]άντι (men are included) is notable here: despite the dispute, and the role the narrator gives subjectivity, everyone will acknowledge the significance of love.

εὐμαρής appears at 96 [7]. 21, Alc. 69. 7 (not with infinitive), Theogn. 845, Pind. *Pyth.* 3. 115, etc. The euphemism at Hdt. 2. 35. 14 suggests that the word had not been exclusively poetic;

fourteen occurrences of πάγχυ in Herodotus suggest the same about that word.

cύνετον: understanding the point is tantamount to perceiving its truth, cf. e.g. Democr. B 293 Diels–Kranz (and cf. Pind. *Pyth.* 3. 80–2). The choice of word again has intellectual point. One would be failing to catch the tone of the language if one supposed that the narrator was merely intending to make others comprehend her point of view sympathetically while continuing to prefer infantry. (Cf. Meyerhoff (1984), 57.)

cυνετόc and ἀcύνετοc occur in a range of texts, e.g. Theogn. 1078, Bacch. 3 [**17**]. 85, Heraclit. fr. 1 Marcovich, Ar. *Eccl.* 204.

ἀ γὰρ κτλ.: the account is developed with a stress on the argument. The tone throughout is, from the perspective of the thought, rhetorical and emphatic. There is no narrative with extension in time: a single moment is dwelt on from various angles, with emotional as well as argumentative force. One may contrast the narrative in Alc. 298 [**10**], and even in Alc. 283.

The opulent description of Helen as far surpassing the beauty of mortals must be relevant in a context where the most beautiful thing on earth is being discussed. The phrase leads the listener to think that the argument will develop in a different direction, with Helen as the object of love (Paris preferred her to manlier bribes). In fact, the line of thought more subtly pursues Helen as subject; the oblique but purposeful movements in the rest of the poem make it likely that this happens through design rather than clumsiness. Helen's own supreme beauty heightens the argument about love's impact on the subject's perception; it also heightens the irony and pathos of her error. The poem is thus led into a far greater complexity.

Cf. Gorg. *Hel.* 4 ἰcόθεον κάλλοc; note Sapph. 23. 4–7.

8. The phrase on Menelaus is given stress by its position at the end of the stanza, separated from its verb. A superlative is likely; it suggests that Helen made a mistake. πανάρ]ιcτον is relatively unlikely: the word has specific point at Hes. *WD* 293; otherwise such formations with superlative are not found in poetry before παγκάκιcτε Soph. *Ant.* 742. For μέγ' adverbial cf. Alc. 348. 3.

9–12. It seems difficult to maintain that Sappho is making no judgement on Helen's act, let alone that she is celebrating it. Even if 'she did not remember at all her dear parents' were to carry no note of criticism, παράγαγ',]αμπτον, and κούφως would seem to imply an error. There is no elaboration of the disaster she caused, even if armies lurk in the background of the poem; the point is not condemnation as such, but a proof of how love can master and mislead the mind. By making Aphrodite (if it is Aphrodite) the subject of παράγαγ', Sappho appears to shift the weight of actual blame, even if mortal weakness plays a part (13–14?); one may compare Hom. *Od.* 4. 261–4 (Bona (1978), 76–8), *h. Aphr.* (but cf. Theogn. 403–7); Gorg. *Hel.* 6, 19, Eur. *Tro.* 940, 948–50. The extreme praise of Helen in 6–7 also ensures an atmosphere of poignancy rather than mere indignation (contrast e.g. Hes. fr. 176. 7 Merkelbach–West).

πλέοι[ca: perhaps the drastic movement of sailing away, here and in other places, accentuates the audacity of the act. Cf. perhaps Alc. 283. 6, Stes. 192. 2, Gorg. *Hel.* 5.

].ιδοc: the horizontal stroke at mid-height does not initially suggest α. The slight descending angle seems unexpected at this height and proximity. However, π]αῖδος seems so probable a supplement that one should accept the α.

φίλων has a dignified quality, but as often in Homer the epithet acquires emotional force (cf., with remembering, *Il.* 22. 390, *Od.* 12. 309). Cf. further Sapph. 44. 11 πάτ[η]ρ φίλος, Tyrt. fr. 10. 5 West, Stes. S104. 18, Pind. *Ol.* 7. 41, etc.

παράγαγ': cf. Archil. fr. 124 (b). 4 West; Theogn. 386 (personification), 404 (daimon).

αὔταν: αὐτόν certainly can mean an unemphatic 'him' at this period (Alc. 42. 16, 129, 19, 326. 8, Tyrt. frr. 11. 37, 12. 39 West, Stes. 200. 1); an emphatic 'herself' followed by τάν would also be conceivable. No doubt the phrase in 12 added point to the argument.

13. The position of γάρ, and the grave accent in 12, seem to recommend the placing of Κύπρις at the start of this line; the name would come with great force after the stanza-end and before the clause-end.

15–16.]με: 17–18 and the obvious supplements in 15–16 indicate that ἄ] is too short. Neuter pronouns would not suit the metre; and ἀναμιμνήσκω active nearly always has a personal subject in Greek of the eighth–fifth centuries (virtually personal at Eur. *El.* 504; later somewhat personifying at Plat. *Theaet.* 209 C 9). If a person reminds the narrator, it must be as a topic rather than literally; this sense seems more awkward with deities, and Helen is a much more effective 'reminder' of the absent Anactoria than love. We should, then, supplement κἄ]μ̄ε, and perhaps suppose that 13–14, even if general in form, contained Helen, maybe as subject.

The narrator turns to her most personal concern as if it has sprung from the preceding thought, just now. The gesture highlights the deliberate artificiality and oblique movement of the poem. There is also pathos in this sudden emergence of feeling, and in the demotion of the narrator from authority to subject (her authority itself is now seen to rest on her experience). The narrator is also a different kind of subject from Helen, not boldly active and in motion, but passive. By a neat reversal, Anactoria becomes in a sense parallel to Helen, the narrator in a sense parallel to those whom Helen left behind. A prolonged, imperfective situation is suggested (cf. 17–20), from the viewpoint of the person remaining, the converse of Helen's perfective act of desertion.

The name is that of a girl (or woman) no doubt familiar to the audience (cf. 219, 253), probably one who has left Sappho's group (cf. 94, 96 [7]). The 'me' is identified on some level with the singer, the 'now' in some way with the present performance, 'not present' at least with the singer's and audience's general habitation. After the generalizing presents and the depiction of the past, the immediacy is striking and poignant; but the line of thought continues.

ἀνέμναιc': despite the momentary sense of 'remind' and the deeper connotations of ἐμνάcθη, Helen's forgetting and Sappho's being made to remember are linked. One may compare the sequence in 94. 7–10; cf. also 96 [7]. 15–16.

οὐ] παρεοίcαc: nothing is said of the act or circumstances of leaving, by forceful contrast with Helen. One could conjecture that the preceding description and psychologizing are known to be entirely foreign to Anactoria's departure; more importantly, the emotional description passes to the person left behind. The simplicity of the phrase is poignantly simple because it comes from the involved narrator.

17–18. The narrator now herself displays the specific preferences contained in the first stanza. It is touching that she herself now speaks from her experience; but the rhetoric of the poetry makes her choice seem natural rather than extraordinary. The charged physical description here contrasts with the neuter κῆν' of 3 and the apparent failure to describe (or name) Paris; the contrast marks our arrival in the narrator's personal territory.

κε βολλοίμαν . . . ἤ, quietly stated, appealingly combines the prosecution of the argument with the heartfelt desire.

ἔρατον, λάμπρον: both the nouns are given epithets to enhance the rhetoric; they also are to be felt as springing from the subject's own perceptions. This in itself furthers the thought, but also gives an ardent lyricism to the moment. λαμπρός is generally used in non-dramatic poetry of armour, fire, heavenly bodies; the application in this context stands out (Pind. *Nem.* 7. 66 is somewhat different).

βᾶμα | κἀμάρυχμα: the nouns concentrate attention on the beautiful features rather than the person herself (contrast the participles at 31 [6]. 3–5). The walk may seem to us an odd companion for the look. To ancient feeling both walk and look include the personality in the physical loveliness. Cf. e.g. Cic. *Cael.* 49 (playing the courtesan) 'non incessu solum . . . non flagrantia oculorum'; Anacr. 360 with Hes. fr. 339 Merkelbach–West, Xen. *Ages.* 6. 7; further e.g. Eur. *Med.* 1164; *CIL* i/2² 1211. 7; Prop. 2. 2. 5–7, 12. 23–4.

The two nouns in -μα together produce a striking effect; cf. 44. 8–9, but here the nouns are more abstract and verbal. For the sense of βῆμα cf. especially Ar. *Knights* 77; ἀμάρυγμα occurs in a formula of the *Catalogue*, Χαρίτων ἀμαρύγματ᾽ ἔχουσα (Hes. fr. 43a. 4 Merkelbach–West etc.), cf. also Hom. *h. Herm.* 45 etc.

19. Cf. Mimn. 14. 1–4 on the Lydian cavalry (attack of Smyrna); note also Waldbaum (1983), 40–2. The militias are now located in the narrator's present, rather than generalized; they are certainly not located in the epic past.

κὰν ὄπλοισι: the short vowel before mute and liquid is adequately defended by 44. 18 (44. 8 and 105. 2 are somewhat different). The phrase, when employed of soldiers, does not usually accompany words of fighting; but here what might seem obvious is given emphasis for its visual significance (cf. Eur. *Suppl.* 1151, with different point). The writing is slightly more graphic than in 1–2, but little scope is given to glamour; if anything, the concreteness is reductive and dismissive.

20. A verb in -μαχέω must be supplemented, and πεσδο-, though it looks a little short, fits better than ἱππο-; it would make 19–20 neatly take up 1. Save for συμμαχέω, verbs in -μαχέω are avoided by poets of the eighth to fifth centuries except for Aristophanes (μονο-

and the different θεο- come in late Euripides). The long word at the end of the stanza probably has a scornfully technical sound. The plural accusatives in 19–20, like the plural genitives in 1, contrast significantly with the single person the narrator wishes to see and imagines.

21. Whether a new poem begins cannot be decided. A poem ends at 32; a second poem would be only 12 or 16 lines long, but 17 was 20, 62 and 63 (2-line stanza) 12 and 10, Alc. 42 (sapphics) probably 16 (and 43 8?). Poems 31 [6]. 17 and 58. 18 make a transition look possible; ἀλλά might in that case seem the likeliest first word (cf. 31 [6]. 9, Alc. 362. 1, 298 [10]. 7). ὄλβιο]ν looks in any case too short, ἀλλ᾽ ἄρα]ν possibly too long.

One can imagine the final 'unexpectedly' linking up with 21–2 (something cannot (or cannot always) be, but one can pray to have a share of something?); πεδέχω is used freely in sense by the Lesbians (55. 2, 63. 5, Alc. 10. 1–2, 70. 3). If a new poem does not start in 21, the reflections in 21–2 must bear on the narrator's deprivation. One's whole sense of the poem would be affected by whether the narrator touched fairly briefly on her own experience at the close, and ended both neatly and wistfully at 20; or whether she moved to dwell on her own suffering at greater length, and to incorporate it into a further large context.

32. ἐξ ἀδοκή[τω, with ἀδοκήτω on its own as in Hipp. *Morb. Sacr.* 17. 3 Grensemann, is a linguistically unlikely expression for this period (contrast Archil. fr. 105. 3 West ἐξ ἀελπτίης); but the adjective could agree with a preceding noun, with only τε and a preposition between. ἀδόκητος is used at Hes. fr. 209. 2 Merkelbach–West, Pind. *Nem.* 7. 31.

The poem, then, presents a drama of independent opinion and argument. The supposed views which it assaults appear as characteristically male, though it asserts a universal position, not one relevant to women alone. There is some graceful mockery of male obsessions; yet within the poem, the narrator appears as a boldly isolated figure, as much as the representative of half the population. The poem does not shun argument or argumentative force (should those interests be thought of as masculine). Its movements, however, avoid the obvious, and its thought is refined. Helen, and the emotion which rules her, are not simply admired. The air of pressing argument is combined with an air of tragedy. The example as deployed shows the capacity of love for creating error and pain. The narrator here seems to be in control of the discourse, not to be tacitly undermined: she is lucidly and terribly aware of the complexity. She herself then emerges as a vulnerable subject too; the movement is touching and subtle. The poem as far as 20 can, and should, be seen both as an oblique movement towards her own state of mind and as a continuing exploration of generalized thought. If it ends with that stanza, it ends both with personal feeling and with a touch of wry polemic.

6: fr. 31 Voigt[15]

This poem contains a celebrated passage about the effect of the beloved's presence on the narrator. The passage is not the whole poem, it is important to remember; but some general points may be made about it here. The depiction of emotion is never linguistically or conceptually straightforward (Wittgenstein would think this an understatement); it is not evident that Sappho's predominantly 'physical' depiction is either less direct or more obvious than other sorts. The most fruitful way to suggest its special characteristics may be through various comparisons.

In Homer, the impact of strong feelings is characteristically described in language that recurs, often frequently (it is not the less impressive for that). Thus even the account of Penelope's reaction at *Od.* 4. 703–5 (loosed knees, inability to speak, tears) consists of a formula and of lines that come in the *Iliad* (17. 695–6). Sappho's description, in its expression, its length, and its structure, is highly individual; it is part of its point to picture an extraordinary response. Other archaic poets, and Sappho herself, write powerfully of the effect of love (e.g. Sapph. 47, 130, Archil. fr. 191 West, Ibyc. 286, 287). They, and she, tend to write colourfully about Eros or at least love doing things, while here Sappho does not mention either, and mostly avoids metaphor (not at 9–10). The sequence of physical

[15] On 31 [6] see n. 7 and Turyn (1929), chs. 1 and 3; Costanza (1950); Beattie (1956*b*); Wills (1967); Privitera (1969); Marcovich (1991*a*); Lefkowitz (1973); Robbins (1980); Race (1983); Di Benedetto (1985); Latacz (1985); Fowler (1987*b*); Murgatroyd (1988); Rösler (1990); De Martino (1992); Marzullo (1996, 1997); Bonanno (1998, and earlier articles).

happenings or states appears to have affinities with the case histories of the Hippocratic *Epidemics*, not simply in content (e.g. 1 α′ speechlessness, cold sweat, 4. 35 sweat, shivering, ἐχλωρίαϲε κάρτα), but in form. Yet even in *Epid*. 1 and 3, the writers seek primarily to record; Sappho's passage pursues the rhetoric of accumulation and extremity (cf. Montefiore (1987), 155). How unusual the poem was in Sappho's own work cannot be known; [Longinus] chooses it for its intensity, but suggests that it is representative (10. 1), perhaps misleadingly.

More extravagant are the Near Eastern complaints adduced by West (1997), 527–8. Medieval and later poetry of love, even when independent of Catullus 51, offers similar evocation of the loss of faculties, of pallor, trembling, proximity to death (early, e.g. Cavalcanti, *Rime*, 31. 11–17; Dante, *Vita N*. e.g. 15 'Ciò che m'incontra' 5–8, cf. (prose) 14. 4, 18. 3; probably drawing directly on Sappho, Parini, *Odi*, 23 ('Per l'inclita Nice'). 5–12, cf. 16. 73–5, 22. 131–210). The language, however, is generally more involved (which is no criticism), and these depictions do not usually cultivate Sappho's abundance or potent simplicity of form. (One may note a partial exception at Vanburgh, *The Relapse*, III. ii, in *Complete Works*, i. 52 Dobrée–Webb; but there is there a strong medical analogy ('hear my Symptoms'; pp. 51–2).) For all its relationships with other literature, in its particular style and tonality Sappho's passage achieves something highly individual.

Metre

See on 1 [4].

1–2. φαίνεταί μοι: the poem begins with emphasis on a personal opinion (cf. 16 [5]. 1–4), one which appears extravagant (ἴϲοϲ θέοιϲιν) and will become surprising. The μοι sounds to express the poet's authority or insight; but the role of the first person becomes more deeply personal.

κῆνοϲ . . . ὤνηρ: in my view, this is general, not specific; no purportedly actual scene, or plurality of scenes, need be in view. Even the gender is not the fundamental point, though the masculine both emphasizes the girl's (or woman's) sexual attractiveness and helps to set the narrator in relief. The argument would be spoiled if the 'anyone' who does not react like the narrator—a notional foil to her—owed his indifference to his sex. The linguistic objections to this line of approach are not significant. Aeolic, like Attic, seems to add article to demonstrative (Alc. 72. 7–8, 141. 3); like Ionic, it is free in adding ἀνήρ (so e.g. Sapph. 105 b. 1; Alc. 6. 12, 76. 11; for generalization (Grimm and Hoog (1968), 852, 855–6) cf. e.g. Hom. *Il.* 9. 320 (note the article), 341, *Od.* 8. 209–11; Hes. *WD* 411; Tyrt. fr. 12. 16 West; Theogn. 744). It would be approaching idiom too abstractly to protest at the article with the generalization (Page (1955), 20). The indicative is satisfactory enough in post-Homeric Greek: cf. e.g. Alc. 305 a. 22–4 (against Sapph. 26. 2–3), Alcm. 1 [1]. 37–9, Sem. fr. 7. 70, 77 West. It may be added that the pattern κῆνος . . . ὄττις allows and even encourages this sense of ὄττις, which it bears in the other two instances of the pattern in the Lesbians (16 [5]. 3–4, 26. 2–4).

The advantages of this view are considerable. If a specific man is indicated, 'that man there', we have a somewhat awkward situation: the generalization in 7–16 ought in that case to be applicable now, with the aorist in 6 referring to the present. Of course, the poem could be proclaiming fictionally the narrator's present fainting, while also reporting it as a generality; but if there is a possible alternative, we should take it. Besides, a poem about 'that man there, whoever he is [*or* inasmuch as he]' seems unlike any other of Sappho's. The same objection would apply to supposing, more obscurely, that κῆνος κτλ. meant 'that man we all know about, inasmuch as he habitually, etc.'. That interpretation would require a word like Catullus' *identidem* to make the point apparent. κῆνος . . . ὄττις would seem a particularly unlucky choice, when the words are bound to be taken by the listener in a different way, either the one adopted above, or else 'that man, whoever he is that . . .'. Further elaboration of the views rejected here, though desirable in a longer treatment, would not much affect the argument.

ἴϲοϲ θέοιϲιν: the reason for the phrase will be unclear to the listener until the narrator starts to speak of herself. However, such expressions denote admirable qualities rather than good fortune: the narrator will not, then, be thought merely to envy such a man's freedom from fainting. For the phrase in Sappho cf. 68 a. 3, 44. 21, 34, 96 [7]. 4.

τοι: address is a vital aspect of the poem. 'The man that sits facing Agallis' (shall we say?) would produce a quite different sort of work. The poetic fiction of contact in address is set against the 'reality' of actual contact; this greatly intensifies the opposition, which many

have perceived, of articulate description and physical collapse. (One
may think, for example, of Brodsky's 'Dorogaja, ja vyšel' (1989)
(*Soč. Iosifa Brodskogo* (St Petersburg, 1997–8), iv. 164), where the
poetic fiction of address is set against the insuperable separation
of poet and addressee.) The urgent intimacy of the form is here
combined with the absence of a name (contr. e.g. 49).
Page's objections to the hiatus of a supposedly short vowel in
a Sapphic stanza appear groundless (cf. Lobel (1925), lxvi–lxx).
Hiatus is hiatus, and the number of examples in this stanza is tiny.
In other forms, where hiatus of long vowels is also commoner, cf.
Alc. 72. 7 (and 347 a. 1, 368. 1; see also Bowie (1981), 116–17). The
argument on length of syllables and the contact of vowels (cf. 1 [4].
1, 11, 16 [5]. 11, etc.) need not be pursued here.

3–4. Physical closeness is emphasized, but also extension in time.
A man is imagined simply sitting, attentively listening (for ὑπ- cf.
e.g. Ar. *Wasps* 318). On the narrator, by contrast, the extreme phy-
sical effects are instantaneous (βρόχε' 7, αὔτικα 10). The description
obliquely implies a relaxed tête-à-tête (cf. Hom. *Il.* 22. 127–8; note
also the situation in Anacr. 358 [13]); in this scene, speech and
laughter receive their natural response—or in the case of this girl,
supernatural.

5–6. καὶ γελαίcαc ἰμέροεν: the description lingers over effectively
into the next stanza. ἰμέροεν stands in chiasmus with ἆδυ; it also
strengthens it, and indicates more clearly the basis of the description
in the narrator's subjectivity. The phrasing in 3–5 may involve an
extension of the Homeric formula ἡδὺ γελάccαc etc. (e.g. *Il.* 2. 270);
ἆδυ is less obviously applied (contrast Alc. 347 a. 3), and γελαίcαc is
given a more striking adverb (cf. Hom. *Il.* 6. 484).
The speech and laughter again evoke personality within sensuous
appeal (cf. on 16 [5]. 17–18). The attractive image of the girl both
causes and contrasts with the violent reaction that follows.
ἐπτόαιcεν: on the understanding of 1–2 suggested, the aorist here
will most satisfactorily refer to the narrator's original falling in love:
cf. the very similar Alc. 283. 3–4, and probably Sapph. 22. 13–14.
The narrator glides arrestingly from generality and imagination to
her own specific experience in the past. (On other views, the aorist
will most likely mean 'has just now', cf. 16 [5]. 15–16: an actual
instantaneous aorist is more doubtful in use and person (cf. Lloyd
(1999)). This clause is thus separate in time from what follows; it

is also different in using more ordinary expression (see above), and in referring to internal organs. The great sequence of description is much better seen as beginning with 7.

The reference of τό will essentially be (again with this view of the opening) to the girl's actions only, not the man's presence; if we took other views and referred it to the whole supposedly enviable scene, we would upset the contrasts between the man and the narrator. The μ' shows the narrator's views at the opening to be based on her passion, though not necessarily invalid for that reason; she appears, however, on the surface of the argument not as less insensitive than such a man (contrast Pind. fr. 123), but as more vulnerable.

μ' ἤ μάν: the lightest conjecture, though it is a little worrying that the particles in this sense do not accompany a main clause (as they do even in Alc. 344). For Ahrens's ἔμαν cf. 48. 2 (suspected of corruption by Lobel), Alc. 283. 3–4 (genitive); in τό μοι μάν, the particle is wrongly placed. An emphatic ἔμοι, as in δῆμοι, would not be unwelcome, if that were possible (cf. e.g. Alc. 129 [8]. 19, Pind. *Ol.* 13. 99, Ar. *Birds* 1058; Hamm (1958), 38–9); otherwise one might desire an ἔμαν capable of emphasis.

καρδίαν ἐν στήθεσιν: cf. e.g. Hom. *Od.* 1. 341 (κῆρ).

7. The description proper begins with the 'long' line. The role of γάρ could be to explain why such a man seems godlike to the narrator (cf. Robbins (1980)). However, this view requires us to skip over τὸ . . . ἐπτόαισεν, which seems very pertinent to 7–16. Perhaps, then, the γάρ gives a reason for thinking 5–6 to be true: the girl's conversation did indeed cause the narrator to fall in love, for any brief look at the girl has now an extreme effect on her. With this form, the objections at Wills (1967), 169, and Robbins (1980), 256, do not seem to have much substance; in any case, 7–9 envisage a situation where response is expected, and the τό is less definite than 'your voice'. At the same time, 7–16 also in fact explain and develop, as it were unofficially, the thought of 1–6.

The Homeric ὡς ἴδεν (cf. esp. *Il.* 14. 294) is made more extreme and instant by βρόχε'; this is also, by a further extremity, made a recurring event. The inability to speak to the girl in these recurrent moments of the present period naturally contrasts with the literal present of performance, when the narrator is fictively addressing the girl. The sentence begins from the impossibility of continuing conversation.

8. εἴκει: cf. especially Plat. *Laws* 734 B 2–3.

9–10. Starting with a new stanza (note μέν), Sappho presents a sequence that fills two stanzas; it begins with the positive converse to the negative on speech in 7–8, and then expands. The abundance of the series is not mere 'vivid' listing: the accumulation has a rhetorical point, as in 44 and 94, and moves to a climax. Cf. also Alc. 208 a. 6–9. The length of the sequence is what gives it its power; the handling of the stanzaic form intensifies the effect. Extremity of impact is sought, not any literal transcription of experience. This first stanza is itself a defined identity; it concentrates on a prolonged state for particular parts of the body. The idiomatic absence of first-person words enables concentration on the physical feelings themselves.

ἄκαν is stylistically unacceptable with πέπαγε or ἔαγε: 'silently my tongue is fixed', or whatever, does not suit Sappho's direct and neat expression. κἀμ would be well supported by the tradition (the corruption in P would be very natural). Tmesis with πέπαγε would be tolerable: we see it at 63. 4, in lighter forms at 42. 2, 48. 2, and in Alcaeus. For the form πέπαγε cf. Alc. 338. 2; it seems more promising in sense and prosody than ἔαγε. (Lucr. 3. 155 need not be evidence for ἔαγε, nor does *infringi* have the same sense there, cf. e.g. Porph. Hor. *Sat.* 1. 3. 47–8; Val. Fl. 3. 236 (note *languescunt*).) Cf. also Fowler (1987*b*).

μέν: for μέν in the purposeful organization of a sequence cf. 2. 2, and also 42. 1, 112. 3, Alc. 362. 1.

λέπτον κτλ.: this clause prevents the stanza from being concentrated wholly on the loss of faculties, and thus avoids too geometrical a neatness. Its writing is particularly refined and forceful. λέπτον does not mean 'slight', as often with heat etc. in the Hippocratic corpus (e.g. *Epid.* 7. 1. 23); rather, it alarmingly exploits the paradox latent in an ordinary metaphor: fire, but invisible and under the skin. The word-order adds to the striking combination. The perfect in this use conveys that it is already spread, in an instant (αὔτικα): cf. Hom. *Od.* 6. 45, 20. 357, *h. Ap.* 284. With this emphasis on the state, the Hippocratic use of ὑποτρέχω is somewhat less pertinent (it does not really mean 'spread' at *Fract.* 27). ὑπα- might denote stealth, but the Homeric parallels, with ἐπι- and ὑπο-, suggest simply 'under'. The sensation is conveyed as from inside: we are not shown, for example, a redness over the skin.

The elision at the end of the line is unexpected: hiatus is found at the end of lines 1 and 2 of the stanza at 1 [4]. 6, 14, 18 (probably), 21, 22, 31 [6]. 2 (cf. Alc. 72. 7 (first line of alcaic stanza); 94. 1, 9, 16). One may, however, compare Alc. 73. 2, 6 (also with δ') after the third line of the alcaic stanza, and Alcm. 1 [1]. 41 (and Sophocles' occasional δ' at the end of trimeters); a special effect may be in view here.

11–12. The structure is elegantly chiastic (cf. Murgatroyd (1988), 477); but in the second half Sappho introduces something more remarkable and precise than 'my ears cannot hear'. The verb looks like a colourful derivative from ῥόμβος 'rushing, whirling', in a highly unusual application (Bergk's ἐπιβρόμεισι or say ἐπιρροίβδεισι (-cδεισι) would be less isolated). The first half resumes the idea of parts of the body losing their function; the abstract heightens the paradox. There is paradox too in the reference back to the moment of sight that began the state (7); there is also point: the narrator cannot continue the scene of social contact with the girl. Similarly, the second half produces a contrast with the man listening in 4; ὐπακούει and ἄκουαι match at the end of stanzas.

ὄρημμ': a notably abstract word, not found elsewhere in poetry or in this sense (singular [Dem.] *Proem.* 55. 1, *al.*).

ἄκουαι: probably an ordinary word for 'ear', cf. Hermipp. fr. 51 Kassel–Austin, etc.

13–16. The subject appears more as a whole in this stanza (note παῖcαν): first-person words and endings return, and particular parts of the body are not singled out. This contributes to the sense of pathos, and the movement towards a climax.

13. The approximate sense is clear, the text irrecoverable. The most important question is whether ψῦχρος formed part of the text. P contains it, the source of the grammarian's text evidently did not (at least in the masculine); [Longinus]' ψύχεται (10. 3) is in the context of his argument much more likely than not to imply it was in the text he used. It is not a probable gloss, and could readily be omitted after the similarly ending ἴδρως. On the other hand, αδεμ' could arise from the omission of a letter in an uncomprehended context; though ἀ is improbable even as a use of the article, grammarians (including Choeroboscus himself) are guilty of much stranger interpretations. Besides this, [Longinus], who is probably transcribing the poem, is a far more reliable witness than the grammatical tradition: the brief quotations are readily corrupted, and then interpreted without reference to a text (Alcm. 1 [1]. 6 offers an instance). κὰδ δέ μ᾽ ἴδρως κακχέεται (Ahrens) seems unsatisfactory: if a preposition repeats a preverb, one would expect it to govern a noun (as at e.g. Sapph. 44. 17); here one would expect ἔμεθεν (note Spitzner's conjecture at Theogn. 1017). Page's conjecture is attractive (κὰδ δέ μ᾽ ἴδρως ψῦχρος ἔχει). Stark's ψῦχρος ἴδρως omits a desirable particle (ψῦχρα δ᾽ (adverb) would be artificial). It may be of significance that cold sweats were later thought, in a strong fever, a fatal sign (Hipp. Aph. 4. 37).

The clause to some extent ties up with that on heat (9–10); but Sappho avoids the epigram of Longinus (ψύχεται καίεται) or of Chaucer, Troilus 1. 420 (pointed out by my wife) 'For hete of cold, for cold of hete, I dye'.

τρόμος κτλ.: the use of a verbal noun, with the narrator as object, is more dramatic than a simple 'I tremble'; one may compare the epic τοὺς δ᾽ ἄρ᾽ ὑπὸ τρόμος εἷλεν (Hom. Il. 5. 862), etc. A single event is conveyed; cf. Archil. fr. 4. 8 West; Sapph. 149; SEG 36 (for 1986), no. 752. 15, 33.

παῖσαν presents an extremity; cf. Dante's 'tutto tremante' (Inf. 5. 136).

χλωροτέρα κτλ.: the narrator is now the grammatical subject, the verb denotes a state; the syntax is energetically varied in this stanza. The adjective no doubt connotes pallor, as in Homer or Hippocrates; quite how it relates (if it relates) to the colour of grass might be disputed, in the light, say, of Longus' echo (1. 17. 4, summer grass), Hipp. Morb. 3. 11 (lizards), and Italian verde (cf. e.g. N. Ginzburg, Lessico famigliare (Turin, 1963), 48 (he had) 'un colorito sempre un po' verdognolo da lucertola', La città e la casa (Turin, 1984), 30 'sei magro, verde e secco'). Again an extreme is sought.

τεθνάκην κτλ. The supreme extremity is reached, and stressed by its position (cf. 94. 1, 95. 5); the exact and limiting ὀλίγω 'πιδεύης actually adds to the intensity. We are as far as possible from the ordinary scene of conversation which is the foil. For the sense one should realize that the perfect of θνήισκω, in parts other than the indicative, often has the meaning of an aorist: cf. e.g. Hom. Il. 6. 164, 24. 225; IG i³. 14. 30.

ἐπιδεύης: least far from this use of the adjective seems Hom. h. Ap. 338 (give me a child) μηδέν τι βίην ἐπιδευέα κείνου. The con-

struction would be easier, and closer to Attic δέω, with ἐπιδεύην; the
possibility of an active seems less remote in the light of Alc. 117 b.
30, 119. 5.

16. The end of the line is provided by the papyrus (the work was not
a regular commentary on one text, μετὰ ταῦτα . . . φηςίν suggests;
cf. P. Oxy. 2506 fr. 5 col. ii. 12–14 (Alcm. 10 (b). 12–14)). The close
of this stanza looks back to the opening of the first, as has long been
observed. The connection marks a contrast between the godlike
man and the woman near to death; it also shows the movement of
the 'I' from a figure of apparent authority to a devastated person
involved, within the situation depicted, in her own physical state.
Cf. 'parve ben' at Dante, *Rime* 67. 67.

17. Presumably Longinus would not have gone on from the descrip-
tion if the poem extended greatly beyond the point of relevance to
him; so probably not much is missing. (Cf. West (1970b), 313.) The
poem evidently moves on to an argument concerning the narrator's
sufferings, not just the girl's beauty. (Compare the movement in
Archil. fr. 13. 5–10 West.) After all that has preceded, the tone of
resignation is, within the poem, a striking gesture. πάν suggests ex-
tremity in itself (anything, however bad); but what precedes gives
it much more force. Fränkel (1962), 199 n. 16 insists that τόλματον
must mean '*can* be endured', perhaps too strongly: cf. e.g. Aesch.
Ag. 408 ἄτλητα τλᾶca, 371 ἀθίκτων, Thuc. 2. 61. 1 μεμπτότεροc. Both
'can' and 'must' have a related significance for our purposes.

The poem clearly involved a range and contrast of tones and feel-
ings rather than monotonal outpouring; 94 seems to have involved
related complexities and oppositions, but with a narrative and more
than one level of speech. We are reminded now that the narrator is
talking and arguing about her experience, not simply reliving it.

The last words could be lacunose rather than corrupt; after all,
the end of 16 was omitted by the despairing scribe.

The poem cannot be judged in its entirety. On one level, it can be
seen as prodigal praise from the narrator for the girl (who might
perfectly well have returned at the close). But the central passage
makes so momentous an impression that the listener must become
involved in the narrator's experience for itself as well as for what
it shows about the girl. That experience is intensely passive, and
the narrator's loss of control and authority is marked by the de-

velopments and contrasts of the poem. Despite the categories of normal and abnormal which the narrator erects at the opening, on the basis of her experience, the experience itself appears as drastic and extraordinary, and a disruption of the ordinary social scene it negates. And yet the narrator herself displays a wise endurance in the last part. The author and narrator are likely to be associated on some level (the poem gives no contrary indication, and the narrator fits well with narrators named as Sappho). However, the literary act of address in the poem is set against the failure of the narrator's actual attempts at contact. This brings out how the articulation of the poem both expresses the experience and is separate from it. Expression and the imposition of shape seem to come together in what appears the last part of the poem; form now elegantly seals off the onset, and the narrator incorporates the experience into some larger structure of the mind.

7: fr. 96 Voigt[16]

The text comes from a parchment codex (see Schubart and Wilamowitz (1907), 11, as against Schubart (1902), 2). The evidence appears to suggest that 94, part of the same double leaf, was not on the preceding page (cf. Turner (1977), ch. 5). If 95 is indeed in the same metre as 96 [7], that is clearly no argument for supposing it part of the same poem; the content makes that seem unlikely. We do not know, then, how much of 96 [7] is missing. In 1–2 it might seem as though the situation is being set out, with the name of Sardis given; it is perfectly possible that line 1 is the second of the poem.

The situation of 94 and 96 [7] is similar: both deal with someone who has now left the group. Poem 94 is focused on the moment of parting, and presents a narrative within which the narrator of the poem, named as Sappho, has a long, and probably the main, speech; the personal relation between the narrator and the girl (or woman) is to the fore of the poem. The speech paints a detailed picture of the way of life which even then was past for the girl. In what we have of this poem, by contrast, the narrator abstains from

[16] On 96 [7] see n. 7 and Schubart (1902), 1–3, 6–12; Schubart and Wilamowitz (1907), 10–11, 15–18; Blass (1902), 471–6; Zuntz (1939), 93–108; Vogliano (1942); Macleod (1983), 18–19; Carey (1978); Janko (1982); Renehan (1983), 15–20; Hague (1984); Fowler (1987a), 68–70; Irwin (1994), esp. 7–8; Fatouros (1997).

portraying her own involvement; she concentrates foremost on the person who has left, and secondarily on others who have been left.

The poem creates forceful oppositions of both place and time. The greatest emphasis is not on the narrator's own world or on a moment of parting, but on the present situation of the woman. This itself is pictured through an elaborate image; the scope and epic resonance of the device further detach the narrator. And yet this seeming distance in the narrator is no absence. The narrator's presence is felt precisely in her restraint; for us now 94 makes this restraint palpable (it is her group the woman is leaving). Her enthusiasm for the woman informs the rhetoric of the simile; her voice treats those left behind with indirect sympathy. The conceptions of both the woman and the situation are created by the subjectivity, or insight, of the narrator (note ποι 17), in an implied drama of communication with those who remain (4–5, 15–16).

Metre

1. $-\cup-\times\times-\cup\cup-\cup-$
2. $\times\times-\cup\cup-\cup-$ (7 $-\cup-\cup-\cup\cup-$)
3. $\times\times-\cup\cup-\cup-\cup--$

Sappho may have written at least one other poem in this metre (95?), but probably not a whole book (cf. 230, and 94, probably from the same book). The expansions of the glyconic are standard enough, as is the three-line form. (For $-\cup-$ at the start of the first line, cf. 98 (b). 3 (Alc. 70. 10, 12 $\times-\cup-$), for $\cup--$ at the end of the third (phalaecian hendecasyllable) cf. 230, and also 154; 94, 95, 98, 99 show three-line stanzas, based round glyconic lines.) An elegant feature is the placing of expansions at the beginning and at the end of this stanza, with the glyconic form itself occurring consecutively, but each time in a different line. More unusual is the absence of pause between the lines of the stanza. Less notable are fr. 112 (lines consisting of 2 arist.) and Alc. 140 (gl+gl+$\times-\cup-$ without pause). There are mostly significant pauses at the end of three-line stanzas in Sappho; in the continuous form of this poem, the close of the stanza can perhaps receive the more emphasis. On the divergence in 7 see n.

1. A concrete reference to the capital of the Lydians, where the woman is no doubt located (cf. 6–7). It is natural to suppose that she has left the group permanently (5, cf. 94); the pre-eminence she enjoys among Lydian women (not girls) makes it sound as if she has now passed from maidenhood. The most obvious assumption is that she has married a Lydian. At all events, the passage indicates the mingling of people as well as artefacts between the places.

2. πόλ]λακι: the poem creates, from the narrator's imagination, a picture of a recurring state. The emphasis, here and clearly in 15, shows how the woman's own mind crosses the boundary of place. The very act of the poem shows a mutual concern from her former companions; in a sense, the woman's longing is a kind of consolation to them.

τυίδε: the 'here' of the narrator and the performance combines with an opposition between Sardis and Mytilene.

3. If ζ had been written before ωομεν, one would expect to see some of the bottom right-hand edge as well as the top (cf. 15, the only other example of ζ in the codex). There may be a vertical trace at the bottom further to the left, as if the letter were τ. The colon after μεν might suggest a first-person plural verb, and a subordinate clause running on from 2; but supplementation is baffling.

4–5. The long syllable before δέ is very likely to be cᾶι (the confusion of αι and ε is common by this time). If ἀριγνωτα is an adjective, its termination would follow epic (cf. Lobeck (1837), 455–8). However, 'famous' is not a plausible standing epithet for a specific goddess; 'like a conspicuous or easily recognized goddess' seems less likely, however θεασικελαν is emended, than 'like the gods' (31 [6]. 1–2 n.; the use of the epithet in 'like the immortal gods' is different). Arignotus is a common enough name (cf. e.g. *LGPN* i. 58, ii. 50, etc.) and the separate feminine termination would be normal, even if the existence of the sixth-century Arignote is dubious (Thesleff (1965), 50–1).

Should the name be nominative or vocative? The absent woman need not be named only once in the poem (which might have just begun); even the recurrence of the name when she has been grammatical subject could be contemplated, cf. Alcm. 1 [1]. 79; Sapph. 15. 11? But the vocative in this vicinity seems much more probable. It could go with the clause that follows (cf. e.g. 131), in which case another name would come in 3; or it could go with the clause that precedes (for the position cf. Alc. 130 b [9]. 4 = 19, 335. 3). In any case, it appears that at least two women are named in the poem as objects of the absent woman's affection (cf. 16). The poem is thus concerned with the loss to the group, not to Sappho in particular, as is more the case in 94 (but note 94. 8). Nor is an exclusive amorous relationship depicted in 15–17 (note μάλιϲτ' here). The principal figure is made to seem more remote from the present locale by not being addressed, when another is.

θέαιϲι in 21 supports θέα⟨ι⟩ϲ' here as a feminine (contrast Alc. 129 [8]. 6). Poem 68. 3 might recommend the masculine in any case, cf. Eur. *Hec.* 356 (but note variant).

μόλπαι: the narrator is becomingly modest. We may note that the present poem itself is part of the environment the woman has lost.

6. A present scene is set against the past; it again springs from the narrator's imagination (rather than the Lydian press), and from her own ardent opinion of the woman. Although the depiction here does not suggest the intimacy and mutual admiration of Sappho's society (4–5), the conception is of external glory, seen from without; this will contrast with the woman's own feelings in 15–17.

7–8. The responsion of 'wilamowitzianus' with glyconic would be acceptable enough in much tragedy. Poem 95. 9 appears to offer a parallel in Sappho, although a vowel there is marked for deletion, and the second line of the presumed stanza-form has three different forms in its three substantial instances. Anacr. 357. 5, and other early examples, are by no means secure. One could certainly not suspect this passage on metrical grounds alone; but the corruption in 4–5 and 8 is worrying. ποτ' is a little strange. One could suppose the enclitic drawn forward, and compare Hom. *Od.* [24]. 88–9 ὅτε κέν ποτ' ἀποφθιμένου βαϲιλῆος | ζώννυνται; Eur. *Alc.* 560, *IA* 376 ὅταν ποτ'; but the emphasis of 'on any occasion when' is hardly called for by the sunset (nor true of the moon). 'When once, so soon as' is hard to parallel, 'sometimes' both unlikely and feeble. If there is corruption, and the metre is involved in it, one might, for example, audaciously imagine ἐμπρέπεται taken up by ⟨πρέ⟩πετ' ἀλίω (cf. 56. 1). West's suggestion for ποτ' alone ((1970*b*), 319 n. 32) uses the hexameter (and one-line) fragment 106; but the epic associations of the simile might justify it.

The setting sun leaves the stage clear for the moon, who takes the costume of the day. ἀελίω and ϲελάννα seem to occupy the same positions in the 'line', and the moon, coming as the final word of the stanza, is given the resounding Homeric epithet of the dawn (cf. 58. 19). ἀελίω | δύντος may have more melancholy suggestions in retrospect; but we should not perhaps go so far as to make Atthis the sun (Macleod (1983), 18, an admirable treatment). That does not quite suit the situation of the poem (if 4–5 are rightly taken). The setting of these images of radiance and fertility at night gives them a romantic attractiveness for modern readers (Leopardi, that moon-worshipper, actually begins 'L'ultimo canto di Saffo' (1822) with the moon). It is hard to know quite how far this corresponds to ancient sensibility; but the passage clearly suggests, in relation to the sun, reversal and strangeness.

βροδοδάκτυλος: the epic flavour of the word is very marked (*Il.* 1. 477 etc., Hes. *WD* 610, cf. Mimn. fr. 12. 3 West, and note Cratin. fr. 351 Kassel–Austin); but it is characteristic of Sappho to twist its application. The colour of the moon is certainly one point to the epithet (cf. e.g. Lloyd-Jones (1985), 277); but Bacch. 19. 18 can turn the word to describe Io, and we should be alert to other points too. A further, punning significance is given by 13, which the word prepares. (A related approach in Irwin (1994), 7–8.) Roses are the first plants mentioned there, produced by the moon's action; βροδοδάκτυλος occupies precisely the same prominent place in the stanza as πολυανθέμοις in the next, which in turn prepares and gains its full point from what follows. One need not be too anxious about the working of the compound in this secondary sense: either it is a loose combination of nouns, as in ἀλλαλόκακος (Alc. 130 b [9]. 7), ἀστύθεμις (Bacch. 4. 3), χειρογάστωρ (Hecat. *FGrHist* 1 F 367), or the first part has an adjectival sense, as in e.g. ἱμερόφωνος (Sapph. 136).

Cελάννα: for the corruption cf. Janko (1982). The personification here, and in Greek conceptions of the sun and moon, is quite sufficient to justify the article.

9. The running over of the stanza carries special force in this metre, where the stanza is one uninterrupted entity. The crucial phrase is thrown into relief, especially πάντα. The enjambment also leads into the flowing of the whole simile over several stanzas. This sweeping design is part of the grandiose and evocative epic effect; one may contrast the parataxis with the same subject in 34. 1–4. The form also enhances the omnipresent glory of the moon, which seems to flood the poem.

For the moon outshining the stars see Nisbet and Hubbard (1970), 163; one should prefer the reading 'Moon', not 'Sun', in the quotation from Wootton.

φάος: the brightness of the moon is placed prominently (cf. the emphasis on radiance in e.g. Pind. *Ol.* 3. 19–20); here the moon again resembles the sun (cf. e.g. *Hom. h. Dem.* 69). It appears as active and dynamic.

10–11. ἀλμύραν to some extent recalls epic (cf. e.g. Hom. *Od.* 12. 236, *al.*, θαλάccηc ἀλμυρὸν ὕδωρ; Sapph. 44. 7, Alc. 334. 2, Pind. *Ol.* 7. 57); so too πολυανθέμοιc (πολυανθήc Hom. *Od.* 14. 353; -εμοc Alc. 286 a. 2, Mimn. fr. 2. 1 West, Pind. *Ol.* 13. 17); so too ἀρούραιc, used to indicate the earth (cf. Hom. *Il.* 7. 421, *Od.* 19. 433, taken up by Aratus). But ἀρούραιc has also the more specific sense of 'fields', as is indicated by the epithet and what follows.

Difference begins to appear, in this independent sentence, between vehicle and tenor. Polarities of place, so important in the tenor, are obliterated by the all-pervading moon (note ἴcωc); the contrast is not only with the woman, but with the total situation for all the women. Cf. Macleod (1983), 18, and, for the wider point, Musil, *Der Mann ohne Eigenschaften*, ed. Frisé (Hamburg, 1978), i. 145 (bk. 1, ch. 38), 'so wie in einem Gleichnis [!], wo . . . aus der Ungleichnis des Gleichen wie aus der Gleichnis des Ungleichen zwei Rauchsäulen aufsteigen . . .'.

12–14. This stanza continues the idea of the active power of the moon: the moon produces the dew (Alcm. 57 etc., cf. Plin. *NH* 2. 152), which causes the flowers to grow (note 73 a. 8–9). The agency is more indirectly expressed (passive 12, parataxis 12–13); and the glory of light is replaced by life-giving power. Again a difference appears between vehicle and tenor, above all in mood and in total situation. The stanza, however, also aims for the sense of imaginative excursion in a Homeric simile (quite compatible with relevance); one is to have too a sense of the epic poet's detachment in the narrator's voice, as well as of the heaping rhetoric so characteristic of Sappho.

The movement to this stanza is carefully prepared (7–8 n.); πολυανθέμοιc at the end of the previous stanza is particularly matched by ἀνθεμώδηc at the end of this.

κάλα sets the note for the stanza; the predicative adjective justifies the article (Lobel (1927), xci–xcii).

κέχυται: the perfect perhaps slightly underlines the idea of what the goddess has accomplished; cf. Hom. *Il.* 12. 284. The following perfect may have more the role of a present, as in 2. 9, Bacch. 10. 40.

The sequence of plants, generated through heavenly power, is related to epic lists of beautiful flowers (cf. Hom. *Il.* 14. 346–9 (divinely produced); *Cypria* fr. 4 Davies; cf. also *h. Dem.* 5–7). The epithets have an epic aura, especially the final epithet which lingers before the return to the tenor of the simile. But the passage is also extremely individual. After the obviously lovely roses, Sappho employs plants rarely mentioned in poetry (cf. Cratin. fr. 105. 6–7 Kassel–Austin, Pherecr. fr. 114. 3, 138. 2, *al.*). The μελίλωτος, a sort of clover, at least has bright flowers (cf. Arnott (1985); (1996), 331–2); but the ἄνθρυςκον has small white flowers at best (cow-parsley is one possibility; cf. Martin (1965), pl. 38). But these plants, which proliferate copiously, suggest vast abundance in wild meadows, and so the fertile power of the moon. ἄπαλ᾽ brings out the sensuous attraction to the touch exactly in plants like cow-parsley; ἀνθεμώδης in part presents a contrast. The latter word, not commonly used as an epithet for actual plants, is employed in an unusual way (contrast e.g. Bacch. 19. 39, [Aesch.] *PV* 455, Eur. *Bacch.* 462).

15–16. The poem does not return to the woman with an 'even so'; rather the δέ marks an addition, and a contrast, to νῦν δὲ Λύδαιςιν ἐμπρέπεται γυναίκεςςιν, with no change of subject. Despite the external image of her beauty making her supreme among her new people, internally she feels grievous longing.

πόλλα is emphasized by its position; but the repeated action is different from the continuous state of her pre-eminence, reinforced by the image of the moonlight. It is part of the restraint, and perceptiveness, of the poem that the longing is not unbroken, but frequently recurring; the woman is not prostrate with misery. Cf. 16 [5]. 15–16.

ζαφοίταις᾽: probably a participle, not present verb (cf. Page (1955), 91–2, against Zuntz (1939), 96–100). If it were a verb, it looks as though there would have to be asyndeton at 17. Further, πόλλα would have to go with this verb; whereas, given the probable meaning of ζαφοίταις᾽, it would go much better with ἐπιμνάςθεις᾽, or rather with the whole sentence. The form of the verb is also uncertain (cf., however, Hamm (1958), 161–2).

The preverb does not have an obvious noun to relate to. The Lydian women are made unlikely by the other uses of the verb; Sardis is a long way apart in the text, and 'go through Sardis' pointless. More likely is 'as she goes about, goes here and there [in Sardis]'; this meaning, though seemingly denied in LSJ *Supp.*, appears to be established by Xen. *Cyr.* 6. 2. 12, and probably *Cyn.*

3. 3, and by *Coll. Alex.* p. 185, *Lyr. Adesp.* 7. 2. 'Roam' is not adequately supported. The word is unemphatic, and down-to-earth after the grandiose images. That suits the concentration on the woman's own point of view, and poignantly suggests the practicality of the new life which is set against regrets for the old. On this interpretation, the passage incidentally implies that for women to move about in a city regularly would not seem unusual to Lesbians.

ἀγάνας: the epithet is from the woman's perspective, and, unlike the description in 4, touchingly quiet.

ἐπιμνάcθειc': the people still matter to her. Cf. 94. 7–8, Hom. *Od.* 8. 460–1, Ap. Rhod. 3. 1069–71, 1109–16, etc. But also, from the viewpoint of the woman, the Mytilenean group is in the past.

Ἄτθιδοc: there is no address, as at 4–5, in this more reflective passage, concentrated on the absent woman. Atthis is spoken of in several poems (49, 90 fr. 10 a. 15, 131); see the introduction.

ἰμέρω⟨ι⟩: it is not linguistically or poetically satisfactory to make this mean 'remembering Atthis with desire'; 'remembering her desire (genitive) for Atthis' (West (1970*b*), 319 n. 33) would be still less plausible. One imagines that the dative went with what follows (instrumental or causal). The position of ποι is not an insuperable obstacle: an important word comes first, and the particle comes second within a small group. For που not coming second in the clause cf. Denniston (1954), 394; Hom. *Il.* 12. 272; Aesch. *Ag.* 1630; τιc at Alc. 362. 2; ποτε at Pind. *Ol.* 7. 30, *Pyth.* 10. 45, etc.

17. λέπταν: the meaning is far from clear. 'Sensitive, delicate'? (Somewhat otherwise Broger (1996), 100; Fatouros (1997), 199.) There might seem to be some characterization here. If βόρηται comes from βαρέω, there would be a relation with λέπταν.

ποι: at the end of the whole depiction, the narrator explicitly indicates that it springs from her imagination, and her knowledge of the people involved.

βόρηται: 'eat' or 'be weighed down'? It is not easy to say without the missing letters. 'Weigh down' suffers the disadvantage that the tradition elsewhere offers βαρ-; note, however, Alc. 326. 9, where the manuscripts of Heraclitus (not P. Oxy. 2306 ii 14) offer χόλαιcι instead of χαλ-. In both places one would have a learned error. 'Eat' (Zuntz (1939), 100–1) suffers the disadvantage of uncertain attestation elsewhere (a papyrus reading at Nic. *Ther.* 395). One evidently eats one's θυμός (or καρδία) rather than one's φρήν; δάκε δὲ φρένας is different (Hom. *Il.* 5. 493, cf. Simon. fr. 25. 3 West²). Accommodating an accusative heart here would be syntactically tricky. Possibly φρένα as an accusative of respect would be preferable, with βόρηται passive; cf. Ar. *Wasps* 286–7 μηδ' οὕτω ϲεαυτὸν | ἔϲθιε (for the accusative cf. Hom. *Od.* 10. 247).

18–20. Whatever was said here, the separation of place is emphatically marked at the start of the stanza; κῆθι matches τυίδε (2). The narrator, in presenting some bleak or consoling wisdom, tactfully uses 'us'. The group is drawn together, and separated from the woman; the narrator avoids dwelling on her own distress.

West makes ingenious suggestions in 18–19 ((1970*b*), 319–20); the one in 18 particularly seems uninviting in expression, and unsuitable for the space.

21–36. Does a new poem begin at 21? A coronis was not written, but one need not be too daunted by the omission (cf. Alc. 130 b [9], with 129 [8] introduction; note Sapph. 99 col. ii. 3 marg.). The precise nature of the alleged connection turns on οὐ. Voigt doubts μ]ὲν οὐκ on grounds of word-order (1971), 109; but cf. Sapph. 16 [5]. 21, Alc. 375. 1, Archil. fr. 197. 1 West, Alcm. 58. 1, Theogn. 1095, Pind. fr. dub. 358. 1. Vogliano's οὖν introduces a particle found in the Lesbians only in a different form, if at all (cf. Alc. 48. 8]κῶν Π), and requires most unlikely sense: a negative is surely needed.

If, then, we do not adopt οὖν, the asyndeton, unusual in these poets, is itself a discouraging sign (cf. 1 [4]. 25, made easier by καί; 44. 13; 94. 3, made easier by καί if real; Alc. 73. 7, made easier by pronouns). More worrying is the difficulty of relating the thought to anything the previous stanza can have said. 'Us', if read in 21, would merely be a deterrent in the light of 18, where 'us' has a different reference. The present second person ἔχηιϲθ' (23) is hard to accommodate meaningfully into what precedes. Presumably it is not the absent woman, so firmly third-person before; if it is one of those remaining, it is hard to imagine a plausible statement that will connect both with the preceding clause and with the preceding stanzas. It also becomes hard to make 26–9 a further scene of the absent woman's past as in 3–5. The possibility that 21–3 are connected with 4 is outweighed by the problems of more immediate coherence; in fact, the abrupt recurrence and correction, with no connecting particle, would be surprising in itself. It is more likely that the clause on human and heavenly beauty (21–3) looks forward (the theme is not uncommon in Sappho); if so, it may be linked to the ministering goddesses of 26–9 (cf. 2. 13–16). A connection of both passages with the earlier stanzas would become all the less compelling. One may add that the coast of Euboea (33) is not startlingly germane to a poem about Lesbos and Lydia; and that 21–3 would make an excellent opening. Since a new poem probably begins here, further comment on the slight remains should be forgone.

Poem 96 [7] displays a remarkably bold and concrete fantasy. The spatial range, sensuous power, and conceptual audacity with which the central image is developed even suggest a relationship with Pindar. Yet all the poems we have considered develop material in a fashion surprising in fullness and arresting in execution: the epiphany, Helen, the onset. One should generally be struck by the inventiveness of the poems within their apparently narrow sphere.

Even on the most elemental level, one can see their range. Thus 1 [4] is in form a prayer, with a narrative of the supernatural in the past, and a divine addressee; the poem is focused on the narrator, yet treats her with a measure of irony. Poem 16 [5] is an argumentative poem; it uses an example from the past, in a fashion not simply narrative, and moves to the specific present situation of the narrator. The problems of subjectivity and the complexity of love complicate, but do not subvert, the poem. Poem 31 [6] also moves to dwell on the narrator, but sooner; it describes her directly and at length, in a depiction of a recurring present, which is set against the specific present of the performance. The narrator finally asserts control over the subjective experience which had overwhelmed the poem; but form and content are in tension throughout. Poem 96 [7] is concentrated on the absent person, and other members of the group; the narrator is a more distant though important presence; the poem moves into and out of an elaborate image. With that imagery, and the free movement of the simile in structure, one can contrast the sequence of literal and parallel experiences in 31 [6], or the intricate and often ironic patterning of Aphrodite's speech in 1 [4].

Consideration of other substantial fragments would enlarge our sense of Sappho's actual breadth more than it displayed repetition. In discussing Sappho, the temptation is to generalize from a few fragments; it is no less desirable to recognize the invention and the varied tonality of a highly imaginative artist.

ALCAEUS

Introduction

THE introduction to the chapter on Sappho dealt with various matters relevant to Alcaeus. The introduction to this chapter will deal with certain historical matters, and will attempt to lay some ground for the proper appreciation of Alcaeus' poetry. We begin with the thorny question of his date.

The most secure item for dating Alcaeus is his brother's mercenary service in the east. He fought for the Babylonians, so before 539, and probably before the death of Nebuchadrezzar II in 562; probably not before c.605. Alc. 48. 10 refers to Babylon and Ascalon: the latest known date this could be related to is the Babylonian expedition of 582 (Jer. 52: 30); 605–4 is another possibility (the reference to Ashkelon in the Babylonian Chronicle for 604 is uncertain). Alc. 350 appears to welcome the brother back, so Alcaeus is an adult at the time.[1]

A papyrus treatise (Alc. 306 A e, *SLG* S282) connects a return of Alcaeus from exile with the war between Astyages and Alyattes (ended by a datable eclipse in 585); but we do not actually know that these figures were mentioned by Alcaeus. Other items are still more problematic. Phrynon is apparently named by the poet at Alc. 167. 17; but the dates of chronographers for Pittacus' supposed duel with this Athenian (607/6, *sim.*), and for Phrynon's Olympic victory (636/5), involve problems of their own and surely have no great claim to respect. Alcaeus himself mentions fighting against Athens, in which he participated (cf. 428, and note 130 b [9]. 10 = 25); but a date around 600 would in itself be far from attractive for Athenian history. Hdt. 5. 94–5 immerses us in difficulties. On any natural reading, he says there was a war between Mytilene and Athens in the Troad which involved both Alcaeus and a son of Peisistratus, established as tyrant of Sigeum before the war. Scholars' dating of this tyranny to no earlier than 540 depends on [Arist.] *Ath. Pol.* 17. 4; but that work's account of the son contains serious difficulties itself. However, since Hippias, Peisistratus' eldest legitimate son, is alive in 490, we cannot happily put the Sigean tyranny as early as

---

[1] On the reference to Ashkelon see Mitchell (1991), 396.

say 560; if we may suppose Peisistratus to be in charge of Athens at the time, and if this is his third period of rule, such a date is the more improbable. Herodotus' difficulties are increased by the 'long time' (5. 94. 2) before the intervention of Periander, for Herodotus a contemporary of Alyattes. We should rest content with locating Alcaeus' activity around the first few decades of the sixth century.[2]

It is important to grasp the radical unreliability of even our earliest information. Herodotus is a very early and promising source; and yet is most likely decades out in his notions of when Alcaeus lived. Even more disquieting is a still earlier source (470s), the kalathoid vase Munich 2416 (*ARV*[2] 385. 288, Brygos Painter?), which depicts Sappho and Alcaeus as being of a similar age. The painter need not have been informed about, or troubled by, chronology; the significant point is that he appears to portray the pair in accordance with the fragment where Alcaeus was taken to be bashfully in love with Sappho (Sapph. 137; cf. Alc. 384). The application and at the very least the later part of the fragment are likely to be inauthentic, but are certainly as early as Aristotle. If such fictional biography and interpretation were current so early as the vase, it would be entirely possible for them to affect chronological conceptions of these poets from the first. Late sources that present exact dates should not be accorded priority over early sources; but if even fifth-century sources are marked by error or fancy, we may reasonably nurse doubts about the entire tradition.[3]

The extant fragments of Alcaeus are dominated by his enemy Pittacus; a brief word on him may be of use. He was elected aisymnetes, perhaps for a limited period (cf. Arist. *Pol.* 1285ᵃ34–5; Theophr. fr. 631 Fortenbaugh; cf. Diog. Laert. 1. 75); he retained the assembly and the boule. Alcaeus speaks of him as being elected τύραννος (348. 3, cf. 75. 12?; 302 b. 7?); but the word is likely to be a hostile designation, one Solon emphatically avoids for himself (frr. 32. 2,

---

[2] For these problems see, among other works, Beloch (1890); Jacoby (1923–), II D. 275–6; Gallavotti (1948), 7–30; Page (1955), 150–60; Servais (1969); Will (1955), 381–91; Davies (1971), 445–5; Rhodes (1976), and (1981), 194; Fehling (1985), 104–8; Viviers (1987); Lapini (1996), esp. ch. 4. At Alc. 167. 17, though it is presented as poetry, something might seem on various counts to have gone badly wrong (inspection of the original only strengthens this impression). It is possible that a gloss or expansion has been incorporated into the poetic text.

[3] On Munich 2416 Sappho and Alcaeus are named; for this vase see Picard (1948), 338–44; Wegner (1973), 168–71; Schefold (1997), 84, 487. On portraits of Alcaeus more widely see Richter (1965), i. 69–70; the 5th-cent. Melian relief British Museum B 367 (Jacobsthal (1931), 57–9, nos. 76–7) does not depict Sappho and Alcaeus.

33. 5–6 West). The roles of Solon and Pittacus may not have been very different, and our category of 'the Greek tyrants' will not be illuminating. Alc. 70. 7 δαπτέτω πόλιν ὠc καὶ πεδὰ Μυρcί[λ]ῳ[has been thought to prove that Pittacus shared power with the (supposed) tyrant Myrsilus before his death; this may be too formalized an inference. Alcaeus certainly claims that Pittacus broke an oath sworn with him and his comrades; but this may be only one view of the matter. We can safely say that Pittacus earlier formed part of an aristocratic faction aimed at overthrowing some person or persons in power; and that he fought with Alcaeus against the Athenians (so before his time of official power). On the other hand, we should be wary of simply accepting the later view of him as benign, early though the belief in his 'wisdom' begins (Simon. 542 [**15**]. 11–13). Presentation of rulers in the tradition is much affected by the picture of the good tyrant as well as the bad, especially when there is a contrast to be made. (Alcaeus and Pittacus appear, with fierce and friendly faces, on a Mytilenean coin of the Roman period.) In the case, say, of the fifth-century Theron (set against Hieron) this tradition seems a palpable distortion. We do not know what actually lies behind Alcaeus' allegation of 'tearing' the people; doubtless property is involved.[4]

Alcaeus' political poems often aim at exhorting a group. Various pieces of evidence ascribe a significant role to his brother Antemenidas. Aristotle says that he and Alcaeus led a group of exiles (προειcτήκεcαν, *Pol.* 1285ᵃ36–7); Diogenes speaks of Pittacus removing the tyrant Melanchrus with Alcaeus' brothers (hence presumably older brothers; possibly Alcaeus was the source (cf. 75?): Diog. Laert. 74). Alc. 306 A e has Alcaeus refer to his brother in connection with his own second exile; the brother seems to be alive, and so would live well into Alcaeus' own career. We may surmise that Alcaeus was an important person in the group, because of his poetry

[4] On Pittacus etc. see among other works Page (1955), 149–243; Andrewes (1956), ch. 8; Berve (1967), 91–5; Mosshammer (1979), ch. 13; Seibert (1979), 20–2; Barceló (1993), 92–4; Osborne (1996), 189–97; note also von der Lahr (1992). (On the tradition of Seven Wise Men see e.g. Martin (1993).) For αἰcυμνήτηc (the word already in Homer) cf. Arist. *Pol.* 1285ᵃ30–1, ᵇ38–9, 1295ᵇ11–14, fr. 524 Rose, Theophr. fr. 631 Fortenbaugh, Nic. Dam. *FGrHist* 90 F 53. No doubt Aristotle and Theophrastus generalize too smoothly. *SEG* 31 (for 1981), 984–5 (Teos) shows eagerness to avoid the popular election of an aisymnetes; here we have a 5th-cent. perspective, but the arrangement is evidently known. The end of Alc. 70. 7 cannot be read as πεδὰ Μύρcι[λ]ο[ν (i.e. directly after Myrsilus' death): so inspection of the original with a microscope confirms (P. Oxy. 1234 fr. 2, in the Bodleian).

and his brother, but that he was not the sole 'leader'. Mytilenean
politics, and thus Alcaeus' life, were vicissitudinous; Myrsilus, like
Peisistratus and Alcaeus, had an exile and return (305, cf. S267).
Ancient scholars appear to have discussed Alcaeus' periods of exile,
at least two, three according to some (Σ on 114, 306 A e). The first
was under the domination of Myrsilus; a later was under Pittacus
(129 [8]). We need not believe, even if Aristotle were saying it, that
the Mytileneans' motive in electing Pittacus was dislike of the ex-
iles. Alc. 70. 9–13 suggest at least that the wider conflicts may have
threatened the unity of the group itself. Alcaeus did not die young:
his poetry mentions his grey chest (50. 2).

Alcaeus' poetry seems at first entirely different from Sappho's,
and, at first, cruder and less interesting. There might be thought an
obvious contrast between her narrowness and his range. This only
obtains up to a point. His poetry shows a more positive interest in
women and love than hers does in men and politics (cf. e.g. 10, 45.
5–8 (note also 41, 296 b); 71, 327, 368?, 380, 434). But politics is
as central a concern of his poetry as love is of hers, and similarly
connected with a first person. Alcaeus shows a dazzling inventive-
ness in his poetic handling of politics; but Sappho is more inventive
with love than is often realized, and exploits various devices little
used in extant Alcaeus (such as narrated conversation). In the light
of the discussion of Sappho above, one might wish to make a con-
trast between Sappho's subtle treatment of her narrator and the
simplicity with which Alcaeus' poems appear to invite acceptance
of the narrator's viewpoint. This contrast would possess consider-
able validity; but the implications need care. Other archaic authors
make it likely that the difference is not due to the social construc-
tion of gender but to the differences felt between love and politics.
(Irony on the self and emphasis on problematic subjectivity are
more at home in ancient poetry about love.) It is also part of the
positive impact sought by Alcaeus' poetry that it displays an almost
heroic energy and resolve amid adversity (e.g. 6). And even these
tones can be subtly mingled with those of a sadder resignation, or
merrier hedonism (e.g. 140, 335). In any case, we should perhaps
resist a tendency to regard subtlety and self-ironization, appealing
as these are to any postmodern aesthetic, as automatically supe-
rior to energy and directness: such a tendency would lead to many
one-sided responses.

More generally, we need to bear two perspectives in mind at once when viewing either poet, a purposeful and an aesthetic. Analogies of a kind are suggested by Kant's *Kritik der Urteilskraft* and Schopenhauer's *Welt als Wille und Vorstellung*: Kant is much concerned with alternative ways of viewing a body (for example), as shaped for a purpose or as not, and Schopenhauer with separate ways of viewing the world, as shaped by Will or otherwise. We need to see most of these poems simultaneously as shaped by a pressing practical will or purpose, which forms part of the work itself, and also as objects of more purely aesthetic contemplation. This practical purpose is not the same thing as the 'author's intention' outside the work; the purpose may be wholly or partly fictional, and the poem may plainly look beyond it (so with the prayer of Sapph. 1 [4], an interesting comparison with the prayer in Alc. 129 [8]). This purposeful, or rhetorical, aspect of the poems must be seen not as artless but as controlling the art for its alleged practical ends. On this model, the rhetorical aspect of, say, Sapph. 16 [5] has often been neglected in considering its detail; with Alcaeus, although the rhetoric is often more devious than is recognized, it is the more purely artistic aspect that has been underplayed. These critical perspectives are simultaneous, it must be repeated, and do not exclude each other. It is not a question of seeking things in Alcaeus that cannot be related to the rhetorical purpose (though these exist), but of remembering a more self-contained aesthetic aspect too. Such a model might enlarge the consideration of other authors besides (Lucretius comes to mind).

Is this approach not grossly unhistorical? Did Alcaeus not write to inflame his comrades? We must not let our critical approach depend on whether the songs were composed for any audience but the group. After all, even a practical purpose outside the work need not be diminished if, as is surely probable, the poet in exile was aware of the value of his songs within the city. If known there, they would promote the views, image, and prominence of the group. On the concrete question of the desired audience, the fact of address cannot logically be used to limit the poems' intended reception; even the most literal views would not take all poems addressed to an individual (e.g. 38 a) as intended for that individual alone.[5]

Yet even if we thought of the songs as written for the group's

[5] Rösler (1980) strongly emphasizes the role of the group; cf. Trumpf (1973), 139. Seibert (1979), 22, uses the word 'propagandistisch'. The later publishing of speeches (whether to real or pretended audiences) perhaps helps remind us of pos-

symposia only, we do not have diaries that tell us how poems were actually received at archaic symposia. Any such knowledge must be based chiefly on the poems; so we cannot exclude what seems to be a part of these texts on the basis of inferred reception. We might argue from some archaic poems to others; but to do so merely strengthens the critical model suggested for Alcaeus. Many poems of, say, Mimnermus or the *Theognidea* have an evident and unpractical aesthetic dimension; such a dimension is clear in Sappho, and still clearer in many of Alcaeus' non-political poems. His listeners evidently appreciated Homer and Hesiod. How could we exclude aesthetic pleasure at the poems themselves as one element in their response to political works, or how limit the art in the poems to tools of persuasion? The imaginative resourcefulness of this and other archaic poetry on politics suggests it is not aimed solely at conviction of the convinced. So even an intentionalist and historicist approach should not circumscribe the works. These points should at least prepare us to perceive the richness of an undervalued poet.

8: fr. 129 Voigt (and Lobel–Page)[6]

This introduction will deal with both 129 [8] and 130 b [9]. These two poems of Alcaeus, the longest fragments save 298 [10], strikingly demonstrate his range in handling a single situation. It is important to see first that it is a single situation. The main papyrus (P. Oxy. 2165) presents four poems in two consecutive columns. There are coronides after 129 [8] and 130 b [9]; not after 130 a, but the metre establishes it as a different poem from 130 b [9] (all blunt endings, not a four-line stanza). (Cf. Gallavotti (1942), 164–5; note Σ on 303 A c. 2.) The poems are connected in subject: 129 [8] and 130 b [9] concern exile, 131. 2 starts φευγον[. Furthermore, the narrator of 129 [8] and 130 b [9] is in a temenos, and the scholiast

sible relations between circulation and address, whatever the material circumstances of circulation.

[6] On 129 [8], 130 b [9], or both, see: Gallavotti (1942), (1948), 9–11, 56–62, 114–29; Deubner (1943); Mazzarino (1943); Vogliano (1943); Goossens (1944), 265–8; Latte (1968); Luppino (1950); Trumpf (1958), 71–2; Robert (1969), 801–31; Quinn (1961); Picard (1962); Burzacchini (1976, 1985); Rösler (1980), 191–203, 272–85; Burnett (1983), 157–63, 176–81; Meyerhoff (1984), 211–35; Huxley (1987); Luppe (1987), 281; Lefkowitz and Lloyd-Jones (1990); West (1990a), 3; Broger (1996), 179–92; Liberman (1999) i. 61–5, ii. 213–16.

adds τὸ τῆς Ἥρας to 130 a. 15 τεῖχος βαςιλήϊον; it seems likely to be the same temenos. The temenos in 129 [8] is for all the Lesbians; the women of Lesbos come for a contest to that in 130 b [9]. The sanctuary in 130 a and 130 b [9] belongs primarily to Hera, and also, in 130 b [9] (28 = 13) to other gods; for Hera in 130 b [9], see Σ Hom. Il. 9. 129–30 (text in Dindorf), which locates the Lesbian beauty-contest in the temenos of Hera, cf. Tümpel (1891), 566. In 129 [8] a goddess of the sanctuary is addressed, probably at the start: this suggests her pre-eminence; Zeus and Dionysus share the sanctuary too. The goddess's name can plausibly be read as Hera in 1; her identity seems confirmed by Sapph. 17, which addresses Hera, groups her with Zeus and Dionysus, and appears to describe the foundation of a cult of theirs on Lesbos. The papyrus must be grouping the poems together because it believes that they are describing the same time and place. Time too, for it will not be merely place that interests them: Σ to Alc. 114 in particular (cf. e.g. Σ to 60) makes apparent the concern of ancient scholars with the chronology of the poems. They had much more Alcaeus to hand than we have; from what we can see, their combination here looks very likely. It would certainly seem unattractive to follow Trumpf ((1958), 56–7, 71–2), and assign 129 [8] and 130 b [9] to separate times.

If we place the poems in the same time and place, obvious and notable differences appear. First, the place. In 129 [8] the sanctity of the great shrine, and its national character, are solemnly employed in a prayer (within the fiction of the poem); in 130 b [9] the poet represents himself as living in a rustic wilderness. He also in 130 b [9] unexpectedly depicts a refined event (the Lesbian beauty contest) occurring at this sanctuary; the transitions and juxtapositions demand that we should see changes of appearance even within the poem. (Both poems are mobile.) One may note too that 130 b [9] creates a vivid sense of Mytilene, in antithesis to the present place; that does not happen in 129 [8].

Second, people. Poem 130 b [9] concentrates on depicting the pains of exile, on which 129 [8] spends little space. Poem 129 [8] makes Pittacus (eventually) its central figure; 130 b [9] does not mention Pittacus, or anyone else in power. Events in the narrator's life from the exile on are important in 130 b [9]; from before it in 129 [8]. The most salient difference, however, is that in 129 [8] the narrator speaks as one of a plurality present in the temenos, and advertises no separate individuality. In 130 b [9] the narrator speaks only of himself, to a friend. With οἶος gone from 10 = 25, he is not actually claiming to be alone (not even 148 need be claiming that; 130 a. 1 is very uncertain). But the change in presentation is impressive. The poet, we must suppose, is depicting the situation under a multiplicity of aspects, or even adjusting its appearance to suit the nature of each poem; this conception certainly seems preferable to separating the poems into different periods. Is it even likely that Alcaeus would be in exile on his own? The writer is exploiting the general range of the narrator in his poetry between the individual suffering and addressing a friend, and the member or leader of a group. For the former compare, in a political setting, 50?, 60, 335, 428 (can he have been the only Mytilenean to flee?).

It would in any case be unpromising to explain the difference in content practically, as the difference between a work inspiring a group who do not need enlightening on their own situation and a work informing a group who need enlightening on Alcaeus' (cf. Rösler (1980), 272–5). The group must be aware of the oath they swore; and they must surely be aware of where Alcaeus is spending his exile (Burzacchini (1985), 374), or at least of the annual beauty contest. Intrinsically too, it is more satisfying to see a literary difference in ethos and emphasis.

The difference between the two poems in character will become more fully apparent from the reading of the comments. Both can be taken too simply and literally: 129 [8] as entirely and actually a curse, 130 b [9] as a work straightforwardly transcribing the experience of solitary exile, or even as an informative letter. The latter, however, strikes one as the more complex and surprising poem. This is an early example of the exile poetry so brilliantly taken up, for example, by Ovid, and by a sad multitude of Russians; but its handling of place, time, and narrator makes it as subtle and potent as any. Poem 129 [8] is remarkable rather for its elemental power; but it too is a more changing, elaborate, and even devious poem than might be thought. Its very sparseness of metaphor or of vivid physicality should be seen, in this writer, not as artlessness but as one particular mode of art. The difference here from his political poetry of allegory, satire, or myth suits the gravity of this poem. So when exploiting this particular place of exile, Alcaeus displays, in both works, the fecundity of his thoughts, and the density of his poems.

Metre

1. $\times - \cup - \times - \cup\cup - \cup -$
2. $\times - \cup - \times - \cup\cup - \cup -$
3. $\times - \cup - \times - \cup - \times$
4. $- \cup\cup - \cup\cup - \cup - -$

This, the alcaic stanza, is the commonest in Alcaeus (reasonably enough). One may think of it as having the intrinsic structure AAA'. In this intrinsic structure 'lines' 3 and 4 are a single colon (cf. West (1982), 33). Line 3 expands the long single-short beginning of 1 and 2; 4 expands their choriambic base and turns their blunt ending to pendant. Line 3 does not look like an independent colon. The validity of this analysis is confirmed by the incidence of pause in Alcaeus after 1 and 2, not after 3: hiatus occurs only after 1 and 2 (72. 7, 12, 325. 1?), overlap of word only after 3 (75. 13, 208. 12? (could be enclitic), 208 A. 4? (73. 6 δ')). A short at the end of the blunt 1 and 2 must then be seen as *brevis in longo* (6. 2, 58. 17, etc.), whereas the last syllable of 3 can be seen as an internal anceps (short 72. 5, 119. 11, *al.*).

However, Alcaeus appears to go beyond this structure, so that one is tempted to think he inherited the stanza. He normally separates 4 from 3 by word-end (47 clear instances); this suggests, though not pause, a strong division. One may compare his treatment of the fourth line in the sapphic stanza (cf. Sapph. 1 [4] *metre*). There results an effective opposition in 3–4 of single-short and double-short rhythms. Line 4 seems to be a point of climax, and often contains a striking phrase: cf. 6. 12, 72. 10, 129 [8]. 16, 20, 298 [10]. 11, 23, 326. 4 (compare 34. 12), 335. 4. Run-over into the next stanza is unusual (119. 5, 129 [8]. 9; not 326. 5), and stanzas are often strongly demarcated as entities.

1. The cέ in 6 strongly implies, as Lobel saw, that the goddess has been named. A̦ιολήιαν̦ κτλ. represent not her name but a title and epithets. In the context of 5–9 the listener expects a name (from previously), not merely a deictic reference. The poem need not have begun with 1; but it is hard to avoid the impression that it did. If so, the name came in 1 or 2; it would not be altogether easy to accommodate. It is tempting to read Ἤρα (Gallavotti) in 1. The tail curving downward from the left, together with a high trace, are compatible with η (cf. 9, 130 b [9]. 5 = 20); the apparent brevis over a would suit the vocative.

The letter which follows a is not like ξ (cf. 3, 20, 21); but it does resemble the first τ of 13. The word might be τᾶι, with the relatively easy errors of the wrong accent and a missing ι ('to whom',

Gallavotti, cf. Luppino (1950), 207 n. 1; 'where' also possible, cf. 130 b [9]. 17 = 32, with 'to you' in 2, perhaps). If so, we would probably need a verb at the start (otherwise Gallavotti).

In any event, we have no ordinary pattern of prayer. A narrative develops, not exclusive to the god addressed; when an imperative appears, it is addressed to all three deities. The god is not here presented as an agent; but for this one might compare Theogn. 11–14; Alc. 296 b. 1–2. Sappho's narrative in 1 [4], though it becomes less numinous in atmosphere, is in some ways closer to the norms of prayer; we see there a different exploitation of religious discourse. The apparent similarity of pattern in Sapph. 17 might be due to literary influence as well as connection in cult.

τόδε Λέcβιο‚ι: the place, shown as present, forms the locale and starting-point for the poem; one may connect Alc. 6, where an image, familiar from life, is made into a scene and beginning for the poem: τόδ' αὖˌτε κῦμα κτλ. The place and thing link the present to the validating and exalting past. (It is fascinating to compare Erenburg's '*Statuja Aphrodity*' (1945), *Sobr. soč.* (9 vols.; Moscow, 1962–7), iii. 468); there the beautiful statue links present and past in quasi-religious experience, but without tradition, and with disruption of religious belief.) And yet the account is the poet's invention, or choice; contrast Sappho's legend on the Atridae (17: Meyerhoff (1984), 219–30). It evokes a nationalism larger even than the poet's own (the whole island!); the unity (ξῦˌνον) contrasts with Pittacus' disloyalty to the group and damage to the city. Both the actions, the Lesbians' and Pittacus', appear in narratives. One has produced an enduring continuity; Pittacus has broken with his own past action, which claimed to fix his conduct.

2. εὖˌδεˌιλον . . . μέγα: aggrandizing adjectives. Note Dioscorid. XVII. 8 Gow–Page (*Ἥρηc ἐν μεγάλωι τεμένει*), possibly deriving from Archilochus. εὐδείελοc is used elsewhere of islands, lands, towns, mountains (so Hom. *Od.* 2. 167, 13. 234, *h. Ap.* 438, Pind. *Ol.* 1. 111, *Pyth.* 4. 76); it is not then altogether expected of τέμενοˌc, and might even refer to another noun. On the meaning of the word cf. Gerber (1982), 167–8; Braswell (1988), 170–1; Broger (1996), 182. It occurs too at Simon. 519 fr. 4. 4.

3. ξῦˌνον: predicative, and emphatically placed. It is not likely to refer to all three gods rather than the Lesbians if the other gods have not yet been named (note 4).

βώμοιϲ: for the creation of an altar (and temenos) as a significant event cf. Bacch. 11. 40–2, 110–12, Pind. *Pyth.* 4. 204 -6, fr. 140 a. 62–5; epigr. ap. [Dem.] 7. 40.

4. ἀθα‚νάτων‚ μακά‚ρων: the gods appear, in a grandiose expression, in what seems to be a climactic part of the stanza. Cf. Hes. *WD* 706 (but spurious?), *Sc.* 79, Theogn. 759.

5. κὰ‚πωνύ‚μαϲϲ‚αν: naming frames the stanza. The stately narrative dwells on the conferring of titles in the past, as if intent on cult and history; it is not a direct litany or ritual act itself. The majesty of the place is created for listeners as if it were new to them; the description of the grove in Sapph. 2, though far more physical, is in this respect akin. But here a kind of tension is produced as the listener waits for the application.

ἀντί‚αον: probably the same title in Sapph. 17. 9. For the meaning assigned by the gloss, cf. the glosses at Aesch. fr. 223 Radt (Hesych. α 5307), Σ Hom. *Il.* 22. 113; note Hom. *Od.* 6. 193, with Garvie (1994), 131–2. But ἀντιάω has other and earlier meanings used of gods. In either case, the title probably bears direct significance here (note 9–11).

‚Δ‚ία: placed next to the emphatic ϲέ, at the junction of lines. The order is notable: although Hera (we may assume) is addressed, and receives the most lavish adornment, she comes after Zeus. Contrast Sapph. 17. 9–10. The order, stressed by τέρ‚το‚ν, is likely to be hierarchical. The shrine might seem to be primarily Hera's, and the goddess to be particularly singled out, but she also takes her place in a divine order based on family. The form of 5–9 conveys a rich and organized religious picture, while also building up a growing tricolon for rhetorical climax.

The religious trio might have old roots: cf. Burkert (1977), 84 (I. 3. 6), n. 10; but gods can also be added to sanctuaries. At all events, what we might imagine as an excitingly primordial trinity would not have appeared in exactly such a light to Alcaeus.

6. Α‚ἰολήιαν‚: a large national unity is suggested, with significance for this context. All that follows in the clause is probably additional glorification rather than more actual titles.

κυδα‚λίμα‚ν: the word is often used in epic of humans (Hom. *Il.* 4. 100 etc.), not of gods; it does not appear elsewhere in elegy, iambic, or lyric. Presumably it has a grandiose resonance.

7. πά‚ν‚των γενέθλαν: Burkert attractively makes πά‚ν‚των mean 'all the Aeolians' ((1985*a*), 401 n. 30, contrast (1977), 211 n. 30). This would be difficult linguistically unless *Α̣ἰολήιαν̣* meant 'of the Aeolians' not 'of Aeolus'. The former seems more natural both in content and in spelling (*ηι* not *η*); the contraction does not seem too extraordinary (cf. Hamm (1958), 29–31, 57–8; Forssman (1975), 18, 25–6). The conception is more relevant to the title, since *πά̣ν̣τ̣ων γενέθλαν* is unlikely to be a title itself. It also seems easier to accommodate into a strophe where Hera looks like Zeus' wife than the notion of her as mother of all. The idea of Hera as originator of a mortal line is surprising, and does not accord with the Hesiodic *Catalogue* (fr. 9 Merkelbach–West; West (1985), 56–7); but it is certainly no more surprising than the idea of her as universal mother. (*Orph. Hymn.* 16. 4 *παντογένεθλε* no doubt derives from this passage; its own conceptions use the Stoic notion of Hera as air.) If this more remarkable conception is Alcaeus', we must suppose that it derives from local tradition about this important goddess; we would perhaps note that even in Homer Hera is the oldest of Cronos' children (*Il.* 4. 59).

8. If *τόνδε* is correct, the word again stresses the immediacy of the setting; it links up with *τόδε* in 1. The demonstrative suggests a quasi-dramatic reference to a statue (cf. Aesch. *Supp.* 217, 220). This hardly makes sense as literal communication by the singer, to comrades or to Hera.

Dionysus appears frequently in Lesbian cult, even in our late epigraphic evidence (*IG* xii/2. 70. 7 (this spelling) etc.). *ὠμήςτ̣αν* is plainly a cult-title (see below); the obscure *κεμήλιον*, if sound, may well be one too. (Not Mycenaean: see Aura Jorro (1985), i. 342.) If so, the pattern seems somewhat strange: not so much the order itself (for proper names may be set in unusual places), as the appearance here of two titles rather than one. The second clearly has point in the context; the first might perhaps serve as support for it, like the elaboration in 6–7.

9. The sentence flows over into the new stanza, unusually. Among other things, the enjambment enhances the magnificence and abundance of the preceding stanza, and intensifies the effect of the sudden request that follows. The title also suggests more ominous powers than *πά̣ν̣των γενέθλαν*. In meaning, myth, or less probably practice, the title would appear to have connections with human sacrifice, a notion which would no doubt appeal (metaphorically)

to the narrator. Cf. P. Oxy. 3711 fr. 1 ii. 17–27, Dosiad. *FGrHist*
458 F 7, Phaen. Hist. fr. 25 Wehrli; Henrichs (1981), 208–24. Even
if connected purely to supposed ritual omophagy, the title would
be grim (cf. P. Oxy. 3711. 27–30; Eur. *Bacch.* 139, *Cret.* fr. 472. 12
Kannicht; Henrichs (1978), 150–2). The poetic usage of ὠμηϲτήϲ
will also affect hearers of a poem. Like ὠμοφάγοc, the word is used
mostly of fierce creatures and monsters (e.g. Hom. *Il.* 11. 454, Hes.
Theog. 300, Bacch. 13. 46–7, oracle ap. Hdt. 5. 92 β 3), once of
Achilles as inhuman (Hom. *Il.* 24. 207). All this sinister suggestion
will gain full point from what ensues.

ἄ‚γ‚[ι]‚τ̓: no ἀλλ' first, as in 38 a. 4, 10, 208 a. 3, Sapph. 43. 8. The
asyndeton is immensely forceful; the poem moves abruptly from
narrative to calling on all three gods.

εὔνοο‚ν: a contrast will appear in 13–14. The word appears first in
Theog. 641, then in Aesch. *Pers.* 226 etc., not in other lyric poetry.

10. ἀμμετ‚έρα[c]: first-person plurals for singulars are no doubt
possible in Lesbian poetry, cf. probably 362. 4, Sapph. 121. 1, 150.
2; ch. 4 n. 8; but we can hardly dissociate this first person from
those in 13 (17, 19) and 24. The narrator speaks as representative
of a group; the poem becomes, for the moment, itself an ἄρα, within
its own fiction or half-fiction of address.

11–12. ἀκούϲατ̓: the act of 'hearing', so crucial in prayer, and the
imperative, end the clause and begin the line (cf. Sapph. 1 [4].
7 ἔκ‚λυεc). The word forms a pattern with the second imperative,
which ends the next line, and again ends the clause.

τῶ‚ν‚δ‚ε: the demonstrative picks up those in 1 and 8 (?), even as
the place is connected with the situation of the band (it is a place
of exile as well as a source of divine aid). The concern of the poem
will now gradually move onto them. Within the poem, the τῶ‚ν‚δ‚ε
μό‚χθων is potently inexplicit; the next phrase spells it out.

ἀργαλέαc probably comments on exile as such, rather than this
particularly grievous exile. Cf. Tyrt. fr. 11. 8 West (Hom. *Il.* 11.
278, Stes. S22. 4), Sol. fr. 4. 38 West, *al.* Emphasis is thrown onto
the word φύγαc, and the phrase advances on τῶ‚ν‚δ‚ε and μό‚χθων.
But here one forcefully placed epithet does what 130 b [9] spends
much of the poem on.

φύγαc: poets do not often use the noun in this sense before the
fifth century (Theogn. 209 = 332b; not Bacchylides or Pindar). It is
not plural here (a slip in LSJ *Supp.*).

12. ϲ[: probably ϲ[άωτε (Lobel). The corrections to the original text usually improve it (corrections above the line are sometimes placed between dots). Line 20 (same point in the stanza) provides an obvious source of corruption; the corruption was not necessarily initiated by the scribe of this papyrus. The construction is unexceptionable (cf. e.g. Soph. *El.* 1356); for exile etc. cf. e.g. Eur. *Med.* 360 ϲωτῆρα κακῶν.

13. The poem turns with dramatic power from help to harm.

τὸν Ὕρραον δὲ παῖδα⌋: the designation is dignified, as befits the moment (cf. e.g. 42. 5, 298 [**10**]. 8). Pittacus' plain name is used at 70. 13, 170. ii. 4, 348. 2, his father's, probably, at 298. 47. The dignity of expression is compatible with a lofty scorn for Pittacus' parentage, within the world of the poems (cf. 469, and κακοπατρίδαν 348. 1, etc.).

πεδελθ⌊έτω: the poem is moving away from direct prayer and from the three divinities. The poem does not make it apparent that the original oath was sworn at this shrine, or by these gods; it would probably have brought out the point, were that the case. Even so, it would have been possible to ask these gods to punish Pittacus (cf. 306 g. 8–12, Zeus to regard Pittacus' perjury); or to send an Erinys. The verb is alarmingly concrete.

14. κήνων: not dead comrades (not previously referred to, and probably not referred to later); not the gods (too abrupt, and not adequately defended by Soph. *Ant.* 1075). Rather, as Mazzarino (1943), 65 n. 1, genitive of the crime to be punished, etc., cf. Kühner–Gerth (1898–1904), i. 380–1, Soph. *Ant.* 1074; it is taken up by the ὼϲ, which now acquires a very satisfactory function. For the plural cf. e.g. Hom. *Od.* 11. 418, 24. 90.

Ἐρ[ίνν]υϲ: the name is forcefully kept until last in its clause. She is the proper god to punish perjury (Hom. *Il.* 19. 259–60, Hes. *WD* 803–4); the wish is intended to sound entirely just. The narrator is not actually calling on the Erinys, in the dark act of an injured parent.

πο⌊τ᾽: the narrative is placed at a distance in the past.

15. τόμοντεϲ: although there seems no specific connection with 1–9 in deities or sanctuary, the atmosphere of religious solemnity carries over from the earlier narrative into this.

ἄ⌊.φ: the bottom of φ is perhaps visible as well as the top.

16. A forceful last 'line': cf. *metre* above. As Deubner felt ((1943),

11–12), the missing infinitive is much more likely to have governed the accusative than to have been governed by it. The emphatic negatives and the designation ἐταίρων bring out Pittacus' act of treachery to the group; group and oath are to stand in flagrant conflict with the fact of the exile and the division now between the exiles and Pittacus. 'We' then included him. ἔταιροι elsewhere in Alcaeus only 150. 4 (cf. Hippon. fr. 115. 16 West; often with πιϲτόϲ in Theognis).

17–20. A whole stanza encapsulates the heroic ethos of the conspirators. The two halves juxtapose the alternatives of being killed and killing, with θάνοντεϲ and κακκτάνοντεϲ both beginning their clauses. The order one would expect is 'to succeed or die' (cf. Aesch. *Th.* 46–8, Hdt. 3. 73. 1, Ephor. *FGrHist* 70 F 216); Alcaeus puts death first, and elaborates it in what follows. This both stresses the group's self-less valour and allows the part of the oath that Pittacus has violated to come next to his breach of it. And the political purpose in fact comes more effectively as an achieved climax than it would have done at the start.

ὐπ᾽ is probably governed by θανόντεϲ; the metaphor of lying prostrate after a defeat at wrestling would be confusing and bathetic.

κείϲεϲθ᾽ gives force to what would otherwise be a more ordinary metaphor in γᾶν ἐπιεμμέγοι (note Hom. *Il.* 3. 57). The concrete actuality of death is and was confronted. Cf. also 296. 4–5.

ἄνδρων: even if this is not alluding to Myrsilus, the absence of proper names contrasts with 28, when the poem has become less exalted.

δᾶμον κτλ.: a ringing 'line'. However selfish Alcaeus really was, we should not deny the idealism of the self-presentation. (Cf. Osborne (1996), 192.) As elsewhere, the poems are concerned with harm allegedly done to the whole city, not merely to Alcaeus' party: cf. 70. 6, 12 (δᾶμον), 348 (and note also 6. 16, 74, 112. 10, 141. 4, 426); Theogn. 43, 50–2 (note δημοϲίωι), and the closely related Sol. fr. 4. 1–6, 16–20, 26 West. What we regard as opposed political tendencies express kindred ideals.

ὐπὲξ ἀχέων ῥύεϲθαι: one can scarcely fail to connect with 11–12, whatever the verb of saving. (On the usual view the same verb ends the two stanzas.) It is a poignant touch that those who are now (τῶ͜ν͜δ͜ε) begging for deliverance were then seeking to bring deliverance to the city themselves.

It is notable for the range of Alcaeus' language that he constructs ῥύεϲθαι in 34. 7 with a bare ablative genitive, here with an unusual preposition (outside epic only once in Herodotus, 3. 116. 1).

21. The poem continues with narrative; the prayer is in abeyance. In the next stanza too we have a statement (οὐ) and a perfect indicative (27); it is a possibility that the final stanza returned to prayer.

What has Pittacus done? Something: the breaking of the oath was not a concern of this poem alone, cf. 306 g (and 167. 1?). From the narrator's perspective, he has not kept faith with his comrades (cf. 16; no doubt they were quarrelsome, cf. 70. 9–12); however, 23–4 emphasize a more public aspect. Pittacus is now 'rending, destroying' the city (we cannot have a historic present in lyric). He is not doing so in company with those he originally swore to kill; τότ' 18 implies their time of power has passed (whatever the supplement), and ποͅτ'implies the oath was sworn long ago. Was his crime to make league with the villains? Support for that notion is found in 70. 7. However, the sequence in 21–5, 'he did not consider this but rather having trampled on the oaths he is rending the city', seems to depict the perjury not as the alliance with enemies but as the present treatment of the city. A lesser point: if Pittacus' crime was to desert to those he swore to slay, how are the others seen to keep their oath? They are still alive, but the hypothesis suggests the conspiracy did not succeed. A delayed success would not only require elaborate stories but cut off the desertion from the destruction, which gives even less credible rhetoric.

From the perspective of the poem, to swear to rescue the city and then to ruin it is a monstrous breach of faith. But Pittacus would deny that he was ruining the city. The passage appears to offer an effective (and possibly sincere) organization of the past into a moral shape rather than an undisputed violation of aristocratic ethics by Pittacus. The point is of considerable interest for Alcaeus' techniques.

κήνων: the word takes up κήνων in 14, and presents a picture of action that contrasts with the action of the oath. It is also a common device in Alcaeus for taking up previous stanzas and moving in another direction: cf. 58. 25 ταῦτα, 72. 7 τούτων, 73. 7–8, 338. 5 τὸν χείμων'; 140. 14 τῶν. The first clause is a variation of the Homeric ἀλλὰ τίη μοι ταῦτα φίλοϲ διελέξατο θυμόϲ; (*Il.* 11. 407 etc.). The genitive might be like that with verbs of heeding (Lobel), or might rather be continuing the metaphor: he did not converse about these things to his heart (*Od.* 11. 174; 4. 114, etc.). The Homeric dismissal is turned to the negative, and sounds extremely casual.

ὁ φύσγων, deliberately out of keeping with the earlier prayer, contrasts with the appellation in 13. It derives from φύσκη 'pudding'; for the rude -ων cf. γάστρων 429, cτίγων, πέδων Ar. frr. 99, 871 Kassel–Austin. The vigorous insult (cf. 429) lasts only a moment; the emphasis is on graver things (otherwise 72. 7–10, which in my view speak of Pittacus' own wild habits). But it serves to initiate a picture set against the religious scene before: the slobbish Pittacus, quite blasé about perjury (note βραιδίωc). The language grows in intensity, and Pittacus in menace, as the stanza proceeds. As in oratory, the contemptible and the terrible can be combined.

On Alcaeus' insults see Davies (1985).

22–4. The line 22 perhaps sets πόcιν with rough bathos against θῦμον: not reflection but contemptuous action.

πόcιν | ἔ]μβαιc: the image for violating oaths is made forceful; it is not particularly inventive in itself, as suits the ethos of this poem. Cf. Hom. *Il.* 4. 157, Hippon. fr. 115. 15 West; Soph. fr. 683. 2–3 Radt, etc. Perjury is a recurring danger in the world of the *Theognidea*, cf. Theogn. 200, 284, etc.

δάπτει: Alcaeus does not use the verb of Pittacus just in this passage: see 70. 8. The primary emphasis of the verb in metaphor seems to be on damaging (by tearing apart), more than on either dividing or eating (cf. e.g. Hom. *Od.* 16. 90; Pind. *Nem.* 8. 23). The word is probably a more colourful version of the φθείρω at Theogn. 45, Sol. 4. 5; it is the opposite of ῥύεcθαι 20.

τὰν πόλιν: takes up δᾶμον from the same point in the previous stanza, and marks the violation and reversal.

ἄμμι: the 'we' of the conspirators is now taken up in the 'we' of the Mytileneans. The dative is probably possessive, cf. 66. 8; 362. 4 (wrongly suspected by Lobel–Page), Sapph. 1 [4]. 26.

]ε͘ίπαιc: the participle εἴπαιc would be surprising but not impossible. Weak forms are found early elsewhere: so Pind. *Ol.* 8. 46 εἴπαιc; 6 [18]. 92, *Nem.* 9. 33, Sol. fr. 34. 6 West, *SEG* 32 (for 1982), no. 908. 1 (Phaestus, second half vi). Cf. Schwyzer (1953–71), i. 745; Sihler (1995), 563; Braswell (1998), 108 (on Homer cf. West (1998–), i, p. xxx). But if the infinitive had been written originally, one would have expected εἶ. It would be very unclear how to accommodate δέδ[(a neuter accusative participle?). παῖc (=πᾶc) is excluded by the accent on εἰ.

25. οὐ κὰν νόμον: the absence of a particle is of interest, in view of the variants in 24. The conventions which Pittacus is defying are likely to transcend the state's politics (cf. Ostwald (1969), pt. 1, ch. 2; note κὰν νόμον 35. 1 and e.g. Pind. *Ol.* 8. 78); but the use remains interesting. One may contrast the ancient tradition created by the Lesbians (1–9).

27. γλαύκαc . . . Ἀθανάαc appears at Theocr. 28. 1, perhaps an ostentatious borrowing from this poem. Cf. Eur. *Hcld.* 754. The relevance of the goddess here would be obscure to us (Athens?).

28. We do not know what was said about Myrsilus here; we do not know whether the ἄνδρων in 18 includes him; we do not know if Myrsilus perished at the hands of Alcaeus' group (332 does not make it clear).

We would need the final stanza to interpret the shaping of the whole poem. Yet whatever happened at the end, the poem moves outside prayer, the second person, the present place; it is not static or uniform. And yet its parts relate. There are three narrative sections, 1–9, 13–20, 21–? (κήνων 21 marks 13–20 as at least a narrative within a narrative). The last two such sections (swearing, perjury) are connected in time and causality; both issue in a present imperfective situation which needs to be resolved: 'our' exile, Pittacus' savagery. The first two (cult, swearing) are connected in solemnity and unity; the third forms a brutal contrast. The prayer provides a present moment, which draws all the elements together, and desires a future that would end the plot and satisfy morality. Divine power may overturn mere political power; in any case cosmic, Lesbian, and moral order shows up the wrongful dominance of Pittacus. For the past is no less a concern of the poem than the future; the poem imposes on events a decisive moral pattern.

9: fr. 130 b Voigt (130. 16–39 Lobel–Page)

For introduction to the poem, see on 129 [8] above.

Metre

1. xx-⏑⏑--⏑⏑-⏑-
2. xx-⏑⏑--⏑⏑-⏑-
3. xx-⏑⏑-⏑--
4. x-⏑⏑--⏑⏑-⏑-

This elegant stanza has the form AABA'. Line 3, though starting in the same way as 1–2, presents a quite different colon, with no expansion of the choriambic core and with a pendant ending. Line 4 recurs to the form of 1–2, save in the one point where 3 had matched them, their disyllabic 'aeolic base' at the start. For the monosyllabic base, cf. e.g. 303 A a (perhaps Sappho), Sapph. 154, and esp. Sapph. 58, 81, etc. There is hiatus after 2 at 18 = 33; elision is not inconceivable at 15 = 30. The distinctness of 3 as a unit if not a line seems to be exploited in 7 = 22. Maas and Pfeiffer both thought of making 3 glyconic, and giving its last syllable to 4 (letter of Pfeiffer to Lobel, 25 Dec. (!) 1941). This unnecessary idea, which is discouraged by the word-end, was partly prompted by the mistaken assumption that 130 a and b were one poem. Dale (1957), 1–2, also favours it, to avoid pause between the third and fourth lines, 'on the analogy of other Lesbian stanzas' (not a strong argument; and what is a line?). Cf. Parker (1970), 90.[7]

1 = 16. The opening as given here is due to Burzacchini (1976). On this reading, Hor. *Odes* 1. 22 would derive its initial *integer uitae* from this beginning (and ultimately its theme from that of exile). Horace's moralizing view of the passage would be misguided. At this date, and without explanation, ἀγνός used of an ordinary male should denote a freedom from ritual pollution, not general moral innocence (cf. Parker (1983), 147–51). In Euripidean passages where the stem is extended to non-ritual morality, the audacious transference is made explicit (*Hipp.* 316–17, *Or.* 1604, *al.*); Soph. *OT* 864 presents an unusual blend of ritual, religion, and general morality. For Aesch. *Supp.* 226, 228 cf. 223; on *Hipp.* 11, if sound, see Barrett (1964), 157. The word should relate rather to the sanctity of Alcaeus' dwelling, and thus, perhaps with ironic congratulation, of himself or his way of life.

This approach seems superior to its rivals. It appears desperate to take refuge in a chaste-tree, even in the company of Lobel. But the correction or variant above the first letter must raise uncertainty. Rösler's ἄλγεινον ((1980), 277 n. 384) does not fit the data in the

---

[7] In his rather charming letter of notes on *P. Oxy.* vol. xviii Pfeiffer writes 'I am sure, there is still room in your waste-paper-basket.' The letter contains no further points on the Alcaeus not published later or by others.

papyrus (cf. Burzacchini (1985), 375); at the very least, however, some alternative reading was known. Even if ἄγνος were correct, the word after βιότοις remains a problem. τοὶς would cause syntactical difficulties if 1 = 16 is, as it must be, the start of the poem. The only possibility would be to put a comma after β[ό]λλας, and make from ἄγνος to ἐςχατίαις᾽ (or φεύγων) one large and implausibly complicated sentence. The accusative of respect τοὶς βιότοις would be unusual (Aesch. *Pers.* 615 is different); but it might be defended by the analogy of the later τοὺς τρόπους, τὸ ἦθος, etc. (cf. e.g. Eur. *Supp.* 187, Ar. *Knights* 1289, *Eccl.* 214, Plat. *Rep.* 535 B 1–2). παῖς (Gallavotti, cf. Burzacchini (1985), 376) is unpromising. One might possibly contemplate τλαῖς (compare τάλαις for the spacing). This would make sense of the markings above the line, and give something to govern βιότοις. It would then become desirable to return to the original reading ἄγνοις; cf. e.g. Eur. *Cret.* fr. 472. 9 Kannicht ἀγνὸν δὲ βίον τείνων, Soph. *El.* 599, Ar. *Wasps* 506. Horace would have to be paraphrasing more loosely, or following a false variant. But neither the article nor the tense would be altogether satisfactory (the aorist would have to mark a moment of acceptance). The line remains enigmatic.

ὁ τάλαις ἔγω: the narrator's self is given prominence at the opening; the emphasis highlights his isolation. With the article, the form suggests not a cry of woe but a more restrained, though vehement, self-pity (cf. esp. Soph. *Aj.* 600, and also *Phil.* 359, Ar. *Thesm.* 925; contrast e.g. Ar. *Lys.* 735; *Clouds* 698; Men. *Sam.* 532; Theogn. 1107). One may note the difference both from the impassioned female opening of Alc. 10 and from Sappho's linguistic restraint in displaying emotion.

2 = 17. ζώω: the poem depicts a prolonged imperfective situation, which awaits resolution.

ἀγροϊωτίκαν falls with disgust; it is helped by its length, its position, and its separation from μοῖραν, to which the listener at first attaches a grander sense. The suffix suggests revulsion from a class (cf. Hamm (1958), 73; note Hom. *Od.* 21. 85). We see a related horror at the unsophisticated country in Alcm. 16, Sapph. 57, Theogn. 54–6; one thinks of late Republican Rome.

3–4 = 18–19. The lines show one place being intensely imagined from another. One participial clause hangs expressively on another:

'when what I really want . . .'. The verb expressively conveys a continuous and unhappy state.

ἀγόρας and β[ό]λλας are shaped in a ring: this gives stress to these institutions of the city. (Perhaps the contrast between ἀγόρας and ἀγροϊωτίκαν is sharpened by the resemblance in sound.) The combination of ἀγορά and βουλή is at this period like a fixed form within which various arrangements could be developed (we should not be too quick to label them). It appears to be still in force, despite the domination of whoever has ousted Alcaeus. Cf. ML 8; *Schwyzer* 410. 6–8, etc.; on consitutions at this period, note Robinson (1997).

It is of some historical or literary interest that later exile poetry dwells relatively infrequently on the loss of political rights.

ἄκουσαι: the narrator's longing is graphically made to be, not for the general state of participation in the institutions, but for a single moment (aorist) of hearing them convoked. One may compare the monologue at the start of the *Acharnians*; there the particulars of beginning the assembly (in which only Dicaeopolis is interested) are used to express wider longings. Cf. also Alcm. 3 [2]. 1–9, again an encapsulation of enthusiasm.

ὦ Ἀγεσιλαΐδα: like Aesimidas (365), this is just as likely to be a patronymic (despite *LGPN* i (1987), 6); neither seems to occur as a name elsewhere. Cf. Theogn. 25 etc. Relatively little is made within the poem of the relationship with the addressee, or the fact of the address (contrast e.g. 38 a, 305 a. 15–31, 335, 428, Archil. frr. 105, 168 West; cf. Archil. fr. 13, 196; note perhaps Alc. 306 c. 5–8, cf. Σ to 60. 3). However, the address is given some weight by its position before the pause at the end of the stanza; it also matches the designation of the narrator at the end of the first line in the stanza, and is perhaps forcefully placed amid a vain wish to hear a summons. The fiction of personal communication in the poem is set against both the isolation which the narrator depicts and the public contact from which he is debarred.

5 = 20. καὶ β[ό]λλας is particularly stressed by its combined position at the beginning of the stanza and the end of the sentence (or possibly clause). Membership of it was no doubt a sign of higher standing than membership of the assembly; the loss is the more deplored and deplorable. After this enjambment, the second stanza presents, not the narrator's present situation, but the more general outrage of what has been done to him, seen in a large perspective of

time. Mytilene is now more to the foreground of the writing than
the place of exile.

τὰ is much more easily referred forward to τούτων than backwards.
This means (probably) an asyndeton here, both explanatory and
angry. Lobel takes the word of possessions rather than rights or
privileges, and so Page ((1955), 174); but that view accounts less
well for the asyndeton and especially for πεδά.

Whether or not Alcaeus would have used πάππος in a poem,
the use of πάτερος rather than κήνω (contrast Isae. 8. 32) creates
a potent rhetoric and the sense of a long chain rudely broken.
The passage rather suggests that Alcaeus' family had always been
members of the boule: this is not only an insistence on citizenship.
The importance of family in Alcaeus' expressed values would be
hard to overstate (cf. e.g. 6. 14, 67. 4, 72. 11–13). There is also an
emphasis on rights here, which carries political significance beyond
the individual narrator.

6–7 = 21–2. ἔχοντες: though the word is common, there looks to be
a contrast with the participle at the same point in line and stanza
at 2 = 17: he now has a rustic's lot, they retain city honours to their
old age. (The perfect suggests that the father at least is still alive.)

πεδὰ κτλ.: the narrator's vexation spills into the clause which
should describe only his elders' happy state. The effect is not to
alienate, but to engage the listener (or reader) in this lively indig-
nation. In the quasi-deictic τωνδέων the indignation for a moment
almost annihilates the very exile, with an animated gesture.

7 = 22: a striking line, marked out by the metre. The epithet is long,
paradoxical, and unusual (cf. Broger (1996), 189–90, and Sapph.
96 [7]. 7–8 n.). For all his wrath, the narrator does not curse, but
dwells with despair and vision on the discords of his people. Re-
lated comment is found 70. 12, 348. 2. The line is relevant to the
narrator's stance on strife later in the poem.

8 = 23: the last line of the stanza takes up the first, and the opening of
the sentence. The first-person pronoun, which falls weightily at the
start, is opposed to two people there; the demonstrative matches
the relative in a forceful structure; there is also a more oblique
connection between πεδά and ἀπύ. A strong verb closes; it indicates
the fateful action, but brings us back to the present.

9–12 = 24–7. This stanza returns to the narrator's place of exile. But
it does not depict a state; it presents a narrative of his original act,

in choosing a place and resigning himself to exile. The narrator is seen as an agent, not only a victim, and his action is commented on. The movement is marked by the recurrence of φεύγων in 11 = 26 after 9 = 24 (hardly carelessness); it comes again at the beginning of the line, but has a different force.

One might wonder if in 9 = 24 a small error had entered the text before the time of the two papyri. Now that we have Π², ἐοίκηca whether transitive or intransitive needs a word of place to go with (cf. Haslam (1986), 124); λυκαιχμίαιc, by virtue of its second element, now looks unlikely to perform that function. And φεύγων ἐcχατίαιc' itself is not wholly satisfactory. One can flee in exile to a place (e.g. Xen. *Mem.* 1. 2. 24); but I have not found any instances of φεύγω, 'I am an exile', with a locative. If one were to consider reading φεύγων. ἐcχατίαιc δ' ὡc, the ignominious φεύγων would be no pointless addition: cf. Soph. *OC* 1292 γῆc ἐκ πατρώιαc ἐξελήλαμαι φυγάc, *al.*

ἐcχατίαιc': probably denoting the region as wild and unurban, rather than an enormous distance from Mytilene. Cf. esp. Lewis (1997a), 291–3. We do not know where the place was (cf. Robert (1969), 801–31; Quinn (1961); Picard (1962)). Presentation of the scene of exile as a wilderness is common in later writing on exile, in prose and verse; less so the twists to come.

The narrator colourfully compares himself to a non-mythological figure. We now know Onomacles to be an Athenian; since the commentary on these lines begins by mentioning Aenus, which concerned Mytilene and Alcaeus, it is probable that he was involved in Athenian fighting with Mytilene (cf. Huxley (1987)). The commentator includes φεύγων τὸν πόλεμον in his lemma (paraphrase is much less likely). The narrator is comparing himself with a well-known enemy of Mytilene, as the ethnic brings out; since the stress is on action, this is likely to suggest a touch of grim, and winning, humour against himself, rather than complaint at his treatment.

ἐοίκηca: the single moment is set against the earlier and later depiction of his life and dwelling, cf. ζώω 2 = 17, οἴκημ⟨μ⟩ι 16 = 31.

λυκαιχμίαιc: the case is not likely to be accusative, in view of -αιχμ-. Such an ending for a dative would be most unusual; even the instance in 15 = 30 below, the most promising example in Alcaeus, is not secure. This disadvantage outweighs the attractions of a straightforward formation in -αιχμία. Stylistically, a dative seems to produce an awkwardly dense sentence, especially with the transmitted text of 9 = 24. A nominative, then, seems the most plausible case; Hesychius' entry takes it as such. A masculine in -ίας is possible enough; the compound is more unexpected (cf. μη-τραλοίας, and Cratinus' φιλοπραγματίας, fr. 382 Kassel–Austin). One might have to suppose that so unperspicuous a word is not being coined now by Alcaeus. If nominative, the word would be in apposition with Onomacles or the narrator or both; perhaps most likely with the narrator, but an interlaced order is more acceptable with proper names. Whether the word justifies the original flight or depicts the present solitude we are hardly in a position to say (-αιχμ- might favour the former). In view of 16 = 31, it is unlikely to describe guerrilla warfare.

11 = 26. The commentary is likely to be giving the actual text here rather than paraphrasing (note the continued indentation). The words must refer to the narrator. Is he avoiding ordinary modes of warfare, but continuing guerrilla warfare (Lefkowitz and Lloyd-Jones (1990)), or simply abandoning fighting? Life is not helped by the irregular metre in 12 = 27, which is generally (and rightly) taken as a sign of corruption. The shifting of the choriamb in Sapph. 96 [7]. 7 is a quite different matter. It is not apparent that an opposition between πόλεμος and cτάcιc could convey an opposition between modes of warfare rather than between types of enemy (clearly not at e.g. Sol. fr. 4. 19 West, where note 21–2). There would be little difficulty, on the other hand, in making them denote the same thing; one notes the loose use of πόλεμος in 305. 15, cf. 305. 10. Furthermore, cτάcιc when applied to fighting is a word of intensely negative connotations (Bacch. fr. 24. 3, Pind. *Pae.* 9 (A1). 15, fr. 109. 3–4, Isocr. *Pan.* 114, 259, etc.). It is hard to see Alcaeus using it in commending the continuation of hostilities; all the more so after 7 = 22. Finally, the narrator depicts himself as keeping clear of trouble (16 = 31); and he seems to be fixed to his sanctuary in a remote spot. It does not sound as if he is engaging in solo guerrilla warfare. ἀναιρέω active seems to mean 'remove, destroy', not 'take up'; but what precedes it seems on metrical grounds to be corrupt. If it is not, or if the original sense was the same, I would prefer to read the clause as a question (cf. Plat. *Phil.* 23 A 6–8); for lively questions in Alcaeus cf. 72. 11–13, *al.* For the punctuation cf. 22 = 37. The argument apart, 'not better' makes more natural sense with the question than with the statement; a quasi-epic use of οὐκ ἄμεινον seems less appealing outside a self-contained οὐ γὰρ ἄμεινον (Hes. *WD* 750, Hdt. 1. 187. 2, etc.). ὀννέλην does not seem the right word for the sense 'give up', as a statement would require; it should denote an action more general in its effect. The narrator may even be claiming that his apparent cowardice is for the public good; one thinks of Cicero. But such a stance would not, of course, be a promise to abstain from violence for ever.

Problematic as the passage is, we can still discern colour and complexity in the narrator's handling of himself, but not real self-subversion. Particularly striking is φεύγων, τὸν, πόλεμον; the phrase is made to look like self-condemnation, but is in fact redeemed. In 428 the narrator may have gone further.

13–16 = 28–31. The stanza begins with more narrative, and ends up with the present situation. Probably 15 = 30 goes with 16 = 31 in time (cf. cυνόδοιcι with 17–20 = 32–5, and also the absence of a particle in 15 = 30). ἐπίβαιc plainly denotes an act prior to the present state of dwelling; so does the verb of motion required by ἐc. In 14 = 29, ἐοίκης[α] μελαίνας fits the space perfectly, and the traces; the previous clause (13 = 28) would supply the designation of place (cf. Eubul. fr. 9. 1–2 Kassel–Austin). Now that we know φεύγων to have been repeated, we might suppose a deliberate sequence in ἐοίκηcα, ἐοίκηcα, οἴκημμι. In 14 = 29 and 16 = 31, as in 9 = 24 and 11 = 26, the words come at the start of cola in the same stanza. We may assume that in 10 = 25 the narrator is fixing his dwelling in the present rustic spot (2 = 17), not in some other place before his voyage to this one (14 = 29). Thus 14–15 = 29–30 do not mark a simple progression in time from the preceding stanza. They are probably going over the same event as in 9–10 = 24–5, but supplying in participles an account of preliminary actions. The emphasis now is on concrete detail. The scene also looks different from the desolate prospect of 9 = 24 and 2 = 17 (preparation of the new scene in 1 = 16 is uncertain). The listener now 'learns' specifically of the temple precincts where the narrator is installed, and is struck (within the poem) by the talk of meetings.

The final line of the stanza suggests a desirable safety attained by prudence, or imposed on rashness. The rest of the poem makes evident already the grim irony of the earthy phrase. It links up with the end of the preceding stanza, on strife and war, but also with the end of the previous two, where the narrator had been driven away, and lamented his exclusion in place. These connections only add to the artistic tension as the poem appears to take a surprising turn. Trumpf (1958), 71 n. 1, actually thinks the change in mood with 13 = 28 shows a different poem beginning there (cf. Hausmann ap. Latte (1968), 486 n. 4). The connection with 21 = 36 would make this difficult (what would the many misfortunes (?) be?); but the reaction is interesting.

Lines 13–14 = 28–9 deploy standard, dignified epithets rather than the colourful language and contemporary reference of the stanza before. The end of the stanza also contrasts with these lines, in a deliberately bathetic movement. For μελαίνας cf. Sapph. 1 [4]. 10 n.; for μακάρων, after epic, e.g. Alc. 5. 7, 117 b. 16, Sapph. 44 A a. 8, Sol. frr. 4. 2, 13. 3 West.

In 15 = 30 the difficulties of text are inextricable. The alteration shows corruption happening at some point; it is all too possible that the change did not suffice to restore the original text. αὔταις (seemingly a dative) is hard to make sense of; to suppose that it means the narrator's life is so miserable he enjoys even the womanish festivals would produce strained writing and an unconvincing meaning (cf. Rösler (1980), 282–3). The form of the dative (short) is a further cause for suspicion; this might, however, be avoided if there were synapheia between the third and fourth lines. (Cf. Gallavotti (1942), 176; the third 'line' of the alcaic stanza provides a parallel for the usual word-end.) Different endings for αὐτ- can be readily imagined; but which it is might depend on the role of the equally surprising μ'. Page wonders if μ is an error for ν; δ (δ' for τ') would be another possibility, since it is hard to see where else a connecting particle might come (a [δ]ή before cυνόδοιcι would probably not be connective, cf. Simon. 543 [16]. 25–7 n.).

cυνόδοιcι: before the second half of the fifth century the word comes in poetry only at Sol. fr. 4. 22 West, Emped. fr. 8. 4 Wright.

κάκων κτλ.: one cannot be certain that a 'proverb' on keeping one's foot out of mud predated and inspired Alcaeus' phrase, or Aeschylus' (*Ch.* 697). One cannot even be certain that such phrases were a current colloquialism in Mytilene: they were not in Athens, to judge from comedy or prose (contrast [Aesch.] *PV* 263–4, Eur. *Hcld.* 109, etc.). Cf. Barrett (1964), 398; Pind. *Ol.* 6 [18]. 8–9 n. But the pragmatic and unelevated quality of the expression is obvious.

17 = 32. The sentence runs on, unexpectedly. The idea of cυνόδοιcι

is given a specific incarnation, in a stanza that forms a highly dis-
tinctive entity. (It does not even look as if there was run-over into
the next.)

Is the narrator conveying pleasure at this beauty contest, or em-
phasizing his isolation from men (for him the only people that
count)? The present place has been acquiring substance, and is
now depicted in a scene which excels in vividness even the depic-
tion of the city meetings in 3–5 = 18–20. The actual sound is set
against the desired sound; the roar of noise fills the place (18 = 33).
It is not a rustic event, to the listener's surprise (within the poem).
This is a famous occurrence in the Lesbian year (cf. Theophr. fr.
564 Fortenbaugh; Σ Hom. *Il.* 9. 129–30), at least as populous as the
agora at Mytilene. ἐλκεσίπεπλοι evokes both the grand cities of epic
(Troy, Hom. *Il.* 6. 442 etc.; Thebes, Hes. fr. 193. 2 Merkelbach–
West) and the elegant deportment of city women (Sapph. 57. 3).
The epic epithet itself, placed at the end of the sentence, is not
found elsewhere in lyric, elegy, iambus, and must primarily en-
hance the dignity of the passage (there is no indication of satire,
and even a light mockery seems hard to substantiate). The descrip-
tion of the cry, adorned with solemn epithets, strongly recalls to
modern readers the description in Sapph. 44. Actual evocation of
Sapphic, or female Mytilenean, poetry is by no means to be ruled
out (cf. perhaps 42 and 283); but the Sappho itself is recalling epic
language in a mythological poem. What roles does the animated
and high-flown passage perform within the poem?

On the one hand, the passage has an obvious attractiveness. The
poet's skill and sympathy in depicting the festival lead one to think,
on the surface of one's mind, that the narrator is bound to delight in
it. His sex might seem anything but an obstacle to enjoyment of the
female καλλιστεία; and the stanza leads on to more solemn sources
of pleasure. The apparent emphasis on his safety encourages this
positive line of thought. This then gives rhetorical power to his
abrupt call for deliverance in 21–2 = 36–7; what does all this beauty
matter to him, deprived of his city? He is not really outside κάκων
but immersed in woes.

On the other hand, the passage itself creates a poignant impres-
sion. Not because women are of no account; but because their festi-
val presents an image of the community from which, in his own sex,
the narrator is shut out. Indeed, the women's ritual gathering brings
the whole of Lesbos harmoniously together; one may contrast the

strife and mutual ill will of the (male) Mytileneans. The narrator's exclusion from his own male community is mirrored by his separation from the women's counter-community here. The alien feminine is emphasized throughout: note the insertion of γυναίκων and the connotations of ὀ]λολύγας (a purely female ritual cry, Deubner (1943), 4–5 and (1941); Pulleyn (1997), 178–81); ἐλκεσίπεπλοι stresses femininity too. περὶ δὲ βρέμει almost puts one in mind of Hom. *Od*. 6. 122, where the cry of the girls at play surrounds the solitary male, ἀμφήλυθε θῆλυς ἀϋτή. For all the rhetorical force and the poignancy of the passage, a faint touch of humour lingers over the narrator's situation, as in the comparison with Onomacles.

ἄχω θεςπεςία: cf. Sapph. 44. 27 ἄχω θεςπεςία, and behind them Hom. *Il*. 13. 834, etc., ἠχῆι θεςπεςίηι. θεςπέςιος, common in epic, is not found elsewhere in elegy, iambus, or lyric before the fifth century; but it occurs several times in Pindar and Bacchylides (Pind. *Isth*. '3/4'. 57, etc.).

ἐνιαυςίας: the word itself comes already in epic (Hom. *Od*. 16. 454, Hes. *WD* 448); for a ritual solemnity of effect cf. e.g. Eur. *Erechth*. fr. 370. 78 Kannicht.

21–2 = 36–7. The narrator now confronts, not in sad longing, but in despairing interrogation, the end to his sorrows. As in 72. 11, the question enters with considerable brusqueness. θέοι probably takes up θέων in 13 = 28 (same position in the stanza). The gods are seen not as part of the narrator's strange sanctuary world, but as sources of deliverance.

The poem has built up the significance of the narrator's present situation, through depicting first that situation, then the past and present of his fathers, the immediate history of his exile, and a moment or tiny imperfective period (the annual festival) within the present situation itself. The poem has built it up too through elaborating the two places and their relation to each other: Mytilene as imagined now, as enjoyed by his family, as the scene of strife; the place of exile as rustic, desolate, as the focus of his choices, as a sort of refuge, and as the locale for an event surprisingly and painfully communal, refined, urban, and yet irrelevant. The narrator has depicted himself in many ways and with many tones, self-pitying, indignant, self-justifying, and not without touches of unlooked-for colour, and humour grim or dry. All now appears to gather in a fine and arresting climax; but we are robbed of the very end.

10: fr. 298 Voigt (*SLG* 262)[8]

The poem had at least 52 lines, and probably more: a scribe would probably not begin a poem with the last line of a column. (On the apparent ending of a poem with the first line at Sapph. 87 (1). 1 cf. Grenfell and Hunt (1922), 44.) Other known lengths of Lesbian poem are: Alc. 130 a: 15 lines; 130 b [9]: 24 (117 b: 40 at least if one poem); Sapph. 1 [4]: 28; 44: over 34, roughly 1½–2 columns; 62: 12; 63: 10. The length of this poem, as of Sapph. 44, might be connected to its use of narrative; but we cannot be sure that this length was unusual.

The poem is connected with a political situation: Pittacus is referred to at 47, and the scholion at the bottom of col. i in Π¹ is obviously expounding the Mytilenean background. It is not clear whether Pittacus is the only target (1–3 n.), nor what he has done; the alleged perjury might be the object again, but the language in 1 does not make this especially probable. Most of the extant poem is concerned with the myth of the Lesser Ajax taking Cassandra by force from Athena's temple. The Achaeans' disastrous failure to slay the sinner (4–7) is the point of connection with the present. The text does not, however, show that the Greeks were actually thinking of punishing Ajax, and this cannot be assumed. At Eur. *Tro.* 71 the Greeks have taken no interest; nor do they seem to, for example, in Quintus Smyrnaeus (e.g. 14. 434–9). The account in the *Iliupersis* (p. 62 Davies), where according to Proclus a plan to stone Ajax is thwarted by his supplication at Athena's altar, need not even be earlier than Alcaeus, let alone be his source; the supplication will certainly not be presupposed here. (On the version in the *Iliupersis* cf. Rösler (1987); Davies (1989), 75–6. Of later versions, particularly important are Soph. *Aias Locr.* (frr. 10a–18 Radt) and Polygnotus as interpreted at Paus. 1. 15. 2 (Stoa Poikile), 10. 26.

---

[8] On 298 [10] see esp.: Eisenberger (1956), 65–7; Lloyd-Jones (1965), 72; Merkelbach (1967, 1968); Barner (1967), 187–201; Lloyd-Jones (1990b); Gallavotti (1969); Huxley (1969); Fowler (1979); Luppe (1979); Rösler (1980), 204–21, (1988); Koenen (1981); van Erp Taalman Kip (1984, 1987); Fowler (1987a), 58–63; Davies (1988b); Mazzoldi (1997); Neblung (1997), 15–17; Liberman (1999), ii. 99–101, 220–1. On the myth of Ajax and Cassandra in art see further: Davreux (1942), 138–211; Kunze (1950), 161–3; Caskey and Beazley (1931–63), iii. 64–5; Touchefeu (1981); Connelly (1993); Anderson (1997), 49–52 (Cycle), 77–80, 189, 199–202.

3 (lesche of Cnidians); note too the version, formally ascribed to a poet or poets, at Liban. (or [Liban.]) *Progymn. ref.* 2. 1–2.)

The depictions of the scene in sixth-century art form an interesting point of comparison with Alcaeus, and will be referred to below (even in Touchefeu (1981) the shield-bands receive insufficient attention). Their treatment of Cassandra as well as Athena is arresting (a female nude in archaic art cannot fail to arrest); in general, artistic and literary treatments of the fall of Troy show a breadth of sympathy which the interpreter of the Alcaeus needs to bear in mind.

From one point of view, the poem may be seen as illustrating the fertility with which Alcaeus handled politics. Rösler (1980), 219, interestingly compares the employment of allegory in other political poems. Both devices can be seen to intensify feelings about the political reality. Defamiliarization might be a useful notion even here; and from one angle the force of the myth is clearly rhetorical and argumentative. Yet even from the rhetorical angle, it is important that the mythological mode of enforcing the thought is in general indirect, in tone as well as matter (one may contrast the allegories). And even the mythological 42, if it is argumentative, would seem more narrowly bound than this poem to its rhetorical point. The length at which 298 [10] tells its story makes in itself a striking difference from 38 a, 42, Sapph. 16 [5].

One could, of course, contrive to find some rhetorical point for everything in the poem. So pity for Trojans in general devastated by the Achaeans in general (12–15) might be held to feed indirectly our indignation at Ajax and so at Pittacus (though the argument of the poem actually separates Ajax and his actions from the Achaeans and theirs). But there is a range to the imaginative and emotional dimensions of the narrative which make the poem a broad and complex work as well as a strongly persuasive. Alcaeus is not altogether segregated aesthetically from the poetic or figurative art which presents such stories with (at the least on the surface) a less immediate point. The power of his narrative art is remarkable: in compressed stanzas, with no speeches or imagery, and epithets only for the goddess, he creates a narrative not only elevated but spaced and nuanced, of striking range in both matter and feeling.

Metre

See on 129 [8].

1–3. The lines are difficult, but need some discussion for under-standing of the poem. It seems apparent from the next stanza that the punishment of the wicked is being spoken of now. τὰ μῆνδικα, however restrained, will hardly accompany a reference to Ajax alone; the plural participle in 1, coupled with the unexpected active singular περβάλοντ' (it seems), suggests a plurality of victims in 1. This passage will either be general, or refer to a group including Pittacus, possibly his faction rather than his family (cf. 68. 3–4; note τὰ μῆνδικα). It might conceivably follow a more general statement in 1 with a specific reference to Pittacus in 2–3. The vehement detailing of the punishment might suggest the passage is not all general. Some form of fastening is involved, most likely around the neck. The scholiast glosses ἀνάγκα as τὴν ἀγχόνην, the rope used in hanging (cf. Σ Arist. *Ach.* 125 c, Σ Eur. *Andr.* 816, *Anec. Ox.* ii. 348 Cramer, etc.); 'so the poet has used ἀνάγκη to mean δεϲμόϲ' (cf. e.g. Σ Ap. Rhod. 4. 200–2 b, 1659; Σ A Alcm. 1 [1]. 14; note the long gloss on 1 above). The original gloss is doubtless encouraged by a re-semblance in the words, and δεϲμόϲ seems to show that the scholiast does not envisage hanging here. Whether stoning is involved in the punishment depends on the interpretation of λαβολίωι (see below); stoning would not normally include a preliminary fastening. Even if stoning is involved, we should not assume that the narrator is calling for the Mytileneans to stone Pittacus as the Achaeans had intended to stone Ajax. Stoning does not seem to have been men-tioned at 4–5, as one would rather have expected on this view. The idea could certainly have appeared in 3 without prompting from the legend (cf. 68. 3).

λαβολίωι: this neuter seems a very strange *nomen actionis* (con-trast Hom. *Il.* 5. 54 ἐκηβολίαι, etc.). If it is not an error for -ίαι, one might wonder if it was an adjective, derived from and paral-lel to λάβολοϲ (cf. e.g. μειλίχιοϲ); cf. λάβολον 68. 3, Hesych. λ 796, Call. *Epigr.* 41. 5 Pfeiffer. The gloss might be λευϲτῶι rather than λευϲμῶι; either would be a literary word (cf. Hesych. λ 758), and λευϲτόϲ could readily be understood from the λιθολευϲτ- quite often used in scholia. And in any case a gloss could be mistaken. It may be noted that this view would not actually exclude a connection with the legend as told in the *Iliupersis*; but the main proposition of 2–3 would be different.

The most promising reading of 2–3 is that adopted by Liberman ((1999), ii. 99): [ἀν]άγκα⟨ν⟩ | ἄμ]φενι λαβολίωι πά[χη]αν. The word-order would be more plausible if λαβολίωι were an adjective. The accusative participle would doubtless agree with the subject of an infinitive at the start of the line. The tone would be rough and ferocious; it is still meant to carry moral authority. The authority will be supported, as often, by an argument, here an argument from example.

4–7. In the contemporary case, the situation is presented as still poised before resolution. The poem moves back to the corresponding point in the past; failure to act then led to the catastrophe for the Achaeans. Ajax is used as an example of the many suffering because of the one in Liban. *Or.* 16. 51; ἀποπλέοντες οἴκαδε supports πλέοντες here.

Ἀχαίοις᾽: the scope of the poem broadens from Mytilene.

πόλυ: the counterfactual is grimly enhanced, in a not un-Homeric fashion. Cf. e.g. *Od.* 9. 228. This negative device is the reverse of the startling counterfactual imaginings discussed by Nesselrath (1992).

κατέκτανον: there is no detail of punishment here; the tone of voice is more restrained than in 2–3.

θεος]ὐλην̣τ̣α seems likely. The stem is plausibly restored at Hipp. fr. 118. 1 West ῥῖνα θεό[ςυλιν . .]εις, cf. comm. A 14 τὴν ἱερόςυλιν ῥῖνα. It is not then found until Philo. ἱεροςυλ- occurs first in comedy and prose (Ar. *Wasps* 845, Eupol. *Dem.* fr. 99. 115 Kassel–Austin, Antiph. 5. 10), and commonly in inscriptions from the fourth century on (*SEG* 12 (for 1955), no. 100. 13, *LSAM* 59. 8, etc.). θεοςυλ-, which occurs again in l. 18, must be a stem in ordinary usage, but one that would not naturally be thought appropriate to dignified poetry. There will, then, be a practical vigour in Alcaeus' employment of the word.

Αἴγαις: we should on present information suppose this to be an Aegae somewhere in Euboea (names can move about an island). Huxley (1969) makes an interesting case for a Lesbian Aegae; but the account of Sapph. 17 on which it is based is very uncertain.

]. ἔτυχον θαλάccac: the curt allusion, probably by implication, will contrast with the ampler description of the storm at some point later in the poem.

8–11. The narrative now moves back, not to the act of Ajax but to the situation before it. It first establishes Cassandra at the statue (doubtless with an imperfect verb); it then moves away to other aspects of the fall (imperfect verbs at 11 and 15); Ajax enters at 16 for his perfective action. The mere delay increases the suspense and the impact of the action, through the literary exploitation of time: the visual depictions show a single moment, and many intensify it by showing Cassandra running in and grasping the statue (e.g. shield-band Delphi 4479 (Touchefeu no. 48), b-f vase Berlin F 1698 (Touchefeu 18), Group E, *ABV* 136. 54). But even in literature the device of beginning from unsubordinated imperfective description is much more striking than it would be to a modern aesthetic (Bacch. 17. 1–7 is less remarkable). The technique increases the disruption of Ajax's act; and it focuses attention on Cassandra as well as Athena. Cf. Virg. *Aen.* 2. 506–25.

At the start of 8 ἀλλ' (Page) does not seem a suitable particle; nor does ἀ μέν] appear apt to the structure and point of the narrative. (Lines 13–15 make against seeing Ajax as the last in a sequence of Greeks.)

]ϵν ναύωι: the location is placed at the start; it is crucial both to the sacrilege and to the concrete experience of the narrative (one thinks of Odysseus' palace). It is also separated from Ἀ]θανάας, which will have defined it even if it did not formally depend on it. The separation highlights both the place and the identity of the god.

Πριάμω πάϊς enhances the dignity of the narrative at its real beginning (cf. 42. 5), and also of Cassandra. The appellation makes her the more tragic too.

πολυλάϊδος: perhaps, as Broger considers possible, a deliberate deviation from the epic ἀγελείη ((1996), 209). The word is not found elsewhere. Its meaning must be of relevance here, when a city is being sacked (note 11). The notion of Athene as giver, and receiver, of much booty points to her expected relationship with the Greek victors, undone in Ajax's sacrilege. The epithet also stresses this female's warlike character, and so marks an opposition between her and Cassandra in the preceding line.

ἐπαππένα: the form is discussed by Slings (1979), at some length. ἐπ- must be introduced; Cassandra has taken hold of the statue's chin (cf. Hom. *Il.* [10]. 454–5, *Od.* 19. 473). The gesture is standard for humans supplicating humans, or gods gods (cf. Neumann (1965), 67–70); in supplicating statues, it is uncommon. One sits low then and embraces the statue at the knees. In some artistic depictions, Cassandra stretches a supplicating hand to Ajax (shield-bands Delphi 4479 (Touchefeu 48); Olymp. B 975 (type XXIX, no. 44 Kunze, scene γ; not in Touchefeu)), but would be too low to touch Athena's chin. This narrative is producing a notable image of quasi-human contact with the goddess; it also affects the depiction of Cassandra, see 21 n.

γενήω: it is the chin rather than the beard that it thought of as being touched in supplication, cf. Hom. *Il.* 1. 501, Richter (1968), pll. viiib–c. LSJ *Supp.* seems mistaken here.

In 11, the last 'line' of the stanza is forcefully exploited: the subject of the verb changes dramatically, and the action is not static but suggests threatening movement. The narrative expands in space: contrast ναύωι in the first line with πόλιν here. δυϲμέ]νεεϲ surely indicates, what the form of the stanza suggests, that the attack is being seen at this moment from the perspective of Cassandra and the Trojans.

πόλιν: the text is perhaps sound, cf. Führer (1976), 245–6; Theogn. 461, 1201, Sol. fr. 12. 8 West. Perhaps Alcaeus, like Sappho, is freer with his language in this mythological narrative.

ἔηπον: 'were moving over, were occupying'? Cf. van Erp Taalman Kip (1984), 6–7, (1987), 115. The next stanza takes up this general statement with more specific actions and results.

12–15. This remarkable stanza creates a background to the main action. Its technique is more compressed and impressionistic than the literary and artistic Iliuperseis (including the *Troades*) which depict a series of terrible events. It shapes our response to Cassandra's disaster, while leaving it in high relief.

Δαΐφοβον: the killing of Deiphobus was a significant event in Iliuperseis: it marked the recovery of Helen. Cf. *Iliupers.* (Procl.) p. 62 ll. 14–15 Davies; r–f cup by Onesimos, Malibu J. Paul Getty Mus. 83.AE.362, 84.AE.80, 85.AE.835 (*BA* 404, 500–490 BC), cf. Anderson (1997), 238. With the small amount of detail possible here (some other victim or the like was mentioned too), the killing will seem more just than appalling (contrast Virg. *Aen.* 6. 494–530). If two victims, the manner may recall Homeric battle narrative at its briskest. The account, however, moves on from the killing of guilty individual men.

The remains of the first letter in 13 suggest o rather than α: cf. ον in 5 and 47. We cannot then say whether the verb in the clause was aorist or imperfect. This was probably the verb (there is little room for a particle in the line, or an adjective in the clause).

Two nouns of sound now become the subject. They are vivid, yet generalized and indirect; the first noun one cannot even associate with women rather than men. The primary force of such cries turns our sympathies towards the Trojans. None the less, the description is not focalized by the Trojans or even Cassandra. ἀ[π]ὺ τείχεος and πέδιον κάτηχε suggest a perspective from outside the city; this shows the extent of the cries. Hom. *Il.* 22. 447, compared in Merkelbach (1967), 89, is not the same: lamentation comes from the wall because it is from there that the Trojans are looking at Hector; there is no reason why cries should come into Troy now from the wall in particular.

οἰμώγα: the word, found in epic, tragedy, Attic prose, is not extant in other lyric, elegy, iambus. This is primarily a matter of the usual interests of genres, threnoi apart (cf. Pind. *Thren.* fr. 128 e (b). 6 (fr. 3 b Cannatà Fera); *Pyth.* 4. 113). Alcaeus, in not particularly epic style, is showing the interest of epic in cries of grief and pain.

At the start of 14, ὄρωρε would be in the wrong tense, ἔλαμψε would be too colourful, and the preverb in ἔνωρτο would be hard to justify; the tense of ἴκοιca does not seem wholly satisfactory.

παίδων ἀΰτα intensifies the pathos. The mass killing of children is most likely suggested here, as is seen on the Mykonos pithos (Mykonos Mus. 2240, vii 2nd quarter; Ervin (1963), pll. 23–8; Anderson (1997), ch. 11). It was probably not actual Greek practice, and will seem a particularly terrible feature of the sack. Cf. Thuc. 7. 29. 5 (and Giotto's 'Massacre of the Innocents' in the Lower Basilica, Assisi). Alcaeus does not single out the individual Astyanax.

On the spacing of Δαρδάνι]ον see 20 n.

πέδιον κάτηχε need not be accounted a reminiscence of Hom. *Il.* 16. 78–89: once given the plain of Troy, the coincidence is not overwhelming. Cf. for κάτηχε rather Aesch. *Pers.* 426–7 οἰμωγὴ . . . κατεῖχε πελαγίαν ἄλα.

16–19. Ajax's entry is exceedingly forceful, after the preparation and delay. The narrative returns to confined space (contrast 15 especially); the scene created earlier is broken in on by the arrival of Ajax. Separating the entry from the deed is an effective use of narrative time in itself; but the separation also means that Athene can engross the stanza. Lines 17–19 provide vigorous rhetorical preparation; they display the extremity of Ajax's folly. The narrator comments on this folly from the perspective of detachment and the future; but the assertion on an individual god other than Zeus, and the emphasis of the narrator's superlative and πάντων, are not altogether Homeric in quality. Cf. *Il.* 16. 688, 20. 264–6; note Alc. 327. 1.

On the spacing of Αἴας δὲ λ] see 20 n.

λ]ύ‚cc‚αν ἦλθ' ὀλόα‚ν‚ ἔχων: cf. Hom. *Il.* 9. 305 Hector (. . . ἄν . . . ἔλθοι) λύccαν ἔχων ὀλοήν. The resemblance of phrase is so striking that one must suppose an echo of epic, very possibly of that passage (to conjecture its use of Ajax in the *Iliupersis* is arbitrary). But the phrase has gained a new force. ὀλόαν is now richly ambiguous: Ajax's emotion brings catastrophe not only to Cassandra but to himself and the Greeks. λύcca is likely to suggest, not simply martial rage as in Homer, but the sense of madness seen in the fifth century (Bacch. 11. 102 etc.; note already Hom. *Il.* 8. 299). The echo marks the perversion of the heroic ethos here.

Πάλλα‚δ‚oc: Athena's name, in the genitive, comes in the second line of the stanza as at 9. The form of her designation is carefully varied from 9, cf. 23 (note 22, cf. 16?). In 9 there was an epithet; now there is an elaborate and emphatic relative clause. The goddess is now set against Ajax in the first line, not Cassandra (8); the placing of θέω‚ν in clause as well as line stresses her hierarchical superiority to him.

θε‚o- probably takes θέω‚ν up in a pointed figure.

In 19 the two papyri have different texts. If we grant a substantial leftward drift to its left-hand margin (see on 20), Π¹ could have had (unmetrically) μακάρων followed by a choriambic superlative, e.g. μακάρων αἰνοτάτα. That supplement would not fit too badly with χέρρεc]ϲι δ' ἄμφο‚ιν in 20. It may be noted that θέων . . . πάντων . . . μακάρων itself gives a somewhat surprising order and interval in respect of μακάρων.

20. The first ν of 20 is roughly aligned in Π¹ with the first c of 11. This means that the first letter seen in Π² would have been pretty roughly aligned in Π¹ with the υ of δυcμέ]νεεc. There has plainly been in Π¹ a substantial Massian movement of the margin to the left; this would be likely even if the unavoidable supplement in 11 were wrong. If it and χέρρεc]ϲι (Page, Treu) or ἐν χέρ]ϲι (West) were right, the movement would be of 3–5 letters. A movement to the left would also be required to reconcile δυcμέ]νεεc and the likely supplements Δαρδάνι]ον 15, Αἴας δὲ λ]ύccαν 16.

The use of two hands is stressed by ἄμφο‚ιν. In the standard iconography of the scene, Ajax takes Cassandra with his left hand, holding a sword with his right. This gesture is more savage, and also suggests more resistance from Cassandra. Passages where the lustful touch with plural hands are less to the purpose. Cf. Burnett (1983), 203–4.

παρθενίκαν, instead of a name, is variously focalized and pointed. It conveys the attraction of Cassandra to Ajax (cf. 42. 8, 10; 45. 5–6). It also conveys the pathos of her plight, and her inferiority in a hierarchy of power. There may perhaps be a contrast with the virgin goddess (for παρθενική of goddesses cf. Simon. 519 fr. 35 (b) 8).

21. παρεςτάκο̣ιςαν: a notable contrast with visual accounts of the story and with normal practice in supplicating statues (see 8–11 n.; and cf. e.g. Ar. *Knights* 30). Even in black-figure vases, the naked Cassandra is a figure of more importance than is sometimes suggested; but in the art she is low down, often small, Ajax sometimes looks down at her (e.g. on the shield-band Olymp. B 975; note also her postures in the Melian terracotta reliefs Berlin 6285, 6283 (Jacobsthal (1931), nos. 65 and 66)). Often she begins to supplicate him. Here she presents a more dignified image. The supreme importance of Athene in the scene does not mean that Cassandra is a 'puppet' (Burnett (1983), 202). Within the concision of his narrative, Alcaeus has subtly created considerable interest in her.

ἀγάλματι: there is no doubt here that the statue is the statue; even in artistic versions, the pose of Ajax would often not make sense if he were actually confronting the goddess in person. However, the statue, not least in supplication, is a potent embodiment of the deity; cf. e.g. Eur. *Hcld.* 112–13. Alcaeus does not seem to encumber his narrative with the story of the statue being pulled from its base: cf. *Iliupers.* (Procl.) p. 62 ll. 23–4 Davies; Paus. 10. 26. 3; Soph. fr. 10c. 8–9 Radt.

22. Preferably 'dragged' (ἔξελκ᾽ is in an unattractive tense; ἔρυςς᾽ would be short in relation to παῖδα] in 23). 'Violated' makes the description of pulling Cassandra from the statue sound in context much too weak. Van Erp Taalman Kip (1987), 117, has the same preference on mythographical grounds (the violation in the temple is attested only much later). The account of Ajax's act, then, is effectively stopped after the most dramatic point, and the one in which he chiefly offends Athena.

23. The stanza again closes with Athena, and a resounding description of her appears to fill the last line. παῖδα] Δίος (Page ap. Lobel (1951), 87) fits well with the supplements of 'hands' in 20; but the traces are far from clear.

πολέμω δότε⟨ρ⟩ραν is a sonorous but multivalent phrase. Other epithets of Athena suggest her prowess in war (so πολεμάδοκος 3. 2, cf. 325. 1), and her inspiration of fighting (so ἐγρεμάχη Phoron. fr. 5. 2 Davies, *Hom. h. Dem.* 424, *IG* i³. 617. 1 (c.525–10); cf. Alc. 206. 1–2). 'Giver of war' sounds a loftier, and more ominous, role: cf. Zeus at Hom. *Il.* 4. 82–4 (ταμίης), *Od.* [24]. 475–6, and the negative epithet of a god ἀλγεςίδωρος (Sapph. 172; cf. Aesch. *Th.* 975 (and Epimen. B 19. 2 Diels–Kranz); Pind. fr. 109. 3–4). Ajax forgets her power even in his own sphere of war; but she will shortly produce disaster in another.

24–36. A substantial problem ensues. There are obeli against 25–31 in Π¹; there could have been obeli against 24 or 32. Line 24 plainly coincides with Π². This suggests that the lines obelized in Π¹ etc. were present in Π², if we suppose that it is whole stanzas which are likely to have been judged spurious. (Spuriousness is what the obeli imply, as Fowler (1979) makes clear.) It is a probable supposition that interpolation would be of whole stanzas. The accidental omission of 8 lines, starting from the second in a stanza and ending after the first, is unlikely to have produced a very convincing join; but such a join would probably have been needed to persuade an ancient critic that the lines missing from some copy were inauthentic. (Fowler (1979), 24–5, notes but does not really meet such points.) It is doubtful whether any argument can be drawn from the position of the scholion in Π², or from the variation between -cι and -cιν at the end of 24. We are not in a position to assert that -cιν implies a vowel to follow, and Sapph. 94. 2–3 suggest otherwise. Lines 24–31, then, are likely to have been present in Π², and obelized in Π¹.

If 25–32 were not present in Π², we should have to combine its headless lines with the openings of 33–6 in Π¹. The openings imported into Π² would exceed the probable χέρρες]ςι or the like in 20 by 3 letters. Koenen (1981) thinks this impossible; the point is accepted by Fowler (1987a), 60–1. It is questionable whether any of the other supplements used in the argument are really certain; but one would have to suppose a fairly drastic movement to the left in Π², say 3 letters in 6 lines. This is not impossible, but unattractive (the instance of such movement in Π¹ is much less drastic). One may then reject the combination on this basis.

Some lesser points may be added. παννύχιος is normally used of animate beings, as subjects of verbs, or of things connected with all-night rituals (dancing Soph. *Ant.* 153 etc.). Hom. *Od.* 2. 434 of a ship travelling (subject) is a venial exception. The use with θυέλλαιc seems curious. The coupling with ἀφάντοι[c seems stylistically unsatisfying; the words do not either support each other well (cf. 345. 2) or stand in clearly distinct categories. We may note that if Alcaeus gives two epithets in asyndeton they involve separate categories (130 b [9]. 20 = 35, 140. 3, 298 [10]. 17–19 (sound?)) or are placed some distance apart (129 [8]. 8–9, 140. 4–5, 350. 1–2), and also are related either to religion or to weapons of war.

Detailed objection has less purchase on the combination of the lines after 24 in Π² with the openings of 25–31 in Π¹ (the view adopted in the text). The lines may be spurious, so that inelegant writing and incorrect forms cannot be excluded. They would be less completely preserved than in the other version, and one certainly cannot assume that ingenuity would be able to restore them through supplements. ἐξαπ[ίν]ᾳc ἐκύκα is not necessarily unsatisfactory (cf. Liberman (1989), 29); and one should not regard the supplement as certain. The reading of Π² in 25 seems less assured now, so that the problem of the opening there diminishes. That problem had, in my opinion, been one of narrow space more than of style. In Π², for example, cμέρδνα πε] would seem a little too long to fit with χέρρεc] in 20, without a substantial shift of margin.

Lines 24–31, then, were thought spurious. We are unaware of the reasons, and cannot see for ourselves how the lines relate to what follows. From this we should infer, not that we can ignore the athetesis, but that we cannot be sure that the lines are genuine. We do not even know on what kinds of grounds atheteses would be made in lyric poems; but the athetesis of lines in Sappho on Cleis, in Hipponax on Bupalus, and the question of [Pind.] *Ol.* 5 might suggest that the atheteses themselves were worth taking seriously (to say nothing of [Dem.] 7 or [Eur.] *Rhesus*). We are in no position to assess the question ourselves; but some points may be briefly mentioned. Lines 38–9 might seem to treat of Athena going to the sea. The actual verb ἀΐξε is anything but certain in 26, though 'sea' is inevitable; conceivably Athena had only been making preparations in 26–7, but her dashing to the sea (if she does) in 38 would still

seem surprising. It looks as if 28–31 may have gone over similar
ground to 4–7 ('αἰ "if"?' Merkelbach (1967), 91). The repetition
would seem somewhat strange, and so too the sequence: she started
stirring up the winds; if . . .; she went to the sea and stirred up . . .
But one cannot be too definite without the lines entire.

Does 306 A h show that a trial of Ajax was narrated in the poem,
and that the lines are genuine? Even if the treatise referred to these
lines, that does not show that they are authentic; and an amplifica-
tion of the story, encouraged by 4–7, seems entirely in accord with
character of such works (note e.g. f and h 14; cf. van Erp Taalman
Kip (1987), 97–8). Certainly there will not have been an extensive
narration here (any narration of it has ended by 34–5). The prose
work does not mention the statue of Athena in line 8; nor is Ajax's
refuge with that statue likely to have found a mention in the poem
as preserved. (Rösler's transposition, though an interesting idea,
has little positively to commend it, and requires a less probable
interpretation of the obeloi.)

The incompleteness and the difficulties of 24–7 deprive us of
solid linguistic arguments for interpolation. ἐκ κτλ., 26–7, actually
looks to be quite impressive (this may prove to be a dreadful re-
velation of bad taste); but that is not much of a positive argument,
particularly when the lines contain a serious problem. The ancient
condemnation and the apparent awkwardness of content, bound up
with duplication of the remaining text, should probably incline one
to accept the athetesis until more evidence appears.

There is at any rate no fixed basis beyond 23 for literary discussion
of the structure, narrative, or detail of the poem. A few detached
points may be appended.

25–6. The mark before δ, above and close to its 'waist', looks be-
neath the microscope like part of a stroke made with the pen; it can-
not belong to an ι. The supposed top of λ is high and anomalous;
the fibres show that there has been no displacement. The marks
might be a lectional sign, but this is not a diagonal line so much as
a blob. φ would be conceivable. All this calls (π)[ε]λ[ι]δνώθεισα into
question, certain as Call. *Hec.* fr. 72. 1 Hollis had seemed to make
it. Van Erp Taalman Kip (1987), 120–1, had found difficulties of
content.

οἴνοπα: until the Hellenistic period (*Suppl. Hell.* 922. 3), the
word is not found elsewhere outside epic (Hom. *Il.* 2. 613, etc.),

save at the parodic Hermipp. fr. 63. 2 Kassel–Austin, Crates *Suppl. Hell.* 351. 1.

ἐκ is plain in the papyrus, and can be seen clearly even from the photograph in Lobel (1951) (there must be some misunderstanding at van Erp Taalman Kip (1987), 122). Lobel rightly found it a strange preverb; it comes above the υκ of ἐκύκα in Π², and one wonders if the letters have intruded from that word. For the separated cύν note Hes. fr. 302. 11–12 Merkelbach–West. But spuriousness might be another explanation.

35. παννύχιος is not found in poetry between epic and tragic lyric (Soph. *Ant.* 153, Eur. *Hcld.* 748, etc). But it occurs at Hdt. 2. 62. 1.

45. ζώει (if rightly read) has been noted as a sign that the poem has returned to the present. It is tempting to refer it to Pittacus (ὦνηρ Merkelbach; cf. Cic. *Cat.* 1. 2); but the change to the second person within the stanza would be abrupt. A related, but less abrupt, change seems probable at 72. 11: both the cύ and the κῆνος ὦνηρ (7–8) seem likely to be Pittacus (note ὀνέτροπε).

47. The reference to Pittacus' father is unmistakable. If the text is sound, one might have to articulate ὦ "Υρραδ' (Gallavotti). But the α of Αἰcιμίδα is long (365), and a long would at the least make the presentation in the papyrus less plausible; ου would be tricky; the following trace might indicate corruption. So Lloyd-Jones's conjecture could well be right. The address comes forcefully after the narrator's long immersion in the past and the indirectness of exemplum. The return to Melanippus at 38 a. 10 is also forceful, though less striking. Helen (also an exemplum?) is herself apostrophized at 42. 3.

We have seen from these few examples how fertile Alcaeus' invention is, and how large a part is played by his imagination and his thought in shaping and transforming experience. The poems can hardly be viewed as unthinking transcription of events and outpouring of hot feeling. We have also seen how intently artistic they are, how their (carefully created) vigour and vividness is combined with a close exploitation of short and highly organized stanzas. Alcaeus is an artist no less than Sappho.

IBYCUS

Introduction

THE problems about Ibycus are entangled with each other. Ibycus came from Rhegium (all accept); he went at some stage to Samos (most accept). His fragments, in order of discovery, comprise, roughly: quoted extracts and references, some mythological, but the longest and most impressive on love (286–8); a very extensive papyrus fragment (S151 [11]), often found dull, which is addressed to a Polycrates but is mostly concerned with the Trojan War; numerous but scrappy pieces of poems and commentaries on papyrus (S152–257 (a)). The questions to be considered are: What was the subject-matter, and quality, of Ibycus' poems? How are they related to their place of composition? When, in date and in his career, did Ibycus go to Samos? Did his poems change when he did so? Did he, for example, move from western mythological narrative to eastern love songs?[1]

Let us ourselves start in Rhegium and eventually proceed to Samos. Rhegium was a primarily Euboean colony carefully placed in a promising spot: on the Italian side of the Straits of Messina, with the length of its walls running along the coast. The wealth and significance it acquired from its position seem to have been considerable. Excavations have naturally been limited by the modern Reggio; but at least one large sacred site has been found. It evidently contained a big sixth-century temple and other buildings, and much imported pottery was found. The lively Chalcidic vases are commonly supposed to have been produced in Rhegium. The city, and its environs on both sides of the straits, would not seem a discouraging setting for a poetic career; at any rate, there would seem to have been people who wanted poems written. Poem 321 describes Ortygia (Syracuse; note also 323; S241). In S227, which appears to be a commentary on Ibycus, a Chalcidian colony is mentioned. S220, from the same papyrus, seems likely to be by

---

[1] On Ibycus in general and some of the problems linked with him see Schneidewin (1833), 1–82; Maas (1916); Vallet (1958), 286–94; Barron (1964, 1984); West (1970b), 206–9; Mosshammer (1979), ch. 16; Jenner (1986); Woodbury (1991d); Carey (1996); MacLachlan (1997), 187–97; other items in n. 13 and in the introduction to Anacreon below.

Ibycus; it would appear to be a victory poem for somebody from (or else competing in) Leontini (3–4), a Chalcidian foundation like Rhegium, on the east side of Sicily. (Rhegium's strongest ties were with Sicily's Chalcidian foundations.) Ibycus, then, is already writing in the west poetry celebrating an individual.[2]

More general features of Ibycus' poetry are likely to be due to his origins, or at any rate with him from the first. His Doric is much more like Stesichorus' than Alcman's. Alcman may use Laconian features avoided by Stesichorus and Ibycus; they sometimes use non-Laconian Doric features (such as infinitives in -εν, Ibyc. S166. 13, cf. S171). But much more important is the Homeric element which Ibycus shares with Stesichorus, most notably the use of genitives in -οιο. This goes with the frequent use of epic adjectives; here Ibycus comes much closer to Stesichorus than the other lyric poets do. The mixture of Ibycus' dialect does not result from the dialect of Rhegium, which is Ionic, as one would expect (with some unusual features). One may add to the dialect the use of triadic structure, which we only know to have appeared hitherto in Stesichorus. There seems some likelihood that Ibycus derives these features from a western tradition. On the other hand, the same kind of dialect will shortly be used by Simonides from Ceos; so the tradition may already have been more widely spread. At any rate, the elements of his poetry do not derive from Samos, but from a tradition he is already using in a western poem, and seems always to have employed. He still uses triadic structures in Samos (S151 [11]) and Sparta (S166).[3]

[2] The chronological sequence (native region before Samos) is accepted for the sake of argument, and is intrinsically plausible; if it were replaced by a purely spatial sequence (the type of poems found acceptable in different places), the same essential arguments would apply. For Rhegium see Vallet (1958), (1996a), and (1996b), 427; note recently Cordiano (1990), 67–9. Nenci and Vallet (1977–) has at the time of writing reached Regalbuto. Chalcidian vases: Rumpf (1927); still seen as likely to be from Rhegium in Boardman (1998), 217 (but the dialect of inscriptions on the vases creates problems). On Kronion in S220 see Treu (1968–9). The poem will be Ibycus': the next poem in the commentary is likely to be his, and is marked only by Callias' name (*P. Oxy.* vol. xxxii, pl. xiv); the papyrus does not look like a commentary on several poets. Gorgias (S226, 289 (*b*)) cannot be localized in Sicily: the name is common. P. Oxy. 4456 might possibly be relevant to Ibycus and Sicily.

[3] For distinctive adjectives used by Homer (not usually Homer alone) see esp. S166. 17, 26, 29, S167. 9, S174. 2, S192 (*b*) 14, S224. 7, S257 (*a*) fr. 2. 6 (ἐλ]?), fr. 27. 12, 287. 6 (ἀεθλοφ.), 288. 2, 298. 3, 303 (*a*). 1, 306, 314. 2, 321. 4. Ibycus goes further than extant Stesichorus in using some epic forms, e.g. datives in -εεσσι (S166. 23, S222. 6; cf. Pind. *Pyth.* 2. 33, *Nem.* 3. 15). The presentation of secondary long *e* is probably an interpretative matter. For evidence on the dialect of Rhegium see

Was he writing in the west large poems that consisted purely of mythological narrative? The papyrus evidence makes this improbable. It was already notable that Ibycus' poems were not cited by title like Stesichorus', and were cited by book number; he wrote only seven bookfuls (*Suda*). In S151 [11] we see extensive use of myth, in a poem to a youth; much of this heroic myth we would not particularly have expected there. Two of the figures named there, Cassandra and Troilus, appear, seemingly as types of beauty, in other fragments (303 (*a*), S224). S176, concerned with games, mentions Heracles, Peleus, Geryon; S222, concerned with the narrator's love, uses Oedipus and Ino in comparison. A poem to one Gorgias told of Zeus' rape of Ganymede (289 (*a*), cf. S226; S233 (*a*). 6, cf. S154, might possibly be connected). A great many of the mythical versions ascribed to Ibycus are related to love (291, 294, 296, 297, 302, 309, 324). This includes 296, seemingly ascribed to a dithyramb by Ibycus; later analogy only indicates a fairly short poem. The hypothesis that Ibycus' references to myth came mainly in songs for individuals looks more and more plausible with each accession of evidence; the notion of long purely narrative poems has virtually no positive support. The myth in Alcm. 1 [1], or that in Alc. 298 [10], or those in Bacchylides and Pindar, only show how an argument from mythological references is no argument at all. If some could ascribe the Ἄθλα ἐπὶ Πελίαι to Ibycus rather than Stesichorus (Stes. 179 (i), apparently a minority view), we cannot safely infer that Ibycus must have written other Stesichorean narratives. A false ascription to Ibycus is made sufficiently intelligible by the similarity of the two in language, and by Ibycus' interest in games, including, probably, this very myth (S176). This is far too slight a base for big conclusions about real Stesichorean narratives by Ibycus. If both poets are cited for a word (328, 335, 336, 340), that hardly proves that the two have been muddled, let alone that their poems were indistinguishable as wholes.[4]

Kunze (1967), 100; Jeffery (1990), 244–5, 454–5 (Chalcidic vases are less certain evidence).

[4] Note 336 (different contexts) and 340 (same use Pind. *Dith*. fr. 70 c. 13, with Σ). S176 (cf. Lobel (1968), 17) looks too rapid to be the Ἄθλα itself, or an extended narrative; cf. Jenner (1986), 61–3. One may note that Stes. 179 (ii) does not suggest Stesichorus' usual pace; if the Ἄθλα itself was anomalously short, the general argument about Ibycus virtually disappears. On 296 note Schwartz's apparatus (Schwartz (1887–91), ii. 293). Also of interest, if by Ibycus, and relevant to S151 [11] is P. Oxy. 4450 (Troy); ἐρασμίαν may be noted.

Another poem, S166, would appear to be written for someone in Sparta; if so, Ibycus was working, temporarily or otherwise, in or for a wealthy mainland state which might possibly have enticed Stesichorus too, and later commissioned Simonides. The poem has various resemblances with S151 [11], written for Samos. In it we see combined various elements that recur generally in the papyrus fragments: a boy of rare beauty is praised (23–7), love is mentioned (7), games appear (36), and myth or religion (15–21); the present performance is spoken of (aulos and song 5). In other poems too a particular boy is praised for beauty in a poem apparently performed in his honour; cf. especially S257 (*a*) fr. 1 (ὕμνοι), cf. 288 (to Euryalus); S257 (*a*) fr. 27 (ὕμν-, the aulos); 289 (*a*). Praise of an individual successful in the games we have seen in S220, and may see in S221 (certainly praise of an individual); cf. also S257 (*a*) fr. 2. Whether the combination of boys and games is peculiar to this poem or occurred in many others we cannot know; it was presumably not present in S151 [11], or victory would be mentioned. But certainly the praise of individuals, and the connections with love and beauty, seem recurring features, which are attested for many individuals besides Polycrates, and are found in poems not written in Samos.[5]

To Samos we finally come. S151 [11] praises a Polycrates. Was this the Samian Polycrates? If it were only a matter of Ibycus, one could hypothesize that ancient scholars had misidentified a Polycrates named in this and perhaps other poems. But the tradition linking Anacreon with the Samian Polycrates goes back to Herodotus (3. 121. 1). The contention that this too was a misidentification is made more difficult by a later reference to Anacreon's work as 'all full of Polycrates' name', which suggests at least some prominence in his writing; Anacreon writes several poems on Samos, or at least an island (353), so not in Teos, Abdera, or Athens. It seems not unduly credulous to accept the identification for Ana-

---

[5] Whether there is some connection between writing for a Spartan and working on Samos (cf. Cartledge (1982)) does not affect the present line of argument. It would be less attractive to suppose that the poem was for Tarentum; cf. Malkin (1994), 128. One wonders where 339 belongs. With S166. 23–6 cf. Eur. *Hec.* 635–7, Cat. 61. 82–6 (and Bacch. fr. 20C. 20–4). For boys note also S173, S174. 10 π]αῖδ' ἐρατ[? (cf. Simon. fr. 27. 5 West), S181. 10. Euryalus, and Gorgias, are not brothers of Polycrates (their names in Hdt. 3. 39. 2); the name Euryalus is extremely rare in historical times. (Paus. 4. 20. 8 is of doubtful historicity.) Note the resemblance in theme between 288 and S257 (*a*) fr. 1. Cic. *Tusc.* 4. 71 (TB2), from the same Hellenistic source as the remark in the *Suda*, might confirm in context that a very substantial part of Ibycus' whole output was concerned with the narrator's love.

creon; and it becomes tempting, though not inevitable, to suppose that Ibycus' Polycrates is the same person.[6]

Polycrates is praised for his beauty. One would naturally suppose that this was a boy; this supposition is strongly supported by the other papyrus fragments referred to above. Furthermore, if the Polycrates were already tyrant, one would not expect here praise for beauty alone: the context separates beauty from valour, and the poem has also depicted mighty rulers. Force is added to this point by the mention of Troilus just before the mention of Polycrates (note S224).

Polycrates' seizure of power should be in the 530s (see the introduction to the commentary on Anacreon). Ibycus thus arrives before that point. Little faith need be reposed in the *Suda*'s indications of date (564–1, TA1). Herodotus describes Polycrates' rise to tyranny in a way which makes it sound unlikely that his father had been tyrant immediately before or at all (3. 39. 1 and esp. 120. 3, however tendentious). The *Suda* (Himerius is less clear) states that Polycrates' father was ruling the island; but this quasi-monarchical assumption should not be thought to carry any weight beside Herodotus. We are bound, however, to deduce from the poem itself that Polycrates belonged to an eminent aristocratic family, so that Herodotus' Mitrobates may be giving a misleading impression of his status, perhaps deliberately (3. 120. 3).[7]

There is no difficulty in supposing that a Samian family was rich enough, or Samos attractive enough, to appeal to the poet. The archaeological record of the island is overwhelming, though varied in emphasis, throughout the first three quarters of the sixth century. The impressive Samian traditions of sculpture and vase-painting continue in this period. Vase-painting produces some very notable

---

[6] See for Anacreon the introduction to the commentary on him below. The idea of a tyrant Polycrates before Polycrates now enjoys little favour.

[7] The epigraphic arguments against ascribing ML 16 to Polycrates' father (dedication by Aeaces as ἐπιστάτης) are greatly weakened by the inscription, if not added later, on the Isches kouros. (Observe the α and θ on Kyrieleis (1996), pl. 30.) There are not, however, such strong sculptural and archaeological arguments in the case of ML 16 for the 540s as there are in the case of the kouros for the early 6th cent. On the *Suda* Mosshammer (1979), 302, judges more soundly than Woodbury (1991*d*), 436, though its expression need not be original. Note that the appearance of Anaximenes with Polycrates in *Metiochus and Parthenope* (Maehler (1976)) suggests that Diogenes (2. 1. 2) or his source has indeed confused Anaximander, though with Anaximenes, not Pythagoras (cf. Jacoby (1923–), II D. 726–7); cf. Anaximand. A 28, 29 Diels–Kranz (and A 17). The original dating involved is thus distinct from datings of Ibycus, Anacreon, and Polycrates in the 560s.

work, both in and before Polycrates' tyranny. From early in the century (probably) comes the massive Isches kouros, made in Samos; whatever the explanation for the smaller and fewer kouroi by the end of the period, we cannot possibly infer aristocratic poverty before Polycrates. From about 560 was built 'Rhoecus'' huge and innovative temple of Hera, together with a vast altar, 38.40 m. long. Foundations of the 'Polycratean' temple were laid in the 530s. Another large building was worked on throughout the century. The great tunnel of Eupalinus, to transport water, was begun probably in the 550s or 540s. The first phase of building on the town walls belongs about this time. The enormous harbour works of this period are not easy to date closely. This rapid summary may suggest the resources of Samos, and the environment to which Ibycus came.[8]

Ibycus' Samian patrons will have been far wealthier even than the families which commissioned his work in the west. It is entirely possible that there were changes in the practical arrangements, for example that he stayed a long while on Samos and wrote mainly for one family, while in the west he might have written occasional poems (e.g. epinicians) for individuals in a number of places. But the nature of his poetry does not seem to have altered greatly. We have already seen the numerous links between S151 [11] and other poems, including poems written in other places and for different families. Even without these poems, intrinsic probability makes it likely that Ibycus had already established the fame which caused him to be invited.[9]

Ibycus and Anacreon both write for this family, but in quite different manners, which are probably connected with their origins, and were assuredly adopted before (or beyond) Samos. It would be

[8] For Samian sculpture see Buschor (1935–61); Richter (1968), 44–50, 90–1, (1970), 35–6, 61, 92, 114; Boardman (1978), 68–72; Stewart (1990), 116–17, 126. Note the fragment of a new type of kore, Blackman (1997), 98–9. For the Isches kouros see Kyrieleis (1996). For the vase-painting see Walter-Karydi (1973). On the Heraion see Walter (1976); Furtwängler and Kienast (1989); Kienast (1992). On the tunnel see Rihll and Tucker (1995) and Kienast (1995); Kienast seems to favour a relatively early date, and perhaps Samos was likely to be in the forefront for such building, as in the case of the 'Rhoecus' temple. For the city wall see Kienast (1978); on the harbour works (which are at present hard to date, within this period) note Tomlinson (1995), 57. Nothing is said here on imported pottery, nor on the causes of Samos' glory (such as others' piety and their own piracy).

[9] Little is to be gained from the acme alleged by Jerome's version of Eusebius (541 BC, TA2). Poem 320 (Cyaras general of the Medes) does not take us far. Cyaras, if he was Cyaxaras, was a contemporary of Alyattes (Hdt. 1. 16. 2); but 320 does not tell us if he is alive.

very rash to assert that Ibycus' poetry was radically influenced by
his contact with the other poet. Love poetry was not learnt from
Anacreon (or not on Samos). One might see in 287 the kind of
drastic metaphor also used by Anacreon (the narrator thrown by
Eros into Aphrodite's nets); the interest in the ageing and possibly
somewhat amusing lover resembles Anacreon too. But we have no
reason to assume that Ibycus is the debtor, if a debt exists. Alcm.
26 and 58 enjoin caution, the more so in view of other connec-
tions between Ibyc. 287 and that poet (cf. Alcm. 1 [**1**]. 47–8, 3 [**2**].
'61–2').[10]

Poem 287 shows Ibycus' characteristic interest in epic language
and double-short rhythm. In metre the difference between Iby-
cus and Anacreon is large and obvious throughout their work. In
general, Ibycus' fragments suggest an interest like Stesichorus' in
runs of double-shorts, whether starting from double-short or long,
and also in single-short groups (as S221. 1–2, S222. 6–7, cf. Stes.
222 (b) [**3**]. 202, 206); the two types of double-short are seen in
S151 [**11**] (cf. 287), compare the *Geryoneis*. The length of double-
short runs, however, is more reminiscent of Alcman (especially
Alcm. 3 [**2**], cf. 17, *al.*); in Alcman too one finds the aeolic cola
seen in Ibyc. S151 [**11**] and also S166. 8 (15, 36) (Sparta?), and in
S221, 286. The choriambic expansion in S151 [**11**]. 8 might pos-
sibly have been learnt from Anacreon; but Lesbos was bound to
interest an amatory poet. Similar points would apply to the brevity
of the stanzas in S151 [**11**] as against S166 (and 286–7).[11]

How Ibycus' poems were performed we cannot say, whether in
chorus or singly (S166. 5 looks intriguing); but whereas Anacreon's
might seem to have been performed to a stringed instrument, played
by the singer (373), in S166 the singer or singers are accompanied
by an auletes, cf. S257 (*a*) fr. 27. 2. Even here there may have been
a fundamental difference; at any rate, the differences between the
poets are much more striking than possible instances of influence.[12]

The general conclusion of this discussion is apparent: one should
certainly not divide Ibycus' poems into two separate groups, or
suppose a radical alteration in the nature of his poetry. The poems
would seem to have mingled praise, love, myth, Homeric diction,
Stesichorean triads, and an emphasis on a narrator identified with

---

[10] S257 (*a*) fr. 1 may show a motif related to Anacr. 346 fr. 1; related points apply.
[11] Choriambic expansion: cf. West (1992), 340 (more cautiously (1982), 52).
[12] On the sambyke see West (1992), 75 n. 120.

the poet. Many of these combinations can be seen in Alcman; some even in Sappho. But the nature of the connections in Ibycus and of the traditions before him, and particularly his closeness to, and distance from, Stesichorus, suggest a more advertised mixing and redirecting of different streams. Socially, culturally, and poetically, Ibycus' work and activity display the roots of Simonides', Bacchylides', and Pindar's; but later developments should not make his own poetry less striking. The long fragment S151 [11] provides our best chance, and our most serious challenge, for getting closer to an understanding of his work.

11: *PMGF* S151[13]

The introduction above indicates that S151 [11] is no anomaly in Ibycus' work, and renders certain lines of approach unrewarding. The use of 'Homeric' language is not a deplorable aberration; notions of parody are no more plausible. Such language is a part of Ibycus' usual style and of his Stesichorean inheritance. As Pindar and Bacchylides reveal, many of these words and phrases become part of the lyric repertoire, and may already have been so; the same is true of the numerous non-Homeric adjectives. The language in fact needs analysis, to single out those words and especially phrases which are likely to have struck the listener as distinctively epic, Homeric, or Iliadic. Strongly Iliadic phrases are placed and used with both care and point.

Antitheses and relationships in this poem between the mythical past and the present, between love and heroism, between the narrator's depiction of his own emotions and his reporting of events, spring naturally from Ibycus' recreation of his genre and its traditions. A map of modern genres like Hamburger's, which uses both time and the lyric first person as primary bases of division between genres (Hamburger (1980)), only makes it the clearer how intriguing are Ibycus' procedure in general and this poem in particular. Is the poem about the first-person subject, his addressee, and the pre-

---

[13] On S151 [11] see Maas (1922); Wilamowitz (1922), 508–13; Page (1951*b*); Barron (1961, 1964, 1969); Maehler (1963), 75–7; Sisti (1966, 1967); West (1966*b*), 152–3, (1975), 307; Robertson (1970); Gianotti (1973); Gostoli (1979); Simonini (1979); Péron (1982); Woodbury (1991*d*); Cingano (1989); Buongiovanni (1990), 121–9; Yatromanolakis (1993); works mentioned in n. 1.

sent, or is it about the past and his epic object? How far is the poem narrative, how far metapoetic? The strange features of the poem are not merely imported from modern and postmodern concerns; nor can they be merely the product of incomplete preservation. The narrator vigorously draws attention to his own peculiar treatment of his topics. It is notable that in doing so, and in speaking of what he will not speak of, he exploits one of the most personal, and most detachedly descriptive, parts of the *Iliad*, the Catalogue of Ships. The poem may rewardingly be treated as operating on two levels: a descriptive one, on which the listener is primarily concerned by the content, particularly, in this fragment, the mythical figures and events described, and a self-referential one, on which the listener is interested by the narrator's own discourse, by his attempts to control his poem, and by the play of *praeteritio*. The interaction and conflict of these levels guide the detailed expression and shaping of the poetry; and they create the interest of the poem.

Metre

str., ant.

1. $-\overline{\smile\smile}-\overline{\smile\smile}-\overline{\smile\smile}-\cup\cup$
2. $-\overline{\smile\smile}-\cup\cup-\overline{\smile\smile}-\cup\cup$
3. $-\overline{\smile\smile}-\overline{\smile\smile}-$
4. $\overline{\smile\smile}-\cup\cup-\cup--$

ep.

1. $--\cup\cup-\cup\cup--$
2. $--\cup\cup-\cup\cup--$
3. $\overline{\smile\smile}-\overline{\smile\smile}-\cup\cup--$
4. $-\cup-\cup\cup-\cup\cup-\cup\cup--$
5. $-\cup\cup--\cup\cup-\cup-$

The metre is triadic, as in S166; the stanzas are shorter than in that poem or in Stesichorus, and recall in length and shape the Aeolic poets and Anacreon. Strophe and antistrophe are differentiated from the epode even more markedly than in Stesichorus. The strophe and antistrophe consist of two sets of 4 da, followed by what is metrically best regarded as an expanded version in a single unit, what looks like 4 da with a single-short close ($-\cup--$). One might interpret this in dactylo-epitrite or aeolic terms; the last two lines of the epode support an aeolic interpretation. All four 'lines' in the papyrus are always followed by word-end, save between 3 and 4 (42); there is elision, not of a particle, between 1 and 2 (1), and no brevis. Pause would in any case not be possible after $\cup\cup$: the frequent substitution of sp for da makes it evident that these are dactyls, not aeolic lines. The strophe and antistrophe are themselves differentiated by their openings: da sp in the extant strophes, sp da in the antistrophes. So triadic is the poet's conception. The epode is different in length. Its earlier lines consist of repeated double-short sets, but beginning from ⏖, and with a pendant ending which suggests pause (note the brevis after 3 at 7). There are 3, not 2, paroemiacs. There follows (4) what might best be seen as an aeolic variation. (Cf. e.g. Sapph. 115; Alc. 367–8; there is no variation in the aeolic base, but no variation of the first ⏑⏑, or contraction of the second and third, either; there may be anaclasis in 47.) It has the same 'da sp' ending as the paroemiacs. Then comes a clearly aeolic line (cf. Sapph. 128, *al.*), which ends like the last line of the strophe, but breaks the dactylic pattern. (See above.) The epode is not only made up of more detached units; its form makes possible the appropriation of unaltered epic phrases, from the end of the hexameter (where 'formulae' are most common). See 7, 21, 31, 33, 34. This is significant, as will appear, for the organization of the poem.

The triads are firmly divided from each other, though 20–2 exploit this division subtly. There might seem to be a stronger break between strophe and antistrophe than between antistrophe and epode (note especially 17 and 30).

1–2. We do not know how much of the poem is missing; my own guess would be a good deal. At any rate, the poem is likely to have started from the present circumstances, from Polycrates. We can reasonably infer from the breaking off (10 onwards) that this recapulation of myth (1–9) was originally introduced for a point relevant in some way to the present occasion. That point is unlikely to be the naval might of Samos: the connection would have to depend on the later part of the fragment, where no allusion is made apparent to the listener. The extent of Samos' navy and imperialism before Polycrates is unclear; even Herodotus' claims on Polycrates' own ambitions should be treated cautiously (3. 122. 2). Lines 10 and 20–2 suggest that there was no detail earlier on Helen's abduction, the Trojans who perished, or the membership of the Argive force. The mention of the Trojan War was thus a brief one; the manneristic disproportion of the interruption and *praeteritio* is the more striking.

Δαρδανίδα Πριάμοιο: Hom. *Il.* 3. 303 Δαρδανίδης Πρίαμος, 5. 159 Πριάμοιο . . . Δαρδανίδαο, *al.*; Pind. *Pyth.* 11. 19.

μέ|γ'] . . . ὄλβιον: a trio of epithets is notable even in Ibycus, who often has two (285. 3 is a special case). These epithets become progressively less standard: μέγα occurs commonly in ἄςτυ μέγα

Πριάμοιο (-ου) (Hom. *Il.* 2. 332 etc.); περικλεές gives an equivalent
to ἄστυ περικλυτόν (Hom. *Od.* 4. 9, *al.*, not of Troy); ὄλβιον is not
a conventional epithet for towns (note Pind. *Ol.* 13. 4, cf. Eumel.
12 Davies; Bacch. 19. 10, cf. 12. 4). The series gives a special force
to the verb of destruction which follows. That verb itself is seldom
used without a personal object (cf. Simonini (1979), 286; even Soph.
OC 842 has been questioned); it increases the suggestions of pathos
which will be drawn out later. Such suggestions are missing from
Simon. fr. 11. 10–13 West. The pathos is intensified by ὄλβιον,
which is most commonly used of people, and which, after Πριάμοιο,
might be thought to recall Hom. *Il.* 24. 543 καὶ cέ, γέρον, τὸ πρὶν
μὲν ἀκούομεν ὄλβιον εἶναι.

3 prepares the development to come, whatever the supplement.
Lines 5–7 and the use of ὄρνυμαι elsewhere recommend a supple-
ment like Ἄργ] rather than ἱππ] (cf. Hom. *Od.* 8. 514–15); for the
tense cf. *Hom. h. Ap.* 29, Mimn. fr. 9. 5–6 West, Pind. *Pyth.* 1. 65–6.

4. The antistrophe ends resoundingly; but the end of the epode will
suggest a different perspective. One would certainly expect Ζη]νός;
but one would also expect the serif at the top right hand of ν to
face the other way. The traces, however, do not much resemble
any letter in the hand (even c). The Διὸς βουλή can be in epic a
phrase with grim connotations: cf. e.g. Hom. *Il.* 1. 12, 12. 241 (with
μεγάλοιο), *Od.* 8. 82 (with μεγάλου, of the Trojan War), Hes. *Theog.*
572, *Cypria* fr. 1. 7 Davies (of the Trojan War; cf. Hes. fr. 204. 96–
101, 115–20 Merkelbach–West). Cf. also Bacch. 11. 121, Priam's
city sacked βουλαῖcι θεῶν; contrast Pind. *Pae.* 6 (D6). 92–8.

5–9. The organization of the epode, and its connection to the anti-
strophe, are highly elaborate. The appearance of the god as cause
at the end of the epode (9) must be related to the appearance of the
god as cause at the end of the antistrophe (4); the fair-haired mortal
at the start of the epode (5) must be related to the golden-haired
goddess at the end of the epode (9). The participial clause 5–7,
following on the participial clause 3–4, already brings in a marked
contrast: a level of causation concerned with the beauty of a woman
rather than with the will of a god. The difference is perhaps marked
by the genitives with epithets in 4 (presumably) and in 5. The end
of the epode gives force and meaning to the change. Whatever the
overt point of introducing the myth, the role and power of beauty
and love must be relevant to the wider themes of the poem.

5. ξα]νθᾱc: of Helen in lyric, Stes. S103. 5, Sapph. 23. 5; of women, e.g. Hom. *Il.* 11. 740, Hes. fr. 26. 31 Merkelbach–West.

6. The epithet for δῆ]ριν contrasts strongly with the epithet for πό]λεμον. Fame is achieved for the Greeks despite and through their suffering; the fame of Troy (2), it is suggested, was simply undone. (Note the contrast with 8–9; those lines suggest that the emphasis of 6–7 is on the Greeks alone.) πολύυμνον stands in relief against the conventionally Homeric δακρ[υό]εντα, and joins with ὑμ]νῆν in 12.

πολύυμνον: unlikely to be invented for the occasion, whatever the date of *Hom. h.* 26. 7; cf. Anacr. 446. Note Pind. *Nem.* 2. 5; Ar. *Knights* 1328, Eur. *Ion* 1074–5, Timoth. 791. 232. The date of Hom. *Od.* [24.] 515 δῆριν ἔχουcι is unknown too.

7. This characteristic epic phrase comes three times with πόλεμος, not synonyms, in the *Iliad*, once in this exact form (*Il.* 17. 512); cf. also Hes. fr. 25. 9 Merkelbach–West. *CEG* i. 47. 2 and Theogn. 890 suggest its familiarity; note also Anacr. 382. But after 6, it will probably recall what was by now the most celebrated poem on this particular strife. The borrowing of an epic line-end, with no alteration even in rhythm, is characteristic of the epodes. The Iliadic language and rhythm sharpen the pointed relation in the stanza of war and love.

8. The poem turns, in a separate main clause, to Troy; a heavy stop is needed at the end of 7 to mark this change in perspective. The Greeks suffered in the war (7), but Troy perished. ταλαπείριο[ν (Hom. *Od.* 6. 193, etc., *h. Ap.* 29, always of strangers or suppliants) strongly suggests sympathy; cf. ταλαίναι at Eur. *Andr.* 292. ἀνέ[β]α gives a graphic personification, quite unlike Homer's style. Cf. Sol. fr. 4. 26–9 West; for ἄ]τα as subject effectively put last cf. e.g. Eur. *Phoen.* 1066.

9. The name of Aphrodite ends with great strength; cf. e.g. Soph. *Ant.* 800. For love destroying the citadel of Troy cf. Theogn. 1231–3 (etc.). That passage suggests that such love may ultimately be connected in the poem with the love which is felt by the narrator for the addressee. (Other fragments and the last triad make an amorous element in the poem appear distinctly plausible.)

χρυ]coέθειραν: not a new word, cf. Archil. fr. 323 West χρυσοέθειρ (and further Nöthiger (1971), 171–2). χρυσοκόμης is used of various male divinites before the fifth century (note also *CEG* i. 308); cf. Alcm. 1 [**1**]. 51–4 of Hagesichora. Unlike the usual χρυσέη for the goddess, this word stresses the link with 5. The beauty of the goddess is strikingly opposed to the disaster she has brought.

10. There is clearly a strong break at the start of this triad, as at 23; this furthers the impression of firm organization underneath.

νῦ]γ: fits the space nicely (as defined by χρυ]); but there are other possibilities for the first visible letter. ἧc suits the space in 11 much better than ἔcτ'. νῦν would probably go principally with ὑμ]νῆν (an unfulfilled conditional earlier is a complicated possibility); in any case, premeditation would be conveyed, and most likely some specific occasion. (Pindar and Bacchylides very often use νῦν of the present celebration or victory, cf. Simon. 519 fr. 80. 4; never of the present point in the poem, save in the postpositive use with an imperative, cf. esp. Pind. *Isth.* 5. 38.) Whatever the supplement, the movement back to the immediate situation is arresting, and suggests the poet is affecting to have wandered capriciously; compare the less formal return, with emphasis on the first person but none on the plan, at Alcm. 1 [1]. 39–40 (the first person is not a poet). The caprice is less openly acknowledged here than in Pindar; cf. Buongiovanni (1990), 121–9. The first person, the narrator, none the less steps to the fore.

οὔτε: the construction already entangles us in a sequence where we become involved in what is denied. The large rhetorical structure in 10–19, running over two stanza divisions, stands far from the norms of Homeric style (*Il.* 9. 379–87 is unusual).

Paris's name (the π and the ν are both likely) matches Helen's in the first line of the preceding stanza. His act, indicated in the epithet, takes up the reference to Aphrodite. The word is used in lyric (Alc. 283. 5, of Paris; Pind. *Ol.* 10. 34). As in the Alcaeus, the narrator shows vehement condemnation; but unlike Alcaeus, he himself may be in another sphere the thrall of beauty.

ἐπιθύμιον: the word is not found elsewhere, but resembles ἀπο-θύμιος, καταθύμιος (Homer onwards). It will be connected in sense with ἐπιθυμέω, etc., first securely attested at Soph. *Trach.* 617, but mostly found in prose and comedy. (The use of ἐπὶ θυμῶι at Hom. *Il.* 13. 485, *al.*, is irrelevant.) The narrator implies his enthusiasm, and perhaps even his love.

Καccάνδραν: the narrator forcefully adds to the guilty Paris an innocent and appealing figure. Her epithet stresses her loveliness, for which cf. Hom. *Il.* 13. 336, 24. 699. Ibyc. 303 (*a*) dwells on her beauty and uses her as an example of fame. Set against Paris's epithet, and in this context, the adjective displays a beauty which was separate from the amorous crime, and was destroyed by it (cf. Aesch. *Ag.* 1156–61). τανίςφυρος occurs at Hes. *Theog.* 364, fr. 43a. 37 Merkelbach–West, etc., Bacch. 3 [**17**]. 60, *al.* How much we are to remember of Cassandra's story is not apparent; but her prophecies about Paris and Troy are pointedly relevant (e.g. Procl. *Cypria* p. 31, ll. 15–16 Davies, Bacch. 23, Pind. *Pae.* 8a (B3), Aesch. *Ag.* 1210, Eur. *Andr.* 293–300). The depiction of the war is again growing complex, and showing an almost Iliadic range of sympathies.

ὑμ]νῆν at least suggests the poems which relate to praise of the honorand: cf. S257 (*a*) fr. 1. 5, fr. 27. 3, 6 (note also S246). The stem very commonly connotes praise, and one might not expect the verb with a mortal of the past as object. The present occasion and Polycrates are much in view.

13. On one level the phrase makes the narrator seem to hasten past the subjects he is dismissing. But on another it forms a kind of climax after the two specific children mentioned. The name of Priam looks back to the presumed start of the account (1): other Trojan names were not mentioned, we can infer from this stanza. The theme, apparent in the *Iliad*, of all the sons he has lost and will lose must surely be implied. This line leads into the generality and sympathy of the final two lines on the Trojans (14–15).

14–15: the supreme calamity. The subject-matter is distinct from that of the strophe; most of those mentioned there did not die at the sack. The event had appeared in 2–3, and again in 8–9; each time the narrator's sympathy grows more marked.

Τρο]ίας: the name of Troy itself comes for the first time, enriched with a Homeric epithet (*Il.* 16. 698, *al.*; Bacch. 9. 46). ἀμ] suits the space (as defined by Τρο]) much better than οὐκ] (ed. pr.) (Nöthiger (1971), 166, seems to consider the latter possible). The whole phrase may well have a close parallel in Stesichorus' full-length account (S89. 11–12): εὐρυ]χόρ[ο]υ Τρο⟨ί⟩ας ἁλώcι[μον ἆμαρ | ⏑⏑–⏑⏑–⏑]ν ἔθηκεν (Epeius). The notable feature in our passage is ἀνώνυμον; the context in the Stesichorus does not suggest sympathy. Here the sense 'removing a name' or 'inglorious' (Maehler (1963), 75 n. 3; Simonini (1979), 289; cf. Eur. *Tro.* 1319, 1322) does not fit ἆμαρ very naturally. The primary sense is suggested by Hom. *Od.* 19. 571 ἠώc . . . δυcώνυμος, and 260, *al.*, οὐκ ὀνομαστήν. The narrator's

242 *Ibycus*

pragmatic refusal to sing of the fall (note the rest of the line) acquires a deeper significance on a different level: the silence expresses the horror.

οὐδϵη[: γ might be possible (cf. Yatromanolakis (1993), 44), but looks less likely, so far as the few undamaged γs suggest. A first-person verb may seem the most promising supposition; in any case, the organizing purpose acquires renewed emphasis from the negative. Like the first epode, this stanza conjoins both the Trojan catastrophe and the heroism that caused it. The end of the sentence (19) makes the complexity explicit.

16. ἀρετάν is expressively made the direct object. Someone's ἀρετά itself, rather than its possessor, is often presented as the object of song in Bacchylides and Pindar; cf. for the syntax Bacch. 5. 31–2, 10. 13–14.

17. ὑπ]ϵράφανον: Hes. *Theog.* 149, al. (ὑπϵρηφανέω Hom. *Il.* 11. 694); Pind. *Pyth.* 2. 28. The word is often said always to be dis-approving, before Plato, but it seems positively coloured at Bacch. 17. 48, and it must be so with ἀρετάν, on a primary level. But even a sense like 'proud' would suggest the ironies of the future; and the negative connotations are unlikely to be banished from a complex context.

18. ναϵς does not fit the space well, as defined by the line before; the word seems unavoidable, so perhaps there has been some mis-spelling. The ships are given emphasis by epithets and position; the author is preparing his allusion to the Catalogue of Ships, and ναϵς at the start of this stanza is taken up by ναῶν at the start of the next but one. As earlier, the phrase κοίλα[ι | ναϵς] πολύγομφοι combines Homeric and non-Homeric elements (κοῖλος of ships Hom. *Il.* 1. 26, etc., Pind. *Ol.* 6 [**18**]. 10; πολύγομφος Hes. *WD* 660, cf. Simon. 543. 10). The standard Homeric element begins the group, as in 1–2. Lines 18–20 also seem to evoke Hom. *Il.* 13. 453–4 ἐνθάδε νῆϵς ἔνϵικαν | σοί τϵ κακὸν κτλ.; but the lyric ἐλϵύσαν is used for ἔνϵικαν, and the context makes Idomeneus' vaunt into a more poised narra-torial statement. (Cf. also 2. 303–4, again an unsympathetic Nestor; within the *Iliad* cf. 24. 542.) Τροί]αι (cf. *Il.* 13. 454; hardly avoid-able) looks back to what precedes, and specifically takes up Τρο]ίας 14, also at the start of a line. κακόν (cf. *Il.* 13. 454), now poignantly balanced by ἐςθ[λούς, acquires a tragic force. The line is detached by pendant endings in 18–19, and given resonance by the pause that follows.

On an entirely different level, the line shows the subject at least straining at the narrator's repressive leash; in particular, ἥρωας ἐςθ[λούς takes up ἠρ]ώων ἀρετάν. He is not in fact supplying details, if 15 implied that; but the language suggests how much there is to say. Details actually follow, but on the leader alone.

The combination ἥρωες ἐςθλοί is not attested elsewhere in archaic poetry.

20–2. Agamemnon is here singled out and magnificently adorned. He appears as a figure of supremacy in power; he is highly relevant to the themes and the implicit argument of the poem.

On the level of the narrator's discourse, the overflowing description shows subject and theme pressing to escape the narrator's professed will.

The poet once again exploits the rhythms of the epode to place common Iliadic line-endings: κρείων Ἀγαμέμνων (Hom. *Il*. 2. 477, 576 etc.; in the *Odyssey* only εὐρὺ κρ. Ἀγ. 3. 248; not 'Hesiod'). The most straightforwardly Homeric language again comes at the start. ἀγὸς ἀνδρῶν occurs only three times in Homer (*Il*. 4. 519, *al*.); it ends the line, but is always preceded by Λυκίων etc. (cf. Pind. *Nem*. 1. 51). The phrase is used more generally, not at the end of the line, at Hes. fr. 196. 1 Merkelbach–West; Ibycus also has in mind the Homeric ἄναξ ἀνδρῶν (note *Il*. 2. 612). The language dwells copiously on Agamemnon's lineage, and includes the non-Homeric Pleisthenes. ἐςθ[λοῦ or ἐςθ[λός (slightly better for the space) probably takes up ἐςθ[λούς, and suggests the general theme of ἀρετά (not a very moral ἀρετά in the case of Atreus).

τῶν] μέν: the supplement fits very neatly, and cannot be avoided. The μέν is primarily emphatic, a use we see much of in the poem. That use is common in epic (e.g. Hom. *Il*. 2. 636, 3. 16, Hes. *Theog*. 479, fr. 43a. 55 Merkelbach–West), but also in Pindar (with pronouns e.g. *Pyth*. 3. 73, 4. 54, *Isth*. 8. 56); it may be part of Ibycus' lyric tradition. However, when μέν emphasizes a pronoun, it invites the consideration of contrasts, and an antithesis between the Greek's glorious leader and the unfortunate Priam springs naturally from the poem so far (note Πλειςθε[νί]δας and Δαρδανίδα).

[ἄ]ρχε: the imperfect evokes the Catalogue of Ships (Hom. *Il*. 2. 494, 576 (NB) etc.), the example which the narrator will shortly be affecting to resist. The Catalogues of Greeks and Trojans one may assume to have been seen by poets in this period as an integrated and impressive part of the *Iliad*; so indeed they are (Visser (1997) seems along the right lines).

Πλεισθε[νί]δας: the ending obviously cannot denote a father or mother here. Cf. e.g. Hom. *Il*. 2. 860 Αἰακίδαο (grandfather), Pind. *Ol*. 13. 67 Αἰολίδα βασιλεῦ (great-grandfather); Eur. *IA* 855 Αἰακοῦ γένεθλον (grandfather). βασιλεὺς Πλεισθενίδας comes at Stes. 219. 2, with whatever meaning (Barron (1969), 145 n. 31, mentions Bacch. 15. 48). The political significance, if any, of Ibycus' genealogy is secondary to the place of Agamemnon's glory in the themes of the poem. Again the epode ends weightily.

ἔκγ[ο]νος is not usually combined with a word for 'child'; as with βασιλ[εὺ]ς ἀγὸς ἀνδρῶν and other aspects of the clause, the words are heaped up and the magnificent lineage stressed.

23–6. First the textual problems. In 26 after διερ.[there are about seven letters missing before τά. Since the metre allows at most one letter, something else must have been put here; even if this were a variant then deleted, the existence of a serious textual problem is indicated. διερ. itself, incidentally, causes problems of reading: if the ink near the foot of ρ is part of a letter, the letter cannot be ο (α would be possible, and could fit the following low stroke). The long syllable at the end of 24, not followed by a vowel, looks a further sign of corruption. The metre would seem to show that the first two 'lines' of strophe and antistrophe are dactyls, not aeolic lines. In ten other places a short syllable ends and is not followed by hiatus, and after one (1) there is elision (the ignoring of digamma is not reason enough to emend); substitution of a spondee for dactyl is frequent in the lines, and suggests these are dactyls, not aeolic cola. (θνατός does not of itself make a short impossible before it: cf. 288. 4 (and 2?), 298, 315. 1; the shortening before a new word is especially easy.) The text, then, is likely to be amiss.

West's αὐτός ((1966*b*), 152–3) is extremely attractive; it restores the metre, and suits the word-order in 25. But what of the sense? West takes ἐμβαίεν ((1975), 307) to mean 'set on the road to fame' (note now the causative perhaps used at Emped. Strasb. d 10 (Martin and Primavesi (1998), 147)); but surely the strong aorist could not be causative. If the word is sound, it must mean 'enter on', with τά as object (see on ἐμβαίεν below). If it does so, with αὐτός, then the narrator is either (*a*) professing that he cannot present a full account or (*b*) professing that he can or (*c*) contemplating the matter in the abstract. (*a*) does not fit αὐτός: to stress 'on his own' implies he could do it with the Muses' aid, and no reason is presented why the narrator would not be helped, which would be a surprising notion. (*c*) means there is no pointed relation to the denial in 15–19, whether a further *praeteritio* (as in (*a*)), or an effectively outrageous contradiction (as in (*b*)); and to what end would the abstract idea be contemplated? (*b*) seems unlikely without at least a further positive statement to go beyond the potential 25–6. Lines 32–45 spring out of 30–1, in a parallel way to 20; it would be awkward to find there the beginning of an account that directly claimed to be full. The description in 23–4 of how the Muses could embark on the tale themselves, in antithesis with 25–6, seems at the least implausibly overdone if the point is merely to stress that the speaker will need their help.

The original text, then, was neither the transmitted text nor this conjecture; but in this unpromising passage it is more important to see the general structure and point. If the corruption lies in θνατός, as deriving from a gloss, the answer could be anything. The narrator must be professing inability to present a full and satisfactory account. He is continuing the sequence of thought in 10–22 as a whole (hence καί, not ἀλλά); he is particularly reinforcing the assertion of 15–19. At the same time, he is averting the appearance which he had teasingly created in 20–2 of intending to give an account of the heroes after all. He offers a hypothetical picture of the Muses starting such an account, which is what he had seemed to be doing himself in 20–2; this picture of course implies that they could do the rest. In 25–6 he shows the mortal unable to carry on and present (or present well) a full account, which is what he is refusing to do now. The poet again seems close to launching an account of some kind at 32; but that is a new stage of teasing, marked by the τ]ῶν μέν which parallels the τῶν] μέν at 20 that opened the preceding stage. The present moment, then, is not chaotic or confused.

Is it not strange to imply that a mortal man could not produce a full account, or a satisfactory full account, when Homer had already done so? Ibycus alludes to Homer throughout 20–35, and not least his passage on the Muses' aid at *Il.* 2. 484–92. The relation to Homer can only intelligibly be seen as ironic, though playfully so and within the fiction of the poem. The probable differences from

Homer in 32–45 imply that Homer's account is neither full nor satisfactory; fullness at least is stressed in the context. Homer's claim to have been informed by the Muses is thus false (Pindar can assail Homer's lies, *Nem.* 7. 23–4). The suggestion of Homer's text that we hear the Muses themselves (cf. *Il.* 2. 484, 761, 1. 1, 11. 218, etc.) is elegantly countered by a notional picture of the Muses acting as poets on this theme, as against the fact of men's, and so of Homer's, inadequacy.

23. μέν may imply a contrast with Polycrates, to whom the mannerist poet will eventually, and briefly, return.

cεcοφι̣[c]μέναι, as Barron notes, looks to Hes. *WD* 649 ((1969), 134), cf. here 18, and perhaps 24. Ibycus' point, however, will be Hesiod's, the importance of the Muses' skill and knowledge. There may be some further point in alluding to Hesiod: Ibycus avoids with care too Homeric an appearance precisely at this juncture. The Hesiodic passage confirms that, even with εὖ, the perfect participle does not lay a great deal of stress on the preceding process. None the less, the conception strikingly presents the Muses themselves as poets. Compare the thematically significant section within the Catalogue, *Il.* 2. 594–600, and Hes. *Theog.* 36–51, *Hom. h. Ap.* 185–93, etc. But cεcοφι̣[c]μέναι | εὖ, of the Muses themselves, and λόγω[ι if right, make them appear more like human poets; that suits the passage (as I see it).

24. Only Ἑλικωνίδε[c] in this line seems fairly certain to be sound.

εὖ: to be taken with cεcοφι̣[c]μέναι rather than with ἐμβαίεν; that would be an odd and condescending collocation. For εὖ following cf. Pind. *Pyth.* 9. 93; Hom. *Od.* 19. 446, Bacch. 3 [**17**]. 94.

Ἑλικωνίδε[c]: Hes. *Theog.* 1, *WD* 658, Pind. *Pae.* 7b (C2). 19, *al.* The origin is probably standard by this time (Pindar needs no noun); Ibycus may well have been aware it was quite un-Homeric.

ἐμβαίεν: an accusative of respect for τά would be thoroughly unconvincing. ἐμβαίνω first takes the accusative, with an external object, at Eur. *El.* 1288. This is not wholly encouraging, especially with λόγωι coming next; but it is not a fatal objection to the word. It suits the context more effectively than, say, ὑμνοίεν. Silk (1974), 157, suggests a connection with ships.

λόγω[ι: if it should be sound, 'in speech', cf. Pind. *Ol.* 3. 16 etc. 'With enumeration' (Wilamowitz (1922), 509) would demand an unattested sense, and would also be prosy.

25. The narrator is on any view more oblique in referring to himself than Homer (*Il.* 2. 488–90, cf. 761), who is so much less personal as a rule. The narrator saves emphasis on himself for the negative (10) and for Polycrates (48). This has more point if the narrator is here speaking of something he is not proposing to do.

27. The dependent construction has a new strophe; the opening word repeats what was doubtless the opening word of the last epode (18) but introduces more detail. All this gives further weight to what the poet will not touch. The listener has a paradoxical sense, as at 20–2, of verbal 'luxury'.

ọ[.... ἀρι]θμός: very slight trace of first *o*. ὄccoc would suit the space. As to the sense of the phrase, the total number seems less suitable to τὰ ἕκαcτα εἴποι than 'the ships, as many as went' (cf. Eur. *IA* 231; Hom. *Il.* 2. 492, with West (1998–) i. 66). In any case, the detailed enumeration in Homer's catalogue is implied. The expression itself is un-Homeric. Cf. 'annoveraste' (the Muses to Homer etc.) in the explicit allusion to the Catalogue at Parini, *Il giorno, Mat.* 858 (= 832 in 1763 version); the whole parodic appeal for aid in 855–64 underlines the expected ideas from which Ibycus is diverging.

ἀπ' Αὐλίδος | Αἰγαῖον: concrete detail not in 17–19, which suggests a more detailed account. Note Hom. *Il.* 2. 303–4. Woodbury's ἐπ' Αὐλίδος ((1991*d*), 416–17) palliates the awkwardness with the end of 28. But the phrase does not stand so easily near or with its noun as in parallel instances (verbal nouns do not count); ἐπί does not seem attractive; considerable awkwardness remains in defining the fleet as that at Aulis while saying it went from Greece to Troy; and the sentence becomes oddly fussy. It seems more likely that ἀπ' Ἄργεος has intruded into 28 from 36, encouraged by the similar line-ending in 27.

ἠλύθọ[ν: the Doric accent implies the plural, as Wilamowitz saw ((1922), 508 n. 2; cf. Stes. S39. 3).

30. An un-Homeric epithet (Hes. *WD* 507, Bacch. 11. 114, Pind. *Nem.* 10. 41 (?), *al.*). The writing here does not show positively the same sympathy for Troy as in the parallel passage 17–19.

If the syntax is rightly restored in 27 and 30, a paratactic turn facilitates the drift into recounting what was being renounced. φῶτες at the end of the stanza balances ναῶν at the beginning, and suggests the whole mass of the Greeks, not only the leaders.

31. The new stanza gives splendid force to this line, which exalts the Greeks at Troy as warriors. The epode again shows an especially strong emphasis on warfare, and epic expression; it is as grandiose as, and even more Iliadic than, the preceding epode. The antithesis of valour and beauty is to be very strongly marked by the language, and connected with sorts of poetry.

χ]αλκάϲπι[δεϲ: the final trace is more likely to be part of ι than of π, which does not usually have much right-hand extension; cf. 11. The resonant compound does not occur in epic, but is used in later lyric (Pind. *Ol.* 9. 54, Bacch. 11. 62, P. Oxy. 2736 fr. 1. 22, *al.*). The pattern in φῶτεϲ | χ]αλκάϲπι[δεϲ, noun, line-end, compound, repeats that in 29–30 with greater strength, thanks to the stanza-end and the content.

υἷεϲ Ἀχα[ι]ῶν: the phrase is archetypally Homeric (e.g. *Il.* 2. 234, 273, 281, 370, 722; four times more common in the *Iliad* than in the *Odyssey*; not in other archaic poetry). But it is here used with more flourish. The poet is again exploiting the rhythmic potential of the epode.

32. τ]ῶν μέν: as in the previous epode (20), the words mark a semblance of transgressive movement beyond the original declaration of silence. The narrator had there given the leader, with abundant detail; he now gives the two outstanding fighters. In this second case, he is also trespassing on the territory of the Catalogue, which gives a special place to the best warriors (and horses), naming Achilles and Ajax. The narrator is not actually entering on the full details of the army; but the author is teasing the listener.

The μέν need not have any further function. Possibly, in spite of its Wackernagelian position, it might presently suggest a contrast with the most fair (cf. e.g. Pind. *Pyth.* 3. 96–9).

πρ[οφ]ερέϲτατοϲ: Homeric (*Od.* 8. 128), but not the phrase used at *Il.* 2. 770 (πόλυ φέρτατοϲ, cf. ὄχ᾽ ἄριϲτοϲ 761, μέγ᾽ ἄριϲτοϲ 768). The poem stresses its divisions by adding α[ἰ]χμᾶι, and especially by not making Achilles, as in Homer, the most beautiful too (*Il.* 2. 673–4). The scholion makes it unlikely there was room to mention Achilles with a πεδά in 38–9.

33. An exclusively Iliadic line-end, again in the epode. One should not introduce historic presents in supplements. A simple ἦνθεν does not seem at all impossible for the space. Pindar and Stesichorus (S39. 3, 222 (b) [3]. 180 ἐνθεῖν) use both ἦλθον (ἦνθον) and ἤλυθον.

34. In Homer's Catalogue, the best men and horses are named partly as a means of emphasizing Achilles at the close; the gap between him and Ajax is important to the poem. (Cf. Alc. 387, Soph. *Aj.* 1340–1.) Here the two are placed as if on an equal footing, and indeed the second is more richly adorned with epithets: two Iliadic phrases are combined (μέγας Τελαμώνιος Αἴας (*Il.* 5. 610 etc.) and μέγας ἄλκιμος Αἴας (*Il.* 12. 349, 362)). The following phrase probably refers to Ajax too, in view of the punctuation at the end of 35.

35. If fire (π is likely), perhaps a comparison rather than the vain defence of the ships (Hom. *Il.* 15. 727–46, 16. 112–23). An arresting close, at any rate.

36. After these names, central to the *Iliad*, come two Greeks foreign to the *Iliad*, and a Trojan, Troilus, mentioned once there (24. 257), but as a famous son of Priam now dead. Other names may have been mentioned in this stanza, but Ibycus clearly wishes to be in some respects markedly un-Iliadic. The divergence is only heightened by the probable use of a Homeric formulation at 36–7 (*Il.* 2. 674 κάλλιστος ἀνὴρ ὑπὸ Ἴλιον ἦλθε), for Ibycus appears to diverge multiply from Homer on the most beautiful Greeks. (For Homer Achilles is first, Nireus second; contrast Eur. *IA* 204–5.) Since we evidently have a superlative in 36, since Cyanippus will hardly have been said only to excel those from Peloponnesian Argos, and since the best fighters have already been mentioned, it is likely that the poem turns to beauty at the start of the stanza. The differences from Homer should throw, within the poem, an ironic light on Homer's authority and claim to inspiration; the very absence of these names from Homer is another blot, since one or both are leaders. Such irony would be part of the fiction of the poem, rather than an actual attack; its basis (some marginal figures) and its setting (wilful *praeteritio*) suggest that the impact of this independence is amusing and mischievous. Such irony is already suggested in 23–6, if the right view has been taken of those lines, for Homer's claims are there implicitly denied. But it is significant that the real movement away from the *Iliad* occurs with the mention of beauty. Despite the Homeric form at the start, the homosexual ethos of the last triad is to be felt as alien to the ethos of the *Iliad*, and contrasted with it. At the same time, the narrator's emphasis on the centrality of love to the Trojan War (5, 9) is given further, and argumentative, significance. The winners in beauty bulk even larger in Ibycus than the winners in prowess; in Homer, the latter were vital, Nireus (for all the anaphora) incidental, and curtly dismissed as insignificant in war (*Il.* 2. 675). On a lighter level, it is to seem pleasing that precisely as the narrator appears to wander most uninhibitedly from his declared intentions he finds his way back to his primary subject.

ἀπ' Ἄργεος: might mean Greece (cf. Hom. *Il.* 2. 287, 348) and so be linked with the superlative, or Argos, from which Cyanippus came.

37. Cyanippus is confirmed by the scholion: for the identification see Barron (1969), 130–1, and also Cingano (1989). It seems most natural (cf. 20, 32, etc.) to suppose that Cyanippus is portrayed as coming at the time of the original expedition. The author mentioned in the scholion seems to think similarly, and further to claim that Ibycus invented this version. Presumably he does not say that he made Aigialeus, Cyanippus' father in some versions, Adrastus' son (as Campbell suggests ((1982–93), iii. 225). It sounds as though Ibycus stated explicitly that Cyanippus was son of Adrastus. This suggests that 38 or 38–9 were still concerned with Cyanippus, 39 or 39–40 with Zeuxippus. Cyanippus is son of Adrastus at Apollod. 1. 19. 13, and so of the right age to come at the beginning of the war; Pausanias (2. 18. 4) and Tryphiodorus (159–61) make him son of Aegialeus, but Paus. 2. 30. 10 suggests a reconciliation with the other version. One might expect him, as king, to be leader of the Argives.

40. καὶ Ζεύξιππος, ὅν] ᾳ suits the space, as far as can be seen (Φοίβωι κυϲαμέν]α does not); it also suits the syntax of 34. For the article cf. 288. 3; it would suit a divine being, as in Pindar and Bacchylides. Barron's other points ((1969), 130) against his original supplement possess little weight (no word-end after the spondee as at the beginning of the other antistrophes, no father or city for Zeuxippus). It seems not implausible, then, that there was a significant break between strophe and antistrophe in sense (as in the other two instances), and thus that the whole of the strophe was devoted to Cyanippus.

For the equally obscure Zeuxippus, king of Sicyon and so a leader, see Barron (1961), Cingano (1979). Again there are chronological complications. Ibycus' own motivation for mentioning him, in this Samian poem, is unlikely to be political.

Hyllis is a nymph elsewhere (Paus. 2. 6. 7, Call. fr. 712 Pfeiffer); in this style χρυϲόϲτροφ[οϲ suggests her divinity. The epithet is not attested before (Soph. *OT* 203–4 uses it in a different sense); it is pronouncedly feminine, even more so than καλλίζωνοϲ, and marks the reappearance of female beauty. (Ibycus' account of the forces had not hitherto included details like Hom. *Il.* 2. 513–15 on Astyoche.) For the ϲτρόφοϲ see Aesch. *Supp.* 457, *Th.* [872] (with Hutchinson (1985), 193).

Troilus, unlike the two Greeks, was a figure well known to Homer, and common in archaic art. See Robertson (1970); Kossatz-Deissmann (1981), 75–95. At Hom. *Il.* 24. 257 he appears as a particularly distinguished warrior; but in archaic art he is only a boy, as in later literature (Pearson (1917), ii. 253; Pfeiffer (1949–53), i. 365; Nisbet and Hubbard (1978), 147–8; add Sen. *Ag.* 747–8). His boyish beauty is referred to by Phrynichus (*TrGF* 3 F13); like Cassandra he was mentioned elsewhere by Ibycus, S224 (cf. Jenner (1998)). Ibycus seems to have referred to him there as a boy (10, cf. 7), to have spoken of Achilles' slaying him, and probably the setting up of his tomb (οἱ must be wrong in 11, θε[οὶ is uncertain). Doubtless he was there too used as an example of beauty. The story of Achilles' slaying him is standard, and appeared in the *Cypria* (Procl., p. 32. 81–2 Davies); whether the story of Achilles' being in love with him is also so early we cannot say (Lycophr. 307–13 etc.; Phrynichus need not imply the story). Within this poem, he is emphatically segregated from Achilles, and the point is rather that Achilles' young victim, within a different scheme of values, is as important as he or more so. (Troilus and his supremacy are dwelt on longer.) We also recur, notably, to Trojans.

A heavy stop after ἐγήνατο seems desirable. The δ' [ἄ]ρα moves the poem on to a new point, and marks a yet further extension of the *praeteritio*, even as the arguments about beauty and supremacy in beauty are advanced. The connection with 13 (Troilus is even a favourite son of Priam in Homer) marks further the narrator's transgression. Here, by contrast with 13, the pathos of Troilus' death is only in the background, and an interest in beauty is to the fore; this is the reverse of the treatment of Priam's daughter Cassandra (11–12).

41–5: first the syntax. The construction of dative for the thing or person compared to and accusative for the area of the comparison (μορφάν) is very common in epic with εἴκελος, ἴκελος, ἐναλίγκιος, ὁμοῖος, etc., cf. e.g. Hom. *Il.* 4. 253, *Od.* 6. 151–2 (with ἔϊσκω), 9. 4, Hes. *WD* 304, *Scut.* 88; Xenoph. fr. 23. 2 West, Ibyc. S166. 26 (cf. *Hom. h. Aphr.* 28). The addition of an epithet to the accusative is unusual; the narrator is dwelling sensuously on the idea of beauty. Stranger is the combination of likening one person to another with a likening inside an image (the first likening is made by the characters within the narrative, the second by the narrator). There is thus an un-epic complexity of comparing. Even more peculiar is the nature of the comparison: is it marking similarity or difference? τρὶς ἄπεφθο[ν] ἤδη seems to make it clear that there is a significant difference between gold and orichalc, and so between the two beauties; on the other hand, μάλ' seems curious unless close likeness is being emphasized. (It is clearly being emphasized at Hom. *Od.* 19. 384 (note also πάντα at *Il.* 5. 181); μάλιστα is of no use, since it could be a true superlative (note also Hom. *Od.* 6. 151–2).) The poet must be deliberately making both points: they said Troilus was in beauty very like Zeuxippus (the narrative starting-point), but yet realized Troilus' unmatched pre-eminence. Even at Call. fr. 75. 30–1 Pfeiffer, where the comparability of the pair is stressed through the comparison with metals, the slight superiority of gold and Cydippe must be suggested (note φαεινῶι in this context). The image is one of connoisseurs expertly separating like and extreme beauties. Cf. in general Theocr. 12. 27–37 (whatever the text at the end). The perplexing intricacy of the language suits the subtle and amorous ethos that the poet is now creating. The simple Homeric idea of the most beautiful is being carried into very un-Homeric territory. That idea was used in Ibycus' poetry about the living: S166. 23–7, 173. 6?; note also 181. 10.

42. Gold, though still related to beauty, now enters the poem in an image; cf. 40, 9. There has been little comparison in the poem so far (35 might be an exception).

Orichalc appears in Stes. 260, Bacch. fr. 51; on its nature cf. Bulloch (1985), 128. Note Plat. *Criti.* 119 c 7–d 1.

43. τρίς gives the most extravagant possible image of perfection. For ἄπεφθό[ν] cf. (with a comparison of metals) Theogn. 1106 (cf. 449), Simon. 592.

ἤδη would not have much point with ἔϊσκον. Presumably it indicates that the gold has already reached the highest state of refinement, and could go no further.

44. Τρῶες Δ[α]ναοί τ': the phrase strikes an Iliadic note at the start of the epode. One might expect the phrase to be used of fighting (cf. Hom. *Il.* 16. 764 etc.); in fact it is used of judging beauty, and the Greeks and Trojans agree, not even showing partiality to their own side. The different currents of Trojan and Greek are here resolved; and it is a Trojan who is most beautiful. The form of the epode is used, after the two preceding epodes, precisely to mark the movement away from warfare and at last even from myth. The first extant epode combined war and love, but in myth, and grimly.

ἐρό[ε]ccαν: Hes. *Theog.* 245, *al.*, *Hom. h. Dem.* 109, *al.*, Alc. 296b. 2, *al.*

46–8. First grammar and the text. The scribe or his exemplar took πεδα to mean μέτεcτι, as is shown by the accentuation πέδα as well as the stop after αἰέν (Doric, and μέν, would prevent anastrophe). But since we have these lines complete, there is no reason to surrender our judgement. 'They have a share in beauty for ever' is quite unconvincing. Why 'have a share'? Hardly in a cosmic and abstract beauty. Nor can one find natural in a poet of this time, or adequately explained in the poem, the idea of the young people keeping their beauty through being celebrated in art. Keats was writing, in a different period, about figures on a work of art treated as if real (cf. Woodbury (1991*d*), 420–1, an admirable statement). One might add that the asyndeton in 48 would be displeasing. It is not, however, a very serious objection to πέδα that μέτεcτι (μέτα) is not attested with this sense or construction so early; cf. Parm. fr. 11. 4 Coxon, Aesch. *Eum.* 575.

κάλλεος, then, will be governed by κλέος (cf. Bacch. 13. 65–6). The appearance of αἰέν as well as ἄφθιτον is not unduly disquieting (cf. Theogn. 245–6).

An epic licence with the name seems at least as plausible as anaclasis, when change and corruption are so easy. Cf. Pind. *Isth.* 2. 36.

If κατά in 48 were to govern both nouns, ὡc would have to go with the preposition. This use is not found before Sophocles; it is a more worrying case than μέτεcτι. It is also not clear what ὡc would mean. Furthermore, the repetition of κλέος is awkward unless it is pointed, as καί would make it; cf. *Hom. h. Ap.* 381, *CEG* i. 344. 2. We should, then, place a comma after ἐξεῖc, and take ὡc to be a conjunction 'as'.

One should understand ἄφθιτόν ἐcτι; understanding the present is grammatically easy, and 'my fame too is because of song' would produce a weak connection and a strained clause. κατά 'because of' (unlike 'in regard to') is satisfactorily attested in Aeschylus (*Supp.* 336 etc.) and Herodotus, and later; it goes here with a somewhat unexpected sort of noun.

The recurrence to the person to be honoured is extremely swift, in comparison with all that has preceded, and even with the space for the mythic beauties. The return and the rapidity must be displaying, not an insult, but a mannered brilliance, and a toying with the areas of Ibycus' sort of song.

The combination of narrator and addressee at the end suits this kind of poem, which is based around the relationship of these two figures, still more than are Pindar and Bacchylides' versions of such praise poetry. The coupling of narrator's and addressee's glory resembles closes in Pindar and Bacchylides, cf. especially Pind. *Ol.* 1. 115–16 (cέ τε . . . ἐμέ τε . . .), Bacch. 3 [**17**]. 93–8; note also Pind. *Ol.* 6 [**18**]. 101–6, and cf. *Hom. h. Ap.* 165–78 (end of Delian Hymn). These passages vary in modesty, but none is so assertive as this. The use of proud statements in closes recalls Hor. *Odes* 3. 30, say, or Ov. *Am.* 3. 15. Such statements, however, come later in the history of poetry; this seems to be the first extant place where a poet directly claims immortality for himself or herself.

This difference from earlier poets is scarcely a matter of their intellectual limitation. Artists were not conceived as of necessity anonymous. Numerous Greek poets from Hesiod on carefully name themselves; even sculptors and vase-painters of the sixth century sometimes sign; Homer's self-effacement springs from epic tradition. Hence it can hardly not have occurred to poets that they, like older poets, might gain posthumous glory (cf. Simon. fr. 20. 14–15 West?), when the eternity of praise produced by poetry was a familiar theme (e.g. Theogn. 242–52, cf. Sapph. 55, and the introduction to her poems above; Pind. *Pyth.* 6. 5–14; note also *CEG* i. 344). Nor is the difference a matter of this author's real character; Ibycus' narrator, like Horace's and Ovid's, seems self-conscious enough elsewhere (and indeed Pindar and Bacchylides are proud enough elsewhere). Decorum, emphasis, and the nature of genre and poem are much more relevant. Not only, in this poem, is the narrator as poet particularly important. We also see here poetry more openly and extensively concerned with the present poem as poem than earlier poetry had been; more so too than the somewhat less exuberant developments by the later epinician poets (one might make analogies between Ibycus and Gorgias' rhetoric). The conclusion marks the poem itself as a primary subject of this self-referential work. The lines also have a role in its design and impact. The level of song and self-reference has hitherto been a somewhat playful element in the poem; now it takes over the language of grandeur. The notable pride of the close is a striking theatrical gesture, which concludes and celebrates the manneristic flamboyance of the poem.

τοῖc μέν: Polycrates is not compared to the supreme Troilus, but to all three beauties; we leave the mythical discussion impetuously. The device that marked expatiation before (20, 32) now also marks return.

πεδά: 'among', as in Pindar and Homer, but metaphorically. The passage indirectly implies the fame bestowed by Homer and other poets; but we see no praise of Homer, as in Simon. fr. 11. 15–18 West, and the emphasis is on the present poet and his powers. The narrator had seemed modest, and more modest than Homer, at 23–7; now he thrusts himself forward.

κάλλεοc: emphatically placed, before καὶ cύ, and separated from κλέοc. The word is likely to resume κάλλι]cτοc (probable in 36); an argument about beauty is felt to run purposefully through. But the martial heroes are left behind. Since Polycrates is a boy, and the narrator quite probably to be thought enamoured, this suits the situation of the poem.

αἰέν: the time of the poem moves not only into the present but into large vistas of the future. Poetry is the force that bridges these divisions of time. Hitherto the descriptive and the self-referential level have been separated; now they coalesce.

The mention of beauty, by this period, makes Polycrates unlikely to have gained his beard. The other poems where Ibycus refers to lovely boys as objects of his praise and love (S173, S257 (a) fr. 1, fr. 27, 289 (a)) provide further confirmation. The address moves us forcefully into the present; but the poet's discourse provides the continuity.

κλέοc ἄφθιτον: the phrase occurs in archaic poetry (*CEG* i. 2. 1, 344. 2); but given the context and the importance of the *Iliad* to the poem, it seems hard to forget that the one place it is used in Homer is of Achilles and his dilemma (*Il.* 9. 413, cf. Finkelberg (1986)).

κατ' ἀοιδάν corresponds to κάλλεος in point and position.

The range and boldness of the poem (or rather fragment) emerge from comparison with Simon. fr. 11 West (if editors are right to join P. Oxy. 3965 frr. 1 and 2). As we have noticed, Simonides' narrator differs from Ibycus' in treating Homer with more reverence and himself with less pride; he is also less complex in his sympathies when treating Troy. His whole relation of Troy and Homer to Plataea and himself stresses links; there is no self-conscious and self-subversive play. Not that Ibycus' poem is simply playful. His polemical handling of the *Iliad* is not only self-advertising; it is connected with the suggested opposition of beauty and valour, of love and war. Is the poem conveying gravely an authorial belief about values (the word 'serious' is full of traps)? We cannot say, not merely because the author's beliefs are inaccessible, but because the poem is so written that pathos and grandeur clash with mischief and self-reference, and evade resolution. By the end there has been no Anacreontic undermining of the narrator; but his final triumph emphasizes self-reference as much as the value of beauty and love. The ultimate 'seriousness' of the poem is left undefined; but the poem stimulates to thought as well as enjoyment.

ANACREON

Introduction

ANACREON is connected with four places, Teos, Abdera, Samos, and Athens. His mobility reflects, not only the impact of Persia, but the interest of the exceptionally rich in attracting poets from elsewhere. There is a more obvious resemblance with Ibycus' and Simonides' career than with that of earlier poets (Stesichorus' date and activities are not clear). The uniform tradition that he came from Teos began early (Hdt. 3. 121. 1, Ar. *Thesm.* 161). Strabo says (14. 1. 30) that it was in Anacreon's time that the Teians left to refound Abdera on the coast of Thrace (it had earlier been founded by Clazomenae). This event happened about 545, when the Persian general Harpagus attacked Teos (Hdt. 1. 168). The date fits well with other dates for Anacreon; if he was then in Teos, he must at least have joined the flight, which Herodotus says was universal, and which necessitated the later refoundation of Teos from Abdera (Pind. *Pae.* 2 (D2). 29–30). There is obviously a considerable possibility that Strabo (or rather his source) gives Anacreon's time because Anacreon mentioned the foundation or Abdera. When the refoundation of Teos occurred is not known (most likely not for several years after 545); the close tie between Teos and Abdera remained into the fifth century.

Teos was a significant Ionian city; Abdera is likely to have been a wealthy place. Anacreon's poetry is often associated primarily with the 'court' of Polycrates (and that of the Pisistratids); but the importance of the earlier period should not be underrated. Some of Anacreon's poems referred to Teos (463; 490 more doubtful?; cf. P. Oxy. 3722 fr. 73. 8–9). Two major and characteristic fragments will be argued below to belong to Abdera, and in one of them he presents himself (it will be argued) as not particularly young. If they at least belong to Abdera, it is not probable that the essential nature of Anacreon's poetry was determined by his environment on Samos. (The misleading associations of the word 'court' should not be allowed to affect the argument.) He will have been invited to Samos because he had already attained a wide renown.[1]

When was he invited, and by whom? A passage of Himerius, with a complicated textual basis, claims that Polycrates' father sent for him to teach his son (Anacr. 491). One may question whether a sixth-century aristocrat would import a bard to educate his child; in any case, the notion is unlikely to have been proved by poems of Anacreon, which would be the only satisfactory source. However, the basic idea that it was the father who sent for him might well have

[1] The career of the celebrated doctor Democedes makes for interesting comparisons with Anacreon's, though Herodotus' account (3. 129. 3–137) raises doubts, not least over the times in 131. 1–2. Our knowledge of Teos and Abdera in the 6th cent. is relatively limited; see esp. Isaac (1986), 73–89, and Graham (1991), (1992). Excavations show the importance of the pre-Teian stage of Abdera, and its continuity with the Teian (cf. French (1992), 53; Blackman (1997), 87). The early coinage of Abdera, and its foundation and refoundation, suggest its wealth (cf. May (1966), 1–2). Artistically, a bronze shield-strap (second half of the 6th cent.?) makes an interesting find. The population of Teos after the Persian Wars was evidently much smaller than Abdera's (Lewis (1997c)). For the newer of the two substantial 5th-cent. inscriptions from Teos see Herrmann (1981). It is possible that the quote on Abdera in Strabo is Anacreon's (Adesp. ia. fr. 3 West). Aristox. fr. 12 Wehrli and probably Athen. 598 c suggest the same opinion as Strabo's.

received support from Anacreon (e.g. from an address). It is made plausible, not so much by the parallel statement about Ibycus (Ibyc. TA1, *Suda*) as by the reference to Polycrates in Ibyc. S151 [11]. 46–8: this would only suit a boy. Hdt. 3. 121. 1–2, in a minority account, has Anacreon present with Polycrates as tyrant, at the end of his reign; even if this is true, it creates no difficulty for Anacreon's arriving when Polycrates was young. The report does indicate that Herodotus supposed Anacreon's Polycrates to be the famous one.[2]

Now, Ibycus was evidently invited before Polycrates' tyranny, and Anacreon may well have been; Polycrates' father is unlikely to have been a tyrant. The *Suda* says he was ruling Samos; but Herodotus, as we have seen (p. 232), makes his ruling at any stage improbable. Is it even plausible that Anacreon would remain with Aeaces if he were a deposed tyrant? It is more likely that we have here a very wealthy and powerful family which at some time (or times) in the century was in sole charge of the island. Polycrates' reign ended *c*.522; if Anacreon came to Samos before his reign began, when Polycrates was young, and also went to Abdera *c*.545 and spent time there, we shall be reluctant to accept that Polycrates' reign began in the 540s, and we shall certainly not want him to be dedicating statues *c*.590–70 (*IG* iv. 565). The grounds for beginning the reign in the 540s are in any case weak.[3]

All Anacreon's poetry was full of mention of Polycrates, says

---

[2] One could not defend the idea of summoning a poet as tutor even by the later example of Apollonius and Ptolemy III (cf. P. Oxy. 1241 ii. 3–5): Apollonius was local and the librarian. There are many later mentions of Anacreon's being with Polycrates when he was tyrant, e.g. Max. Tyr. 37. 5. The mentions themselves often palpably derive from biographical fiction or Herodotus; we cannot say how far the essential idea derives, directly or indirectly, from Anacreon. The best support for it is the Herodotus, and perhaps Strabo's πᾶca . . . πλήρης (Anacr. 483); we should probably accept it, with due caution.

[3] On Polycrates see Berve (1967), i. 107–114; Mitchell (1975); Shipley (1987), chs. 4 and 5; Osborne (1996), 272–80; see further the introduction and commentary on Ibycus. Polycrates' rule should ideally begin several years before Cambyses' accession in 530 (cf. Hdt. 3. 39 and Mitchell (1975), 81); but if possible not too long before, so as to fit with Thuc. 1. 13. 6. Positive argument for the 540s (Shipley (1987), 74–80) depends on Arist. *Pol.* 1313ᵇ24; but Aristotle makes only some of τῶν περὶ Cάμον ἔργων Polycratean, and in any case later attribution to a famous figure is at least as likely as deliberate suppression by Herodotus. (On the dating of the ἔργα see the introduction to the commentary on Ibycus.) For *IG* iv. 565 (Shipley (1987), 74) see Jeffery (1990), 156, 168; the name is common enough when evidence for names becomes more abundant (e.g. *IG* i³. 1187. 38). The tyranny of Syloson from the same family earlier in the century has been doubted (Osborne (1996), 272; cf. Polyaen. *Strat.* 6. 45); for other items on the family, including new material for dating ML 16, see again the introduction to the commentary on Ibycus. The

Strabo (14. 1. 16). Whatever allowance we make for hyperbole and mistaken identification, this must suggest some appearances of the name. No instance has yet been found; but note 483 (Himerius), P. Oxy. 3722 fr. 16. 12–22. We need not assume that such appearances came in substantial Ibycean songs of praise. Anacr. 352, 353, 416 probably belong to Samos, and 353 at least refers to the political situation, in which a faction overruns the city. We do not know whether it was written before or during the tyranny.[4]

The final place clearly connected with Anacreon is Athens, to which Hipparchus invited him ([Plat.] (?) *Hipparch.* 228 c 1–2; [Arist.] *Ath. Pol.* 18. 1). He is commonly assumed to have done so after Polycrates' death (*c*.522); but the use of a penteconter to fetch Anacreon, even if authentic, might suggest honour more than rescue. The invitation was probably designed for the prestige of the family and perhaps the city, and did not only reflect Hipparchus' alleged interest in poetry (and love!). Hipparchus, after all, gave his name on his herms (*Hipparch.* 228 E 7–229 B 1, *CEG* i. 304). Simonides was also invited (not to touch on rhapsodes). The poetic luminaries no doubt corresponded to the remarkable building programme which glorified Athens and the Pisistratids.

Anacreon was felt to be enough of an adornment to the city for his name and figure to appear on red-figure vases; he is named on one of *c*.520–10 (London E 18, cup by Oltos, *ARV*² 62. 86), and one of *c*.510–500 (Syracuse 26967, lekythos by Gales Painter, *ARV*² 36. 2), and his name appears on a lyre in another *c*.500 (Copenhagen inv. 13365, calyx-krater fragments by Kleophrades Painter, *ARV*² 185. 32, *Para.* 340). One of these vases, then, will be painted during the tyranny, two after, and at least one in Anacreon's lifetime. Even when allowance is made for the kinship of his subject-matter with that of vases, the portrayal of a contemporary individual on vases is highly unexpected; Alcaeus and even Sappho were portrayed from a greater distance in time. Hipparchus died in 514, Hippias was expelled in 510; Anacreon wrote poetry which

original involvement of brothers, as with Alcaeus, is interesting for the political role of families at the time (Hdt. 3. 39. 2).

[4] Shipley (1987), 92, assumes the latter, but the former seems at least as likely. The faction presumably is not supported by Anacreon, despite Page (1966), 30. Neither Strab. 13. 1. 54 nor Anacr. 402 (Max. Tyr.) throws much light on Strab. 14. 1. 16; the πᾶcα makes πλήρηc more emphatic than e.g. μεcτά at Dion. Hal. *Rhet.* 11. 5. Heracl. Pont. fr. 60 Wehrli clearly affords little support for assigning Artemon to Samos.

praised another distinguished Athenian family, that of Critias (Plat. *Charm.* 157 E 4–7). He is said to have loved, i.e. he may have written love poetry naming, a Critias whose puberty might well go back to before 510. This would cast an interesting light on his activity under the Pisistratids. In any case, the connection with the house of Critias shows a link with grand families that would parallel Anacreon's original invitation by Aeaces father of Polycrates.[5]

There is no good evidence that Anacreon visited Thessaly. Two epigrams ascribed to him (*FGE* XIII and VII) mention or probably mention Thessalian royalty of the first half of the fifth century; there is no reason to think them genuine. Unusual longevity need no more be credited than the fatal grape-pip; but the available dates and some references to old age (esp. 395) indicate a life of substantial duration. If the move to Abdera (*c.*545) happened in his adult life, if he reached, say, 40 there (cf. on 417 [**14**]), and had left Samos by 522, one might be reluctant to credit his living very much beyond 500.[6]

Anacreon is the first known poet to write lyric in Ionic, if one sets aside the epodic forms of Archilochus and Hipponax. There was, however, a vast tradition of Ionic poetry. Should we see Anacreon's language as the language of that tradition, or as the language of Teos and Abdera, or as neither? There can be no doubt that his language is in its essence a literary one. So, like elegy, iambus, and non-Lesbian lyric, in first and second declensions he uses both long and short dative plurals, the former with or without *v*. The fifth-century Teian inscriptions, as we would expect, use only long forms with *v* (nos. 261 and 262 in McCabe and Plunkett (1985); ML 30, *SEG* xxxi (for 1981) 985). But further, Anacreon includes from time to time forms not only strikingly alien from contemporary Ionic, but also unknown in elegiac and iambic poetry: P. Oxy. 3722

---

[5] For the vases (and others often associated with them) see Caskey and Beazley (1931–63), ii. 57–61; Richter (1965), i. 77; Herington (1985), 198–9; Kurtz and Boardman (1986), 47–70; Price (1990); Rosenmeyer (1997a), 29–33; Schefold (1997), 76–9, 481. For Critias cf. Davies (1971), 324–6. On the Pisistratids see Lewis (1988).

[6] Naturally our categories of old age etc. are not particularly relevant to 417 [**14**] and other fragments (cf. Cameron (1995), ch. 7); the age of 30 for marriage may be. Two other epigrams ascribed to Anacreon appear also on inscriptions (*CEG* i. 312–13); but they are in any case too late for Anacreon. Page's inferences from them may be doubted ((1981), 138–9). Cf. Hansen (1983–9), i. 167–8.

fr. 5. 3 (ἄρμ') ἐλάαι (epic); 3722 fr. 16. 12 κλεεν[ν- (lyric); 3722 fr. 29.
2 (=380) μειδιόων (epic).⁷
On the other hand, he sometimes uses the form Δεόνυcοc (first
syllable a long diphthong: 357. 11, 365. 2, contr. 410. 3 and prob.
411 (b)). This form for the god, derived from local language, would
surprise in any Ionic literature. Again, he differs markedly from
iambic and elegiac poets, and from lyric including Pindar, in pre-
ferring to add the article with the possessive pronoun (357. 10,
358 [13]. 6, 360. 3, P. Oxy. 3695 fr. 12. 1 (not 370, where the text is
uncertain, nor 432. 2)). Addition is much rarer in lyric poets includ-
ing Pindar, and in iambic and elegiac poets. Anacreon is no doubt
moving here towards ordinary speech. The two big fifth-century
Teian inscriptions essentially confirm this, though in insisting on
the patterns γένοc τὸ κένο, γῆν τὴν Τηίην they themselves are prob-
ably deploying relatively old or solemn language (261a 5, 262a 4–5,
etc.). Anacreon's language, then, is a literary one, not a reproduc-
tion of local speech; but in it he can draw both on literature other
than elegy and iambus and on the spoken language of his own time
and place. His language is rich and diverse.⁸

Anacreon particularly uses in his metres iambo-trochaic, aeolo-
choriambic, and anacreontic-ionic. He brings the third group into
new prominence and is the first known to use anacreontics. He
tends to use only one of these three types of rhythm in a poem
(contrast Alcman). His stanzas, though sometimes as long as 6 lines,
are reminiscent of the Lesbian poets in their brevity; but they are
often characterized by the striking repetition of relatively simple

⁷ The first quotation is assumed to be, the second and third are certainly, from
Anacreon; the reading in the second is clear. -άω verbs themselves are few in elegy
and iambus, but such a form as -άαι would be unexpected there. One may notice
also 378 πτερύγεccι; such datives are found in elegy but not iambus (cf. West (1974),
95–8). Save for the article, long first-declension dative plurals, with ν, predominate
in Ionic, long second, with ν, in the Ionic of Asia Minor, cf. Thumb, Kieckers, and
Scherer (1932–59), ii. 268, 270–1. One should note that the actual stone *LSAM* 50
(Miletus), where there are more complicated rules for the absence of ν, dates from
the 2nd cent. BC, though it copies out 5th-cent. material.

⁸ For Δεόνυcοc see Thumb, Kieckers, and Scherer (1932–59), ii. 274, 275–6, 281
(Anacr. 365 (Samos) is probably an inference from Anacreon, cf. e.g. Ibyc. 328,
341 (ii)?). Note Alcaeus' use of Aeolic Ζόννυccοc (129 [8]. 9). The preference for
the article with possessive adjectives was observed by Lobel (see Haslam (1986), 5).
For the order in the inscriptions cf. ML 8 C 3–4, 5–6 (Chios, 6th cent.; formal?),
contr. *Schwyzer* 723. 1 (Miletus, 7th cent.). It is inconsistent with Anacr. 352 if
rightly restored; it may well be adopted at P. Oxy. 3695 fr. 12. 1, but not in the other
instances in Anacreon, or archaic poetry generally (Sapph. 160, if sound, would be
an exception).

units. Their origins may be popular, but one cannot necessarily
make inferences to their effect (related forms and features, within
larger strophes, recur in tragedy). But the simplicity and slickness
in themselves heighten by antithesis the frequent irony and self-
deprecation of the content.[9]

What is the relationship in Anacreon's poetry between the author
and the narrator? First, should they be thought of as formally, no-
tionally the same person? One cannot prove even that the narrators
of the different poems are to be thought the same person as each
other; but recurring features make this a natural supposition (absur-
dity, age, the individuals loved, even δηῦτε). The whole tradition of
archaic poetry would encourage listeners to identify, formally, this
narrator and the poet Anacreon. In many poets (notably Sappho,
Solon, Theognis, Hipponax) such identity is shown by the use of
the author's own name; in others (notably Ibycus) references to the
speaker as poet make it evident; in others (notably Alcaeus) any
alternative is obviously improbable. (Poems which clearly show the
listener a different narrator, like Alcm. 1 [1] or Alc. 10, are another
matter.) In some fragments of Anacreon himself the first person
looks intrinsically likely to be the poet (353, so 416). Artemon,
attacked in elaborate detail in 388, is probably real, and most prob-
ably presented as a rival in love (372, P. Oxy. 3722 fr. 27; cf. Cat. 37,
39); this would suggest that the narrator in the love poems is not
seen as a fiction, which is the likeliest alternative to the poet.

In the poems, we shall see evident gaps between the engaged nar-
rator and the detached author, which create humour (as in Ovid's
Amores). These gaps are wider than in Sappho, where there is
less humour; for this very reason, it is important to insist on the
formal identity. (The term 'narrator' obscures it.) The humour is
different, not only from the third-person humour of 388, but from
the humour produced in Alcm. 1 [1] by the gap between author and
narrator, where the narrator is a different person from the author.
The formal identification makes possible an element of formal self-
consciousness and self-mockery which creates a distinctive tone.
For Greeks, humour about others can be aggressive and ridicule
mortifying; humour about oneself creates a tone of charming mod-
esty and genial nonchalance.

---

[9] Anacreon's metres are discussed by West (1982), 56–9. Anacreontics and ionics
are evidently related for him, whatever their genesis, cf. 395. 5, 11 (cf. 356 (*a*). 5,
(*b*). 5) with e.g. 358 [13]. 3, 7.

The relation of reality and fiction will be complicated. Only the first audience, if they, would know about the actualities of Anacreon's amorous and convivial existence; but at the very least some elements of the poems must be seen as in some senses unreal. Most importantly for the poems, ridiculous exaggeration (347 fr. 1 [**12**]) or self-deception (417 [**14**]) from the narrator must imply that the author does not take the same view of the situation. (Hence the surface of the poem must be mistaken, the narrator and author not actually inseparable.) In concrete situation, calls for restraint from fellow drinkers (356 (*b*)), accounts of what a Lesbian girl is doing now (358 [**13**]), addresses to an unknowing boy (360) or scornful girl (417 [**14**]): these can only be thought literal on strange views of this poetry as improvised or as suddenly applied to the circumstances of the symposium (which at least some of them do not fit). Some elements, again, will not be fictitious. If narrator and author are even formally identified, references to the narrator's old age (e.g. 395) must imply the author's; references to Samos (353), say, as the narrator's locale must imply it is the author's too. In between, we ourselves have little idea of the historicity of, say, Smerdies (there are more grounds for supposing Eurypyle real). Even the audience might not have been able to associate, say, the Thracian filly with any particular person; it is tempting to imagine they saw such characters as fictitious. There is some significant mixture in the poems of reality and fiction, of identity and gaps in the relationship of narrator and author.

How is this relationship received by the audience? Walton's aesthetic theory of mimesis might make us want to see the formal identity of narrator and author as a kind of game, or make-believe; this instance would actually be playful and fun, a sportive contract of half-pretence. The love poetry at least seems informed by a constant awareness that none of the narrator's emotional postures is taken seriously by the author. This is not only the background for perfective moments of humour where the contract is ruptured; it is also itself entertaining, and a source of the imperfective humorous atmosphere that pervades the poems.[10]

This is at any rate a way of regarding the poems which provides a route into them. If we could read more Anacreon, we might well

---

[10] Walton (1990). This particular type of problem does not appear to concern him greatly.

see a wider range in his humour and further complications in his first person.

The three poems treated here, though relatively short and relatively well preserved, will receive fairly ample discussion. It is not only that they present considerable difficulties of interpretation. Their particular complexity and sophistication call for close analysis.

12: *PMG* 347 fr. 1 (frr. 71–2 Gentili)[11]

Lobel very plausibly connected this poem with references to Anacreon's chiding the Thracian boy Smerdies, whom he loved, for having his hair cut. See 402, 414, 422, 471; 346 fr. 14, 366, 503, P. Oxy. 4454 fr. 3. 3. There appears to be a reference to Thrace here (10); one would naturally take cτόλοκροc (3) as masculine (Hesych. κ 3370 is not satisfactory evidence for a feminine in -oc). The person whose hair has been cut despite Anacreon's efforts is not likely to be the woman who so laments (a possibility considered but declined by Evans (1963), 23). It is no serious obstacle that Aelian *Var. Hist.* 9. 4 speaks of 'the poem' on the loss and Favorinus (fr. 19 Barigazzi) quotes a fragment (414) in a different metre: one poem on the theme was especially famous. (Max. Tyr. 18. 9 p. 102 Trapp suggests, but does not prove, that there was more than one poem.) The connection seems hard to resist.

According to Athenaeus (540 E) and Aelian (*Var. hist.* 9. 4), Polycrates loved Smerdies too, and cut his hair (or had it cut) in jealousy. But it is evident from Aelian's account, and from Favorinus fr. 19 Barigazzi, that the motivation was ascribed by Anacreon to Smerdies himself (the charge was transferred out of prudent restraint, says Aelian). It sounds as though Polycrates was not mentioned at all (it is not indeed obvious where he would fit in). The story will thus be a product of that urge to enrich the biographies of lyric poets which we see e.g. at Max. Tyr. 21. 2, and probably see even in the scene of Anacreon with Polycrates reported at Hdt. 3. 121. 1. Poem 417 [14], it will be suggested below, most naturally

[11] On 347 fr. 1 [12] see esp. Latte (1955), 495–6; Peek (1955–6), 200–2; Gentili (1958*a*), 206–18; Evans (1963); Woodbury (1991*c*), 590–1; Gow and Page (1965), ii. 45; Führer (1967), 99, 130–2; Emley (1971); Vox (1990), 99–102; MacLachlan (1997), 206.

belongs to Anacreon's time in Abdera; if that is plausible, it inclines one to think the same in the present instance. Since Smerdies is or may be a known individual, this case is itself less strong than the other; but he is at any rate a free agent, not a slave, and it is notable that there should be poems about two such Thracians. The story on Polycrates seems to be treated with varying degrees of scepticism or credulity (credulity Gow and Page (1965), ii. 45); it is not clear that anyone has taken scepticism quite this far.

One speculative point may be added. If the Thracian boy is no longer seen as a page, one may wonder whether the cutting of his hair has anything to do with his being Thracian. Theocritus implies that a Thracian haircut is something peculiar (14. 46); the peculiarity evidently goes back to the archaic period, where the Thracians are ἀκρόκομοι (*Il.* 4. 533, Hippon. fr. 115. 6 West), whatever that means. (Gow's notes, (1952), ii. 259–60, Gow and Page (1965), ii. 45, seem rather unsatisfactory and inconsistent.) At Antip. Sid. xv. 6 Gow–Page Κίκονα Θρηικὸς Ϲμερδιέω πλόκαμον, one might expect the first epithet to add a further point, which a reference to hairstyle would supply. It might also be useful to have a reason for the boy's decision: it is plainly not maturity or grief (cf. Apollod. Car. fr. 18 Kassel–Austin). This may be pertinent to the poem's last part.

The poem is most often thought to be two poems. On any view, it displays (or they display) an extravagance and vigour, a concreteness and imaginative scope, too often forgotten in images of Anacreon.

Metre

1. $- \cup - \times - \cup - -$
2. $\underset{=}{\cup} - \times - \cup - -$
3. $- \cup - \times - \cup - -$
4. $- \cup - \times - \cup -$

Three trochaic dimeters acatalectic, followed by a catalectic (blunt). The same metre as 417 [**14**]; see there for further details. Lobel prefers stanzas of two tetrameters (Lobel and Roberts (1954), 62). But the hiatus at 417 [**14**]. 6 does not prove this; and it seems precarious to draw conclusions from 418, which would not have word-end after line 1 of this stanza. Even an ordinary tetrameter would have a caesura at this point; and 418 is probably a first line (Hephaestion; content). We may well, then, have to do with a different metre there. The 'inconvenient width of column' which is alleged to account for the arrangement in the papyrus has not affected papyrus presentation of trochaic tetrameters, e.g. in Archilochus. At all events, the important point, obscured by Page's presentation of 417 [**14**], is that these are stanzas.

1. The past beauty of the hair itself seems not to be evoked lengthily, at least at this point. The attractive description pointedly transfers to a boy Archilochus' description of a woman, ἡ δέ οἱ κόμη | ὤμουc κατεcκίαζε καὶ μετάφρενα (fr. 31 West, cit. Lobel). The boy's hair does not spread so opulently (contrast Pind. *Pyth.* 4. 82–3); but Anacreon enriches the expression with an epithet, and one full of significance.

The pattern of an adjective at the end of one line agreeing with a noun at the end of the next appears characteristic, cf. 348. 2–3, 7–8, 356. 4–5.

3, 4–8. νῦν δὲ δή: the change of stanzas is exploited for a drastic contrast of times (cf. 388. 10; Sapph. 96 [**7**]. 6; e.g. Theogn. 961). The μέν of 3 is linked with δ' in 4, not 8, as ἡ shows; but there is no strong contrast between the boy and his hair, though they are effectively (and suitably) separated from each other. (Note the relative clause with τοι in 1–2.) Lines 3 and 4–8 are strongly differentiated in style. The first is extremely brief, with no verb; the second has two subordinate clauses, and spreads itself over the division of stanzas. The first announces the present state; the second describes the past event. The second is an ornate and would-be pathetic third-person narrative; the first looks like a blunt insult. This clause (3) is undignified and surprising; the effect and apparent tone comically undercut the tragic and indignant impact sought by the narrator.

cτολοκρόc is probably an adjective, and probably means 'cropped'. The conception is not the drastic one of Ov. *Am.* 1. 14. 2, Apul. *Met.* 2. 8. 5–6.

4–6. The adjectives are not mere adornment, but vital to the mood and point.

αὐχμηράc must refer to a barber's hands: the boy's would not be rough, and the hair could not fall into them if he cut it himself. The barber's hands are squalid because of his social standing, and perhaps his profession. (It may be relevant that Mandelstam says, 'Vlast' otvratitel'na, kak ruki bradobreja', 'power is as repulsive as a barber's hands', 'Ariost' (1933), l. 22, *Sobr. soč.* (Moscow, 1991), i. 193.) The function of the word is to contrast implicitly with the hair;

the word is often used of ill-kept hair, and is a general opposite to λιπαρός (Xen. *Mem.* 2. 1. 31). It contrasts also with ἁβρόν (1). But we do not see people directly here, only hair and hands. ἀθρόη conveys the magnitude of this moment of disaster (it is not portrayed as a prolonged session); it also suggests the beautiful abundance of the hair, and marks the distortion of the clause in 1–2.

μέλαιναν is not a mere standard epithet for 'earth', as often in lyric poetry (Sapph. 1 [4]. 10 n.; ἐρεμνήν *Hom. h. Herm.* 427 (date?)); Anacreon chooses 'dust' instead of 'earth', and so creates an ugly picture (cf. Peek (1955–6), 200). The word also gestures towards the tragic description of Hector's head, once beautiful, defiled in the dust (Hom. *Il.* 22. 401–4, cf. MacLachlan (1997), 206; no other Iliadic description is so relevant).

The moment of falling (aorist) is also dwelt on, with elaborating horror. The plain πεcοῦca is taken up in the richer κατερρύη, which suggests the liquid luxuriance of the hair. The writing is of remarkable power, but the power fuels the absurdity.

7. τλημον .c: scholars have accepted Lobel's cautious preference for ω rather than o, on grounds of space. However, there would only be about 1 mm. of difference, if, in the absence of vo elsewhere, one may judge from the spacing of μο (τλημο- here; 14, fr. 2. 5). Neither reading really fills the expected space; and spacing in this papyrus can be unpredictable. The slight trace does not decide. In the archaic poets, and Pindar and Bacchylides, adverbs in -ωc usually belong to a limited and frequently recurring set; however, νηλέωc 417 [**14**]. 3 is something of an exception. The adverb does not go very suitably with περιπεcοῦc'; however, one might take it with κατερρύη, although the run-over between stanzas then becomes more drastic than is expected in Anacreon. (Cf. Antiph. *Tetr.* β γ 6 διά–ἀπέθανε; Eur. *Tro.* 40.) Yet an epithet, 'accursed', for cιδήρου seems altogether more stylish and effective, and positively desirable for the surface of the rhetoric: the last clause falls a little flatly otherwise. Cf. Soph. *Trach.* 886–7 (cit. Lobel); Call. fr. 110. 48–50 Pfeiffer.

The flowing of the sentence over the boundary between stanzas is an expressive device, as in 388; but the engaged adjective prepares for the narrator's direct statement of his feelings in the next sentence.

τομῆι cιδήρου: the language, building on 5–6, hints at violent death; cf. Soph. *Trach.* 886–7, Eur. *Or.* 1101.

8. περιπεcοῦc̣': 'encountering', but with a hint of the more physical encountering of a weapon; cf. Ar. *Wasps* 523 (not 'falling upon', as is indicated by Antiph. *Tetr.* B γ 6, cf. 7). The stem of *πεcοῦc'* from the opening participial clause (4) is taken up with a different sense in the closing one; this is made to appear an elaborate period.

ἐγὼ δ᾽: the narrator returns to a state, his own, the real centre of the poem and the source of its perspective.

ἄcηιcι must be a strong word: see on Sapph. 1 [4]. 3.

9. τείρομαι expresses a painful state with force. The clause is to be compared with that on cύ in 3; Smerdies feels no woe, and is not considered as a thinking subject.

τί γάρ τιc ἔρξηι: not a shrug of the shoulders (Latte (1955), 495), but a gesture of despair (note γάρ). The words might in theory refer to a generality which applies to the past, before the cutting: what is anyone to do in such a situation (cf. Call. fr. 110. 47 Pfeiffer)? This would ease the reference of τυχών; but the participial clause is too specific for generality, and the γάρ would become difficult.

10. Θρήικηc: Lobel gave Θρη[[ι]]κηc as the papyrus' reading. θ seems clear under the microscope. Even in this papyrus, it would be surprising if there were no letter between κ and η (despite κυ 18). There are two traces before η, of which the lower looks too high to be the lower right-hand stroke of κ, and both look too far away to be part of κ (despite 18, where the two pieces of papyrus may have been too widely separated). The traces are more naturally taken as the top of ι and the beginning of a stroke of deletion.

The ρ too appears to be deleted: the continuation of the downward diagonal to the left of the vertical argues against a redrawing of ρ. It would seem, then, that we have to do here, not simply with scribal carelessness, but with two distinct variants. ὑπερθήκηc, 'postponement', was considered by Lobel (Lobel and Roberts (1954), 63 n. 1); it gives intelligible sense, and, although the word is not found elsewhere, the formation is probably acceptable (cf. e.g. ἐπιθήκη Hes. *WD* 380, προcθήκη Aesch. *Ag.* 500). However, ὑπερτίθημι etc. are not used with this meaning before Hellenistic documents and prose. The point and the close do not well suit the overwrought tone of this and the following stanzas. We should at present prefer ὑπὲρ Θρήικηc.

ὑπέρ Θρήικηc is most likely to refer, as it is Smerdies' country, not the narrator's, not to the narrator's motive, but to his plea (cf. e.g. Hom. *Il.* 24. 466–7, ὑπέρ with λίccεο). This suggests that τυχών at least includes the idea of obtaining what one requests, somewhat as in the Herodotean idiom (5. 44. 1 etc.). That would have advantages: ἔρξηι does not refer to an earlier possible action with the object of preventing the haircut. τυχών, then, should not be too closely tied to it; in 10 itself the failure of the plea is the most important point, and 'even for the sake of Thrace' enhances it. But all this could make little sense unless the narrator's plea, mentioning Thrace, had been spoken of earlier in the poem. (Cf. the plea at Ov. *Am.* 1. 14. 27–30.) One needs some idea of an attempt or request for τυχών to relate to (in Herodotus' phrases, a word of asking appears). μηδ' ὑπέρ Θρήικηc, with its emphatic μηδέ, demands some prior (or at the least some subsequent) account.

There would be no real difficulty in Smerdies' cutting his hair because of Thracian custom. An earlier appeal might have drawn some point from it (e.g. Thracians all do this, I know, but for the sake of your fatherland itself . . .).

11–18. Lobel thought that the poem continued here; the general opinion has been that a new poem begins. But the poem would begin very abruptly, with no explanation of who 'the' woman is, or what is her plight. This is essentially an aesthetic point. One can find dramatic beginnings, where the listener is plunged into the middle of some situation that will presently become clear (e.g. Archil. fr. 172 West; Alc. 10; cf. Arist. *Lys.* 1). This one makes no such impression of opacity for effect; it is as if the writer is taking up something already referred to. Even if we granted that ἀρίγνωτον made it clear the woman was a prostitute (Latte (1955), 496), the oddity of the article remains; one may contrast 346. 13. The reference can hardly be to something just said in the symposium; whatever the actual knowledge of an archaic audience, the poems are not so written that they could only be followed by a listener present then. At any rate, there seems no clear instance of such a poem, and there are many poems where knowledge that would not be needed by an intimate is included for the comprehension of other listeners. As an opening, this would be anomalous.

On the other hand, if the lines are not the beginning of the poem, 12 will have something to take up, and the identity of the woman can be made clear; this seems the more promising as it has already seemed desirable to postulate some significant narrative before the extant fragment (10 n.). The calamity she laments will now need no explanation; the tone of wild lament will follow on perfectly from what precedes. The asyndeton is common after a question (δή rarely connects, save with a pronoun, in lyric, elegiac, and iambic poetry of this period).

Who is the woman? Some female that has already been referred to in connection with Smerdies. It could in theory be a woman who is in love with him too (cf. e.g. Hor. *Odes* 3. 20); or a female relation, say a sister, by whom the narrator had also appealed to the boy. If it were objected that the poem is growing too much, we do not have any poem of Anacreon's that is certainly complete, and if we did it would not impose limits on all the rest. The Cologne poems of Archilochus and Alcaeus are reminders that archaic poems could be long and, in the former case, involved. On such a view, the passage would move in a sequence from cύ to ἐγώ to the woman, with the οἰκτρὰ δή emphasizing her reaction. But why should this woman's reaction be given more prominence, space, and extremity than the narrator's?

What of Lobel's suggestion that the woman is Thrace? The articular phrase would then take up Θρήικης from the previous sentence. The obvious awkwardness is that this female is presented in emphatically human guise: a woman, blaming the δαίμων, seeking destruction. Now countries, like personifications, are not so emphatically divine as ordinary goddesses. Two γυναῖκε are allotted Europe and Asia in the Persian queen's dream (Aesch. *Pers.* 181, cf. 182–3, 184 τῶν νῦν ἐκπρεπεστάτα); they are sisters, and thus presumably are the eponymous nymphs (185–6; Andron *FGrHist.* 10 F 7 (Thrace is their sister too)). Personifications can be referred to as women in comedy (Ar. *Lys.* 1118, *Plut.* 441, fr. 466. 4 Kassel–Austin; Henioch. fr. 5. 15 Kassel–Austin). *Plut.* 441, and the context, confirm that this is not simply a matter of humorous expression (cf. Dante, *Canz.* 104). Certainly it would be unsatisfactory to suppose that the expression in 12 here is to be explained by a jocular manner. That would not fit either 14 or the surface of the narrator's tone. The character of Anacreon's genre might still be relevant. We would have simply to posit, with some encouragement from outside, that the designation is possible in a genre free in fantasy (cf. 358 [13]. 1–4 n.); it would be assisted by, and would assist, the allegorical narrative of 11–18. (So too with the queen's dream in Aeschylus.) This poem would be actively exploiting marginalities of status, for surprising and exaggerated effect. But if we posit this possibility, is the reference intelligible when it first appears? Intelligibility would be greatly helped if there had been considerable mention of Thrace earlier; but the expression in 10 already makes this likely.

The result of this discussion is that the poem is more likely to continue at 11 than to end at 10. Identification of the woman is uncertain in the absence of the rest; but, with considerable doubt, one might think that Thrace is the most promising possibility. On any identification, the poem appears an elaborate structure, amusingly raised on slender foundations. The narrator also affects to objectify and enhance his own emotion by presenting the still intenser emotion and voice of another; this only heightens his absurd subjectivity. If the woman is Thrace, we see a remarkable scope and audacity of imagination.

11. οἰκτρά sets the tone for the lament that will follow. There may be some intellectual content to φρονεῖν (cf. Lobel in Lobel and Roberts (1954), 63), especially if Smerdies' nationality has caused the disaster.

ἀκού[ω, 'I hear that', is much the most natural supplement. The phrasing has obvious point if it places a distance between the narrator and the fantasy he reports.

12. ἀρίγνωτον: at least on the surface, 'famous', cf. Pind. *Nem.* 5. 12 (ἀριγνῶτες).

13. The narrator seems to have turned to narrating, but still in a strongly emotional fashion. πολλάκιc δὲ δή matches οἰκτρὰ δή; the repetition of the lament increases the pathos. Cf. Sapph. 94. 3, Cic. *Mil.* 93.

14. A notion of metaphysical force closes the stanza: accusation of a personal δαίμων here shows the intensity of grief.

15. The opening of the speech begins with the new stanza, in keeping with Anacreon's firm separations. One may contrast Sapph. 1 [4]. 15, 18, 94. 4, Archil. fr. 196a. 10 West.

For a country to be hurled into the sea might be destruction rather than death; but the wish expressed here would still correspond to the elaborate wishes in epic and tragedy that one had died or might die (so Hom. *Il.* 6. 344–8, Aesch. *Ag.* 1448–53, Eur. *Alc.* 864–

7). The idea of death takes up and responds to the suggestion of death in 3–8; again there are strong epic echoes. Especially close is Hom. *Il.* 6. 344–8, where the mother is mentioned. Thrace may, like Helen, feel guilt as well as grief.

ὡ]ϲ ἂν εὖ πάθοιμι: with extreme extravagance, the killing is presented as a great pleasure or benefit. Within the speech, the line leads surprisingly into what follows.

μῆτερ: Aphrodite turns to Dione in her pain (Hom. *Il.* 5. 370–4); compare also the mortal Creusa at Eur. *Ion* 893. The address to the mother, even in apostrophe, sounds much wilder here than speaking about her in the third person: the mother is asked to destroy her daughter. The idea of the mother, not a wind, hurling the speaker into the sea, is itself stronger than Hom. *Il.* 6. 346–7 or *Od.* 20. 63–5 (note also Ar. *Lys.* 973–7); cf. Eur. *Andr.* 293–8. The birth of the speaker is to be reversed.

The mention of family probably suggests the aspect of the eponymous nymph, as in Aesch. *Pers.* 185–6 (cf. also Hippias *FGrHist* 6 F 10). A place in myth is enough to make reference to a mother acceptable, whether or not Parthenope or another was to be thought of specifically (Andron *FGrHist* 10 F 7, Jacoby (1923–) I a. 481). But that suggestion in this context heightens the play between immortality and mortality (cf. more seriously Virg. *Aen.* 12. 879–84).

16–18. Words to go with the sea are piled up to dwell on the destruction the speaker desires, and to depict through their abundance her unrestrained feeling. The Homeric π]ορφυ[ρ]έοιϲι adds mock grandeur to the close of the stanza (cf. especially Hom. *Od.* 13. 84–5, and note Alc. 45. 2).

φέρουϲα: perhaps more natural when the speaker is not actually human.

The speech must have gone on for a further stanza at least. There is another vehement female speaker at 432, possibly not the narrator of the poem (cf. P. Oxy. 3695 fr. 18; note, from a different poem, 354). One may also compare, in lyric, the vigorous female speaker in Stes. 222 (b) [**3**]; her hypothetical wish for death (cf. Anacr. 411 (*a*)) is expressed in much more restrained and less colourful language. Even Simonides' Danae (543) [**16**] is more restrained; but she, like the speaker of Alc. 10, suggests the emotional possibilities available to the genre. Note later Bacch. fr. 2 etc.

The poem (or poems) shows Anacreon drawing forceful yet comic poetry out of triviality. The concrete particulars of the cutting; the language and literature of violent death; opulent fantasy; contrasts in diction and syntax, contrasts between people, and between times: all appear to be fused in an elaborate yet integrated structure. The resource and richness of the poetry are part of the absurdity and the exuberant joke; yet they also impress and exhilarate. This is no circumscribed or tamely agreeable poet.

13: *PMG* 358 (fr. 13 Gentili)[12]

This is usually assumed to be a complete poem; but one could easily imagine it continuing, for example with reflections on the incident. Neither Athenaeus nor Chamaeleon as quoted implies that the poem has ended; 'Sappho's' stanza is not a reply to this poem (contrast Arist. *Rhet.* 1, 1367ᵃ7–13, Sapph. 137). At most, one might think that if the poem continued, it did not continue to describe the girl.

The poem is commonly supposed to be set at a symposium; but there is no evidence for this in the text. Furthermore, a situation in which a girl can not only scorn a man's advances but concern herself with 'some other' girl (see below) does not harmonize with anything we know of symposia. Rather, the listener is not prompted (at least in what we have) to assign a specific locale to this fiction any more than to that of 417 [**14**]. In time, there is a narrative sequence between the first stanza and the second. But the poem lacks a clear sense of decisive action; its eventlessness is part of its charm. The present tenses assist this floating quality. The narrative impulse begun by προκαλεῖται is finally thwarted in the matching verb χάϲκει, which depicts an imperfective situation.

It is important that the poem is not addressed to the 'beloved'. Contrast 346 fr. 1 (including 13), 347 fr. 1 [**12**]. 3, 360, 363, 366, 414, 417 [**14**], P. Oxy. 3695 fr. 12 (probably), 3722 fr. 3. 5 μ]έμφεαι?, 4454 fr. 3. 3 (probably); otherwise 357, 359, and esp. 378. Through

---

[12] On 358 [**13**] see esp. Wilamowitz (1913), 116–17; Harvey (1957), 213; Wigodsky (1962); Giangrande (1967), 111–12, (1973, 1976); West (1970*b*), 209; Gentili (1973); Campbell (1973–4); Easterling (1977), 329–31, 334–5; Dover (1978), 182–4; Campbell (1983), 21–2; Woodbury (1991*e*); Marcovich (1991*b*); Renehan (1984, cf. 1993); Davidson (1987); Goldhill (1987), 16–18; Vox (1990), 54–6, 82–3; Pelliccia (1991, cf. 1995); Urios-Aparisi (1993); Burzacchini (1995), 100–2; MacLachlan (1997), 207–8; Williamson (1998), 78–81.

this form the narrator becomes wrier, less engaged; our view of the girl becomes more direct, the play of subjectivities more vivid.

Metre

1. $-\,-\,-\,\cup\,\cup\,-\,\cup\,-$
2. $-\,-\,-\,\cup\,\cup\,-\,\cup\,-$
3. $-\,-\,-\,\cup\,\cup\,-\,\cup\,-$
4. $-\,-\,-\,\cup\,\cup\,-\,-$

Three glyconics, with a pherecratean as clausula. The same stanza, it seems, 360, 361; related stanzas 348, 357, 359 (perhaps at 357. 5 omission as well as transposition has occurred, i.e. there is a stanza 2 gl pher). The final pherecratean can clearly stand out (8). It is notable that Anacreon greatly prefers two longs in the aeolic base: 60 examples in gl or pher, as against 3 of $-\cup$, 2 or 3 of $\cup-$. Anacreon seems more meticulous than the Lesbian poets and the Attic tragedians, who use $-\cup$ freely in the base. ($\cup-$ is less popular, $\cup\cup$ is much less popular with the Lesbians and absent from the Athenians; in Aristophanes the ratio of $--$ to $-\cup$ is 3:1 (Parker (1997), 73–4; for tragedy see Itsumi (1984), 67). Anacreon's practice recalls (or helps to cause?) the refinements which Roman poets came to use in such metres.

1–4. The poem opens (1–2) with a graphic scene of god and mortal, created by metaphor. The conjunction and the action are amusing; one may compare 396. 2 (cf. 346 fr. 4. 1) and 413. The interaction here is not comically violent, but (on the surface) humorously mild. δηὖτε makes it improbable that in 1–2 an action of the girl's is evoked (cf. Pelliccia (1991), 30 n. 3); a literal invitation (cf. Ar. *Clouds* 997 etc.), or even a literal game of ball, would not suit the next stanza well. Rather, as in 378, a striking metaphor is followed by a more prosaic situation. The girl is in some ways linked to Eros in glamour and colour; but there is also a marked descent into the literal and mortal. In a chiastic pattern, and an opposition of successive lines, Ἔρως is set next to νήνι, and the epithet describing divinity is answered by an epithet describing fashion. In the last line of the stanza the literal is mixed with the divine. One would usually challenge someone to contest with oneself; but it is the girl, not the god, the narrator is to play with.

This whole stanza is seen in retrospect from the second stanza as a sort of statement about the narrator; but the narrator plays only a passive part in it. He is to seem passive throughout the pair of stanzas. This stanza to some extent conveys too his subjective viewpoint, on his feelings and the girl; but as a subject he is less emphasized and visible. The invention and humour of the language certainly cannot be confined to the representation of emotion; the listener enjoys the detachment of the god, and the detachment of the author.

1. **cφαίρηι**: Eros is presented in art before at least the late fifth century as an attractive boy or youth, not as a very small child (cf. Greifenhagen (1957); Hermary, Cassimatis, and Vollkommer (1986); note χρυcοκόμηc). He is here using a toy employed in games by beardless males of various ages: cf. e.g. Hom. *Od.* 8. 370–80 (echoed here), Ar. fr. 145 Kassel–Austin, the late archaic statue-base reliefs Athens NM 3476–7. Astragaloi (398) are associated more particularly with boys of an age for school (e.g. [Plat.] *Alcib. I* 110B 1–3, Asclep. XXVII. 7 Gow–Page; Hom. *Il.* 23. 88). One cannot be sure whether the present image here parodies the shooting of arrows, which Eros is already firing on a red-figure lekythos by the Brygos Painter of *c.*490 (Fort Worth AP 84. 16; no. 332 in Hermary).

δηῦτε: Alcm. 59, Sapph. 130. 1, Ibyc. 287. 1 suggest that it was a standard way of opening a love poem to begin with the metaphorical action of Eros, once again, on the speaker. Here and in 413 (Hephaestion) Anacreon parodies this device, with unserious metaphors (cf. 376). In the Sappho, and probably the Ibycus, the δηῦτε suggests suffering; here, the mildness of the assault, and the age of the narrator, suggest something pleasingly incorrigible. Cf. 356 (*a*) 6, 394 (*b*) (uncharitable), 400, 428. It seems a favourite device; but even Sappho had used it not without humour (1 [4]. 15–18, cf. 22. 11?).

πορφυρέηι: the Homeric allusion (*Od.* 8. 373) adds elevation. All the epithets in the stanza relate to colour.

2. **βάλλων**: more knowledge of ancient ball-games might (or might not) add something.

χρυcοκόμηc: a familiar epithet before Anacreon (Hes. *Theog.* 947, Alcm. S1, Alc. 327. 3); always used of gods.

3. **ποικιλοcαμβάλωι**: a much more unusual adjective (cf. χρυcεοcάμ-βαλοc Eur. *Or.* 1468; *IA* 1042). cάμβαλον was used on Lesbos (Sapph. 110. 2, cf. Alc. 303. 1?); but one can have no confidence that it was not an East Ionic form too. Sandals are quite rare in archaic art;

but we see a fancy-looking pair on Phrasikleia (Athens NM 4889, illustr. Stewart (1990), ii, pls. 121–2). The poet is preparing the idea of the girl's sophistication. However fetching the item, it is striking that a word is not chosen to convey the girl's beauty more directly. This increases our detachment.

4. cυμπαίζειν hints at the activity of youth (παιδ-); youth links the god and the girl but not the narrator (more preparation). We do not know how standard a metaphor 'play' was for amorous sport at this time. It may come in Aristophanes, does come at Xen. *Symp.* 9. 2, and is common in Hellenistic poetry (Theocr. 11. 77 etc.).

προκαλεῖται: 'challenge' is more probable than 'invite' for this period and style (and note Plat. *Symp.* 217 B 7–C 1 for cυμ-). Eros shows a forceful attitude, which is matched, in this narrative, by the girl rather than by the narrator.

5–8. Is it another female or another set of hair at which the girl gapes? It might be thought that τὴν μὲν ἐμὴν κόμην is so emphatic that it demands another κόμη to take it up; but the article is expected in Anacreon (cf. esp. 360. 3 and also 357. 10, P. Oxy. 3695 fr. 12. 1, with Haslam (1986), 5), ἐμήν is necessary to the sense, and μέν, which is quite sufficiently accounted for by the turning from one person to another, need carry no remarkable weight (cf. 347 fr. 1 [**12**]. 3, 4–8 n.; 362. 1, 417 [**14**]. 5 n., *al.*). In poetry, ἄλλην τινά with no noun and no gentive could not refer to a thing. In prose, this could happen: cf. e.g. Hdt. 2. 115. 6 ἐκ τῆς ἐμῆς γῆς ἐc ἄλλην τινὰ μετορμίζεcθαι, Plat. *Phaed.* 79 B 9–10. But even in such examples, there is no possibility of referring the phrase to a person; they would not show that a reader or listener could prefer an impersonal understanding when a personal understanding is readily available. There are perhaps further difficulties with applying ἄλλην to hair. To make τινά in effect do the work of τινός is by no means easy; and the hypothesis of a contrast between the hair on the narrator's head and his pubic hair (Giangrande (1967), 111–12) ill sorts with τὴν μὲν ἐμὴν κόμην. At all events, language strongly recommends applying ἄλλην τινά to a person.

What is the point of the last line and of the γάρ clauses? χάcκει will denote gaping in admiration (Aesch. *Ag.* 920, Ar. *Knights* 651) or desire (Sol. fr. 13. 36 West, Arist. *Ach.* 10, *Wasps* 695). Admiration will especially suit the contrast with καταμέμφεται; but in the context an amorous admiration is bound to be suggested. There is little to support the idea that love for another woman, as opposed to a man, would be something scandalous or hilarious; or even that it would make love for a man impossible. The girl finds the narrator unattractive because he is old (λευκὴ γάρ). Her coming from the particularly smart island of Lesbos increases her scorn; the pattern of some girls' lives in Lesbos, though not peculiar to Lesbos, may also explain her adoration for another girl. The first γάρ clause should go with the whole sentence. There is a little humour at the expense of the girl, in χάσκει; but the prime target is the narrator. The fundamental point is not that the girl's love is homosexual; that merely adds a pleasing touch. It accentuates that the narrator is not in the same rank of the amorous hierarchy as the girl he loves; her love goes to an equal. As in the first stanza, there is a descent, but not merely a literary one; the descent in the hierarchy of beauty from the sandalled girl to the narrator generates the action, or lack of it.

The two γάρ clauses delay the crucial καταμέμφεται. They highlight a contrast between the narrator and the girl; this is furthered by the opposition between the longer first γάρ clause, with its epic adjective, and the extremely short second clause, with its stark λευκή. The whole involved structure suitably accompanies the messiness of reality.

5. εὐκτίτου: the epic adjective is placed in the same position as the epic πορφυρέηι in the preceding stanza (1); this helps the sense of matching downward movement in the poem. The word is in epic a lesser variant of ἐϋκτίμενος, applied to many places including Lesbos (Hom. *Il.* 9. 129 (271), *Od.* 4. 342). Save in Bacchylides and perhaps Simonides (S414. 14), both are rare outside epic (Stesichorus uses ἐϋκτίμενος, S118. 7).

6–7. Λέσβου: emphasized by position (end of clause, beginning of line); it perhaps matches effectively λευκή, in the same part of the next line, and of the same length (and initial letter).

κόμην, | λευκὴ γάρ: the contrast with the god is evident (note 418); it is assisted by the difference in form between the compound χρυσοκόμης and the separate adjective in this small γάρ clause. The narrator is very different from the god he pictures inspiring him. We now see him from outside, and from the girl's perspective; but it is amusing to hear his admission too. As an admission, however,

it is entertainingly oblique: it is his hair rather than him she finds
fault with.

The white hair of age is exploited at 395. 1–2.

For such short verbless γάρ clauses, remote from the style of epic,
cf. Alcm. 1 [**1**]. 98 n.

καταμέμφεται need not indicate an actual speech (cf. Homer's
use of ἐπιμέμφομαι, Aesch. *Ch.* 40, fr. 99. 8 Radt). To suppose one
perhaps introduces too fussy a narrative, and the two verbs in 7 and
8 should correspond: χάσκει should not denote a momentary action.

8. The final pherecratean has an elegant and self-contained quality.
Two subjectivities clash; for the narrator the second woman is an
unknown and unimportant ἄλλην τινά, for the first woman she is
the object of lavish devotion. The narrator should perhaps be seen
to present that devotion with a certain petulant mockery; he cer-
tainly does not depict her passion with the same subjective richness
as his own. The expression in any case highlights amusingly the
painfulness of the narrator's failure.

14: *PMG* 417 (fr. 78 Gentili)[13]

The fragment is quoted as a convincing example of ἀλληγορία, ex-
pressing one thing in terms of another. This term is used in an
ancient commentary on Anacreon, P. Oxy. 3722 fr. 20. 8 (presum-
ably), and fr. 52. 4, where 401 seems to be referred to (with a rude
sense?). (Cf. Σ Bacch., fr. 7. 2.) The larger context in Heraclitus
does not assure us that the poem is complete; nor can the excel-
lence of 12 as a close prove that this is the close of the whole poem
(one would like to think it was). On the other hand, Heraclitus'
elucidation of the poem, which makes the girl more knowing than
the fragment seems to, probably rests not on more material but on
a misreading of the extant lines.

The weight in this poem, unlike Alc. 6, falls not on the vivid
exploitation of known experience but on the dexterous handling of
a literary equivalence. Unmarried girls had long been associated
with young horses. (Cf. e.g. Alcm. 1 [**1**], Semon. fr. 5 West (?), and

---

[13] On 417 [**14**] see esp. Wilamowitz (1913), 116–20; Harvey (1957), 211–13; Silk
(1974), 124, 126; Nisbet and Hubbard (1978), 78; Campbell (1983), 20–1; Goldhill
(1987), 15–16; Vox (1990), 67–70, 83–4; Burzacchini (1995), 102–3; Henderson
(1998), 23–4.

ἀδμής etc. in Homer; note, incidentally, the horse in P. Oxy. 4454
fr. 1.) Lovers were often likened to charioteers (e.g. Theogn. 257–
60, 1249–52, 1268–70). But the finesse and mobility with which
the poem (or fragment) handles its imagery have not been fully
perceived.

The humour of the poem is mostly taken to be directed against
the girl; but the subversion of the narrator is much more significant.
The subtlety and skill of the poem will be seen to work more against
the narrator than as part of him, for all his vaunts of expertise. It
might be thought that such subversion, and such humour against
the male, were twentieth-century anachronism. But the narrator is
characteristically subverted in Anacreon, and there is much weighty
evidence in the poem itself, when it is read carefully. Indeed, this
poem inclines one to wonder whether the comparison of a girl to
a young animal in 408 really was for the listener simply mockery
of the girl (the language seems not without tenderness; note also
P. Oxy. 3722 fr. 82. 18). At all events, essential to this poem is the
element of address and of amatory rhetoric (cf. Gross (1985), ch.
2); but Archil. fr. 23 West, well compared by Vox (1990), in fact
brings out how differently Anacreon's narrator is treated.

Metre

1. $- \cup - \times - \cup - -$
2. $- \cup - \times - \cup - -$
3. $- \cup - \times - \cup - -$
4. $- \cup - \times - \cup -$

See on 347 fr. 1 [12], which employs the same metre: three acatalectic
trochaic dimeters, followed by a catalectic. There is word-end after each
line, and hiatus after 6 (line 2 in stanza); the elision of a postpositive at the
junction of lines 3 and 4 (4, 8 if ϲ' is rightly added) is probably compatible
with pause: cf. 353. 2 (after pendant; 357 is more problematic). Cf. further
on Alcm. 1 [1]. 41, Sapph. 31 [6]. 10. The last line can probably stand out
when required, like a clausular pherecratean (358 [13]. 8).

1–4. The imagery intensifies as the poem proceeds; the recognition
of stanzas makes this clearer. Looking askance (2) might be thought
an implausible sign of equine ill will or fear (my daughter, who
knows about horses, confirms these doubts). But even if it were
a plausible sign, it could not be displayed while running away.

πῶλε, and to a lesser extent φεύγεις, prepare the development of the imagery, but do not go far themselves.

πῶλε: this word is the fount of the allegory. But the word itself is commonly used to denote young people in Euripides; Aesch. *Th.* 454–5 (πωλικῶν) and *Ch.* 794 indicate that this is not a Euripidean invention. The scope of the poem will not, then, be apparent to the listener from the first.

Θρηικίη: the word will denote the origin of the girl, not, or not only, of the notional horse. (Thracian horses, despite Rhesus, are not so famous as to give the epithet point on its own.) This Thracian girl, free to choose, young, with no lover, will not be a slave or a prostitute; she seems in no lower category than the girl from Lesbos. Furthermore, this unnamed person in a fictional situation is likely to be a fiction herself, not an individual known to the audience; so her origin should seem intelligible to listeners, and not be a curious contingent fact. What place of performance would make this kind of contact with Thracians seem natural? Samos and Athens, like Mytilene, were interested in Thrace (and especially its precious metals); but the likeliest setting is Abdera, to which the Teians moved (see introduction). Abdera was actually in Thrace (note Pind. *Pae.* 2 (D2). 25); this seems the most promising locale for such contact. Miltiades' marriage with the Thracian king's daughter (Hdt. 6. 39. 2; Davies (1971), 302) throws an interesting light on relations between the two peoples; compare later the sister of Nymphodorus of Abdera (Thuc. 2. 29. 1; Graham (1992), 66). See further on 347 fr. 1 [12]; Anacr. fr. eleg. 5 West is obscure.

τί δή: the question produces an animated start (cf. P. Oxy. 3722 fr. 17 col. ii. 7). It also presents a quasi-realistic form for the narrator's attempt to persuade the girl: cf. e.g. Theocr. 3. 6–7 (cf. 11. 19); Ap. Rhod. 3. 975; Ov. *Met.* 3. 384–5 (in Echo's interpretation). It also opens the ironies of the poem; the listener will be led to wonder if the girl may have a different reason for her aversion from that alleged by the narrator.

2. A sign of hostility, perhaps, more than of suspicion. Cf. Sol. fr. 34. 4–5 West; Call. *Aet.* fr. 1. 37–8 Massimilla. A vivid amatory scene is conveyed to the listener through the second-person description.

3. νηλέως suggests the narrator's pleading (note 354 perhaps for the air of vigorous dialogue); but it is an amusingly extravagant word, too strong for its verb. It is doubtless elevated in register; but what

we know of its usage, and what we do not know of sixth-century literature, discourage confidence that it is intended to recall the *Iliad*. Harvey's treatment ((1957), 211–13) goes further astray by insisting on relevance to the foal and by positing the sense 'stubbornly', or at any rate not the sense 'without pity'.

φεύγεις has an element of physicality even when applied to lovers (cf. e.g. Theogn. 1287, Sapph. 1 [4]. 21); but 1–2 suggest that the idea of fleeing is not strong on the primary level.

δοκεῖς δέ: there is parataxis here, and a certain hysteron proteron, in relation to φεύγεις. This brings out the actual leap in what are presented as two aspects of the same thing. The narrator asserts a thought in the addressee, and asserts that it is the cause of her action. Even the former assertion seems bold, bolder than in 360 (the listener may wonder even there); but as a reason for the action, the alleged thought sounds decidedly implausible. Would a young person avoid someone's advances through an opinion that he was deficient in sexual technique? At any rate, the alert listener will imagine alternative possibilities; and will recall that the claim to expertise is the characteristic suit of the lover without the appeals of youth (cf. e.g. Arist. *Eccl.* 895–6, with cοφόν).

The interpretation 'you seem to me' (μ(οι)) is now rightly rejected as less fitting to the next stanza. The δέ shows that τί governs δοκεῖς too (otherwise Vox (1990), 69).

4. εἰδέναι should not be deprived of all sense of 'know', in this context (note 449). There is an air of injured pride here about the supposed insult (note 402 (*c*). 2, P. Oxy. 3722 fr. 2. 7; Archil. fr. 23. 14 West); οὐδέν is rather vehement. The persuasion moves further from dramatic plausibility.

The final cοφόν, and its line, set up the next stanza and the climax. On one level, the ensuing imagery of horsemanship will lend rhetorical support to the concentration on technique: within such an image only technique is relevant.

5–8. In this stanza, the potential of the image is realized, in a manner meant to be more suggestive sexually than poetically. The narrator assures the addressee of his skill; but precisely the image of the untamed horse implies how unwelcome these activities would be to the object (cf. e.g. Hom. *h. Ap.* 231–2, [Aesch.] *PV* 1009–10). On the level of dramatic realism, the address becomes absurd. On another level, we see the narrator displaying a knowing manner towards and an aggressive mastery over the callow female; but the hypothetical and unlikely character of his imaginings is made apparent by the situation and the syntax. The stanza presents a perfective resolution to an imperfective situation which the narrator regards as unsatisfactory; but the resolution is merely notional.

The imagery does not point to any specific sexual position (so Henderson (1991), 165 n. 67); the passage should be distinguished from those which use an image of riding to denote the *woman* astride the man (cf. further Adams (1982), 165–6; Cameron (1995), 515–16). The author is developing the general, and traditional, analogy between ending a maiden's virginity and taming a horse; even the connection between sexual climax and winning a race is not pressed to the full at 8. The passage naturally sounds naughty, as the very device of 'concealment' ensures (cf. Goldhill (1987), 15–16); it is not heavy-handedly obscene. Its humour, on this level, lies not so much in particular double meanings as in the entertainingly extended application of the metaphor; it demands a full sense of the comic paradox in the device (the girl is not really a foal).

5. ἴϲθι τοι: the phrase continues the tone of conversation, and so highlights the disparities. The asyndeton in fact marks idiomatically the continuity with the preceding question. The unusual combination ἴϲθι τοι seems to display a loud and overbearing attempt at authority (cf. Soph. *Ant.* 473 (Creon), *El.* 298 (Clytemnestra)); it follows on from the emphatic οὐδέν. (Perhaps there is even a pointed turn in εἰδέναι . . . ἴϲθι.) It seems hard to deny that there is something amusing in this strenuous self-assertion.

καλῶϲ receives great stress from its position; the word is full of ironies. Superficially, it continues the argument about ϲοφία. But would the acts be done καλῶϲ from the perspective of the girl? One might even wonder if we should contrast the adverb καλῶϲ with the adjective καλόϲ, which the narrator will not use of himself.

μέν, brought to the front, marks the two items as a kind of series; it is often used with this sort of force in the Mytilenean poets (e.g. Alc. 362. 1).

6. χαλινόν: the previously untamed horse must be forced to accept the bit, δαμαϲίφρονα χρυϲόν (Pind. *Ol.* 13. 79, cf. 65–8); a newly tamed horse may not do so readily (Xen. *Eq.* 3. 2). The bit is often used as an image of compulsion (e.g. [Aesch.] *PV* 671–2). It does not sound attractive for the filly.

7. ἡνίας δ' ἔχων again emphasizes control.

8. Not the end but the progress of the 'race' is envisaged. The moment of turning illustrates both control and skill. For the sexual act as a race, see Brown (1987), 311.

9–10. νῦν δέ presents the girl's unconcerned maidenhood not as temporary but as the actual state of affairs which contrasts with the preceding fantasies of a resolution.

The comparison here opens out wonderfully to convey through the image a winning picture of the girl's existence. Young horses running freely are a natural image of liberty: cf. esp. Lermontov, '*Uznik*' ('The Prisoner' (1837), *Sobr. soč.* (Moscow, 1964), i. 30), 13–16 (a contrast with the prisoner); note also Hom. *Il.* 6. 508 (=15. 264), Enn. *Ann.* 536 Skutsch, Virg. *Aen.* 11. 492–3. The epic passages depict too the joy and beauty of the horse. The image here suggests, first, the attractiveness of the girl's existence for the girl; maidenhood is often seen as a time of enchanted ease (e.g. Soph. *Trach.* 143–52). The imagery does not make it seem likely within the poem that the girl would wish to change her lot for subjection to the narrator; its lyricism may, indeed, promote sympathy for her from the listener. The image also suggests the attractiveness of the girl to the narrator. In doing so, it indicates that she is unattainable by him: free and, within the image, at a distance. This aspect of distance, within the image, is accentuated by the continuing device of address. The address now becomes still less of a dramatic reality; in so far as the sense of drama remains, the address becomes still more absurd.

λειμῶνας: the plural here adds to the sense of large freedom; contrast the narrow place in the preceding line. For meadows as the place for young horses, cf. e.g. Virg. *Georg.* 3. 75. Cf. also Nisbet and Hubbard (1978), 82.

κοῦφα κτλ.: the preceding line portrayed static enjoyment; this portrays youthful and carefree movement.

cκιρτῶcα: this spontaneous, purposeless motion contrasts with the earnest discipline that would be imposed by the narrator. Cf. Plat. *Phaedr.* 254 A 3–4.

παίζειc: the stem connects with παῖc. The listener should sense that it could not be used of love here, as it is in 358 [**13**]. 4, so rigorous is the image of 'love' in what precedes and follows. Note

Plat. *Laws* 653 D 7–E 3 on the joyful and playful movements of youth; note too Antiph. B 49 Diels–Kranz, ad fin.

11–12. The lines on one level offer the girl an unlikely-sounding reason for her continuing virginity, and an unpromising lover. The absence of a skilled man is presented by the narrator as a misfortune for her; and the narrator affects to assume that if a skilled man were wanted it would be he. In this general form, and after the idyll of 9–10, his chances sound still more remote than before. Does the narrator on a different level score a triumph over the girl through his wit and the complicity of the male listener in his innuendo? The wit, on my view of the text, is not explosive enough, nor favourable enough to the narrator, to achieve a quasi-narrative reversal. Better to say that it helps the poem to dissolve in agreeable humour; the author prevails over the narrator.

δεξιόν takes up ϲοφόν, with still more idea of dexterity at a craft.

ἱπποπείρην: perhaps an extension of ordinary language: there are no compounds of -πείραϲ (or -οϲ) in this sense, but ἱππογνώμων (Aesch. fr. 243. 3 Radt) might have been an ordinary word, cf. ἀργυρογνώμων. None the less, the length and type of the word (the only true compound in the poem) give it a resounding weight. It appears superficially to support δεξιόν, maybe with a suitable suggestion of technical language; but of course it does more too. The narrator now more overtly implies experience (a converse of youth). The witty undertone of the word probably suggests not so much successful assault as an attempt; cf. relatively early examples like Pind. *Pyth.* 2. 34, Ar. *Knights* 517 (cf. *Plut.* 149–50). The sense 'attempt' at any rate could hardly be excluded. The wit, then, rather than establishing the knowing aggression of the narrator, points to his failure.

ἐπεμβάτην: Silk attractively conjectures ἐπαμβάτην ((1974), 126). However, the earlier image is of a chariot race (8); the idea of one horse mounting another does not so well suit the conception here and earlier of skilled control. The case for pronouncing ἐπεμβάτην corrupt does not in any case seem strong. Eur. *Supp.* 685 etc., sufficiently confirm the existence and use of the word; the noun ἐπαμβάτηϲ in the desired primary sense is perhaps a little more questionable (cf. Aesch. *Cho.* 280). The passage is less loudly bawdy than might be supposed.

These discussions have brought out the remarkable refinement of detail in Anacreon's writing: a refinement well seen, for example, in his use of adjectives, compound, epic, and plain. The refinement, however, we have seen to be put at the service of larger strategies within the poem; these strategies and their direction have not perhaps been fully appreciated. The range and imagination shown by these few fragments are much greater than at first appeared; so too is their vigour. Sappho, similarly lauded for her art, forms an interesting point of comparison; but the more humorous poet pushes the possibilities of image and conception further. It is notable that the papyrus fragment 347 fr. 1 [12], on the interpretation followed here, enlarges our notion of Anacreon and an Anacreontic poem considerably beyond what quoted fragments had suggested. The arresting start ὠοί, τίc τρόποc οὗτοc; from a newer papyrus (P. Oxy. 3722 fr. 17 col. ii. 7) again reminds us not to limit or soften our picture too readily. He is an exciting as well as an elegant author.

SIMONIDES

Introduction

SIMONIDES came from Ceos. The island flourished in the sixth century: testimonies are a large kouros (*c.*530, 2.07 m. high), a very large lion (*c.*540, 6.40 m. long), and various sacred buildings, such as the temple of Athena at Carthaea. The Ceans' closeness to Athens and distance from Asia no doubt encouraged their participation in the Greek navy of 480, as early as Artemisium according to Herodotus (8. 1. 2, cf. 46. 3). A later fifth-century inscription attempts to restrict lavish funerals, and so suggests upper-class display (*IG* xii/5. 593 (*Schwyzer* 766)); the law itself is thought to come from the sixth century. Another inscription records victors, including fifth-century victors, in panhellenic games (*IG* xii/5. 608); some Cean victors were sung by Bacchylides (1, 2, 6, 7, 8?; cf. 17 (dithyramb for Ceans)). But only Simon. 621 suggests poetry written by Simonides for Ceans. It is conceivable that some of his poems about Artemisium and Salamis were for Ceos; but Pind.

Pyth. 1. 75–8, probably alluding to Simonides, speak of Athens and Sparta as the obvious places to commission poems on Salamis and Plataea.[1]

Some of Simonides' poems were for patrons in places near to Ceos, not in the first rank of wealth: a paean for Andros (519 fr. 35. 11), epinicians and laments for Euboeans (Carystus and Eretria, 509 (?), 518 (Eualcidas, d. 498), 530). Others were for cities that were reasonably near but were plainly major states in wealth and achievement: most notably Athens. The sources that tell of Anacreon's period with Hipparchus in Athens (d. 514) also tell of Simonides', though with less external support. Athens, as we have seen, is the likely recipient of poetry about Salamis, and indeed Artemisium. For other probable or possible signs of poetry for Athenians see 519 frr. 35, 120 (*b*), fr. 86 West. He also seems to have written an epinician for a Corinthian family.[2]

Simonides' range was much wider: not only Sparta, but both Thessaly and the west. For Sparta, we have poems celebrating Spartan achievements in the Persian Wars: probably the imposing elegy on Plataea (10–17 West; note Pind. loc. cit. and Simon. fr. 11. 25–8 West), and a lyric lament (presumably) for the dead of Thermopylae (531). (Note also *SLG* 319.) In the west, tyrants are particularly important: Anaxilas (epinician 515; date probably 480); Hieron (580; regent of Gela 485–78, tyrant of Syracuse 478–66). In Thessaly, Simonides wrote for various powerful families epinicians and laments (510, 511, 521, 528, 529), and different sorts of poems: an amorous elegy (fr. 22 West), a lyric poem on ἀρετή (542 [15]). It is not easy to sort out the members of the families or even the families themselves (Theocritus actually appears to separate, probably wrongly, Scopadae and Creondae, 16. 36–9). The Scopas to whom 542 [15] was addressed was seen by Phaenias as a ruler (fr. 14 Wehrli); Antiochus and Aleuas are said to have been rulers, the former of all Thessaly (Aeschin. Socr. fr. 10 p. 44 Krauss). Thuc. 1. 111. 1 mentions an Echecratidas as king of Thessaly; the name is

---

[1] For the lion see Manthos (1991), 115 pl. 4 (in general see the notes and photographs there by L. G. Mendoni); for the kouros (Athens 3686), Boardman (1978), pl. 144; on the archaic temples of Ceos see Schuller (1985), 361–83. Ekschmitt (1993), 277–83, conveniently summarizes the archaeology of Ceos. No Aegean islands further from Athens than Tenos, Naxos, Melos appear in Hdt. 8. 46 or ML 27. On *IG* xii. 5. 608 see Schmidt (1999).

[2] See Barrett (1978); note also 545, 596. Simonides' life: Stella (1946); Molyneux (1992); Parsons (1996*b*); Poltera (1997), 543–4.

the same as that of Antiochus' father and of Simonides' 'beloved' (fr. 22 West).[3]

Even from this selective account, it is apparent that Simonides wrote for a good many of the richest and most powerful states and individuals in the Greek world. It is notable too that poems for specific occasions bulk so large in our evidence, above all poems for funerals and celebrations of victory in games: great family events. State events, paeans, and probably celebrations of military victory are notable too. We need not necessarily think of prolonged service under particular patrons, such as one might suppose with Anacreon. One might bear in mind rather the more short-term commissions and visits of Pindar and Bacchylides. In 480 and shortly after we know that Simonides is writing for Rhegium, Sparta, and Athens. He may of course have resided for longer periods at particular places (Pisistratid Athens?); but the idea of a 'court poet' must be viewed with special caution, notably in regard to Syracuse. Simonides' tomb was said to be not at Syracuse but at Acragas; he had written an epinician for Xenocrates of Acragas in 476 or earlier. The story, for example, of his reconciling Hieron and Theron (Timaeus *FGrHist* 566 F 93) belongs with the fictions about Stesichorus' and Ibycus' political importance; it is hardly to be credited. Xenophon's *Hieron* (which is like an extended version of the anecdotes) actually begins ἀφίκετό ποτε πρὸς Ἱέρωνα.[4]

One cannot be sure how wide a period the poems for Thessalians cover. Simonides wrote poetry both for Scopas and when Scopas died, probably in an accident (529). He wrote a lament for Antiochus, who died while his mother was alive, and love poetry to a young Echecratidas, doubtless a member of this family and possibly Antiochus' son. But any intervals in time are compatible with separate visits, as say in the case of Pindar and Aegina. Poetry not about specific events might be commissioned too, like say Pindar's encomium for Hieron; at his symposia, Scopas will not have liked only the drink.[5]

---

[3] On Thessaly and Thessalian rulers see esp. Helly (1995).

[4] For tales of Simonides and Hieron (and his wife) cf. P. Hibeh 17, etc.

[5] Simonides' ξεινίη with the seer Megistias of Acarnania (Hdt. 7. 228. 4) does not fit readily into a career of continuous laureate residencies. The earliest direct evidence on the disaster of the Scopadae is Call. fr. 64. 11–14 Pfeiffer; even Page is insufficiently sceptical about Simonides' supposed escape ((1962), 243–4). We should not be too confident even that all the family perished (Favorinus in 521): someone must have commissioned the lament! The notion that the Echecratidas of

The poet has now attained, in the spectacular instance of Simonides, an international status. He does not appear to write as part of a community, nor in a local tradition; from outside, he appreciates, and adds prestige to, the traditions and communities he writes for. What scale of time should one envisage? The clearest evidence suggests poetry for a figure nearer home some time before 497; poetry for a western dynast *c.*480, for Sicilians before 475 and between probably 478 and 466, for Corinthians probably in the 470s (or later); poetry for Athens and Sparta in the aftermath of 480–79. Some of the Thessalian poetry may have been written before 498. If invited by Hipparchus, Simonides would have won fame before 514. We may readily suppose that Simonides is older than Pindar; it is not Pindar who gets the grand commissions after the Persian Wars, and his earliest dated poem is 498. At the other end, we have no reason positively to connect Simonides with the 460s, and Pindar's last dated poem is 446. Further precision is not to be had. Ancient birth-dates, and death-dates, are a highly unreliable category of evidence. They were typically based on guesswork long after the time; those for the lyric poets are especially suspicious. It is conceivable that Simonides' birth-date is based on a datable poem in which Simonides stated his age; but since an epigram which seems to fulfil just this function is clearly spurious (xxviii Page), that must be a very dubious hope. The most proper course is to ignore both the birth-date of *c.*556 and the rival date (mentioned in the *Suda*) of *c.*532, however the divergence between them is to be explained.[6]

In metre, Simonides follows on from the tradition of Stesichorus and Ibycus. He sometimes uses Stesichorus' dactylo-epitrite,

fr. 22 West is Antiochus' father seems unlikely; it seems implausible to separate him from the boy and the amorous fantasy of 13–14 (note 11–12), and to imagine a man who died in adulthood as a lovely boy in the next world. Cf. West (1993), 12–13; note Hunter (1993). An ordinary island, not excluded by the text, would cause fewer difficulties.

[6] The chronology implied in the accounts of Simonides' presence in Athens before 514 is given some plausibility by Arist. *Wasps* 1410, where Lasus and Simonides are contemporaries (unlikely to be Philocleon's mistake), and Hdt. 7. 6. 3, where Lasus and Hipparchus are. (Cf. Privitera (1965), 47–50; the Aristophanes passage is test. 63 in Ieranò (1997).) πολλά in Hdt. 5. 102. 3 (Eualcidas) does not mean 'often': cf. 1. 90. 1, 2. 135. 6, 8. 124. 3. There naturally remains a considerable likelihood that the poem for Eualcidas takes us before 500 (cf. Poltera (1997), 543). On dating the poetry for Aleuas before 498 (Pind. *Pyth.* 10) see Molyneux (1992), 134. The sources on Thargelia, however, inspire little confidence. Whether fr. 89 West, declaring Simonides' age, is genuine, one cannot be certain.

and he sometimes at least uses triads (543 [**16**], 649 (*f*); the non-triadic 542 [**15**] is reasonably short and not a public poem). He wrote some poems that were definitely and only aeolic, some that were definitely and only dactylo-epitrite (to judge from 581), some (see especially 531) that combined the types. One appears to see a conscious drawing together of Stesichorean and other traditions; the divisions between the types are very clear in Pindar and Bacchylides. In the two large fragments, we see Simonides approaching the composition of stanzas, and handling aeolic cola, in a far more complicated and ambitious fashion than earlier extant poets. As in other areas, he seems a poet intensely aware of traditions, and one ready to combine them in novel ways and to extend them in adventurous innovation.

In dialect, for which the papyrus fragments 519 offer the best evidence, Simonides continues the form employed by Stesichorus and Ibycus. As in them, genitives in -οιο are lavishly employed (Pindar and Bacchylides are more restrained); on the other hand, the forms πάρειτι (519 fr. 35 (*b*). 5, cf. 555. 1?) and Ποτ[⟨ε⟩ιδ]ᾶνος (519 fr. 77. 6) go further in the direction of West Greek than Pindar and Bacchylides seem usually to do. For Simonides, unlike Anacreon, dialect has nothing to do with his area of origin. He is following a tradition that was associated, at least through Ibycus, with the occasional poetry to which most of his lyric belonged. Lyric does not here stand against elegy as even notionally a more localized type of poetry. But within Simonides' own *œuvre*, the dialect differentiates, at a fundamental level, the two main types of poetry he writes.[7]

This is the most extraordinary of Simonides' combinations, his cultivation of both the main separate divisions of archaic poetry. Anacreon may have written elegiac and iambic poetry, but Simonides seems the first to practise both lyric and elegy or iambus on a substantial scale. His audacity was not imitated by Pindar or Bacchylides. His mastery of both lyric and elegy was made salient to Greeks of the time: he conspicuously treated the battles of 480–79 in both types of verse (for whatever reasons). Indeed, the same

---

[7] On Simonides' dialect see Poltera (1997), 503–33 (in relation to his successors, not his predecessors). Bacch. 27. 36 (P. Oxy. 2364) has φατί, but 13. 48 ἐφίηςι (ἐφίητι Pind. *Isth.* 2. 9). The aeolic τελέςςαις (519 fr. 92. 3) is already paralleled at Stes. P. Oxy. 3876 ('ined.' in *PMGF*) fr. 62. 5. The Ionic of the elegiac poetry is not of course guided by the dialect of Ceos.

battles or the same audiences in some cases appear to have received
the attention of both his muses.[8]

Poem 581, in paraphrasing and attacking an Ionic dactylic ori-
ginal (whatever its extent), displays for us, and perhaps for origi-
nal listeners, the more colourful use of language and freer use of
rhythm available to lyric. Poem 579 treats Hesiod in a related way.[9]
Simonides' lyric is firmly differentiated stylistically from his elegy
(earlier elegy and lyric substantiate the comparison). For example,
the length of sentences or half-sentences is much more varied in
his lyric than it is in elegy (apart from Archilochus), which aims at
a more even flow. Cf. e.g. 542 [**15**]. 21–5 and 26, 34–8, 543 [**16**]. 7–
17. His lyric deploys rhetorical figures in a much more flamboyant
manner than elegy: cf. e.g. 526. 2 (cf. *SLG* 414 (*d*). 12–13), 531. 3,
543 [**16**]. 21–2. Language appears to be much more freely handled
in his lyric than in what remains of his elegy, and in earlier elegy:
so the abstract subjects of 521. 3–4, 543 [**16**]. 23, the transferences
of 531. 3 (contrast fr. 16. 1 West), 542 [**15**]. 3, 543 [**16**]. 22, or the
use of compounds.[10] The constant change of rhythm in his lyric of
itself makes the language feel more unpredictable, and can throw
the individual word or phrase into more startling relief. Even when
the conceptions of the elegiac poetry seem most imaginative, as in
fr. 21 or 22 West, the diction and the lines remain relatively smooth
and aim less at striking surprise. And yet Simonides, as we shall
see, also causes these two types of writing to interact fruitfully.

The freedom and daring of his lyric are admirably exhibited
by the two large fragments of it to be discussed. The austerity
and intellectualism of the one and the intense narrative imagina-
tion of the other display his range. The case of the near-complete
542 [**15**] shows further a willingness to select and exclude, to write
a quite distinctive kind of poem against the visible background of
his own and other people's poetry. The overt sophistication, the
self-consciousness and the audacity with which his work handles
poetry and tradition, make Simonides, if not postmodern to us,
at least in terms of his own time inescapably and challengingly
modern. Ibycus had himself formed a new combination of genres
into a relatively cohesive body of poetry, and had played arrestingly
with the epic genre and with self-reference; Anacreon had to some

---

[8] Certainly Artemisium; Thermopylae (531; VI Page); probably Spartans (see
above).   [9] Contrast the spareness of Gottfried, *Tristan* 38–40.
[10] Note the distribution of hapax legomena in Poltera's list ((1997), 391–401).

extent subverted tradition in irony, within the poems. Simonides reworks the past with a larger ambition and a wider scope of creation. This is not of course a point to the detriment of Anacreon and Ibycus, any more than of Bacchylides and Pindar, who derive a tradition from Simonides rather than matching his own innovation. But it is notable that Simonides' lyric appears a significant source of inspiration and point of reference even for the further modernity of the later fifth century.

15: *PMG* 542[11]

This poem is elaborately considered in Plato, where Protagoras is made to attack the work for self-contradiction (cf. 1–3 and 11–13). In this attack, and in Socrates' defence, we see a Platonic and Socratic game (the length of Socrates' account is particularly cheeky). We also see an image, neither wholly unserious nor wholly committed, of fifth- and fourth-century criticism (note 347 A 6–B 2). Finally, the poem itself is made into a thematic reflection of an encounter with an earlier coφóc and of strife for truth (one might think of *mise en abyme*). The Platonic passage greatly distorts the poem; but the choice of poem for this extended discussion signals how the work stands closer to sophistic and post-sophistic intellectualism than does most archaic lyric.

Although the scholarly disussion takes its impetus from the quoting author, it is in this case more profitable to concentrate on the actual words preserved. (In fact a keener feeling for Plato should prevent the use of him to reconstruct more words of Simonides.) However, placing too much emphasis on Plato is less of a danger at present than reposing the weight of intepretation on the passage missing after 3. This gap can be exploited to make the poem occasional. Yet its contents are purely conjectural; and the greater and latter part of the poem, which must have made its own impact, looks as if it were general and not focused on a particular situation (even if we allow for the lacunae after 18 and 30). Furthermore, the poem

[11] On 542 [15] see esp. Wilamowitz (1913), 159–91; Blass (1872); Gundert (1977); Woodbury (1991*a*); Fränkel (1960*a*), 72–4, (1962), 350–6; Gentili (1964); Parry (1965); Donlan (1969); Easterling (1974), 41–3; Babut (1975); Taylor (1975), 141–8; Dickie (1978); Schütrumpf (1987); Giuliano (1991); Carson (1992*a*); Rutherford (1992), 150–2; Most (1994); Henry (1999).

cannot plausibly be read as praising the triumph, or consoling the failure or misfortune, of the aristocrats it addresses: 'true excellence is impossible, but abstention from badness is commendable' is no message for such an occasion. Bacchylides and Pindar help to make apparent the difference of this poem from such occasional poetry. Bacch. 14 could be inspired by this poem, but it well illustrates how the content is altered, subordinated, and placed in a different structure to accommodate it to praise (notice too 10. 50–6). If there were some connection to a specific happening of a different kind, the poem remains striking for its abstraction.

One way to view this abstraction is as a cross-fertilization of genres. The *Works and Days*, and more especially elegy, provide analogies for extended generalized discussion; Sol. fr. 13 West offers a notable instance. Simonides overtly imitates Hesiod at 579, and was remarkable for writing elegy as well as lyric. A striking extension of lyric boundaries seems more likely than unconscious contamination. (The tiny generalizing scolia *PMG* 889, 890, etc. scarcely affect the picture.) As with much elegy, or say many poems of Anacreon, no specific occurrence is required to account for the creation of the poem. One may no doubt imagine solo performance, at a symposium; but this last point does not take us far.

The poem differs even from its non-lyric forerunners in argumentative manner and shape. Disagreement with a predecessor has antecedents; more important is the sense here of a firm and purposeful development of thought. Hesiod and Solon follow older patterns of utterance; Simonides is not Parmenides, but his organization and persuasive force are arresting. It is partly a matter of his exploiting the stanzaic form to structure the exposition; lyric form is made to do, and offer, something different.

One cannot exclude the possibility that Simonides' approach to form had been anticipated by others; but that possibility is far more significant for the ideas of the poem. Scholarship has been increasingly inclined to deny their originality. An intriguing twist is provided by 541, which handles similar material, and is most likely to be by Simonides (for Lobel's reasons (Lobel and Turner (1959), 91–4); note also Johnstone (1997), contrast Bacch. 17. 116, Eur. *IA* 1300). We know far too little of earlier writers to assert originality; it is even precarious to use the later Pindar and Bacchylides in denying it (cf. Schütrumpf (1987), 20). A more answerable question is what impression the poem makes on the listener within the drama of the poem. As we shall see, in the earlier part of the poem the narrator is highlighting the independence and boldness of his position. In the later part, he moves to a less strenuous manner; this confers on his position, as now developed, a beguiling plausibility. Within its confines the poem should strike the listener, through its prominent and animated narrator, as impressive in its persuasion and challenging in some aspects of its thought. The listener is not merely soothed by platitudes. And even beyond the poem as performed or read, originality would not be essential to the stimulation of reflection.

Metre

1. −∪∪−∪∪−∪−∪−−
2. ∪∪−−−∪−∪∪−∪−
3.   −∪−∪∪−∪−⏝−∪−
4. ∪∪−∪−−∪−∪∪−∪−
5.   −∪−∪∪−∪−
6. ∪∪−∪−−∪−∪∪−
7. −−∪−−∪−∪∪−
8. ∪−−∪−−−∪−∪∪−
9.   −−∪−∪−−

The metre is a version of aeolic like those used by Pindar and Bacchylides. It develops the central pattern of single-short sequence, followed by choriambic or 'dactylic' core, followed by single short, though some of these elements can be omitted, and a colon can begin its 'single-short' section with ∪∪−: cf. Bacch. 18. 1, Pind. *Ol.* 4. str. 1, *Pyth.* 6 str. 3, *Nem.* 6 str. 5, ep. 6, Pind. *Pae.* 6 (D6) str. 9 (the last similar to str. 6 here). No two cola are the same (contrast 521), and we are far from the short and easily grasped stanzas of the Mytilenean poets. This stanza opens with an expanded version of the 'ibycean' (cf. Ibyc. 286. 1–3; Simon. 575. 1), which in this context may be considered aeolic. But in the rest of the stanza there are no other sequences of successive double-short. This is unlike most other Simonidean fragments of more than three lines (not 579, on Ἀρετά); one may plausibly suppose that a certain weightiness is designed. The opening line is pendant, and stands distinct. Then follow three pairs. In the first two (str. 2–3, 4–5) the pair, joined without pause, has a first colon that begins ∪∪− and ends −∪−∪∪−∪−, and a second that begins or consists of −∪−∪∪−∪− and ends ∪−; 5 is a shorter version of 3, 4 a version of 2 with one more syllable. The third pair need not be joined without pause, though a pause precedes; after 16 and 26 but not 36 there is a strong break in sense. Str. 6 again begins ∪∪−, but ends −∪−∪∪−: it is 4 without the final ⏑-. Str. 7 also ends ⏑⏑-; it is like 3 and 5, but with more before and less after. What are usually printed as the last three lines (ἐκὼν . . . | μηδὲν . . . | δ' . . .) should perhaps be taken as another pair of cola. For ἀνάγκαι, if pendant, would suggest pause; while δ' would not necessarily conflict with this in earlier lyric (not Bacchylides or Pindar), it and τοῖcιν in 39 together make it more inviting to run the last two 'lines' into one, with --⏑⏑-⏑-- to close. (It now becomes easier to deal with 18.) This renders it tempting to remove the isolated 2 ba in the first 'line', and make them part of the single-short sequence in a colon that goes on -⏑-⏑⏑- (cf. Pind. *Pyth.* 7. str. 3; Soph. *Aj.* 1185–223 [**19**], *metre*). This then means that the first colon (str. 8) again ends ⏑⏑-, like str. 6 and 7; the final colon will be pendant, like the opening colon only. This is a cohesive and elegant structure, but much more intricate than anything in earlier poetry.

1. ἄνδρ' ἀγαθόν: two poems by Theognis may begin thus (173, cf. 319). But ἀλαθέωc immediately introduces a more challenging type of language. It may go closely with ἀγαθόc (so Arist. *EN* 1100[b]21–2; cf. Anon. Iambl. 4. 6 Diels–Kranz; Thuc. 6. 92. 4 (ὀρθῶc)); or it may, more easily, go with the whole infinitive phrase. In either case, it indicates that words are not being applied by normal criteria; and it suggests the narrator's independence. The emphasis falls on this word, not γενέcθαι: that gives little scope for giving γενέcθαι, 'be' more than 'become', large and subtle significance. (Socrates wisely finds a different job for ἀλαθέωc to do, *Prot.* 342 D 6–A 7.) Note 598 on truth and appearance.

Whether μέν refers forwards, and if so to what, cannot be known for certain without the missing lines; Socrates' exegesis is not to be trusted (342 C 7–D 6).

2. χαλεπόν stands out sharply; it starts the metrical colon, has no verb, and is surrounded by elaborations of the difficult ideal. The word does not actually mean 'impossible' (cf. 541. 7); and the sentence itself does not make clear that this is implied (cf. Easterling (1974), 42, and Most (1994), 137–8). At any rate, immodest Greek aristocrats would not have thought it was; note 579. 5–7 (522, 526. 2, 541. 6); fr. 15. 3 West; Hom. *Il.* 15. 641–3 etc. (and e.g. Bacch. 1. 181–2, Theogn. 463–4 for the idea of difficulty). But the poem is already preparing its arresting claim.

Henry (1999) argues, interestingly, that the whole phrase means 'it is hard for a truly good man to come to be': mind and limbs, he objects, can hardly be made after birth. But χαλεπόν with infinitive in poetry should indicate difficulty for a specific person, even when there is an accusative and infinitive (cf. Hom. *Il.* 16. 620–1, *Od.* 23. 80–1). Henry's Platonic examples themselves, seen in their context, in fact involve difficulty for individuals (*Rep.* 502 c 1–2, 528 b 6–7, *Laws* 711 d 1–2). The objection seems to stress too strongly the sense 'become', and the physical formation of hands and feet (see below); it is needlessly strict.

As 541. 7 and Protagoras' argument show, there is no reason for any link to be made at this point to Pittacus.

χερсὶν κτλ.: rhetorically piled up (cf. Most (1994), 138). The datives should be taken with what precedes; 'square in hands and feet' would be rather awkward. Physical and mental attributes are forcefully combined. For ἀγαθός and ἀρετή used physically cf. e.g. Tyrt. fr. 12. 2 West, Sol. fr. 27. 8 West, Xenoph. fr. 2. 15–17 West, Pind. *Pyth.* 10. 23. It might sound as if only aristocrats would qualify; but not even they will do so.

3. τετράγωνον: Pythagorean connections need not be supposed, let alone a canon of four virtues, which scarcely suits 2 (cf. Giuliano (1991), 110). It is enough to suppose the idea of exact craftsmanship, which enables us to take the whole phrase τετράγωνον . . . τετυγμένον together, and to give a point to the otherwise otiose τετυγμένον. Cf. the metaphorical *quadrare* and e.g. Colum. 11. 2. 13. As Aristotle notes, the metaphor is not particularly colourful (*Rhet.* 1411ᵇ24–8): in its 'sound-world', to use a musical analogy, the poem is austere.

ἄνευ ψόγου is primarily applicable to the tenor; it means 'without cause for blame', cf. Eur. fr. 417. 1 Nauck; the theme is taken up in 24.

4. How much is missing here, the rest of this stanza, or another stanza too? Both Protagoras' ὀλίγον δὲ τοῦ ποιήματος εἰς τὸ πρόσθεν προελθών (339 d 4–5) and Socrates' ὀλίγα διελθών (344 b 6) suit their rhetorical purposes (note ἐπελάθετο and διὰ πάντος τοῦ ἄισματος). At *Hipp. Min.* 371 d 2 ὀλίγον πρότερον . . . παραχρῆμα refers to a gap of 45 lines in the first instance (cf. 370 b 1); this might, or might not, be a different case. Used of conversation such phrases can refer back 5, or 14, Stephanus pages (*Euthyphr.* 14 a 11, *Phaedr.* 277 d 3–4). Socrates' claim to go through the whole τύπος of the poem (344 b 2) involves at least a little sharp practice, when his treatment of the rest is considered, in respect of the 6 lines certainly omitted; 344 b 6–7 reinforce this impression. Whether he is being more wilful, here as in other matters, cannot be determined. It will be most reasonable to posit that only 6 lines are missing, but to bear it in mind that 15 may be.

What was in the missing passage? 339 A 7 (πρὸς . . . Θετταλοῦ makes it likely that the poem had an addressee, and plausible that the addressee's name or his father's appeared within the poem (it could have been surmised subsequently). Such a name could have appeared in 19–20 or 31–4 (not 36); but one would expect an earlier first appearance. The address might have been limited to the name itself, a common enough practice in archaic poetry, especially elegy (Alc. 130 b [9]. 19 n.; Theogn. 39, 43, etc., Semon. fr. 1. 1 West (prob.)). We may suppose the material was not generalization directly on the theme of 11–40. If it had been, probably Plato would have included it, though the needs of Protagoras' and Socrates' arguments might have encouraged the omission. A particular situation for Scopas might conceivably have been mentioned (see the introduction to the poem); but there are many other possibilities.

11–13. οὐδέ presumably means 'but not', whether or not it is linked to μέν (1). It is not, however, the strongest adversative particle; this will prove significant.

μοι is 'in my judgement' (Kühner–Gerth (1898–1904), i. 421); not '(in harmony) with me' (there is no ϲυν-), nor '(suitably) to me' (there is no sense). The narrator's independence is strongly marked here; perhaps one should read ἐμοί (cf. 21, 36; Eur. *Med.* 580, Sapph. 16 [5]. 3, Pind. *Ol.* 1. 52, Hdt. 1. 182. 1, etc.; Eur. *Andr.* 1053).

ἐμμελέωϲ: there need not be a strong sense of metaphor; but such metaphor as there is increases the self-referentiality.

νέμεται is difficult. 'Is thought to be true' is without parallels, and does not suit the context effectively. One may suspect νέμεται is used for ἀνανέμω (and other compounds), in the usage 'read, read out' (Soph. fr. 144. 2 Radt, probably with νέμω; *CEG* i. 108. 2 middle, *SEG* 35 (for 1985) no. 1009, Theocr. 18. 48) or, as here, 'recite, repeat' (Hdt. 1. 173. 5, middle). See also Lightfoot (1999), 134–5; Catenacci (1999). Cf. *Prot.* 343 A 5–B 7 (for ὑμνέω cf. 317 A 5–6, *Laws* 9, 871 A 1, etc.).

τὸ Πιττάκειον, ϲοφοῦ: the explicit reference to a source, and characterization of that source, appear highly characteristic of Simonides. Cf. 564. 4, 581, fr. 19 West; P. Oxy. 3965, randomly preserved, twice presents description of Homer (frr. 11. 15–18, 20.

13–15 West). The feature might then have seemed more naturally at home in elegy, cf. the similar Sol. fr. 20 West (Callin. fr. 6 West?); later lyric occasionally takes up explicit reference and naming, cf. Bacch. 5. 191–4, Pind. *Ol.* 9. 1–2, *Pyth.* 2. 55, 4. 277–8, *Nem.* 7. 21–4, *Isthm.* '3/4'. 55–7, 6. 66–8, *Pae.* 7b (C2). 11, frr. 265, 347. The effect here is forcefully intellectual, and marks a link to the later fifth century; one may compare the generalized disagreement in Sapph. fr. 16 [5] and the implicit dissension with Homer in Ibyc. S151 [11].

cοφοῦ: the narrator is courteous (cf. Plat. *Rep.* 331 E 6—on Simonides); but by implication he magnifies himself: he disagrees both with common opinion and a wise predecessor. Whether the canonical collection of Seven Wise Men existed yet is not known; Plat. *Tim.* 20 D 8 might seem to make against Fehling's contention that Plato invented it (otherwise Fehling (1985), 19).

εἰρημένον: placed at the end of the clause like νέμεται; it perhaps sets the original simple act of speech (cf. φάτ') against the later tedious repetitions (cf. *Prot.* 371 A 5–6).

χαλεπὸν κτλ.: the original form of Pittacus' remark is not known. One may probably infer from 342 B 5–7 and *Crat.* 384 A 8–B 1 that Plato did not suppose this remark to be the same as χαλεπὰ τὰ καλά, and that he did not know the story which connected Pittacus with the first and Solon with the second (Σ Plat. *Crat.* 384 B, *Hipp. Maj.* 304 E, cf. Greene (1938), 178; Bühler (1987), 299–300). However, his knowledge of Pittacus' saying seems to be derived from the poem; Simonides could still have derived it from the other saying.

φάτ' does not necessarily emphasize a difference from writing, cf. Bacch. 5. 191 (metre requires the past), Pind. *Pyth.* 4. 278. The asyndeton can be for explanation or from brevity.

What is the relation of these lines to the earlier ones? However large the gap, one cannot think that Simonides did not notice the contradiction or hoped it would not be noticed. Contradictions noticed by deconstructive critics are often not invisible to the writer, and Socrates' fall and the applause may be overplayed, like his own reaction (339 E 1–3). So close a relation as this between the starts of stanzas cannot be accidental: the same basic three words χαλεπὸν ἐcθλὸν ἔμμεναι are as it were varied and expanded on in the first stanza. We can hardly escape the contradiction by stressing the difference between γενέcθαι and ἔμμεναι. The former is not emphasized (see above), and no listener could possibly catch the point. Nor can we escape it by saying that χαλεπόν has a different meaning (i.e. implication) in the two passages. The problem is not one of opinion but of form. How are we to reconcile with acceptable utterance a sequence which formally asserts and denies the same proposition, and which ascribes the opinion both to the narrator and to another, so that the second utterance cannot be seen as a straightforward retraction of the first (as in Hes. *WD* 11–13)? The passage is crucially different from, though related to, Aesch. *Ag.* 750–62, Soph. *Trach.* 1–7, Pushkin, 'Mozart i Sal'eri' (1830), 1–3: in those places the old or common saying is not formally affirmed then denied by the speaker. Also different and related is Pind. *Nem.* 6. 1–7, where the narrator produces a series of statements on divine and moral kinship and difference in which each contrasts with the statement before but does not actually contradict it. But that last passage, with its strategies of surprise, gives us a clue. This passage too pursues such a strategy, but more drastically. The narrator at first seems to issue a blatant and startling self-contradiction; his ascribing the rejected opinion to another marks and stresses the change for the listener. One expects a dissenter from 'it is hard to be excellent' to think it is easy to be excellent (note 541. 7); such a change would be especially remarkable in view of the emphasis in 1–3. In fact the dissent turns out to be in an opposite direction: no mortal can be excellent. This view only advances further on that in 1–3. What follows shows further that the poet does not shrink from the surprise of formal self-contradiction. No mortal can be excellent; a mortal in misfortune is the opposite of excellent; all men in good fortune are excellent. Formally the third statement contradicts the first, and the ἔμμεναι in the second excludes the possibility of escaping formal contradiction through subtlety with ἔμμεναι in the first. The whole passage is not an ingenious exercise in logic; it treats the discourse and the listener audaciously, and through its audacity dramatizes the boldness of thought and gives life to a cohesive outlook.

14–16. θεός: it would ordinarily appear odd to predicate excellence of a deity; but the verb is not ἔχει (contrast Plat. *Phaedr.* 278 D 4). The optative denotes what is actually a counterfactual situation (cf. e.g. Sol. fr. 24. 9 West): only a god would have the immunity from ill fortune to have this honour, were it available to him.

The asyndeton appears for the same reasons as in the preceding clause (such asyndetic groups are common); it intensifies the abrupt manner and the surprise. Note 526. 3.

ἔχοι γέρας: the language, in this context, suggests a specific honour that would separate a man or men from other men (cf. e.g. Aesch. *Supp.* 986, Hdt. 9. 27. 5). This marks the counterfactual, and quasi-aristocratic, character of the thought. ἔχειν is a very common verb for γέρας, which is given and possessed.

ἄνδρα is opposed to θεός; the word had not appeared in the version of 13, unlike that of 1. It now comes back with new meaning; it is separated from κακόν in meaning and position. Forcefully placed contrasts of 'gods' and 'men' are notable in Simonides' quoted lyric fragments: 526, 527, cf. 525, 581. 5–6, fr. 11. 28 West, and also e.g. fr. 20. 5, 11 West.

κακὸν ἔμμεναι opposes ἐςθλὸν ἔμμεναι at the same point of the last colon but one. The double negative οὐκ ἔςτι μὴ οὐ is far more striking and impressive than οὐκ ἔςτιν ἐςθλὸν ἔμμεναι would have been. The thought itself is disturbing. The passage is not talking merely about social prestige, as the connection with 1–3 makes clear. (Cf. Dickie (1978), 26–7; but there is surely considerable irony even in the passages he cites.) The idea that one cannot be excellent in adversity, continued in 18, is hardly commonplace; the passage considerably exceeds even Hom. *Od.* 17. 332–3 (note 'half', and *slavery*).

ἀμάχανος (Bacch. 1. 171 etc.) reinforces the idea of the inescapable in οὐκ ἔςτι. Cf. 541 8–9.

cυμφορά: 17–18 suggest bad fortune more than, say, strong desire as in 541. 9–10; c]υμφορά refers similarly to fortune at the related Bacch. 14. 3.

καθέληι: a very strong word to end the sentence, more usually employed of literal destruction (not at the pertinent Eur. *HF* 1396 καὶ τοὺς cθένοντας γὰρ καθαιροῦςιν τύχαι). A non-human subject is frequent from Homer on (*Od.* 2. 100). The subjunctive stresses the commonness of the occurrence.

17. Still more surprising than the impossibility of excellence in bad fortune seems the necessity of excellence in good. Not only does it appear to contradict 11–13 more directly, but it seems a notion that few resentful aristocrats would accept. How should we sort out the immediate point and the wider context? On the one hand, the emphasis throughout on the perfect man, and the idea of truly being ἀγαθός in the first line, mean that the assertion at any rate cannot give a strong sense to ἀγαθός. (And later on, voluntary wrongdoing (28–9) and folly (37–8) are obviously common.) On the other hand, the parallel assertion about being κακός must at least be taken as a truth about personal qualities, since on it depends the argument that true excellence cannot be reached. Between these two points, there is, in a poem, considerable scope: the line allows one to hear undertones of scorn, or even irony, in the depiction of this undemanding excellence, and the conflict with the general position encourages suspicion. Such undertones need not invalidate the wider argument about perfection. It is both a provocative and an open utterance.

The wider argument is based on the notion that all suffer misfortune, which is implicit in the contrast with a god. This misfortune inevitably causes action which falls short of true or unflawed excellence. The language in 16 is extreme, to show the inevitability of the cause; in 18 it is weaker, to show its universality. In 18 faring ill forms part of a simple polarity, and it is natural to suppose that everyone will have good and bad (the aorist πράξαις encourages the idea of transient fortune). When all allowances are made, the tight relation forged between fortune and excellence, and the picture of all people changing their worth and 'moral' category, go beyond the notion of man's fluctuating lot. They are so presented as to strike and disquiet.

εὖ at the end of this clause is taken up by ἀγαθός at the end of the next. The connection of the words gives an appearance of grim logic. The reference cannot be to good deeds, as 14–16 indicate; the tautology of 17–18 would also be odious.

πᾶς ἀνήρ helps the argument and the provocation; a mere τις would be much less forceful.

κακός is effectively set next to ἀγαθός, at the start of a new colon and clause; the clash drives home the instability of the individual's 'moral' position.

19–20. It is normally supposed that Plato's words at 345 C 3 offer a lightly altered version of Simonides' (Manuwald (1999), 345–6, is more doubtful). But ἐπὶ πλεῖστον and kindred phrases are never found in poetry ([Eur.] *Rhes.* 946–7 is different); they are often found in prose. Furthermore, as καί and the context suggest, the phrase in Plato is referring to time (cf. 343 B 8): that is, it presupposes Socrates' peculiar account of the passage. It is also an idea of suspiciously Platonic colouring that the nearest approach to ἀρετή is made by those humans whom the gods love. Cf. *Men.* 99 E 5–100 A 1, *Rep.* 383 C 3–5 (382 E 3), 501 B 9–C 2; *Symp.* 212 A 5–7. The καὶ τοῦτο and the τείνει at *Prot.* 345 B 8 should be observed. We cannot know what kind of basis 345 C 3 had in Simonides' words, or whether it was simply inspired by 14 (cf. 344 C 1–3). The point is important for our interpretation of the whole poem, and for the degree of its pessimism.

τὰ ἐπίοντά γε τοῦ ἄιсματος (345 C 4–5), 'what follows', create an impression that 1 line rather than 10 has been omitted. It is reasonable to accept this; there is no ὀλίγα διελθών here (343 B 6). τοὔνεκεν would follow on very well from this stanza.

21–3. The present stanza is the only complete one. The first half-sentence (21–5) is long; it elaborates, and suits, the fruitless search; it contrasts with the dry and pithy half-sentence that follows.

τοὔνεκεν starts the stanza with a strong sense of logical progression. The epic form τοὔνεκ- (Hom. *Il.* 5. 822, etc.) is found once in elegy (Theogn. 488, not 854), once in lyric, besides Corinna (Pind. *Ol.* 1. 65).

οὔ ποτ': a vigorous negative marks the engagement of the first person. Cf. Pind. *Nem.* 8. 35; Soph. *Ant.* 207–8 etc.

ἐγώ: the pronoun takes up that at the start of the preceding stanza. There is some suggestion of the 'I, and any reasonable person' found in tragic choruses; but the rest of the poem shows that, as with similar cases in Pindar, the 'I' is not merely representative.

τὸ μὴ γενέϲθαι | δυνατὸν διζήμενοϲ brings out the absurdity trenchantly. The phrasing takes up the language of impossibility in 14–15, and the whole line of argument. τὸ μὴ ἐόν would have been much less purposeful.

διζήμενοϲ: the idea of the search is after this developed in space and time. One may compare Theogn. 415–16, Parmen. fr. 5. 2 Wright, and especially Heaney's version of Diogenes' search in 'The Haw Lantern' (*The Haw Lantern* (London, 1987), 7; cf. Diog. Laert. 6. 41).

κενεὰν κτλ.: the search, not to be undertaken, produces in the main clause a lavish negated image of wasted life and vain hopes. The point is argumentative; but the poetry also throws emphasis onto the narrator, as he affects to consider the consequences for himself, and contends vehemently.

κενεός so commonly goes with hope that one imagines it does here too. However, the preposition dividing the synonymous adjectives seems slightly curious (contrast Bacch. 5. 12); one might just wonder whether it went with μοῖραν. In any case, the emphasis is notably strong, and the familiar language of authoritative wisdom is evoked (Hes. *WD* 498, Semon. fr. 1. 6–7 West, etc., cf. Simon. fr. 19. 4–5 West).

μοῖραν αἰῶνος βαλέω: the extreme language has a point (the vain search would take a lifetime, cf. Protag. B 4 Diels–Kranz). 'Part' seems too specific. βαλέω suggests a wanton caprice, μοῖραν an interference with what had been planned (or apportioned).

24–5. πανάμωμον ἄνθρωπον stands out at the start of a new period, after a substantial clause which separates it from the phrase it is in apposition to (τὸ . . . δυνατόν). The change from the generalizing neuter increases the impressive effect. ἄνευ ψόγου is here strengthened and heightened by παν- (cf. Semon. fr. 4 West, contr. Theogn. 799). Simonides is especially fond of this prefix; it is found with a negative in epic, Parmenides, Pindar (*Pae.* 8a (B3). 14).

εὐρυεδέος: the epithet is put first, before the relative. It magnifies the search, and the surprise. The adjective recurs, with -ους, at *SLG* 395 (*b*). 2 (Simonides?); the variant in some of Plutarch's manuscripts derives from the Homeric χθονὸς εὐρυοδείης (*Il.* 16. 635 etc.).

ὅσοι κτλ.: a version of epic phraseology, turned to the first person plural (cf. Soph. *Phil.* 709). The closest parallel is Hes. fr. 211. 13 Merkelbach–West χθονὸ]ς ὅς[ς]ο[ι καρ]πὸν [ἔ]δουςιν; in view of Simon. fr. 19 West, we may note that Hom. *Il.* 6. 142 (cf. 21. 465) comes in a particularly famous passage. αἰνύμεθα imports an epic verb not used in lyric, elegy, or iambus elsewhere, and perhaps more elevated in sense than ἔδουςι; the epic-style epithet also aggrandizes the passage (cf. *Hom. h. Ap.* 365). The grandeur of language supports the rhetoric of size, and continues the strange negative poetry of the search; but it is also deflated by the brusqueness of the next clause. The elevated language for mankind is itself at ironic odds with the depreciation of man in the content, and the implicit contrast with the gods. The first person plural tempers the depreciation with humility.

For the move from ἄνθρωπον to ὅcοι see Kühner–Gerth (1898–1904), i. 55–6; it is effective here.

26: a line of brilliant dryness. The finding is syntactically subordinated to the message, and thus formally made to sound possible, when the actual point is that no message or finding will or can take place. The presuppositions of the humour need not be too closely scrutinized. It is as if the narrator might achieve the result of a search (cf. Hom. *Il.* 5. 168, Cratin. fr. 144 Kassel–Austin, etc.), but without searching. The movement implied in ἀπαγγελέω is necessary to the result.

ὔμμιν can hardly denote the human race; the message would not make sense. An address to listeners in general would be anomalous. Presumably it denotes the family of Scopas. The form of address in 4–10 may have made this easier, and a plural pronoun might even have appeared there (cf. Pind. *Ol.* 8. 15, *Pyth.* 7. 17–18). The present audience comes into the poem again, but not in respect of a particular situation. The ethos of the narrator is again enhanced; he is here coolly humorous with these patrons, not effusive.

27. The narrator suddenly changes to a genial attitude: the converse of the moral pessimism he had seemed to present, but an essentially coherent development. πάντας . . . ὅcτιc contrasts with the lonely, and non-existent, perfect man (24), who also started a colon with παν-.

ἐπαίνημι καὶ φιλέω: the declaration of one's own likes and dislikes suits the more personal among archaic narrators, though the declarations are meant to carry authority (Archil. fr. 114 West, Anacr. 416 (note ἐγώ and πάντας ὅcοι), fr. eleg. 2 West (note ὅcτιc)). ἐπαίνημι carries more suggestion of the poet's role. The rare, aeolic form (Pind. fr. 155. 3) avoids a jingle in the eager pair of verbs; it may well come from Hes. *WD* 683.

28–30. ἑκών: the word is given emphasis by its position in period and sentence (before ὅcτιc); it is answered by ἀνάγκαι. The argument looks back to 14–18; but now a virtue is recognized that is not simply the product of circumstances (contrast 17). This is not an ethic which is based on intention; it simply excludes acts alleged to be wholly unintended. This would not strike a contemporary listener as surprising (cf. Most (1994), 141); rather, an attractively evident phrasing is substituted for the provocative expression of 17–18. 'Necessity' is carefully not defined. The negative terms in which the clause is couched correspond to 3 and 24; but there is now a more definite emphasis on deplorable action. This point will become more important later.

ἀνάγκαι is connected to 14–16; but there is a livelier sense of personification than in 16.

οὐδὲ θεοί: cf. 581. 6 καὶ βρότεοι, 584. 4 οὐδὲ θεῶν. In 14 the gods had been used to show the impossibility of human perfection; here they are used, more encouragingly, to excuse human imperfection. Cf. Eur. *Hipp.* 458. At Eur. *Alc.* 978–9 Zeus and Ananke act together; at e.g. Pind. *Isth.* 8. 31–5a Zeus evidently could not escape what was (conditionally) fated. Cf. Schreckenberg (1964), 72–81. The concise statement makes an authoritative and imposing end to the stanza.

31–4. The first word that is certainly Simonides' is ἄγαν: even μηδ' might have been adjusted from another negative to suit Plato's syntax. What precedes in Plato is not only unmetrical but an unreliable guide. In particular, οὐ . . . φιλόψογος, like the inserted οὐ γάρ εἰμι φιλόμωμος (346 C 7), is part of Socrates' strained attempt to show that this passage is about Simonides' attack on Pittacus; one cannot assume either is even a paraphrase of Simonides' words. The expression is not at all uncharacteristic of Plato: for φιλο- with εἶναι cf. e.g. *Lys.* 211 E 8, *Menex.* 244 E 3, *Tim.* 24 C 7–8. ἐξαρκεῖ is also characteristic of Plato; it recurs at 346 D 7. It should at least correspond to something in Simonides. The verb itself would be possible in this sense (cf. Pind. *Ol.* 9. 3, Heracl. fr. 23 Marcovich); but one might wonder whether the expression would be stylistically in place.

34–5. ἀπάλαμνος: the sense 'physically feeble' might suit 2 and ὑγιής; but it is not adequately attested. It does not fit the Plato well. 'Idle' (Hes. *WD* 20) is not appropriate. We should rather suppose the sense 'unrestrained, unseemly, αἰσχρός' (Sol. fr. 27. 12 West, Theogn. 281, 481, cf. Pind. *Ol.* 2. 57). The negative with ἄγαν amounts to 'not at all', cf. Aesch. *Supp.* 409, Eur. *Med.* 583, etc. The meaning fits admirably with 29 and the whole passage.

ὀνησίπολιν: Hermann's conjecture is only an interpretation of the paradosis; his τ' is also a great improvement on the implausible γ'. Compounds so formed are found already in Homer (so φθισίμβροτος *Il.* 13. 339, *al.*, τερψίμβροτος *Od.* 12. 269, 274); in lyric cf. Stes. 250 ἀρχεσίμολπον, Ibyc. 303 (*a*). 2 ἐρασιπλόκαμον, and note in iambic

Hippon. 135 ἀνακεικίφαλλος. They are eagerly produced by Bacchylides and Pindar (*Ol.* 14. 14, *Pyth.* 9. 86, *Pae.* 1 (D1). 8, etc.; cf. Eustath. *Proem. Pind.* 16). The word gives resounding force to the conception, in style and meaning. There is nothing particularly democratic in the idea; cf. e.g. Hes. *WD* 219–37, Pind. *Ol.* 13. 6–7. In the present context, δίκη appears principally as a matter of restraint.

36–40. ὑγιής: after the grandiose expression, a simple word, available to prose and comedy. It gives an attractive straightforwardness to the notion. ὑγιὴς ἀνήρ matches in its opening rhythm and its position in the period the unreal πανάμωμον ἄνθρωπον (24).

οὔ νιν ἐγώ: the missing words might have been omitted by Plato, if say an address. An omission before οὔ would be particularly attractive on this hypothesis. The brevity would in any case justify asyndeton. The narrator pushes himself and his opinion to the fore, but with an air of obvious good sense. μωμήςομαι takes up πανάμωμος in 24; although such a man is not 'blameless', in the rhetoric of the context 'blaming' such a worthy man now sounds wrong. The narrator is seeking to sound plausible now rather than startling.

ἀλιθίων: fifth-century usage (including ἠλιθιάζω) strongly suggests that this is not a very elevated word: 'stupid' rather than 'foolish'. The tone of the clause is delightfully dry. The narrator again adopts a less extreme position than he had seemed to, on the surface, in 18–19. There is a worthlessness, too, which is not determined by circumstances, as 34–5 imply. The narrator sounds here somewhat less generous than he had in 27–9: even this version of merit is commended by its relative paucity. The impression is assisted by the singular of 34–6 as against the plural in 27. There is now a sort of moral aristocracy in the narrator's conception, and in his presentation of himself: we hear the tones of the *Theognidea*, but without the personal despondency.

πάντα κτλ.: the statement sounds, and is meant to sound, self-evidently true; but the narrator is taking up 27–9, from the last part of the previous stanza, and taking up especially the implications of the negative formulation. The absence of what is αἰσχρόν is enough to qualify for the desirable category; Socrates catches much of this point (346 D 1–347 A 1). The neuter plural, and the use of καλός rather than ἀγαθός, makes the statement sound more plausible than

if πάντες and ἀγαθοί had been used. The abstraction also gives a
lofty power to the final utterance, which τοι assists. It matches the
end of the preceding stanza (29–30), but in less theological colours.
τοῖσιν: manuscripts have very slight authority on such a ν. The
alteration is scarcely a conjecture.

The poem develops and changes remarkably, both in its argument
and in the narrator's tone. It proceeds broadly from extremity and
severity to a more moderate and positive stance; but the latter ap-
pears to the listener to be grounded in the former. The detail of
the poem both modifies the antithesis and intensifies the surprise
at particular moments; the narrator does not shrink from the bold-
est gestures in expression and argument. The poem pursues an air
of difficulty: its precise position is often made purposefully hard
for the listener to grasp, while the argumentative and authorita-
tive manner assures the listener of its coherence. It provides an
absorbing and demanding intellectual experience.

16: *PMG* 543[12]

As will be seen from the discussion of the metre, the poem must
be incomplete. It is at least missing nearly the equivalent of a stro-
phe, and probably much more. The poem might have been solely
mythological (cf. 539, 562), or have adorned a victory or a death.
Even if Danae's crisis was not resolved explicitly within the poem
(cf. e.g. Bacch. 5. 176–8), the listener will have been aware of the
sequel (cf. 6 n.). The fragment, then, will have played a part in still
more complex structures, poetic and mythological.

In itself the fragment imagines this part of the myth with extraor-
dinary intensity. The physicality of the strange event is strongly
presented through the language: the artificial darkness, the water
that does not touch the humans. The sleeping and tiny baby is
sensuously evoked, in a fashion beyond the scope of the red-figure
vases. But we see all this from various perspectives. We imagine the
scene visually; but we also see these things as objects of Danae's
emotion. That emotion invites us to share it, and to reflect on its im-

[12] On 543 [16] see esp. Wilamowitz (1886), 144–50; Davison (1968a); Page (1951c),
133–40; Führer (1976), no. 4 (111–64); West (1981); Burnett (1985), 11–14; Rosen-
meyer (1991); Carson (1992b), 57–9.

plications; we also observe it more distantly, particularly in the light of our foreknowledge. The introductory narrative, and the device of the speech, promote both these responses. Most of the speech does not, despite its opening, present Danae's emotion by making her talk about it; it is more inventive and subtle. It creates a deeply conceived situation. Danae is in the closest contact with her son; but he is also cut off from her. The very paradox of her speaking to him is brought out and made poignant.

There is an elaborate exploitation of hierarchy and of difference. The child is in some ways hierarchically beneath the woman who loves him; he does not understand, but that lack of understanding is variously regarded. His consciousness is not explored in itself (one might contrast say the third of Rilke's *Duineser Elegien*, or even Perseus' upstretched arm in the Providence Painter's lekythos (Toledo (Ohio) 69. 369, *c*.480–70) and his behaviour in Aesch. fr. 47a Radt). He serves as the object of Danae's interpretations and thoughts, and the foil to her involvement. And yet his calm infects the knowing listener.

Danae herself will arouse complex responses in the Greek male listener; distance through knowledge and through gender from her female terrors will be mixed with the powerful impact of her female love and suffering. The distinctively female quality of her experience and of her emotional force is articulated more strongly than in the woman's monologue of Stesichorus (222 (b) [3]). At the summit of hierarchy is Zeus. The listener's sympathy will be drawn, on one level, into an indignation which Danae does not express. Despite actual knowledge, the listener's imagination is led into the possibility of criticizing the god, from the perspective of ignorance about the future. Poem and story do not end here; but it would be curious to feel no sense of religious challenge, however temporary.

As we shall see, fifth-century Attic red-figure depictions of Danae have much to offer the reader of the fragment. (For them see Maffre (1981, 1986); Beazley in Caskey and Beazley (1931–63), ii. 11–13.) Whether they are influenced by Simonides is unknowable; only a lekythos by the Icarus Painter (Providence, Rhode Island School of Design 25. 084, *ARV*² 697. 18, *c*.460) shows Danae and Perseus in mid-sea. It is hard to think Aeschylus was not aware of Simonides in his *Dictyulci* (on its date see most recently Goins (1997)). In any case, the passionate speech of Danae there, and the contrasted cheerfulness of the child, show a dramatized and extended form of what the lyric here concentrates in its speech. We may surely see in this fragment seeds of Euripidean monologue, monody, and female pathos (the archaic backgounds to Euripides' work are commonly underplayed). Here too lies the starting-point for Pindar's intensity of mythical imagination.

Metre

1.	⏑⏑–⏑–
2.	––⏑⏑–
3.	⏑⏑–⏑† †⏑–
4.	–––⏑⏑–––⏑–
5.	⏑–⏑–⏑⏑––⏑⏑–
6.	––⏑⏑–⏑⏑–⏑⏑–⏑–
7.	–––⏑⏑–⏑⏑–⏑–
8–9.	⏑⏑––⏑⏑–––⏑–
9–10.	––⏑⏑–⏑⏑–⏑⏑–⏑⏑––
11–12.	† †–⏑⏑–⏑–† †
13.	––⏑–⏑⏑–⏑–
14–15.	⏑––⏑⏑–––⏑⏑–⏑⏑–
15–16.	–⏑⏑––––⏑⏑–
17.	–⏑⏑–⏑⏑–⏑––⏑–⟨　⟩
18.	–⏑–––⏑⏑–⏑–
19.	–⏑⏑––⏑–
20.	–⏑⏑–⏑––
21–2.	⏑⏑–––⏑⏑–⏑–⏑–
22.	⏑–⏑–⏑⏑–⏑–
23.	⏑⏑–⏑–⏑–⏑–
24.	––⏑⏑–⏑–
25.	–⏑⏑–⏑⏑–⏑⏑–⏑–
26–7.	––⏑⏑–––⏑–

The metre presents enormous problems. Dionysius' comments must be seen in the light of the whole of his chs. 19 and 26. From them various points follow: metrical units will often not match units of sense, the metrical units will be varied and of varied length. It is intrinsically unlikely even that all colon division will follow word-end, as in most suggested schemes; and hiatus shows that there are is one very short period (2). It may also perhaps be supposed that the division between stanzas will not correspond to obvious breaks in sense; this would make against division of stanzas after 7 and after 20 (so West (1981)). Speeches can certainly begin anywhere in a stanza, as Bacchylides and Pindar indicate. The papyri of Bacchylides suggest that Dionysius' copy had a reasonable view of the colometry.

It is evident that the metre is basically aeolic: see above on 542 [**15**] (*metre*). The fluidity of the type means there are different points at which boundaries can be fixed. The tradition of Dionysius, here especially impoverished, cannot be relied upon for the text; that is evident from the two lines quoted by Athenaeus. The text given suggests one way of making metrical sense out of what is transmitted; it is fairly similar to Page's and West's, but makes some use of the points mentioned above. For those reasons a colon is hesitantly ended after παρει- (5), rather than παρειαῖc. In 542 [**15**]. 23, 26, 27 the choriambic base ends, and this would here be extended to a doubled choriambic base; in 542 [**15**] there is a similar run of blunt endings. For those reasons too κέλομαι . . . πόν- (21–2) is made a colon (◡◡–––◡◡–◡–◡–), not . . . βρέφοc | (or πόντοc |); and ἢ νόcφι . . . μοι is made into one colon.

In 14–16 the division βαθεῖαν . . . ἀλέγειc | οὐδ᾿ . . . πορφυρέαι | is made on metrical grounds. A choriamb (οὐδ᾿ ἀνέμου) is quite often 'prefixed' to an aeolic colon (555. 2, Bacch. 16 str. 12, ep. 12, Pind. *Pae.* 2 (D2) ep. 2, *Nem.* 2. 5, etc.). A clear suffixed choriamb, as in | κύματοc . . . ἀνέμου |, would be rarer (Pind. *Nem.* 6 str. 3 is the clearest example); it might be a Pindaric innovation. To have an isolated hemiepes | κύματοc οὐκ ἀλέγειc | would seem less welcome than the colon ––◡◡–◡◡– in combination, cf. 520. 5 (and 555. 2). With φθόγγον πορφυρέαι cf. 2 (and e.g. Pind. *Isthm.* 8. 6).

Dionysius implies that the poem was triadic; he does not necessarily imply that more than two stanzas are included (antistrophe and epode, thought Schneidewin ((1835), 69). It is not apparent that any responsion exists in the passage. Page cautiously suggested that ὅτε . . . †μηνⳠ responded to ἔποc . . . μοι ((1951c), 135). This might be so, but would mean that Dionysius had included, at the very end and without necessity, lines where cola and sense go exactly together. A licence of responsion (ἄνεμοc = cυγγνω-) is discouraging when the areas that respond are so very slight. The length of the last syllable is quite uncertain; the first line-ending is very common in aeolic; the supposed complete agreeing colon is the shortest possible, a string of syllables found 10 other times in the extract. Even the period-end after εὔχομαι need not be real. The coincidence is not so overwhelming as to make us ignore the difficulties.

The extract ends the treatise with a flourish; but Dionysius' chief aim is not to set a puzzle. Although he has no doubt selected judiciously, his point is presumably that the rhythmic identity of cola and of stanzas becomes invisible when set out by sense. The size of stanza is considerable, even on Page's hypothesis, but would not surprise in Bacchylides or Pindar (Bacch. 4, 5, 11, 19 etc.; note Simon. 519 fr. 4 and 541). Wherever the stanzas began and ended, we see stanza-building of a novel complexity. The complexity and variety seem greater than in 542 [**15**].

1–7. The narrator establishes the imperfective situation on which the whole passage is built: the situation is unresolved and looks towards resolution. The depiction of Danae sets up specific points that will be taken up and given fresh meaning in the speech. The wind and waves do not appear primarily so as to present the physical scene to the listener; they appear as sources of Danae's emotion. The motion of the sea, and the wind, recur in 13–17 as things that do not stir Perseus; Danae's own fear is the essential counterpoint, and this too will be directly taken up from the narrative (δείματι 4, τοι δεινόν 18). The narrative also directs a response to Danae as a woman: her prostration by fear, her weeping, and her embrace of her child would all affect the listener differently if the figure were a man.

The grammatical structure is unclear. If 1 begins a new sentence, with οὐκ in 5, then the asyndeton, in such a context, is displeasing; ὅτε, and ἐπεί 'when', never begin an asyndetic sentence in Pindar or Bacchylides. If 1–7 are all governed by ὅτε, with οὐδ' in 5, then we have a very elaborate clause leading in to the verb of speaking with τε (contr. Bacch. 5. 76–80, 84–6, 17. 16–20, 50–2, 71–4, Pind. *Isth.* 6. 50–2). West's examples with a series of events ((1981), 37 n. 11) are not really parallel. More plausibly, something preceded the ὅτε, whether the subject of βάλλε (so οὐκ) or a main clause to a sentence ending with ἔρειπεν (so οὐδ'). The former makes an undesirably involved sentence with so unexplanatory a 'when' clause (contr. e.g. Pind. *Ol.* 1. 36–42), and perhaps implies an odd omission by Dionysius (even if the name itself was the subject, one would need to explain the superfluous explanation).

2. δαιδαλέαι: epithet of a chest in Bacch. 5. 140; cf. Epicharm. fr. 85. 6 Austin. The chest is decorated, and has elegant legs, on several vases; the decoration is notably elaborate on the Providence Painter's lekythos (Toledo (Ohio) 69. 369, c.480–470). The epithet has a conventional appearance; it will be set against Danae's intensely subjective description (10). However, the short line highlights the adjective; it conveys a contrast between the civilized luxury associated with this royal object and the wild forces of nature amid which it is surprisingly found. The effect at Bacch. 5. 140 is different, but connected.

3–4. μήν is unsuitable (and the dialect in any case requires some change). μιν is an easy phonetic alteration; the Doric νιν should probably be preferred, but μιν appears often enough in papyri and manuscripts of these poets (519 fr. 53. 10 (both forms), fr. 62 (*b*). 3, fr. 92. 8, Bacch. 11. 111, etc.). However, λάρνακι | ἐν δαιδαλέαι then becomes awkwardly isolated: with the 'her' inserted within 3–5, and an emphatic phrase put at the start, the activity of the elements is located within the chest. Page takes 'blowing on the chest' together ((1951*c*), 140), but this puts τε in an unpromising and muddling position. The participles could be taken as 'the blowing of the wind' etc., but the change in tense of the participles makes this subterfuge unattractive. 'Her, being in a chest' is much less easy if the μιν is placed so. A word for 'her' is not necessarily required at all. In short, one should hesitate to introduce this order by conjecture. This means that the argument for responsion is weakened. It might even be that the νιν should be moved to follow ὅτε (cf. Pind. *Ol.* 1. 26): in the text of Dionysius the verse colometry was not observed, so such an error would be easier.

πνέων, κινηθεῖcα: straightforward language, when compared with 13–16. κινηθεῖcα indicates that the sea has been drastically stirred up by the wind, cf. Hom. *Il.* 2. 144–7, 4. 423 (note the tense), Sol. fr. 12. 1–2 West. Nouns and participles seem to be arranged in a neat and brisk chiasmus.

δείματι has much better authority than δεῖμα. As is soon apparent, Danae's fear is not only for herself. On the Deepdene Painter's stamnos (NY Metr. 17. 230. 37, *ARV*² 498. 1, *c.* 470–60), where she is holding her hand to her mouth in a gesture of fear, her other hand is on Perseus' head.

5. ἔρειπεν: a drastic metaphor of destruction, cf. Bacch. 11. 68; for the use and the tense cf. the present at Eur. *Supp.* 613. The word is heightened by the pause and enjambment (shown by the hiatus).

οὐδ' ἀδιάντοιcι: there is a certain grim detachment in the expression, which suits the narrator's role; it is compatible with sympathy. Cf. the different forces of the litotes at Hom. *Od.* 4. 493–4 (Proteus to Menelaus), Eur. *Ion* 1458 (Creusa on her past). ἀδίαντος occurs in Bacchylides (17. 122) and Pindar (*Nem.* 7. 73); it is not extant elsewhere, as an adjective.

6. ἀμφὶ κτλ.: the loving gesture will add force to the combination of closeness and separation in the speech. The pathos of a mother's embrace is more elaborately exploited at Eur. *Tro.* 757–62.

Περcεῖ: the name contrasts with the mother's own τέκος in the next line (cf. βρέφος 21). It also reminds the listener of the adult hero (a familiar, and no doubt the most familiar, connotation of the name); it thus suggests an ironic perspective on the present fears. Simonides could merely have written 'the child'.

7. ὦ τέκος: the emphasis is on the baby from the start; but the address will shortly become paradoxical.

οἷον ἔχω πόνον: a poignantly simple utterance. But it becomes the foil to the much longer description of the child. For the contrast in length, note Bacch. 16. 30 after 23–9.

8. cὺ δ' ἀωτεῖc: the firm rhetorical structure accentuates that the child is separated from real communication. This is not a universal point about the difficulties of communicating, but the development of an untypical situation. (Cf. Rosenmeyer (1991), 27.) ἀωτέω, γαλαθηνός (*Od.* 4. 336), κνώccω all come in Homer; the words for 'sleep', and probably γαλαθηνός applied to a human (cf. 553. 2), remove the diction from the everyday, and intensify the presentation of the baby. See for γαλαθηνός Athen. 396 c–f; Poltera (1997), 451.

The picture of a baby oblivious of its woes occurs movingly at Soph. *Aj.* 552–9; cf. also the baby oblivious of danger at Stat. *Theb.* 4. 793–800. But here Perseus is more completely cut off from the situation and from his mother's words by a young baby's deep sleep. The mother's dejection is contrasted with the child's unperturbed gaze on a fragment of a bell-krater by the Phiale Painter (Oxford 1917. 62, *ARV*² 1018. 75, c.450–440); but Perseus is not asleep on any vase, even the Icarus Painter's lekythos (see the introduction to the poem).

9. ἦτορι is preferable. ἤθει is unlikely to mean 'habit, way' in the singular by this period; it rather denotes character, spirit. On the other hand, a word for 'heart' or the like could be used in the dative to support the adjective, with very little specific sense (cf. e.g. Aesch. *Supp.* 606, 775, *Ch.* 303); it may also convey sensually the child's satisfaction with his feed (cf. ἦτορ at Hom. *Il.* 9. 705–6, Hes. *WD* 593; note too Bacch. fr. 4. 77–8). For the word-end after ἦτορι postulated in the scansion cf. the end of 4.

κνώccειc: the 'distraction' in P's κνόω- is a great oddity. Simonides is said to have made the common monosyllable πῦρ disyllabic (587, cf. Hes. *Theog.* 145 ἔειc?); this seems another matter. It is sanguine to believe P when a superior source shows the usual form. The corruption would merely be a duplication of the ω.

10–12. Danae portrays the chest as it seems to her from inside it;

the narrator (2) had portrayed it from without. As in 550, a significant object is elaborately portrayed; but the poet is now intensely evoking the character's experience of that object. The chest is of course closed by a lid, as 13 suggests, and the recovery by the fishermen demands. It has a lid on several vases, even if on the Icarus Painter's lekythos (above) representation demands an open chest.

The text cannot possibly be recovered; but some points may help our understanding. P is usually taken to have read δνόφωι; but its abbreviation must surely mean -ων (cf. e.g. Tsereteli (1896), pls. 24, 30). However, the dative, as in M, must be presumed right, unless another dative noun was omitted to govern the genitive (plural Aesch. *Cho.* 52). The matter is not crucial for the sense. The heart of the problem is νυκτὶ λαμπεῖ. The reason for the κυανέωι δνόφωι will surely be enclosure in the chest; it would be distracting and confusing for Simonides to mention that the scene occurred at night, and for Danae to regard the night as an unusual source of terror. The νυκτί then will bear some relation to the darkness encountered within the chest. Why should something or somebody be shining amid this darkness? Hardly Perseus (λάμπεις). The text would have had to offer some explanation of the babe's luminosity; and the idea interrupts the sequence of thought, which concerns Perseus' indifference. In any case, such bold fantasies are not to be suspended from what we know of Simonides and from an unreliable manuscript tradition. And hardly the chest. νυκτιλαμπεῖ, 'agleam in the night', on account of the bronze bolts (Page (1951c), 137–8), seems to presuppose an actual night, to attach too much importance to bolts, and to view the chest from an external perspective. A mixture of light entering from outside with metaphorical night within seems hard to understand from a single adjective, and unhelpful to the rhetoric. (The difficulty is not removed by the carpenter on the Gallatin Painter's hydria (Boston 13. 200, *ARV²* 247. 1, *c.*490), who seems to be making Danae a hole.) It must be borne in mind that νύξ is not ordinarily used in Greek poetry as a metaphor for darkness, save for that of death or unconsciousness.

Ilgen's ἀλαμπεῖ seems much more promising (cf. Bacch. 13. 175); but problems still arise. We need Bergk's τ' ἀλ.; but the τε . . . τε is unsatisfactory, whether it means 'both . . . and' or provides a sequence δούρατι . . . νυκτί τ' ἀλ. κ. τε δνόφωι. Nor is the νυκτὶ κ. τε δνόφωι satisfying in itself. τε with explanatory apposition does not seem to be a feature of Pindar or Bacchylides' style as it is of Aeschylus'.

At this point we may note χαλκεογόμφωι, which should go with δούρατι, not with any word for darkness. In the kindred poets Ibycus and Bacchylides, the presence of two epithets would not surprise, and what we have suggests Simonides' similarity here too (511 (*a*). 5–6, 555. 2, 3, 586. 3 (the third adjective is of a different kind)). In consequence, something must also be done with δέ.

A line of thought which might deal with several problems, including the use of νύξ, would be to read something like ὥτε νυκτὸс ἀλαμπέϊ κυανέωι δνόφωι (ἀλαμπέοс would also be possible). The corruption of ωιωτε to ωδε is easily explained, as is the attraction of νυκτόс to the wrong case and the consequent insertion of τε. One need not be too rigid in separating metaphor from reality (cf. e.g. Pind. *Isth*. '3/4'. 36–36b); but one could take ὥτε especially with νυκτόс, cf. Bacch. 17. 103–5 . . . сέλαс | ὥτε πυρόс (not ἀπὸ πυρόс).

This conjecture would require 11–12 not to form a fresh main clause. It is conceivable that ταδ' εἰс hides a second-person verb; but yet another word for sleep might not be welcome, especially after the bare opening cὺ δ' ἀωτεῖс. The rhetoric seems to encourage a subordinate clause, such as is generally posited. ταθείс, as West suggests ((1981), 31), might seem to require a good length (cf. τανύομαι). His tentative ἀλείс suits a baby's posture, but appears somewhat isolated and ineffective. Bergk's сταλείс, which West prefers, requires the unattractive view of νυκτί. The truth is scarcely to be ascertained; the line of conjecture above might suggest, but does not demand, something like καλ⟨υφθ⟩είс (note αὐλέαν following).

ἀτερπέϊ: used of dismaying places in Hom. *Od*. 7. 279, 11. 94, cf. [Aesch.] *PV* 31. The word partly serves to mark that this is a perverted kind of δούρατι. At Aesch. 47a. 828 Radt κατὰ ναῦν is used, but in paradoxical combination with ὕφαλοс (cf. Arat. 425). One may contrast the straightforward appellation λάρνακι in 1.

χαλκεογόμφωι: γόμφοι are seen as a prime feature of ships (note Aesch. *Supp*. 440). The epithet is not solely ornamental; it belongs with the play here on ships. χαλκεο-, rather than πολυ- (Hes. *WD* 660, Ibyc. S151 [**11**]. 18), stresses in the context that nails do not merely join the wood, but firmly confine the pair.

κυανέωι reinforces and advances on ἀλαμπέϊ (if that word is correct). It suggests not merely an absence of shining light, but a rich or deep darkness. It may be relevant that the stem is used of water

(567. 4, Bacch. 13. 124, Eur. _IT_ 7); for its employment with an emphasis on blackness cf. Simon. fr. 21. 7 West, Theogn. 709, Pind. fr. 33 c. 6.

13–17. Waves and sea are taken up in reverse order from the narrative (3–4).

ἅλμαν is preferable to ἄχναν (Page). In a tumultuous sea (4) not only spray would be going over the chest; and the matter would be too trivial for the context. With Page's own text, the word is not suitable to βαθεῖαν 'deep' (is West (1981), 31, thinking of βαρεῖαν?). The grammar of the prepositional phrase attached to the noun is somewhat awkward: the noun is not verbal, the phrase does not state an origin. The genitive absolute appears a somewhat weak addition to the sentence in style. One might then feel some inclination to take the prepositional phrase and the genitive absolute together: in this context the combination of 'above' and 'going by' would seem to make sense (as it needs to on most other views). Cf. Pind. _Pyth._ 8. 77 for ὕπερθε with a verb of motion. This view would invite us to make βαθεῖαν genitive (cf. βαθυπλόκαμος). Vases suggest that the word would not be unsuitable to the baby; the beauty of the child would be germane (cf. 17), and it is notable that the mother speaks of the hair rather than of the head, as one might expect. βαθεῖαν would be apt enough to the sea (cf. Pind. _Nem._ 4. 36); whether it is so apt with ὕπερθε might be questioned (Hom. _Od._ 12. 214 is different). The chest is not permanently submerged (contr. Aesch. fr. 47a. 28 Radt): the water is produced by the passing wave.

The order sets the negatives οὐκ and οὐδ' effectively close. The phrase οὐκ ἀλεγ- as a rule implies, not ignorance of the object or incapacity to feel, but a chosen indifference. Danae's language here treats Perseus almost as if he were conscious and aware; babyhood, sleep, and the situation produce paradox.

φθόγγον: φθόγγος (-ή) and its compounds are often used of birds, animals, and musical instruments (at Pind. _Isth._ 6. 34 the bowstring is treated as if it were an instrument, cf. Hom. _Od._ 21. 411). They are not generally used of meaningless noises. The word presents the wind as a hostile being; cf. Hom. _Il._ 14. 398–9. πνέων 3, by contrast, scarcely personifies (cf. 595. 1–2). The brevity on the wind is no less forceful here than the fullness on the waves. The word also connects with 19–20: the wind's and the mother's voices alike are unheard by the child.

πορφύρέαι κτλ.: the sentence ends with a picture of the child. We see this partly through the mother's affectionate eyes; but the scene, and its strangeness, are also physically depicted for the listener. The still stranger and more vivid scene in Pind. *Ol.* 6 [**18**]. 53–6 furnishes an interesting comparison.

πορφύρέαι: a conventional-sounding epithet (cf. e.g. Hom. *Il.* 24. 644–5, *Od.* 4. 115), but with a point. The princely child is in an appalling situation, and the luxury is ironically incongruous. The epithet has a related significance at Pind. *Pyth.* 4. 114.

χλανίδι: the child is wrapped in a cloth, as κείμενος ἐν strongly suggests; whether one thinks of it as a cloak or a blanket in this case scarcely matters. He is often wrapped in such a cloth on vases, e.g. the Eucharides Painter's cup, Ferrara T. 503 (*ARV*² 231. 79, *c*.490).

πρόcωπον καλόν: the reading of M is unlikely to possess authority. It would be a natural scribal reaction to the repetition to eliminate one πρόcωπον (whether or not consciously), and to follow familiar word-order. Note the more surprising happening at Eur. *Andr.* 1187. Where πρόcωπον stood originally, one can hardly determine; the order adjective second, though the less frequent, is entirely acceptable, and implies the easier corruption.

The phrase 'dear face' is not a paralleled or plausible address. Page's contention ((1951c), 136) that it is 'a *vocative in apposition*... to the whole of the preceding picture' founders on πρόcωπον, which cannot mean 'a sight'. One πρόcωπον must have displaced a participle (cf. e.g. A at Eur. *Med.* 994). Ahrens's προφαίνων is palaeographically attractive; but there are many possibilities, including its opposite.

καλόν is a common epithet for 'face' (Hom. *Il.* 19. 285 etc.); but it gains a different force on the mother's lips. Cf. Eur. *Supp.* 1137.

18–20. A short and pointed sentence now follows the rich elaboration of 8–17. The paradox of calm, and the fiction of address, are now brought out more sharply by counterfactual imaginings and pointed language. In 19 it is to sound almost as if *x*=*x* were an impossible condition; but τοι is of course dative, and τὸ δεινόν is perhaps on a primary level specific (cf. e.g. Soph. *El.* 376, Ar. *Frogs* 593, Thuc. 3. 45. 1). The play on words is promoted by their ordering and by γε. Such play is very characteristic of the later fifth century, not least with this word (cf. Gorg. B 6 Diels–Kranz,

Ar. *Wasps* 26–7, Eur. *Or.* 413); especially close is Lys. 6. 50. For the form cf. Eur. *Tro.* 466 (cf. Bacch. 3 [**17**]. 47 n.). Cf. in general Fehling (1969).

καί: if Perseus understood, he would not only be listening with alarm to the sea and storm, he would be listening to his mother too. If he were not wrapped in fearless slumber, he would hear her; but the words suggest the remoter notion of his understanding language. λεπτόν brings out its impossibility. The whole sentence displays the unreality of Danae's talking to him. But this unreality includes a pathetic reality: mothers do talk to babies, as the coming evocation of lullabies underlines, and the felt lack of actual communication makes this talking sad. The λεπτόν also touchingly evokes the actual, especially in Danae's mouth. The word is far more suggestive for a baby's ear than μικρόν would have been; the whole phrase stands in for a more obvious (ὑπ)άκουες. Pathos and intellectualism here combine, as in Euripides.

21. Danae now resumes the ordinary communication of a mother. She uses her words to bid him sleep (as he is already doing), despite the danger to which her previous words (ἐμῶν ῥημάτων) would have alerted him if heeded. The simple language of 21 suggests a very humble species of song, the lullaby (cf. Theocr. 24. 7–9; Athen. 618 E, Auson. 27. 9*b*. 91 Green; on Σ *Pers.* 3. 16 see Kißel (1990), 391 n. 35; see also Wærn (1960)).

κέλομαι belongs only to the second-person imperative; a colon should follow βρέφος. Hence the absence of μέν with εὗδε: cf. Fehling (1969), 207–8; note also Eur. *Hcld.* 755–6, *Supp.* 834–5. κέλομαι, like κελεύω, is often much gentler than 'order' (cf. Hom. *Il.* 23. 894, *Od.* 17. 400; *IG* i³. 78. 32–3). The particle δ' is required by sense and style.

εὗδε: a more basic word than those in 8–9—and with more scope for exploitation in imagery.

22. With sublime rhetoric, the simple language generates through metaphor a huge movement in range. One might perhaps think that in her language, instead of finding her baby's action anomalous, Danae now wants to shape everything else to fit that action. (Not that she is to be seen literally as deceiving herself, cf. Rosenmeyer (1991), 24–5.) At all events, her language extends beyond the child in two passionate expansions, first to the sea, then to her whole trouble, explicitly portrayed as immeasurable. One may call to mind

318 Simonides

the complex relations and contrasts of sea and human experience in Shakespeare's *Pericles*.

εὐδέτω: the metaphor is common enough both for sea (e.g. Hom. *Od.* 12. 169) and for troubles (see Collard (1975), ii. 403). But the second involves the bolder extension.

ἄμετρον κακόν: Homer's ἀμέτρητος πόνος (*Od.* 23. 249). The language returns to, and advances on, the οἷον . . . πόνον with which Danae began (7). One may compare the vehement speech at Bacch. fr. 2. There are not sufficient grounds to impugn the form ἄμετρος (Poltera (1997), 370); but one may note that Dionysius' treatise gave some incentive to introduce it by mistake (it comes even at the start of ch. 26).

23–4. Danae continues her thought about the situation, but moves from wild imperative to earnest prayer; a different addressee is introduced, and a third and crucial person in the story. The tentative, yet pleading, language intensifies the pathos. The abstract noun, τις, ἐκ σέο are less direct than an imperative μεταβούλευσον (the abstract in the address to Zeus at Pind. *Nem.* 10. 76–7 has a very different effect).

μεταβουλία: in effect P's reading. The noun is not found elsewhere (likewise Sophocles' μετάγνοια, *El.* 581). The word mixes the external result and the inward change; nouns in -βουλία can be used of the conduct or plan itself (ϲυμβ.; δυϲβ. Aesch. *Ag.* 1609). ἐκ can be used even when there is some internal emphasis (Soph. *Ant.* 95; note the mixture at *El.* 619). The noun does not connote regret in the same way as the later μετάγνοια, μεταμέλεια, μετάνοια. It is notable that Danae sees what is happening as planned by Zeus, despite his 'love'; the storm may be seen as encouraging this view (cf. e.g. Hes. *WD* 665–8). (The listener will naturally suppose that Danae knows the gold was Zeus, as at Aesch. fr. 47a. 783–4 Radt. Involved explanations to the contrary seem unlikely; story and speech make Hor. *Odes* 3. 27 a different case.)

φανείη: a decisive moment is hoped for, and will appear.

πάτερ: it is the listener rather than Danae who sees the pointedness of this title; such sharpness would not suit the surface of her prayer, and irony would not suit its ethos. A further, and more pathetic, point for the listener is that Danae's plight has been inflicted on her by her own father, and she can only call on the god (himself her oppressor). But Danae herself has not railed against, or men-

tioned, Acrisius. At Aesch. fr. 47a. 781 πατήρ (of Acrisius) carries
considerable force, at least for the spectator. Danae's encounters
with Acrisius, intense on the earlier vases, and Acrisius' shockingly
unpaternal action, are central in artistic treatments (Danae seems
especially spirited on the Gallatin Painter's hydria (10–12 n.)); cf.
also Sophocles' *Acrisius*, esp. fr. 64 Radt.

25–7. The text and meaning first. ὅτι δή seems unsatisfactory. The
transmitted ἤ does not fit with ὅτι; postpositive δή is rarely a con-
nective in lyric, elegiac, or iambus save with a pronoun (Archil. frr.
23. 10 West, 196a. 8, 22, Alc. 72. 12, etc.; Pind. *Nem.* 10. 75 is
an exception). Mehlhorn's ὅττι δέ introduces by conjecture a form
not found in lyric poets save Sappho, Alcaeus, and Corinna (even
the pronoun ὅτι occurs a good deal in Pindar and Bacchylides; *Lyr.
Adesp. PMG* 1020. 1 is extremely doubtful). ὅτι (pronoun) δέ would
introduce what in a conjecture would be unwelcome metre. One
might consider εἰ δέ τι (the sense suggested this before I noticed
Schaefer's conjecture). The reading gives a common construction
with cυγγιγνώcκω etc., and one which need not sound so blunt an
admission of audacity: cf. e.g. Ar. *Wasps* 958–9, Xen. *Mem.* 2. 2. 14.
ἤ helps this nuance.

On any view, what is audacious or unjust about what Danae has
said? θαρcαλέοc used negatively is a strong word, denoting shameless
transgression of hierarchy (Hom. *Od.* 17. 449, 19. 91). Although on
her understanding of Zeus' plan the listener would not see him in a
favourable light, this is not brought out explicitly, and the acknow-
ledged fault of her words can hardly lie in negative implications.
And however much we allow for humility, her request for a change
can scarcely be thought unjust. It is more likely that the description
relates to what she is about to say. Such a point would not concern
Dionysius unduly in making his excerpt: his interest was in the
metre. The likeliest view of the opening implies the same attitude
in Dionysius; and note how he breaks off in Eur. fr. 102. 7 Austin
at 26. 13 (cf. 12). Danae is about to make a prayer (or vaunt) of
some spirit, we may surmise: for example, that Zeus will not betray
their son.

Danae addresses Zeus with bitter blame at Aesch. fr. 47a. 783–4
Radt; Nonnus brings out, in his own fashion, the hard treatment
received by Danae (*Dion.* 25. 119–22). Creusa's monody attacks
Apollo with extreme anger (Eur. *Ion* 859–922); Helen is scarcely

less vehement to Aphrodite (Hom. *Il.* 3. 399–412), and Menelaus
has vigorously exclaimed at Zeus (365–8). Bacchylides' Croesus
strongly reproaches the gods (3 [**17**]. 37–9). One can hardly see
Danae's restraint here as inevitable. Whatever she is going to say,
the striking caution, the fear of injustice by *her*, the apologetic
cύγγνωθί μοι must suggest to male listeners a touching and remark-
able subservience to hierarchy in the woman. Such words from
a man would not have this pathos. None the less, the view sug-
gested here would mean that she was not so angelically meek as
would otherwise be thought, and that the irony of the god's appar-
ent behaviour was about to be sharpened by a forceful utterance.
The disturbing implications may have been totally cancelled by the
treatment of the happy ending to come; but one would need the rest
of the poem to be sure.

νόϲφι: used at Ibyc. S221. 2, (preposition) Bacch. 1. 170.

cύγγνωθί μοι: the language in this context implies substantial
impiety, real or apparent, cf. e.g. Ar. *Clouds* 1478–80, Eur. *Hipp.*
117, *IT* 1400 (*Ion* 1440 is deliberately peculiar), and note Soph.
Ant. 65–6, *El.* 400. Cf. Pulleyn (1997), 66–9. The imperative here
has a very different relation to hierarchy from that in 21.

The speech shows a remarkable range of language and feeling. The
length, character, and mood of sentences differ forcefully, and this
mobility and range greatly contribute to the impact of the speech.
We do not find quite the large sweep and abrupt transitions of say
Catullus' Ariadne; restraint is actually an important part of the
pathos. Yet in the later part of the speech, the sense of firm and
orderly organization felt in 7–20 gives way to more volatile and
impassioned writing as the speech rises in elevation and meaning.
This in turn contributes to a sense of shape and power in the
whole passage. So much has been put into this little space. Change,
surprise, development emerge as essential features of these two
quite different fragments.

BACCHYLIDES

Introduction

BACCHYLIDES came from the same city on Ceos as Simonides; it is said by some sources that he was Simonides' nephew, but it is not clear on what reliable evidence this could rest, let alone that it actually rests on any. Dates for Bacchylides' poems suggest that he was at least as old as Pindar. Fr. 20 B is for the future Alexander I, who seems to be young (6); he may have been around 30 when he began his rule *c.*495, and the poem should certainly precede that date, perhaps by a good deal. Pind. frr. 120–1 could belong to the same period, but θραcύμηδεc 120. 2 might suggest a later date. Pindar's earliest datable epinician is 498 (*Pyth.* 10); we also hear of an entry in the Athenian dithyramb competition of 497/6 (fr. 74 a). Our information for Pindar is so much fuller that we can have some confidence Pindar's extant poetry starts around this time, no confidence that Bacchylides' does so. Bacchylides' latest datable poem happens to be 452 (6), Pindar's is 446.[1]

Bacchylides' areas of activities may be compared with those of Simonides and Pindar; the topic is revealing both for Bacchylides and for the geography of Greek poetry. It must be remembered that much less is preserved of Bacchylides than of Pindar, and that he wrote far fewer epinicians (1–14 B are extant). Bacchylides' native Ceos is an important source of patronage (1, 2, 6, 7, 8, 17), as Thebes is for Pindar. As in Simonides and Pindar, Sicily is prominent (3 [**17**], 4, 5, 20 C), and Magna Graecia appears too (Metapontion, 11). There are poems for Thessalians (14, 14 B); this region,

[1] It is usually supposed that Bacchylides' mother was Simonides' sister, which requires a less usual sense for ἀδελφιδοῦc (Strab. 10. 5. 6, Steph. Byz. s.v. ᾽Ιουλίc; Syrian. in Hermog. *Id.* 1, i p. 47 Rabe; Molyneux (1992), 97–9, with lit.). But the very text which names Bacchylides' grandfather, and so implies his father was not Simonides' brother, reduces the claim about the relationship (cυγγενήc: *Suda* β 59). This suggests that the *Suda*'s source saw a discrepancy. Its information about Bacchylides' father and grandfather seems at least as attractive (cf. Maehler (1982–97), i/1. 6 n. 2) as the claim that the two poets were uncle and nephew. Dates for Alexander I: see Hammond, Griffith, and Walbank (1972–88), ii. 59–60, 103–4. Schmidt (1999) shows convincingly, in an important article, that *IG* xii/5. 608 cannot be used to date poems 1 and 2 to the 450s. However, in view of fr. 20 B, one may regard with some scepticism Eusebius' mention of Bacchylides as alive in 431. This scepticism is reinforced, not by the hypothesis of corruption in our sources for Eusebius, but by doubts on the reliability of the chronographic tradition.

important for Simonides, appears rarely in Pindar (the early*Pyth.*
10; *Thren.* fr. 128 e = fr. 2 Cannatà Fera; fr. 255 is questionable;
for Macedonia see above). An Athenian receives an epinician from
Bacchylides (10); and Athens is important for its dithyramb com-
petition (18 (probably), 19, 23?). Pindar also entered at least twice,
once in 497/6 (frr. 74 a–76); but there are only three epinicians
by him for Athenians (*Pyth.* 7, *Nem.* 2, fr. 6 c), at least one early
(note also *Thren.* fr. 137 (62 Cannatà Fera)). An absence of Spar-
tan epinicians by Bacchylides, as by Pindar, is hardly a surprise;
Bacchylides wrote a dithyramb for Sparta (20), and Pindar wrote a
poem for a dance there (fr. 112). Cities in the north-east Pelopon-
nese employ Bacchylides, Phlius (9) and Asine (fr. 4). In Pindar,
apart from Argos (*Nem.* 10, *Pae.* 18 (S7), *Dith.* 1 (fr. 70 a)?), Sparta
(above), and Stymphalus (*Ol.* 6 [**18**]?), only the wealthy Corinth
appears from the Peloponnese, and that only for one person (*Ol.*
13, fr. 122). Corinthians had probably employed Simonides (see the
introduction to the commentary on him). Wherever *Ol.* 6 [**18**] was
performed, the idea of using Pindar might well be connected with
the victor's Syracusan citizenship. Aegina, which patronized Pin-
dar on such a large scale, is represented in Bacchylides too (12, 13).[2]

As regards the areas of patronage, the most striking point is the
absence of east Greece from Bacchylides, apart from the excep-
tional, and not very eastern, Ceos. (Aegina is of course west of
Athens.) Even in the slighter remains of Simonides, Andros and
two Euboean cities appear. In Pindar, besides Ceos (*Pae.* 4 (D4))
and Rhodes (*Ol.* 7, fr. 2), we find only Tenedos (*Nem.* 11, fr. 123),
Abdera (*Pae.* 2 (D2)), perhaps Naxos (*Pae.* 12 (G1)). Athens or
Athenians are not now particularly interested in making commis-
sions; their attitude to foreign poets may be altering. As regards
Bacchylides, the differences from Simonides and Pindar are not
very remarkable. He may perhaps seem to have cultivated an area
of the Peloponnese quite accessible to Ceos, in a way that Pindar
did not. The statement that he was exiled in the Peloponnese (Plut.
Exil. 605 c) may or may not be true. Conversely, it is natural that we
should not see Boeotian cities in Bacchylides (in Pindar, there are,
Thebes apart, sporadic commissions). Much further afield, Cyrene
is not found in Bacchylides (Pind. *Pyth.* 4, 5, 9). Broadly speaking,
however, we see with him a range akin to that of Simonides and

---

[2] For Asine see Barrett (1954). Pind. fr. 6 a presents us, rather interestingly, with
a poem for a Megarian.

Pindar; he too is an international poet. Most notably, the supreme patron of poets Hieron of Syracuse makes much use of Bacchylides as well as Pindar. One should not infer from Bacch. 3 [**17**] that he was preferred to Pindar, who was not asked for a poem that year, especially if Pindar was asked to write for another Syracusan then (*Ol.* 6 [**18**]). But Bacchylides was evidently perceived by Hieron to have the same general kind of standing as Pindar, and as Simonides, from the first (476 BC: Pind. *Ol.* 1, Bacch. 5).[3]

The tradition of epinician goes back to Ibycus and Simonides. It would thus be rash to explain resemblances between Bacchylides' and Pindar's epinicians as the former's imitation of the latter. The exiguous remains of earlier epinician, and still more the language and metre of Simonides, point to the general importance of the tradition. The common place of origin shared by Bacchylides and Simonides creates an unusually significant biographical argument for supposing that the latter was a powerful influence on the former. Specific probable examples of influence support the supposition: e.g. Bacch. 14, cf. Simon. 542 [**15**]; 11. 8, cf. Simon. 559. 2; 13. 205–6, cf. Simon. 531. 5, fr. 20. 15 West; 17. 122, cf. Simon. 543 [**16**]. 5; fr. 14. 4–5, cf. Simon. 541. 5.[4]

In any case, it would be dangerous for Pindar to make radical originality our only criterion of worth. In at least some tangible respects, neither Pindar nor Bacchylides matches or even continues the extreme innovations of Simonides. Most obviously of all, neither creates a reputation in elegy as well as lyric. Bacchylides at any rate ventures in some 'personal' lyric poems into Ionic dialect and Anacreontic metre (fr. 20 A, cf. frr. 17, 19). Otherwise, Bacchylides and Pindar cultivate both aeolic and dactylo-epitrite, for the most part in separate poems, and occasionally use iambics; the range seems to derive from Simonides. The elaborate species of aeolic apparently devised by Simonides is taken over by both; Pindar is more elaborate than Bacchylides, but Simonides 543 [**16**] seems

---

[3] Bacch. 13 is written for the same Aeginetan victory as Pind. *Nem.* 5; the family will have been important, as it commissioned two further poems (*Isth.* 5–6). Whatever the explanation for the virtual absence of east Greece from Pindar and Bacchylides, it is not lack of interest in athletics, as P. Oxy. 222 makes clear. Bacchylides' exile is thought to be supported by Pindar's paean for Ceos (Maehler (1982–97), i/1. 8–9); but the commission by that enterprising island need not be explained only by the absence of Bacchylides, and could itself be the source of an invention. (Apollonius' exile is fictitious.)

[4] On the authorship of Simon. 541 see the introduction to Simon. 542 [**15**], last paragraph.

as complicated as Pindar. In dactylo-epitrite, Bacchylides shows certain refinements less strictly observed by Pindar. For example, Bacchylides normally avoids short anceps save before a period-end of e or e⁻. Pindar's usage is less precise; Simonides did not anticipate Bacchylides. This is sophisticated rather than audacious change.[5]

In their dialect, Pindar and Bacchylides essentially adopt Simonides' language, itself traditional. They restrict some Homeric elements (as well as some markedly West Greek ones); in particular they would seem to use genitives in -οιο a good deal less freely. For us, it is more important that Bacchylides and Pindar continue and extend Simonides' use of epithets, itself an extension of Ibycus, Stesichorus, Homer. The context of such a tradition makes it inept to complain that ornamental epithets are frequent in Bacchylides. Their distribution is in any case carefully handled; and the evidence suggests that it is largely from Simonides on that the tradition acquires a dynamic character. Epic style had been characterized by the frequent use of epithets, which were predominantly traditional, and distinctively epic. Lyric had always been interested in these epithets; Stesichorus had used frequent epithets as a fixed feature of style, and predominantly the epic epithets. By the time of Bacchylides and Pindar, we see this strand of lyric still using frequent epithets; these, however, are not only epic epithets, but, in abundance, equally striking compounds which are probably inventions of lyric, and in formation or meaning characteristic of this specific genre. Many must be devised by the poet for the particular passage. The tradition, then, becomes one of free innovation.[6]

---

[5] Three 'non-Bacchylidean' instances in Simonides (581. 5, 584. 1–2), even from a minute sample. See Barrett (1956) and West (1982), 74, for more detail on the feature; in general for dactylo-epitrite see West (1982), 69–76. Some of the refinements in Bacchylides follow tradition; the important critical point is the aesthetic difference they produce together from the metrically less meticulous Pindar.

[6] For 5th-cent. compounds in comparison with Homer's see Williger (1928), 1–9; for Pindar and Bacchylides, note Hummel (1997); for Bacchylides' use of compounds in context see Segal (1998*b*). Cf. the introduction to the commentary on Simonides, n. 10; Simon. 542 [15]. 24–5, 34–5, 543 [16]. 10 nn.; contrast Ibyc. S151 [11], but note e.g. on Stes. S15. ii. 5–6 in the introduction to the commentary on Stesichorus. Old English, for example, provides a poetic tradition of which the free invention of compounds appears to be a fixed part. The distinction between compounds used previously in lyric and compounds devised by the poet will not always have been evident to listeners; but the general impression of innovation is clearly important. Note Eustath. *Proem. Pind.* 16. So far as can be seen, Bacchylides appears more restricted than Pindar in limiting the -οιο ending to proper names, compounds, and

It follows from all this that Bacchylides and Pindar can most profitably be viewed, stemmatically, as brothers. Together they illustrate their common tradition or conventions; influence of Pindar on Bacchylides (or the reverse) is hard to demonstrate. Furthermore, the importance of individuality in the tradition, and of an appearance of originality and mannerism in Pindar especially, make comparison of the two poets in actual originality confused and unhelpful; the poems are more important than the literary biography. And Pindar's unique power of language makes comparison in poetic quality unduly detrimental to Bacchylides. We would not view earlier poets unfavourably for failing to match Pindar; only if Bacchylides were known to be Pindar's disciple would the point be sensible (if then). One can actually gain a fresher idea of Bacchylides' poems by viewing them against the background of earlier lyric as well as of Pindar. There is no startling drop from earlier lyric in liveliness or art; Bacchylides' poems finely sustain the craft and the attractiveness of the genre.[7]

This assertion will be confirmed by the detailed consideration of a particular poem; but one or two general points will continue the argument. First, we can use Bacchylides' handling of narrative to illustrate the liveliness and variety of his works, within the lyric tradition. The large structures show a remarkable range of strategies. Outside epinician, which must inevitably speak of its occasion, he can begin a dithyramb with an elaborate self-referential prelude (19, cf. Pind. frr. 70 b, 75, etc.), or efface a narrator's voice entirely in a dialogue gesturing towards Attic tragedy (18). He can begin a paean with narrative, and continue it almost to the close, reducing the elements of the paean-form to the merest vestige at the end (17, contrast Simon. 519 frr. 35 (b). 12, 61 (a). 2, 78. 10, Pind. *Pae.* 2 (D2). 1–5, 5 (D5). 1, 6 (D6). 1–18, etc.). Even in epinician, the narrative within a narrative of 5 offers a very striking device; notable too are the elaborate structure and shifting focuses of the myth in 11.[8]

very common nouns (1. 9; 13. 63, cf. Pind. *Pyth.* 6. 39; 13. 121 cf. Pind. *Ol.* 10. 56, etc.). For -οιο and -ου in Simonides, Pindar, and Bacchylides see Nöthiger (1971), 45–6; Poltera (1997), 514–15, 519.

[7] In Bacchylides note the emphasis on novelty at 19. 9.

[8] Related points still apply to the narrative of 17 if the poem is a dithyramb, as is argued by Zimmermann (1992), 91–3. On the form of 18 see Zimmermann (1992), 95–7.

Internally, Bacchylides in his narrative can deploy an appearance of leisurely Stesichorean fullness (so 17), and, like a Stesichorus in small compass, evoke the heroic amplitude of martial epic (so 13). His narrative can also hasten to a crisis with alarming rapidity (so 16). Pathetic situations can be lingered on, in a manner reminiscent of Simon. 543 [**16**], but more forcefully (so 3 [**17**] especially). The narrative can, like that, in Alc. 298 [**10**], be firmly attached to an argumentative point (so 3 [**17**] again). Without displaying the mannerism of Pindar or Ibycus, Bacchylides can stop ostentatiously before the crucial point of his story (so 5, 16, 18), and present sequences of narrative from striking perspectives in time and point of view (so 5, 18). Even in these large terms, one can see how variously and interestingly Bacchylides exploits the possibilities of the lyric tradition, and creates narratives no less arresting and purposeful than those of his predecessors.

We may go further by taking another area: here the false historical antithesis of an original Pindar and an unoriginal Bacchylides can lead with particular ease to an aesthetic misconception of Bacchylides. This is the area of epinician first-person narrators. The greater prominence and vigour of the first person in Pindar's epinicians might be thought too simply to display a more original handling of the genre. The nature of the genre makes the historical supposition already appear questionable a priori. In other genres, such as paean or dithyramb, the first person represents sometimes the poet, sometimes the performing chorus (paean: Pind. *Pae.* 6 (D6). 5–6, 10–11; *Pae.* 2 (D2) and 4 (D4); dithyramb: Bacch. 19. 11–14; Pind. fr. 75. 7–9). In epinician, the first person is always the poet, although the poems are performed by a chorus (this bald statement will be defended in the introduction to the commentary on Pindar). So essential is it to epinician that the poem should present itself as a personal communication from the poet, who is portrayed as a guest-friend of the victor (and his family, and his city). It is very unlikely that this fixed convention with the epinician narrator was introduced by Bacchylides and Pindar, either independently of or in dependence on one another. One would not think it obvious, then, that a more prominent first person was necessarily a Pindaric innovation.[9]

---

[9] Poet as ξένος: Bacch. 5. 11, 12. 5, 13. 224, in Pind. e.g. *Nem.* 7. 61–5. Even without Pindar's epinicians, we could establish that at least some of Bacchylides' were performed by a chorus: cf. 13. 190–1 νίκαν . . . μέλπετ' ὦ νέοι | Π]υθέα. The

Earlier poetry helps us to be more positive. The remains of Simonidean and Ibycean epinician are exiguous; but a fragment of an epinician by Simonides shows a highly emotional use of the first person (519 fr. 92. 6–7). This seems to be the narrator. Ibyc. S221, very possibly an epinician, also presents a vehement and engaged narrator; in any case, the whole complex of Ibycus' poetry makes such a narrator seem plausible in his epinicians. And lively narrators have connections beyond epinician. This is especially obvious in the case of the choral narrator in Pind. *Parth.* 2, who is linked to Alcman's choral narrators; but the same is true of Pindaric narrators in other genres, and indeed in epinician (Alcm. 1 [**1**] and Simon. 542 [**15**] are very relevant to epinician).[10]

Thus Pindar's own use is likely to have its roots in tradition. The earlier discussion would incline one to suppose (and certainly to think possible) that the gestures often shared by Pindar and Bacchylides at moments of self-reference, and plainly connected, spring from a common tradition rather than Bacchylides' imitation (cf. e.g. 5. 42 and the similar 8. 19–20 with Pind. *Ol.* 2. 92, 6 [**18**]. 20–1, *Nem.* 11. 24–6). These connections also remind us not to exaggerate the interval here beween Bacchylides and Pindar. Bacchylides is by no means devoid of self-reference (cf. 1. 159, 3 [**17**]. 85, 96–8, 4. 7–8, 5. 11–14, 15–33, 42, 195–7, 8. 17–20, 9. 4–6, 10. 10, 49, 51–2, 11. 24, 12. 3, 13. 103, 221–31). There are also many ways besides self-reference for narrators to make their presence felt; Bacchylides uses some animated devices that do not appear in Pindar (cf. e.g. 3. [**17**]. 10 n.). None the less, the presence of Bacchylides' narrator is less emphatic and obtrusive than that of Pindar's; one should not, however, infer that Bacchylides is uninterested, or uninteresting. His quieter approach to the narrator positively suits the specific ethos of his poems. Thus he, unlike Pindar, repeatedly uses a specific type of third-person phrase to denote himself, with varied images: see 3 [**17**]. 97–8 n. The effect is

reference there to the present occasion, with the separation of speaker and performer, is indicated by 19. 8–11, and further confirmed by Pind. *Pae.* 6 (D6). 121–2. (Note also for Bacch. 19. 8 Pind. *Nem.* 4. 44.) Carey (1989), 550–1, (1991), 190, notes 13. 190–1 themselves; they are not discussed in Heath and Lefkowitz's rejoinder (1991). For Pind. *Pae.* 6 (D6). 5–6 cf. Radt (1958), 105–8; D'Alessio (1994), 124–5.

[10] Simon. 519 fr. 84. 12 is of interest, whatever its genre (note also S387. 10). For the narrator (poet) in Ibycus' epinician note also S165; S223 (*a*). ii. 6 might also be relevant. Interestingly, the first person plural in Simon. 519 fr. 35 (*b*) (paean) seems to represent the chorus.

arch and elegant (though not modest). This well exemplifies how Bacchylides' handling of his narrator forms a distinctive version of the tradition. One could add, for instance, that the self-referential simile in 5. 16–30, given its application in 31–3, is a less abrupt and strident device than Pindar's parataxis with the same image at *Ol*. 2. 86–8, *Nem*. 3. 80–2; it is clearly not feebler, but creates a different tonality. Bacchylides' restrained, refined, and far from colourless treatment of the narrator matches his treatment of the addressee, which we shall shortly be exploring.[11]

So Bacchylides' lyric predecessors lay the best foundations for the fuller appreciation of a major lyric poet of the fifth century. He has often been announced to be in need of reclamation; but much remains to be done, even now, in the close analysis which is required to support such opinions properly. The following attempt may help to give some idea of his real stature.

17: poem 3[12]

The poem is formally a celebration of Hieron I's chariot victory at Olympia in 468; but it gives most space and emphasis to his dedication of a golden tripod or tripods at Delphi. One may compare Pind. *Pyth*. 1, which dwells chiefly on Hieron's 'new' city Aetna; *Pyth*. 3 seems to be written on no recent victory at all. The present poem does not mention the victory at Cumae, which may have been

---

[11] Note that the end to the early 13 (221–31) uses a more emphatically first-person form than the third-person periphrases. Only there, in fact, and at the rather different 5. 31 do Bacchylides' epinicians use the emphatic ἐγώ, ἐμέ, etc. for the narrator.

[12] On poem 3 [17] see esp. Kenyon (1897), 14–29; Housman (1972), 443–5; Wilamowitz (1970), 326–7; Schaefer (1901); Dessoulavy (1903); Jebb (1905), 194–7, 253–67, 452–63; Gentili (1958*b*), ch. 2; Fränkel (1962), 527–33; Segal (1998*a*), (1998*b*), 109–114; Snell (1973), 202–3; Lefkowitz (1976), 125–42; Maehler (1982–97), i/2. 32–63 (the fundamental commentary); Carson (1984); Burkert (1985*b*); Burnett (1985), ch. 3; Murgatroyd (1986); Krummen (1990), 285; Irigoin, Duchemin, and Bardollet (1993), 95–108. On Hieron and Syracuse: e.g. Wilamowitz (1901); Andrewes (1956), 128–36; Berve (1967), i. 147–52; Finley (1968), ch. 4; Kraay (1976), 209–15; Gabba and Vallet (1980), i. 3, plans 14–15, 654–93; Carratelli (1985), e.g. illustr. after p. 194; Wescoat (1989), esp. 84–98; Holloway (1991), 97–102, 112–15, 121–30; Asheri (1992), 148–54; McGlew (1993), 137–45, 178–9; Luraghi (1994); Panvini (1996), chs. 4, 5; lit. on dedications 17–18 n. below. Further on Croesus: see the introduction to the commentary on Sappho above, and refs. in Burkert (1985*b*); and e.g. Asheri (1989), 320–1; Hall (1989), 65; Mellink (1991), 643–55; Kuhrt (1995), ii. 567–72; on the fall of Sardis note Greenewalt and Rautman (1998), 487–97.

the reason for the dedication: piety and wealth are the point. But the poem does not merely continue Hieron's display, spectacular as this was, and important as was such display in general to the Deinomenids (so Polyzelus' famous bronze charioteer in the Delphi Museum). The dedication is drawn into a powerful sequence of thought, which is developed in narrative and reflection.

How far is this sequence (see the conclusion after the notes) addressed to Hieron in his particular circumstances? Are there reflections on death and old age because he was old and dangerously ill? The assumption seems not implausible. Hieron died a year or so later; his illness was sufficiently severe for Pindar to refer to it in *Pyth.* 1. 50–6, and to make it a principal subject of *Pyth.* 3. (Later reports of the nature of Hieron's and of Gelon's illness (Σ Pind. *Pyth.* 1. 89 a, b (Arist. fr. 486 Rose); Plut. *Pyth. Or.* 403 c) may not have been derived from satisfactory sources: what would these have been?) Hieron is likely to have been in his forties at least (88 n.): enough for old age to be a possible description (cf. Cameron (1995), ch. 7).

But it is not simply a question of acquiring sufficient information to decode the message of Bacchylides to Hieron. The poem is a literary text for public performance; it is a significant part of its surface that it does not touch at all directly on Hieron's condition. In poems 3 [**17**], 4, and 5 Bacchylides avoids the specific references to Hieron's life so prominent in Pindar's poems to him (fr. 20 c, from a 'personal' poem, at least alludes to the founding of Aetna). Remarks on health and fame after death occur, for example, at the end of poem 1, to a boy. And yet, even if Hieron's illness did not seem particularly perilous at this time, and his years not particularly advanced, the argument of the poem on old age and death must still have carried a weightiness and pertinence which it would not have had, or not had in the same way, if addressed to a fit young man. Various specific points will support this notion. But the corollary is that the poem derives some of its character from facing painful matters both unflinchingly and obliquely. The obliqueness is not simply necessary tact to a tyrant, as Pindar shows. Bacchylides as a writer is deeply interested in obliqueness (cf. 85): 5. 161–78 or the end of 18 form obvious examples. As a poet for patrons he is reserved on personal things. Yet the specific situation, and still more the specific shaping of the poem, help to turn what might in themselves seem pastable commonplaces into a profound and individual poem.

Metre

str., ant.

1. ⏓ – ◡ ⏒ × ⏒ ◡ – ◡ – –
2. ⏓ – ◡◡ – ◡◡ – ◡ – –
3. ⏒ – ◡◡ – ◡◡ – ◡ –
4. ◡ – ◡ – ⏓ – ◡◡ – ◡ – –

ep.

1. ⏓ – ◡◡ – ◡◡ – –
2. – ◡ – ⏒ – ◡ –
3. – ◡ – ⏒ – ◡ –
4. – – ◡ ⏒ – – ◡ –
5. ⏒ ◡ – ⏒ – ◡ – ⏒ – ◡ –
6. – ◡ – ⏒ – ◡ –

The scheme of the poem is notable for the brevity of the stanzas, and for the marked differentiation between the epode and the strophe and antistrophe. If one measures dactylo-epitrite stanzas with D and E as 1, d¹, d², e as 0.5, the epode is the shortest dactylo-epitrite stanza in a 'public' poem (6.5; fr. 20 B 6, fr. 20 C 6.5). Poem 14 str. is the only other under 8 (7); the average in 'public' poems, even including some incomplete stanzas, is 10.5. The strophe, unusually, is substantially shorter than the epode. Its 4 lines are matched in aeolic poems only in the epode of the single-triad 2; the average in 'public' poems is 11. *SLG* 320 and 323 (probably Simonides) might offer some background if themselves less problematic. The stanzas in poem 3 [**17**] at all events have a forceful concision. A possible further point to the brevity may become increasingly apparent in the later part of the poem: a hinted personal quality as the shadowed personal argument is discerned. The distinction of epode from strophe is extreme: dactylo-epitrite is set against aeolic, a combination found in only one other epinician (Pind. *Ol.* 13 (464)). The dactylo-epitrite shows various unusual features in detail (as if it were part of a structure with the aeolic strophe, not merely an anomalous insert). Cf. Barrett (1956), 249–50. But after the opening, which gestures towards aeolic as the opening of the strophe gestures towards single-short, the epode is resolutely single-short and epitrite. The epode is thus very strongly demarcated (Maehler (1985), 395, lays too much weight on the openings). We shall see how this demarcation is exploited in the poem.

In its individual structure (ABBC), the strophe has at its centre two similar cola with expanded double-short core. The initial 'O- of 4 will be regarded by the listener at that point as simply part of the next colon; catalexis without pause would not be attractive, and later too the syllable is always short. But the usual placing of the word-end after that syllable (not 3, 35, 91) may create a teasing appearance of identity between str. 2 and str. 3. The first line, by contrast with str. 2–3, is entirely single-short (ia ia ba). The last colon str. 4, not preceded by pause, has a lengthened single-short opening and only a choriambic base; it thus joins the two types str. 1 and str. 2–3. The epode is notably uniform and the endings of its three periods parallel; but the periods are kept distinct (ep. 1–2 ×D-E; 3–4 E-E; 5–6 E-eE). The first period opens with single-short; the first part of the third period (ep. 5) is conspicuously longer than the first part of the second (ep. 3). The absence of link-syllable following ep. 5, and the word-end there (after the opening triad), drive home the shape.

1–4. The stanzas of the first triad are firmly demarcated by pause; this happens in no other triad. The unusual metrical design is drawn to the listener's attention; so is the small scale of the stanzas.

A compound epithet comes in every colon (cf. Segal (1998*b*), 109). The first, a hapax (Maehler (1982–79), i/2. 40), makes an especially resonant beginning, cf. 1. 1 (cf. Pind. *Ol.* 2. 1), 17. 1, Pind. *Ol.* 13. 1, *Pyth.* 2. 1 (of Syracuse), fr. 144. The last, 'Ο[λυ]μπιοδρόμους, a magnificently polysyllabic hapax, is strengthened by another epithet; the single-short rhythm, striking in the shape of the stanza, gives it further weight. There is also a significant massing and movement of names. The poem begins imposingly from Sicily rather than Syracuse (contrast poem 4, Pind. *Pyth.* 2, *Nem.* 1 (Sicily first in 12–18)). Hieron's role as hierophant of the goddesses (Pind. *Ol.* 6 [**18**]. 94–5 n.), and Gelon's temples, are only secondary in the rhetoric. The singing is to begin from the divinities, cf. 5. 178–86, Pind. *Ol.* 6 [**18**]. 88–90, and from the place, cf. 4. 1–3, Pind. *Nem.* 10. 1–20; but it proceeds to its point in the name of Hieron. Note the placing of the name at 5. 16, Pind. *Ol.* 2. 95; here Bacchylides more obliquely makes the song praise the horses (cf. fr. 20 C. 8–9).

Further words in this poem not found in other authors are εὐρυδίνης (6), ὑψιδαίδαλτος (18), χαλκοτειχής (32) (cf. πλείσταρχος (12) not as a name; not μεγαίνητος (64) or μελαμφαρής (13–14)). The first (and sometimes second) part of these compounds appears in other words peculiar to Bacchylides or Pindar. At least the majority of such words will have been invented in the lyric tradition, and some (probably many) will have been invented by Bacchylides. It is notable that the present hapaxes come mostly in the first part of the poem. In poem 5 the hapaxes are spread more evenly over the poem; in this poem there are especially marked differences of style between the various parts.

The address to the Muse elegantly varies the Homeric pattern by using a particular name, with a compound epithet, cf. Alcm. 27 (*Μῶc'* as well, no epithet), Bacch. 5. 176, 12. 1–2. Bacchylides uses *Μοῦca* in address only at the Homeric 15. 47, whereas Pindar in address often uses *Μοῖca* and never a Muse's name, or compound epithet (*πότνια Nem.* 3. 1; fr. 94 b. 1 dubious). *γλυκύδωρε* (5. 4, 11. 1) will become more significant at the end of the poem; its suggestion of quasi-sensuous joy is part of the epinician ethos.

5–8. Despite Snell–Maehler's note, *cεύον*]*το* looks both too long for the space and no better for it than *φέρον*]*το*: cf. 18. 10, 5. 104; 13. 144, 17. 97. *ἵεν*]*το*, though it looks too short, is not so far out. An aorist might be more natural in itself (note 9), and more suitable to *cύν* with an uncapitalized *νίκαι* and *ἀγ*]*λαΐαι*.

Should they be capitalized, as they now generally are? *ὑπερόχωι* is not an obviously suitable epithet for a goddess (cf. Schaefer (1901), 23–4): the superlative with genitive at Pind. *Pyth.* 2. 38 is quite different; contrast Bacch. 17. 68–9. On the other hand, the adjective is eminently suitable to 'victory'; *ἀγλαΐα* 'triumph, glory' is suitably akin in meaning to *νίκη*. Note 12. 36–7. The emphasis throughout the antistrophe is on victory, which had not explicitly been declared in the strophe.

παρ' εὐρυδίναν | [Ἀλφεόν]: the same epithet at 5. 38, cf. 8. 26–7, 9. 39. The turn, though stylized, creates a more vivid version of *Ὀ*[*λυ*]*μπιοδρόμους*.

Δεινομένεος . . . τ[: as with Olympia, Hieron's name is now conveyed by a different name. Cf. 4. 13 after 3, 6. 12–13 after 1, Pind. *Pyth.* 2. 18 after 5, etc. Hieron has appeared in the genitive at the end of the preceding stanza, and seems to appear as object now, and to be spoken of more. He finally comes into his own in the epode, as subject.

ἔθη | καν: 'caused Hieron to', cf. Eur. *Med.* 717–18, *HF* 221 (cf. Bond (1981), 222–3), and earlier e.g. Hom. *Il.* 16. 222–3. Maehler's objection that the phrase only refers to compulsion ((1982–97), i/2. 42) does not apply to the first two passages, and in any case seems too strict. The alternative, to make *κυρῆcαι* a consecutive infinitive dependent on *ὄλβιον* as complement, is extremely strained, especially for this author; Pind. *Pyth.* 9. 6–8 would only form an analogy if we imposed the same construction there.

[ὄ]λβιον leads into what follows (cf. 22).

9. The shout of the public inspires the listeners' (inward) applause. The universal cry may perhaps be assigned most naturally to the moment of victory rather than of the herald's announcement, and so connected with the horses' action. Cf. 9. 35 etc.

10. The development of the sentence does not suit a momentary cry, or even the awards ceremony; after the sentence, there would be no obvious point for a speech to stop. The narrator, then, is speaking; but one may still see the exclamation as partly reflecting the emotions of the crowd. Cf. φεῦ at 17. 119, Hor. *Odes* 1. 5. 5, etc. Such vivacious words, in direct speech and out of it, are characteristic of Bacchylides (16. 30, cf. 9. 15, 5. 152, fr. 2. 1), not of Pindar (fr. 182 is unusual), nor of earlier lyric, as opposed to elegy and iambus (cf. Alcm. 3 [2]. '77' (26. 2); Sapph. 168 and *Scol.* 907. 1 are unusual). Cf. ἆ μάκαρ at Hippon. fr. 117. 6 West. τρίς also suggests a spontaneous exclamation produced by the moment, and so the crowd as well as the narrator: cf. e.g. Hes. fr. 211. 7 Merkelbach–West, Ar. *Peace* 242, Men. *Dysc.* 603. Note ὦ μακα.[at the start of a stanza at *SLG* 323. 16 (probably Simonides), cf. Eur. *Bacch.* 73; compare the more restrained Bacch. 5. 50–3. The grounds for the exclamation extend further than we expected, and we are led from the specific moment in the recent past to a larger picture of the broader present (Hieron's conduct). The conception of good fortune (10, cf. 8) is also extended and refined.

11. First in the ampler picture of Hieron comes his kingship. Pindar and Bacchylides present him as a king (Pind. *Ol.* 1. 23, 114, Pyth. 3. 70, etc.; 70 n. below, Pind. *Ol.* 6 [**18**]. 93 n.). The gift of Zeus indicates tradition and legitimacy: cf. Hes. *Theog.* 96. Kingship is naturally a standard extreme of felicity: cf. e.g. Pind. *Ol.* 1. 113–14, *Nem.* 4. 83–5, Plat. *Theaet.* 174 D 3–E 2, 175 C 4 (as self-evident? and a lyric quotation?).

λαχών commonly of the gifts of gods: cf. e.g. 6. 1–2, 19. 3–4.

12. πλείσταρχον Ἑλλάνων: Hieron is outstanding among the Greeks, a theme important later (63), and important for the myth of the foreign ruler (24) Croesus. Cf. also for the ranking of Hieron Pind. *Pyth.* 1. 48–50, 2. 58–61; one finds the notion even in Herodotus (3. 125. 2). For the particular point here Aetna and

Gela do not need to be specifically borne in mind, nor does it even need to be established whether πλειϲτο- implies population. Compounds from superlatives, occasionally found in tragic lyric (Aesch. *Supp.* 709, Soph. *Aj.* 935), are a speciality of Pindar and Bacchylides (ἀριϲτο-, μεγιϲτο-, πλειϲτο- (Pind. *Ol.* 6 [**18**]. 69); cf. Hummel (1997), and Hom. *Il.* 18. 54 δυϲαριϲτοτόκεια). In the first stanza the superlative had belonged to Sicily.

πλείϲταρχον would not make good or pointed sense with A''s γένοϲ.

13–14. The kingship (11–12) is the precondition of the wealth; the visible employment of the wealth is exemplified by the four-horse team (note Hdt. 6. 35. 1, Thuc. 6. 16. 2). Wealth is a theme particularly common with Hieron and other kings (cf. e.g. Pind. *Ol.* 2. 53–6, *Pyth.* 5. 1–4); on the idea of ignoble hoarding see Bundy (1986), 83–91, Theocr. 16. 22–33. The darkness suggests not only miserly concealment but the contemptible obscurity of those uninterested in the glories of fame (cf. e.g. 13. 175–81).

οἶδε indicates ability and character, which go beyond the merely passive receiving from Zeus.

πυργωθέντα: the only word in the poem beginning with three longs; it carries great force. More of πύργοϲ may be heard than in πυργοκεράτα (fr. 39). The image suggests not an avaricious heaping (Epicur. fr. 480 Usener etc.), but a monumental achievement, which ought scarcely to be hidden.

μελαμ | φαρέϊ gives a graphic ugliness to the darkness, which becomes more than a mere absence. Contrast e.g. Pind. fr. 42. 7, and even *Parth.* 1. 9–10. For the word cf. *TrGF* Adesp. 660. 6 Kannicht–Snell; and note Aesch. *Eum.* 370.

15–16. The idea of rule leads naturally to the displays of generous wealth in Hieron's kingdom. For Hieron's festivals cf. Pind. *Ol.* 6 [**18**]. 94–6. The festivals are for the glory, and benefit, of the citizens (cf. [Xen.] *Ath. Pol.* 2. 9; Thuc. 2. 38. 1); the narrator shows his appreciation of Hieron's kindness to foreign guests too (cf. Pind. *Pyth.* 3. 71 and e.g. *Ol.* 1. 16–17, 103–5, Bacch. 5. 14).

βρύει: a colourful verb popular with Bacchylides and Aeschylus, found in Simonides (519 fr. 77. 3), and probably Anacreon (P. Oxy. 4454 fr. 3. 4, cf. Anacr. 346 fr. 11 + 3 + 6. 20), but not in Pindar. Poem 6. 9 (cf. Eubul. fr. 56. 6 Kassel–Austin) suggests that the literal sense may be felt in Bacchylides, as often elsewhere. There seems no marked difference of meaning between genitive and dative in a figurative sense at least (cf. e.g. Aesch. *Ag.* 169, *Ch.* 588 (Hermann); Eur. fr. 1086. 1 Nauck): the variation in the papyrus can be allowed. βρύει . . . βρύουϲι itself shows a desire for variation.

βρύει, βρύουϲι are emphatically present, and depict as continuous a repeated situation (note βουθύτοιϲ ἑορταῖϲ).

Pindar several times sets anaphora at the beginning of consecutive lines, especially at the start of stanzas, with a forceful artistry not cultivated in archaic lyric (Anacr. 359, with variation, is expressive and jocular). For the start cf. *Ol.* 2. 61–2 (cf. *Nem.* 10. 87–8), *Pyth.* 2. 49–50 (cf. *Isth.* 5. 52–3), 4. 70–1, *Nem.* 1. 63–4, 11. 6–7 (contrast Alc. 283. 15–16, Sapph. 94. 12, 16, Anacr. 388. 7–8). In this confined stanza, the effect is especially striking; the cumulative meaning of the anaphora, and the sense of the verb, convey both Hieron's opulence and the narrator's exalted enthusiasm. Despite 21, Eur. *Bacch.* 107 βρύετε βρύετε does not give sufficient ground to suppose ritual language here; the parallel remains of interest for the tone.

The expression in 16 is both devious and vivid; a straightforward idea is defamiliarized. The metonymous ἀγυιαί stresses the city as well as the ruler.

17–18. The reference to Delphi is only gradually made clear; the name itself (that of the people) is kept climactically for the end (21). After the anaphora of the μέν clause, the δέ clause is syntactically involved, and flows over the stanza, for the first time in the poem. The dedication of a tripod, or tripods, by Hieron at Delphi forms the starting-point for the poem's central invention, one which boldly moves us to Delphi in an Olympian poem. The parallel references to water (6–7, 20) underline the relation.

Hieron appears to have set up a large tripod of pure gold before the east front of the temple at Delphi, next to, and in emulation of, the tripod set up by Gelon (Homolle (1897), 588–90, (1898); Theopomp. *FGrHist* 115 F 193, etc.). Object and location were plainly spectacular. Whether Hieron also erected smaller gold tripods in front of the temple is uncertain; ὑψι- seems to tell against their inclusion here. The large tripods of Gelon and Hieron would sufficiently justify the poet's form of words here and at 63–6. But we cannot argue that the form of words must spring from cunning: it is also part of Bacchylides' literary strategy to present directly in 15–21 not Hieron's actions but their results. (On the tripods cf. further Jebb (1905), 452–7; Dittenberger (1915–24), i. 33–8; Courby (1927), 249–54; Gentili (1958*b*), 72, 84; Ebert (1972), 60–3; Page (1981), 247–50; Jeffery (1990), 266.)

λάμπει: with exciting indirectness and physicality together, the narrator shows the present continuous shining, not the past act of dedication. The word, elaborated in ὑπὸ μαρμαρυγαῖc, contrasts with the μελαμ|φαρέϊ cκότωι of 13–14. The literal shining moves into the metaphor of conspicuousness and glory (though 'literal' and 'metaphor' divide too much).

ὁ χρυ|cόc: the article is given sense by what follows (cf. e.g. Pind. *Isth.* 2. 33); this makes the introduction of the topic the more abrupt. 'Gold' is the subject rather than 'golden tripods'; again the poetry both avoids the obvious and seeks the concrete. Gold will be a recurring element (65, 87).

ὑψιδαιδάλτων: the two parts of the compound should be related. The foremost adornment is on the top part of the tripod, and that part is high up because the tripods are so tall. Cf. ὑψιπέτηλος, etc. (δαιδάλλω means 'adorn' rather than 'create richly'.) For a highly elaborate top part to these works of art cf. the middle and late sixth-century examples Berlin Inv. F. 768 and Belgrade Inv. br. 137/I (illustrated e.g. Bruns (1947), 32; Vulić (1933), 467–8), and for the principle e.g. the tripods on the Berlin Painter's hydria in the Vatican (*ARV*² 209. 166) and Myson's calyx krater in the British Museum, E 458 (*ARV*² 239. 16). The resonant compound stresses the conspicuousness of these particular tripods; for the latter element cf. χρυcοδαίδαλτοc (Ar. *Eccl.* 972 etc.). The content of the word suggests it is likely to have been invented for this occasion. Bigness and height are important aspects of kingly wealth in the poem; cf. 13 and on 32.

19–22. πάροιθε ναοῦ: the prominence of the phrase in the stanza highlights the prominence of the objects visually, which promotes the argument. The religious ναοῦ is advanced on by the name of the god at the start of the next period (20); this will be crucial to the argument.

μέγι[c]τον: the grove partakes of the grandeur of the shrine.

Mention of the spring here helps to suggest the numinous beauty of the place: cf. 11. 118–19.

Δέλφοι: compare the forceful appearance of the name of Olympia, 4.

διέπουcι: the reverence of the Delphians supports the religious atmosphere. In Syracuse and Delphi, unlike Sardis later, all is harmonious and as it should be.

θεόν, θε̱[ό]ν: an imitation of sacral language or of religious agitation may form part of the background here: cf. Norden (1916), 136–7; Fehling (1969), 169–70; Maehler (1982–97), i/2. 46; add Soph. fr. 314. 100 Radt, Virg. *Ecl.* 5. 64, etc. (Note the perversion at Eur. *Andr.* 1031.) The animation of the language remains arresting: Pindar's epinicians do not show anything fully parallel (cf. *Pyth.* 2. 49–50; *Isth.* 2. 11 (quotation); *Isth.* 6. 44), but the expression would be natural enough in Euripides' lyric. The asyndeton heightens the abruptness of this utterance, after the long sentence before.

ἀγλαϊζέτω· ὁ: the bold crasis, unexpected in this style, perhaps enhances the roughness. The third-person imperative, rather than a statement ('one should . . .'), furthers the pious vivacity. Contrast the expression at 1. 163–5, 14. 18.

[ὄ]λβων: 'wealth' becomes figurative (cf. Eur. fr. 137 Nauck), and also suggests the sense 'good fortune' (cf. 5. 50 etc.). Croesus' dialogue with Solon in Hdt. 1. 30–3 reflects on the stem more argumentatively and searchingly; but even here the word takes up 8 and 10, and gives the sense of advancing the argument. The statement offers a universal, timeless 'present', which can contain the time long past to which the poem now proceeds.

23–5. The narrative begins with an epode; in poem 5 it begins with an antistrophe. ἐπεί marks a connection of argument, not a connection through a person or (as would be natural here) a place; the asyndeton at 5. 56 serves a related function. ποτε establishes a distance in time, as it does when the mythical narratives begin at 5. 56 (cf. 11. 40, Pind. *Pyth.* 9. 5, 10. 31, etc.). But here the distance is less than eighty years, and the mention of the Persians in 27 must surely recall the link with the last eighty years of Greek history.

Croesus qualifies for a quasi-mythical narrative by virtue of his distance in place, which corresponds to the mythical distance in time (cf. Racine's preface to *Bajazet*). The distance also makes possible the extraordinary end to the story. It is striking, none the less, that Bacchylides rather than Pindar takes the daring step of making his formal 'myth' a historical event. (Pind. fr. 270 proves nothing, any more than *Pyth.* 1. 94.) Bacchylides is at least equally

ready to take risks (one may notice his taking on the story of the
Iliad in 13); besides this, it may be significant that he shows closer
links than Pindar with Attic drama. Athenian dramatists had been
expanding mythical tragedy to include oriental themes (Aeschy-
lus, Phrynichus, the apparent depiction of a tragedy discussed by
Beazley (1955)). The depiction of Croesus on Myson's amphora
(Louvre G 197, *ARV* ² 238. 1, *c*.490–480) suggests the unusual sta-
tus of the story even at that date. At all events, the recent depictions
of Orientals in Attic drama, and still more the significance of the
distance in place, should make us cautious of accepting that Croe-
sus is depicted 'as a Greek'. In fact, we shall see that his foreignness
is strongly emphasized in Bacchylides' treatment.

καί indicates the link with Hieron, the unsurpassed Greek bene-
factor of Delphi; but the rhetorical accumulation of the temporal
clause in 25–7 also creates the sense 'even'. Croesus' preservation
was utterly surprising.

δαμασίππου: the epithet connects Lydia and Croesus to Syracuse
and Hieron. Cf. 69 n., and for Syracuse e.g. Pind. *Pyth.* 2. 2. It also
evokes the vanished might of Lydian chariots (Sapph. 16 [5]. 19 n.).
The formation from (or as if from) the sigmatic aorist is characteris-
tic of Simonides, Bacchylides, Pindar (note δαμασίμβροτος at Simon.
616 and Bacch. 13. 50); it here defamiliarizes the epic ἱππόδαμος.

ἀρχαγέταν underlines the connection with Hieron.

πεπ[: πεπ[ρωμέναν seems promising. If so, the narrator removes
the actual fall of Sardis from the scope of criticism by invoking fate
combined with Zeus. A related strategy is used by the Pythia in
Hdt. 1. 91. 1. The action of Apollo is still set against that of Zeus.
For the relation of gods and destiny cf. 17. 23–8.

26–8. The proper names are massed in 23–9, and especially 26–9,
as say in 15. 1–7. Here they offer a striking combination: the names
of a foreign race, person, and city, little associated with mythology,
are joined with the august and familiar gods. The effect is different
from that of gods helping the poets' patrons. More specifically,
Zeus' action here in destroying Sardis contrasts with his gift to
Hieron (11–12). The bare name Κροῖσον, after the periphrasis in
23–4, is expressively set against the name of Apollo (with epithet).
Compare the names of Zeus (with epithet) and his son Minos at 17.
67–8 (cf. 74–5), after the periphrases for Minos at 20, 39, 50.

If the supplement χρυσά[ορος is correct, this stock epithet for the god (Hom. *Il.* 5. 509) might here suggest the superior wealth of the gods, or might evoke Hom. *Il.* 15. 245–7, where Apollo declares his protection of Hector. But in view of Bacchylides' general use of divine epithets one can hardly be confident.

29–31. φύλαξ' Ἀπόλλων: at the start of the new triad, the words end, and give verb and subject to, a long sentence and reverse the gloom of the epode; they fall with tremendous weight. It does not matter that the divine name is prepared in 28. φύλαξ' is a milder word than ἐξήρπαξεν (Hom. *Il.* 20. 443; cf. e.g. *Il.* 10. 291), and does not specify details: the nature of the climax is only indicated broadly. With the decisive event marked out, the narrator goes back to build up an imperfective situation.

ἄελπτον: the astonishing reversal of Croesus' glory is only intimated briefly here.

ἆμαρ recalls the Homeric νηλεὲς ἦμαρ etc., and conveys already a decisive moment; but more is to come in Croesus' thoughts and the narrative.

πολυδ[άκρυο]ν, which fits the space well, is better taken with ἆμαρ than with δ[ουλοςύ]ναν (as by Maehler). Much weeping in or at slavery would not suit Croesus as it would a woman (cf. Hom. *Il.* 6. 455), and if slavery had an epithet here, one would expect it to be 'shameful' or the like. The day of disaster itself may fitly be given this epithet (cf. 40–7). It fits well with ἔτι and the sequence of time. The horrors of the sack are only conveyed generally now; elaboration comes with Croesus' own description. The arrangement is both oblique in narrative and pointed in rhetoric.

οὐκ κτλ.: the negative and the simple verb have a stern pride which partly depicts Croesus' thoughts but also compels our admiration. One can see a connection with the Greeks who ten years before had fought to avert slavery at the Persians' hands (e.g. *IG* i³. 503/4 A 4); what follows will be far distant from Greek behaviour. There is also irony in οὐκ ἔμελλε: Croesus' intentions will be achieved, but in a wholly different manner. Compare the different irony of human plans at 16. 19–20. To anyone who knew this poem, Hdt. 1. 89. 1 would in turn seem pointedly ironical.

31–5. The Nabonidus Chronicle (ii. 16–17) may but need not state that Cyrus killed the king of Lydia (Smith (1924), 112, 116; Grayson (1975), 107; cf. Cargill (1977); Burkert (1985*b*), 5–7; Mellink (1991), 653). The pyre already appears on Myson's amphora

(Louvre G 197; *ARV*² 238. 1), and there too it seems lit at the behest of the king, rather than of Cyrus (Hdt. 1. 86. 2). Croesus is pouring a libation: the self-immolation is perhaps conceived as a sacrifice. Herodotus, in ascribing motives to Cyrus, appears to use this last element: either it was a sacrifice, or the fulfilment of a vow, or an experiment to see if a god would save him (again borrowed from Bacchylides' simpler version?). Thus: Bacchylides did not invent the notion that the immolation was Croesus' choice, but he has chosen not to make it a religious act; that suits Croesus' anger with the gods in his speech, and the whole argument of the story.

On the amphora no women are present on the pyre with Croesus (in Herodotus Lydian children are included). The constraints of artistic design mean it would be rash to deduce that Bacchylides has invented the females (Maehler (1982–97), i/2. 34, 37, cautiously). Even if he has, they are not merely figures of contrast. To create a pyre to perish on is not, in historical times, normal Greek behaviour; it is the sort of action Greeks and Romans readily associated with foreigners. To add one's family is an extremity that marks out still further the alien ruler; it appears in various Greek accounts of recent and remote events: cf. Hdt. 7. 107 (Boges in 477; Herodotus admires); Diod. 2. 27. 2 ('Sardanapallus', cf. Ctes. *FGrHist* 688 F 1 q); Burkert (1985*b*), 9–10. Livy's account of the fall of Saguntum is interesting precisely because he moves closer to this model, and makes some men perish on the pyre, some burn themselves with their families (21. 14. 1, 4; contrast Diod. 25. 15, Zonar. 8. 21 (Dio vol. i p. 190 Boissevain), App. *Hisp.* 44–5; nothing in Polyb. 3. 17. 9–10). Such passages actually make it notable that Croesus does not here destroy his riches in the flames: that would confuse the argument, and focus the poem too strongly on material prosperity. It is certainly evident that Croesus is being cast very much as an 'Oriental' here; he is not for that reason despised.

32. χαλκοτειχέος: Croesus' fabulous wealth, like Alcinous', excels anything possible for Greek mortals (Hom. *Od.* 7. 86; cf. Pind. *Pae.* 8 (B2). 68). The placing of the word next to πυράν is forceful.

π[ροπάροι]θεν seems very decidedly too long for the space, which is determined by 34–40; in this it is unlike the supplements in 29–31. Nor do the traces before θ suit it. 'In front of the courtyard' seems in any case a slightly odd expression, perhaps adequately justified by Eur. *Or.* 1277 and the mention of the walls. We should not, then, press any connections with 19, though the lavish pyre may be seen as a counterpart to the creations of fortunate wealth (cf. 49–52 n.).

33. cὐ[ν ἀλόχωι] again looks too long. The wife is mentioned at 50 but not 60; it is not quite certain that she is mentioned here.

34–6. ἐπέβαιν': the tense underlines the imperfectivity of the whole situation.

θ]υγατράcι: in view of 60 (and 50), it is unlikely that the poem mentioned sons as well. This might be because Bacchylides knew the story of Atys (not of the other son?). Such an explanation would not conflict, however, with the significant roles performed by the daughters within the narrative.

δυρομέναιc: at this point the narrator does not separate the girls' grief at their coming fate and at the disaster to the city. The expression (cf. Hom. *Od.* 14. 174) suggests woe rather than alarm. The girls are of course contrasted with Croesus, but they also stir the listeners' involvement. In retrospect (60) we see in their reaction the irony of their ignorance, cf. 17. 92–6. ὀδύρομαι and δύρομαι do not occur in Pindar, μύρομαι doubtfully in *Parth.* 2. 97; ὀδύρομαι occurs at Bacch. fr. 11. 9, μύρομαι at 5. 163.

χέρας κτλ.: the standard gesture for prayer (West (1997), 42–3) comes repeatedly in Bacchylides (11. 100, 13. 138, 15. 45, 17. 72–3). But here it accentuates the bold perversion of prayer. Contrast even Eur. *HF* 498.

37. The speech begins at the start of the epode, as the narrative did. The device shows an avoidance of the obvious; but the greater length of the epode, the different metre, the connection of the two moments, create a natural emphasis (cf. Maehler (1985), 395).

37–9. At Hdt. 1. 87. 1 Croesus calls on Apollo to rescue him. Here he raises his hands, and calls on divine power, but speaks of Apollo in the third person. The use of the third person, with ποῦ, expresses Apollo's absence and failure to act; the address to the δαίμων expresses Croesus' emotional communication with the gods he wishes to condemn. At Eur. *HF* 338–47 Amphitryon addresses Zeus, who has failed to help; Hippolytus furiously asks Zeus if he can see what is happening (*Hipp.* 1363–9); in Bulgakov's *Master i Margarita* Matthew even tells God, self-defeatingly, 'you are deaf' (ch. 16, *Sobr. soč.* (5 vols.; Moscow, 1989–90), v. 174). Croesus' address presents a different shade. Except where a particular god

is clearly indicated, addresses to the δαίμων are usually made when
disaster has struck or is looming, and are commonly accompanied
by a negative epithet or a remark that the power has violently
attacked or greatly deprived the speaker. Cf. Alcm. 116 (ὀλέ), Aesch.
Pers. 472 (στυγνέ), 515–6, *Ag.* 1468, Soph. fr. 210. 37 Radt, *OT*
1311, Eur. *Alc.* 384, *IT* 156, Ar. *Clouds* 1264 (σκληρέ), *Peace* 1250.
At *Clouds* 1264 (and so probably at Eur. *Andr.* 1056) the speaker
goes on to address another, specific god. In our passage too, the
δαίμων is not a nameable god; the epithet ὑπέρ[βι]ε is very likely to
be negative, to denote brutal and excessive use of power. However
conceived, the δαίμων is sufficiently connected to the gods in general
to receive the reproaches of Croesus. But it is the destructive, not
the beneficent, side of the divine which seems most actual, and it is
with that that he communicates.

Assaults on the gods vary in intensity of tone, and in elevation
(Euripides' Amphitryon is less passionate, Creusa less elevated;
Bulgakov's Matthew is outstandingly undignified). Here passion,
concision, and sublime eloquence are at their highest. The two
questions match each other exactly in metre; the second is made
even more forceful by its position at the start of a period. The
passage is bold as well as emotional. Divine criticism is pushed to
the furthest point, but within the redemptive shape of the story;
to this shape it gives tremendous force and depth. Polydeuces' im-
passioned but uncritical prayer in Pind. *Nem.* 10. 76–9 (cf. Führer
(1967), 133–5) shows how far Pindar stands from such theological
audacity. The connections to tragedy are apparent, especially to
Aeschylus (but not in my view *Ag.* 182), and to Euripides (note
Tro. 1060–80 etc.).

ποῦ of course implies 'nowhere' (cf. e.g. [Aesch.] *PV* 546), and in
the first question perhaps suggests uselessness too (cf. e.g. Hom. *Il.*
13. 219, Eur. *Hel.* 453). In the second question the idea of absence
is more literal and terrible; cf. Dostoevsky, *Bratja Karamzovy*, bk.
7, ch. 2 (*Sobr. soč.* (30 vols.; Leningrad, 1972–90), xiv. 307), 'Wher-
ever (*Gde že*) was Providence and its finger?', and especially Hardy,
Tess ch. 11 (Oxford edn. (1983), 102) 'But, might some say, where
was Tess's guardian angel? where was the providence of her simple
faith? Perhaps . . . he was talking', etc. The second question is
made ironic by the name of Apollo at 29, and 58–60 will reinforce
the point. Apollo's role in predicting and advising makes him es-

pecially liable to criticism (Aesch. fr. 350 Radt etc.), and to ironic complications.

40–6. ἀ[ε]ικελίωc κτλ. (45–6) certainly give one of the horrors attendant on the fall of a city. It is natural to suppose that 41–5 (to Πακτωλόc) do so too, though it is possible that this theme began only in 43. The familiar constituents turn into accusations against the gods; the asyndeton in 45 indicates a strident series.

40. We do not know how strong the emphasis on the physical building is (note the plural in the sense of 'family' at Pind. *Ol.* 2. 45). But the mention of Alyattes must stress the royal line which is now ended, as well as suggesting the wealth of that ruler, with his famous tomb. ἔρρουc]ιν fits the space, but that is only a necessary condition.

43. ἄcτυ: there is likely to have been a contrast for the listener with the description of Syracuse in 15–16. βρυ- there may even have created a connection or contrast with μυρίων in 41.

44–6.]δίναc | Πακτωλόc: the point is likely to be the staining of the river with blood (13. 165, 27. 36). Kenyon's supplement fits the space better than Blass's, unless we suppose a considerable leftward shift in the margin. One might contrast the scenes at Delphi's and Olympia's rivers, though -δίναc is a standard element. The riches brought by the gold-bearing river may have been underlined by the first part of the compound.

ἀ[ε]ικελίωc κτλ.: there may have been an implicit opposition between the killing of males (blood) and the enslavement of women; but the emphasis certainly falls on the female sex. Female pathos runs through the whole narrative. It is especially striking that Croesus should lay this stress on the women. Since his own womenfolk are with him, and since he is still free to act, these γυνα[ῖ|κεc are probably the womenfolk of others. It is natural to link their ἐϋκτίτων μεγάρων and his own palace (32; 40?) and especially to compare those women and his own (no males in his household are mentioned). This utterance implies that he is not, in his way, without feeling for his own women; the emphatic ἀ[ε]ικελίωc suggests to the listener that his decision on their death is grounded in fierce morality and pride.

47. Speeches in Pindar sometimes end flowing over into the first period of a stanza (*Pyth.* 4. 155 (cf. 232), 8. 55, *Nem.* 10. 78). But the effect is not the same as with the detached and climactic sentence here. Without particles, it forms a culmination to the whole sequence, and the cue for action. The asyndeton, of which there may have been much in the speech, gives particular energy and abruptness to the conclusion. The first half of the line points to the second (death once hated is now dear); it also underlines the overturning of Croesus' mental world in the catastrophe. The paradoxical expression has links with Simonides (543 [**16**]. 18), and points forward to Euripides; indeed at *Tro.* 466 one should perhaps read οὕτω φίλα τὰ μὴ φίλ'. γλύκιστον is clearly stronger than φίλα. Even allowing for the freedom with which Bacchylides and Pindar use γλυκύς, the paradox of the last two words is extreme. It expresses absolute disruption, not simply an unthinking heroism.

48. ἀβ[ρο]βάταν is difficult; the difficulty does not seem quite to be seen e.g. by Schmitt (1975). It can hardly stand without a noun unless it is itself some technical word; at Aesch. *Pers.* 1072 γοᾶϲθ' ἀβροβάται it is somewhat strange as an adjective, but is unlikely to mean 'attendant' (Xerxes has no attendant, and Xerxes should not at this point be asking the chorus to become attendants). Some word for a dignitary would be conceivable there and here (the lighter of Myson's pyre has a name); but this all seems a little strained. A misunderstanding of Aeschylus by Bacchylides would be slightly more promising, but not much. The text may be corrupt, then (A¹ was itself originally corrupt and need not have been corrected rightly). Housman's τόθ' ἀβροβάταν ⟨ἐπέταν⟩ κέλευϲεν introduces the desired noun, at considerable cost. Purely to enlarge the field of possibility, one might consider ἀκρότατον. It would mean 'very high' (cf. Pind. *Ol.* 6 [**18**]. 70 n.), rather than 'the outmost part of' (cf. δι- 54, τὰ περιέϲχατα Hdt. 1. 86. 5). If ἀβροβατ- is kept, Bacchylides seems to be stressing again the foreign character of the scene.

49–52. δόμον: Pindar refers to Coronis' pyre as τείχει . . . ξυλίνωι (*Pyth.* 3. 38); the Danaids refer to their ship as a λινορραφὴϲ . . . δόμοϲ (Aesch. *Supp.* 135). The word here can hardly avoid connections with real houses (32, 40, 46). The pyre is what Croesus has come to after the splendour embodied in his palace. It is a kind of perversion of the tallness and heaping (note 33) associated in the poem with great wealth (13, 18). Even in adversity Croesus performs lavish gestures.

The girls are recurring characters in the narrative. Here, not as in 34–5, their cry is clearly one of terror at the imminent catastrophe.

One role of the cry is to make that apparent ending to the situation come closer; another is to generate the listener's own (notional) alarm. Their behaviour, particularly in turning to their mother, is meant to suit their gender and age (note the paradoxical 5. 139); and the generalization ἔχθιϲτοϲ marks a contrast with Croesus' remarkable γλύκιϲτον (47). But it would be unresponsive in the listener to feel only hierarchical scorn; θνατοῖϲιν shows the narrator's vision is wider.

ἀνὰ . . . ἔβαλλον: cf. Ar. *Frogs* 789. The 'up' suggests at least here a relatively young age for the girls, or else a lower hierarchical position (note the relative heights of the figures even on the Brygos Painter's skyphos Vienna inv. 3710 (*ARV*² 380. 171)). In either case, the object is pathos. For a child instinctively turning to the mother, who cannot help, cf. Sen. *Tro.* 792–3; ancient literature and art treat the ages of young people with fluidity. One should contrast with this raising of the arms the angry gesture of Croesus at 35–6.

The tense is different from that of ἔκ[λα]γον. The point might be that the first verb conveys an instantaneous reaction, the second highlights imperfectivity in relation to the death (cf. 17. 92–6?). But Bacchylides often combines aorists and imperfects, or uses imperfects where aorists might have been expected: cf. e.g. 5. 115, 139–40, 11. 48–55, 85–91, 110–12 (cf. e.g. Pind. *Pyth.* 9. 123). So one must be cautious. The point is relevant to 56 too.

ὁ γὰρ προφανὴϲ κτλ.: the narrator's generalization is a characteristic device of Bacchylides and Pindar (Alcm. 1 [1]. 16–17, 36–9 suggest a lyric tradition). In this passage, as say at Pind. *Nem.* 1. 53–4, it creates space before the peripeteia; but it also introduces the narrator's voice and wisdom, and underlines the relation of the narrative to larger things. προφανήϲ brings out irony within the story, and the general theme of mortal ignorance of the future. As at Bacch. 1. 176, or in Simon. 542 [15], the narrator's comment shows his wise detachment from the race he belongs to, as well as from the event. The internal narrator's generalization at 5. 129–35 is more self-defensive, and more tightly integrated (136). Similar things may be said of Alcaeus' narrator in 298 [10].

53–4. Even after ἀλλ', the narrator continues to bring the disaster closer. λαμπρόν, added to the Homeric phrase (*Il.* 6. 182), is in the context alarmingly vivid; it also perverts the glorious brightness of wealth (17).

55-6. Ζεύς: the monosyllable begins line and clause with effective brevity. One can hardly be confident that Bacchylides has himself added the god of Olympia here (Maehler (1982–97) i. 2. 35, 37): rain is Zeus' province, and the rescue by Apollo in Herodotus suits the special line of argument there (cf. 1. 91. 3). Within the poem, it is important that Zeus and Apollo now act in concert, not as in 26, 29.

If [μελαγκευ]θές, 'concealing through its blackness', should be right, the contrast with ξανθά[ν and λαμπρόν is effective. For ξανθά[ν cf. fr. 4. 65, and 18. 56.

Again the epode is a point of particular weight in the narrative; there is a definite pause at the end of it, as heaven brings in its own resolution of the situation, and a decisive reversal.

57-8. The comment refers forward more than backward, though Herodotus distances himself even from the sudden rain (hence the stress on his 'source' at 1. 87. 1). The idea occurs several times in Bacchylides and Pindar (17. 117–18, Pind. *Ol.* 13. 83, *Pyth.* 10. 48–50), mostly with the word ἄπιστον. Cf. Bundy (1986), 2–3; the idea of climax is more promising than that of imminent praise (note the first and second examples above). The emphasis on belief also presents a narrator pious rather than naïve; the third example is overtly first-person. The declaration here has some functions specific to the context. It marks the story of this recent figure as outside ordinary experience, as myth. It also matches the comment in 51–2, and sets the wise narrator's knowing perception of mortals against his humble acceptance of the illimitable divine.

Apollo's title gives the name even more weight than that of Zeus at 55, or than his own at 29. He must come to the fore in this sequence to stress the causality of reward.

59. The destination suits Apollo: the Hyperboreans are his protégés (Pind. *Ol.* 3. 16, *Pyth.* 10. 34–6). Bacchylides again exploits the striking brevity of his stanza, and gives the event in the strophe with forceful concision. There is no elaboration on the Hyperboreans as in Pindar. On them cf. Brown (1992).

γ]έρον|τα contrasts with κούραις. The two words also present two particularly helpless categories of people delivered by the god. γ]έρον|τα has thematic point (see on 88–9). Croesus is not portrayed as old by Myson. His old age had not been mentioned before

by Bacchylides; one may (in my opinion) compare the end of the
Antigone.

60. The explicit mention of the daughters produces a pleasing sense
of elaborate plotting; it also conveys again the breadth of the nar-
rator's sympathies.

κατ[έν]αϲϲε suggests the 'ever after', not merely the happiness of
escape. A state of felicity has been restored.

61–6. The connection of 61–6 with 17–22 is strongly marked; but
this is not a straightforward ring as at 11. 110–12, cf. 40–2. Un-
less 41–2 mentioned Croesus' dedications, which is not particu-
larly likely, the narrative now climactically makes explicit what
had in fact underlain it (cf. especially 38–9). Hieron's dedications
now appear again, and are explicitly ranked as unsurpassed among
Greek offerings, but beneath those of the Oriental, past, and quasi-
mythical Croesus. Cf. 5. 4–5. As at 17–22, Hieron appears not as
the target of admonition (however unnecessary), but as an example
of the ideal conduct. The link here does not directly promise Hi-
eron the same kind of divine deliverance (for example from death);
the formal accent turns out to be on praise. γ]έρον|τα may create
a connection with Hieron; but the miraculous nature of Croesus'
rescue also creates a certain incommensurability. The application
to Hieron's future is left hanging, subtly and poignantly, and the
poem in fact develops less optimistically than the myth suggests.
(Myths are examples, but are also different.)

61. δι' εὐϲέβειαν: the start of the antistrophe comes with great force,
separating event from cause, and returning to the theme which the
narrative was to establish. The stem is given no less strength at
Soph. *Phil.* 1441–4.

For Croesus' dedications at Delphi see Hdt. 1. 51 (for Gyges'
1. 14. 1–2); there is archaeological evidence of his contribution at
Ephesus (Lessing and Oberleitner (1978), 15). See also Mellink
(1967), 172, for a rich later excavation; and the introduction to
the commentary on Sappho above. The supremacy of Lydia over
Greece here would not seem remarkable to Greeks.

62. ἀγαθέαν: a standard epithet for the place in Bacchylides and
Pindar (Bacch. 5. 41 etc.), derived from epic; it is highly relevant
here.

⟨ἀπ⟩έπεμψε: editors, rightly rejecting Kenyon's ἐπ-, have been
seduced by the neatness of ἀν- (cf. Housman (1972), ii. 444). But

ἀπ- is the obvious prefix for sending offerings (cf. e.g. Hdt. 8. 121. 2,
Thuc. 4. 134. 1). Jebb (1905), 261, implies that ἀπ- would only suit
'a Lydian point of view'; but ἀποπέμπω is often used of offerings
etc. within Greece, or even of things sent to the speaker's city (e.g.
Ar. *Ach.* 113, Isocr. *Paneg.* 31). ἀν- is not justified by sending inland
or upward (the steepness of Delphi will scarcely be alluded to in
so undetailed a passage). Polybius' use of ἀναπέμπω, however it is
to be viewed, is scarcely relevant here (Jebb is misled by the word
'metropolis' in LSJ'). For Ar. *Thesm.* 583, 1045 see Deubner (1932),
54. A''s omissions, encouraged by the dispensability of syllables or
particles, are adequately explained by a sequence like αναπεπ: cf.
the next line and e.g. 5. 193.

64. The address to Hieron comes with great force; it is the first in the
poem. The subject of an epinician poem is most commonly spoken
about in the third person, and address is intrinsically striking. In
poem 5 an arresting address begins; but from the first antistrophe
on, references to Hieron are third-person. In *Ol.* 1, for example,
Hieron is not addressed until 106. The addresses at 6. 10–16 and
13. 67–76 seem to be the only other addresses of victors extant in
Bacchylides. In this poem address continues (74, 92); the narrator's
emotional involvement is to mark all this part of the poem.

μεγαίνητε Ἱέρων: the conjectures to remove the implausible
lengthened final vowel are so unwelcome (-ητ' ὤ Wilamowitz, etc.)
that one might just wonder whether to introduce two lesser licences
with μεγαίνητος. The lengthening of -ος before a name, analogous
to the hiatus before a name at 92, *al.*, is paralleled at Pind. *Ol.*
6 [**18**]. 77, *Pyth.* 3. 6 (-ν is different; note for -ς Bacch. 17. 90). For
the nominative instead of the vocative, especially common with an
adjective, or an adjective and noun together, cf. e.g. Hom. *Il.* 4.
189, Pind. *Nem.* 3. 76, fr. 157, Eur. *Andr.* 348, *Hel.* 1399. The cor-
ruption would be self-explanatory. The epithet gives emphasis to
praise, not hope, for Hieron.

θελήσει: the subject of πέμψαι, as of θελήσει, can only be [ο]ὔ|
τι[ς] . . . βροτῶν. Presumably, then, the reluctance to utter is due to
a fear of certain ridicule. The tone, though encomiastic, is contained
by a certain negativity and obliqueness (cf. Pind. *Pyth.* 2. 58–61).
'You, Hieron, have given more gold than anyone' would not sound
the same.

65–6. As suits the address and the argument, the expression is much more direct than in 17–21, which did not mention Hieron's act of sending the gold. Theopomp. *FGrHist* 115 F 193 (Phaenias fr. 11 Wehrli), oversimplifying, presents Gyges, Croesus, Gelon, Hieron as the givers of gold to Delphi: before, Delphi had had none. Herodotus' emphasis on gold is also notable (1. 14. 1, cf. 51). Cf. Maaß (1993), 138–48.

βροτῶν: cf. 8. 22–5 οὔτιϲ ἀνθρώπων κ[αθ' Ἕλλα]ναϲ κτλ. (and 4. 15, fr. 20 C. 21–4). Here 'mortals' comes at the end, separated from the Greeks at the beginning, to whom it is limited; the arrangement gives stress to Hieron's glory, and creates a parallel with the θνατῶν used in regard to Croesus (61).

67–8. The idea of praise (not of any reward) is developed. πάρεϲτιν appears as a sort of converse to [ο]ὔ|τι[ϲ] . . . θελήϲει (cf. Maehler (1982–97), i/2. 53); but it is not the donor himself who would do the praising. After the superlatives and the address of the negative sentence, the positive sentence is deliberately restrained in its praise, as if it gave an understated minimum that almost anyone would accept as true. The tone particularly suits Hieron's own ethos (69, 70 nn.).

εὖ λέ]γειν is itself a fairly abstracted rather than a clamorous expression. Cf. εὖ ἀκούειν at Pind. *Pyth.* 1. 99, *Nem.* 1. 32; but note also Bacch. 9. 72.

φθόνωι πιαίνεται: imaginative language is devoted to the unjust envy that resists the demand of merit for praise. Cf. 5. 188–9, 13. 199–205. πιαίνεται connotes here an unhealthy but engrossing diet, cf. Pind. *Pyth.* 2. 54–6, Aesch. *Ag.* 276. For φθόνοϲ in Pindar see Bulman (1992).

69. φίλιππον . . . ἀ[ρ]ήϊον: the terms are moderate, but in their very plainness enhance the active and warlike image of Hieron, parallel to that of Syracuse, which Bacchylides and Pindar often present. Cf. e.g. 5. 1–2, 34, Pind. *Ol.* 1. 23, *Pyth.* 2. 1–2. Hieron is decidedly not shown as an armchair sportsman.

70. ϲκᾱπτρ[ο]ν: cf. Pind. *Ol.* 6 [18]. 93, and for the strong emphasis on Hieron's kingship e.g. *Ol.* 1. 12, 113–14, *Pyth.* 2. 13–14, 3. 70 (τύραννον 85 is a mere synonym, like πρύτανι at *Pyth.* 2. 58); note too Bacch. 4. 3 ἀϲτύθεμιν. Naturally Herodotus (3. 125. 2), Xenophon (*Hieron*), Aristotle (*Pol.* 1312ᵃ39–ᵇ16 etc.), Strabo (5. 4. 9), Plutarch (*Them.* 24. 7, *Pyth. Or.* 403 C), etc. think of him as a 'tyrant' (contrast e.g. Polyb. 5. 88. 4, Diod. 11. 38. 3, 66. 1, and note App. *Sic.* fr. 2. 4 Viereck–Roos for Hieron II as 'tyrant'). But

the address to Gelon ὦ βαcιλεῦ Cυρηκοcίων at Hdt. 7. 161. 2 strongly
indicates that Gelon and Hieron wished to be thought of as kings
(contrast 154. 1, 156. 3, Thuc. 6. 4. 2). Cf. Ϝαναcc[of Polyzalus
at Gela (*SEG* 3 (1927–9). 396; Wade-Gery (1933), 101–4, Jeffrey
(1990), 266). The poetry is not merely creating a convention of
its own. The stylish restraint of Gelon's and Hieron's inscriptions
need not at all conflict with the title; one would not in any case
expect to find an individual's name on coins (and one does not on
Group II coins from Gela either, cf. Jenkins (1970)). For cτρατα[γ]έ
at Bacch. 5. 1–2 cf. 17. 120–1 etc. Otherwise on this question:
e.g. Wilamowitz (1901), 1275–9 (too legalistic and Mommsenian);
Asheri (1992), 149.

Διό[c takes up 11; but the vocabulary (cκᾶπτρ[ο]ν) is again more
direct, and there are no superlatives. The name, advancing on that
of Ares, resoundingly ends the triad.

71. The arrangement of triads allows the narrator's special concern
to receive prominence, despite the syntax. The point is Hieron's
culture, as well as the poet's praise; cf. Pind. *Ol.* 1. 14–15.

73–6 encourage caution in the addressee rather than confidence;
this is in the context a notable development.

74. The commentary suggests an imperative (Lobel (1956), 49;
Lloyd-Jones (1958), 17); we would need more of the context to be
sure that cκοπεῖc was wrong, but the evidence makes cκόπει appear
more probable.

βραχ[: probably the explanation ὅτι ὀλιγοχρο-[belongs here (Lo-
bel). The brevity of life is likely to be the underlying point; βραχ[
might have been accusative, say after an imperative, but the δ' in 75
makes this less probable.

75. The narrator, with aloof wisdom, comments on the infatuations
of hope; cf. 9. 18, 13. 157–8 (contrast 220–1), and e.g. Sem. fr. 1.
6–10 West, Sol. fr. 13. 33–6 West.

76–7. There is a considerable disparity in space between the guar-
anteed πτερό]εccα and the expected ἐφαμ]ερίων. It might be noted
that the repetition from ἐφάμερον in 73 would not be altogether wel-
come in this author, whereas that line might furnish an easy source
of corruption.

The remark Bacchylides gives to Apollo might not have been
original itself, though [Epich.] fr. 267 Kaibel does not prove it.

There could have been a poetic source in which it was made to or by Admetus, but this is uncertain (Σ Ar. *Wasps* 1238 a (Steinhausen (1910), 6, 8, 14), Ar. fr. 444 Kassel–Austin). The saying will at the least have been adapted (note βαθύπλουτον); and the figure of Admetus is significant in the poem. He was another person whom Apollo famously delivered from death: cf. Eur. *Alc.* 11–12, 30–4, Aesch. *Eum.* 723–4; the story is exploited in Herodotus' version of Croesus (1. 91. 2–3). Yet for all Apollo's deliverance, Admetus must still accept mortal uncertainty: θνατὸν εὖντα, the immortal begins. Any hope which the example might offer Hieron would thus be muted, as well as mythical, and would be overborne by the explicit advice against thinking to know the future. The profound, balanced, positive speech of the god is opposed to the ignorant, impassioned, life-renouncing speech of Croesus. The narrator takes into his discourse the complex and paradoxical wisdom of the god, which enhances his own authority. The epode, anticipated by one line, is made the home for material of particular weight.

78. διδύμουc: in comparison with [Epicharmus]' version (ὡc πολὺν ζήcων χρόνον χὢc ὀλίγον, οὕτωc διανοοῦ), Bacchylides' sets up the paradox elaborately. Two contradictory opinions ('two' emphasized by word-order and stanza-end) cannot be nursed simultaneously, if the opinions are literally held. But this strange state of mind is to be set against the *naïveté* of winged hope; it also counterbalances any extreme of gloom. These clashing quasi-beliefs remove one from irrational emotion and action. Cf., without the contradiction, Epicur. *Ep. Men.* 127. ἀέξειν implies a conscious effort.

79–80. αὔριον ὄψεαι | μοῦνον κτλ.: the word-order is effective and discouraging. More common is the idea that one may not see tomorrow, e.g. Eur. *Alc.* 783–4, Hor. *Epist.* 1. 4. 13 (*crede*). The point here is about mental enjoyment as well as the actual use of wealth.

81–2. The figure, fifty years from now, is concrete, but lavish. Various Oriental monarchs in Herodotus reign for around fifty years; Amasis had recently ruled for 44. βαθύπλουτον, and the appearance of the number in poetry, remind one of Anacr. 361, which speaks of great wealth and reigning for 150 years, and alludes to a long-lived king of rich Tartessus. ὅcια δρῶν shows that part of the point is to act piously, for so long a time actually gives great scope for disaster (cf. Bacch. fr. 25), whether the gods cause it as punishment or mitigate it as reward. Herodotus takes up the idea, and combines it with Sol. fr. 27 West, at 1. 30. 2–3. Hieron has already shown his piety in his offerings at Delphi.

βαθύπλουτον: the word may hint at the risks and responsibilities of great wealth; but more important is the optimistic conception (within this γνώμα) that the long life will in fact turn out to be prosperous.

τελεῖc does not refer, as we might have expected, to the final moment which proves one to have been happy; the accusative of duration ἔτεα shows that it denotes, more cheerfully, a process of continuous accomplishment. The thought is made to sound more positive than the emphasis on brevity in 74; but the idea remains, not a statement, but one half of a contradictory pair of 'beliefs'. Hieron himself will not have envisaged another fifty years.

83. The depth of the elaborate sentence 78–82 is resolved into a beautifully simple imperative in two parts.

84. κερδέων is transformed beyond the material (cf. e.g. Pind. *Isth.* 1. 51, with ὕψιcτον, after 45, 47); at the same time, it draws on its own natural semantic range (cf. e.g. ἀκέρδεια at Pind. *Ol.* 1. 53 for the results of impiety). The sentence is strongly linked to 22; one contrasts the excited vehemence of the mortal narrator in that part of the poem with the god's cool tone here. The speech and epode end harmoniously together.

85. The narrator resumes the speaking voice, with an emphatic γαρύω. Yet the exciting absence of connection itself implies a connection between the god's words and the narrator's. Particularly after 74, φρονέοντι will refer to Hieron (cf. Pind. *Pyth.* 4. 142, fr. 105 a. 1); contrast cυνέτοιcιν and ξυνετοῖc at Pind. *Ol.* 2. 85, Eur. *IT* 1092 (cf. Theogn. 681–2), and the article at *Nem.* 4. 31. cυνετά refers forward, principally; but it also reflects on the passage before, no less challenging to the mind. The remark does not mean simply that Hieron has no real need to be informed (note 74); the narrator implies the intelligence and moral understanding of both his addressee and himself. Not everyone will comprehend: such is the pose. One may contrast the determination of Sappho's narrator that all should 'understand' her (16 [5]. 5–6). The remark implies too the special relevance of the whole section to Hieron, and a personal communication.

Krummen (1990), 285, interestingly sees a reference to mysteries and eschatology here and elsewhere in the poem; but ὅϲια δρῶν should not be detached from its place in the argument.

85–7. This passage (designated (1)) is more than an instance of the broad term 'priamel' (for which see Race (1982)). At (2) Simon. 541. 3–5 (see introduction to 542 [**15**]), (3) Pind. *Ol.* 1. 1–8, (4) 3. 42–5, we notice striking recurrences and connections: the mention of particular things, water (1, 2, 3, 4, placed first in 3 and 4), other elements (αἰθήρ; note the fire in 3), gold (1, 2, 3, 4); resemblances of phrasing (ἄριϲτον 3, ἀριϲτεύει 4; ἀμίαντοϲ 1, οὐ μιαίνεται 2); a notable obscurity (especially 1, 3, 4), and bold movements between things of seemingly different kinds. Sapph. 16 [**5**]. 1–4 brings out how different a priamel can be. Evidently we have to do with a type of passage particular to these poets. It is significant for some aspects of their self-presentation that an appearance of difficulty, here explicitly signalled, should form part of this convention. The use of the elements makes such passages the more elevated; the traditional gold gains a special force in this poem.

What is the argument? The sequence in 85–9 as a whole contrasts things free from change and corruption with man, in whom occur irreversible change and decay. Gold appears in (2) as free from corruption; in (3) and (4) it appears as the best form of wealth, just as water there appears as 'best'. Now, the purity and value of gold go closely together, as in Ibyc. S151 [**11**]. 42–3; and movement between them is made especially easy by the interrelation of the four passages. In (1), the latest example, the sequence indicates that the incorruptibility of gold is the main and underlying point; but this is made more oblique by dwelling, in terms themselves oblique, on the value of gold, which in unmiserly hands brings festivity, victory, joy. The singling out of gold suits the poem; the static truth about gold poignantly contrasts with the forces that affect human pleasure.

The placing of the dominant noun is carefully varied in these lines; so is the syntax of the predicate (adjective, verb, noun). The most important member, 88–90, is sadly extended, by contrast with these brisk clauses on the things that do not change.

βαθύϲ adds to the grandeur; it is itself both arresting and conventional within the genre (Ibyc. S223 (*a*). ii. 6–7, Bacch. 5. 16).

πόντου is essential to the argument (Hippocr. *Airs* 8. 5); it also adds to the largeness of the passage.

88. π[. .]εντα: αρ would fit the space, but, despite Jebb (1905), 265, ρο would do so too (cf. 11. 118). Does the passage speak of a second life after the first, beginning with youth, or of sudden rejuvenation? The former would be defended by Eur. *HF* 656–64, and would fit the argument well (cf. 90–1). However, it is not clear that παρίημι could mean 'finish' rather than 'wait for a period, allow a time to pass'; at Soph. *OC* 1229 the verb is πάρειμι, as the whole stanza shows. And if immortality were the idea, it would be indicated more emphatically. Rejuvenation, then, which is more naturally placed during old age than before it (Hom. *Il.* 9. 445–6 etc.). παρέντα would be 'letting go, forgetting' the old age already on one; the more determined προέντα would not be without attractions, if there were better evidence for the active in a suitable sense. The thought of a second youth and of escaping death go naturally together as a pair: cf. Theogn. 1009–11, and e.g. Mimn. fr. 2. 4–5 West. In denying one, the narrator is tactfully suggesting denial of the other too, as the continuation shows. The passage in one direction appears to take up the εὔφραινε θυμόν of Apollo's speech; but in the other direction, and more emphatically, it indicates the transience of life. The narrator is looking back also to 73–4; somewhat more sternly than the god, he is not encouraging two simultaneous 'beliefs' about the length of life, but facing its irrevocable movement.

The negative implications of this movement were relevant to Hieron, who must at least have been over 40, had been ill for some years, and was to die a year or two later. He is likely to have been at least around 20 when put in charge of Gela by his brother in 485 (so at least around 37 now), and at least around 30 when married to his first wife, before Himera in 480 (so at least around 43 now). (On his wives see Philist. *FGrHist* 556 F 50, Timae. 566 F 97. Timae. F 21 could be referred to Hieron's death (so Jacoby (1923–), III b. 544), and so suggest Deinomenes was under say 17 in 466; but chronology and the role of Aetna in *Nem.* 9 make it more likely that it refers to guardianship of Deinomenes in 476/5 (cf. Thuc. 2. 80. 6 etc.).)

The initial ἀνδρί matches θνατόν 78. It is the mortal, not the god, who dwells on the divine law which confines humans (οὐ θέμις).

89. γῆρας comes forcefully at the start of the stanza; ἥβαν begins the next period and ends the sentence, grimly. πολιόν and θάλ[εια]ν also match each other. γῆραϲ recalls the [γ]έρον|τα Croesus (59–60); Hieron, it is here implied, will receive no such treatment.

90–1. ἀρετᾶ[c] . . . **φέγγοc:** the ring encompasses and dominates the sentence. ἀρετᾶ[c] stands out as the leading noun, like αἰθήρ, ὕδωρ, χρυ|cόc, ἀνδρί; βροτῶν is relegated to second place. φέγγοc helps it to have some of the elemental quality of the earlier things; οὐ μινύθει recalls οὐ cάπεται in syntax, and joins ἀρετά to the series that had seemed over when ἀνδρί appeared. c[ώμ]ατι is made to seem an inferior irrelevance. After the low point reached by ἀνδρὶ κτλ., a resounding and unprovisional redemption is achieved; it is achieved, as ἀλλὰ κτλ. reveal, by the narrator precisely in his role as poet, and in the present utterance. The line of thought is a common one in these poets (Pind. *Pyth.* 3. 114–15 etc.; note also Simon. 531. 8–9); but the drama of the poem's sequence makes it a powerful and hard-won moment.

c[ώμ]ατι: for the use of cῶμα in antitheses on mortality cf. e.g. Pind. *Parth.* 1. 14–15, *Thren.* fr. 131 b. 1–2 (fr. 59. 2–3 Cannatà Fera).

92. Μοῦcα: the goddess is immortal (contrast βροτῶν), and so implies the eternity of fame through poetry, though composed by a mortal. Cf. 9. 84, 87. τρ[έφει supports this understanding; cf. 13. 61–2 and, in context, Pind. *Ol.* 10. 95–6.

Ἱέρων: the simple vocative, without epithets, comes with force and frankness at the end of the poem (cf. Pind. *Ol.* 1. 107). It matches the open laudation (contrast 63–6). The name comes at the same point in the stanza as at 4 and 64 (Maehler); the hiatus marks the special type of word (cf. 2. 7, 16. 5). τρ[έφειc] would suit the space; but the word-order is unattractive. Although commas around vocatives are artificial, one would expect the order of either Soph. *OC* 101 ἀλλά μοι, θεαί or Theog. 341 ἀλλά, Ζεῦ, τέλεcόν μοι, Ὀλύμπιε, καίριον εὐχήν.

ὄλβου: the crucial word ends the stanza (cf. 22).

93–4. κάλλιcτ' . . . **ἄνθεα:** the emphasis is not now on quantity but on quality. The general phrasing can encompass both the victory and the tripods. ὄλβου . . . ἄνθεα is a striking expression; it is notable that ἄνθοc with a genitive is often used of song in Bacchylides and Pindar (Bacch. 16. 8–9, fr. 4. 63, Pind. *Ol.* 6 [18]. 105, 9. 48–9, *Pae.* 12 (G1). 4–5). Hieron's displays of wealth are already something beautiful; they demand, as the next clause implies, the answering beauties of song.

πράξα[ντι] δ' εὖ: unambiguous achievement, simply expressed, that requires recognition. Cf. 5. 190; 13. 65–6.

95. Instead of a positive personal statement, the negative stresses the moral obligation, and replaces adulation with litotes. The requirement for glory is taken for granted. κόcμ[ον continues the fame already implicit in ἐπεδ[είξ]αο θνατοῖc.

96–8. The poem ends with a difficult passage, which is of much importance for the narrator's self-presentation. There are two interlocking problems: †καλων†, and the question whether Bacchylides will be praised or Hieron. The latter is more fundamental, and will be considered first. If Hieron is to be praised, as one might naturally suppose, χάριν will have to denote the poem (so Fränkel (1962), 530 n. 44, followed by Maehler (1982–97), i/2. 60–1). Parallels for this usage of the singular (as probably of the plural) are suspicious. All appear in the accusative. A dative, genitive, or possessive pronoun accompanies them (most often of what is praised, as at Bacch. 14. 19, Pind. *Pyth.* 11. 11–12, *Nem.* 1. 6); they could be taken as 'for the sake of', or 'because of' (the extension with adjective at Pind. *Ol.* 10. 78 does not affect the basic sense). The verb usually has an object already; at Pind. *Pyth.* 2. 70–1 the accusative χάριν would be the wrong case for an object of ἄντομαι in this sense, at *Pyth.* 10. 64 the verb is normally intransitive elsewhere, at *Nem.* 7. 75–6 an economic sense is made primary by the context (the genitive plural at *Isth.* 1. 6 is probably metaphorical too). We may doubt, then, whether the usage is adequately attested. καί would also be awkward. It is not attractive for it to denote Bacchylides in addition to Simonides and Pindar; even earlier poets in general could not be clearly understood from the context. An 'even' of false modesty is implausible too (note μελιγλώccου). A lesser disadvantage of this view of χάριν is that ὑμνέω would not, as elsewhere in Pindar and Bacchylides and as usual in poets, have an external object, what is sung of.

We are driven to take Bacchylides as the object of praise. καί encourages us: the context suggests that it denotes Bacchylides in addition to Hieron. This matching of patron's and poet's glory is found in other closes: see on Ibyc. S151 [**11**]. 46–8 (note Pind. *Ol.* 1. 115–16). Those closes, and Bacch. 4. 7–8, 5. 13–14, 16–30, 9.

4, 10. 10–13, 19. 11–14 make the pride here credible. Why should
Bacchylides be *sung* of? The main point is the reversal: the singer
too will be sung. What of χάριν? The standard view would make it
the object of ὑμνήcει. 'The beauty of (the songs of) the nightingale'
would be tolerable in itself (not 'charm', which can be used to
import illegitimately a certain conception of Bacchylides). χάριc is
not unambiguously used by Bacchylides or Pindar to mean 'beauty',
as it is in earlier poets; but at 23. 7 (P. Oxy. 2368) the meaning looks
quite likely (possibly of song), and one may note χαρίεν at Pind.
Pyth. 5. 107 (of song), cf. *Ol*. 1. 30. This meaning for the word
is much more satisfactory than the meaning required by the other
view, and also lets ὑμνέω be used normally. It is preferable too to
personifying Χάριν, which does not belong to a poet in Pindar or
Bacchylides; even Theocr. 16 does not support the singular. But
there is perhaps another possibility.

The letter after the gap in 96 must be κ or χ: κ is possible enough,
although the distance between its right-hand tips would be some-
what small. But the genitive is hard to justify. There is little help
in genitives after ἀλήθεια referring to events, or in Hom. *Od*. 11.
506–7 (note 505). 'The truth about beautiful things' would in any
case be unappealing; and the other instances of cὺν ἀλαθείαι make
the self-contained phrase much more desirable (8. 20–1, 9. 85, cf.
5. 187, 11. 26–7, 13. 202, 204). καλέων (Jurenka), with synizesis,
produces an unsuitable verb; κλέων (Fränkel) could do with an ob-
ject; λακών (Housman) is not attested in these poets, or altogether
apt in meaning. More promising might be to produce a different
object for ὑμνήcει. We would then make χάριν mean 'because of, to
the honour of', a construction not only clearly attested but common
in contexts of singing praises (cf. 14. 19–22, Pind. *Pyth*. 11. 9–12,
Nem. 1. 4–6, *Pae*. 9 (A1). 36–7); μελιγλώccου would give χάριν its
more usual position in this sense. A¹ often puts the wrong case (e.g.
9. 46), and καλά 'fine things' would make a satisfactory parallel with
Hieron, answering κάλλιcτ', but claiming less.

However we emend, the main import of the last lines is now clear.
One may see the emphasis on the poet as doing several things. It
suits the epinician ethos to have the narrator no servile sycophant,
but a proud individual speaking his mind; and at the end of sub-
stantial epinician poems straightforward praise of the victor is most
often avoided as too crude in tone. Self-referentiality is also impor-
tant to the genre. In this poem the elegance of manner seals off with

a light touch the arduous argument and disturbing content. Atten-
tion is directed to the poetry as art: one may contrast ὑμνήϲει here
with ὕμνει in the opening stanza, μελιγλώϲϲου with γλυκύδωρε. At
the same time, consciousness of the artistic achievement obliquely
reinforces the argument on Hieron's eternal praise.
   The manner of self-reference (cf. Nünlist (1998), 351) accords
with other passages in Bacchylides. The comparison with another
bird, the eagle, in 5. 16–30 is used by Pindar, and was probably
conventional for the genre (note Ibyc. S223 (*a*). ii. 7); but 4. 7–8
ἀδυεπὴϲ . . . Οὐρ[αν]ίαϲ ἀλέκτωρ, 10. 10 ναϲιῶτιν . . . λιγύφθογγον
μέλιϲϲαν, and 19. 11 εὐαίνετε Κηΐα μέριμνα show an ornateness and
poise not characteristic of Pindar's self-reference. In this passage
the phrasing combines a vivid and attractive image of the poet with
a graceful distance.

μελιγλώϲϲου: used again at fr. 4. 63, and by the Pindaric poet
at Ar. *Birds* 908. The word develops the epic, and lyric, μελίγηρυϲ
(Hom. *Od.* 12. 187, *al.*; Alcm. 26. 1, Pind. *Ol.* 11. 4, *al.*); cf. Pind.
Ol. 6 [**18**]. 21 n.

The organization of the poem may now be summarily resumed.
The opening exultant celebration of Hieron is succeeded by a kind
of myth; the disaster of Croesus' situation there contrasts with Hi-
eron's state, but Croesus' final deliverance does not lead into the
straightforwardly encouraging application that we might have ex-
pected. More celebration of Hieron, in a different key, leads into
complex reflections on mortality; these partly suggest a complica-
tion of the simple [ὄ]λβιον and τρὶϲ εὐδαίμ[ων of the beginning. Issues
are faced here, but not with the passionate simplicity of Croesus'
speech, in thought or expression. The final resolution is through the
great achievements of Hieron, which remain central, and through
the actual poem, which turns in upon itself. The poem is very much
a sequence and an argument. Like other major epinician poems, it
deploys the generic ingredients of narrative, generality, a specific
situation, and the relationship between narrator and addressee to
create an entity, dense, subtle, and unique.

PINDAR

Introduction

PINDAR's city of Thebes was no cultural desert, for all the jibes on Boeotians. In the sixth century the sanctuary of the Ptoion, under the rule of Thebes, shows an extraordinary quantity of fine kouroi (principally from Boeotia). Sculpture in the later sixth century and the fifth century shows some stelai of good quality; various close links are apparent with Ionic and Attic sculpture. Among other impressive artefacts is an extremely accomplished bronze bull 12.55 cm. long, full of character (Athens NM 10565). One would not expect any particular glories in the field of pottery, now completely dominated by Athens; but Boeotian pottery of the period, while not attempting anything like the Attic level of artistry, often reveals a salient energy and humour. Fine vases were imported, besides, from Athens to Thebes. The various Theban festivals for which Pindar wrote poems must have been aesthetically memorable occasions. Pindar's poetry for Thebes and Thebans illustrates too the rich religious life of the city, with its famous cults and its fabled past; and it demonstrates the importance in the festivals of aristocratic families striving for renown.[1]

[1] Cf. *Parth.* 2, and probably 1 (Schachter (1981–), i. 83–5; he is surprised by the family element); *Isth.* '3/4'. 79–90b, with the agon (Schachter (1981–), ii. 20–30). See also *Pyth.* 11. 1–8, *Hymn* 1, *Pae.* 7 (D7), 9 (A1), fr. 66 (F3), *Dith.* 2, frr. 71, 94 c, 109, 194, 215?; *Isth.* 1, 7 (note 14–15), fr. 195. For the sculpture at the Ptoion, see Ducat (1971); for the reliefs see Schild-Xenidou (1972), 2–45, 152–78; further, for Attic and Ionic connections, see Heimberg (1973), 15–22, Stewart (1990), i. 248. Bull: Schmaltz (1980), 87–8. Pottery: Ure (1927), Waiblinger (1974), 25–48, Maffre (1975), 428–520. Attic vases in Thebes: Symeonoglou (1985), 248; see ibid. 104–48, 213–309 for the city in general. For the finds at the shrine of the Cabiri see Wolters, Bruns, *et al.* (1940–). Note also for the appeal, and spread, of Boeotian art e.g. the charming and accomplished domestic terracotta groups probably from Tanagra (*c.*475–450) found in Lipari, tombs 2514 and 2516. Synoptic accounts of Theban and Boeotian art: Demand (1982), ch. 7; van Effenterre (1989), 163–84.

It might be helpful for any closer study of Pindar to list, without completeness, which poems are covered by which 20th-cent. commentaries, other than commentaries on the whole of Pindar, and original editions of papyrus fragments (for which see Snell and Maehler (1987–9), ii, pp. vi–vii); one or two works are mentioned which cover several poems and are akin to commentaries in some respects. *Ol.* 1: Gerber (1982); Kirkwood (1982); Verdenius (1987–8); Fisker (1989); Instone (1996); also Krummen (1990); *Ol.* 2: Kirkwood (1982); Willcock (1995); *Ol.* 3: Verdenius (1987–8); also Krummen (1990); *Ol.* 6: Kirkwood (1982); *Ol.* 7: Kirkwood (1982);

Pindar's dated poems run from 498 to 446. In the course of this period Thebes' fortunes were drastically reversed. After the disaster of Plataea, in which it sided with the Persians, it seems to have lost its position as leader of the Boeotian League (if the league still existed); from 458 Boeotia was in some sense under Athenian domination. Yet, although 479–447 is undoubtedly a low point in Thebes' career, it is difficult to tell quite how radically existence changed for the worse, for the surviving people of high birth. The paucity of evidence is not necessarily a sign of prostration. *Isth.* 4 records the loss of four members of an aristocratic family in a battle (Plataea?: *Isth.* '3/4'. 34–5b); but a member of the family is still able to afford a four-horse chariot team. Pindar's Theban poems show cultic and aristocratic life continuing with vigour. At any rate, Athens and Thebes were two of the northernmost homes of poetry so far in mainland Greece. For all the vast difference between their fortunes in the course of this period, by the start of it the two cities had brought up the two greatest poets in the first half of the fifth century.[2]

It seems likely that Pindar claimed to belong to the Aegeidae

Verdenius (1987–8); Willcock (1995); also Young (1968); *Ol.* 10: Verdenius (1987–8); *Ol.* 11: Kirkwood (1982); Verdenius (1987–8); Willcock (1995); also Bundy (1986); *Ol.* 12: Kirkwood (1982); Verdenius (1987–8); *Ol.* 14: Kirkwood (1982); Verdenius (1987–8); *Pyth.* (all): Schroeder (1922); Gentili *et al.* (1995); also Burton (1962); *Pyth.* 1: Kirkwood (1982); *Pyth.* 2: Kirkwood (1982); Carey (1981); also Most (1985); *Pyth.* 3: Young (1968); *Pyth.* 4: Kirkwood (1982); Braswell (1988); *Pyth.* 5: Krummen (1990); *Pyth.* 7: Willcock (1995); *Pyth.* 8: Kirkwood (1982); Pfeijffer (1999); *Pyth.* 9: Carey (1981); Kirkwood (1982); Instone (1996); *Pyth.* 10: Kirkwood (1982); also Köhnken (1971); *Pyth.* 11: Young (1968); *Pyth.* 12: Köhnken (1971); *Nem.*: W. B. Henry is at work on a selection; I have not seen Waring (1984) (note also Bury (1890)); *Nem.* 1: Carey (1981); Kirkwood (1982); Braswell (1992); *Nem.* 2: Instone (1996); *Nem.* 3: Instone (1996); Pfeijffer (1999); *Nem.* 4: Willcock (1995); also Köhnken (1971); *Nem.* 5: Pfeijffer (1999); *Nem.* 6: Gerber (1999); *Nem.* 7: Carey (1981); Kirkwood (1982); also Köhnken (1971); Most (1985); *Nem.* 8: Köhnken (1971); *Nem.* 9: Braswell (1998); *Nem.* 11: Verdenius (1987–8); *Isth.* (all): Thummer (1968–9); Privitera (1982) (note also Bury (1892)); *Isth.* 1: Kirkwood (1982); Instone (1996); also Bundy (1986); *Isth.* 2: Verdenius (1987–8); *Isth.* 3: Willcock (1995); *Isth.* 4: Willcock (1995); also Köhnken (1971); Krummen (1990); *Isth.* 6: Kirkwood (1982); *Isth.* 7: Willcock (1995); *Isth.* 8: Carey (1981); *Hymn* 1 Kirkwood (1982); *Paeans*: Bona (1988); Rutherford (2000); *Paean* 2: Radt (1958); 6: Radt (1958); Kirkwood (1982); *Dithyrambs*: van der Weiden (1991); fr. 70 b: Kirkwood (1982); *Encomia*: van Groningen (1960); frr. 123, 124 a and b: Kirkwood (1982); *Threnoi*: Cannatà Fera (1990); frr. 131 b, 133 (frr. 59. 2–5, 65 Cannatà Fera): Kirkwood (1982); hymn to Pan: Lehnus (1979).

[2] For the history see Buck (1979), chs. 7–9; Demand (1982), ch. 2; Hornblower (1991–), i. 172; Lewis (1992), 96–7, 115–16, with Lewis (1997*a*), 20 n. 43.

(*Pyth.* 5. 72–81), a widespread Doric 'clan' that began in Thebes. If his son had a leading role in a Theban ritual (fr. 94 c), that might imply social distinction and perhaps distinguished origins. But the notion of noble birth may not have been particularly precise. Much more important is the image projected in his poems, as in Bacchylides', of a man who can be the friend of the families he writes for. Like Simonides and Bacchylides, he is a figure of international range (see the introduction to the commentary on Bacchylides, above). The types of poem he writes resemble theirs: principally 'public' poems for various rituals and celebrations, and also 'private' poems for important people's parties. (The opposition of public and private is unsatisfactory.) The genres he was classed as writing in also overlap with theirs: epinicians (Simonides, Bacchylides), paeans (Simon., Bacch.), dithyrambs (Simon., Bacch.), partheneia (Simon., Bacch.: so [Plut.] *Mus.* 1136 F), threnoi (Simon.), hymns (Bacch.), hyporchemata (Bacch.), prosodia (Bacch.), perhaps encomia (Bacch.?). Pindar's debt to Simonides (or certainly to the associated tradition) looks fundamental. Particularly interesting is a fragment like Simon. 526: many specific features suggest links with Pindar (cf. e.g. 526. 2 with *Pyth.* 3. 30, and *Nem.* 7. 3, fr. 232), but the whole style, manner, and thought would seem, if the lines came in Pindar, intensely Pindaric. Pindar turns all he appropriates from tradition into a way of speaking which within the poem strikes the listener as fresh and utterly personal.[3]

In dialect he essentially follows his tradition. Mostly the papyri

---

[3] The *Suda* (c 439) ascribes ἐγκώμια to Simonides; but, whatever the value of the source, it is likely to mean epinicians, which it does not mention. Cf. P. Oxy. 2438. 17. For possible 'encomia' by Bacchylides cf. frr. 20–20 G. One may naturally ignore the additions to Pindar's works in the *Suda* (π 1617) beyond the works in P. Oxy. 2438, the *Vita Ambrosiana*, and the quotations and papyri; cf. Gallo (1968), 42–5. For those 'genres' of which we have substantial remains in Pindar, the idea of definite types of poem appears broadly desirable, despite ancient and modern disputes on particular lyric poems and the occurrence of complicated occasions. The idea is often reinforced by internal evidence (note e.g. *Thren.* 3. 1–2 (fr. 56 Cannatà Fera) for paeans, and the whole fragment; *Dith.* fr. 70 b. 1–3 for dithyrambs, cf. also e.g. van der Weiden (1991), 15–16). Cf. Fowler (1987a), ch. 3; D'Alessio (1997); Rutherford (2000), 3–136. The odd term 'clan' is used in this chapter to denote large patrilineal groups with a mythical common ancestor, notably those two exceptional sets the Aegeidae and the Iamidae. What exactly the Aegeidae were even in Sparta is not wholly clear. The appearance of the name in Simon. 519 fr. 134 is interesting for its aristocratic currency. The date of Pindar's birth does not seem to have been established for antiquity by the context of fr. 193 or by any other work: so P. Oxy. 2438 suggests. It was thus unknown.

of Pindar and Bacchylides have Bacchylides eschewing Aeolic (i.e. Lesbian) features which Pindar adopts (participles in -οιϲα, -αιϲ, Μοῖϲα, etc.). Even if they are right, Pindar's use of such features will go back to earlier Doric lyric. A few things, most notably the use a number of times of ἐν 'for' ἐϲ, may plausibly be seen as borrowings from his own dialect. In metre Pindar again broadly follows tradition. Not only do the two main classes of dactylo-epitrite and elaborated aeolic, used also by Bacchylides, go back to Simonides; the idiosyncratic version of iambics seen in *Ol.* 2 and fr. 75 is used by Bacchylides, probably goes back to Simonides (541 is probably his), and is not visible earlier. Pindar's aeolic stanzas can look much more complicated than Bacchylides'; but Simon. 543 [16] (and its choice by Dionysius) warns us against underestimating the complexity of the earlier poet. Pindar and Bacchylides can include purely iambic periods in aeolic stanzas (Bacch. 3 str. 1, 16 str. 9, Pind. *Nem.* 3 str. 2, *Isth.* 8 str. 10), and Pindar can produce more thoroughgoing mixtures of aeolic and iambic periods (cf. especially *Ol.* 1). Although we may not see such mixture in Simon. 542 [15] or 543 [16] (see on 542 [15] *metre*), Simon. 519 fr. 35 (*b*). 6 confirms it would be extremely rash to exclude it from Simonides (note, from the other direction, 541. 6–7). The same line of Simonides shows a series of 4 short syllables (note also 10?), something which Pindar is interested in, but Bacchylides avoids. At any rate, Pindar is building his stanzas from Simonidean materials, and extending a Simonidean approach to metre.[4]

---

[4] For the iambics see West (1980); (1982), 60–76, for the metre of these poets in general. The iambics use freely the syncopated form –◡◡◡ which Aeschylus rarely if ever employs (e.g. Simon. 541. 8–9; cf. Hutchinson (1985), 93, 132). At least for the sake of argument, one should not class as iambic elements within a period which could (and usually should) be regarded as expansions of single-short sections in aeolic cola. For series of short syllables note the experimental Anacr. 378 (Ibyc. 285. 3 is doubtful); the ◡◡◡ 'aeolic base', one may note, is common in Pindar and Bacchylides, and not found before (◡◡– is frequent in Simon. 542 [15]). Pindar employs 'd¹' and 'd²' much more freely than Bacchylides in dactylo-epitrite (only 3 examples, 2 at the beginning of stanzas). On dialect, for the Aeolic forms mentioned see Verdier (1972); they appear, or seem to, in papyri of Simonides (Poltera (1997), 511, 527), and participles in -οιϲα are certainly standard in papyri of Alcman and Stesichorus. The primary evidence of metre, where available, can suggest complications. Pindar's ἐϲλόϲ in itself looks straightforwardly borrowed from Lesbian poetry (ἐϲθλ- in papyri of Stes. Ibyc. Simon. Bacch.). But the short scansion in several places might seem to indicate, there at least, ἐθλόϲ, an alternative simplification of the cluster; the simplification would be made more natural by the Boeotian τθ for ϲθ already present in *CEG* i. 110 (*c*.500?), cf. Stratt. fr. 49. 3 Kassel–Austin, etc. The retention of ἐν with accusative as well as dative is found in various dialects besides

A full account of Pindar would give much space to genres other than epinician (Pindar's fragments, like Bacchylides, are still rather underused by Pindarists). In the present confines, however, the most useful preliminary might be to dwell on some aspects of the genre which is best preserved and can be best understood. The prime concern here will be with the genre in Pindar's time, and in Pindar's work; by the end we shall be looking only at Pindar's particular approach.

One essential aspect of the epinician poem is the fame it brings, which Pindar and Bacchylides refer to with great frequency (Bacch. 9. 1–9, Pind. *Ol.* 6 [**18**]. 10 n., *Nem.* 5. 2–5, etc.). The poem is the equivalent of the statues dedicated in Olympia 'for mortals to see' (*CEG* i. 399 (i) 2). The fame is to exceed the limitations of the original performance both in time and in space; thus the later circulation, and the intrinsic artistry, of the poem are essential to its practical purpose.[5]

The poem is originally performed on a specific, and complex, occasion. That occasion, at least in presentation, extends out of other events. The glory at the games themselves consisted principally of the herald's announcement of the victor, whose city was named, and of the giving of a garland; at the Olympian and Nemean games the setting was by the altar of Zeus (Bacch. 10. 29–30, 13. 58–60). The elements of city and of religion are significant here. Both the announcement and the garland are much used in Pindar's poems; the song itself announces the victory and is the equivalent of a garland.[6]

At the place of the games there was celebratory feasting with friends (*Ol.* 9. 1–4), certainly involving at least a traditional song of triumph; there was also singing by choirs, in some cases local choirs

Boeotian, but not in literature. On another aspect of Pindar's dialect see Forssman (1966) (not wholly convincing).

[5] See Ebert (1972), 69–71, for the problems of the phrase from *CEG* i. 399 (carved later by the same cutter); these do not affect the conception of such statues which is implied.

[6] *Pyth.* 9. 1–4, *Nem.* 4. 73–5, etc.; *Ol.* 6 [**18**]. 86 n., *Pyth.* 8. 19–20, *al.* Note also Bacch. 13. 230–1, and 4. 16–18. For the herald and the garland cf. also e.g. Hdt. 6. 103. 2–3, Thuc. 5. 50. 4 (cf. Xen. *Hell.* 3. 2. 21), Σ Pind. *Ol.* [5]. 13 a, Poll. 3. 152; for the combination note further e.g. *IG* xii/2. 505. 9–15, 18–23. On garlands see Blech (1982), 109–81; note also Krause (1838), 157–82. Naming of city (and father): Pind. *Pyth.* 1. 30–3, *Isth.* '3/4'. 11–13, *Ol.* [5]. 8 (compare Σ 18 with Σ 16). For the 'naming complex' in Pindar cf. Hamilton (1974), 15. On the involvement of the city in the victory, and various other aspects, note Eur. fr. 282 Nauck.

(*Nem.* 10. 33–5; Bacch. 6. 4–9, cf. 4. 4–6). A few of Bacchylides' and Pindar's epinicians are actually written for this locale (most clearly Bacch. 2, 7, Pind. *Ol.* 8). Bacch. 7 is written for the day of the garland-giving itself, with which *Ol.* 8 is also connected (*Ol.* 8. 9–10, cf. Poll. 3. 152). Bacch. 2 and 7 are matched by another piece for the later celebration at home.

That later celebration is parallel to the earlier one. In both cases, various elements enter in. Firstly, the element of friendship and personal relations. The performers are or are part of a κῶμος (*Ol.* 4. 9 etc.), the song is an ἐγκώμιος or ἐπικώμιος ὕμνος; the poet is presented as a guest-friend of the victor or his family. The occasion is at least connected to the symposium, a setting for much private poetry, and the narrator will often speak as if he is a friend. But the poet is also presented as a guest-friend of the city, which the poem praises; the city is fundamental to the genre, and most commonly the myth is connected to the city.[7]

Important, finally, are the gods. The performance may sometimes have taken place in front of the victor's house (Bacch. 6. 14–15, Pind. *Nem.* 1. 19–24, *al.*); on occasion it was combined with a religious festival, or took place in a temple. Reception by a god is often desired. δέκομαι here denotes both the benevolent welcoming of the victor (and his friends), and the favourable acceptance of a kind of dedication, whether of the garland, other offering, or the revel itself. Sometimes the offering appears actual (*Pyth.* 12. 5; *Ol.* [5]. 1–3); sometimes the subject is a personified city or an abstraction. The object can be a person even in formally cultic poems (*Pae.* 5 (D5). 44–8; 6. 5–6 (subject Delphi)). At all events, the gods are crucial within the world constructed by the poem. The god of the festival and others have granted the victory (e.g. Bacch. 8. 26–32, Pind. *Pyth.* 4. 66–7, *Isth.* 2. 18);

---

[7] This was of course harder for, say, Sicily. The poet as friend of victor or family: e.g. *Ol.* 13. 97, *Pyth.* 10. 64–6, *Nem.* 1. 19–24, 7. 61–3, cf. Bacch. 13. 224–7 (friend of same man as at Pind. *Isth.* 6. 66–71), note also (chorus), *Parth.* 2. 38–41; friend of city: e.g. *Ol.* 9. 21–2, 11. 16–19, 13. 3, *Nem.* 5. 8, cf. Bacch. 12. 4–7. On ξενία with the victor cf. e.g. Crotty (1982), ch. 3 (also on relations to symposiastic poetry); Hubbard (1985), 156–8; Kurke (1991), ch. 6. Wine on the occasion is implied at *Nem.* 9. 48–53 (cf. Braswell (1998), 137–42), but Pindar does not dwell on such things much save indirectly; contrast Simon. 512 (cf. *SLG* 328. 5). ἐγκώμιος (ἐπικώμιος) is used by Pindar as if a technical word in relation to the genre (note esp. *Ol.* 10. 77, 13. 29, *Pyth.* 10. 53–4, *Nem.* 6. 32, 8. 50; cf. P. Oxy. 2438. 17). But it does not appear in Bacchylides, who uses ἐπινίκια as if a technical word (2. 13, cf. Aesch. *Ag.* 174, Pind. *Ol.* 8. 75, *Nem.* 4. 78).

the relation of man and gods usually concerns every part of the poem.[8]

The actual mode of delivery is a contentious matter, already touched on in regard to Bacchylides. In my view, (1) the first person in the epinician poems always denotes the poet, or if plural at least includes him; but (2) the poems are performed by a group of young men, not certainly dancing. The combination of poetic narrator and choral perfomer is extremely probable for *Pae.* 6 (D6) or *Dith.* fr. 75. Since choruses by convention so commonly present themselves as a single individual, in Pindar and elsewhere, this combination is not actually stranger than one which would otherwise have to be accepted sometimes for the epinicians: that of poetic narrator and deputizing performer. As to (1), other genres by Bacchylides and Pindar make it very clear that their narrator is sometimes a chorus (Bacch. 17. 130–2, 19. 8–14; Pind. *Pae.* 2 (D2). 24–31, 4 (D4). 21–7, *Parth.* 2. 6–12, 33–5, etc.). For the epinician there is far more material; and yet, while innumerable passages indicate that the narrator is a poet, only a very few can reasonably be thought to indicate that the narrator is not, and those few contain suspicious features which call their credit into question. This contrast makes it very likely that the narrator of the epinicians always denotes the poet; at most the one plausible exception would have to be explained, if real, by the unusual circumstances of the poem.[9]

---

[8] For prayers and wishes with δέκομαι see *Ol.* 4. 6–9, 8. 9–10, 13. 29, *Pyth.* 8. 1–5 ('Ηϲυχία) (cf. 18–20), 12. 1–6, *Nem.* 4. 11–12; *Ol.* [5.] 1–3. Cf. *Nem.* 11. 1–7, *Pae.* 5 (D5). 44–7, 6 (D6). 1–6 (cf. 126–31); Ar. *Wasps* 877.

[9] Passages which speak of the poet sending the poem, and so indicate that the poet is distinct from the performer: Bacch. 5. 10–12, 197; Pind. *Ol.* 9. 21–5, *Nem.* 3. 76–80; cf. *Ol.* 7. 1–10, *Isth.* 2. 47–8, *Ol.* 6 [18]. 85–91 n., and, in personal poems, Bacch. fr. 20 B. 3–4, 20 C. 6–7, Pind. fr. 124 a. 1–2. Passages implying that the first person is a poet: e.g. *Ol.* 7. 7–10, 9. 21–7, 10. 1–6, *Pyth.* 11. 38–45, *Nem.* 5. 1–3, *Isth.* 2. 45–8, Bacch. 5. 9–12, 16–33, 9. 1–6, 13. 221–31. (In Pind. *Nem.* 1. 19–24 the singer, as a foreigner, is less likely to be the chorus than the poet.) In *Nem.* 7. 85 (Aeacus, of course) the transmitted text is inconsistent with 61 (the view that in one poem the first person can take features of either poet or chorus is not itself clearly enough established). Otherwise Carey (1981), 173. In *Pyth.* 5. 72–81, a more problematic passage, the speaker is connected with a clan known to be connected with Thebes (*Isth.* 7. 12–15; cf. Arist. fr. 532 Rose, Ephor. *FGrHist* 70 F 16, Jacoby (1923–), II C. 44–5). The emphasis on the speaker in the passage would be somewhat surprising if he is the chorus, unless the chorus were drawn (rather unexpectedly) only from the Aegeidae; and even so, it would be odd to differentiate the Aegeidae from other Spartans as the source of the Carneia. If the poem is taking place at the Carneia (so Krummen (1990), 130–41), there is no problem in ϲεβίζομεν, which would perhaps be inclusive, cf. *Ol.* 1. 16 (and cf. e.g. Bacch. 2. 9)? If it is not, the present must be general and refer to or include the Theban department of the clan (its celebration

One could not apply a similar argument against (2); for if by convention the narrator is the poet, references to the actual singers need not be expected. But in fact there are a good number. One can escape these by maintaining that the reference is always to separate singing by the young men at a later stage in the revel. In some cases, however, the connection to the present poem seems very strong. In others there is such emphasis on artistry that the separate songs would have to become the main aesthetic event of the occasion; other evidence, and intrinsic probability, indicate that the main aesthetic event was Pindar's poem. The rhetoric of imperatives and the like in other contexts shows that imperatives, and so forth, to the singers need not be referred outside the poem; one is even positively encouraged to refer them inside it by the obvious kinship of passages. Furthermore, there is very little that could even be seen as positive evidence either for solo performance or for reference to other songs devised or improvised on the same occasion. The singing of a traditional triumph-song mentioned at *Ol.* 9. 1–4 of the revel at Olympia would not answer the requirements that would be placed upon it.[10]

of the principal Doric festival would not be unlikely if it wished to stress its Dorian connections). The praising of Cyrene in these celebrations would be a polite fiction: cf. Eur. *Alc.* 445–51 (and for ϲεβίζομεν note Aesch. *Supp.* 1024). *Ol.* 10. 78–83 are relevant even if 'we' is not including a chorus, cf. 78 with *Pyth.* 5. 78. The text in *Pyth.* 5. 72 is corrupt; this is important for the problem. For the interweaving in 79–80 cf. Bacch. 13. 147–8. On Carneia and Aegidae note Lübbert (1883) (information e.g. on name Pindar out of date). These issues: Lefkowitz (1991), (1995); Bremer (1990); West (1992), 346; D'Alessio (1994); Krummen (1990), 98–151; Instone (1996), 15; Aloni (1998), ch. 7; etc. Rutherford (2000), 335–6, contemplates making the ἀοίδιμον Πιερίδων προφάταν of *Pae.* 6 (D6). 6 the member of a chorus rather than the poet; but this seems doubtful.

[10] If *Ol.* 1. 16 implies that Pindar is playing on his own (and not conceptually playing for a chorus), it is a reference to the composition, conceived to take place while playing the lyre; cf. Bacch. frr. 20 B. 3–4, 20 C. 2–7, and Pind. *Ol.* 6 [18]. 103 n. below (note also e.g. *Nem.* 10. 21–2). *Nem.* 2 does not seem to refer to songs by young men (ὦ πολῖται 24); it is plausible to see the citizens' songs, or repetition of this song, as purely imaginary; there is clearly some interplay with the beginning. Cf. Fränkel (1962), 488 n. 6; Heath (1988), 192; Instone (1996), 144–5, 151. Pindar's song as main artistic event e.g. *Ol.* 14. 16–18 (for Pindar's centrality note also *Pyth.* 3. 73, *Isth.* 6. 57–8); song of young men as main artistic event: *Pyth.* 5. 98–107 (note χαρίεν), *Isth.* 8. 1–4 (note εὔδοξον). Difficulty of separating them: *Pyth.* 10. 4–6 (ἀνδρῶν; for ἐπικωμίαν here cf. 53–4, surely connected (and *Nem.* 8. 48–51), and note κλυτάν); *Nem.* 3. 1–12 (note μελιγαρύων τέκτονεϲ | ὕμνων 4–5, and the syntax of 11–12, 'undertake it together with'), cf. 65–6. Note that Bacch. 13. 190–8 implies the young men do not sing a traditional triumph song (though the content might, on a solo hypothesis, be imaginary).

The presence in epinician of quite numerous references to the performers' singing, and even to their garlands, combined with proportionately numerous references to dancing in other genres, inclines me to accept that in epinician the singers did not dance. Dancing may not have been so necessary at komoi as it was in cultic ritual. By contrast, the music was certainly important, and Pindar accordingly makes many references both to features of the specific music for a poem and to the usual sounds of voices, lyre, and auloi. The instruments appear at least sometimes in combination: a considerable noise is produced (too much background, one wonders, for a solo performer?).[11]

The relation of epinician to other public genres would be more easily explored if we had more in those genres. The difference seems most radical in some probably innovative non-epinician poems of Bacchylides' (17, 18). Pind. *Parth.* 2 well illustrates more complicated possibilities: it obviously takes up the tradition of Alcman, yet also speaks of a family's victories; its narrator is distinctively choral and feminine, yet she deploys gestures, and adopts roles, of the epinician authorial narrator.

The structure of epinicians has been much and subtly discussed; yet the basic patterns are unlikely to have been peculiar to that genre. Alcm. 1 [1] appears to contain the last part of a section of myth, followed by transitional gnomai, emphasis on the present subject of song, and praise of individual humans; Alcm. 3 [2] shows a definite proem. Pindar's paeans show plenty of mythical narrative (like Bacch. fr. 4), and open with a section on the present circumstances and the task of the narrator. In *Pae.* 6 (D6), 9 (A1), and also 4 (D4), the opening section seems to have the length one would expect in an epinician. In 6 we see three stanzas of myth, a pattern recalling some epinicians, especially for Aegina; three stanzas follow, in the text we have (they concern, indeed, Aegina). Bacch. fr.

---

[11] Music: West (1992), 344–7; Instone (1996), 13. In allowing Heath's contention on dancing (1988), 184–7, one would have to accept that χορεύων at *Isth.* 1. 7 was strictly appropriate only to the member of the pair it appeared in; in Ar. fr. 505. 2–3 Kassel–Austin the reference would have to be to comic choruses. On other genres, cf. esp. Bacch. 16. 8–12, 17. 130, Pind. *Pae.* 6 (D6). 7–10, *Dith.* fr. 75. 1, *Parth.* 2. 39 (most of these appear, significantly, in particularly well-represented poems). Bacch. 14. 12–16 are interesting in suggesting that χοροί are in place at feasts. C. S. Lewis's 'Pindar Sang' (1949, *Poems* (London 1964), 15–17) intriguingly presents Pindar singing while a chorus simply dances (the greatest attraction for the audience). The poem is also critically stimulating in its unsuccessful attempt to combine utterances from different works of Pindar into a new whole.

4 had a no less substantial section after the myth. The openings of
non-epinician poems by Pindar and Bacchylides often recall those
of epinicians: so Pind. *Hymn* 1 (cf. *Isth.* 7, *Nem.* 10), *Pae.* 2 (D2;
with 2. 4 cf. *Isth.* '3/4'. 21), 6 (D6; cf. *Ol.* 8; 12; [5]), 7b (C2; cf. *Ol.*
3), Bacch. 19 (cf. Pind. *Isth.* '3/4'. 19). City and gods are crucial
to both classes of poem. Families and individuals can be important
in non-epinician public poems by these poets and others, as can a
poetic narrator; the victory itself need not be the most important
subject of epinicians. Yet for all the interconnections, the epinician
is given a highly particular quality, among public poems, by the
place at its hub of a past but recent moment, achieved and granted,
and by the set role of the poetic narrator, and the formality of the in-
tention to praise. The earlier history of the genre in Ibycus remains
pertinent, and the connections of the form with personal poetry.[12]

Pindar presents epinician as a distinct type of poetry. He shows
it as an institution, and mode, which goes back to the mythical past
(*Ol.* 10. 76–83, *Nem.* 8. 50–1). He would not in any case name
contemporary or recent poets; but he is well aware of literary and
social changes for poetry (*Isth.* 2, *Dith.* 2 fr. 70 b), and he is keen, like
the Athenian Aristophanes, to advertise and commend originality
(*Ol.* 3. 4–6, 9. 48–9, *Nem.* 8. 20–1, *Pae.* 7b (C2). 10–17). The notion
that his type of poetry, or his values, were part of a vanishing world
might have surprised him.[13]

Comments related to genre are called forth from the narrator by
one main sort of moment: the explicit cutting short of a subject.
These passages are a particularly rewarding group. The first thing
to be noted is the range and complication of the approaches to genre
they imply. (They cannot be taken as the statement of Pindar's ac-
tual views even when serious in tone; but they affect the appearance
of the genre.) The motivation to stop the myth or the praise can
be, sometimes in combination: the concrete limits of time on such
poems (*Isth.* 1. 60–2 (with generic suggestion), cf. *Pyth.* 4. 247 (!),

---

[12] For the structure of Pindar's epinicia see, besides much else, Schadewaldt
(1928); Hamilton (1974); Greengard (1980); Race (1992); Rutherford (1997a). The
problem in *Pae.* 6 (D6) brought to light by Rutherford (1997b), (2000), 306–38, and
D'Alessio (1997) greatly affects one's view of its structure.

[13] On *Isth.* 2 note the discussion of Kurke (1991), ch. 10 (with literature). For
the mythical origins of other genres cf. *Thren.* 3. 5–12 (Cannatà Fera fr. 56; cf.
Schröder (1999), 9–12); note also Bacch. 20. 1–6 (Dunbar (1995), 757); Ar. *Frogs*
397–8. In naming other poets, Simonides comes nearer to his own time than Pindar
or Bacchylides (Stesichorus at 564. 4). In Pindar the only clear allusion to Simonides
or Bacchylides is the complimentary *Pae.* 4 (D4). 23–4.

Nem. 4. 33–4); or the danger for this genre of sating the ill-willed (*Nem.* 10. 19–20, cf. *Ol.* 2. 95–8); or a generic rule (τεθμός, *Nem.* 4. 33–4). Or the narrator can think this the best way to approach this genre (*Pyth.* 10. 53–4 ἐγκωμίων . . . ἄωτος ὕμνων); or one which shows his artistic independence and innovation (*Pyth.* 4. 247–8; note e.g. *Nem.* 8. 19–21); or one which will appeal to the discerning (cοφοῖς, *Pyth.* 9. 76–9). The poet can thus be under practical constraint from the genre, or prescribed to by its poetic laws, or he can choose and can fashion anew.

The passages also exploit contradictions within the genre, on the subject of relevance. On the one hand, epinician by convention ranges widely; on the other, it has by conception the specific object of praise. In *Pyth.* 10. 53–4 it is implied that epinician (or the best epinician) has a multiplicity of diverse λόγοι; the myth on Perseus is included. At *Pyth.* 11. 38–45, however, the narrator marvels at his wandering off course on to the irrelevant myth; his Muse's financial contract requires her to sing for the victor's family (cf. *Isth.* 6. 56–9). The playfulness should be obvious; but the robust humour draws on and points to the complications of the generic recipe. In *Nem.* 3, after an elaborate introduction on the desire of victory for song, and on the Aeginetan chorus, the narrator harangues his heart for wandering on to the myth of Heracles, instead of the Aeginetan Aeacus and his line (26–31): the city is the criterion here.[14]

The whole type of passage appears to be, in its basis, a standardized procedure: various images recur, some shared with Bacchylides (5. 176–8; 10. 51–2). Cf. also Alcm. 1 [1]. 39–40. But these are not devices for unobtrusive modulation. Pindar's narrator calls atten-

[14] *Pyth.* 11. 41–5 cannot at any rate be saying that the variety is generic and it is only now time to return (cf. Burton (1962), 69–70); that view does not fit 38–40 (the participial clauses and such parallels as *Nem.* 3. 26–7, Bacch. 10. 51–2 make it unlikely that the question expects a 'no'). ἄλλοτ' ἄλλαι does not suit very well the two connected people that follow (note 45), nor the contrast with what precedes (cf. Wilamowitz (1922), 261 n. 2). One might feel some temptation to make 41–5 an indignant question, after 37–40; the dative would be used in the same way as on the standard view, but the ᾗς gain more point from the question (wandering not suitable in praising either). At *Nem.* 4. 33, *Isth.* 6. 19–21 would not support the notion of a purely personal rule for τεθμός. Note the emphasis on speed in the aesthetic *Pyth.* 10. 51–4 (ταχύ, θύνει); an air of rapidity is important to the presentation of these poems (cf. e.g. *Nem.* 10. 46, with its effective parenthesis; *Ol.* 6 [18]. 23 n.). The type of passage is discussed e.g. at Bundy (1986), 75–6, without an appreciation of its complexities; some other aspects in Race (1990), ch. 2. The range of reasons is not exhausted above; of interest too for our purposes is the universal aesthetic approach to κόρος at *Nem.* 7. 52–3, from Hom. *Il.* 13. 636–9.

tion to his genre at points of juncture between different types of material, displaying that difference, or the underlying complications of the genre; he emphasizes the thwarting of narrative expectation; he dwells disconcertingly on the pressures of time, as if he had not been noticing; he plays with his own poem, and obtrudes his own audacity. The effect is often flagrantly disruptive; the manner can be outrageously sportive, or stunningly self-assertive. In the poem that most recalls Homer and especially Stesichorus, the moment emphasizes the extraordinary mannerism of Pindar's narrative, and its refusal of completeness and satisfying closure. More widely, the genre becomes the opposite of flowing genres that (in appearance) immerse the listener in a story, and display the poet and the poetic process only with great discretion. Pindar's epinician, by contrast, has a remarkably strong and overt metapoetic element. Central to it is the lively figure of the poet-narrator, a figure who is fundamental to the conception of the genre in his connected role as giver of praise. The vivacity, energy, and pride which form part of his characterization make the metapoetic concrete and compelling.[15]

It should be stressed, to avert misapprehension, that that characterization has many other roles to perform. The same is true of Pindar's style. Mobile, surprising, it continuously draws attention to itself; yet this is quite compatible with the primary involvement of the listener in the content. Gnomic passages should be seen as exciting in their very difficulty and abruptness, and yet also as pointed and full of meaning. The narrative, often highly manneristic, is yet both purposeful thematically and imaginatively inspiring. These features can be seen in other types of poem too; the metapoetic interest which in Pindar appears especially important to the epinician genre makes part of wider complexities which inform all his writing. Even the choral narrator is made to create another arresting figure and another source of combinations. But the detail of Pindar's writing and organization is best explored in the consideration of a particular poem. They are all too individual to be mere 'examples'; but the Sixth Olympian might be a good place for the nervous or the sceptical to begin a closer reading of the poet.

[15] On the relation of *Pyth.* 4 to Stesichorus cf. e.g. Segal (1986), 4–5, and Braswell (1988), 160–1. Note esp. the negotiation on rule and possessions with Pelias (131–68), vital to Pindar's themes, which calls to mind 222 (b) [3]. In 'mannerism' is understood, particularly, paraded strangeness of proportion, cultivated in its own right (but not only for its own sake); one may bear in mind the earlier applications of the term to architecture, painting, etc.

18: *Olympian* 6[16]

Olympian 6 [**18**] derives its particular identity from the particular career of its recipient; yet the poet's mind has created from it no less extraordinary a construction than the more ostentatiously intellectual *Olympian* 1. The poem was probably written after the foundation of Aetna (476), for Hieron is priest of Zeus Aitnaios, 94–6 (cf. Boeckh (1811–21), iii. 151–2); either 472 or 468 would be possible. Hagesias lived in Syracuse (18 etc.). On the paternal side of his ancestry, he was one of the Iamidae, a clan of seers claiming descent from Iamus and centred, in cult, on Olympia. On the maternal side, his family came from Stymphalus in Arcadia. Since only his maternal ancestors come from there (77), he is unlikely to have emigrated himself from Stymphalus to Syracuse. Syracusan citizenship may not begin with his generation, and may indeed go a long way back (cf. 6). However, he is also a citizen of Stymphalus, it seems (7, 99), and it is his maternal family that have organized the performance (87–8). The performance takes place in Stymphalus, so 103–5 are generally taken to show: the κῶμος has yet to travel to Syracuse. (Cf. first Hermann (1817), 295–6 (without this argument), Boeckh (1811–21), iii. 153.) That view is provisionally

---

[16] On this poem, and on the Iamidae, see especially: Schmid (1616), 164–77; Heyne (1817), i. 65–101; Hermann (1817), 290–6; Boeckh (1811–21), i. 374–81, iii. 151–64; Dissen and Schneidewin (1847), i. 31–8, ii. 71–86; Donaldson (1841), 32–42; Cookesley (1851), i. 118–30; Hartung (1855–6), i. 231–4; Mommsen (1864*b*), 55–67; Metzger (1880), 122–35; Gildersleeve (1885), 171–81; Wellmann (1886), 107–12; Wilamowitz (1886), 162–85, (1922), 307–10; Christ (1896), 40–9; Fennell (1893–9), i. 58–71; Schroeder (1900), 112–21; Garrod (1907), 146–7; Hiller von Gärtringen (1913), 74–5; Hepding (1914); Weniger (1915); Jacoby (1923–), iii b (Suppl.). 445; Ahlert (1942), 68–71; Fernández Galiano (1948), 169; Kakridis (1970); Pearson (1931); Farnell (1932), iii. 40–9; Norwood (1941); Chantraine (1953); Woodbury (1991*b*); Beattie (1956*a*); Peek (1958); Dover (1987); Löffler (1963), 13, 25–9; von der Mühll (1976*b*); Binder (1964), 134–5; Pavese (1964), 307–8; Parke (1967), 173–80; Slater (1969), 88–91; Stern (1970); Friis Johansen (1973); Péron (1974), 62–6; Nash (1975); Ruck (1975–6); Bourriot (1976), i. 357–89; Roussel (1976), 53, 74, 77 n. 35; Carne-Ross (1979); Rubin (1980–1); Bonelli (1987), 77–84; McDiarmid (1987); Heath (1988), 191; Burnett (1989), 284 n. 9; Carey (1989), 556–7; Froidefond (1989), 29–48; Lefkowitz (1991), 182–3, 195–7; Heath and Lefkowitz (1991), 182–3; Too (1991); Garner (1992); Parker (1996), 63 n. 26; Sancassano (1996–7), 86–7; Salvador (1997). For Stymphalus cf. Jost (1985), 99–109 (and pl. A), 358–60; Williams *et al.* (1997), on the later site, which may at the least prove significant for Stymphalian religion.

accepted in what follows; but a temerarious alternative is mentioned on 103–5.

Hagesias, as a seer, must have been important in Hieron's state; he would seem to have played a significant role in the battle of Cumae (474; cf. 9–11, 16–18). He must have enjoyed the favour of Hieron, whether or not the scholion about his friendship with Hieron (165) draws on Timaeus, like that on Chromius (Σ *Nem.* 9. 95 a). The laudation of Hieron in this poem of itself illustrates either his favour or his predominance (92–6). Even though the performance takes place in Arcadia, Syracuse receives more praise; the Stymphalian audience may not actually have been as important as other listeners or readers. If so, this is of some significance for the immediate reception of Pindar's works.

The success of Hagesias and his clan displays the possibilities of the time. Seers had always been mobile (cf. Löffler (1963), 12–13); and there were celebrated but relatively static clans of seers, like the Branchidae of Miletus. The Iamidae, however, move around the Greek world at an impressively high level. Herodotus gives us the story of an Iamid who was patronized by the tyrant of Sybaris, and then received land for him and his descendants from Croton (5. 44. 2–45. 5); he tells of how another forced the Spartans to make him and his brother citizens (9. 33–5). He may play an important role in Simonides' poem on Plataea (fr. 14 West). The great value of these seers is in war; but the interest of rich rulers and powerful states in exploiting famous foreigners connects this group of seers to the poets. Polycrates may have had dealings with the Branchidae (cf. P. Oxy. 3722 fr. 16. 15–17); but it was an Elean seer he had with him (Hdt. 3. 132. 2). At all events, the Iamidae were a striking and unusual phenomenon.

Pindar is often said to show a fascination in the poem with the number two: seer and warrior, Apollo and Poseidon, Stymphalus and Syracuse are the most striking instances (so first Gildersleeve (1885), 171–2, with many examples, convincing and unconvincing). This pattern, though notably abstract, must surely make itself felt to a thoughtful listener; but the matter is not so simple as a recurrence of pairs. In the first place, the emphasis on plurality is part of a rhetorical point, the abundance of glorious features. This point is established at the start (4–7); it is apparent in ἀμφότερον used of seer and warrior at 17, and implicit in the pair of divine antecedents at 58–9; even at 100–2 the emphasis is really on praise more than prudence. All these places, in epodes 1, 3, 5, involve the same metrically striking area (ep. 2–3). Secondly, at least some of these pairs form part of dynamic structures within the poem. The pair Apollo and Poseidon leads on, within the narrative, to a culmination: the patronage of the Iamidae by the still greater god Zeus (70). The pair Stymphalus and Syracuse emerges fully after the development of another pair: Hagesias' paternal line, which reaches a culmination in Olympia, and his maternal line, which is rooted in Stymphalus. The division between Arcadia and Elis is minimized by Pindar, but Olympia and Stymphalus are important places, set against each other, in 61–91. The appearance of another place in 92, Syracuse, is made to constitute both a significant movement and a climax.

Syracuse is also the place where Hagesias actually lives; the return to this actuality forms part of another large structure in the poem. In this structure, another figure plays a central part: the narrator. The narrator as a person forms a dominating presence in the parts of the poem outside the narrative of Iamus (1–28, 72–105, 59 per cent of the poem). His contributions, while usually bringing the poem as poem to the fore, can evoke the present performance, in a tone of lively address (so 87–91), or take the poem beyond the literal reality into a region of vivid imagery (so 1–3). Vivacious address and fantasy can also be boldly combined (22–8). The narrator can draw myth and the present together within his discourse (12–21); he can display himself as a figure with an ancestry, parallel to but different from Hagesias (84–7; he does not present himself there as an Aegeid, though that clan resembles the Iamidae in internationalism). All this, however, is not merely a random variety. In the last triad the narrator comes back from metaphor to concrete and present realities; likewise, the treatment of Hagesias leaves the past, and myth, and comes to his permanent present and the immediate future. Such a pattern is indeed related to the common organization of the epinician; but it looks quite distinctive in this poem. This is thanks to various particular features of the work: the special circumstances of Hagesias' background and of the performance; linked with this, the special role of places in the poem, and the importance of journeying; the distribution within the poem of metapoetic imagery centred on the narrator, and the unusually forceful presentation of the actual execution of the poem (and what preceded it, 85–91). The design of the poem grows out of its circumstances and what the author's mind has evolved from them.

Intricate structure and conspicuous organization are no less apparent within the central narrative. That is not just because its themes are densely and deftly treated, or because the very story is seen to depend, as will appear, on a specifically poetic imagination. The narrative of Iamus' birth is also set out with an interwoven and elaborate plotting that we would not expect in this genre. One wider consequence is that the world of myth acquires a particularly full existence for the involved listener; this affects the larger structuring of 'worlds' within the poem. Another and connected consequence is the emphasis on the divine which results from the structure: we are shown the human sphere both in separation from, and irradiated by, the action of gods. The particular nature of the interventions within the narrative differentiate the mythical world from the present; the fact of intervention forms a link which binds the mythical world and the present together, as the poem is concerned to bring out. The eternity of the gods underlies and unites the temporal sequences and temporal structure of the poem.

Metre

str., ant.

1. $--\cup---\cup---\cup\cup-\cup\cup-$
2. $-\cup\cup-\cup\cup---\cup\cup-$
3. $-\cup\cup-\cup\cup---\cup--$
4. $-\cup---\cup---\cup\cup-\cup\cup--$
5. $--\cup---\cup\cup-\cup\cup-\cup-$
6. $\cup---\cup---\cup---\cup\cup-\cup\cup--$
7. $-\cup\cup-\cup\cup---\cup---\cup--\cup--$

ep.

1. $-\cup\cup-\cup\cup---\cup---\cup\cup-\cup\cup-$
2. $-\cup---\cup---\cup\cup-\cup\cup-\cup\cup---\cup\cup-$
3. $-\cup\cup---\cup\cup---\cup---\cup-$
4. $-\cup---\cup-\underline{\cup}-\cup\cup-\cup\cup-$
5. $-\cup\cup-\cup\cup---\cup\cup-\cup\cup-$
6. $-\cup\cup-\cup\cup---\cup\cup-\cup\cup-$
7. $-\cup--\cup---\cup---\cup--$

In the standard notation for dactylo-epitrite: str. 1 -E-D, 2 D-d¹ (d West), 3 D-e-, 4 E-D-, 5 beg. - e-D, 6 end E-D-, 7 D-e-E-; ep. 1 D-e-D, 2 E-d¹ d² d²-d¹ (E-D²-d West), 3 d¹-d¹- (d-d- West) E, 4 E-D, 5 D-D, 6 D-D, 7 ee-E-.

The first thing to remark about the metre is the handling of blunt and pendant closes at period-end. Pindar's dactylo-epitrite generally shows an enthusiasm for the less full, more restless blunt closes which is not evident in Bacchylides. In Bacchylides every close in a stanza can be pendant (11 str., 13 str.), as in Stes. 222 (b) [3] (str., ep.). In Pindar the proportion of blunt to pendant is almost 3 : 1, and common patterns are for all closes to be blunt (*Nem.* 1 str., ep., 8 ep., 10 str., ep.) or all but the last (*Ol.* 3 str., ep., 6 ep., 7 str., ep., *Pyth.* 1 ep., 4 ep., 9 ep., *Isth.* 1 ep., 6 str.). It is characteristic that it should be the epode of *Ol.* 6 [18] that takes a form where blunt endings persist. As in *Pyth.* 1, 4, 9, the strophe, as more varied in its closes, is contrasted with the epode. This contrast is marked the more here because the latter part of the first period in the strophe and, more notably, the whole of the second, coincide in rhythm with the later part of the matching periods in the epode ($-\cup----\cup\cup-\cup\cup-$ and $-\cup\cup-\cup\cup---\cup\cup-$). The openings of strophe and epode contrast; the closes match (e–E–). The latter point is not unremarkable: there is so extensive a match at the ends of strophe and epode only in *Ol.* 3.

At one point in the epode (2–3) the usual patterns are modified for so substantial a sequence ($-\cup\cup-\cup\cup-\cup\cup---\cup\cup-$ | $-\cup\cup---\cup\cup-$) that the listener is almost thrown off course. This is more notable than a simple extension or abridgement of D (e.g. *Pyth.* 3. 4, 23). It must particularly underline the point of first occurrence, the short and significant speech of Adrastus (16–17). An emphatic purpose can be seen in the first appearance of the related, though more limited, sequence at *Pyth.* 1. 20, where the entrance of Aetna is marked out. Later occurrences in the poem are also significant. The strophe appears to show some audacity too, at the end of 5 and the beginning of 6. The aeolic-style extension at the end of 5 is matched at *Nem.* 8. 14 (Schroeder (1900), 112), and the opening of 6 might be likened, in aeolic terms, to *Nem.* 8. 1 (but cf. Stes. 222 b [3]. 210). The moment in the strophe is not so striking as that in the epode, nor is any expressive aim. One might be tempted to think the period-end illusory; but it would be wild to attempt removal of all the indications of pause (12 (12–13 n.), 26, 33, 68, 75). Hermann essays an interesting compromise ((1817), 291–3); cf. West (1982), 73.

1. The poem begins, as often in Pindar, by contemplating beginning. The point presently emerges as the need to find a splendid opening, and dissolves in the narrator's despair or delight at the multitude of possibilities. The underlying rhetoric of διαπόρηϲιϲ in beginning praise and of manifold opportunities for it was familiar and presumably traditional in this self-reflexive poetry: see Pind. *Hy.* 1 fr. 29 (with [Lucian] *Enc. Dem.* 18–19), cf. *Hom. h. Ap.* 19–27, and note the standardized language at Pind. *Isth.* '3/4'. 19 (most likely an opening), cf. Bacch. 5. 31–4 (and 19. 1–11). Pindar, how-

ever, leads into the theme obliquely, with a powerful image of his activity.

The participial clause is the most important part of the first sentence; this is already apparent from the bulk of its detail, and especially from the opening χρυϲέαϲ. The word makes a striking start in itself, cf. *Pyth.* 1. 1 (and Greengard (1980), 66), especially as gold has a conspicuous and traditional place in the genre as an image of imperishable supremacy (Bacch. 3 [**17**]. 85–7 n.). It receives further emphasis through its wide separation from its noun, which waits for the start of the next period and the end of the clause. But it derives its chief significance from the solid detail of the sentence. What might otherwise seem an airy epithet is turned into a conception of wild luxury, golden pillars for a house; this in turn transforms the image from sober comparison into glorious fantasy. The ordinary world must be altered to become a fit image for poem and victor. One may compare the role of χρυϲέα, perhaps somewhat less imposing, in the parallel passage fr. 194. 1–3. The treasure-house of praise announced at the start of *Pyth.* 6 (1–18) is also disjoined from the ordinary reality of the vehicle: it will not perish (10–14). At *Nem.* 7. 77–9 fantastic metaphorical garlands of gold, ivory, and coral are disjoined from the real variety.

εὐτειχεῖ: cf. *Nem.* 7. 46, *al.*; Hom. *Il.* 16. 57, Theogn. 1210, of cities. Cf. Sotiriou (1998), 21, 41.

προθύρωι: the πρόθυρον is a porch, with pillars at the opening, and walls; in Olynthian houses it is set into the front wall of the house, and forms a recess of about 2 m. before the front door (Robinson and Graham (1938), 154–6). εὐτειχεῖ emphasizes the solidity of the construction. ὑπο- is used in relation to what the pillars support; cf. *Ol.* 8. 26–7.

θαλάμου should in my view be corrected into θαλάμων. One should not have a πρόθυρον to only a room or part of a house, and this one is to be a πρόϲωπον . . . τηλαυγέϲ. The plural 'rooms, halls' is often used to denote a house (e.g. Pind. *Pyth.* 4. 160 (cf. Braswell (1988), 220); Soph. *El.* 190, Eur. *Ion* 476–7). The singular is not so used, and it would be surprising if it were; *Ol.* [5.] 13 ϲταδίων θαλάμων . . . ἄλϲοϲ naturally does not show that it can. The singular can be used of goddesses' abodes, *Nem.* 11. 3, fr. 75. 14, both with possessives; but μέγαρον could not be a temple in poetry, and προθύρωι would not be apt. For πρόθυρον with a word for house in the genitive cf. Aesch. *Ch.* 966, Hdt. 3. 140. 1.

2. ὡc ὅτε is equivalent to ὡc, cf. *Nem.* 9. 16, *Isth.* 6. 1, *al.* The opening device of comparison is presented with explicit pomp, cf. e.g. *Ol.* 7. 1, Bacch. 12. 1.

θαητόν is emphatically placed; in the argument, it prepares for τηλαυγέc, emphatically placed too.

μέγαρον frequently means 'house', cf. e.g. *Nem.* 1. 31 (Braswell (1988), 220), Bacch. 17. 101.

3. πάξομεν: a more concrete verb than 'make'. It is of course the poet, not the poet and chorus, who constructs the edifice. The verb is most likely to be subjunctive, as the parallel passages suggest: *Pyth.* 1. 60, fr. 194. 2, cf. *Nem.* 9. 1. Cf. Hummel (1993), 264–5. It falls with vigorous emphasis at the end of the sentence and the start of the period.

ἀρχομένου δ' ἔργου: the sentence, in parataxis, justifies the participial clause of the preceding sentence and specifically χρυcέαc. ἀρχομένου makes the connection with the poem more overt. The actual link is not with the order in which the builder would work but with the front as the beginning when one 'reads' or approaches the house. Cf. for the general principle *Pyth.* 6. 14–18. The opening of the poem is made to sound more visibly dominating than by προοίμιον and κρηπῖδ' at *Pyth.* 7. 1–3/4.

4. χρή expresses not only justification, but the narrator's pondering (what shall it be?). The assurance of πάξομεν is subtly modulated.

τηλαυγέc: the word comes several times in Pindar, and is used by Bacchylides too (17. 5); cf. Ar. *Birds* 1092, 1711. The separation from the noun throws further emphasis onto this final adjective, which joins up with the opening χρυcέαc; χρυcέαc activates -αυγέc, in which light is not always important (e.g. *Pae.* 7 (D7). 11).

The whole passage 1–4 implies that houses can be splendid objects of display. Despite what is often inferred from the archaeological evidence, the conception is perfectly possible for pre-Hellenistic Greeks; cf. e.g. Dem. 3. 25–6, 29 (the assertions about the fifth century are naturally dubious), 21. 158. The ethos of conspicuous luxury, not absent from Alcman, is important to epinician.

4–7. After the abundance of words in the first sentence and the simple syntax of the next, a sentence develops of more elaborate construction, but with some relatively pithy members. A conditional clause introduces from an oblique angle the claims of Hagesias to praise. They appear, formally, from the viewpoint of poetic

strategy; they are couched in general terms. The optative expresses
generality rather than incredulity: cf. *Ol.* 11. 4 and Bacch. 5. 190
(standard wording in a related statement), and e.g. *Pyth.* 1. 81. The
three areas indicated in 4–6 all form part of the poem, and their
order bears a relation to the sequence of the poem; the narrator is
to some degree presenting a plan while affecting to contemplate a
start. But the trio only makes the proportions of the poem more
surprising. The first area, the victory, makes an allusive appear-
ance in the next stanza, a subordinated appearance in the second
strophe (25–7), and a generalized appearance after the myth (75–6,
cf. 81–2); it is the middle area, the seership, which unexpectedly
dominates the poem.

'Ολυμπιονίκας: a technical and valued title, like Πυθιονίκας (-ος),
and 'Ισθμιο- (Pindar but not Bacchylides loftily abstains from the
last). Herodotus uses them, with syntax like that here (5. 47. 1,
8. 47 (cf. *Pyth.* 10. 13)); they are seen in fifth- and sixth-century
inscriptions (*IG* i³. 1213, Lang, *Ath. Agora* 21 (1976), 12 c 5 (nasty),
L 12. 1), and are converted into proper names (*Pyth.* 11. 43; Andoc.
Myst. 11; *IG* i³. 84. 37, cf. Hornblower (1991–), ii. 487). Pindar and
Bacchylides like setting the words proudly at or near the beginning
of poems: cf. *Ol.* 3. 3, 4. 8, 8. 18, 10. 1, 11. 7, 13. 1, *Pyth.* 6. 5, 8. 5,
9. 1, Bacch. 4. 5, 11. 13. In the present context, the appearance of
the appetizing word is teasingly indirect; the implied praise comes
through no less strongly, but the tone is devious.

μὲν . . . τε . . . τε: the form with two τες accentuates the piling up
of nouns. The second and third members are longer than the first,
and build up in shape to the climactic question.

βωμῶι: the pretence of generality becomes ever more strained
as the details accumulate. The phrasing joins the passage to 70
(here too Διός goes with βωμῶι). Neither passage offers so detailed
a depiction of the empyromancy as *Ol.* 8. 1–7; the connection with
the victor's actual activity or status seems to make a description
actually less suitable for the poem. We cannot know how actively
the Syracusan pursued his hereditary right at Olympia. For this
mode of divination at Olympia see (with works in n. 16 above) Hdt.
8. 134. 1, Σ Pind. *Ol.* 6. 111 b, d, e. See further e.g. Stengel (1910),
97–8; Halliday (1913), 185.

Πίσαι is linked to 'Ολυμπιονίκας in content and to the place-name
Cυρακοccᾶν in position.

cυνοικιcτήρ: the meaning is not clear to us. One could hardly emend to -ητήρ: the cυν- would have little point. The scholia suggest (8 a–b) that some Iamidae (better would be, some Iamid) participated in the original foundation; Wilamowitz (1922), 307, suggests that Gelon's expansion of the city was seen as a new foundation, in which Hagesias joined. The second seems a doubtful idea (one may contrast Camarina, Thuc. 6. 3): if Hagesias' role is to have been distinctive, the refoundation must have been not merely a metaphor but a formal affair, complete with seer. Perhaps, as the Corinthians in general remained 'the founders' of Corcyra (Thuc. 1. 25. 1), the Iamidae in general could be called 'co-founders' of Syracuse; the singular used of one Iamid would be more difficult, but might possibly be justified by the appearance of the genos and of hereditary position in the context. It would seem, at any rate, that Pindar is going to some lengths to include Syracuse among Hagesias' glories.

κλεινάν: often used elsewhere in Pindar of the city where the work is sung, *Ol.* 3. 2, 9. 14, *Pyth.* 9. 70, *Nem.* 1. 2, *Isth.* 9. 1, *Dith.* fr. 76. 2 (otherwise of the locales of games). Stymphalus is not mentioned here, or praised in 7.

τίνα: the question effectively conveys innumerability and suggests the perplexity of choice; cf. *Ol.* 2. 98–100, and *Hom. h. Ap.* 19 πῶς τ᾽ ἄρ c᾽ ὑμνήcω, πάντωc εὔυμνον ἐόντα;

φύγοι with a genial touch presents the praise as something to escape, like arrows; ἀφθόνων and ἱμερταῖc, rather like μαλθακᾶc and εὐκλέαc at *Ol.* 2. 90, bring out the paradox. The poet thus complicates the writing a little at its point of climax.

ὕμνον: an abundance of ὕμνοι can be devoted to one occasion; cf. *Pyth.* 6. 7, Bacch. 16. 4.

κεῖνοc ἀνήρ takes up the preceding description, and does not formally denote Hagesias. Cf. e.g. *Ol.* 1. 55. The beginning of the period and the end of the clause give further weight to the phrase.

ἀφθόνων ἀcτῶν: it is implied that Hagesias' fellow citizens, despite the ubiquitous urge to envy, rejoice in his and the city's triumph. Cf. e.g. *Isth.* '3/4'. 3; *Pyth.* 9. 93–6.

ἱμερταῖc ἀοιδαῖc: the stanza ends self-referentially, but not quite directly, calling attention to the beauty of the present performance and poem. Cf. *Isth.* 6. 9.

8–9. The question of the narrator's opening is lost from view, as the game of indirectness is ended. ἴcτω is used both to show the supposed mystification as finished and to signal the extraordinary lot of Hagesias (cf. *Nem.* 9. 45).

ἐν κτλ.: we do not have the evidence to pronounce this a colloquialism. It does not appear elsewhere, to my knowledge; even if it had once been colloquial, it might have been borrowed from earlier literature (a possibility with fr. 169. 36 and [Aesch.] *PV* 135, cf. Alcm. 1 [1]. 15). Modern idioms are not a safe guide. Cf. Alc. 130 b [9]. 13–16=28–31. We can say that the phrase has an earthy quality which suits the moment of identification, and makes it blunter. It also clashes effectively with the numinous δαιμόνιον, for which cf. e.g. *Ol.* 9. 110, *Pae.* 8a (B3). 11, Bacch. 9. 25–6.

Cωcτράτου υἱόc: the name at last appears (cf. Hamilton (1974), 47); it comes at the end of a sentence and the start of a period. Names are similarly handled to effect at e.g. *Ol.* 10. 55, *Pyth.* 6. 32, *Nem.* 2. 10 Τιμονόου παῖδ᾽. The delay has particular force here; but Pindar and Bacchylides often deliberately keep the victor's name or patronymic for near the beginning or end of first antistrophe, or epode, or second strophe (*Ol.* 4, 11, *Nem.* 2, 4, 6, Bacch. 5; *Ol.* 7, 8, 12, *Pyth.* 7, *Isth.* 1, Bacch. 9, cf. *Ol.* 10, *Pyth.* 11, *Nem.* 8, *Isth.* 5, Bacch. 14; *Nem.* 10, cf. *Ol.* 13, *Isth.* 7). The delay in *Pyth.* 1 is grandiose (end of second antistrophe). In *Pyth.* 3 (name middle of fourth antistrophe, identity end of third epode) it advertises the unusual nature of the poem. *Isth.* 8 and Bacch. 6 make the name the first word; the self-consciousness is evident in Bacch. 6.

ἀκίνδυνοι: the thought of 9–11 takes up the last part of 4–7, and comments on the celebration. The idea of actual danger, as opposed to toil and expense, is not normally applied directly to the present games (contrast e.g. *Ol.* 1. 81; note *Ol.* [5]. 15–16). It is not that mule-carts are uniquely perilous; rather the narrator is suggesting a link with Hagesias' actions in battle, which will appear more explicitly at 12–18.

10. ἀνδράcιν: cf. *Hom. h. Ap.* 142.

ναυcί: the antithesis is not a normal one, nor can the ships be naturally explained unless there is an oblique reference to the battle of Cumae, or, less plausibly, miscellaneous naval battles. (Contrast e.g. Hartung (1855–6), i. 232.) *Nem.* 9. 34–5, of Chromius, is related; *Nem.* 5. 9 (Aegina) provides no counter-example. The Homeric κοίλαιc strengthens the heroic suggestion; the epithet for ships does not occur outside Homer (including *h. Ap.* 405, of one ship), save with obvious evocation of Homer at Ibyc. S151 [**11**]. 17 and Eur. *Cyc.* 487. The word is not an epithet at Hdt. 8. 119. Epinician is eager to forge connections between prowess in games and in battle: cf. e.g. *Pyth.* 8. 25–7, *Nem.* 2. 13–15, *Isth.* 1. 50–1.

11. τίμιαι: honour and danger (negated) frame the sentence; τίμιαι is stressed further by the placing of the pause at the start of the period.

μέμνανται: more usually it is emphasized in Pindar that memory needs song (e.g. *Nem.* 7. 11–13, *Isth.* 7. 16–19; contrast *Isth.* '3/4'. 48). Here the role of song has already been implied; the emphasis has moved for the present to Hagesias' achievements.

The language in this half-sentence (πολλοὶ . . . ποναθῆι) is forcefully simple. The bare καλὸν εἴ τι ποναθῆι is a standard sort of phrase in the genre, cf. e.g. *Pyth.* 9. 93, *Nem.* 9. 6, Bacch. 9. 82; but see also Pind. *Pae.* 2 (D2). 66, fr. 121. 4.

12. Ἁγησία: after a brief flight of epinician generality, we now return heavily to Hagesias. His own name appears, for the first time, and the narrator addresses him. The victor is usually addressed, if at all, in the last part of the poem; *Pyth.* 2. 18, 5. 5, *Nem.* 1. 29, 10. 37, *Isth* 5. 17 depart from the general pattern.

12–17. The directness of second-person praise is tempered by a characteristic device. The creation of the praise is assigned to another (it is ready-made), and the narrator displays a kind of ingenious erudition. Pindar and Bacchylides several times refer to utterances by or to figures of myth which have a bearing on the present (*Pyth.* 4. 9–11, 6. 19–23, 8. 38–42, 9. 94, cf. fr. 2. 2–3, fr. 43; Bacch. 3 [**17**]. 76–7). These mythical quotations resemble the citations in these authors and Simonides of remarks by poets and Wise Men, and have an almost learned appearance. But some of them may formally conceal poetic quotation or reference too (just as *Isth.* 2. 9–11 might actually be derived from Alc. 360). For *Pyth.* 6. 19–27, the Hesiodic Χείρωνος Ὑποθῆκαι might well be the source; however, Σ 22 does not cite a parallel to the specific remark. The present case is the clearest: Σ 26 runs ποθέω· ὁ Ἀσκληπιάδης φησὶ ταῦτα εἰληφέναι ἐκ τῆς κυκλικῆς Θηβαΐδος (F7 Davies). Asclepiades (1st cent. BC) is said to say that Pindar has 'taken' the speech from the *Thebaid*; if the lemma is mistaken, as often happens, he might have said rather that ἀμφότερον κτλ., or the whole episode, was taken from that poem. εἰληφέναι need not imply a literal quotation, cf. Σ

Ol. 7. 64 (τοῦτο), Σ Ap. Rhod. 1. 57–64 a (cf. Pind. *Thren.* 6 (fr. 57 Cannatà Fera)); ὀφθαλμόν could hardly have been used in the archaic epic. Various passages, like Hes. fr. 25. 37–8 Merkelbach– West and especially *CEG* ii. 519. 2 ἀμφότερον μάντιν τε ἀγαθὸν καὶ δορὶ μα̣[χ, lend plausibility to the notion that 17 follows an epic original closely (contrast *Nem.* 10. 9, and 9. 26). At all events, the further layer of allusiveness will have been apparent to the listener.

12–13. **ἐνδίκου:** ἀπὸ γλώccαc on its own normally contrasts speech with action or with writing (e.g. Theogn. 63, Cratin. fr. 128. 2 Kassel–Austin, Thuc. 7. 10. 1). The addition of a significant attribute, as in Herwerden's ἐνδίκου, would be desirable; cf. *Pyth.* 3. 2 (note κοινόν). It is not apparent that the phrase on its own could simply emphasize the speech, like διὰ cτόμα (the instances of which might themselves be questioned); nor would the emphasis, just after ἐν δίκαι, be particularly wanted. Snell's conjecture ἐνδίκαc is made with designs on the period-end; cf. e.g. 59, *Nem.* 5. 9.

μάντιν: this connection with Hagesias is made at once; in this immediate context it is the attribute to be added, Amphiaraus' valour, which is more striking and important.

Ἀμφιάρηον: cf. on the legend Braswell (1998), 27–41, with literature mentioned there. On the questions of cult see also Petrakos (1968); Parker (1996), 146–9.

14. There is no mention of Zeus here, as at *Nem.* 9. 24–7, 10. 8–9; the benevolence of that intervention is clear from the former passage (note 9. 19–20). The whole scene here is made merely human, and desolate, by contrast with the story of Iamus. The glory of Amphiaraus is not dwelt on in this poem either (cf. Soph. *El.* 837–41 etc.). The moment ends the stanza imposingly.

κατὰ . . . ἔμαρψεν: the verb encloses the sentence grimly. Cf. ἔμαρψαν at Soph. *OC* 1681, contrast ὑπέδεκτο at *Nem.* 10. 8.

φαιδίμαc: the word is used elsewhere only of gods, men, and parts of their bodies (and of Apollo's bow, *Hom. h. Ap.* 4). The application to the horses is arresting, and forms an implicit contrast with the darkness of earth and the abyss.

15. The text is corrupt. *Nem.* 9. 24 would seem to guarantee the formal opposition between seven other leaders and Amphiaraus, although Amphiaraus was one of the Seven; cf. *Aetna* 578 *septemque duces raptumque profundo* (*profundi* Goodyear (1965), 202, with the same result). For other ways to avoid more elaborate conclusions

see Lee (1986), 169–70; Erbse (1974), 191; Braswell (1998), 91–
2. Also relevant is the existence of a place at Thebes called Ἑπτὰ
Πύραι; cf. Schachter (1981–), iii. 22–4. But the grammar of πυρᾶν
νεκρῶν τελεcθέντων does not cohere: the genitive πυρᾶν dependent on
νεκρῶν would be most unsatisfactory in this author, even with ἑπτά,
and we may safely assume there are no sound instances of mascu-
line participles used as feminine (cf. Barrett (1964), 366–7). Even if
the participle were emended to a feminine, the dependent genitive
would not satisfy; even if πυρᾶν were changed to πυρᾶι (Bernhardy),
τελέω here in the sense 'end' would be quite unacceptable in Pin-
dar's style. Braswell ((1998), 91) suggests the meaning 'arranged
for cremation'; but like other proposals this does not in my view
seem particularly plausible or inviting. No convincing substitute
for τελεcθέντων has been found.

Ταλαϊονίδαc: the patronymic recalls that Amphiaraus had slain
Adrastus' father in the earlier quarrel, described at 9. 13–17 (cf. Σ
30 b), and in the *Cycle* (*Theb.* F9 Davies). This makes Adrastus'
esteem and love the more poignant.

16–17. On the relation to the *Thebaid* see 12–17 n. Amphiaraus'
valour was most likely seen in action in the *Thebaid*: cf. F5 Davies.

ἐν Θήβαιc: in *Theb.* F6A Davies Adrastus leaves Thebes wearing
εἵματα λυγρά; since these will be clothes put on specially (cf. e.g.
Od. 16. 457), he will not be fleeing the battlefield, despite Σ Hom.
Il. 23. 346. A scene of burial at Thebes is thus conceivable, and
clothes of mourning would suit it (cf. Welcker (1865–82), ii. 369).
At all events, the Seven are buried at Thebes in *Nem.* 9. 22 (cf.
Hom. *Il.* 14. 114, with Σ). This passage might, then, be stressing
that Adrastus utters these words at the funeral of the others, and
before departing for home. The placing of ἐν Θήβαιc in this clause
makes it less likely that Pindar is polemicizing against the Athenian
tale that the Seven were buried at Eleusis (so Jacoby (1923–), iii b
(Suppl.). 445; cf. further Collard (1975), i. 5–6, ii. 433–6).

ποθέω: the brief speech comes forcefully after the long anticipa-
tion. It opens with a verb of emotion, cf. e.g. *Pae.* 4 (D4). 40. The
word may include, besides general longing, the point that Amphia-
raus alone has been absent from the burial (note νεκρ-). At any
rate, we see in Adrastus' perspective a different angle from special
dispensation (*Nem.* 9) or oracular status (*Pyth.* 8. 38–56).

ὀφθαλμόν: a strong word (cf. *Ol.* 2. 9–10); but the speaker concentrates, heroically, on warfare. Cf. e.g. Hom. *Il.* 23. 12. ἐμᾶc too is both emotional and heroic.

μάρναcθαι: if ἀμφότερον κτλ. draw closely on the *Thebaid*, the deviation from hexametric rhythm in the last word heightens still further the complex metrical impact of the passage.

καί: the movement back to now is made more arresting by the period-end; the καί is not even prepared by a τε (as at *Ol.* 9. 65, *Pae.* 2 (D2). 25).

18. κώμου: the present occasion and mood are contrasted with those of the mythological scene.

Cυρακοcίωι: the difference of place is also brought out. Here too it is notable that Stymphalus is not mentioned.

19–21. With much ado, the narrator asseverates the applicability of Adrastus' saying to Hagesias. The present and past are being strikingly juxtaposed and related. The narrator here dwells on his own nature, speaks dramatically of swearing an oath, and alludes to his role as poet, which is being realized now. The present is thus made vivid; but an element of convention and fiction is important too. The narrator's character is such as to make his judgement valid and his candour exemplary; it does not show an interesting idiosyncracy, like say Anacreon's, but a model restraint. Cf. e.g. *Nem.* 7. 66–7, and note fr. 210. The swearing of an oath is also a conventional device in the genre (see the introduction to the commentary on Bacchylides). It is commonly introduced with an unneeded vehemence and an elaborate emphasis on the ritual (note μέγαν here, and the hand on the ground in Bacch. 5. 42, 8. 19); these endow the present with a degree of fiction. The last clause entangles this and another fiction: the Muses, with a legal turn, refer the matter to the narrator to judge. Cf., and contrast, *Ol.* 11. 16–17. The entanglement, and the inversion of hierarchy, create a gently amusing effect at the close.

19. The metre creates an elegantly balanced line, not unsuited to the nature portrayed. The stem φιλονικ- looks prosaic, but appears in Simon. 541. 11.

20. μέγαν ὅρκον ὀμόccαιc: cf. Hom. *Il.* 1. 233 etc., Sapph. 44 A a. 4.
γε is used more sparingly by Pindar and Bacchylides than by many authors, and carries considerable weight. Cf. e.g. *Nem.* 8. 10. καί too adds to the emphatic quality.

21. μαρτυρήcω: one might reasonably think that this future, like those at *Ol.* 2. 92 and Bacch. 8. 20, is little different from the present in the closely related passage Bacch. 5. 42. But καί does not suit the present; and the future of μαρτυρέω is often used of someone willing to bear witness, as it were at the right moment in the trial: cf. e.g. *Ol.* 13. 108, Aesch. *Ag.* 1505–6, *Eum.* 576, Soph. *Ant.* 515, Plat. *Ap.* 21 A 7–8, Aeschin. 2. 126; for the conception cf. Pind. *Ol.* 4. 3, *Parth.* 2. 38–9. The idea of intention is in fact vital to making sense of Pindar's futures; cf. e.g. *Ol.* 8. 54–9, 13. 91, *Pyth.* 2. 83–5, 3. 107–9; *Ol.* 7. 20, *Pyth.* 9. 1, *Isth.* 1. 15–16 (note ἦ . . . ἤ); note further Eur. *El.* 180, *HF* 673. Cf. Bundy (1986), 21–2; Slater (1969) ; Hummel (1993), 228–36.

μελίφθογγοι: Pindar presents numerous compounds in μελι- to vary the epic (and lyric) μελίγηρυc; the impulse is probably generic, cf. Bacch. 3 **[17]**. 97 (with n.), Lasus 702. 2; Sapph. 185?

The end of the epode matches the end of the strophe; it contrasts with the end of the antistrophe, sombre and in the past.

22–8. An address to Hagesias' charioteer, who actually did the racing, excitingly intrudes. It might seem that we were about to come to the victory itself, which has been variously overshadowed so far; cf. *Pyth.* 5. 45–53. But it at once becomes apparent that we are dealing, not with the recent past, but with the immediate future (contrast Silk (1974), 170–1). The mule-cart is hijacked by the poetry and its unreal discourse; even more notably, the metaphorical mules come to appear as different from the victorious mules, but parallel (they have learnt from them). Elaborate interplay between reality and metaphor, narrator and victor, is certainly characteristic of Pindar; but this is not just a standard instance. Pindar's narrator often presents his poetic movements as a journey or voyage; uses metaphors for his poetry from sport, sometimes the victor's sport; speaks of a poetic chariot, an idea with associations beyond the games (as in Parmenides). In one place a patron (friend) is said to have yoked the chariot of the Muses for him (*Pyth.* 10. 64–6). Such passages, especially when making transitions, sometimes contain vivacious self-addresses, addresses to the Muse, or anonymous commands (e.g. *Ol.* 2. 89–90, *Nem.* 3. 26–8, 5. 19–20 (τιc)). But here there are some differences.

Most importantly, the address is not confined to the poet's sphere; it draws in the actual charioteer, who must have been present at the performance. The effect will have been more audacious, and vigorously humorous, than we realize in reading. This remarkable passage in fact brings out how in the other passages too Pindar is not merely trying to assimilate his narrator to the athletes (cf. Steiner (1986), ch. 10). He is also relishing and exploiting their unlikeness, with, as often, an animated sense of play.

The mule-cart stands apart from the usual poetic four-horse chariot; in general, the metapoetic sports are a limited group. But the precise resonance is disputable. The mule-cart race, an innovation of 500, was discontinued in 440 or 436, and was not part of the later victory list (see P. Oxy. 222); scholars scorn it (e.g. Finley and Pleket (1976), 42). Anaxilas of Rhegium, however, proclaimed his victory in the race through coins and probably poetry (Robinson (1946), 17–18), and Simonides (515) was no doubt doing his best for the animals. As for metaphor, Pindar likens a private poem to an ὄχημα (fr. 124. 1), which he may intend to be the Sicilian speciality of a mule-cart (fr. 106. 5–6, Crit. fr. 2. 3 West; note also Pind. fr. 140 b. 8). Yet the listener is at any rate made aware of a striking and intriguing variation.

22. ὦ Φίντις: the narrator turns from the third person to the second. The address to Aeneas at 87–8 will be seen as parallel. The charioteer, like the wrestling trainer, can be an important person in the celebrations; cf. *Pyth.* 5. 45–53 (a close relation of Arcesilaus), *Isth.* 2. 20–8.

ἀλλά: as if an abrupt turning to business, cf. e.g. *Nem.* 10. 21. Since the goal will not actually be the victory itself, the appearance is a little teasing.

ἤδη has a certain urgency: it is high time now, there must be no delay. Cf. e.g. fr. 194. 2, Aesch. *Eum.* 605, Eur. *IT.* 1079.

cθένος ἡμιόνων: there is surely an air of self-consciousness here; cf. *Pyth.* 2. 11–12 καταζευγνύῃι | cθένος ἵππιον. Precisely by relating mule-carts to horse-chariots, Pindar is bringing their special quality to mind.

23. τάχος: a concern with speed, as with brevity and compression, is common in Pindar's transitions. Cf. *Pyth.* 4. 247, 10. 51, *Nem.* 4. 34. This professed concern enhances the ethos of the poetry (cf. *Pyth.* 10. 53–4); here it is made part of a spirited metaphorical scene, and taken up at the end (28).

καθαρᾶι: the narrator wants a clear run (cf. *Isth.* 5. 23); this is a journey, not a race.

25. γένος is marked out by *καί* and the enjambment. It is unusual for Pindar to devote the main narrative of his epinician to the mythical ancestors of his victor; cf. *Ol.* 2. 35–47 (short), *Pyth.* 5. 55–103 (not mythical, and the founder of the city). A main cause of the difference will be the unusual nature of this 'clan'. Even here the large body of the Iamidae is emphasized (ἀνδρῶν), not only the origin of one individual (ἀνδρός Hartung).

κεῖναι: the horses of real chariot teams (not Pherenicus) are rarely given so much personality. Even in *Nem.* 9. 52–3 their action is figurative.

ἀγεμονεῦσαι: they will not need to be guided, as would be usual.

26. ταύταν is emphasized by position and separation. Although later the initial journey will be to Sparta (28), the way to the Iamidae is still to Olympia, the centre of their activity (cf. 5). ἐν Ὀλυμπίαι is thus significant for the argument, and placed before ἐπεί.

27. δέξαντο: the animals are not commonly said to receive the garlands. The mention of Hagesias' triumph takes place in a subordinate and surprising context; not that the ingenious mannerism diminishes its impact.

χρή gives what the narrator must do, as at 4: another contemplated start. With χρὴ τοίνυν he bustles energetically. The gates are to be opened so that the mules can begin their journey. Cf. πύλαι . . . κελεύθων at Parm. fr. 1. 11 Coxon (on the situation cf. Tarán (1965), 13–14 etc.). The sentence is effectively simple and pithy; but the opening of gates of song is an inspiring conception. One thinks of Alc. 296 b. 3, the opening of the gates of spring (imitated at Pind. fr. 75. 14–15). There is probably an incidental play between ἀναπιτνάμεν and Πιτάναν.

28. Another pressing statement. δεῖ now appears instead of χρή, for the only time in Pindar. The closing ἐν ὥραι and cάμερον both dwell on time, in tones of hurry and stress. cάμερον both enters into the situation as if it were real and marks its unreality; in fact they arrive at Sparta in the very act of mentioning it. The air of game in the whole passage is not lost here.

cάμερον: the long syllable with final ν is a licence found in Bacchylides too; cf. e.g. *Nem.* 1. 51, Bacch. 10. 10.

παρ᾽ Εὐρώτα πόρον brings out the distance to be travelled; it also provides a contrast with the Alpheius (34, 58), and marks the difference in place from Elis and Arcadia (cf. e.g. *Isth.* 5. 33, Simon. fr. 11. 28 West).

29–35. The mythical narrative proper begins with the second antistrophe, a common enough point (see Hamilton (1974), 36). It tells not only of Iamus' origins but of his mother's. This is no awkward 'doublet' (cf. Wilamowitz (1886), 178). First, an appearance of mythological density is valued in itself, especially in the narrative intricacy of this poem; likewise the origin of Cyrene's father is given at *Pyth.* 9. 15–17. That passage too, however, is also thematically relevant to its poem. Here one can hardly think insignificant the correspondence of the beginning and end of the stanza, intercourse with Poseidon and with Apollo. The role of Poseidon is vital to the subsequent narrative, and to the poem, particularly in the pairing with Apollo. The intercourse is important too. Other correspondences between the accounts of Pitane and Evadne are the hiding (κρύψε 31) and the failure to hide (36 οὐδ' ἔλαθ' . . . κλέπτοιϲα), and the mention of the time of pregnancy in this context (32, 36). But there is an essential difference between the passages in the evocation of the woman's experience. μιχθεῖϲα . . . τεκέμεν (29–30) is utterly standardized and unemotional language (cf. e.g. *Ol.* 7. 71, *Pyth.* 9. 84, *Pae.* 9 (A1). 42–3; Alc. 327. 2–3, Bacch. 17. 30–1); Pitane's subsequent arrangements are related with no reference to her feelings (32–3). Evadne's encounter with the god, her giving birth, and her next action are described with striking expressions and detail, and with some indication of her emotions (35, 39–41, 44). In plot, all goes smoothly after the birth of Evadne; things are much more complicated after the birth of Iamus. The narrative on Pitane thus sets the narrative on Evadne and Iamus in effective relief.

It matters less to us how or why this part of the story developed before Pindar. One might certainly suspect that the family tree has at some stage undergone secondary expansion. It looks as though two places of origin for the clan are being combined (as in the narrative about Zeus in Call. *H.* 1); and the scholia know of a version in which Iamus' father is Poseidon (59 b). Gods do not commonly beget mortal girls. The motif of sending the child away is treated elsewhere by Pindar, with Jason and Orestes (*Pyth.* 4. 111–15, 11. 15–22, 34–6, cf. Eur. *Cresph.* fr. 448a. 15–18 Kannicht (66 Austin)); but the invention need not be his here any more than there. More particularly, the wish to give Iamus a Spartan ancestry has been interestingly linked with the Iamid seer Teisamenus' becoming a Spartan (Hdt. 9. 33–6, cf. Wilamowitz (1886), 179–82). However, this would not obliterate the positive functions that Sparta possesses in the poem of Pindar, who was under no obligation to bring it in. Sparta creates a surprise after the mention of Olympia in 26, and increases the movement in a narrative full of journeying; opposition with that distinct and distant locale facilitates the blending of Elis and Arcadia.

Pindar's narrative ingeniously blurs those last two regions; the Arcadian origin of the Olympian Iamus suits the Arcadian Hagesias most conveniently. In 34 Arcadia and the Alpheus are connected, in 57–70 we pass easily from the Alpheus to Olympia. In fact, the Alpheus comes into southern Arcadia, but does not approach the northern region, where Aepytus, like Stymphalus, appears to belong. Aepytus' famous tomb is certainly situated in the north-east near Cyllene, as is his father's kingdom (Hom. *Il.* 2. 604, Paus. 8. 4. 4, 16. 2–3; cf. Wentzel (1894); West (1985), 93, 154). The blurring might better suit, perhaps, a Syracusan than a Stymphalian audience; cf. Ov. *Met.* 5. 585–600, with Haupt and Ehwald (1966), 295. The term 'Arcadians' assists the treatment; we are hindered from understanding the full effect by our ignorance of what Phaesane (34) conveyed to the audience. Istros, *FGrHist* 334 F 41, knew of a Phaesane in Elis; but one cannot depend on Didymus that no other places of the name existed (Σ 55 a). How far in all this Pindaric invention or choice extends, we have not the means to say; but we may certainly register that the narrative is concerned to unite Hagesias' Arcadian and Olympian connections.

29. ἄ: Pitane now turns from a place into the eponymous nymph; her father was Eurotas, also simply a place just now (Sosib. *FGrHist* 595 F 21, with Jacoby (1923–) III b. 655–6). The change with Pitane, however characteristic it may be thought of Pindar, remains striking here.

λέγεται: a common type of expression for introducing a story, or a new part of one; cf. e.g. *Nem.* 1. 34, Alc. 42. 1, Bacch. 5. 57. Here the effect is to show, after 24–8, other sources for the narrative than simply the narrator (cf. *Ol.* 9. 49 after 48–9). The less emotional section of the narrative also receives a little distancing.

30. ἰόπλοκον: the same corruption at *Isth.* 7. 23. The epithet is

used by Bacchylides too (9. 72, 17. 37); its first part might acquire
more significance, on a second hearing, from the development of
the narrative (note especially 55).

31. The phrase does not convey even the physical sensation with
particular force (contrast Eur. *Ion* 15). ὠδῖνα, though hardly 'child'
before birth, is here weak and generalized (contrast fr. 33 d. 3–4, and
43 here). Yet the combination κρύψε . . . κόλποις, and the different
senses of κόλποις, make the brief sentence and self-contained line
arrestingly concrete. Contrast the separation of *uestis* and *uterum* at
Ov. *Met.* 2. 460–3, and the straightforward and comic effect of that
passage.

παρθενίαν evokes the normal world and the need for secrecy; the
metonymy focuses attention on the condition rather than on the
person as a subject. The word underlines the link with the narrative
to come (note πρῶτον 35).

32–3. κυρίωι δ᾽ ἐν μηνί: the actual moment of birth is not dwelt on.

πέμποις᾽ ἀμφιπόλους . . . πορϲαίνειν adds to the impression of
elaborate arrangement and circumstantial narrative.

ἥρωϊ . . . Εἰλατίδαι: his name comes only later (36). This central
character of the subsequent narrative is introduced with pomp; the
relative clause accentuates his royal status (cf. 47). Cf. Bacch. 3
[**17**]. 23–4.

βρέφος: the absence of the child's sex here and the emphasis on
its babyhood (contrast 30, 41) reinforce the connection with the
later narrative.

35. γλυκείας: the union with the god is remarkably depicted as
voluptuous for the girl (cf. ἀδείας at *Pyth.* 9. 41); one may con-
trast say Bacch. 1. 118, and compare *Pyth.* 9. 16. ἔψαυϲ᾽ carries
suggestions of sensuality and attained knowledge. Cf. *Pyth.* 4. 92,
Nem. 5. 42, and also e.g. *Pyth.* 9. 36, Ov. *Met.* 3. 353–5 (girls too).
The colouring suits not only the sensuousness of epinician but the
benign ethos of the narrative.

36. οὐδ᾽ ἔλαθ᾽: a grim turn to the narrative after the close to the
antistrophe. Cf. the even grimmer *Pyth.* 3. 27. The phrase and its
position evoke the epic, cf. Hom. *Il.* 17. 1, 20. 112. The whole
period and sentence counters 31; the conative κλέπτοιϲα contrasts
with the success of κρύψε.

In concealing their pregnancy by gods from their father or foster-
father, Pitane and Evadne are naturally concealing what seems to

be sexual misconduct on their part, as Coronis conceals her guilty
liaison (*Pyth.* 3. 13). Creusa and Auge in Euripides do the same
(*Ion* 14–15, *Tel.* fr. 103. 4–7 Austin). Here the narrative conveys the
irony: the god's parentage (θεοῖο), when revealed by an authoritative
source, will bring joy. Cf. the significant θεοῦ at *Pyth.* 3. 15.
The mention of the god takes up the end of the antistrophe and
is itself taken up at the end of the stanza: the god acts (41–2).
After this opening clause of the stanza, which mentions Evadne,
Aepytus, and Apollo, Aepytus is made the subject of the next main
clause, Evadne of the next, Apollo of the last. In this shaping of
the stanza Apollo is made to control and dominate the narrative;
cf. 49–50, 61–2. From another perspective, a sequence of μέν s and
δέ s accentuates the birth and culminates in Iamus (also mentioned
in this sentence), at the start of the next stanza and the new triad.
Cf. 71. This interweaving and this handling of the stanzaic form
organize an apparently straightforward stretch of narrative with
much subtlety.

37–8. The syntax is involved: the first participial clause splits up
the main clause, and other participles follow. Lines 39–41 are much
simpler and smoother in structure. The style in 37–8 suits the
animated movement and the king's conscientious arrangement. In
contrast stands the magical simplicity of the scene of birth (on
the surface). The surrounding and subordination of the clause on
emotion express Aepytus' self-control; but the unusual metrical
moment highlights his vehement feeling. This is taken up in the
focalized ταύτας περ' ἀτλάτου πάθας which closes. The narrative,
quieter hitherto, is now acquiring a forceful dynamic.

Πυθῶνάδ': the divine father's seat (cf. 36) is an ironic, as well as a
distant, destination.

ἐν θυμῶι πιέcαιc: a noble repression of emotion, unlike Pelias'
(*Pyth.* 4. 96–7). The aspect is decisively perfective. The grammat-
ical structure effectively reverses the structure more frequent with
this verb in such contexts: emotion etc. as subject, person as object
(e.g. *Nem.* 1. 53, Eur. fr. 665 Nauck). ὀξείαι too is transformed. It
is often used of emotion etc. (e.g. *Nem.* 1. 53, 11. 48); here it is
expressively applied to a word for discipline, and conveys both the
pain and the force of the effort.

οὐ φατόν: immense, cf. *Isth.* 7. 37; *Nem.* 1. 47.

ἰών: the addition is Homeric (*Il.* 15. 219 etc.); it contributes to the stir and style of the passage. Whether it can form part of the play with *ἰ*- is doubtful: not only is the play not yet visible, but the word is relatively inconspicuous (contrast 30). Furthermore, Pindar would presumably have thought of the words *Ϝίος, Ϝίον* as possessing *Ϝ* (cf. 30, *Isth.* 7. 23), even if the letter could be ignored in verse. There is nothing implausible in a mythical name *Ϝίαμος*. Cf. e.g. *Ϝιολα, ϜιολαϜος, Ϝιολας* on Corinthian and Laconian vases; Iolaus' *Ϝ* is often active in Pindar. The point about *Ϝ*, at least, applies also to *ἴμεν* in 63; cf. McDiarmid (1987), 377 n. 35.

μαντευσόμενος: there are no close parallels for such an enquiry of the oracle, but that by Cydippe's father is not wholly unrelated (Call. fr. 75. 19–20 Pfeiffer). In any case, the situation is an urgent crisis in which Aepytus wishes to act wisely; cf. *Ol.* 7. 31. For the oracles in Pindar see Parke and Wormell (1956), ii. 61–4. Prophecy is of course thematic in this poem, and Apollo's powers are passed to his son (cf. 41).

ἀτλάτου πάθας: Aepytus' own line is not concerned, but the shame he finds intolerable; cf. e.g. Aesch. *Supp.* 956. Proetus considers suicide when his daughters go mad, Bacch. 11. 85–91. Otherwise Bonelli (1987), 77.

39–41. Here for the first time in the poem the ornamental epithets are lavishly strewn; hitherto there have been only *εὐτειχεῖ* 1, *κλεινᾶν* 6, *ἱμερταῖς* 7, *κοίλαις* 10, *φαιδίμας* 14, *μελίφθογγοι* 21 (none in the second strophe), *ἰόπλοκον* 30, *γλυκείας* 35, all well spaced. *φοινικόκροκος* occurs only here; *φοινικο*- derives from epic (Hom. *Od.* 11. 124), and is popular with Pindar and Bacchylides. Cf. Eur. *Hec.* 471 *ἀνθοκρόκοισι*. The stylistic effect contributes to the complex mixture in the passage of luxury and simplicity. The king's daughter is engaged on tasks that would be thought humble in Pindar's time; but this is itself an epic feature (Hom. *Od.* 10. 105–8, *h. Dem.* 105–7, etc.), and her clothes and vessel are costly. The pastoral locale for the birth may seem both epic and attractive (cf. e.g. Hom. *Il.* 4. 474–6); but there is also a contrast between the bright and glamorous possessions and the dark copse. The structure and metre of 40 sharpen this contrast (cf. 19). The scene even has the potential to seem sordid as well as dismal, no fit setting for the inspired child; 45, and 54, help to realize this potential. Simon. 543 [**16**] pursues related complications. For all the complexity, the narrative flows with a primal inevitability to its wonderful culmination at the start of a new period, τίκτε.

The abundant colours of the scene of course contrast with the colourless, and predominantly mental, 37–8. But so far we have only human colour and natural darkness; a more deeply magical scene is to come (55–6).

τίκτε: the verb has probably no specific imperfective force, cf. e.g. *Pyth.* 3. 101, 9. 16, Bacch. 13. 97, Hom. *Il.* 16. 180. But the plain statement is developed in what follows (41–4).

θεόφρονα κοῦρον: he is still not named. The designation progresses from θεοῖο γόνον at the start of the stanza. The epithet is used of Cadmus at *Theb.* F2. 3 Davies; but here it is converted to mean 'prophetic', cf. *Suppl. Hell.* 443. 4. (The semantics of this development are not altogether clear.)

τᾶι: the emphasis seems to fall on Apollo's helping the mother rather than the child; cf. πραΰμητιν. Benevolent divinity is actually present at the apparently lonely scene; Evadne does not realize (44–5).

ὁ χρυσοκόμας: the title is standard (*Ol.* 7. 32; with Ἀπόλλων *Pae.* 5 (D5). 41, Bacch. 4. 2); but here the divine colour is opposed to mere mortal brightness, especially the silver of the preceding line. Anacreon uses the epithet in a related fashion at 358 [**13**]. 2.

42. πραΰμητιν: only here.

παρέστασέν τε: the order in πραΰμητίν τ᾽ κτλ. is certainly unusual, with the word common to both parts, παρέστασεν, beginning the second group. The same principle appears at fr. 42. 3 καλῶν μὲν ὦν μοῖράν τε τερπνῶν. ἐν (Peek (1958)) would only suit if there were various additions in colourful profusion; 'among' or 'in' would not be apt. The word-end with the conjecture would be acceptable, if not particularly welcome; cf. Parker (1966), 8.

The Fates naturally belong here, cf. *Nem.* 7. 1 (Carey (1981), 138), *Pae.* 12 (G1). 16–17, Plat. *Smp.* 206 D 2. At the end of the triad they suggest the tremendous destiny of Iamus. Their name contrasts and connects significantly with that of Aphrodite at the end of the preceding stanza (cf. e.g. the meaningful placing at Eur. *Hel.* 1121, 1136). From that pleasure birth and mighty consequences come.

43. Wilamowitz's ὠδίνεσσ᾽ ἐραταῖς is quite unwanted ((1922), 308 n. 1). Pindar does not elide the ending -εσσι. The second ὑπό is not of accompanying circumstances: the ὠδῖνος is something from which the child emerges, cf. *Nem.* 1. 36. Pindar commonly repeats a preposition with τε; the pair is less notable than that in *Ol.* 14. 17–18 (cf. Mommsen (1864*b*), 197); cf. also *Nem.* 9. 44 (with Braswell (1998), 130–1); *Pyth.* 4. 281–2; not to mention *Ol.* 1. 88. For A's omission of τ' cf. 17, *Ol.* 9. 21, 89, Young (1970), 103. ἐρατᾶc (ἐρατόν Bergk) is now secured by *Pae.* 12 (G1). 13–14, where we hear of Leto's τερπνᾶc | ὠδῖνοc (contrast e.g. fr. 33 d. 3–4, *Hom. h. Ap.* 91–2). These epithets dwell on the moment of release and birth. A connection is made here with the related γλυκείαc at 35; the benign atmosphere of this scene is enhanced. There will be a striking contrast with the next clause.

Ἴαμοc: after the long prepositional phrase the name comes with great effect to end the period; cf. παῖc Διόc at *Nem.* 1. 35.

44–5. ἐc φάοc is also effectively placed at the start of the period. The enjambment and the absence of epithet (contrast *Nem.* 1. 35, *Pae.* 12 (G1). 15) help suggest, with the final αὐτίκα, a sudden marvellous escape. One may perhaps contrast the sudden engulfment in earth of Amphiaraus and his bright horses (14); certainly the scenes and moods of death and birth are opposed.

τὸν μέν κτλ.: starting within the same period, and with no announcement of subject, a brief clause presents an abrupt reversal. Aepytus' emotions had been treated with amplitude; here one word conveys Evadne's grief in leaving her child. κνίζω in Pindar can refer to various types of agitating emotion, often strong (e.g. *Pyth.* 11. 23). The word contrasts with ἐρατᾶc; λεῖπε contrasts poignantly with τίκτε, which has the same shape, the same place in its period, and begins the same metrical sequence. (Its tense may be influenced by Homer, e.g. *Il.* 21. 201.) χάμαι makes the abandonment more ugly; the careful exposures of drama look different. There would be little mystery in an unmarried girl leaving her baby: cf. e.g. Ar. *Clouds* 530–1 (and Patterson (1985), 115–16). Here, however, the phrasing and the enjambment seem to render the action at once pitiable and startling.

45–7. The narrative here and at 55 is engendered by two plays on the name of Iamus, both set at the same point in their different periods (an indication that this position is significant). Cf. 37–8 n. Pindar elsewhere has a story to explain a name or word, *Ol.* 9. 44–6, *Isth.* 6. 49–53 (with a merely incidental further play on αἰ- at 52). Here the second story is made the cause of the name, 56–7;

the first is added exuberantly. The first, moreover, could only be thought of as created in poetry, and of a particularly daring kind. ἀμεμφεῖ | ἰῶι μελιccᾶν is not merely a metaphor presented explicitly as a paradox (a tragic rather than a Pindaric figure): it is a reversal of nature through language, so that the venom given by snakes is not harmful. Cf. *Ol.* 1. 31–2 (the conception of paradoxical reversal), 12. 13–15 (the expression: the τίμα would have been ἀκλεής). One may think of how copiously imaginative play on words can appear to create events in *Finnegans Wake* (e.g. from the shipping forecast, p. 324, ed. Faber 1975); but there the effect is subversive, comic, anarchic, here solemnity and fertile ingenuity combine. The poet's mind comes boldly to the fore in a part of the poem where the narrator directs little attention to himself.

The most obvious parallel for the two snakes that nurture Iamus are the two that nurture Erichthonius (Eur. *Ion* 21–6 etc.; cf. Burkert (1966), 11). Snakes have a different impact from the female mammals that suckle abandoned children from pity (Binder (1964), 125–49). Even Erichthonius' snakes were terrifying. Snakes sent to harm babies are more prominent in myth and poetry: so the two snakes sent by a goddess (θεόπομποι) against Heracles and Iphicles (*Nem.* 1. 38–43, with Moret (1992), *Pae.* 20 (S1). 7–9), and the snake which, as a sign, kills Archemorus (Sim. 553; Bacch. 9. 12–13); one can note too the snakes which for heaven's purposes kill Laocoon's son or sons (cf. Bacch. fr. 9; Early Lucanian red-figure bell-krater by the Pisticci Painter (Basel Lu. 70, *LCS* suppl. 2, 154 (3, 6). 33a, 430–425 BC); *Suppl. Hell.* 562. 10–12). Here the gods (46) intervene to save. Snakes and honey have manifold and varied religious significance; this enhances the mystery and depth of the happening.

γλαυκῶπες: the epithet is used of the snake at *Pyth.* 4. 249. The form and usage of course vary the epic divine epithet γλαυκῶπις.

δαιμόνων βουλαῖσιν: the same resounding phrase, even more prominently placed, at *Isth.* '3/4'. 37 (cf. Bacch. 11. 121). The gods in general are now involved. There may perhaps be a link here to the striking δαιμόνιον of 8: the gods' favour extends down the generations.

δράκοντες: the word is effectively delayed after the preparing numeral and adjective at the start (45). μελιccᾶν is opposed.

καδόμενοι ends the sentence beautifully; the serpents' action contrasts with the mother's.

47–9. From beasts and the divine we move back abruptly to a bustling human world. βαcιλεύc at once marks social status; the life and structure of the household is vividly captured in what follows. The prophecy is not given as Apollo's statement (cf. e.g. *Ol.* 7. 32–3; Call. fr. 75. 21–37 Pfeiffer); it appears only indirectly through Aepytus' statement. None the less, this human world too has been turned upside down by the divine; events, and Aepytus' feelings, have been completely altered. The narrative has points in common both with Creon's reversal in the *Antigone* and with Charisius' in the *Epitrepontes* (878–903).

πετραέccαc: a Homeric epithet for Delphi (*Il.* 9. 405, *h. Ap.* 183, etc.). It interacts effectively with ἐλαύνων, suggesting a demanding journey. It also gives solemnity to the holy place, by contrast with the palace.

ἐλαύνων: the motif and the animation of journeying are thematically and poetically important; the link with the metaphorical drive of the second strophe is evident. The placing of the participle between πετραέccαc and ἵκετ᾽ ἐκ Πυθῶνοc adds to the stylistic and syntactic complication: the same was seen in 37–8, on Aepytus.

ἅπανταc indicates Aepytus' eagerness, and the futility of his enquiries.

τέκοι evokes Aepytus' utterance, cf. Goodwin (1889), 281–2; Kühner–Gerth (1898–1904), ii. 548–9. The indirect speech is continued more openly in the next clause. Aepytus' remarks do not turn from reported speech to direct, like Aphrodite's in Sapph. 1 [4]. Direct speech, which Pindar uses cautiously, is kept in the poem for the momentous utterances of Adrastus and Apollo; cf. e.g. *Ol.* 13. 75–82 as against Athena's speech 67–9. Indirect speech suits the agitation of the scene here, and the effective indirectness of the prophecy. Even Teiresias' prophecy at *Nem.* 1. 61–72 is rendered in *oratio obliqua*; but this prophecy is doubly indirect, a report of Aepytus' report of Apollo.

Φοίβου: Apollo appears forcefully again at the end of a stanza, as father not as originator of the prophecy. The name matches Εὐάδνα, and gives the less obvious and more remarkable half of the parentage; hence (from Aepytus' perspective) the emphatic πατρόc in 50.

γεγάκειν: the form is striking; contrast γεγάμεν *Ol.* 9. 110. Cf. Hesych. γ 229 Latte γεγακώc (Diels's conjecture at Emped. fr. 15. 10 Wright is dubious). The form of the infinitive is parallel to but more surprising than the perfect participles in -οντας, with epic precedent, at *Pyth.* 4. 179, 183. With the infinitive epic influence is not in question, and Doric or other dialect influence is not particularly likely (cf. Thumb, Kieckers, and Scherer (1932–59), i. 203, 275). Here Lesbian poetry remains the most plausible inspiration; cf. Sapph. 31 [6]. 15, 94. 1, Hamm (1958), 170–1 (otherwise, by implication, Braswell (1988), 266–7, affected by Strunk (1957), 104–8). The unusual form must highlight this word at the end of the stanza; it takes up τέκοι, but not inertly. The ideas of being born, and alive, are important.

50–1. πατρός: the divine origin of Iamus is proudly marked at the start of the stanza; but the stanza also ends, touchingly, with μάτηρ. The divine origin propels rhetorically the mention of Iamus' exalted status and the eternity of his line (50–1).

The prophecy announces the birth and opens a glorious window on the future. It has obvious points in common with the prophecies at *Ol.* 8. 42–6, *Pyth.* 4. esp. 50–6, 9. 51–65, *Nem.* 1. 62–72, *Isth.* 6. 52–4, *Pae.* 10 (a) (A2). This one is unusual for its indirectness: apart from the handling of speech (47–9 n.), it presents a formally subordinate justification for Aepytus' questions; the narrative that resumes after it concerns the principal issue of the child's whereabouts. The prophecy is also unusual in dwelling on an everlasting future, into which the present of the narrator is subsumed. In other words, the author is manneristically setting in a narrative recess a spectacular and particularly important element.

περὶ θνατῶν . . . ἔξοχον: the supremacy rings the clause, a more glorious supremacy than Amphiaraus' (16–17). The expressions have an epic resonance, without quite following the epic phrases.

μάντιν: the thematic word appears itself within the report of a prophecy from the god who assures the greatness of the prophet.

ἐπιχθονίοις: the dative here suggests a divine perspective behind Aepytus' own.

οὐδέ ποτ' ἐκλείψειν: the use of the verb, and the language, here are thoroughly un-Homeric; cf. *Il.* 20. 307–8, *Od.* 15. 532–3.

52–3. μάνυε is a more significant word than the expected 'spoke', and underlines the prophecy. Cf. e.g. Bacch. 10. 13.

τοὶ δ' κτλ.: the extreme simplicity and brevity of the sentence mimics the vehement denials of the slaves, as far as εὔχοντο, and

then presents bluntly a surprising and alarming situation (cf. e.g.
Pyth. 6. 33–4).

εὔχοντο: the verb, unusually, denotes a claim about the past that
is not a boast. Pindar may have in mind the disputatious (and
disputed) passage Hom. *Il.* 18. 499. The two imperfect verbs may
make a background for the pluperfect in 54.

πεμπταῖον γεγενημένον: the verb appears in a more ordinary and
worrying context than at 49. It also stands in apparently ironic
opposition to γενεάν in 51, from the same root, again at the end of a
sentence. Paris was reared by the bear for five days, in Apollod. 3.
12. 5.

53–4. ἀλλ’ . . . γάρ is adversative, and sets aside what precedes; the
train of thought is that, for all the ignorance, enquiry, appearance
of danger, there he was, lying concealed, etc.

ἔν | : cf. for the period-end after the preverb Bacch. 5. 74 (prob-
able); *Isth.* '3/4'. 18 (not quite so probable, the less if *Isth.* 3 is a
separate poem); with a disyllable *Ol.* 1. 57. Cf. Willcock (1995), 91.
The usage here is the more remarkable in that ἀλλ’ . . . γάρ pre-
vents the preverb from being treated as an adverb: only a close-knit
group like noun and article could separate them (Alcm. 17. 7). But
there is enough evidence to make us chary of accepting Hermann's
ἀλλά (with the preposition ἀπὸ κοινοῦ). It is also unusual for a new
sentence to start two syllables before the end of a period; besides 17
and 102 here, cf. *Pyth.* 10. 59, *Nem.* 4. 31, 47, 5. 50, 10. 51, 57 (none
narrative; mostly ἐπεί etc.). The effect of the two things together is
to make the transition more surprising.

54. At first the image seems almost squalid; the baby has been
preserved, but in an unlovely, uncivilized place. The scene is not
transformed until the participial clause. The action of the snakes
had had definite and zealous agents, and had been presented with a
decisive aorist (46). Here the pluperfect is employed to emphasize
a state; it is an unusual tense for Pindar (cf. *Isth.* 2. 39, an unusual
situation). No agent is given; the adversative, not explanatory, par-
ticles, the participial clause, and 45, make it plainly not Evadne.
Instead of a moment of rescue, we are shown an imperfective vi-
sion of the unmoving child.

The singulars cχοίνωι and βατιᾶι, one derived from the epic (Hom.
Od. 5. 463), one no doubt from everyday language, paint the scene

broadly. The rough suggestions of βατιᾶι will be cancelled in the next clause.

ἀπειρίτωι is somewhat awkward. ἀπειράτωι, from πειράω, will not scan (or provide a suitable meaning). It is hazardous to postulate an essentially unattested ἀπείρᾰτος from περαίνω: Pindar actually has elsewhere the standard ἀπε(ί)ραντος. The promising meaning 'impenetrable' does not match extant examples of ἀπέραντος. We seem to be thrown back on ἀπειρίτωι, an epic word which seems to mean 'boundless, innumerable', and to be treated as a synonym of ἀπειρέςιος. A recursion beyond epic to a distant conjectured original 'impassable' does not seem especially likely (cf. Schulze (1892), 116 n. 3, with Chantraine (1968), i. 96). The implied infinity of ἀπείριτος and ἀπειρέςιος need not be taken too seriously, cf. e.g. *Hom. h. Aphr.* 120 (crowd), Stes. 255 (dogs' howling); but the word does not seem particularly telling (cf. now Günther (1998), 132–3). One would have to suppose that a vast and desolate scene is portrayed. Perhaps if βατιά is an everyday word for a limited patch of brambles (cf. ϲποδιή, ἰωνιά, etc.), the adjective counters the restrictive and reductive appearance of the word in effective paradox.

55–6. The stem Ϝι- appears again, in a sudden moment of astounding poetry. The colours of royal luxury (39–40) are replaced by colours at once natural and divine. The idea of the colours shining through the flowers is remarkable for Greek poetry in itself; cf. perhaps Asclep. v. 4 Gow–Page. The expression of it draws different areas into unexpected harmony: 'wetness' and softness, flowers and a baby's skin. At the same time the combinations through metaphor and metonymy surprise: 'rays of flowers', 'drenched by rays'. This etymology too will appear to the listener to spring from poetic imagination: the physical union of body with flowers presents a far more powerful account of the name than if Iamus had merely been found among violets. As with the snakes, the suggestions of the image cannot be fully analysed; but this only makes more profound the evocation of the divine birth.

ἴων: Theophr. *Hist. Plant.* 6. 6. 3 divides ἴα into black and white (cf. Amigues (1993), 187); Pindar seems to exploit a related division here.

παμπορφύροις: the colours are strong (cf. Carne-Ross (1979), 39).

βεβρεγμένος: cf. Emped. fr. 14. 4 Wright ἀργέτι δεύεται αὐγῆι. Zenodotus would seem to have taken exception to the metaphor, and so emended (Σ 92 (a)); cf. Anacr. 408; Pfeiffer (1968–76), i. 117–19.

ἁβρόν: cf. Eur. (?) *Med.* 1075 for this sensuousness.

τὸ καί: cf. Call. fr. 75. 38 Pfeiffer Ὑδρούσσαν τῶι καί μιν ἐφήμισαν. The Homeric use of τό, not found elsewhere in Pindar, strengthens the gravity. Cf. Hom. *Il.* 12. 9, 17. 404, Soph. *Phil.* 142.

κατέφαμιξεν: the word comes only here before Polybius; φημίζω is used by Hesiod and Aeschylus, ἐπιφημίζω is found mostly in Attic prose. The unusual word probably indicates a solemn pronouncement, and glances at the use of (-)φημιζ- for naming; cf. Plat. *Tim.* 73 D 5, *al.*, Arat. 442, Rhian. 25. 5 Powell, Call. fr. 75. 15 Pfeiffer, 38 (see above). καλεῖcθαι is a Homeric future.

χρόνωι cύμπαντι: eternity is prominent, and will end this whole portion of the story (57); the mother dwells on it like the father (51). The immortal fame is here for the son, not only his descendants; but it will be achieved through them.

μάτηρ: not only the finding of the child is implied, but the mother's recovery of the child she had abandoned; the word is strikingly placed (cf. *Ol.* 2. 80). The plot is elaborately and sympathetically completed, with an oblique touch. And yet from a different perspective, the passage is not mannerist: it is the name that most concerns the narrator.

57–9. τοῦτ' ὄνομ' ἀθάνατον: the name begins the stanza and ends the section of narrative. ἀθάνατον, besides celebrating glory, suggests Iamus' links to gods, and difference from them.

τερπνᾶc δ' κτλ.: as in *Pyth.* 3 (or the Homeric *Hymn to Apollo*, as we have it), we pass on from the birth to later deeds. In *Pyth.* 3. 45–6 the transition is smooth; here it is abrupt. The birth and the later episode belong together in the narrative argument; but there is also an effective contrast between the youth and the baby, and a connection with the young Evadne, just mentioned (56). τερπνᾶc joins up with γλυκείαc in 35, Ἥβαc with Ἀφροδίταc. The whole phrase could be used of a man sleeping with a virgin, as in the closely similar *Pyth.* 9. 109–11, and some have been surprised by λάβεν; but the male plucks the fruit of his youth for himself (cf. *Pyth.* 6. 48), and his concern is not with love. The youth of Pelops and Theseus is more physically evoked (*Ol.* 1. 67–8; Bacch. 18. 54–7); but here too, as the structural parallel with *Ol.* 1. 67–8 suggests, we are to sense the excitement of the youthful hero's quest for glory.

χρυcοcτεφάνοιο: used of Hebe at *Pyth.* 9. 109 and Hes. *Theog.*
17, of Aphrodite at Sapph. 33. 1 and Hes. fr. 26. 13 Merkelbach–
West, *al.*

Ἀλφεῶι κτλ.: the place for the prayer is particularly suited to Po-
seidon, who is a god of rivers too. Obviously akin is Bellerophon's
entering the sea to pray to Poseidon (Plut. *Mul. virt.* 248 A, *cit.*
Kakridis (1970), 172); Pelops' going near the sea with the same
purpose, at night, looks related too (*Ol.* 1. 71). In Pindar's narra-
tive, the Alpheus is by Iamus' home, and so is the most easily ac-
cessible water (34). The emphasis on Poseidon helps the structure
of the poem; for the duality must be maintained, despite Apollo's
predominance (cf. also 103–5). The role of the two gods has been
carefully built into the design of the narrative; ὃν πρόγονον 59 un-
derlines the connection with 29. Nor is the connection with two
gods at all awkward; cf. *Pae.* 9 (A1). 41–9 on Poseidon's, as well as
Apollo's, honouring of Teneros, Apollo's prophetic son. Whether
or not Pindar has invented the scene, we should not see it as some-
thing merely left over from an earlier account, where Iamus set out
for Olympia or was the son of Poseidon (Wilamowitz (1886), 176;
Kakridis (1970), 172). The idea that Pindar 'could not unify' a pre-
packaged incident with his narrative should seem incredible now.
The atmosphere of the scene is plainly important: μέccωι stresses
the dramatic locale; Ἀλφεῶι μέccωι καταβαίc at the start and νυκτὸc
ὑπαίθριοc at the end ring the description with the impressive setting.

καταβαίc: Amphiaraus' fatal engulfment by earth may perhaps
be contrasted.

The unusual metre at this part of the epode marks out Iamus'
invocation of the two gods.

εὐρυβίαν: used of Poseidon at *Pyth.* 2. 12. The word is found
in epic (*Hom. h. Dem.*, Hes. *Theog.*), not in earlier lyric, elegy, or
iambus, and is popular with Pindar and Bacchylides. The epithets
given to the two male gods set them against Hebe in the same
sentence.

59. ὃν πρόγονον: emphatically placed. Apollo is referred to more
allusively, and his paternity is saved for 62.

τοξοφόρον: of Apollo at *Hom. h. Ap.* 13, 26.

θεοδμάταc: the word is popular with Pindar and Bacchylides, and
later with Euripides (Pind. fr. 33 c. 1 of Delos); before, it is extant
only at Hom. *Il.* 8. 519. Pindar uses Delos in addressing Apollo

at *Pyth.* 1. 39; the epithet here indicates how ornate the passage is becoming.

cκoπόν: a usage not seen before Pindar, cf. e.g. *Pae.* 6 (D6). 94, and perhaps Aesch. *Supp.* 381, Soph. *Aj.* 945.

60. λαοτρόφον τιμάν τιν': the τιν' indicates that Iamus is asking for some undefined but honourable position of importance to the state, rather than specifically for kingship (cf. Braswell (1988), 198). There are various τιμαί; cf. *Parth.* 1. 6, Bacch. 14. 6–7. The passage exploits the mortal's ignorance and the perspective of time. λαοτροφον should not refer to the people maintaining the seer, as the passage is not insulting (cf. von der Mühll (1976*b*)); nor would the people naturally be said to τρέφειν the honour. Iamus is generous as well as concerned for his own glory; the words are carefully arranged in the line. The utility of seers to peoples is evident from the Iamidae, and implicit in Adrastus' lament. Cf. *Ol.* [5.] 4.

έâι κεφαλâι stresses and dignifies the self; cf. *Ol.* 7. 67–8.

61. νυκτὸc ὑπαίθριοc: the mildly paradoxical phrase returns the sentence from the prayer to the place. The light and colour of the earlier scenes with Iamus are opposed to the mysterious darkness.

ἀντεφθέγξατο: preverb and verb convey the wonder of the heard response.

ἀρτιεπήc: the voice speaks clearly out of the darkness, but only the voice; Zeus is seen directly by Polydeuces (*Nem.* 10. 79). The word comes in epic, Hes. *Theog.* 29, *al.*, and perhaps at Simon. fr. 22. 18 West.

62. πατρία ὄcca: the words in the clause have been beautifully arranged; the name of father begins the line. Cf. 50, and the position of ὃν πρόγονον (59). πατρία at the start of the period is matched by τέκοc at the end.

μεταύδαcεν: μεταλλάω, a Homeric word, could hardly not be taken to mean 'ask', or 'search for'; μεταλλατόν at *Pyth.* 4. 164 uses the latter meaning, and both appear in later poets (so Timon *Suppl. Hell.* 822. 4, Ap. Rhod. 4. 1471). We should not invent original meanings for the word to which Pindar had access; in any case, 'look at' (for instance) is not very suitable here (Ebeling (1871–80), i. 1077 (Mutzbauer), drawing on Bühler (1859)). μετάλλαccεν, 'was moving him to a different place' (cf. Christ (1896), 46), does not find a parallel at Plat. *Tim.* 19 A 5. The sense would really be apt only if the god were physically transporting Iamus, which the speech precludes. The best conjecture is Bergk's (and Garrod's (1907), 146–7) μεταύδαϲεν. If Apollonius can make it take the accusative like αὐδάω (2. 54), that seems reason enough to think that Pindar could be as bold (cf. *Pyth.* 4. 36?).

Apollo is given direct speech, unlike Iamus in 60 (contrast Pelops). The god's speech is all the more impressive for its brevity, cf. e.g. *Ol.* 13. 67–9 (also ending the triad), *Pyth.* 3. 40–2. It is itself practical (like Athena's), and transitional. The momentous τέκοϲ comes in unemphatically; one may contrast the start of Zeus' speech at *Nem.* 10. 80 ἐϲϲί μοι υἱόϲ (itself part of an argument). The speech contrasts with Adrastus' (16–17); the human's impotent lament for the dead prophet is set against the god's brisk creation of a new one. The moment does not merely affirm Iamus' lineage. The unseen god guiding the mortal clearly in the darkness provides a powerful image of the nature of prophecy. This point is reinforced by 66.

ὄρϲο: ὄρϲο and ὄρϲεο begin speeches in Homer, and usually demand movement (not necessarily rising). Here the construction combines δεῦρο (Hom. *Od.* 22. 395) and ἴμεν (*Od.* 6. 255); Iamus' first movement is to join his father, his next to follow his voice.

τέκοϲ: it seems reasonable to think that τέκοϲ is a variant; it should probably be preferred, as rarer and more liable to be replaced by its rival (cf. Eur. *Tro.* 248 (Q), 581 (P^ac), *Phoen.* 1565 (R)). Homeric usage provides sufficient justification for it here, without suggesting an importation by reminiscence: cf. e.g. *Il.* 3. 162, 21. 331, *h. Dem.* 460; Bacch. fr. 2. 1.

πάγκοινον: Iamus has been thinking only of his own people, but Olympia will presently be a place common to all Greece (cf. 69).

φάμαϲ ὄπιϲθεν: the phrase lingers at the end of the triad; the actual following of the divine voice in the darkness is left undescribed.

64–70. This strophe, though less intense as narrative than what has preceded it, is what the narrative has been leading up to, the institution of the Iamids' prophecy. The stanza is particularly rich in what might be called ornamental epithets; grandeur and gravity are enhanced. The whole stanza forms a single elaborate sentence; the structure holds the whole together, although another verb is added at 70.

64. ἵκοντο: it is important that Olympia is a different place from

Iamus' home; but the situation does not suggest a long journey to the listener, like that from Sparta to Arcadia.

The bare verb, with no subject stated, is highly effective.

ὑψηλοῖο πέτραν ἀλίβατον Κρονίου: the epithets evoke a dramatic setting for the consecration. ἠλίβατος is a standard epithet for πέτρη in epic (e.g. Hom. *Il.* 15. 273); it may be used by Simonides (519 fr. 37. 2, cf. 4).

65. ὤπασε θησαυρόν: it is a generous gift to the son; the doubleness increases the munificence. θησαυρός is already used metaphorically by Hesiod (*WD* 719–20), with intricate play.

66. μαντοσύνας: the thematic word begins the line and is followed by a pause; it also answers the vagueness of 60.

τόκα μέν: not 'now this form of divination, now that'. It would be pointless to mention temporal alternation. Rather, the first form of divination is only for now ('then' in the narrative); the second is for when Heracles comes. τότ᾽ (70) picks up εὖτ᾽ ἄν, cf. e.g. fr. 33 d. 3–5, Hes. *WD* 458–9 εὖτ᾽ ἄν . . ., δὴ τότ᾽; τότ᾽ αὖ also looks back to τόκα μέν, with αὖ underlining, as often, the opposition of μέν and δέ, and the difference of time (cf. e.g. *Isth.* '3/4'. 36). It might be thought that θησαυρὸν δίδυμον made against the first form at any rate not continuing into the second period; but θησαυρός may denote something valuable rather than abundant, cf. Collard (1975), ii. 368, and add for things e.g. Hes. *WD* 719–20, Theogn. 409–10. In any case, there will be abundance in the use each form is put to. Both are given to Iamus himself, so that he receives a twofold gift.

On the view that the two forms of divination continue for ever, the meaning of φωνάν has been disputed: chance utterances (Weniger (1915), 84–7), birds (Parke (1967), 177–8), the voice of Apollo (Löffler (1963), 28, cf. Boeckh (1811–21), iii. 159; Dissen and Schneidewin (1847), ii. 80). The scholia, notably, have no information to offer on this point, unlike the empyromancy (111 c–e, 119); nor do other sources. Apollo would be inappropriate for the later period. As a reference to birds, this seems oddly opaque (a difficulty felt by Heyne (1817), i. 75). ψευδέων ἄγνωστον is far more effective of a god, all-knowing, but unable to speak falsehood, than of birds or remarks. If we allow a temporal separation between the two forms, we can refer the phrase to Apollo after all. Apollo is preferable to Zeus in 66–7 (despite λόγον at *Ol.* 8. 4): πατρί . . . Ζηνός (note the placing of both) makes its sound as if a new deity is being introduced; we have just heard of Apollo's voice; and Apollo is famous for pronouncing no falsehood, so that the allusion is natural (cf. e.g. *Pyth.* 3. 29, Aesch. fr. 350. 5–6 Radt). The narrative thus reinforces in Iamus' practice the prophet's connection with Apollo; it also makes the Iamids pre-date even Heracles' Olympic games. A quasi-scholarly, and imaginative, handling of chronology may be seen at *Ol.* 10. 49–51. The present passage suggests a contrast between the lonely scene of god and mortal, in what is made to appear a rugged setting, and the future popularity of the site (64, 69); the provisional form of prophecy is grounded in the preceding action (61–3).

ἄγνωcτον: usual and earliest recoverable spelling, cf. *IG* ii². 1632. 185 (*c*.323/2 BC), *al.*; West (1990*b*), xliii; Dover (1993), 308.

εὖτ' ἄν: Heracles' great arrival is still in the future. Pindar's exploitation of these strange perspectives is illustrated, for example, by the hidden Rhodes of *Ol.* 7. 54–68.

67. θραcυμάχανοc: the application to lions at *Nem.* 4. 62 suggests that the word is not particularly abstruse in meaning here. In Pindar's mythology, Heracles has just fought a war against Augeas: 69 n., cf. Call. frr. 76–7a, 131 Pfeiffer. For -μάχανοc (and perhaps θραcυ-) cf. Simon. 575. 2, Bacch. 18. 8, Phrynich. *TrGF* 3 F 6; θραcυμήδηc is used of Heracles at Bacch. 16. 15.

68. Ἡρακλέηc: the name is effectively placed, after the anticipation produced by the separated epithet; a designation of Zeus appears at the other end of the line. Heracles' mortal 'lineage' comes before that climactic word; cf. for the expression *Ol.* 2. 45. Heracles, like the Iamidae, belongs to a mighty race; his father (cf. 50, 62) is even greater than Iamus' (and will become his patron).

69. The myth forms the central narrative of *Ol.* 10 (24–77), and the starting-point (19–22) for that in *Ol.* 3 (on which see Krummen (1990)); it comes at the start of *Ol.* 2 (3–4). Here the foundation of the Olympic festival and the games is made formally subordinate to the institution of the empyromancy, which it parallels. None the less, the importance of the games is conveyed by the rhetoric of the superlatives, and implies, outside the narrative, the glory of Hagesias' victory; this will shortly be developed.

πλειcτόμβροτον: cf. Bacch. 3 [**17**]. 12 n. Compounds in -μβροτοc are seen in epic (τερψί- (also Bacch. and probably Pind. (P. Oxy. 2736 fr. 2 (*a*), 5, Lavecchia and Martinelli (1999), 2)), φαεcί- (also

Bacch., Pind.), φθιcί-, ληcί-). They are much used by Pindar and
Bacchylides (ἀλεξί-, δαμαcί- (cf. Simon. 616), ἐναρί-, θελξί-, λυcί-,
μεληcί-, ὀπιθό-, πειcί-). Cf. Simon. 542 [**15**]. 34–5 n.

70. Ζηνός: the name appears climactically in the last period, sur-
passing the name of Apollo in the last periods at 35 and 49. It also
joins us to the beginning of the poem (5).

ἀκροτάτωι: not 'the topmost part of' (ἐπί already implies 'on the
top of'); rather, 'most high', cf. e.g. Sapph. 105 a. 1–2 (cf. Hom. *Il.*
2. 312, Ibyc. 317 (*a*). 1), Soph. *OT* 876. The impressive superlative
follows on from those in 69. The altar was formed from the heaped
ash of sacrifice; its height in the time of Pindar cannot be known.
On the altar see Paus. 5. 13. 8–11; Weniger (1913); Schleif (1934);
Yavis (1949), 210–13; Herrmann (1972), 67–8; Burkert (1977), 95;
Bacch. 13. 58, etc.

χρηcτήριον means not a sacrificial victim (a feeble injunction) but
the seat of an oracle, a building. The metaphor is used here in bold
paradox of the divination from the victims sacrificed on the altar
of ash.

71. The narrative triumphantly reaches its goal at the start of the
stanza. γένος Ἰαμιδᾶν shows that the narrator has at last got to
ἀνδρῶν . . . γένος (24–5); the proper name can now be filled in.
In its position at the end of the first period in the strophe it corre-
sponds to Ἴαμος (43). The panhellenic fame builds on 63 and 69;
cf. *Ol.* 1. 116, *Pyth.* 7. 7–8, Bacch. 13. 82–3. Families and races are
commonly famous in Pindar: cf. e.g. *Nem.* 2. 18, 10. 37, *Dith.* 2 fr.
70 b. 30. The sentence does not touch explicitly on the spreading,
or as scholars say 'swarming', of the Iamidae: the emphasis is on
origins, in birth and place. (See the introduction to the poem.) The
Iamidae are presented as all descended from Iamus, as the Branchi-
dae were from Branchus; so the prophetic gift runs in the line of
Melampus, Hom. *Od.* 15. 225–56.

72–4. ὄλβος ἄμ' ἕcπετο: the fame of the Iamidae was accompanied
(note ἄμ') by prosperity, the ideal combination. The narrative is
finished off, and the time before the present covered, with sudden
rapidity. The asyndeton, infrequent with Bacchylides and Pindar in
narrative proper, shows an emergence from the flow of the narrative
manner. Cf. *Ol.* 1. 89, and e.g. 13. 91, *Pyth.* 10. 51. The expression
too is now abstract; cf. e.g. *Pyth.* 5. 55.

The subject of ἔρχονται is usually taken to be the Iamidae; but en-

tering on the road, rather than travelling along it, becomes difficult
to explain. 'Honouring' ἀρετάc also seems a slightly weak expres-
sion to use of the glorious clan. One might suggest that τιμῶντεc
means 'those who honour', and refers especially to poets like Pin-
dar. (Heyne (1817), i. 77, at least seems to see the statement as
general, despite the translation (not by him?), ii. 19; cf. Schmid
(1616), 161.) The path is clear and evident (φανεράν); not only is it
clearly right in the abstract to praise excellence, but the fame (and
success) of the Iamidae illustrates how in actual cases the praise of
excellence will be seen as obviously fitting. ἄλλων acquires a pointed
meaning, in contrast with τιμῶντεc. The whole passage is linked,
on this view, to 9–11, with its distinctive emphasis on the natural
glory of fine deeds (note ἀρεταί . . . τίμιαι). It is also linked further
to 23–5, already recalled in γένοc Ἰαμιδᾶν. ἐc φανερὰν ὁδόν echoes
κελεύθωι . . . ἐν καθαρᾶι (23); but the journey is now generalized
and extended (Hagesias too), and φανεράν carries more meaning for
the tenor. Honouring is a natural occupation for poets, cf. e.g. *Nem.*
9. 10, 54, *Isth.* '3/4'. 55–7, Bacch. 4. 13. Participles as nouns fre-
quently lack an article in Pindar: e.g. *Ol.* 2. 57, 8. 77–8 (E. Schmid),
13. 17, *Nem.* 1. 27, 32, *Isth.* '3/4'. 5, cf. *Ol.* [5]. 16, Bacch fr. 20 B. 16.
This view, if correct, indicates both how difficult Pindar's gnomic
passages are, and how specifically suited to the poem.

ὄλβοc and ἀρετάc are placed at either end of the period, so as to
underline the implication, already apparent in ἄμ', that the Iamidae
have both of this desirable pair. πλοῦτοc and ἀρετᾶι are significantly
placed in the grammar at *Pyth.* 5. 1–2, cf. Bacch. 1. 160. φανερὰν . . .
τεκμαίρει form a plain ring in their line, helped by the enjambment.
The object of τεκμαίρει is carefully left vague. While the verb
superficially refers to the preceding proposition as a whole, the idea
of manifest proof, by the easiest of glides, confirms φανεράν, and
suggests the clear manifestation of excellence itself (cf. *Nem.* 6. 8).
χρῆμ' ἕκαστον generalizes, from the Iamidae and to victors; cf. *Ol.*
9. 104 and, in my opinion, Bacch. 8. 20–1. The confidence and
universality are related to the argumentative manner of Sapph. 16
[5]. 5–6.

The asyndeton with τεκμαίρει and μῶμοc is found in many non-
narrative passages of Pindar and Bacchylides, especially before or
after short sentences. Cf. e.g. *Pyth.* 1. 88, *Isth.* 5. 14–16, 52, *Pae.* 2
(D2). 28, Bacch. 1. 172, 178. The effect is arresting here, immedi-
ately after the narrative. But the poem is notably sparse in gnomic

generalizations, and μῶμος κτλ. develops into a longer sentence which draws us back to the emphatically particular.

κρέμαται suggests both a danger and an oppressive presence; cf. e.g. *Isth.* 8. 14, Simon. 520. 4; *Isth.* 2. 43. μῶμος is made the looming subject; in the relative clause of this very sentence, the narrator already combats the adversary. That adversary gives dynamism and drama to the genre. Note the early Ibyc. S221.

φθονεόντων: the verb, not the adjective φθονερός, contemptuously adds their motive, after a separation.

75. δωδέκατον: the twelve laps of the course at Olympia are mentioned elsewhere for chariot races, *Ol.* 2. 50, 3. 33, *Pyth.* 5. 33. Cf. Lee (1986). The phrasing unobtrusively assimilates the mule-cart to four-horse chariots, and dramatically sets πρώτοις against δωδέκατον. The final lap of the race is imagined, where the victory first looks apparent but is still being won (cf. Bacch. 5. 45). περί is probably used with the turn into the twelfth lap in view.

76. Imminent victory confers a quasi-physical beauty, in the eyes of those watching. The underlying idea of glory is suggested by αἰδοία and εὐκλέα, cf. *Ol.* 7. 89–90. The sensual extension of the language is seen again at *Ol.* 1. 18–19 (note also 1. 30); the connection forged at *Nem.* 3. 19 is relevant too. στάζω is a concrete and sensuous verb characteristic of the genre, and suitable here; cf. e.g. *Isth.* '3/4'. 90b and note Simon. 519 fr. 79. 9, Bacch. 13. 229.

77. The Olympic victory remains the underlying theme of the long ensuing sentence; the discreet obliqueness does not remove this significance. But the most prominent concern of the poetry is now Hagesias' Arcadian origins.

The figure of Hermes creates an ingenious transition. He was born on Mt. Cyllene, near Stymphalus, and was also a god of contests, Agonios and Enagonios, cf. *Pyth.* 2. 10, *Isth.* 1. 60, Simon. 555. 1; *IG* xii/2. 96, 3, etc. Cf. also Jost (1985), 33–5, 102–3 (the bearing of Aesch. frr. 273, 273a Radt is disputed). Stymphalus itself may have been less particularly associated with Hermes than say Pheneus; but the expression ὑπὸ Κυλλάνας ὄρος . . . ναιετάοντες, and the evocation of Hom. *Il.* 2. 603–8 (ὑπὸ Κυλλήνης ὄρος 603), helps to smooth over any such difficulty. (All the more so if the audience were Syracusan.) The Iamid connection would run in the paternal line; the general context, and the opposition of the Iamids in the first period of the stanza to the maternal relatives at the end of the last, strongly suggest that Hagesias' paternal relatives, by contrast, are not from Stymphalus. The importance explictly attached to the maternal line (of males!) is seen elsewhere in Pindar, e.g. *Nem.* 10. 37; Aeneas' activity encourages it here.

εἰ δ': no uncertainty is implied, cf. e.g. *Ol.* 3. 42.

ὅρος: the Homeric allusion confirms the unusual lengthening of a syllable in ς before a proper name, cf. *Pyth.* 3. 6, and also Bacch. 3 [17]. 64 n.

Ἀγησία: the direct use of the name in address resumes 12, so far the only appearance of the name, or of address to Hagesias. There he was seen in his roles as an Iamid and a Syracusan.

78. θεῶν κάρυκα: an indirect description appears first, as often.

λιταῖς: Chantraine (1953) makes this another noun in asyndeton, here and at *Pyth.* 4. 217 (cf. Braswell (1988), 300-1; Hummel (1993), 365). However, the noun does not well suit ἐδώρησαν; a 'sacral formula' appears less convincing at *Pyth.* 4. 217 (the notion is needed to justify the asyndeton). It seems rash to dismiss fr. 21 and other evidence for the adjective. For the form cf. ἄλλιτος, πολύλλιτος in Hellenistic poetry.

79. πολλὰ δὴ πολλαῖσιν: cf. *Nem.* 8. 8. Behind Hagesias' triumph lies the fervent piety of generations. A long tradition is conveyed on the maternal side too.

ὅς κτλ.: the title is elaborated; the two parts of the relative clause (79–80), at a striking point for the metre, display the neatness of idea, with the essential word at the start of each. In the same region of the last epode came Apollo and Poseidon; the maternal line too has its gods.

80. εὐάνορα: the epithet is changed from its Homeric application to wine and bronze, and praises the population like εὔανδρος, cf. *Ol.* 1. 24 (Peloponnese), etc.

τιμᾶι: cf. e.g. Soph. *Ant.* 1137-8 (Dionysus and Thebes).

κεῖνος: after the long conditional clause, and the attributes of Hermes, the pronoun appears with climactic force. The address of 77 is similarly renewed and strengthened in the apodosis. The mention of the father Sostratus brings the paternal line into this section too.

81. Zeus appears, in majestic periphrasis, as god of the Iamids (70), as well as god of the games in question (cf. *Ol.* 8. 83-4, *Isth.* 2. 18,

7. 38, etc.). In this joining of gods, the paternal line is made parallel to the maternal.

βαρυγδούπωι: cf. *Ol.* 8. 44 (of Zeus), *Pyth.* 4. 210. The epithet for Zeus combines the epic βαρύκτυπος and ἐρίγδουπος (Hes. *Theog.* 388 etc. (Poseidon 818, as Pind. *Ol.* 1. 72 etc.), Sem. fr. 1. 1 West; Hom. *Il.* 7. 411, etc.). Compounds in βαρυ- are popular with Bacchylides and Pindar (cf. Lasus 702. 3); of Zeus, *Pyth.* 6. 24, *Isth.* 8. 22, Bacch. 7. 4?; cf. Soph. *Ant.* 1117.

κραίνει is present, because the celebrations are a prime part of the felicity; the aorist would be more usual in such a context (cf. *Isth.* 2. 18, etc.); but the topic, on my view, is about to pass to the present poem.

82–4. A first-person statement appears, with characteristic abruptness. Asyndeton is common with first-person utterances, and increases their trenchancy; cf. e.g. *Ol.* 4. 17, 13. 91, *Pyth.* 11. 50, *Nem.* 5. 14, 16, 20.

This passage is extremely difficult, as well as corrupt, and has been much debated. First a word on the papyrus, which seemed to indicate an ancient interpretation. One might doubt, however, the high point read by Grenfell after γλωσσαι (Grenfell and Hunt (1919), 159). Together with the supposed circumflex (which would be incorrect and on the second vowel) it may more intelligibly be taken as a roughly written 'diaeresis'. A 'diaeresis' is similarly used in 80, where Grenfell's high point ignores the existence of another dot, separated by a clear gap from the top of ι. That dot itself is somewhat roughly made; cf. also 85 (a ligature is less likely) and for the placing 93. For the use of the 'diaeresis' cf. also Sapph. 96 [**7**]. 2, Ibyc. S151 [**11**]. 5, Bacch. 3 [**17**]. 23; Hope and Worp (1998), 297–8, etc. It would be easy to see how the erroneous punctuation had arisen in the medieval manuscripts.

To come to the actual sense: δόξαν 'conception or perception' (of a whetstone) is very obscure; and 'opinion' (of Hagesias' ancestry) is quite unsuited to Pindar's confident mythologizing. The meaning 'glory, fame' for δόξα is much the commonest in Pindar, and seems the most promising avenue to explore; it is explored by the two important contributions of Beattie (1956a) and Dover (1987). Both take δόξαν ἔχω to mean 'I have a reputation', though Beattie alone makes ἐπί mean 'for' (possible, though one would expect the genitive after δόξα in Pindar). On this view of δόξαν ἔχω, τιν' is not comfortable, whether mock-modest (uncharacteristic) or 'informative' (unnatural); the latter understanding is not helped by the highly unattractive notion of making Metopa the δόξα (Dover). A further difficulty is the relative clause. Beattie is compelled to change ἅ μ' to ἀλλ'; but to make the narrator glad at the complementary inspiration by Metopa produces a lame sequence and a clause which ἐθέλοντα does not fit in tone. Dover keeps a relative clause. Its main point would then be that Metopa is a glory to the narrator; but the main point should be that he is attracted to glorify Hagesias because their peoples are related. Cf. *Nem.* 4. 21 οὐκ ἀέκοντες, *Isth.* 8. 16–18. It is also strange on this view that the narrator should explicitly be made willing; we should surely rather relate ἐθέλοντα and the genealogical connection.

At this point we may consider the relation of the tongue and the whetstone. πρός and the bare dative are the commonest constructions with whetstones (πρός+dat. Aesch. *Ag.* 1535–6; dative Soph. *Aj.* 820, Hermipp. fr. 47. 5 Kassel–Austin); ἐπί is clearly suitable too. (Hipp. *Acut. Append.* 66 refers to a mortar.) It would be stranger to have a whetstone on the tongue which it sharpens. Generally, tongue-sharpening expedients fail to persuade. We may note in this context that transposition is not a common error in the manuscripts of Pindar (*Isth.* 7 and 8 are a special case). If one had γλώccαι, λιγυρὰν ἀκονάν, the epithet (which the style would demand) would not suit the context: we would need 'sharp'. But if the tongue is itself the whetstone, it would seems curious for the tongue to incite the narrator, especially in the context of his own reputation.

One might then consider whether the δόξα is rather glory for Hagesias: I have glory on the whetstone of my tongue for you. The whetstone becomes the instrument of the narrator's art; we are freed from an unwelome τιν'. The passage coheres well with the distinctive present in the line before. One could either read τίν or emend to τοι. With τίν one might wonder whether the emphatic form should be used non-initially, and whether an emphatic form is in place. The position is acceptable (cf. e.g. *Pyth.* 2. 66), and examples of it in fact make one ask how emphatic the non-enclitic forms have to be: cf. e.g. Alcm. 5 fr. 29. 5, Stes. S13. 5, Ibyc. S221. 1, Bacch. 16. 2, Soph. *Aj.* 701. Here, however, one could say that the relative clause justifies the emphasis: for *you* I am sharpening a glory which exerts on me a special attraction. Hagesias' Arcadian descent not only wins the favour of Hermes but makes the narrator particularly keen to glorify him. If one remained unhappy, one might, as I should prefer, emend to τοι (cf. *Pyth.* 4. 148 for the correption). The postpositive pronoun can accompany the verb, cf. 27, *Ol.* 7. 38, *Pyth.* 9. 36, *Nem.* 3. 39, 4. 3, 10. 79, *al.*; for other non-Wackernagelian positions cf. e.g. *Ol.* 1. 57b, *Nem.* 1. 16, 10. 34; Hajdú (1989). Individuals can naturally have their own δόξα, cf. e.g. *Pyth.* 9. 105, *Isth.* '3/4'. 15–16. For ἔχω cf. *Ol.* 2. 83–5. The weapon is now being sharpened, cf. Aesch. *Ag.* 1535–6.

At the end of the line the obscurity of three genitives should be avoided (for the dative cf. e.g. 70). ἀκόναι λιγυρᾶc helps to explain the error, but λιγυρᾶι would be somewhat preferable in style (cf. e.g. *Nem.* 6. 28b–29). The shift of image in 83 takes place in a separate clause, and relates to the tenor; it is unlike that at e.g. *Isth.* 7. 19. The change is positively effective as we move from the narrator's action to his subjectivity. προcέλκει gives more point to ἐθέλοντα (as Beattie says), and more natural grammar. The almost amorous attraction is not primarily that of fresh water. The πνοαί are flowing in the air (cf. *Pyth.* 1. 22 of smoke), and καλλι- primarily describes them. The lavish emotion of the narrator turns attention onto himself.

The asyndeton in 84, though partly explanatory, recalls the first-person descriptions e.g. at *Nem.* 7. 61, *Pae.* 2 (D2). 29. The narrator's statement is to sound formally like a surprising pronouncement about his grandmother; the word at least resembles in type the ordinary μητροπάτωρ used by Herodotus, and μητρομήτωρ appears ordinary language in Aelian's context (*Nat. anim.* 11. 16). The narrator is actually taking his own 'maternal' origins further back than Iamus; the sequence of mothers Metope and Thebe recalls Pitane and Evadne. Although the mother is figurative, the narrator is setting himself on an equal footing with Hagesias. (μάτρωεc ἄνδρεc (77) and ματρομάτωρ come in the last periods of their stanzas.) One cannot imagine Bacchylides talking with such insistently personal emphasis; Pindar can dwell emphatically on his origins, both in family and city (cf. *Pyth.* 5. 72–81, *Isth.* 1. 1, 8. 16–18). Cf. e.g. *Nem.* 11. 33–7 for such material, *Pae.* 2 (D2). 28–9 for such language, deployed for people other than the poet. The particular link found here probably existed already, at least in a broad way. Later mentions of Metope's marriage to Asopus father of Thebe do not depend on Pindar (Σ 144 b–e, h, Diod. Sic. 4. 72. 1, Apollod. 3. 12. 6), and Metope was a river in the region of Stymphalus (cf. Ael. *Var. hist.* 2. 33). The parallel strategy with Thebe and Aegina (*Isth.* 8. 15–22) had been used in a political context, according to Herodotus (5. 80. 1–2; cf. Bacch. 9. 53–6, West (1985), 100); mythological adroitness had many functions in the period.

εὐανθής: adorning epithets are richly strewn in 78–87, and not only for mythological figures. The whole passage is to be grandiose, by contrast with the following sentence (ὄτρυνον κτλ.). This word, used by Homer, Sappho, 'Theognis', etc., is not elsewhere an epithet of a person; it attractively suggests the river (cf. Donaldson (1841), 40). Rivers too are important in the account of Iamus.

Μετώπα: a semi-divine name closes stanza and triad; of course εὐανθὴς Μέτωπα sounds less awesome than the Μοίρας who ended the second triad.

85–91. This stanza is singularly controversial; the treatment must be brisk.

Aeneas is to tell his companions to sing of Hera; whether or not the singing to her is real, one imagines the companions would be such as to sing, in other words would constitute a chorus. When are they to sing? At a separate part of the κῶμος performed at Hera's temple, or now? (For the former possibility see Heath and Lefkowitz (1991), 182–3; Dissen and Schneidewin (1847), ii. 84.) The meaning of the postpositive νῦν may be disputed, but ὄτρυνον νῦν looks like a pressing command to a pressing command, which one would not expect to refer to a later occasion (or later part of this occasion). Cf. *Ol.* 2. 89, *Pyth.* 4. 263, etc. Line 92 sounds less plausible for the occasion in the temple; and it comes straight after the mention of Aeneas as both Pindar's messenger and a mixing-bowl of songs. It does not sound to describe, however notionally, subsequent singing unscripted by Pindar. ('Pindar' will be a clearer term than 'the narrator' for the present.) The two imperatives ὄτρυνον and εἶπον are obviously parallel, as is the utterance they want requested. Furthermore, if ἐςςὶ γὰρ κτλ. is merely an interposed interruption, the resumption of the order to order would seem awkward and overdone, supposing that these singers are merely to take part at a later stage. The γάρ clause can be justified on this hypothesis (your rendition gives an authentic basis for judgement); but it works much more happily if the present song and Aeneas' communication with the singers are closely united. The whole passage runs much more effectively if the companions' song and Pindar's are not separate entities and themes.

The real nature of the passage emerges from parallels, which make plausible the following propositions. (*a*) The reference to singing of the goddess *first* in a sequence of actions presents a piece of pious good manners; an act of worship is not being called for. (*b*) The goddess is chosen because she is especially suitable to the Arcadian chorus, and their Arcadian and Stymphalian nationality is here set against Pindar's Boeotian and Theban nationality; in other words, the choice is especially relevant to the situation. (*c*) κελαδῆcαι and μεμνᾶcθαι do not refer to a later occasion; they are either fulfilled in the act of uttering them, or are vague. Cf. Bacch. 3. 1–4 (Muse told to sing of Sicilian goddesses and Hieron's horses: *a b c*); 5. 176–80 (Muse told to stop story and sing about Zeus, because god of Olympia, about the Alpheus, etc.: *a b c*); 11. 24 (*c*); 14. 19–22 (must sing now (νῦν χρή) of grove of Poseidon, god of these games, and of Cleoptolemus: *a b c*); Pind. *Ol.* 1. 8–11 (*b c*); 7. 13–14 (*b c*); *Pyth.* 5. 25–6 (ascribe all to god; love Carrhotus best, who . . .: *a*); 6. 23–7 (Zeus first, before main point: (*a*)); 8. 56–60 (*b* (*c*)); *Nem.* 9. 9–10 (honour for Adrastus, founder of games: *a b* (*c*)); *Isth.* 1. 52–67 (reference to present evident, note 59: *b c*).

This passage makes something audacious from common patterns. The pious preliminary, itself relevant to the theme of nationality, is succeeded by a lively demand for the singers to assess what they are singing. The initial injunction on singing can naturally be taken up in 92, since the present song has concerned the preceding sentence. This understanding makes far more spirited and cohesive sense of the passage, and fits with the other passages much better, than suppositions of a soloist and separate hymns in temples.

Aeneas acts as a messenger; the chorus, his companions, are evidently Arcadian; Pindar is in Thebes. It is natural to deduce that Aeneas is Arcadian, and that he has taken Pindar's poem to Stymphalus and (γλυκὺc κρατὴρ κτλ.) trained the chorus as well as being postman. (Cf. Σ 148 a, 149 a, Σ Lycophr. 433.) Nicasippus appears a similarly important figure at *Isth.* 2. 47–8. The distribution of the name Aeneas would not of itself compel the conclusion that he was Arcadian; however, a Hagesias and an Aeneas, both from Stymphalus, participate in Xenophon's expedition (*Anab.* 4. 1. 27, 7. 13), and an Aeneas of Stymphalus of course leads the Arcadians in 366 (*Hell.* 7. 3. 1). It is tempting to suppose that the present

Aeneas is a Stymphalian aristocrat related to Hagesias. We know also of a third-century Iamid son of Aeneas described as from Elis (Paus. 6. 2. 4, 8. 10. 5); possibly there were further connections between the maternal and paternal branches of Hagesias' family. Two general points may be made about the whole stanza. First, the metaphorical representation of the poet's activity now yields to the actualities. The narrator is not now travelling over Greece; he is fixed in Thebes. His address to a person present at the performance is not, like that to Phintis, part of an imaginative flight; he is now presenting, more closely than usual, the actual circumstances of rehearsing the poem. (Too (1991), 259–60, sees that the two addresses are connected.) The fiction of the chorus uttering his words is now taken to the limit of paradoxical transparency. The introduction to the poem has already indicated the place of this movement to reality in the shape of the whole work. The local effect in this stanza is particularly remarkable. The narrator diverts the flow of poetry vigorously; he plays with conventions and language; he is jestingly proud, and jovially affectionate. Self-reference and the genre are handled with delightful daring.

85. πλάξιππον: the epithet comes in epic (e.g. Hom. *Il.* 2. 104 (Pelops); Hes. *Scut.* 24 Boeotians). It is also used by Bacchylides (5. 97) and again by Pindar at *Isth.* 2. 21, perhaps at *Pae.* 1 (D1). 7 of Thebes; cf. διωξίππου of Cyrene at *Pyth.* 9. 4, ἀ]ναξίππου of Larisa at Bacch. 14 B. 10. The word presents a more energetic figure than flowery Metopa.

ἐρατεινόν: in epic, often of places (e.g. Hom. *Il.* 2. 532); also used at Theogn. 984 (cf. Pind. fr. 122. 7). Cf. Hes. *WD* 739 πολυηράτωι ὕδατι. The effect here is both sensuous and emotional.

86. πίομαι: cf. Hom. *Il.* 2. 825. The future, like some other first-person futures in Pindar (e.g. *Pyth.* 2. 84, 3. 107–9), does not relate only to the performance of the poem yet could be replaced by a present. As often, intention is expressed (hence the importance of the first person); but the intention principally concerns the participial clause. The narrator moves on from simply asserting his origin, and returns to the subject of his poetry.

ἀνδράσιν αἰχματαῖσι: cf. Hom. *Il.* 17. 740, *al.*, Hes. fr. 196. 1 Merkelbach–West, Theogn. 868. The heroic phrase, though formally general, especially suits Hagesias. It evokes his career in Syracuse, and the narrator's earlier affirmation on his behalf (19–21).

πλέκων: the poetry is the equivalent, as often, of the victor's garland; cf. *Ol.* 1. 100–3, *Nem.* 7. 77–9, *Isth.* 8. 66a–67. ἀοιδαῖc ἐν εὐπλε[κ has different associations at *Pae.* 3 (D3). 12.

87. ποικίλον: artistry is emphasized by the enjambment; it is essential to the coming argument. The stem is a common one in Pindar for lauding song (e.g. *Nem.* 5. 42; *Ol.* 4. 2, *Pyth.* 9. 77–8, *Nem.* 4. 14); cf. also Ibyc. S257 (*a*) fr. 27. 3. A more audacious word would have suited the rhetoric less well.

88. Αἰνέα: the name begins the period. The effect in performance will have been arresting.

Παρθενίαν: for the Stymphalian cult cf. Paus. 8. 22. 2, Burkert (1977), 211; one may have reservations on whether there were really three temples to correspond to the three titles (Παῖc, Τελεία, Χήρα). Hera was worshipped as Παρθένοc in various other places; the ὄροc Παρθένιον seems too far south to be relevant to Stymphalus directly (Σ 149 g, along with numerous guesses and bits of lore).

89–90. ἀρχαῖον includes a suggestion that the slur is out of date; cf. ἦν ὅτε in fr. 83. There is thus a mild opposition between ἀρχαῖον and ἀλαθέcιν, as between ὄνειδοc and λόγοιc.

ἀλαθέcιν | λόγοιc: the phrase must be seen as referring to this very clause; no other view will suit both words. The implicit claim to be escaping is itself seen as a poetic utterance; through its (representative) artistry he would be escaping. The ingenuity helps the argument.

φεύγομεν: a present referring to this very moment. The effect would be lost if the decision were being made later.

Βοιωτίαν ὗν: the final phrase has been built up to by the elaborate conception of the sentence, the delaying μέν clause, and the preparatory ἀρχαῖον ὄνειδοc. The connection with Θήβαν at the beginning of the stanza is at last made clear. There is a marked fall from the pomp of genealogical myth, and a contrast between the dismissive contempt of the jibe and the fervent patriotism seen in ματρομάτωρ ἐμά and in 85–6. The final monosyllable ὗν is trenchant, and the form is alien to Bacchylides and Pindar (4 examples of cῦc, including the reference to the saying in fr. 83). The phrase is placed as it were in inverted commas, despite a secondary and comic play on fleeing the animal; it is made to sound much more out of place in the language than the proverb in 100–1. cυοβοιωτοί is used by Cratin. fr. 77 Kassel–Austin. Nonn. *Dion.* 13. 124–6 provides a myth which connects the phrase with the proverb on the pig who competed with Athena (for beauty in Nonnus); this would certainly explain the feminine in Pindar. The point here is the uncultivated dullness which was ascribed to the ancient Boeotians (even now cf. Boardman (1998), 109–10); on this see Göbel (1915), 57–61; Arnott (1996), 673–4.

90–1. Wilamowitz's ἔϲτι ((1886), 168) is not much supported by the papyrus' incomplete correction. A first-person εἶπον would not give a desirable tense; nor would it be nearly so purposeful to stress the accuracy of the poem as a messenger about the narrator.

Aeneas is heaped with praises in asyndeton; the cola grow, with two, three, and four words. The tone is warmly laudatory; the second two metaphors, applied to a human, have a latent grotesquerie, which provides a touch of genial humour.

ἀγγελ- (and κᾶρυξ), when used in relation to poetry in Pindar and Bacchylides, usually involve a journey (not at *Ol.* 7. 21), and the report of some definite point (probably not at *Ol.* 9. 25). The latter idea is in any case absent here; but this may be most readily explained if Aeneas is a different kind of messenger, one to the chorus.

ἠϋκόμων: an epic adjective (Hom. *Il.* 1. 36 (Leto), etc.), also used at *Pyth.* 5. 45.

ϲκυτάλα: this striking word clashes effectively with those that surround it; it must in this context of messages carry some idea of the Spartan device. It had appeared in Archil. fr. 185. 2 West, though it may not be used of a person there; its obscurity there extracted a treatise from Aristophanes of Byzantium (pp. 132–3 Slater).

κρατήρ: the idea can naturally be used in relation to poetry (ἀοιδᾶν), cf. *Nem.* 3. 76–80, 9. 49–52 (note γλυκύν), *Isth.* 5. 25, 6. 1–3 (and fr. 181). The image is felt to be extended from the occasion of celebration. The application of the word itself to a person is more unexpected; cf. Ar. *Ach.* 937, in a context of wholesale comic equation. It gains a special aptness for one who prepares the singing, as a drink is prepared.

ἀγαφθέγκτων ἀοιδᾶν takes up ποικίλον ὕμνον 87, but now stresses the audible performance. The phrase at the end of the last strophe also answers ἱμερταῖϲ ἀοιδαῖϲ from the end of the first (cf. Metzger (1880), 135). The epithet is more conspicuous here: it is found nowhere else. It will be modelled on epic ἀγάστονος, but ἀγα- will now have the sense 'well', not 'loud', cf. *Pyth.* 5. 81 ἀγακτιμέναν, and εὔφθογγον Theogn. 534 (εὐφώνοις *Pyth.* 1. 38, *al.*).

92. A bare and simple sentence brings the poem suddenly back to Syracuse (6, 18), where Hagesias actually lives, and where he is returning to (99). There is no loss of magnificence in this reversion from the past and myth; the stanza glorifies the city and especially its ruler. Comparison with what is said of Arcadia, and said to the individuals Phintis and Aeneas, suggests that this is an awaited highlight of the poem. Mention of the ruler and friend makes us look back to the first myth and see Hieron as a more fortunate Adrastus, Hagesias as a person of particular importance in his city.

We do not know whether there is a special reason for the mention of Ortygia; at *Pyth.* 2. 5–6 it seems essentially a synecdoche for Syracuse, and to Syracuse τάν refers here. There need not be a special reason even at *Nem.* 1. 1–6.

93. The main logical emphasis falls on this participial clause; but the gods receive more space and colour. διέπων is matched by ἀμφέπει (used with σκᾶπτον at *Ol.* 1. 12); the latter is weightier in rhythm and exclusively poetic.

καθαρῶι σκάπτωι: an unexpected combination. See on Bacch. 3 [17]. 70 for Hieron's kingly rule; in the context of this poem the mention recalls not only Adrastus but the wise king Aepytus (34, 47).

94–5. ἄρτια μηδόμενος: the phrase evokes Hom. *Il.* 14. 91–4 (ἄρτια βάζειν, of one who is σκηπτοῦχος). Although neither word appears here in quite the epic sense, the phrase sounds like the first half of an epic hexameter. ἄρτιος has the same moral force as in Sol. fr. 4. 32, 39 West; it takes up καθαρῶι.

φοινικόπεζαν probably has no special cultic significance. It is based on the epic ἀργυρόπεζα (*Il.* 1. 538 etc., of Thetis; *Pyth.* 9. 9 of Aphrodite; cf. Ibyc. S167. 9); it is used of Hecate at *Pae.* 2 (D2). 76. Cf. φοινικοκράδεμνος at Bacch. 11. 97–8, 13. 222 (Leto, Muses). λευκίππου likewise is applied to the Dawn at Bacch. fr. 20 C. 22 and to various mortal groups or places by Pindar (fr. 202, etc.); cf. Stes. 256, Ibyc. 285. 1 (Moliones). In this poem, φοινικο- recalls 39, and the opposition with white recalls 39–40, of the mythical figure (silver was white to Greeks). Such employment of colour had been one of the most memorable features of the narrative.

θυγατρόc suggests the title *Κόρη* without using it; Bacch. 3 [**17**].
2 comes closer to it. Hieron was by heredity the hierophantes of
the goddesses; cf. Hdt. 7. 153. 1–4, Σ 158 c (Didymus; Philist.
FGrHist 556 F 49, Tim. 566 F 96), Jacoby (1923–), iii b. 505,
Zuntz (1971), 72 n. 5. Hagesias and Hieron are linked in the august
religious offices they derive from their lineage.

96–8. Ζηνὸc Αἰτναίου forms a climax, as at *Nem.* 1. 6; *κράτοc* stresses
his supremacy with an impressive periphrasis. Zeus has occurred
at important points in the poem as Iamus' god, and the god of
Olympia (5, 68, 70, 81). The scholia speak of a festival (162 a),
which Didymus thought contemporary (Σ *Nem.* 1. 7 b); assuredly
doubtful is the report of Hieron inheriting the priesthood of Zeus
from Telines too (Σ *Ol.* 6. 158 a). But the phrase certainly glances
at Hieron's foundation of Aetna.

ἀδύλογοι: cf. Sapph. 73 a. 4; Pind. *Ol.* 10. 93 ἀδυεπήc τε λύρα.

νιν: the reference of this pronoun is connected with the applica-
tion of the following sentence. Hagesias is obviously impossible in
grammar. Syracuse is preferable to Hieron, since the present oc-
casion can either be denoted by this sentence or form an implicit
instance of its content; Hieron's victories in the games, however
dutiful the poet to the monarch, are much less relevant here. The
same applies to the ὄλβον of 98; for the present occasion is part of the
city's felicity in a way that it is not of its ruler's. Cf. e.g. *Ol.* 7. 93–4,
13. 24–8; Simon. 511 (*b*). 7–8?; Ebert (1972), 11, 59, 68. So far, we
ought to agree with the conclusion of Friis Johansen (1973), 4–6,
if for separate reasons from his. However, for the subject of δέξαιτο
one should, with some hesitation, prefer Time not only to Hieron
but to Syracuse; so Wilamowitz does ((1886), 169; he misses its
divinity ('die zukunft')). Against Hieron, apart from the preceding
arguments, one would expect the subject of a wish or prayer about
accepting the κῶμοc to be a divinity (or personification), a city, or a
place. *Pyth.* 5. 22 δέδεξαι is different, since not only is it a statement
and perfect, but the κῶμοc is one Arcesilaus has obtained as a reward
for his own victory. Against Syracuse, there is some awkwardness
to passing in parallel clauses from Syracuse as a potential victim
to Syracuse as a divinity. But the main argument against either is
that the subject of the two optatives should be the same if that
is acceptable; and it is acceptable. Even with ἐφέρπων, χρόνοc can
be personified and so deified: cf., in similar passages, *Ol.* 8. 28–9

(ὁ . . . ἐπαντέλλων; cf. Bacch. 5. 36), *Nem.* 7. 67–8 (ὁ . . . λοιπός; cf. *Ol.* 4. 12), and also *Ol.* 10. 7–8, *Pyth.* 1. 46, *Pae.* 2 (D2). 27 (and *Nem.* 4. 41–3); for further personification and deity cf. e.g. *Ol.* 2. 17, 10. 51–5, *Nem.* 1. 46–7, frr. 33, 159, Bacch. 7. 1, 13. 205–7, fr. 20 A. 18–20, Simon. 531. 5, fr. 88. 1–2 West, Pherecyd. B 1 Diels–Kranz (and Orphic cosmogonies), Soph. *El.* 179, *OT* 1213, Eur. *Supp.* 785–8, fr. 303. 3–5 Nauck. (This notional divinity should in my view be emphasized more than in Gerber (1962).) Reference to divinity is normal in such contexts as these wishes for the future, which are a recurring device in epinicia (cf. *Ol.* 4. 12–13, 13. 24–6, *Pyth.* 1. 56–7, 5. 118–21, 10. 17–21, Bacch. 5. 36). θράccοι already involves a measure of personification (cf. *Isth.* 7. 39). The notion of Time accepting the revel need not be dwelt on anxiously, any more than that at *Pyth.* 8. 1–5; the device lightly marks the futurity of the occasion. Time's acceptance in the near future would also be a token of his later forbearance towards Syracuse's good fortune.

The wish can hardly be for the subject, especially if quasi-divine, to lay on a celebration; it would in any case be peculiar to wish that there may be a celebration, rather than to say there will be one. Much the most natural explanation for εὐηράτοιc is that φιλοφροcύναιc denotes friendly festivities. Cf. *Thren.* 4. 14 (fr. 1 Cannata Ferà), Ion fr. 26. 11 West (Hdt. 3. 51. 1, 5. 18. 1, etc.), and e.g. Bacch. 11. 12; for adjectives like εὐήρατοc of parties etc. cf. e.g. Bacch. fr. 4. 79, Hom. *Od.* 8. 61. (φιλοφροcύναιc itself, as 'friendli-ness', would not be particularly suitable to a deified city in relation to a citizen; φιλόφρον at *Pyth.* 8. 1 describes a deified abstraction, and an apt one (cf. Ar. *Birds* 1321), Aesch. *Pers.* 96 denotes an abstraction's deceptive behaviour.) cύν perhaps most probably de-notes an occasion, cf. e.g. *Pyth.* 8. 66, *Nem.* 2. 24 (note Bacch. 9. 103). The vagueness of the present participles, in any case vague in relation to each other, would scarcely matter, especially in this future context.

γινώcκοντι: the next clause, and the connection of other such prayers to present good fortune, make desirable a reference to the present moment, rather than a general statement about Syracuse's fame. The bold personification appears at *Ol.* 7. 83; cf., with a different metonymy, *Ol.* 13. 1–4. The personification revivifies a standard way of denoting choral music; cf. e.g. *Ol.* 2. 47, *Pyth.* 8. 31. λύραι is forcefully placed too, at the start of the period with anticipatory epithet. The present mention of Syracuse, even if at Stymphalus, is giving her glory.

μή: asyndeton with a wish or imperative is especially common, e.g. *Pyth.* 1. 29, 10. 21, *Isth.* 1. 3. This is relevant to 101.

θράccoι: θραύcoι is not possible, and would be somewhat odd as a corruption of θραύcαι. The combination of the scholion and the existence of the recherché form θράccω suggests θράccoι as the likely answer.

One cannot make any inferences from so standard a remark as this to crises for Syracuse, let alone for Hagesias. Σ 165 says that Hagesias died when Hieron was deposed. But it is certainly mistaken in regard to Hieron; it can hardly be significant for 472 or 468. Cf. Friis Johansen (1973), 2–3.

εὐηράτοιc: not found before Pindar (cf. *Pyth.* 9. 8), but used also at *Ol.* [5.] 9.

κῶμον: the stanza ends, like the last, with a word linked to the present occasion; but unusually for such a wish and for a poem of this length, the actual occasion in view is a still more glorious one in the future.

99. Stymphalus reappears at the start of the new stanza; the naming matches that of Syracuse in the first period of the previous stanza. The separation of stanzas here enhances the significance of the literal movement between places. We now have the final journey in the poem, and the largest, as Hagesias returns. The scenes in the poem, and on the usual view the very scene of the poem, are left behind too: everything was set in mainland Greece, the occasion and the central part of the main narrative in Arcadia. Yet, despite the emphasis on the voyage, Stymphalus still belongs to Hagesias; the poem is drawing strands together and stressing plurality.

οἴκοθεν οἴκαδ᾽: the opening of the final stanza recalls the construction of a house at the opening of the first; but here the 'homes' are less metaphorical. The words also bridge this stanza and the last, and announce the themes of this one. The phrase creates a slight paradox, as it does not at *Ol.* 7. 4: an individual notionally has only one home.

Cτυμφαλίων: the city is more directly presented than at 84; it is not named elsewhere.

τειχέων: literal masonry is evoked, contrast 1.

100–1. μᾱτέρ᾽: the basis for this aggrandization is not apparent; but since Arcadia would never be a mythological entity, the language is less mythologizing than that of 84; it is also less personal to Hagesias than that was to Pindar. Yet even this degree of personification creates a suggestion of pathos at the end of the sentence. εὐμήλοιο: of places in epic (Hom. *Od.* 15. 406, *al.*); cf. of Arcadia πολύμηλος at *Hom. h. Herm.* 2, μηλοτρόφος at Bacch. 11. 94, εὔμηλος at Theocr. 22. 157. πολύμηλος is used of Sicily at *Ol.* 1. 12, cf. *Ol.* 7. 63 (Rhodes), etc. The epithet gives the idea of Arcadia dignity and a little substance.

ἀγαθαὶ κτλ.: the narrator deploys a well-worn saying of proverbial type (cf. Headlam (1922), 35; Diggle (1970), 124–5). When opposed to the grandiose enumeration of Hagesias' claims to fame in the opening (4–6), this treatment of his two cities seems strikingly homely; the more so as the context seems so unexpected for the saying. The effect is complicated and made more subtle by the writing. In proverbial utterances, the original image loses its vividness; here it is restored by the graphic χειμερίαι, ἐκ, ἀπεcκίμφθαι. The connection with the actual voyage increases the force, and ingenuity (contrast χειμερίαι | νυκτί with 103–4). The traditional θοάc adds weight. And yet the underlying saying becomes most visible at the end, with the anchors and the mention of a number. The saying is made more positive and less canny: the original form of the saying is probably something like 'a ship harbouring on one anchor isn't safe' (cf. together e.g. Eur. *Phaeth.* 124–5 Diggle, Herod. 1. 41–2, Call. fr. 91 Pfeiffer), or at least 'better two anchors than one' (cf. e.g. Prop. 2. 22. 41). 'Two anchors are good' is less direct and sounds wiser. The passage is hardly embarrassed stylization of the unsuitable; there is an element of game here. Also present is the grave awareness in this genre of the general fragility of fortune. Hieron's health is likely to have been frail; but a sly pointer to the handiness of an Arcadian bolt-hole seems too crudely prudential, and too little supported in the rest of the work, to be poetically acceptable. See Péron (1974), 63–4. The following sentence suggests that the accent is rather on praise.

The lines, which highlight the abstract idea of plurality in the poem, appear at a metrically notable point.

θοάc: common of ships in epic and elegy, e.g. Hom. *Il.* 1. 300, Hes. *WD* 631, Archil. fr. 4. 6 West; cf. Pind. *Ol.* 12. 3–4 (with Archil. fr. 106. 1 West), *al.* The designation resembles ναυcὶ κοίλαιc at the start of the poem (10); but the resemblance brings out the difference between the passages in elevation.

ναόc: one may notice how different is the real and metaphorical journeying prominent in the passage on the mule-cart (22–8). **ἀπεςκίμφθαι:** Pindar uses forms in ςκίμπτω, found in Homer (*Il.* 16. 612, *al.*); Hipp. *Morb.* 1. 20 is probably corrupt.

102. Cf. *Pae.* 2 (D2). 56–7 τοκεῦcι⟨ν⟩ φέρειν βαθύδοξον αἶcαν. The narrator wishes Hagesias a share that is glorious in the things of Stymphalus and of Syracuse. τῶνδε, especially when παρέχοι is present, must be what αἶcα is a share of, cf. e.g. *Pyth.* 9. 56a, Hom. *Il.* 18. 327, Emped. fr. 53. 5 Wright. The pronouns are used with an expressive sense of place; the employment of two different pronouns contrasts with Pindar's frequent τά τε καὶ τά, etc. (*Ol.* 2. 53, *Pyth.* 7. 21, *Nem.* 1. 30 (with Braswell (1992), 52), *Isth.* '3/4'. 51, 5. 52, *Pae.* 6 (D6). 132). Glory now comes to the fore again, as in the opening; the stem recalls those different sources of glory, the Iamid line (71) and the Olympic victory (76).

103–5. The narrator turns from θεόc and a wish to the majestic invocation of a specific god. It is his first prayer in the poem. It recalls Iamus' prayer for honour to Poseidon and Apollo (given epithets and titles), within the narrative and not in direct speech. The circumstances, and the relation of the speaker to the god, are now much less extraordinary. One thinks too of the prayers of Iamus' Arcadian ancestors to Hermes (given titles). From the listener's and narrator's perspective the prayer concerns not the remote past but the near future. Poseidon reappears in the poem to help the victor himself, and the narrator.

Epinicians close with prayers only in about 13 per cent of instances; in paeans a prayer or wish of a god might seem a more standard close, even apart from refrains (cf. especially *Pae.* 1, 5, 6 (D1, D5, D6), Bacch. 17 (?)). Cf. Rutherford (1997a), 44–6. When prayers do close epinicians, they address the god in less stately and elaborate a manner than this one. Cf. *Ol.* 8. 84–8, 13. 115, *Pyth.* 5. 122–4, 8. 98–100, *Nem.* 9. 53–5, *Isth.* 7. 49–51 (the nearest), and also Bacch. 5. 199–200. There are, by contrast, many elaborate prayers at openings and elsewhere (e.g. *Ol.* 14. 1–17, *Pyth.* 1. 39–40); cf. Race (1990), chs. 4 and 5. This poem, after numerous lighter moments (especially in the final strophe), rises excitingly to an impressive solemnity.

The lines appear to determine that the poem was not performed in Syracuse. However, one might note, first, that the final sentence, or *envoi*, of *Isth*. 2 is written from the perspective of the time of or just after composition; admittedly it refers to the composition by implication, but so would ἐμῶν . . . ὕμνων, on the hypothesis that this too was a sort of *envoi*. Cf., at the other end of the poem, as if just before composition, Bacch. 19. 8–11, frr. 20 B. 3–4, 20 C. 2–7 (both these on sending); Pind. *Ol*. 1. 17–19?, *Pyth*. 10. 4–6 (this at least as if before performance). Cf. also perhaps Alcm. 14 (*a*). Second, *Pyth*. 9. 73 δέξεται is evidently written from this perspective before the performance: ἀγγέλλων 2 in my view implies the poem was not performed at Delphi (cf. Carey (1981), 65, 85–6), and δέξεται is not a first-person future or an extension of one. It might be, then, that the poem was performed in Syracuse; the strangeness of the Arcadian choir travelling to perform it is counterbalanced by the strangeness, on the other view, of the κῶμος travelling to Syracuse after the performance. The idea of a secondary performance there, not formally envisaged in the rest of the poem, would introduce a literary strangeness.

δέσποτα: this word and δέσποινα are not used of gods in epic, but several times so in Pindar and Bacchylides; cf. Sapph. 95. 8 ὦ δέσποτ᾽ (Hermes). In Pindar and Bacchylides they are accompanied by genitives; ποντόμεδον includes this function.

ποντόμεδον: first extant in *IG* i³. 828. 2–3 (*c*.480–475?), then in Aesch. *Th*. 131; that inscription also uses χρυσοτριαίνας, which appears in an elaborate invocation to Poseidon in choral lyric, *SLG* 443. 6–7 (and perhaps in Stes. P. Oxy. 3876 ('ined.' in *PMGF*) fr. 72. 7).

εὐθύν: a straight voyage, without complications. Cf. *Nem*. 7. 29. One may connect the unimpeded journey sought in 23; but that was metaphorical, here the journey is real. The request itself is phrased in relatively simple language. Such prayers for safe voyages are already an established theme of poetry, cf. especially Sapph. 5. 1 with *SLG* 286 col. iii. 2 (the start of a poem), Sol. fr. 19. 3–6 West (perhaps the end of one).

χρυσαλακάτοιο κτλ.: the address is continued, even more ornately. The epic title for Zeus 'husband of Hera' is extended to other gods here and at *Pyth*. 4. 87–8 (Ares). There the epithet χαλκάρματος describes the male, as usually with the periphrasis in epic; here it describes the female, as at *Il*. [10]. 5, Tyrt. fr. 2. 12 West. No

epithet is used at *Nem.* 7. 95 (Zeus). χρυσαλακάτοιο itself displays
a related extension of epic language: the word is used of Artemis
in epic (Hom. *Il.* 16. 183, etc.; cf. Bacch. 11. 38), of any female
divinity in Pindar (*Nem.* 5. 36 etc.; cf. Bacch. 9. 1).

ἐμῶν: emphatically placed. The final moment draws on various
patterns: the coupling of the victor's glory (102) with the poet's
(Ibyc. S151 [11]. 46–8 n.); a journey which parts the narrator (note
85–7) and another or others (Sol. fr. 19 West, see above; cf. *Isth.* 2.
47–8); perhaps the closing prayer on poetry to a god already being
spoken of (*Hom. h.* 6. 19–21, cf. Call. fr. 9. 13–14 Massimilla, Ov.
Fast. 3. 833–4, 5. 377–8). Despite all this, the sudden movement to
the narrator is an effective surprise, within the prayer to Poseidon
and after the exalted address and a petition for physical safety. After
the opening of the poem, the narrator's oath (19–21), the poetic
journey (22–8), the presentation of the narrator and his activity in
82–91, self-reference closes the poem.

ἄεξ' . . . ἄνθος: the metaphors are both standard, cf. e.g. *Ol.* 8. 88
(a close); 9. 48, Bacch. 16. 8–9, fr. 4. 63 (all with genitives of poems),
P. Oxy. 2636 i. 19–20. But here the combination reinvigorates them,
as is shown by Pind. *Dith.* 1 (fr. 70 a). 14 ἀέ]ξετ' ἔτι, Μοῖcαι, θάλοc
ἀοιδᾶν; cf. *Pae.* 12 (G1). 4–5. The narrator now avoids metaphors
of poetic journeying. These would weaken the surprise, and the
implicit contrast with the poet who is not coming (in 85–7, note
ὕμνον with epithet).

εὔτερπεc: the word comes only here in classical poetry; it ob-
liquely suggests the Muse (Hes. *Theog.* 77), cf. 91. εὐτερπὲc ἄνθος
lightly recalls εὐανθής from the ending of the triad before; the con-
nection marks the distance from the mythological entanglements of
the first person there. More importantly, all three stanzas in this last
triad end with reference to song and celebration; so in the first triad,
the strophe ended with lovely song, the epode with the Muses. The
arching shape simultaneously stresses the idea of art and reinforces
the impression of artistic structuring.

Extreme artistry is apparent on every level of the poem; the com-
mentary has brought out the subtlety, the elegance, and the ex-
pressiveness of Pindar's language in the details of syntax, diction,
handling of the verse, and so forth. Such art would be found any-
where in Pindar; but the poem remains, like Pindar's other poems,
highly individual. One aspect of the art in this poem is the range

of differentiated tones and types of writing; but the poem remains highly cohesive.

The cohesiveness is not only seen in the large structure of the poem but is illustrated by the multitudinous smaller connections that have been traced or suggested; the differences of writing within the poem become significant and pointed. To those sceptical on principle one may stress that these poems present themselves as elaborately crafted and demanding works. Much classical music would provide a sufficient answer to the objection that all connections must be clear in performance to most of the audience.

The individuality is seen straightforwardly in the attenuation of the gnomic element in the poem (whereas in *Ol.* 13, say, the role of the narrator is unusually small). Other features of the poem have been marked out as uncommon in degree (such as the treatment of the performance). But the individual character of the work is not simply a matter of measurable difference, and we can only really seize it through careful and responsive reading of this poem, and others. One can point to the particularly robust handling in this poem of the narrator and his environment, in concrete actualities and in audacious metaphor; to the far-reaching treatment of the victor's lineage; the density of the narrative, in counterpoint with transcendence; to the remarkable extent to which the whole poem, and not least the most numinous moments of the narrative, are seen to take origin from the poet's imagination. One can point too to the specific and indelible creations of that combinatory imagination here: the opening as a porch with golden pillars, the mules transporting the narrator, the snakes nurturing the child with honey, the child illuminated by the rays of flowers, the voice of the god in the darkness. But only during the experience of attentive reading itself, in its detail and its wholeness, can we adequately grasp this astonishing work of art. The notes may perhaps have helped to further that experience, and to suggest some approaches for the reading of other poems.

TRAGEDY

Introduction

THE choral songs of Attic tragedy present a remarkable adaptation of the lyric tradition; but they are too seldom considered from this perspective. Whatever the prehistory of tragedy, from the time of its establishment as a major literary form one surely may and should view its lyrical element against the background of earlier and contemporary lyric poetry. The evidence of comedy is particularly significant here, since this genre can refer to and quote from texts in other genres much more freely than does its austerer sister. The grander flights of comic song show a heavy debt to earlier lyric; this strongly implies the relevance of that lyric to dramatic song of a more elevated kind. Even Homer, the general fount of Greek poetic language, is much less important to comic song, precisely because it is earlier lyric, not epic, that constitutes the generic tradition. So too the comic use of earlier elegy and iambus is kept for non-lyric metres. Also of interest is the significance attached in comedy to dramatic songs as aesthetic entities and as part of the poet's individual achievement.[1]

Tragic lyric, however, is far more centrally related to earlier lyric poetry than is the lyric of comedy, much of which reflects the more emphatically Athenian and contemporary concerns and language of that genre. In their very dialect, the lyric portions of tragedy,

[1] On Aristophanes and lyric see Kugelmeier (1996), esp. ch. iv. Some striking examples of quotation (often adapted): *Knights* 406 (Simon. 512), 1264–6 (Pind. fr. 89 a), *Clouds* 598 (Pind. fr. 325), *Peace* 775–9, 796–800 (Stes. 210–12, beginnings of stanzas), *Birds* 251 (Alcm. 26. 3); note also *Birds* 1372 (Anacr. 378, although Cinesias singing; beginning of stanza). Homer: *Wasps* 1521 (cf. Hippon. fr. 128. 4 West), *Peace* 805 (*Od.* 11. 421), *Birds* 250. The language of Cratin. frr. 171. 63, 237. 1 Kassel–Austin, notably recalls that of Pindar, cf. *Ol.* 9. 47, *Nem.* 10. 21, fr. 6a (e), *Pae.* 13 (a) (S5). 17; *Ol.* 1. 3–4, etc. Dramatic lyrics: e.g. Ar. *Knights* 529–30, *Wasps* 219–20, 268–9, *Thesm.* 40–2, 95–133, *Frogs* 1249–56, 1298–300 (the attitude to originality is like that seen in Pindar and Aristophanes on themselves). Interesting too is the conjunction of Simonides and Aeschylus (and Euripides), or of Sophocles, Phrynichus (lyric), Simonides, Pindar, or of Phrynichus, Stesichorus, Pindar simply as poets in *Clouds* 1355–6, 1361–72, Ion fr. 8 von Blumenthal, Tim. *FGrHist* 566 F 32. Herington (1985) performs the great service of confronting the question of the literary background to tragedy; but there is much more to be said. The articles in *Arion* 3/1 (1994–5) and 4/1 (1996) contain a good deal that is relevant here, esp. Henrichs (1994–5) and Calame (1994–5).

unlike those of comedy, have a prominent (if superficial) Doric element (notably long α and first-declension genitive plurals in -ᾶν). Whatever the original reason for this, it can hardly have failed to suggest in the fifth century the common dialect of choral lyric. Fifth-century tragic and choral lyric can broadly be said, in their use of compounds and other features, to employ a common and distinctive language.[2]

Although tragedy is more reserved than comedy in its use of other texts (with the partial exception of Homer), there are some plain exploitations of specific passages in earlier lyric: so of Bacch. 27. 34–43 at Eur. *IA* 1058–75. More typically, there is an evident relationship between passages or topoi or devices in choral lyric and in the lyric of tragedy, which tragedy is as a rule unlikely to have originated; but the exact nature of the derivation cannot be determined. The opening or near-opening addresses Soph. *Ant.* 101 ἀκτὶc ἀελίου, Eur. *Med.* 1252 ἀκτὶc ἁλίου must bear some relation to that at Pind. *Pae.* 9 (A1). 1 ἀκτὶc ἀελίου. The near-opening address to Φάτιc at Soph. *Aj.* 173–4 as μᾶτερ αἰcχύναc ἐμᾶc must be a perversion of the kind of expression seen at Pind. *Pae.* 9 (A1). 2, and also of the kind of address to Φήμα seen at Bacch. 2. 1. The whole phenomenon of opening addresses to deities is deeply grounded in lyric tradition, and especially choral lyric; one can even see in lyric poetry anticipations of, or pointers to, the Euripidean development of elaborate opening addresses to other creatures or things. Soph. *Aj.* 173–81 and Pind. *Pae.* 9 (A1). 1–10 also illustrate the pattern, related in the two genres, of opening with a string of questions (cf. *Isth.* 7. 1–15; Bacch. 18 (NB). 1–11). A more specific example is the nest of topoi, adapted by Sophocles and Euripides, on the different skills, attainments, desires of different people. This already has the air of standard expression in Bacchylides and Pindar themselves.[3]

---

[2] Compounds: Williger (1928), esp. 1–8. But note, for example, that compounds in -cι- are much less prominent in tragedy. For compounds in Euripides see Breitenbach (1934), 61–103 (comparisons 66–71, 76–7, etc.). Also of interest is the further limitation in tragedy of non-Doric features, notably the genitive in -οιο (infrequent in Aeschylus and Euripides, probably never in Sophocles). In comedy, the Doric α at e.g. Ar. *Clouds* 571 or *Lys.* 263 is the exception.

[3] Bacch. 27 and *IA*: note also Pind. *Isth.* 8. 47–8, but the device of reported speech within direct speech points to a specific connection (the particular setting suggested by Barrett in Maehler (1982–97), ii. 281, takes too little account of the presents). See also Soph. *Aj.* [19]. 1195–6 n. At *Aj.* 173 editors print φάτιc. Addresses: e.g. Eur. *IT* 1089–93 (halcyon), *Hel.* 1451–5 (oar); cf. Alc. 359 and Sapph. 63 (though Homeric), Pind. *Nem.* 8. 1–3 (though divine). Topoi of different paths to glory, etc.: Bacch. 10.

The discussion here confines itself to choruses and dwells particularly on choral lyric. The newer form of tragic monody had various connections with Simonides, Bacchylides, and others, besides the influence of later lyric on its development by Euripides. Lyric dialogue provides a notable invasion of the lyric mode by the dramatic. But in this limited space we should concentrate on the particularly fundamental area of choral odes; choral lyric, especially in its fifth-century form, provides the most obvious and immediate point of comparison. One must, of course, allow for the possibility of influence by tragedy from the first half of the fifth century on Bacchylides and Pindar. The possibility is more plausible with Bacchylides; but it hardly affects basic characteristics of the genre or general aspects of the two poets' style, particularly in view of their relation to Simonides. Some of the less well-preserved forms of choral lyric might have been still more relevant to tragedy: the pessimism of e.g. Simon. 521, and the vocabulary and refrain in Pind. *Thren.* 5 (frr. 2, 3 Cannatà Fera), suggest, without proving, the interest that choral lament might have had for this question. However, its meagre remains appear to suggest something more restrained than most tragic lamentation.[4]

Now that the general connection of choral and tragic lyric has been indicated, we can consider the divergences between tragic lyric and its nearest relation. Style will be a good place to begin. The general pattern is easily grasped. Tragic lyric is far richer than Bacchylides and Pindar, or earlier lyric, in emotive devices and in obtrusive artistry. The cries, the immediate repetition of words, the strings of adjectives in asyndeton: all these should immediately strike anyone who turns from non-dramatic to tragic lyric. Striking too is the relationship in tragic choruses between salient rhetorical figures and the structure of the verse: their appearance at the beginnings of stanzas, of successive lines, and so forth. A bare stream of examples may best make the point, with line and stanza divisions

35–45 (–51), 14. 6–11, frr. 20 C. 19–20, 34, Pind. *Ol.* 9. 104–7, *Pyth.* 10. 59–62, *Nem.* 1. 25, 7. 5–6, 8. 37–9, *Isth.* 1. 47–51, *Parth.* 1. 6–10, Soph. *Phil.* 137–40 (note also *OT* 380–1; 502–3, with Pind. fr. 61. 1–2), Eur. *Bacch.* 905–12. Related passages, like Sol. fr. 13. 43–66 West, are less akin in wording. Naturally, even the more scurrilous element in comic lyric has in fact some connections with earlier lyric poetry; cf. e.g. Anacr. 388 and Ar. *Ach.* 850.

[4] In the case of laments refrains, seen also in Aeschylus, might be a connected adaptation of ritual tradition. They are also found, notably, in paeans (e.g. Pind. *Pae.* 21 (S2)), as an extension of the ritual cries; but not in epinicians.

marked where significant (the instances could be multiplied indefinitely): Aesch. *Pers.* 256 ἄνια ἄνια (start of ode), 550 | Ξέρξης μὲν ἄγαγεν, ποποῖ, | Ξέρξης δ' ἀπώλεcεν, τοτοῖ, | Ξέρξης δέ κτλ. (with responsion 560–2; an extreme instance), *Th.* 166 || ἰὼ παναλκεῖc θεοί, | ἰὼ κτλ., *Ag.* 194 κακόcχολοι, νήcτιδεc, δύcορμοι, κτλ., 690 ἑλέναυc ἕλανδροc ἑλέπτολιc, 1490 ἰὼ ⟨ἰὼ⟩ βαcιλεῦ βαcιλεῦ, *Ch.* 55 ἄμαχον ἀδάματον ἀπόλεμον, [*PV*] 904 ἀπόλεμοc ὅδε γ' ὁ πόλεμοc, ἄπορα πόριμοc, Soph. *Trach.* 655 || ἀφίκοιτ' ἀφίκοιτο, *OT* 483 || δεινά με νῦν, δεινὰ ταράccει, 661 ἄθεοc ἄφιλοc, *El.* 489 πολύπουc καὶ πολύχειρ, *OC* 220 ὤ· ἰοὺ ἰού, 1237 πρόπαντα | κακὰ κακῶν ξυνοικεῖ ||, Eur. *Alc.* 472 | νέαι νέου, *Hipp.* 1124–7 | εἴδομεν εἴδομεν . . . | ὤ . . . | ὤ . . . *Andr.* 1036 | ὤ δαῖμον, ὤ Φοῖβε, πῶc πείθομαι; ||, *Hec.* 629–30 (start of ode) ἐμοὶ χρῆν . . ., | ἐμοὶ χρῆν . . ., *Supp.* 622–3 | εἰδείηc ἂν φίλων, | εἰδείηc ἂν τύχαc, 966 ἄπαιc ἄτεκνοc, *El.* 585 (start of single stanza) ἔμολεc ἔμολεc, ὤ, *HF* 126–7 γέρων γέροντα . . . νέα νέωι, 763 || χοροὶ χοροί (responding to 772 θεοὶ θεοί), *Tro.* 1085 | ἄθαπτοc ἄνυδροc, *Ion* 690 | ἄτοποc ἄτοπα, *Hel.* 1134 γέρας οὐ γέρας, *Or.* 1305 λιποπάτορα λιπογάμετον (cf. Stes. 223. 4–5), *Phoen.* 243–7 | κοινὰ . . ., | κοινὰ . . . | κοινὸν . . ., κοινὰ . . ., 1030 ἔφερες ἔφερες ἄχεα πατρίδι | φόνια· φόνιοc, *Bacch.* 986 ἐc ὄρος ἐc ὄρος ἔμολ' ἔμολεν, *Phaeth.* 94 Diggle | βαρὺν βαρεῖα φόβον ἔπεμψεν οἴκοιc ||.[5]

One could hardly dispute that this phenomenon must be at least partially connected to the higher emotional temperature of tragedy. Most of the above examples commend the further conclusion that the exploitation of the verse must be at least partially expressive, must emphasize and highlight the emotional impact of the devices. Various qualifications should be registered at once; they do not affect the basic connection of emotion and figures. It is not suggested that emotion is all that matters in tragic lyric; indeed, the emotional element in the odes is often in fruitful tension with other elements, like the choral narrator's moderation. Nor is it suggested that the emotion, or the figures, are at a constant level. In Aeschylus' lyric, particularly, the density and type of conspicuous figures and other emotive devices vary considerably. None the less, the variation there for the most part relates to emotional pitch and the nature and emotional state of the chorus (he makes barbarians and women especially susceptible). The centrality of emotion for the style is

---

[5] For the basic difference cf. Fehling (1969), 101–2. Kranz (1933), ch. 4, is rewarding on the expression of tragic choruses, as on many other aspects ((1910) less so). For figures in Euripides see Breitenbach (1934), ch. 3.

in fact particularly evident in this author. It need not have been equally so, one may add, in all tragedy of his time; we should be inhibited from supposing this by the considerable differences from Phrynichus' lyric apparent in the slight evidence. We should be inhibited still more from seeing Aeschylus' approach as the reflection of a particularly primal world in Athens.[6]

At the other end of the century, Euripides' plays from 412 on might be thought to take some features to an extreme which was to be explained not by emotion but by music or mannerism. Yet even if this were so, emotional impact must be seen as the natural effect of such devices within tragedy, which Euripides would be modifying. That is apparent enough from an earlier passage like *Erechth.* fr. 370. 41–3 Kannicht (monody). A further complication is that in the second half of the century such devices, at any rate in dialogue, come to suggest connections with prose rhetoric. But this does not remove a connection with emotional force; indeed, in this respect as in others the prose writers active in the later fifth century may themselves have been affected by poetry from its first half.[7]

Closer consideration of non-dramatic lyric supports the general connection of figures and emotion. The commentaries above should have made it clear that the relative paucity of strongly marked figures in lyric is no sign of a want of artistry, and still less of an innocence of the figures. On the contrary, seventh- and sixth-century century lyric can employ some unusual devices in revealingly unusual contexts. At Alc. 10 ἔμε δείλαν, ἔμε παίcαν κακοτάτων πεδέχοιcαν the notable anaphora with asyndeton of the first-person pronoun appears in the mouth of a female speaker, in an obsessive metre unusual for Alcaeus; whatever the impact of the piece on the listener, the passionate agitation of the speaker shows the relevance of the passage for tragedy. Danae's threefold anaphora at Simon. 543 [**16**]. 21–2 is germane. Revealing too are places where Anacreon uses extremely striking figures to convey a speaker's extreme feeling, but

---

[6] Fehling's arguments about anadiplosis in Aeschylus ((1969), 170) would not be adequate to support an explanation of the figures that considered only musical art and ignored emotion. The more restricted use of such figures in Aeschylus' dialogue can readily be explained by the greater potential of dance and music for emotional exploitation. On music in tragedy see West (1992), 350–5; for dance note esp. the red-figure vase Basle Inv. BS 415 (Simon (1982), 8–9). On Phrynichus see Lloyd-Jones (1990*a*).

[7] Anadiplosis is actually less frequent in Timoth. 791 than in Euripides (129; for separated repetition cf. 76, 154–5, 157). The feature is naturally parodied by Aristophanes in Euripides (*Frogs* 1335, 1352–5); but not in Cinesias (*Birds* 1372–400).

with comic exaggeration: so 346. 12 λεωφ]όρε λεωφόρ' Ἡρο[τ]ίμη, or the polyptoton starting three lines in 359. Tragedy will make such emotionalism both important and earnest.[8]

In certain respects Pindar and Bacchylides themselves display both an intensification of expression and an increase in the prominence of verbal artistry. One significant area for the former is the use of the superlative. In non-epic poetry before the fifth century the range of superlatives and, for the most part, the frequency of their use are severely limited; in Pindar, Bacchylides, and tragedy these greatly expand. But superlatives are a less flagrantly emotional device. Pindar and Bacchylides are also much more interested than earlier poetry in tying rhetorical figures to the metrical structure, particularly to the starts of periods and the starts and ends of stanzas. Artistry is thus more saliently displayed, by a means which is of great importance in tragedy. The two poets' actual use of prominent rhetorical figures shows a perceptible expansion and increase in relation to lyric before Simonides and Anacreon; but the gulf from tragedy remains enormous. The distinctive elements of tragic lyric thus have in certain ways a context in wider developments of the fifth century; but the interval in emotional heat is clear.[9]

The area of metre can only be touched on impressionistically. The most startling innovation is that tragic songs, rather than repeating a stanzaic or triadic form indefinitely, always change to a new form after one pair (or triad). This creates immense scope for contrast

---

[8] Whether the repeated exclamation at Alcm. 26. 2 was also first-person humour we have too little of the fragment to decide. The extended repetitions in the questions of Sapph. 1 [4]. 15–20 clearly have a mocking element. The anadiplosis at Sapph. 114. 1 appears in an emotional and unusual context.

[9] Some examples of the relation of figures and metrical form: Bacch. 3 [**17**]. 15–16 n., 6. 1–2, Pind. *Ol*. 9. 105, 10. 27–8, *Pyth*. 3. 107 (cf. *Nem*. 3. 72–3), 10. 66 (contr. *Nem*. 4. 22), *Nem*. 8. 39, fr. 122. 15. Other striking uses of figures: Bacch. 18. 42 (cf. Aesch. *Ch*. 398), Pind. *Ol*. 1. 31 ἄπιϲτον . . . πιϲτόν (cf. fr. 233), *Pyth*. 8. 95, 9. 6a–7 πολυ- καὶ πολυ-, 105–25 (unusually rich in figures), *Isth*. 7. 48 γλυκὺ πικροτάτα, fr. 76. 1 three epithets, but joined by καί, fr. 143. 1–2 three adjectives in ἀ-, but string avoided. Many other instances have a proverbial, Hesiodic, or traditional quality. On exclamations and on anadiplosis in Pindar and Bacchylides see Bacch. 3 [**17**]. 19–22 n. As to superlatives, in range of words and usage Homer is extremely limited. An eloquent indication: if one excludes ἀκρότατοϲ, Pindar has more superlatives in -τατ- than the whole of the *Iliad* (55 to 44); the number of his superlatives, including compounds, in -ιϲτ- (about 85) is almost matched in *Iliad* 1–2 alone. In lyric, and most elegy and iambus, superlatives are infrequent, and certain words and types of phrase are heavily cultivated; so even in Alcaeus, where they are unusually frequent (6. 7, 38 a. 6, 58. 15, 296 a. 1, 298. 18, 327, 335. 3, 347 a. 4, 367. 2, 387. 1). For Pindar note e.g. *Pyth*. 1. 21, 26, 'elative' as so often (cf. Dornseiff (1921), 78–80).

and subtle relationships; meaning and feeling are important here as well as more abstract design. The stanzas are usually sealed off from one another firmly, with no run-over as in Pindar and Bacchylides (or the Lesbian poets). Pind. *Parth.* 1. 6, 2. 11, 16, 41, and occasional exceptions in tragedy (e.g. Aesch. *Supp.* 582, Eur. *Hec.* 649) indicate that this is not a necessity imposed by dance, even if dance accentuates its effect: the structural divisions are starkly emphasized.[10]

Within the stanza, the metrical difference from Simonides, Bacchylides, and Pindar is most marked in Aeschylus. Iambics, relatively marginal in them, are for him the primary, 'default' metre; dactylo-epitrites do not appear at all. He is particularly interested in accumulated repetitions of the same short metrical unit. The genealogy of this procedure is disputable (popular?), and both Anacreon and comedy are pertinent; but the effect in Aeschylus' contexts is to heighten emotion strongly, even obsessively, in a fashion quite unlike the choral poets. Sophocles and Euripides are more reserved with such metrical repetition, and sometimes when they use it may be evoking Aeschylus. But they too are quite different from Pindar. Dactylo-epitrite stanzas, with their flowing and less sharply defined sequences, do not occupy a central position (see on Eur. *Med.* 627–62 [20], *metre*). Aeolic is not extended in the manner of Pindar or Simonides (Bacchylides is perhaps less different here). Sophocles often pursues complexity of mixture but the individual cola are still much more limited and more easily grouped than in Simonides or Pindar. Sophocles' and Euripides' stanzas are certainly more elaborate and varied than those of the Lesbians, Anacreon, Ibycus, even Alcman; but a certain perspicuity and crispness is needed for their vivid structures and their forceful changes.[11]

The discussion comes now to some larger aspects of choruses related to genre. Non-dramatic choral lyric, including Alcman, refers very frequently to the singing and the instruments of the perfor-

---

[10] Comedy sometimes has four or three (or eight) identical or virtually identical stanzas; it rarely places two different choral pairs together without interruption (*Thesm.* 959–1000, *Wasps* 291–315 (with dialogue), cf. *Plut.* 290–315; there are three or four cases with slight interruption).

[11] Obsessive repetition in Aeschylus: e.g. *Th.* 295–300, *Ch.* 327–30, *Eum.* 328–9; cf. also e.g. [*PV*] 115, Soph. *El.* 504–6, 508–9 (cf. Bacch. 16. 9 for rhythm), Eur. *Tro.* 560–3. Phrynichus' few fragments (*TrGF* 3) seem to present a very different metrical picture from Aeschylus; F9 is probably dactylo-epitrite. See on Soph. *Aj.* 1185–222, *metre*, for sequences of short syllables, used with more emotional point than in Pindar.

mance; the songs are partly about themselves, and like to underline the fact of the present occasion. Tragic (like comic) choruses are full of references to song, dance, music, and to cries of lament; the spectacle of the chorus is brought out by the words. But in tragedy the area is more complicated than in non-dramatic lyric. The fact of the chorus' singing and dancing is not on the whole self-explanatory, as it might be in a paean. The chorus in tragedy rarely performs an institutionalized song, like the song that summons the dead Darius (Aesch. *Pers.* 619–88, 697). The wedding-song at Eur. *Phaeth.* 227–44 Diggle, unlike those of comedy, is actually assigned to a secondary chorus. The numerous laments of tragic choruses are not usually the official funerary lamentation. The chorus' singing and dancing are made a part of the dramatic fiction, by a curious contract; one should contrast the austerity of tragedy over any explicit reference to acting, which is not part of the fictional world.

Set types of song (such as paeans) are often referred to and exploited by choruses in contrast or analogy to their own singing; indeed, a great many of the references to singing and the like are to the past or the future, or at least go beyond the present occasion. The devices and language of choral lyric are relevant here; but tragedy offers something distinctive. The moment of performance is not only emphasized: it is often marked as unusual, and often drawn into complex relations with other moments and sorts of song. The elements of the genre and the performance become part of a subtle and powerful art of allusion. Euripides' *Heracles* provides an outstandingly rich example.[12]

[12] So Eur. *HF* 110–11, 348–58 (cf. Pind. *Thren.* 3 fr. 56 Cannatà Fera; 356–7 related to choral lyric), 673–700 (here paeans as analogy, as against earlier Linussong; with 673–7 cf. Pind. *Pyth.* 9. 89a–90), 751–3, 761, 763–4, 781–97, 875–9, 889–92, 1025–7, 1054. Some other examples: *Tro.* 511–57 illustrates powerfully contrasts between past song and the present. The chorus in the *Bacchae*, who hymn Dionysus in the parodos, often imagine their future dancing (cf. *Phoen.* 234–8, *Erechth.* fr. 370. 5–10 Kannicht); cf. e.g. 412–16 for some of the complexities. The parodos of the *Phaethon* sets the singing and sounds of the world at dawn against the wedding-song the chorus wishes to sing. The lamentation of the chorus at [Aesch.] *PV* 397–401 is presented by the ode as one part of the whole world's lament. At Soph. *Trach.* 202–24 a song is ordered and sung, but extends beyond the stage; contrast the ironic future reference at 640–2. The chorus's famous question at *OT* 895–6 contrasts with the quasi-hymnic future at the end of the previous stanza. Cf. on these matters Wilson and Taplin (1993), esp. 169–70; see also Henrichs (1994–5). Such reference is found in actors' lyric too, and it also reflects on the present moment; cf. e.g. Eur. *Tro.* 125–6. Among many interesting passages in choral lyric are Bacch. 11. 9–14, 17. 124–32, Pind. *Pyth.* 1. 1–20, *Pae.* 2 (D2). 96–106; in comedy, e.g. Ar. *Knights* 405–6, *Lys.* 541–2 (cf. Henderson (1987), 138).

The most important generic feature of tragic choruses is the narrator. Although a first person plural is sometimes employed, the first person singular is far commoner. This device derives from choral lyric, and justifies us in retaining for the speaker the term 'narrator'. (It is not implied that the speaker is invariably conceived as (notionally) singular, though the first person plural need not prove a plural speaker.) Within the larger drama, the narrator of the songs is an internal narrator.[13]

Various types and aspects of non-dramatic narrators, seen in earlier chapters, are of interest for tragedy. Non-dramatic lyric often stresses, so to speak, the biological classification of the narrator: maiden, woman, ageing man; the narrator's utterance often particularly suits this role. The narrator can also be made to voice general wisdom, which may carry the stamp of authority (subversion sometimes occurs). Yet even a seemingly typical or representative 'I' often belongs in fact to a defined person; in particular, such 'I's in Pindar are usually accompanied or immediately followed by mention or suggestion of the narrator's role as poet.[14]

The non-dramatic narrator may be emphatically separate from the author (as in Alcm. 1 [**1**] and 3 [**2**]); the narrator may be formally connected to the author, but still be undermined or questioned, particularly in the poetry of love. The pathos, or comedy, of powerlessness can also be exploited (as in Sappho, Alcaeus, Ibycus, Anacreon). Non-authorial narrators too can be given a quasipoetic role, as at Alcm. 1 [**1**]. 39–40, Pind. *Pae.* 2 (D2). 3–4 (cf. *Isth.* '3/4'. 21).

Non-dramatic narrators are often central figures; but even narrators linked to the author may sometimes adopt a role formally subordinate to a main figure or figures. In epinician the narrator is on one level both subordinate to the man he is celebrating and a foil to his achievements of action. But the conception of the poetry, especially in Pindar, gives him a highly prominent role, and he is not separated from the victor in spirit: they enjoy a sympathetic

---

[13] For the first person in tragedy see Kaimio (1970); the figures on p. 251 for first-person singular and plural in lyric parts, excluding internal address, would convert into percentages for the singular as 81% in Aeschylus, 91% in Sophocles, 89% in Euripides. Eur. *Hec.* 914–49 offers a striking instance of the length to which the conception of a singular narrator can be taken.

[14] Cf. e.g. *Ol.* 1. 52–3 (cf. 35–6), *Pyth.* 3. 108–15 (where Schroeder (1922), 31–2, is curiously limited), *Nem.* 1. 31–4, 8. 35–9. *Pyth.* 2. 83–5 is an unusual passage in other respects too; but even here note 81, 86.

relationship, and share heroic values. The narrator's commendations of caution are blended with support for, and even embodiment of, the exceptional. (Metaphor can further blur the interval between the two figures.) In Alcman's partheneia the non-authorial narrator is in some respects the central figure, but less glorious than the leading girls; in values there is little sense of a division between the narrator and her leader.[15]

The chorus in tragedy has no formal connection with the author; in comedy the parabasis often provides an institutionalized link, with the chorus speaking for (rarely as) the poet. In tragedy the separation from the author is crucial. The chorus is denied any intrinsic assistance to its authority, in a type of work where conflicting views and approaches to life are given voluble voice. Spectators, like the jury in a trial, must assess all views critically (but not necessarily reach a verdict). The event will often decide, in the end. The status of the chorus provides further complication, most clearly in Euripides and Sophocles (Aeschylus is more varied). In those two authors, at least, the chorus rarely equal the main characters in rank, or have more than a marginal role in the action. Their biological standing (very often women, or old men) frequently underlines their passivity, or else marks out by contrast an unusually active female protagonist. And yet within the demarcated lyrical sections they are (the narrator is) a central figure, naturally. The narrator's views are typically cautious, sensible, humane, and often resemble the wise stances of the narrators in choral lyric; the generic tradition, and various devices, lend weight to his or her utterance. But these utterances are frequently at odds with the more extreme attitudes and behaviour of main characters in the action.[16]

---

[15] 'A division in values' would be too weighty for Alcm. 3 [2].

[16] Enhancements, or apparent enhancements, of the narrator's authority, often descending from lyric: didactic confidence (Aesch. *Ch.* 603–4, cf. Sapph. 16 [5]. 5–6), φαμί (Aesch. *Eum* 553, Eur. *Hcld.* 608, *Med.* 1090, cf. Bacch. 1. 159); claims to be a μάντις (Soph. *OT* 1086–7 (here at least an ironic emphasis of ignorance), *El.* 472–3, *OC* 1080; cf. Pind. *Dith.* fr. 75. 13, *Parth.* 1. 5–6, note the literal disclaimer at Aesch. *Ag.* 1130–1). A meditative, and even intellectual, quality marks some narrators (cf. e.g. Simon. 542 [15]: so Aesch. *Ag.* 164, 757–8, Eur. *Alc.* 962–6 (on *Medea* see below; cf. the playful Ar. *Wasps* 1265–6). A manner like that of a poet can be included here, cf. e.g. Aesch. *Ag.* 105–7, and further Eur. *HF* (n. 12), *Tro.* 511–14; poets and others can also be attacked, with intellectual vigour (e.g. *Ion* 1090–3). Interesting is the anti-intellectual stance of the narrator in the *Bacchae* (cf. e.g. 430–1, 890–6, with Thuc. 3. 37. 4); the language at 395–7 has its relation to the less egalitarian epinician narrator (e.g. Pind. *Ol.* 9. 37–8), but the situation of the play (a novel cult, rejected by the ruler) could be thought to fill the position with paradox. The

It is not obvious in such cases that the chorus must be right (the genre would be dull if it were); often events actually show them to be mistaken. The listener must ponder. The fusion of drama and lyric, and the exploitation of various possibilities within lyric, lead overall to a form that challenges the spectator, and to an interesting version of Bakhtinian polyphony (a plurality of independent voices, consciousnesses, personal worlds). In tragedy the sharp conflicts of the spoken dialogue (or of lyric dialogue) may create a multiplicity of perspectives more directly and energetically. But such multiplicity is created in an equally thought-provoking fashion through the choral odes, with their distinctive language, their range and reflectiveness, and the unusual standing of their narrator. Even where there is no conflict, the choral odes enlarge the field of vision.[17]

A particularly marked characteristic of odes in tragedy, as compared to the spoken portions, is the breadth and freedom with which they range. The generalizing passages of Euripidean speeches, though themselves an interesting generic development, hardly compare with the imaginative excursiveness of choral odes. This feature is derived from lyric, and most especially choral lyric. Narrative, with a connection or point, is a significant element in tragic choruses, and here the general links with lyric are evident. Even the details have many connections; for example, in the introduction of the narrative at Soph. *Trach.* 497–507 the nervous piety of the *praeteritio* and the particular form of the epic questions have obvious affinities with Pindar and Bacchylides. But more widely the

---

generalizing 'I' is another device deriving from lyric that lends force (cf. e.g. Eur. *Alc.* 472–6); its quality, more fully typical than in epinician, suits the nature of these non-authorial narrators (but main characters in tragedy sometimes use it too). The parodos, like the opening of partheneia (Alcm. 3 [2]. 1–10, Pind. *Parth.* 2. 6–35), naturally provides a striking moment at which to emphasize the chorus's age or sex, cf. e.g. Aesch. *Ag.* 73–82, Eur. *HF* 107–114, *Cresph.* 448a. 45–8 Kannicht (and Ar. *Ach.* 210–24 etc.). A passage like *Hipp.* 121–8 or *Hel.* 179–84 performs this function among others. As to comedy, for our purposes questions about Aristophanes and Callistratus do not matter (cf. Halliwell (1980) and Macdowell (1982)).

[17] The narrator's judgement is awry e.g. at Soph. *Ant.* 853–5, as Teiresias will show. The narrator's ungenerous behaviour to Oedipus at *OC* 229–36 turns out to be mistaken (cf. still 1483–4). The chorus of the *PV* provides an excellent illustration (from divine beings!) of a choral narrator disapproving audacity, but without fierce antagonism, cf. e.g. 178–80, 542–3. Note the character's perspective on the narrator's stance at Soph. *OT* 688–9. On these questions cf. recently Gould (1996); Goldhill (1996) (and Taplin (1996), 191–4); Mastronarde (1998). For Bakhtin's *poliphonija* see esp. (1929), 14, (1963), 208–9.

recurrent impulse to move away from the situation in hand comes
from the lyric genre.[18]

Such movement is a standard feature of choral lyric. In choral
lyric, unlike tragic odes, the specific occasion normally encourages
beginning as well as ending reasonably near the 'home' subject;
Sophocles and Euripides in particular are fond of beginning at a
distance. Even so, a short poem like Pind. *Ol.* 12 has a shape like
a tragic ode (with address to the victor at the beginning of the last
stanza); an unusual poem like *Pyth.* 3 illustrates the possibilities for
deferring the given situation. Sapph. 16 [**5**] provides a conspicuous
example of starting at a distance from it. Relevant to the closes of
tragic odes is the sudden return to the addressee at the end of Ibyc.
S151 [**11**]. But such specific points of structure merely underline
the general kinship.[19]

The ranging of tragic lyric gains a distinctive significance and
effect from its context within a play. The main drama is tightly
confined, in time, place, and subject (more so in time and place
even than comedy). By taking the listener into other places, times,
subject-matter, the odes greatly enrich the main drama; they give
it new settings, and extend the listener's thought and perception.
At the same time, the excursive manner enhances by contrast the
fierce concentration of the rest.[20]

These points give some indication of how deeply tragic lyric is
indebted to the lyric tradition, and how radically it transforms it.
Cultural history here takes a noteworthy turn. The development of
lyric had been away from a plurality of local traditions; Pindar and
Bacchylides come from different places, and write the same sorts
of poems for patrons in a wide range of cities. Athenian drama is
strongly local in its production, audience, and authorship (Ion is

---

[18] Easterling (1982), 133–4 stresses the relation of Soph. *Trach.* 497–530 to Pindar
and Bacchylides in other respects. The repeated questions, with no address, at 503–
4 are closer to Pind. *Pyth.* 4. 70–1 than to Homer; cf. also *Ol.* 10. 60–4. For the
pious silence cf. e.g. *Ol.* 9. 35–42, fr. 81. The parodos of the *Agamemnon* in some
ways recalls Stesichorus; but the suppression of the ending uses, the interspersed
meditation hugely expands, devices from later poets (cf. e.g. Pind. *Ol.* 13. 91, *Pyth.*
3. 21–3).   [19] *Pyth.* 3 may well be used at Eur. *Alc.* 121–30.
[20] It is a sort of converse to a device in Turner: he often enhances an atmospher-
ically indefinite scene by contrast with sharply defined objects in the foreground.
The similes of the *Iliad* offer a closer analogy; there too a movement of imaginative
excursion often intensifies the austere and claustrophobic main narrative. This point
is not in the least inconsistent with the manifold thematic connections and contrasts
between narrative and simile, which indirectness only makes more suggestive; the
same applies to choruses.

unusual); it also presents a drastic combination and reworking of the lyric and other genres into something highly idiosyncratic. Yet its poets remain the successors to Alcman, Simonides, Pindar.[21]

19: Sophocles, *Ajax*, 1185–1222[22]

This song diverges remarkably from its surroundings in its vista of time. Teucer, leaving in haste to arrange Ajax's burial, has charged the chorus itself with helping to guard Ajax's body from his enemies, a dangerous task (1182–4). This pressing crisis is left aside in the ode, which presents a long perspective of time: the interminable war at Troy. It reaches back to the remote past of the invention of war. Even Ajax's death, when finally referred to (1214–15), appears not as the crucial event in itself, but as something that intensifies the narrator's pessimism about return. The whole present situation appears merely as part of a huge imperfective continuum, the perfective end of which is desired.

In place, too, the song produces an expansion of scope. The action has been focused, not simply on the stage, but on a body; Ajax's child has just been made the suppliant of his father, in an emotive tableau (1171–81), Tecmessa stands by. But the song does not touch directly on that body at all; it begins with the entity of 'Troy', which extends far beyond the stage, and ends with a longing vision of Attica.

All this, though highly effective, is no random excursion. The ode is closely linked to the first stanza of the ode at 596–645. The difference in context is notable. The shaping of the play is marked, not simply by its characters' different perspectives (Segal (1995), ch. 1), but by a distinction between their evaluation of Ajax and their

---

[21] The relation of Aeschylus' and Pindar's style is sometimes considered; the relation of Sophocles' and Pindar's would be a subtler subject. It would involve, among other areas, defamiliarization, self-conscious use of tradition, and the impact of the individual word.

[22] On this chorus see Hermann and Erfurdt (1848), 147–53; Wunder (1857), 129–31; Lobeck (1866), 376–9; Blaydes (1875), 262–70; Campbell (1879–81), ii. 104–6, (1907), 78; Schneidewin and Nauck (1882), 161–3; Schneidewin, Nauck, and Radermacher (1913), 163–5; Wilamowitz (1921), 511; Kamerbeek (1963), 227–33; Stanford (1963), 205–9; Pohlsander (1964), 23–4; Dawe (1968), 13, (1973–8), i. 167–8; Ronnet (1969), 145–6; Dale (1971–83), ii. 20–1; Burton (1980), 36–8; Segal (1981), 145–6; Itsumi (1982), 70 n. 40; Gardiner (1987), 71–2; Lloyd-Jones and Wilson (1990*b*), 35–7; Garvie (1998), 232–4.

individual outlook onto the action from the basis of their own future and past: between an emphasis on the object and on the subject. The earlier passage had followed a clash of personal outlooks between Tecmessa and Ajax, but no one had doubted a high valuation of Ajax. In the present part of the play evaluations of Ajax are in fierce dispute. In this antagonistic setting is placed an ode which does not question Ajax's greatness, but provides a drastically different outlook on what is happening. The ode may prompt the listener to reflect on the sources of Ajax's 'greatness'; but its primary interest is not so much that it generates criticism of him. Rather it broadens the whole range of the thought, and it offers the fascination of a beguiling approach quite unlike Ajax's or even Teucer's (one might modify Gould (1999), 109–10). But the narrator himself is not to be perceived without a certain degree of detachment. Rich material, much of it deriving from lyric, is here fashioned into a touching and emotional poem; the poem is deliberately deprived of the intensity that belongs to the main tragedy.

Metre

str. and ant. 1

1. ⏑⏑⏑ ⏑⏑⏑ –⏑⏑–
2.   –⏑⏑––⏑⏑–⏑––
3. –⏑–⏑͞–⏑⏑–⏑–⏑–
4.   ––––⏑⏑–
5. –⏑–⏑⏑–⏑–
6. ––⏑⏑–⏑–––

str. and ant. 2

1. ⏑͞–⏑––⏑⏑–
2. –⏑⏑––⏑⏑–
3. –⏑⏑––⏑⏑––
4. ––⏑⏑––⏑⏑–
5. –⏑⏑––⏑⏑––⏑⏑––
6. ⏑––⏑––⏑⏑–⏑––
7. ––⏑⏑–⏑––
8. ⏑–⏑⏑–⏑–
9. –⏑⏑–⏑–
10.   ͞⏑––⏑⏑––

The first strophe opens with a series of short syllables; cf. Pind. *Pyth.* 2. 1, but here the connotations are more emotive. Cf. *OC* 1447, and *Aj.* 608 at the end of a stanza; that strophe is closely connected with this passage, as was noted. Cf. further Aesch. *Ch.* 25, *Eum.* 158, and the group [Aesch.] *PV* 904, Soph. *El.* 823, *OC* 1222 (cf. 1237), Eur. *Andr.* 491. The short syllables evolve into a colon of asclepiad type (cf. 228, *Ant.* 785 for the base (Parker (1997), 71)). The form may derive from Anacr. 378 (cf. Parker (1997), 78–9); there the emotion is mocked. After 1–2 the cola grow shorter: after the three –◡◡– of the first colon, there comes (3) an aeolic colon with only one, followed and preceded, as in 1–2, by single short. A 'wilamowitzian' comes next (4): the –◡◡– is now followed by nothing; then a glyconic (5). The stanza swells out somewhat to close; the dragged ending is here full of expressive force, especially in the antistrophe. Cf. for the effect *Trach.* 849–50 = 860–1. Note the feature near the start of the stanza already mentioned, at 597.

In the second strophic pair the opening colon of the first pair is expanded and varied. There are two matching periods (1–3, 4–5); in each there are five –◡◡–, the last culminating in a pendant close (cf. *OC* 510). The base is a single syllable in 4–5 (cf. Ar. *Frogs* 1347), and ×–◡– (or ×–◡) in 1–3. The expansion and repetition suggest in the second strophe an increase of intensity in the narrator, as his vision narrows. The extremity of 1205 (6) confirms this approach. In the second antistrophe the first and second periods stand in forceful contrast (πρὶν μέν, νῦν δ'). Although Sophocles likes to exploit ambiguities of ionic and choriambic, the important thing here seems the connection of 1–3 with 4–5 and of 1–3 with the opening of the first strophic pair.

In the antistrophe there is a strong break before 6–10. In the strophe there are more connections backwards from 6–10; but the change introduces a climax. What seems like a repeated bacchiac proves to be part of the 'single-short' section of an aeolic colon (Simon. 542 [**15**]. 29, *metre*; cf. also Pind. *Nem.* 6. 1, Eur. *El.* 864, Soph. *OC* 525 (where the base ◡– – responds to, and is a variant of, – – –, cf. 515, 518, 520); Parker (1997), 340). After that colon come more aeolic cola, which get ever shorter (7 hagesichorean, 8 telesillean, 9 dodrans A); in the strophe the diminishing distinct phrases suit the narrator's picture of his pitiful state. The slight expansion in the final phrase (pherecratean), with a disyllabic base, perhaps suits the aggrandizing gesture of self-pity. The metrical units are syntactically less detached in the antistrophe. The strong break at 1215 (5) has led to a contemplation of home; the effect of 6–10 in the strophe is overcome and reversed.

1185. τίc: the opening with an agitated question is a device that suits the manner of tragedy, but has connections with choral lyric (see the introduction to 'Tragedy' above). In Sophocles cf. e.g. *OT* 152, 463, *Phil.* 135–6. The lyric immediately preceding opens with questions, of a wishful sort (879–87); the connection marks the broader scope of the present song (cf. 888, and 1197 n.). The questions here particularly resemble in tone the longing question that starts the ode at Eur. *Bacch.* 862–912 (cf. *Erechth.* fr. 370. 5–10 Kannicht); still closer is the climactic question (probably) reached at the end of Alc. 130 b [9] (note πόλλων). Cf. also the passionate question at Eur. *Hec.* 929–32 (the Greek longing for home).

ἄρα: enlivening, cf. Denniston (1954), 39–40, and Eur. *Supp.* 623, *Bacch.* 987.

νέατος: the use 'last' is a development not found before Sophocles (*Ant.* 627, 807–9) and Euripides (*Tro.* 201–2). As those passages suggest, the question 'what will be the final number' is a more convoluted way of saying 'which year will be last?'; the two questions τίς and ἐς πότε become entangled with each other. The syntax combines vigour and complication.

ἐς πότε should be preceded by a comma, not only because the sense of ἀριθμός changes for the second question but because the underlying question is the same (contrast *Ant.* 401). This is a more devious version of anadiplosis. Even the rhetorically simpler πότε is here varied to ἐς πότε (cf. Aeschin. 3. 99, rather than Aesch. *Ch.* 1075–6).

1186. πολυπλάγκτων: the word itself, here imaginatively applied, had come in Homer (*Il.* 11. 308, etc.), elegy (Theogn. 1257), lyric (Bacch. 11. 35, 13. 181), and in Aeschylus (*Supp.* 572). The men, despite Aesch. *Ag.* 194, could hardly be said to have spent the years at Troy in much wandering (for 'at Troy' cf. 1190; 414–15). And there is only a secondary thematic link to the wanderings of 888. The prime reference must be to the motion of the years (cf. *Ant.* 607–8 (Wunder)); the idea of length implied through πολυ- would be given subjective colour by notions of protraction, futility, and vicissitude (cf. Eur. *Hipp.* 1110). This view, then, does not require that -πλάγκτος should mean simply 'move', a view uncertainly supported by Bacch. 13. 181 (other views are possible) or by Parmen. fr. 17. 1 Coxon (there is a variant); cf. also Holmes (1998), 448.

ἐτέων: the time is defined more specifically than in the related passage at 414–15, and more dauntingly than at 600–5. The mythical data of the Trojan War are deployed here; so they are, more directly, in the related passage Eur. *Andr.* 304–6, cf. Soph. *Phil.* 715.

ἀριθμός: the word in this context communicates the measured sequence of time painfully mounting; despite the question here, one may contrast the use of ἀνήριθμοc at 604–5, cf. *OT* 168, 179, *El.* 232. The concrete sense of ἀριθμόc implied by λήξει is seen in earlier lyric, Ibyc. S151 [**11**]. 27 (n.).

1187–9: the question is syntactically complete, but the sentence runs on expressively for the rest of the stanza.

ἄπαυcτον: first extant Parmen. 8. 27 Coxon, Aesch. *Supp.* 574; not in Pindar or Bacchylides.

αἰέν goes with ἄπαυcτον, cf. Eur. *Supp.* 82, Soph. *El.* 1239, *OT* 905. The phrase, placed at the start of the participial clause, conveys the narrator's feeling about the experience hitherto; but the main clause suggests a more pessimistic undertone: the warfare will never cease.

ἐμοί: the form sets the narrator's emotions in some relief.

δορυccοήτων: a deviation from the standard δορυccόοc (Hes. *Scut.* 54, Theogn. 987, Aesch. *Supp.* 182, Eur. *Hcld.* 774, etc.; note Bacch. 17. 90). It is the toil of war the narrator has principally in mind, rather than the present task.

μόχθων ἄταν: as we had ἐτέων ἀριθμόc rather than ἔτεα, so we have μόχθων ἄταν rather than μόχθουc. The phrases intensify, and the fullness promotes, the expressive design of the sentence. The sense of folly stands in the background for ἄταν.

1190. The text contains too many rarities and oddities to be credible, even in the lightly emended form presented by Lloyd-Jones and Wilson ((1990*a*), 48, ἂν τὰν εὐρώδη Τροΐαν, cf. (1990*b*), 35–6). If there were no other problems, the correspondence of glyconic to 'wilamowitzian' would be endurable (cf. Itsumi (1982), 72–3; Diggle (1994), 195, 473). Yet the numerous examples in Euripides do not start before the *Supplices*, and the few examples in Sophocles are late (*Phil.* 1082, 1124). (*Trach.* 960 (λέγουc-)=969, tel=shortened wil, would be an abnormal case anyway and is altered by Lloyd-Jones and Wilson themselves.) To gain this undemanding degree of correspondence, we have to accept an apocope of ἀνά not found elsewhere in Sophocles, credit a peculiar formation unlike the numerous -ώδηc compounds of drama, and give the common word Τροία a scansion which is standard in Pindar, but is found in tragedy only in the late [Eur.] *Rhes.* 231, 360. Since there are only four words in the line, this seems a suspicious level of anomaly.

1191. δύcτανον: an epithet intensifies the gloom and swells the sentence; contrast e.g. Ar. *Ach.* 855.

ὄνειδοc: the reason for the shame is not spelt out, as is often the case with ὄνειδοc, αἰcχύνη, etc.; cf. e.g. Eur. *Tro.* 171, *Phoen.* 821. The most obvious reason might be the Greeks' lack of success so far (Wunder); but that in itself does not seem particularly creditable to Ajax or consonant with the play. At least part of the thought, even if obliquely, will be the irrational folly of war, especially evident in a war so large and long. This prepares for the next stanza.

Ἑλλάνων: the word forms a climax; but this narrator does not show the matching sympathy for the Trojans seen in Homer, Ibyc. S151 [11], and choruses in Euripides (cf. *Andr.* 301–7, 1010–46, conversely *Hec.* 647–57). Line 1210 takes the point up. The figure of Tecmessa, present on stage, makes this a significant matter in the play (note 1168–84). The chorus, revealingly, show sympathy for this individual Phrygian (525–6, 903, etc.), unlike Ajax and even Teucer.

1192–4. The chorus embark abruptly on a vain wish; they contemplate a figure in the distant past. The ideas are characteristic of the wistful and imaginative thought-world of much tragedy; but tragic lyric often uses such a movement to an impossible wish at the start of a new stanza. Cf. Aesch. *Ch.* 345–7 (str. 3), ([*PV*] 152–7), Eur. *Alc.* 455–8 (str. 2), *Supp.* 786–8 (ant. 1), *Phoen.* 801–5 (ant.). Strophic form unites with expansion of range and vehemence of expression. Here the effect includes a movement into generality too. The imagining of a figure in the past often begins a stanza or ode (*Inach.* fr. 269c Radt, 1–20, [Aesch.] *PV* 887–93).

The subject of the wish is delayed intriguingly until after the first period and the two alternatives of air and underworld. Places other than the surface of the earth are natural destinations for those who eagerly desire, or are eagerly desired, not to be on it; cf. e.g. Eur. *Ion* 1238–9, *Phaeth.* 270–3 Diggle, Plat. *Laws* 905 A 5–6, Virg. *Aen.* 12. 892–3; Eur. *HF* 650–4 (hostile wish). The conception is made more vivid and striking here by epithets which set a region not meant for mortals against the region to which they must all come. For πολύκοινον cf. παγκοίνου at Soph. *El.* 137–8; the present compound has a touch of sombre litotes. It occurs also at Pind. *Pyth.* 2. 41. For μέγαν cf. *Ant.* 420–1, *OC* 1471.

Ἀίδαν forms an impressive close to the period.

1195–6. Invention as a motif has a long poetic tradition: cf. Kleingünther (1933), esp. chs. 1–2; Davies (1986*b*), esp. for ἔδειξεν. For

curses on inventors, and the invention of war, cf. Leo (1912), 151–
4, and also Smith (1913), 376–7; Murgatroyd (1980), 151. Note
further for war etc. Hdt. 1. 68. 4, cf. Call. fr. 110. 48–50 Pfeiffer.
Detestation of war or longing for peace is expressed several times
by choruses; cf. Eur. *Erechth.* fr. 369 Kannicht, 370. 5–10, *Cresph.*
fr. 453, *Bacch.* 419–20. More argumentative is *Hel.* 1151–63 (ant.
2). Frr. 369 and 453 Kannicht are very clearly based on choral lyric,
and echo specific passages (see Bacch. fr. 4. 61–80; for fr. 453. 1 cf.
Pind. *Ol.* 13. 7, for 453. 10–11 Pind. fr. 109. 3–4, and Bacch. fr. 24.
3). Note also Ar. *Ach.* 971–87, *Peace* 1127–39, *Thesm.* 1146–7. The
tradition is here made to suit the choral narrator well; this is not to
deny its power to provoke thought.

cτυγερῶν at the start of the clause, separated from its noun, con-
tinues the depiction of the narrator's feeling.

ὅπλων . . . Ἄρη instead of simply Ἄρη shows a fullness with the
genitive seen at the same point in the strophe; the expression is un-
usual with this metonymy. κοινὸν Ἄρη at the end of this period takes
up πολύκοινον Ἅιδαν at the end of the last. Both use metonymy and
(-)κοινος. The connection hints grimly at the fate that war inflicts
on the Greeks, because one man did not undergo that fate first.
κοινόν here is unlikely to denote primarily a common expedition:
ἔδειξεν and 1198 suggest War rather than the Trojan War (the in-
vention of panhellenic expeditions is hardly plausible). Rather this
is something which the Greeks all do, a sad bond. The senses of
a common expedition, of war among Greeks, of public disaster as
against the individual inventor (cf. Eur. *Hec.* 640–2), may all lie in
the background. In any case, the generality is sufficient to include
the experience of the audience, and to cause them to reflect.

1197. ὦ: as the strophe is corrupt, one cannot be certain that ἰώ
is wrong. The form of base might be defended by Eur. *Or.* 816
⏑–⏑–⏑⏑–⏑– (= ––––⏑⏑–⏑–), and other unusual bases (note 1205
below); cf. West (1982), 66 n. 80 ('enneasyllable'). ἰώ need not be
matched by an ἰώ in the antistrophe, cf. e.g. Soph.*Trach.* 856, *El.*
1232; and note e.g. Aesch. *Ag.* 1167 ἰὼ πόνοι πόνοι. But the change
is too easy to be resisted.

The emotional exclamation is effectively made not to end the
stanza (cf. e.g. *OC* 1471), but to fuel the impressive last statement.
Exclamations with πόνοι are common in tragedy, but usually of
woes more central to the plays (Aesch. *Th.* 739–40, *Supp.* 126, *Ch.*

466, Eur. *Hipp*. 1344; more generally *Hipp*. 367). The figure with πόνος goes back to Simon. 520. 3; cf. e.g. Eur. *Or*. 816–18. One should contrast the more trivial and exaggerated use by the weary semichorus at 866. The metaphor of birth creates a forceful picture, not of connected woes within a family, but of the disastrous causal chain of wars in the world.

1198. A forcefully brief clause to end.

κεῖνος: the word is taken up from the start of the last period but one, with intensified indignation.

ἔπερσεν: the word is often used widely, e.g. Phrynich. *TrGF* 3 F 6, Eur. *Hipp*. 541, *HF* 700. But the military connotations of the word have an extra point here, and enhance the paradox of one man doing this to mankind. This, and nothing more recent, was the decisive event in the past.

ἀνθρώπους: the word goes beyond Ἑλλάνων at the end of the strophe, and Ἕλλασιν in 1196. Cf. Hdt. 1. 68. 4 (and Antiph. fr. 121. 2 Kassel-Austin, etc.). The rhythm heightens the force of the word.

1199. The opposition of war and the party is an essential part of the poetic tradition on peace: cf. Bacch. fr. 4. 68, 79, Eur. *Erechth*. fr. 369. 2–3 Kannicht (garlands), *Cresph*. fr. 453. 8, Ar. *Ach*. 1071–149, etc. However, the movement to this point after 1198 and the preceding strophe seems a striking descent: from mankind to the narrator, and from woe and destruction to the loss of parties. The change of focus is only reinforced by the continuity of agent: ἐκεῖνος at the start takes up κεῖνος in 1198. Concern with these ordinary pleasures suits a tragic chorus; cf. Soph. *Phil*. 712–17, Eur. *Hcld*. 892–3 (cf. 894–5). What stands at the centre of much lyric poetry stands at the margins of this genre. Here it creates a certain bathos, so that one should be charmed as well as touched; 1205 confirms this. We are not utterly remote from the deprived chorus of Eur. *Cycl*. 63–6.

We have to choose between altering strophe and antistrophe. If the lines are an extended asclepiad, the base ⌣–⌣– would be preferable (cf. Parker (1997), 71, and on 1197 above). And one should prefer an extended asclepiad to ionics. One cannot exclude Sophoclean ambiguities, but such asclepiad forms often appear in groups (so within *Ant*. 944–50, *Phil*. 707–15, cf. *OC* 510, 517); the shape of the ode, especially the following lines and the opening of str. 1, makes an asclepiad form seem more probable and inviting here. Hence we should keep οὔτε, and read αἰὲν νυχίου in 1211, an easy change (*eneen* for *enen*).

1200. βαθειᾶν: a relative rather than a generic epithet. Cf. Pherecr. fr. 152. 4 Kassel–Austin.

κυλίκων: part of the poetry of parties, as well as the actuality; cf. Sapph. 2. 13, Alc. 346. 5, Bacch. fr. 20 B. 7, Pind. fr. 124. 4, etc.

1201. νεῖμεν: the man from the past is like an inverted deity, prescribing the lot of even the narrator in the future.

ἐμοί: the pronoun again receives a measure of emphasis, to contrast with the wider scope of ant. 1.

τέρψιν: the word is strongly emphasized by its repetition at 1204 and at 1215, in exactly the same point in the stanza as this, with a repeated question. The stem, and even the noun, need not denote pleasure of the senses rather than joy; but they are quite often associated with feasting, as here, cf. Archil. fr. 13. 2 West, Pind. *Pyth.* 9. 19, Eur. *Med.* 202, *Bacch.* 423, Philox. Leuc. 836 (*c*). 3, etc. Ajax's use of τέρπειν at 475 is much more general; but there is a contrast between his view there and the narrator's here: the narrator passively persists in a state with no delight. Ajax's death is explicitly mentioned in the sentence before 1215; there is also a contrast there with 967 (if it is genuine). ἠράσθη in 967 confirms that τερπνός in 967 has some colour. Finally, there is a connection between our chorus and 521, where Tecmessa's appeal to the debt created by sexual pleasure (τερπνὸν . . . τι) is of no interest to Ajax. These echoes will not be consciously noticed by all the audience; but they underline essential contrasts.

ὁμιλεῖν: the exepegetic infinitive is so used with this verb at Pind. *Nem.* 10. 72; but here there is an elaborate interplay. The verb suggests the social pleasures which the narrator is denied (cf. Pind. *Pyth.* 6. 52/3); he does not even consort with the pleasure itself.

1202. γλυκὺν αὐλῶν ὄτοβον: the expression is closely akin to Bacch. 2. 12 γλυκεῖαν αὐλῶν καναχάν. For ὄτοβ- cf. [Aesch.] *PV* 574; the stem occurs elsewhere at Hes. *Theog.* 709, several times in Aeschylus, and at Soph. *OC* 1475, but not in lyric poetry.

1203–4. δύσμορος: the epithet for the inventor seems satisfactory in sense; he is not forgotten. But δύσμορος is rarely used in attack, as at *OC* 804, and Blaydes's δυσμόρωι may very well be right. The added designation is characteristic of Sophocles' choral narrators, cf. e.g. *El.* 1407–8, *OT* 665, *Trach.* 949. Ajax has applied the term emphatically to himself for very different reasons (372); cf., recently, 905, 923, applied to Ajax because of his death.

οὔτ᾽ κτλ.: the syntax with the three accusatives is varied: first an object (τέρψιν) with an appended infinitive, then a simple object (ὄτοβον), and now, probably, an infinitive with internal object. ἐννυχίαν τέρψιν is an evocative description of a pleasurable sleep rather than of love: 1205 must be introducing a new topic. The pleasures of the sleep lost in war are far more richly described in Bacch. fr. 4. 75–7 than in non-lyrical references to the point (e.g. Aesch. *Ag.* 335–7, Ar. *Peace* 347, Tib. 1. 1. 4, Luc. 4. 395). With the striking expression contrast e.g. Pind. *Pyth.* 11. 25 ἔννυχοι . . . κοῖται, Ibyc. S257 (*a*) fr. 1. 15–16 ἀ]γρύπνο[υ]ϲ ἰαύων | νύκτας (cf. Hom. *Il.* 9. 329).

1205. A fresh main clause or sentence expresses the narrator's greatest sorrow incisively.

ἐρώτων δ᾽, ἐρώτων . . . ὤμοι: the extreme expression for the loss of sex does not engage our impassioned sorrow; there must be an element of wry distance in the spectator's sympathetic response. (Hermann's 'nimis cupide', in suspicion of the text, is an interesting comment (Hermann and Erfurdt (1848), 149).) One may contrast the temperate enthusiasm e.g. of Eur. *Hcld.* 894–5. The emotive device of anadiplosis, so characteristic of tragic lyric, is discussed in the introduction to 'Tragedy'; from this play note 396–7, 414, 620 (627). The exclamation ὤμοι seems generally uncommon from Sophoclean choruses; it has been used by this one (probably) at 227, 610, 900–1, 909, 946, but in far graver contexts. Ajax's attitude to the importance of love was extremely different; the presence of Tecmessa and his son on stage sharpens the antithesis.

1206–10. The sentence, after its initial verb, accumulates a series of phrases, in a rhetoric less tightly bound together than the accumulated οὔτεϲ and the parallel members of the first half of the stanza.

After all the negatives, the narrator offers a picture of his actual nights. The generalizing present and ἀεί make the picture eminently imperfective and extended in time.

κεῖμαι κτλ.: ἀμέριμνοϲ οὕτωϲ connects the picture with the chorus' present appearance, in a visual and pathetic gesture; idioms like οὕτωϲ εἰκῆι can hardly prevail against the deictic suggestions of the context. The whole depiction resembles the pathetic depiction of

Philoctetes, cf. *Phil.* 183–6 (with κεῖται and ἀμερίμνητα (Page)). This first phrase recalls Ajax's description of himself (426–7).

ἀεὶ κτλ.: whatever the realities of military service (the problem sounds superable), the passage must recall the Herald of the *Agamemnon*, a lowly man contrasted with the stately and gloomy hero. This passage is made more lyrical in style than *Ag.* 560–2; the origin of the dew is not specified, and insects are naturally excluded.

The treatment of the narrator's hair contrasts with the garlanding he is deprived of (1199). A contrast may also be suggested between abundant dew and abundant wine (cf. 1200). In any case, ἀεί and πυκιναῖc go effectively together.

λυγρᾶc μνήματα Τροίαc: a haunting phrase to close. The point can scarcely be that the wetness of the narrator's hair reminds him he is in Troy (had he forgotten?), nor that it will remain wet as a reminder when he has left it. Nor can the phrase simply denote memories from a future standpoint. The idea is the more imaginative one that the narrator himself lying there neglected is a kind of memorial to the fighting at Troy. The long fighting at Troy already requires commemoration; the phrase hints too at the thought or fantasy of his continuing there for ever, in death. κεῖμαι is made to acquire connections both to death and to monumentality; note 899, 913, and the present tableau of Ajax's corpse. The present language is joined to, and contrasted with, the real βροτοῖc ἀείμνηcτον τάφον which they desire for Ajax (1166–7; contr. 426–7). Relevant here is Hom. *Il.* 4. 173–82, where Agamemnon envisages Menelaus' bones rotting as he lies (κειμένου) in Troy, the war having failed, and men thinking of the war through his tomb (cf. also 7. 84–91). Relevant too is the language of inscriptions, where statues, altars, etc. are a μνῆμα of fighting or a place, e.g. *CEG* i. 177. 4, 272, 390. 1 (cf. also Pind. *Thren.* 3. 5 (fr. 5 b Cannatà Fera)). In a more comic vein, cf. I. Svevo, *La coscienza di Zeno* (1923; ed. Milan 1988, p. 131) 'perché avrei dovuto divenire addirittura il monumento ambulante della vittoria di Guido?'

Troy is thought of only in the sufferings it causes Greeks; λυγρᾶc strikingly brings out for the listener the narrator's one-sided perspective, and his ignorance of the future. Ajax has addressed the landscape as hostile to the Greeks, including himself (418–20); the authenticity of 862–3 is uncertain. The name Τροίαc ends the stanza, matching the Ἑλλάνων ending str. 1 and the ἀνθρώπουc ending ant.

1; it emphasizes again, for the listener, the narrator's perspective and its limitations.

1211. νυχίου maintains the sequence of thought. Some features of the night remain perpetually the same; but one aspect, the terror of attack, has grown worse. The discourse has still not turned to their danger at the moment. The introduction of Ajax none the less marks a return, at a common point in stasima, to the primary subject of the play. The listener will feel the difference from 596–645: there str. 1 dealt with the narrator's lot along the same lines; but the start of ant. 1 already turned to Ajax.

The fear of death, not least from fellow Greeks, is a dominating characteristic of this chorus. It displays, indirectly, Ajax's present isolation; it also shows a dependence on him in the chorus which is the reverse of his own lack of dependence, even on the gods (770–5). For all this see the chorus's opening anapaests, 134–71; 245–56 (stoning with Ajax feared), 606–7; cf. also 1021–3 for Teucer's related plight. Such characteristics appear in many tragic choruses (unlike those of comedy); cf. *Phil.* 135–43, 154–8, etc., Eur. *Andr.* 143–6 (fear, of their rulers), *Ion* 1229–49 (death with Creusa feared), *Or.* 1539–40, contrast *Hcld.* 356, 766–7 (Athenians of a different sort!).

1212. προβολά: the word comes mainly in prose, and, like πρόβλημα (1219), is not extant in poetry before tragedy, cf. *Phil.* 1455 (different sense), Eur. *Or.* 1487. πρόβλημα, however, had been used by Aeschylus (*Th.* 540, 676), and is used by Herodotus; Xenophon and the Hippocratic corpus employ it much less than προβολή. This suggests that προβολή is a striking word to find in tragic lyric, all the more for being predicated of the adorned proper name. Less notable is the similarly used πύργου ῥῦμα at 159 (cf. Aesch. *Eum.* 701). The combination δείματος... καὶ βελέων, itself striking, brings out the physical and metaphorical range of προβολά. Its military suggestions, along with βελέων, call to mind Ajax's wider role as defender of the Greeks; this will come to the fore in the next scene (1273–6 etc.).

1213. θούριος Αἴας: the name comes as a climax to the sentence and period. The phrase, with this placing, has a Homeric quality, like φαίδιμος Αἴας (*Il.* 5. 617 etc.), the more so because the chorus have already used the present phrase at 212. However, the epithet is not itself found before tragedy, or in Bacchylides and Pindar. It is a variation of Homeric θοῦροc, which is not used of people (often of Ares, as θούριοc at 613 here; θούριοc of people e.g. Aesch. *Pers.* 74). Its suggestions of vigorous speed suit Ajax, cf. 301, 305; it complements προβολά and contrasts with the inertness of 1214–15.

1214. In the context, both νῦν δ᾽ and οὗτοc include a suggestion of the scene now visible. Cf. 970, 1060, 1087.

ἀνεῖται: the expression seems in itself a colourful way of saying that someone is doomed to misfortune or death, dedicated to a malevolent divinity. Cf. Eur. *Phoen.* 947 for the extended ἀνίημι, and e.g. Soph. *El.* 1156–7, Lys. 2. 78 for allocation; cf. further Pind. *Pyth.* 3. 34, Aesch. *Pers.* 354 for the daimon. The use of the perfect is notable, now that Ajax has already died; his evil fate continues. It is still more notable that this expression is used when the argument makes us expect 'he is dead'. The expression is not calculated to imply his near-deity. Rather, it skirts over the fact of his death. The ode does not touch directly on the dead body before the audience; it is the narrator's body that receives the pathetic description (and connections with death). The perspective of the narrator and the distance of the ode from the action are remarkably conveyed at the very point when the action makes a brief appearance. The passive form absolves Ajax from responsibility. He is not blamed for the consequences of his suicide. δαίμονι performs the same functions; cf. 534.

cτυγερῶι: the word was used at 1195, of warfare in general; this may underline the movement that has taken place from that extreme generality to the plot. The word had not been used before in the play (cτυγναῖc 561).

1215–16. τίc μοι κτλ.: the occurrence of τέρψιc at the same point as τέρψιν in the strophe is bound to be significant, and to affect the understanding of the word. Cf. e.g. θάρcοc at *El.* 479 = 495; the device is important in Pindar and Bacchylides. The fate of Ajax, just mentioned, brings the thought to a fuller pessimism; the loss of τέρψιc described in str. 2 will last for ever. The question looks back to the opening of str. 1, and again is still more pessimistic. The rhetorical form is also more passionate and direct; the figure is that used for the exclamation, less generalized, in 1205. For the figure of repetition separated by a postpositive, as here and at 1205, cf. Alc. 374 (humorously overdone), Pind. *Isth.* 6. 44, and e.g. Soph.

Ant . 1273, *OT* 1189, *Ichn*. fr. 314. 247 Radt, Eur. *Cycl*. 361, *El*. 594, Ar. *Lys*. 666; note in dialogue Soph. *OC* 982.

μοι: μοι . . . Αἴαc, οὗτοc . . . μοι form a sequence. It is himself that the narrator is concerned with; the movement from Ajax's doom to the narrator's pleasure shows his perspective drastically.

ἐπέcται: 'will remain', cf. Hom. *Od*. 4. 756, *Hom. h. Dem*. 263. Ar. *Birds* 597 is less relevant, but affects Dawe's argument against the word ((1968), 13).

1217. The climax of despair in 1215–16 issues in the half-relief of a fantastic wish. This is not a practical hope for the distant future, but a vain wish for now, as the parallels show. Wishes for impossible (or unlikely) motion, often accompanied by metamorphosis, are frequent in tragic lyric after Aeschylus (but cf. Aesch. *Supp*. 779–83), and have their origins in lyric poetry: cf. Alcm. 26 (note εἴην 2), Anacr. 346 fr. 11 + 3 + 6. 16 (whatever the syntax of the optative; cf. also 347 fr. 1 [12]. 15–18). See Soph. *Trach*. 954–8, *OC* 1044–53, 1081–4, fr. 476 Radt, Eur. *Hipp*. 732–51, *Andr*. 861–5, *IT* 1138–52 (note 1095), *Hel*. 1478–86, *Phoen*. 226–38, *Bacch*. 402–11.

Here, as often, the mood is nostalgic; metamorphosis would not suit the temper of the song, and a sea voyage is envisaged. The emphasis is on place, often described in these passages; the syntax is more tightly contained than is commonly the case in them, and προcείποιμεν keeps the narrator's desire strongly to the fore. The whole sentence moves the discourse suddenly and expressively away from the gloomy environment conjured up in the rest of the ode; the effect is the opposite of that at 596–8, where Salamis begins the ode. The geographical progress of the sentence ends with the place where the tragedy is being performed, present for the audience, distant and unattainable for the narrator. Euripides does similar things at *Hec*. 466–74, *Tro*. 208–9.

ὑλᾶεν: Hom. *Il*. 17. 748 etc. The descriptive words in this clause are not particularly specific, but evocative.

πόντωι: ἔπεcτι wants a dative expressed.

ἁλίκλυcτον: cf. ἁλίπλακτοc of Salamis at 598. This word is not found elsewhere in the fifth or earlier centuries; it varies the epic περίκλυcτοc (Hes. *Theog*. 199 (Cyprus) etc.).

πλάκα: a vague rather than a precise word, tragic usage suggests (cf. e.g. *OC* 1563, *Trach*. 273, Eur. *Ion* 1267). The accusative probably indicates, in this author, previous motion. The narrator imagines reaching the cape; from that point the coast runs up northwards towards Athens, and Salamis. Note Ar. *Clouds* 401.

The lengthening before the mute and liquid takes place within a close-knit group of words; tragic lyric does not frequently allow itself even this small liberty, cf. *El.* 853, Eur. *Alc.* 101, *al.*; Barrett (1964), 310, 435 (and Hutchinson (1985), 219). Essentially, tragic lyric does not adopt the free treatment of mute and liquid seen in choral lyric, but attributes almost the same importance to word-end as tragic dialogue. Even lengthening within a word is a departure from Attic speech.

Couνίου: the place-name ends the clause and period, and matches Ἀθάνας. On the place, and its buildings, see Tataki (1978); Travlos (1988), 404–29.

ἱεράς: the epithet, a common one for places from epic on, is so placed with the article as to build up for the name at the other end of the clause.

προσείποιμεν: cf. Aesch. *Ag.* 810–11 (and 503–4, 508); Eur. *Ion* 1613. The word conveys an emotional moment.

Ἀθάνας: the name contrasts with that of the city of Troy at the end of the strophe. The particularity contrasts with the mention of Greeks at the end of str. 1. There is also a connection, finally, with the beginning of the ode at 596, which only mentions Salamis.

The chorus are commonly said to be Salaminian sailors. They seem to have sailed Ajax's own ship (201, cf. 902); their sailing then, though referred to again at 356–7, does not mean that they should be conceived only as 'sailors', for they are involved in fighting now. Their address to Salamis at 596–8 suggests, but does not demand, that Salamis is their homeland; at 202 they are said to be from the race of the Erechtheidae, i.e. to be Athenian in origin. It seems unlikely that the racial identity of Salaminians and Athenians is simply assumed; 861, if genuine, need not imply this (cf. March (1991–3), 25). One must surely connect the *genos* of the Salaminioi (for whom see Ferguson (1938); Osborne (1994), 154–9; Parker (1996), 308–16; Lambert (1999)); it is notable that one of their two divisions is entitled 'from Sounion' (the actual history does not matter here). Now, various attempts had been made, especially in the sixth century, to appropriate the Salaminian hero Ajax somehow: cf. Hdt. 5. 66. 2, 6. 35. 1, Plut. *Sol.* 10, etc.; Eurysaces is conspicuous in this play and in the cult of the Salaminioi. However, the origin of the chorus in this play seems to present a different means of making the Salaminioi Athenian from those connected with Ajax and his family. It could be Sophocles' invention.

Whether Athens is central to the meaning of the play is another matter. Athenian tragedy seizes opportunities to glorify Athens, but it is possible to have glory without centrality. The bearing on the play of Ajax's Attic cult is an important question here (cf. Henrichs (1993) etc.).

20: Euripides, *Medea*, 627–662[23]

As the discussion of the metre will indicate, the odes in the *Medea* are closely linked as a group. This interconnection, and the contrasts it brings, are plainly shown in the obvious echo and change of view on the question of whether there are female poets (424–8, 1081–9). Here the narrator's language has changed from that of the first ode, where she has represented womankind and claims that Jason's behaviour will upset hierarchies and stock notions of gender (her own view on gender is judicious, 429–30). Now her concerns are more prudential, her approach less emphatically female. Some changes in the chorus are caused by the action: it is important that by the end of the play the narrator is horrified at Medea's deeds. But the present change cannot plausibly be attributed to a change of heart induced by the intervening scene, one of argument between Jason and Medea. On the contrary, the chorus condemned and condemns Jason, and that scene would make natural a vehement response here. But instead the narrator shows in the first pair, by contrast with Medea's bitter and vigorous assault, a nervous and cautious wisdom. In the second strophe she is emotional but not aggressive, contemplating a hypothetical fate with horror. Only at the end does she attack Jason, more obliquely than Medea had done, but with sound feeling. The manner suits a choral narrator;

---

[23] On this ode see Musgrave (1778), i. 419, iv. 67; Matthiae (1813–37), vi. 481–3; Porson (1826), 455–7; Elmsley (1828), 354–8; Hermann (1828), 202–4; Pflugk and Klotz (1867), 89–92; Paley (1872–80), i. 116–18; Weil (1879), 148–61; Wecklein (1909), 76–8, 132–3; Verrall (1881), 58–60; von Arnim (1886), 51–4; Headlam (1897), 81–2; Page (1938), 117–20; North (1966), 73–4; Elliott (1969), 85; Meridor (1986); van Looy (1992), 136; Boedeker (1997), 141; Ciani and Susanetti (1997), 186–7; note also on the chorus in the *Medea* Knox (1979), 314–15; Seibert (1979), 301–3; Pucci (1980), 117; Hose (1990–1), ii. 76–89, esp. 82–3, 194 (note also i. 53–9); Williamson (1990), 28–9; Friedrich (1993), 233–5; Gould (1996), 229–31.

but the contrast with Medea, and the change from the previous
ode, prompt reflection not only on gender but on approaches to
existence.

The approaches are affected by experience; the narrator speaks,
with alarm, from outside these misfortunes, while thinking what
they would be like. Certainly the lyric language, the theology,
and the narrator's imagination, add intensity to our perception
of Medea's suffering. But the perspective from outside produces
too a sensible and moral disquiet at Medea's extreme passion, and
interestingly blends that passion with Jason's behaviour.

As so often, Medea's misfortune is emphatically split into the
pain of rejected love and the pain of exile; in relation to exile the
narrator's sympathy is strong and leads to firm detestation of Jason's
conduct. The notion of exile is one that alters in the play. Here it
comes in its 'earliest' form, that of Medea's loss of Colchis, with
its effects; the next scene will immediately arrange the altogether
'later' form of Medea's escape and reception in Athens, one which
eventually makes her departure a terrible triumph.

Love and exile are themes of 'private' lyric poetry; but it ac-
customs us more to the perspective of the victim, not an outsider.
Consciousness of such poetry heightens awareness of the particular
angle taken by this song.

Metre

str. and ant. 1

1. ⏑–∪∪–∪––
2.   –∪–––∪–
3. –∪∪–∪∪–⏑
4.   –∪∪–∪∪––
5. –∪–––∪∪–∪∪––
6. –∪–––∪∪–∪∪––
7.   –∪–––∪̇––
8.   –∪–∪––

str. and ant. 2

1. –∪∪––∪∪–
2.   –∪∪–∪––
3. ∪∪–∪∪–∪–∪–∪–∪––
4. –∪∪–∪∪–
5. ∪∪–∪∪–∪–∪––
6. –∪–––∪∪–

7.   ◡－－◡̆－◡◡－

8.   ◡－－◡◡－◡－－

The choral odes of the *Medea* mostly exploit in a single way drama's metrical difference between strophic pairs. There are five odes with two strophic pairs. The last, the climactic dochmiac lyric 1251–92, diverges effectively. The rest have the first pair only in straightforward dactylo-epitrite (straightforward save for the ending). The second pair bears vary-ing relations to dactylo-epitrite, but is always markedly different from the first. This difference in metre reinforces a division of content. The second pair is marked off from the first by greater intensity, whether through rhetorical figures or address to characters; in 431–45 and 846–65 the nar-rator turns more directly to the plot. The general pattern of a straightfor-ward dactylo-epitrite pair followed by a different pair or epode is found a number of times in drama, which never has two consecutive straight-forwardly dactylo-epitrite stanzas (unless responding). Cf. [Aesch.] *PV* 526–60, 887–907, Soph. *Aj.* 172–200, *Trach.* 94–140, Eur. *Andr.* 766–801, *Tro.* 799–819, [*Rhes.*] 224–41. But the cohesion between the *Medea*'s odes is remarkable; indeed, all the odes in question begin ×d×e (or ×d×E).

The dactylo-epitrite metre is surely likely to evoke, among other things, its appearances in stately choral lyric, the more so as Aeschylus (though probably not Phrynichus) had avoided the form. Note the allusions to choral lyric in Ar. *Knights* 1264–5, *Peace* 775–80, 796; Eur. *El.* 862–5. The rhythm in the first pair is 1–2 ⌣d-E, 3–4 d⌣d-, 5 e- d-, 6–8 e- d- e-E-, cr (=e) ba (cf. 420, *Andr.* 776 etc.).

The second pair starts with a distinctively different rhythm. Lines 1–2 may be viewed as wil+arist, but in a special form (cf. e.g. *HF* 637–8) which recalls the asclepiad. Lines 3 and 5 present types of enoplian (see Itsumi (1991–3), 245–6; Diggle (1994), 205–6); the form provides an altered echo of the alternation of double- and single-short common in dactylo-epitrite; cf. 989, *Tro.* 833 (followed by hemiepes), [Aesch.] *PV* 546 (and its context). Line 4 is (with this text) a hemiepes, a common means of evoking dactylo-epitrite in such a second strophic pair. Lines 6 and 7 are two 'wilamowitziani', which resume the opening of the stanza (cf. Itsumi (1982), 73; for the word-end see Willink (1986), 214). A hipponactean (8) adapts the form of 6 and 7 into a close.

627. ἔρωτες: the word takes up Medea's exclamation at 330 φεῦ φεῦ βροτοῖς ἔρωτες ὡς κακὸν μέγα; but it does so in a more elaborate and measured structure. The division of types of love is found at *IA* 543–57, a closely related stanza, or *Hipp.* 443–6; but the thoughtful tone of this passage is distinctive.

The idea of divinity is scarcely apparent in the μέν clause.

ὑπὲρ μὲν ἄγαν: a pre-verb in tmesis (Page (1938), 117) would not make sense here; ὑπέρ must here be treated as modifying ἄγαν, cf. e.g. Aesch. *Pers.* 794 ὑπερπόλλουϲ ἄγαν, ὑπέρευ, etc. It is regarded here as sufficiently distinct for the interposition of a postpositive; cf. Hom. *Il.* 17. 309 διὰ δ᾽ ἀμπερέϲ. There is a mimetic extravagance in the expression, as often in such cases: cf. Fraenkel (1950), ii. 197. The insistence on due limits in love suits the choral narrators of tragedy (cf. esp. *IA* 543–57); but it has connections too with the narrators of choral lyric: cf. esp. Pind. *Nem.* 11. 47–8 (ἔρωτεϲ metaphorically connected with love, as the language shows; cf. e.g. *Pyth.* 3. 19–20, *Nem.* 8. 1–7).

628. οὐκ εὐδοξίαν: the narrator expresses her point with a restrained negative.

629. ἀρετάν: the Ἔρωταϲ at 844–5 are παντοίαϲ ἀρετᾶϲ ξυνέργουϲ. In that stanza, Love is a source of Athens' harmonious art and beauty; the world of Corinth is to be contrasted.

παρέδωκαν: cf. Pind. *Pyth.* 2. 52. On the giving of ἀρετή note *Ol.* 7. 43–4. Simon. 541. 9–10, cf. 6–7, assert the same notion of love more directly.

630. ἀνδράϲιν: since the narrator prays to avoid such love herself (and perhaps suggests personal experience in 631), it is most plausible to suppose the word, as often, denotes mortals rather than males (note e.g. 1257). This would fit well with θεόϲ 631. Even so, it is striking that the narrator is not talking about female experience alone, all the more so after the first pair of the last ode, in which the narrator spoke as representative of her sex (410–30). Is the narrator referring to the excessive passion of Medea, or to the passion which Jason thinks Medea is ascribing to him (cf. 555–6, and Medea herself at 623–4)? Surely both. Lines 640–1 refer to a desire for new partners; on the other hand, 633–5 echo Jason's prominent description of Love assailing Medea (530–1), and the sex of the speaker referring to herself makes it the more natural to think there of the woman. The chorus has shown itself on the side of Medea in the dispute (cf. e.g. 576–9), and will do so again at the end of the ode. But the generality of this strophic pair, the emphasis on external causes, the absence of vehement partisanship, create at this point an air of cautious wisdom.

εἰ δ᾽ . . . ἔλθοι: the clause matches ἐλθόντεϲ (627–8). But the coming now has more sense of will (cf. *Hipp.* 529, 542, 557); the optative presents the favourable possibility with canny caution, but not downright disbelief (contrast the imperfect at *Hel.* 1105). Cf. e.g. *Alc.* 540, *Or.* 775, 780.

ἅλιc: emphasis on the right measure (and no more) is highly characteristic of Sophocles' and Euripides' choruses. Cf. e.g. 159, *Hcld.* 619, *IT* 420–1, *Ion* 490–1, *IA* 543, 554, Soph. *OT* 685, *El.* 140, *Phil.*177, *OC* 1211–12, 1695. We may see connections on the one hand to the language of minor characters like the Nurse in the *Medea* (121–30; note even *Hipp.* 443), and on the other to the narrators of choral lyric. Cf. e.g. Pind. *Ol.* 13. 47–8, *Pyth.* 11. 52–3, *Nem.* 1. 31, *Pae.* 4 (D4). 35–52.

631. Κύπριc: the divine name falls with emphasis at the start of the period and the end of the clause; the element of divinity is brought out by the clause that follows.

οὐκ ἄλλα κτλ.: the enthusiasm for love is apt to a chorus (cf. e.g. *Hcld.* 894–5), but more striking in a female one. The words sound more related to the speaker's experience than at *Hel.* 1105–6.

εὔχαριc: cf. *Hcld.* 894; the word occurs in prose (e.g. Plat. *Rep.* 486 D 9, Xen. *Hell.* 4. 8. 22). ἄχαριc appears already at Sapph. 49. 2.

633. The discourse suddenly becomes personal, as the narrator addresses the goddess, about herself. The vocative and the first person are placed next to each other. The narrator's wish has something in common with Sapph. 1 [4]. 1–4; but that is actually a prayer for success in love. The manner of the wish here goes back especially to choral lyric (e.g. Pind. *Nem.* 8. 35, *Pae.* 2 (D2). 26–7). However, the anxious contrast implied with the protagonists gives such utterances a special quality in tragedy. Cf. e.g. *Alc.* 976–7, *Hipp.* 528–9, [Aesch.] *PV* 526–35, 894–900. The narrator takes up the conception of 627–30, but now nervously speaks as if any attack from Aphrodite would be unwelcome.

The image of Love's arrows had appeared in 531, and is probably by now an established conception (cf. Anacr. 358 [13]. 1 n.; Eur. *IA* 547–9). It is here replaced by the idea of Aphrodite's arrows, which is more alarming because less familiar and less readily demythologized. Cf. Pind. *Pyth.* 4. 213; Eur. *Hipp.* 531–2.

χρυcέων: underlines the divinity (cf. e.g. *Hec.* 465), in a different manner from Anacreon 358 [13].

634–5. ἀφείηc: the ἐπ- of the manuscripts with a bare ablative genitive would not be impossible (note *Alc.* 268–9); but Naber's conjecture is too easy to be resisted.

ἱμέρωι χρίϲαϲ': the metaphorical and the mental are powerfully blended. The malevolent action of the goddess is graphically conveyed.

ἄφυκτον οἰϲτόν: the stanza closes with an echo of Jason's τόξοιϲ ἀφύκτοιϲ (531). There the adjective assisted Jason's argument that Medea had no choice; here it emphasizes human vulnerability (cf. Soph. *Ant.* 787–90). The single arrow combines with ποτ' and the tense of the optative to portray a single terrible moment.

636–7. ϲτέργοι suits a deity (cf. e.g. Ar. *Frogs* 229), δώρημα κάλλιϲτον θεῶν subjects ϲωφροϲύνα too to the gods; both make the human passive. Even this desirable quality of mind is not presented as the product of mortal will. Such wishes about one's future behaviour have links with choral lyric too, cf. e.g. Pind. *Pyth.* 11. 50–1, *Nem.* 8. 35–6 (both involving gods); but the context makes this wish more anxious. The type of love denoted by ϲτέργοι itself contrasts with the passions the narrator desires to avoid.

Cωφροϲύνα: the language might be thought particularly suitable to a woman rather than an adult man; but *IA* 543–6 and fr. 503 suggest that it is less specific (cf. also e.g. *Hyps.* fr. 60. 44–5 Cockle). Given the preceding stanza and what follows, the reference is not so much to chastity in itself as to the wise avoidance of the extreme and dangerous forms of love.

δώρημα κτλ.: a striking valuation, as at Aesch. *Ag.* 927–8, and an attractively ardent expansion. The opening sentence of the stanza is effectively short and simple, by contrast with what follows.

638–42 begin from the conjugal strife caused by passion outside marriage; the strife is primary in the syntax and the style, and the passion is enclosed in the inserted clause θυμὸν κτλ. This emphasis suits the play (cf. already 14–15), and particularly the preceding scene. Each noun has an epithet. For ἀμφιλόγουϲ cf. Soph. *Ant.* 111; the form ἀκόρεϲτοϲ occurs at Lyr. Adesp. *PMG* 973, several times in tragic lyric, and at Xen. *Symp.* 8. 15. μηδέ ποτ' takes up μήποτ' (633), but the focus has now shifted from one person's feeling to an involved domestic situation.

θυμὸν ἐκπλήξαϲ': the expression is much less elaborate and graphic than in 633–5. Aphrodite's deed is stressed more by the active here than that of love by the passive in 8 ἔρωτι θυμὸν ἐκπλαγεῖϲ'

'Iácovoc; cf. Alc. 283. 3–4 and probably Sapph. 16 [5]. 11 on He-
len. In my opinion, the θυμός must be taken from the context,
especially 636–7, to be principally the narrator's rather than her
husband's (otherwise Meridor (1986)); but Jason's passion is very
much in view.

ἑτέροις ἐπὶ λέκτροις: the narrator speaks from the perspective
of a married woman, cf. e.g. *Andr.* 469–70. For the expression cf.
Andr. 487.

προσβάλοι: the domestic turmoil is the prime affliction. The god-
dess is not now addressed, but viewed with more distanced alarm;
the narrator now stands further from the experience of love.

δεινά: the narrator now thinks only of Aphrodite's terrible power,
cf. *Hipp.* 563; *Phoen.* 798; Simon. 541. 10, Soph. *Trach.* 497.

Κύπρις: the name of the goddess is saved for the end of the clause.

643–5. ἀπτολέμους: the question of discord is put to the fore, in a
forceful word. The adjective itself goes back to Homer (*Il.* 2. 201,
etc.); it is used at Pind. *Pyth.* 5. 66, and several times in tragedy
(Eur. *Ion* 216, etc.). For domestic war cf. Soph. *El.* 219.

σεβίζους': the narrator hopes that Aphrodite will honour all har-
monious unions as a matter of principle; the first stanza makes this
seem dubious. For such general 'honouring' cf. e.g. *Supp.* 378–
9, Aesch. *Ch.* 629, 637; for honouring by gods, e.g. Aesch. *Eum.*
1001–2, Pind. *Ol.* 6 [**18**]. 80 n. The listener should contrast καινὰ
λέχη σεβίζει (155), used by the chorus of Jason.

ὀξύφρων: this is the only compound adjective in the ode in which
the first part is nominal rather than a mere prefix. Compounds in
-φρων are common in tragic and earlier lyric, cf. e.g. *Phoen.* 658,
672, Aesch. *Th.* 730, Soph. *Aj.* 930, Alcm. 3 [**2**]. '82', Alc. 69. 7,
Pind. *Pyth.* 2. 51; none the less, the word stands out in the texture
of the ode. The word occurs nowhere else in archaic or classical
literature. It is set at the front of its clause, and presents a forceful
image of the skilled judgement wanted from the goddess of passion.

κρίνοι: it is difficult to make the word refer to the allotting of
marriages. κρίνω 'allot' seems to be used of a prize or victory or some
special distinction (Soph. *Aj.* 443, Pind. *Pyth.* 8. 84, *Isth.* 5. 11,
Bacch. 11. 6–7), and does not really suit the allotting of marriages in
general. κρίνοι, then, might rather mean 'make a judgement about'
(*Hec.* 1240; Thuc. 8. 2. 2), with the purpose of choosing those to af-
flict or not afflict. ('Sort, separate', with such a purpose, would also

be possible (cf. Hom. *Il.* 2. 362, 16. 198–9); 'choose' itself would be more awkward with the general λέχη γυναικῶν.) In the context, this approach seems intelligible; Aphrodite is to act with respect for marriages now peaceful. ὀξύφρων would reinforce the wish for discrimination effectively. It is welcome not to have a disconcerting shift from a viewpoint within marriage in 638–42 to one before it in 643–4, and not to imply after 638–42 that initial compatibility would prevent later attacks by love.

λέχη: three different words have been used in the last four lines for this central conception (λέκτροις, εὐνάς, λέχη). It connotes in the play both marriage and its sexual aspect, dwelt on especially but not always from a female perspective or as a female preoccupation; cf. e.g. 240 (230–47), 443–4, 555, 568, 591–4, 697, 953, 999, 1338, 1367–9. εὐνάς and λέχη here are pointedly less sexual than λέκτροις had been in the negative clause.

γυναικῶν: the narrator in the final word of the stanza speaks of women in general, but not men, by contrast with the reference to mankind in 630. This clause, unlike 627–30, is a wish, and fits into a first-person structure. It is not, then, that the original generalization has become a more limited generalization; rather, the narrator's persona has expanded in scope. The explanation of this expansion is given by the preceding ode; there, the 'I', going beyond the 'I' that represents a nation in Pindar's *Paeans* (cf. e.g. Eur. *Ion* 211), is made to represent a whole sex. Cf. 415 and especially 422 τὰν ἐμὰν ὑμνεῦσαι ἀπιστοσύναν. The polemical rationality of the earlier ode has now changed to an anxious wish for self-protection.

The generality of the wish makes it appear the less likely to be fulfilled; indeed, it is generated by a specific case where previous harmony has not been respected. The echo at 1290–2 shows the hopelessness of the wish in more general terms.

645. The narrator continues her wish for herself; this time the general proposition on which her wish is based appears after it (652–3), rather than before it (627–32). The overall structure is apparent: comment on love, followed by comment on exile. The previous ode has stressed the parallelism of Medea's loss of marriage and of home and homeland (435–8, 441–5). The relative brevity of the section on exile here (this stanza) does not show it to be unimportant; the much stronger emotion makes the brevity intensity.

The transition is none the less forcefully abrupt. The double exclamation makes a passionate start: cf. *Hec.* 475–6 at the start of a stanza (ὤμοι), and further e.g. Soph. *Phil.* 176–7; note also Enn. *Trag.* 87 Jocelyn. The exclamation takes up Medea's own at 166 ὦ πάτερ, ὦ πόλις; cf. also 328. The verbal connection forms part of the contrast between Medea, who has neither city nor home, and the chorus, who have both: cf. 253–8, and 1021–2, where a related contrast is made with the children.

646. ἄπολις γενοίμαν: the nominal expression intensifies the horror by imagining the state. Cf. 255. The word, not attested before the fifth century, is frequent in tragedy and in prose (e.g. Hdt. 7. 104. 2, Isocr. *Pac.* 44). Tragedians often incorporate it in pathetic figures: cf. e.g. *Hec.* 669, 810–11, *IT* 220, Soph. *Phil.* 1018.

647–9. The textual problem is above all one of metre. Musgrave's conjecture here, and the manuscripts' reading in the antistrophe, produce $-\cup\cup\cup\cup-$ or (with synizesis) $-\cup\cup\cup-$. The sense seems more or less satisfactory; one might only question whether the life or having it could be described as constituting a single ἄχος. (For *Ion* 763–4 cf. 776–7 and the whole context.) But the metre is so improbable that one should prefer a different reading. A hypodochmiac (cf. e.g. Soph. *Inach.* fr. 296 c Radt 36, 39 $\cup\cup\cup\cup\cup-$) would be quite out of place here. $-\cup---$ appears in various contexts (cf. e.g. Soph. *OT* 1097, Eur. *HF* 133, *Phaeth.* 235 Diggle; Ar. *Lys.* 804 $-\cup\cup\cup--$ (cr sp)). But a trochaic context would be irrelevant, even were the final resolution permissible; in an aeolic context the resolutions would be very doubtful; as an evocation of dactylo-epitrite the double resolution (or ed²) would be impossible for the listener to grasp. On the other hand, a hemiepes would suit admirably the suggestion of dactylo-epitrite natural in such a stanza; nor would a dodrans (with synizesis) be inappropriate.

If, then, we read οἰκτροτάτων, we lose the extreme parallelism of having genitives in both stanzas dependent on the superlatives; but some parallelism remains with the two superlatives, and the matter is of subordinate importance. Willink's -όν γ' (Kovacs (1994), 352) actually retains the parallelism, but the singular is not ideal, and the γ' looks an awkward stopgap (the examples in Denniston (1954), 138–9 are different). As to the sense with οἰκτροτάτων, one might or might not have a comma after αἰῶ. With it, the genitive would have to hang in unconvincing apposition to ἀμηχανίας; without it, the genitive would depend on ἀμηχανίας, as at *Hipp.* 162–4, which leads to an involved but not impossible clause. ('A life of woes' would not be plausible in Euripides.) The omission of a comma is thus to be preferred; but somewhat easier style would be produced by οἰκτροτάτων τ'. The τ' would join οἰκτροτάτων ἀχέων to ἀμηχανίας. For the antistrophe, see on 658.

On any view of the metre of 649, it seems surprising that the pendant enoplian form of 647–8 does not end a period. One should rather introduce with Stinton (Kovacs (1994), 352) the form αἰῶ used by Aeschylus in lyric (*Ch*. 350, cf. *Ag*. 229), but removed by scribes.

At all events, the narrator speaks of exile in an elaborate and emotive phrase, far removed from the particularities of Alc. fr. 130 b [9], or of *Phoen*. 388–407. The description is more extreme than that of the strife produced by love, 638–9.

δυσπέρατον: cf. [Aesch.] *PV* 59 (Wecklein). The word, with ἔχουσαν, conveys a prolonged period of unhappiness. -περατος comes in Aesch. *Supp*. 1049; cf. Eur. *Hipp*. 678, 883.

τόν: the usage belongs particularly to the lyric of tragedy, cf. [Aesch.] *PV* 537, Soph. *El*. 166–7.

οἰκτροτάτων: on superlatives see the introduction to 'Tragedy', above; here the correspondence (cf. 658) throws them into relief. This particular superlative comes already at Pind. *Pyth*. 3. 42, cf. e.g. Eur. *Hec*. 912.

650. The thought of such a terrible period leads the narrator to desire instead the moment of death. The utterance recalls Medea's on her desertion (146–7); but she has now moved beyond that passive reaction. The wish passes to Creon (1210), and is there turned into reality. In general, such passionate wishes are not confined to the actors in tragedy; cf. e.g. *Hipp*. 364–5. They have their roots in earlier literature, including lyric: cf. especially Stes. 222 (b) [3]. 213–17 (n.). The expression here, as suits this moment in the ode, deploys the emotive figure of anadiplosis; for this see the introduction to 'Tragedy'. Cf. *Andr*. 1208 θανεῖν, θανεῖν.

651–2. ἁμέραν κτλ.: in my view of this difficult phrase, the narrator would wish to die, not merely before that happened, but at the end of this very day. So Stesichorus' queen wishes to die αὐτίκα . . . πρίν ποκα ταῦτ' ἐςιδεῖν (222 (b) [3]. 213–14). The emphasis here is on this day being the narrator's last, rather than on her completing it (contrast *Andr*. 101–2). Since the idea of today as one's last day is

common, the expression is actually less unexpected than the idea at
Bacch. 3 [**17**]. 79–80 that tomorrow should be seen as one's last day.
Other opinions do not seem possible interpretations of the Greek.
'Day' can be used to mean one's life, cf. e.g. *Ion* 720, Alcm. 1 [**1**].
38 n.; but 'this day' could scarcely be understood so. 'Finishing my
life' would also be a banal addition here. ἀμέραν τάνδ᾿ could in itself
denote the day of exile (cf. e.g. Eur. *Cyc.* 437, [*Rhes.*] 464); but it
is impossibly contorted to take the lines to mean, with Hermann
((1828), 203–4) 'finishing that day—may I die rather, i.e. may I die
rather than finishing that day!' And why 'finish'?

652–3. μόχθων κτλ.: the general statement recalls the opening gen-
eral passage in phrasing; οὐκ ἄλλος echoes οὐκ ἄλλα 632. But the echo
underlines the extremity of this present statement, as against the
balanced restraint of the statement on love. The thought that exile
is the greatest of woes is not surprising (cf. e.g. *El.* 1313–14; note
Med. 329 with *Phoen.* 405–6). μόχθων δ᾿ οὐκ ἄλλος ὕπερθεν creates a
density of expression characteristic of tragic lyric.

γᾶς πατρίας near the end of the stanza takes up and intensifies
πάτρις from the start; note perhaps the sudden and striking high
notes for γᾶς πατρ- in the music of *IA* 793. The final στέρεσθαι
produces a dark close, as the same stem does to other stanzas:
Supp. 793, *El.* 736, *HF* 137; contrast the order at Pind. *Ol.* 12. 16.

654–5. With pithy abruptness, the narrator shows the truth of the
general statement (652–3) from the present situation; the asyndeton
after εἴδομεν gives the utterance force. The verb is used elsewhere
too to stress a chorus's own perception (which the audience has
shared in): cf. *Hipp.* 1124, Soph. *El.* 853. But here the word is
extended into an opposition between direct perception and hearsay.
Most commonly, this opposition is used in tragedy in relation to
surprising events; sometimes it is used to emphasize the speaker's
own misfortunes. Cf. e.g. Eur. *HF* 798–806, *IT* 900–1, Soph. *Phil.*
676–801 (Pind. *Pyth.* 1. 26); Eur. *Hcld.* 5, *Tro.* 481–3. Here the
point is vigorously argumentative; cf. e.g. *Hcld.* 903–9, or (less
markedly) *Andr.* 486, and further e.g. Sapph. 16 [**5**]. 5–6.

The idea of having a story from others 'to ponder on', even in the
negative, increases the intellectual and reflective character of the
speaker. For the intellectualism frequently seen in this chorus and
thematic in this play, note the paradoxical defence of childlessness
at 1090–115, which has links with Antiph. B 49 Diels–Kranz *fin.*;

cf. Eur. *Ion* 488–91, contrast the manner of *Supp.* 786–93, 822–3. One may also contrast the passages where female choruses explain how they have acquired knowledge indirectly, and so display their distinctive and circumscribed world (*IA* 173–8; *Ion* 507–8). However, the intellectualism here becomes, when the narrator turns to Medea, an ironically dry form for the sympathy and indignation she feels.

656–7. cé: the pronoun brings in not only the story of the play but contact with its protagonist. Previously the narrator had addressed the goddess (633–5) and apostrophized her home and country (645); now there is engaged human communication, in significant contrast to the lack of feeling that is being described. The absence of a name, as at 431, adds force to the moment (cf. *Hcld.* 619, *Andr.* 1041; contrast the ostentatiously casual second person at *El.* 745–6). Medea is present on stage.

The meaning of the lines depends on the form of the verb we read for ὤκτειρεν. The narrator has stressed that 'we have seen': a past thus seems more suitable than a future. The direct application of the statement about the native land (652–3) is not Medea's banishment from Corinth, of which she is not a native, but her departure from Colchis. Cf. 34–5 ἔγνωκε . . . οἷον πατρώιας μὴ ἀπολείπεcθαι χθονός, 253–5 (note ἄπολιc, before Creon's announcement). The ode thus reverts, with the freedom of odes, to a problem faced by Medea from the start of the play; the banishment is only indirectly implied. The reading which metre seems to dictate in 658, δεινότατον, suits a single disaster, desertion by Jason (cf. the same phrase at *El.* 1226); this would be less appropriate for Medea after leaving Corinth too. The following attack on Jason (659–62) fits a reference to the desertion particularly well.

πόλιc, on this view, should refer principally to Corinth, rather than cities in general. But φίλων τιc itself suggests that we do not have here the grandiose generality of e.g. Simon. 526. 2, or Soph. *Ant.* 953–4. The figure with the negatives here rather conveys the sadness and the paradox of what it describes. The accent in παθοῦcαν δεινότατον παθέων naturally falls on δεινότατον, and makes the combination of main clause and participial clause a surprise.

φίλων τιc may seem at first to dwell only on Medea's abandonment of her former φίλοι as an expatriate. Cf. e.g. *Andr.* 138–9. But the next sentence makes it apparent that the narrator is preparing to assault the φίλος she did have in Corinth; the word forms the thread that connects 656–62. It has been emphasized by Jason's own use of it in his final line in the preceding scene (622); and it will come, as a surprise, in Aegeus' first speech in the next scene (664).

659–61. The narrator does here (more generally) what the Nurse had declined to do (83): she curses those like Jason. The curse is made the more vigorous by asyndeton. The narrator takes up the frank choral criticism of 577–8, but in the general tones of wisdom.

ἀχάριστος: the word, and its derivative verb, when used of people habitually denote ingratitude or the like; one should take it here as primarily 'because he is thankless, thankless person that he is'. 'Horribly' is hard to justify as a sense for the word; 'without favour' (Paley) is somewhat obscure in reference, too.

μή: the negative expression of the lines presents an attractive image of φιλία, as opposed to a picture of treachery. The idea is now expanded beyond the realm of marriage.

τιμᾶν: 'honour' amounts to treating φίλοι as φίλοι. Cf. 696, *Ion* 700–1 (whatever the text).

καθαρᾶν κτλ.: elaborate language develops the idea of good conduct. It is noteworthy that Paley (1872–80), i. 117, thinks the expression 'singularly Pindaric'; cf. *Pyth.* 9. 39–39a, and also *Ol.* 4. 16. *PMG* 889 (scolion) wishes one could open the breast to discern the true friend; here the notion is the more striking one of a duty to open what sounds naturally secret. The noun κλῇδα makes the phrase more striking than Eur. *Tro.* 662. Jason's furtiveness has been debated in the preceding scene (586–90). Since καθαρ- is predicative, an accusative by enallage seems too complicated; the genitive stresses the idea of innocence winningly.

662. The narrator ends by emphasizing herself; cf. e.g. *Hcld.* 926–7, Soph. *Aj.* 200, *Ant.* 372–5. In *Ant.* 372–5 the narrator wishes to have no dealings with the wicked. Here the clause is effectively curt, by contrast with what precedes; it displays robust and firm moral feeling. After the 'never' of the anxious wishes to avoid disastrous passion (633, 638), we have the 'never' of assured statement. The 'I' has a typical quality (see the introduction to 'Tragedy', n. 12); but it remains connected to the moral outlook displayed by this particular speaker, in this ode and earlier (cf. 179–80). Most of the ode has in a sense been general; but most of it has also been about the narrator.

These two odes are notably different in style. The Euripides is much more straightforward in its syntax and plain in its language; its conceptions are no less imaginative. These particular narrators are very different in the responses they call forth. In the narrator of the Sophocles, one had little sense of wisdom, though vigorous common sense was shown on war. One saw a lavish self-pity and a somewhat endearing valuation of pleasure. In the narrator of the Euripides, there appeared more concern with morality, and the moral subject. A persona was created that seemed attractive in its discipline, anxiety, firmness. Both these poems had a sombre tonality; but the Sophocles is spoken more out of the subject's experience. That experience consisted more of waiting vainly for a decisive event than, as in the *Medea*, of fearing one. The two odes illustrate the actual variety of tragic lyric; but they also exhibit moods, stances, and structures characteristic of the genre. The discussion has displayed the intricate relation of the songs to their settings; but it has brought out also their aesthetic value as poetic entities. Contemplation of these aspects is enhanced by considering the odes within the lyric tradition that they metamorphose.

Bibliography

ADAMS, J. (1982), *The Latin Sexual Vocabulary* (London).

ADRIANI, A., *et al.* (eds.) (1970–88), *Himera* i–iii (Rome).

AHLERT, P. (1942), *Mädchen und Frauen in Pindars Dichtung* (*Philologus*, suppl. 34.1 (Leipzig).

ALLEGRO, N., and VASSALLO, S. (1992), 'Himera: Nuove ricerche nella città bassa (1989–92)', *Kokalos*, 38: 79–150.

—— *et al.* (1991), 'Il santuario di Athena sul piano di Himera', in C. A. Di Stefano (ed.), *Di terra in terra: Nuove scoperte archeologiche nella provinzia di Palermo* (Palermo), 65–84.

—— *et al.* (1993–4), 'Himera 1989–93: Ricerche dell'Istituto di Archeologia nell'area della città', *Kokalos*, 39–40: 1119–33.

ALLEN, T. W. (1898–9), *Codices Graeci et Latini Photographice Depicti*, iii. *Plato, Codex Oxoniensis Clarkianus 39*, with preface by T. W. Allen (2 vols.; Leiden.).

ALONI, A. (1998), *Cantare glorie di eroi: Comunicazione e performance poetica nella Grecia arcaica* (Turin).

AMIGUES, S. (1993), *Théophraste, Recherches sur les plantes, III, livres V–VI* (Paris).

ANCHER, G. P. (1978), 'P. Lille 111 c et P. Lille 76 abc (+73)', *ZPE* 30: 27–35.

ANDERSON, M. J. (1997), *The Fall of Troy in Early Greek Poetry and Art* (Oxford).

ANDREWES, A. (1956), *The Greek Tyrants* (London).

ARENA, R. (1994), 'Tra linguistica ed epigrafia', *ZPE* 103: 155–8.

ARIGHETTI, G. (1980), 'Civiltà letteraria della Sicilia antica fino al V sec. a. C.', in E. Gabba and G. Vallet (eds.), *La Sicilia antica*, ii/1. *La Sicilia greca dal VI secolo a.C. alle guerre puniche* (Naples).

—— (1994), 'Stesicoro e il suo pubblico', *MD* 32: 9–30.

ARNIM, H. VON (1886), *Ausgewählte Tragödien des Euripides*, iii. *Medea²* (Berlin).

ARNOTT, W. G. (1985), 'Μελίλωτος, Melilotus', *BICS* 32: 79–82.

—— (1996), *Alexis: The Fragments* (Cambridge).

ASHERI, D. (1989), *Erodoto, Le Storie*, i² (Milan).

—— (1992), 'Sicily, 478–431 B.C.', *CAH* v². 147–70.

AUJAC, G. (1974), 'Recherches sur la tradition du περὶ cυνθέcεωc ὀνομάτων de Denys d'Halicarnasse', *Revue d'histoire des textes*, 4: 1–44.

—— and LEBEL, M. (1981), *Dionyse d'Halicarnasse: Opuscules rhétoriques*, iii. *La Composition stylistique* (Paris).

AURA JORRO, F. (1985), *Diccionario Micénico* (10 vols.; Madrid).

AUSFELD, C. (1903), 'De Graecorum precationibus quaestiones', *Jahrbücher für classische Philologie*, suppl. 28 (Leipzig), 502–47.

BABUT, D. (1975), 'Simonide moraliste', *RÉG* 88: 21–62.

BAKHTIN, M. M. (1929), *Problemy poetiki Dostoevskogo* (repr. Kiev 1994).

—— (1963), *Problemy tvorčestva Dostoevskogo* (repr. Kiev 1994).

BARCELÓ, P. (1993), *Basileia, Monarchia, Tyrannis: Untersuchungen zu Entwicklung und Beurteilung von Alleinherrschaft im vorhellenistischen Griechenland* (*Historia* Einzelschriften 79; Stuttgart).

BARNER, W. (1967), *Neuere Alkaios-Papyri aus Oxyrhynchos* (Spudasmata 14; Hildesheim).

BARRETT, W. S. (1954), 'Bacchylides, Asine, and Apollo Pythaieus', *Hermes*, 82: 421–44.

—— (1956), 'Dactylo-epitrites in Bacchylides', *Hermes*, 84: 248–53.

—— (1961), review of *The Oxyrhynchus Papyri*, xxiv (1957), in *Gnomon*, 33: 683–92.

—— (1964), *Euripides*, Hippolytos*: Edited with Introduction and Commentary* (Oxford).

—— (1978), 'The Oligaithidai and their Victories (Pindar, *Olympian* 13; *SLG* 339, 340)', in R. D. Dawe, J. Diggle, and P. E. Easterling (eds.), *Dionysiaca: Nine Studies in Greek Poetry by Former Pupils Presented to Sir Denys Page on his Seventieth Birthday* (Cambridge), 1–20.

BARRON, J. P. (1961), 'The Son of Hyllis', *CR* 11: 185–7.

—— (1964), 'The Sixth-century Tyranny at Samos', *CQ* 14: 210–29.

—— (1969), 'Ibycus: To Polycrates', *BICS* 16, 119–49.

—— (1984), 'Ibycus: Gorgias and Other Poems', *BICS* 31: 13–24.

BAURAIN, CL. (1980), 'Kinyras: La fin de l'âge du bronze à Chypre et la tradition antique', *BCH* 104: 277–308.

BEATTIE, A. J. (1956a), 'Pindar, *Ol.* 6. 82 f.', *CR* 6: 1–2.

—— (1956b), 'Sappho Fr. 31', *Mnemosyne*, 9: 103–11.

BEAZLEY, J. D. (1955), 'Hydria-fragments in Corinth', *Hesperia*, 24: 305–19.

BECK, W. (1988), 'The Cause of the War in the "Lille Stesichorus"', *ZPE* 73: 8–12.

BELOCH, J. (1890), 'Wann lebten Alkaeos und Sappho?', *RhM* 45: 465–73.

BERVE, H. (1967), *Die Tyrannis bei den Griechen* (2 vols.; Munich).

BETANCOURT, P. P. (1977), *The Aeolic Style in Architecture* (Princeton).

BIANCHETTI, S. (1987), *Falaride e Pseudofalaride: Storia e legenda* (Rome).

BINDER, G. (1964), *Die Aussetzung des Königskindes: Kyros und Romulus* (Meisenheim am Glan).

BLACKMAN, D. (1997), 'Archaeology in Greece 1996–7', *AR* 1996–7: 1–125.

470   Bibliography

BLASS, F. (1872), 'Das Simonideische Gedicht im Protagoras des Platon',
   RhM 27: 326–32.
—— (1879), 'Das ägyptische Fragment des Alkmans (mit Facsimile)', *Hermes*, 13: 15–32.
—— (1885), 'Zu Bergk's Poetae Lyrici, ed. IV vol. III', *RhM* 40: 1–24.
—— (1902), 'Die Berliner Fragmente der Sappho', *Hermes*, 37: 456–79.
BLAYDES, F. H. M. (1875), *The Ajax of Sophocles* (London and Edinburgh).
BLECH, M. (1982), *Studien zum Kranz bei den Griechen* (Berlin and New
   York).
BLÜMEL, W. (1982), *Die aiolischen Dialekte: Phonologie und Morphologie
   der inschriftlichen Texte aus generativer Sicht* (Göttingen).
BOARDMAN, J. (1963), 'Artemis Orthia and Chronology', *BSA* 58: 1–7.
—— (1978), *Greek Sculpture: The Archaic Period* (London).
—— (1994), 'Settlements for Trade and Land in North Africa: Problems of
   Identity', in G. R. Tsetskhladze and F. De Angelis (eds.), *The Archaeo-
   logy of Greek Colonization: Essays in Honour of Sir John Boardman*
   (Oxford), 137–49.
—— (1998), *Early Greek Vase Painting: 11th–6th Centuries BC* (London).
BODENSTEDT, F. (1981), *Die Elektronmünzen von Phokaia und Mytilene*
   (Tübingen).
BOECKH, A. (1811–21), *Pindari Opera Quae Supersunt* (3 vols.; Leipzig).
BOEDEKER, D. (1997), 'Becoming Medea: Assimilation in Euripides', in
   J. J. Clauss and S. I. Johnston (eds.), *Medea: Essays on Medea in Myth,
   Literature, Philosophy, and Art* (Princeton), 127–48.
BONA, G. (1978), 'Elena, la più bella di tutti i mortali (Nota a Saffo, fr. 16
   Voigt e a hom. hy. ad Aphr. 33–44)', in E. Livrea and G. A. Privitera
   (eds.), *Studi in onore di Anthos Ardizzoni* (2 vols.; Rome), i. 73–89.
—— (1988), *Pindaro: I Peani. Testo, traduzione, scoli e commento* (Cuneo).
BONACASA, N. (1982), 'Il Temenos di Himera', in N. Bonacasa (ed.), *Sec-
   ondo quaderno imerese*, 47–60.
BONANNO, M. G. (1973), 'Osservazioni sul tema della giusta reciprocità
   amorosa da Saffo ai comici', *QUCC* 16: 110–20.
—— (1998), 'Seconda e ultima postilla a Saffo 31,9 V. (γλῶcca ἔαγε)',
   QUCC 60: 143–8.
BOND, G. W. (1981), *Euripides, Heracles, with Introduction and Commen-
   tary* (Oxford).
BONELLI, G. (1980), 'Saffo, I, 1: Analisi estetica', *AC* 49: 23–44.
—— (1987), *Il mondo poetico di Pindaro* (Turin).
BORING, T. A. (1979), *Literacy in Ancient Sparta* (*Mnemosyne*, suppl. 54;
   Leiden etc.).
BOTER, G. (1989), *The Textual Tradition of Plato's Republic* (*Mnemosyne*,
   suppl. 107; Leiden etc.).

BOURRIOT, F. (1976), *Recherches sur la nature du génos: Étude d'histoire sociale athénienne—periodes archaïque et classique* (2 vols.; Paris).

BOUVRIE THORSEN, S. DES (1978), 'The Interpretation of Sappho's Fragment 16 L.–P.', *SO* 53: 5–23.

BOWIE, A. M. (1981), *The Poetic Dialect of Sappho and Alcaeus* (Salem).

BOYAVAL, B., and MEILLIER, CL. (1984), *Album des papyrus littéraires (CRIPEL* suppl.; Paris).

BRASWELL, B. K. (1988), *A Commentary on the* Fourth Pythian Ode *of Pindar* (Texte und Kommentare, 14; Berlin); separate *Index of Passages Cited* compiled by M. Somazzi (Fribourg, 1992).

—— (1992), *A Commentary on Pindar,* Nemean One (Fribourg).

—— (1998), *A Commentary on Pindar,* Nemean Nine (Texte und Kommentare, 19; Berlin and New York).

BRAUN, T. F. R. G. (1982), 'The Greeks in Egypt', in *CAH*² iii/3. 32–56.

BREITENBACH, W. (1934), *Untersuchungen zur Sprache der euripideischen Lyrik* (Tübinger Beiträge zur Altertumswissenschaft, 20; Stuttgart).

BREMER, J. M. (1987), 'Stesichorus: The Lille Papyrus', in J. Bremer, A. M. van Erp Taalman Kip, and S. R. Slings, *Some Recently Found Greek Poems: Text and Commentary* (*Mnemosyne,* suppl. 99; Leiden), 128–74.

—— (1990), 'Pindar's Paradoxical ἐγώ and a Recent Controversy about the Performance of his Epinicia', in S. R. Slings (ed.), *The Poet's I in Archaic Greek Lyric* (Amsterdam), 42–58.

BROGER, A. (1996), *Das Epitheton bei Sappho und Alkaios: Eine sprachwissenschaftliche Untersuchung* (Innsbrucker Beiträge zur Sprachwissenschaft, 88; Innsbruck).

BROWN, C. G. (1992), 'The Hyperboreans and Nemesis in Pindar's *Tenth Pythian*', *Phoenix,* 46: 95–107.

BROWN, R. D. (1987), *Lucretius on Love and Sex: A Commentary on De Rerum Natura IV, 1030–1287, with Prolegomena, Text, and Translation* (Columbia Studies in Classical Tradition, 15; Leiden etc.).

BRUGNONE, A. (1997), 'Legge di Himera sulla ridistribuzione della terra', *PP* 52: 262–305.

BRUNS, G. (1947), *Antike Bronzen* (Berlin).

BRUSCHI, L. (1994), 'Alcmane, fr. 26. 64–72 C. = 3 D.', *ZPE* 101: 38–48.

BUCHHOLZ, H.-G. (1975), *Methymna: Archäologische Beiträge zur Topographie und Geschichte von Nordlesbos* (Mainz am Rhein).

BUCK, R. J. (1979), *A History of Boeotia* (Edmonton).

BÜHLER, G. (1859), 'μεταλλάω', *Kuhns Zeitschrift für vergleichende Sprachforschung,* 8: 365–9.

BÜHLER, W. (1968), 'Ein neues Archilochosfragment und ein neues Wort für Menander aus einer Oxforder Kyrillhandschrift', *Hermes,* 96: 232–8.

—— (1987), *Zenobii Athoi Proverbia,* i. *Prolegomena* (Göttingen).

BULLOCH, A. W. (1985), *Callimachus: The Fifth Hymn* (Cambridge).

BULMAN, P. (1992), Phthonos *in Pindar* (Univ. of California Publications, Classical Studies, 35; Berkeley etc.).

BUNDY, E. L. (1986 [orig. 1962]), *Studia Pindarica* (Berkeley and Los Angeles).

BUONGIOVANNI, A. M. (1990), 'Marginalia Pindarica', *SIFC* 8: 121–36.

BURKERT, W. (1966), 'Kekropidensage und Arrhephoria', *Hermes*, 94: 1–25.

——(1976), 'Das hunderttorige Theben', *WS* 89: 5–21.

——(1977), *Griechische Religion der archaischen und klassischen Epoche* (Stuttgart etc.).

——(1985*a*), *Greek Religion: Archaic and Classical*, trans. J. Raffan (Oxford).

——(1985*b*), 'Das Ende des Kroisos: Vorstufen einer herodoteischen Geschichtserzählung', in C. Schäublin (ed.), *Catalepton: Festschrift für Bernhard Wyss zum 80. Geburtstag* (Basle), 4–15.

——(1987), 'The Making of Homer in the Sixth Century BC: Rhapsodes versus Stesichorus', in *Papers on the Amasis Painter and his World* (Malibu), 43–62.

BURNETT, A. P. (1983), *Three Archaic Poets: Archilochus, Alcaeus, Sappho* (London).

——(1985), *The Art of Bacchylides* (Cambridge, Mass., and London).

——(1988), 'Jocasta in the West: The Lille Stesichorus', *CA* 7: 107–54.

——(1989), 'Performing Pindar's Odes', *CP* 84: 283–93.

BURTON, R. W. B. (1980), *The Chorus in Sophocles' Tragedies* (Oxford).

——(1962), *Pindar's Pythian Odes: Essays in Interpretation* (Oxford).

BURY, J. B. (1890), Πινδάρου ἐπινίκιοι Νεμεονίκαιc . . . (London).

——(1892), Πινδάρου ἐπινίκιοι ᾽Icθμιονίκαιc . . . (London).

BURZACCHINI, G. (1976), 'Alc. 130b~Hor. Carm. I 22', *QUCC* 22: 39–58.

——(1985), 'Some Further Observations on Alcaeus Fr. 130B Voigt', *PLLS* 5: 373–81.

——(1995), 'Lirica arcaica (I)', in U. Mattioli (ed.), *Senectus: La vecchiaia nel mondo classico* (2 vols.; Bologna), i. 69–124.

BUSCHOR, E. (1935–61), *Altsamische Standbilder* (5 vols.; Berlin).

CALAME, CL. (1967), 'Sappho fr. 96, 15–17 LP', *QUCC* 4: 101–6.

——(1970), *Etymologicum Genuinum . . . les citations de poètes lyriques* (Rome).

——(1977), *Les Chœurs de jeunes filles en Grèce archaïque* (2 vols.; Rome).

——(1983), *Alcman: Introduction, texte critique, témoinages, traduction et commentaire* (Rome).

——(1994–5), 'From Choral Poetry to Tragic Stasimon', *Arion*, 3/1. 136–54.

——(1999 [orig. 1992, in Italian]), *The Poetics of Eros in Ancient Greece*, trans. J. Lloyd (Princeton).

CAMERON, AL. (1995), *Callimachus and his Critics* (Princeton).

CAMERON, ARCH. (1939), 'Sappho's Prayer to Aphrodite', *Harvard Theological Review*, 32, 1–17.

—— (1964), 'Sappho and Aphrodite Again', *Harvard Theological Review* 57, 237–9.

CAMPBELL, D. A. (1982), *Greek Lyric Poetry: A Selection of Early Greek Lyric, Elegiac and Iambic Poetry*² (London).

—— (1982–93), *Greek Lyric, with an English Translation* (5 vols.; Cambridge, Mass., and London).

—— (1983), *The Golden Lyre: The Themes of the Greek Lyric Poets* (London).

—— (1987), 'Three Notes on Alcman 1 P. (= 3 Calame)', *QUCC* 26: 67–72.

CAMPBELL, L. (1879–81), *Sophocles: Edited with English Notes and Introductions*² (2 vols.; Oxford).

—— (1907), *Paralipomena Sophoclea: Supplementary Notes on the Text and Interpretation of Sophocles* (London).

CAMPBELL, M. (1973–4), 'Anacr. fr. 358 P.', *Museum Criticum*, 8–9: 168–9.

CANNATÀ FERA, M. (1990), *Pindaro, Trenodie: Introduzione, testo critico, traduzione e commento* (Rome).

CAREY, C. (1978), 'Sappho Fr. 96 LP', *CQ*, NS 28: 366–71.

—— (1981), *A Commentary on Five Odes of Pindar: Pythian 2, Pythian 9, Nemean 1, Nemean 7, Isthmian 8* (New York).

—— (1989), 'The Performance of the Victory Ode', *AJP* 110: 545–63.

—— (1991), 'The Victory Ode in Pindar: The Case for the Chorus', *CP* 85: 192–200.

—— (1996), 'Ibycus', *OCD*³. 744.

CARGILL, J. (1977), 'The Nabonidus Chronicle and the Fall of Lydia: Consensus with Feet of Clay', *Amer. Journ. of Anc. Hist.* 2: 97–116.

CARNE-ROSS, D. S. (1979 [orig. 1976]), 'Weaving with Points of Gold: Pindar's Sixth Olympian', in id., *Instaurations: Essays in and out of Literature, Pindar to Pound* (Berkeley etc.), 29–60.

CARRATELLI, G. PUGLIESE (1985), *Sikanie: Storia e civiltà della Sicilia greca*² (Milan).

—— (ed.) (1996), *The Western Greeks: Classical Civilization in the Western Mediterranean* (London).

CARSON, A. (1984), 'The Burners: A Reading of Bacchylides' Third Epinician Ode', *Phoenix*, 38: 111–19.

—— (1992a), 'How Not to Read a Poem: Unmixing Simonides from *Protagoras*', *CP* 87: 110–30.

—— (1992b), 'Simonides Painter', in R. Hexter and D. Selden (eds.), *Innovations of Antiquity* (New York and London), 51–64.

—— (1999), *Autobiography of Red: A Novel in Verse* (London).

CARTLEDGE, P. (1979), *Sparta and Lakonia: A Regional History 1300–362 BC* (London).

——(1982), 'Sparta and Samos: A Special Relationship?', *CQ*, NS 32: 243–65.

——(1987), *Agesilaos and the Crisis of Sparta* (London).

CASKEY, L. D., and BEAZLEY, J. D. (1931–63), *Attic Vase Paintings in the Museum of Fine Arts, Boston* (3 vols.; Boston).

CATAUDELLA, Q. (1972), 'Sugli scoli A e B al *Partenio* I di Alcmane', in id., *Intorno ai lirici greci* (Rome), 21–41.

CATENACCI, C. (1999), '*Ἀπονέμειν*/"leggere" (Pind. *Isthm.* 2, 47; Soph. fr. 144 Radt; Aristoph. *Av.* 1289)', *QUCC* 62: 49–61.

CATLING, H. W. (1977), 'Excavations at the Menelaion, Sparta, 1973–76', *AR* 1976–7: 24–42.

CAVANAGH, W., CROUWEL, J., CATLING, R. W. V., and SHIPLEY, G. (1996), *Continuity and Change in a Greek Rural Landscape: The Laconia Survey*, ii. *Archaeological Data* (*ABSA* suppl. 27; London).

CELLERINI, A. (1988), *Introduzione all'Etymologicum Gudianum* (*Bolletino dei classici*, suppl. 6; Rome).

CHANTRAINE, P. (1953), 'Un tour archaïque chez Pindare (*Ol.*, VI, 78; *Pyth.*, IV, 217)', *RPh* 27: 16–20.

——(1968), *Dictionnaire étymologique de la langue grecque: Histoire des mots* (2 vols.; Paris).

——(1986–8), *Grammaire homérique*⁶ (2 vols.; Paris).

CHRIST, W. (1896), *Pindari Carmina Prolegomenis et Commentariis Instructa* (Leipzig).

CIANI, M. G., and SUSANETTI, D. (1997), *Euripide: Medea* (Venice).

CINGANO, E. (1989), 'Tra epos e storia: La genealogia di Cianippo e dei Biantidi in Ibico (Supp. Lyr. Gr. 151 Page), e nelle fonti mitographiche greche', *ZPE* 79: 27–38.

CLASSEN, J., and STEUP, J. (1892–1922), *Thukydides*³⁻⁵ (Berlin).

COLE, T. (1988), *Epiploke: Rhythmical Continuity and Poetic Structure in Greek Lyric* (Cambridge, Mass.).

COLLARD, C. (1975), *Euripides, Supplices: Edited with Introduction and Commentary* (2 vols.; Groningen).

COLVIN, S. J. (1999), *Dialect in Aristophanes and the Politics of Language in Ancient Greek Literature* (Oxford).

CONNELLY, J. B. (1993), 'Narrative and Image in Attic Vase Painting: Ajax and Kassandra at the Trojan Palladion', in P. J. Holliday (ed.), *Narrative and Event in Ancient Art* (Cambridge), 88–129.

CONTE, G. B. (1991 [orig. 1986]), 'L'amore senza elegia', in id., *Generi e lettori: Lucrezio, l'elegia d'amore, l'enciclopedia di Plinio* (Milan), 53–94.

COOKESLEY, G. G. (1851), *Pindari Carmina*² (2 vols.; Eton).

CORDIANO, G. (1990), 'Note sulla storia di Reggio magno-greca', *QUCC* 36: 67–81.

COSTANZA, S. (1950), *Risonanze dell'ode di Saffo fainetai moi kēnos da Pindaro a Catullo e Orazio* (Messina and Florence).

COULSON, W. D. E., and LEONARD, A., Jr. (1981), *Cities of the Delta*, pt. 1. *Naukratis: Preliminary Report on the 1977–78 and 1980 Seasons* (Malibu).

COURBY, F. (1927), *Fouilles de Delphes*, ii. *La Terrasse du temple* (Paris).

CROTTY, K. (1982), *Song and Action: The Victory Odes of Pindar* (Baltimore and London).

DALE, A. M. (1957), 'Greek Metric 1936–57', *Lustrum*, 2: 5–51.

——(1971–83), *Metrical Analyses of Tragic Choruses* (3 vols.; *BICS* suppl. 21; London).

D'ALESSIO, G. B. (1994), 'First-person Problems in Pindar', *BICS* 39: 117–39.

——(1997), 'Pindar's *Prosodia* and the Classification of Pindaric Papyrus Fragments', *ZPE* 118: 23–60.

D'ALFONSO, F. (1994), *Stesicoro e la performance: Studio sulle modalità esecutive dei carmi stesicorei* (Rome).

DAVID, E. (1989), 'Laughter in Spartan Society', in A. Powell (ed.), *Classical Sparta: Techniques behind her Success* (London), 1–25.

DAVIDSON, J. F. (1987), 'Anacreon, Homer and the Young Woman from Lesbos', *Mnemosyne*, 40, 132–7.

DAVIES, J. K. (1971), *Athenian Propertied Families* (Oxford).

DAVIES, M. (1979), 'A Commentary on Stesichorus' (2 vols.; diss. D.Phil., Oxford).

——(1984), 'ΧΑΡΙΣ and the verb ΕΦΙΖΩ in Alcman's Second Partheneion', *Maia*, 36: 15–16.

——(1985), 'Conventional Topics of Invective in Alcaeus', *Prometheus*, 11: 31–9.

——(1986a), 'Alcman and the Lover as Suppliant', *ZPE* 64: 13–14.

——(1986b), 'The Motif of the πρῶτος εὑρετής in Alcman', *ZPE* 65: 25–7.

——(1988a), 'Monody, Choral Lyric, and the Tyranny of the Hand-book', *CQ*, NS 38: 52–64.

——(1988b), 'The "Cologne Alcaeus" and Paradigmatic Allusiveness', *ZPE* 72: 39–42.

——(1989), *The Epic Cycle* (Bristol).

——(1991–), *Poetarum Melicorum Graecorum Fragmenta* (Oxford).

DAVISON, J. A. (1968a) [orig. 1935 and 1952], 'Simonides fr. 13 Diehl', in id., *From Archilochus to Pindar* (London and New York), 257–76.

——(1968b [orig. 1938]), 'Alcman's Partheneion', in id., *From Archilochus to Pindar* (London and New York 1968), 146–72.

DAVREUX, J. (1942), *La Légende de la prophétesse Cassandre d'après les textes et les monuments* (Paris).

DAWE, R. D. (1968), 'Emendations in Sophocles', *PCPS* 14: 8–18.

—— (1973–8), *Studies on the Text of Sophocles* (3 vols.; Leiden).

—— (1996), *Sophoclis Ajax³* (Stuttgart and Leipzig).

DAWKINS, R. M. (ed.) (1929), *The Sanctuary of Artemis Orthia at Sparta* (London).

DELIVORRIAS, A. (1984), 'Aphrodite', *LIMC* ii/1. 2–150 (ii/2. 2–153).

DEMAND, N. H. (1982), *Thebes in the Fifth Century: Heracles Resurgent* (London etc.).

DE MARTINO, F. (1992), 'Saffo, senza miracoli (appunti sul fr. 31 Voigt)', in M. Capasso (ed.), *Papiri letterari greci e latini* (Lecce), 63–88.

DEMOS, M. (1999), *Lyric Quotations in Plato* (Lanham and Oxford).

DENNISTON, J. D. (1954), *The Greek Particles²* (Oxford).

DESSOULAVY, P. (1903), *Bacchylide et la IIIme ode* (Neuchâtel).

DEUBNER, L. (1932), *Attische Feste* (Berlin).

—— (1941), *Ololyge und Verwandtes* (*APAW*, Phil.-hist. Kl. 1; Berlin).

—— (1943), *Zu den neuen Bruchstücken des Alkaios* (*APAW*, Phil.-hist. Kl. 7; Berlin).

DI BENEDETTO, V. (1985), 'Intorno al linguaggio erotico di Saffo', *Hermes*, 113: 145–56.

DICKIE, M. (1978), 'The Argument and Form of Simonides 542 *PMG*', *HSCP* 82: 21–33.

DIEHL, E. (1964), *Die Hydria: Formgeschichte und Verwendung im Kult des Altertums* (Mainz).

DIELS, H. (1896), 'Alkmans Partheneion', *Hermes*, 31: 339–74.

DIGGLE, J. (1970), *Euripides, Phaethon: Edited with Prolegomena and Commentary* (Cambridge).

—— (1979), 'Stesichorus, P. Lille 76. 220', *ZPE* 35: 32.

—— (1981–94), *Euripides, Fabulae* (3 vols.; Oxford).

—— (1994), *Euripidea: Collected Essays* (Oxford).

—— (1997), 'Notes on Fragments of Euripides', *CQ*, NS 47: 98–108.

DIHLE, A. (1959), 'Ptolemaios 78', *RE* xxiii/2. 1862–3.

DISSEN, L., and SCHNEIDEWIN, F. G. (1847), *Pindari Carmina Quae Supersunt²* (2 vols.; Göttingen and Erfurdt).

DITTENBERGER, W. (1915–24), *Sylloge Inscriptionum Graecarum³* (4 vols.; Leipzig).

DOCHERTY, T. (1996), *Alterities: Criticism, History, Representation* (Oxford).

DONALDSON, J. W. (1841), *Pindar's Epinician or Triumphal Odes . . .* (London).

DONLAN, W. (1969), 'An Interpretation of Simonides fr. 4D and P. Oxy. 2432', *TAPA* 100: 71–95.

DORNSEIFF, FR. (1921), *Pindars Stil* (Berlin).

DOVER, K. J. (1968), *Aristophanes,* Clouds*: Edited with Introduction and Commentary* (Oxford).

—— (1978), *Greek Homosexuality* (Oxford).

—— (1987 [orig. 1959]), 'Pindar, *Olympian Odes* 6. 82–6', in id., *Greek and the Greeks,* i (Oxford), 130–2.

—— (1993), *Aristophanes,* Frogs*: Edited with an Introduction and Commentary* (Oxford).

DUBOIS, L. (1989), *Inscriptions grecques dialectales de Sicilie* (Coll. de l'Éc. Fr. 119; Rome).

DUBOIS, P. (1995), *Sappho is Burning* (Chicago and London).

DUCAT, J. (1971), *Les Kouroi du Ptoion: Le Sanctuaire d'Apollon Ptoieus à l'époque archaïque* (Paris).

DUNBAR, N. (1995), *Aristophanes,* Birds*: Edited with Introduction and Commentary* (Oxford).

EASTERLING, P. E. (1974), 'Alcman 58 and Simonides 37', *PCPS* 20: 37–43.

—— (1977), 'Literary Traditions and the Transformations of Cupid', *Didaskalos,* 5: 318–37.

—— (1982), *Sophocles,* Trachiniae (Cambridge).

EBELING, H. (1871–80), *Lexicon Homericum* (2 vols.; Leipzig).

EBERT, J. (1972), *Griechische Epigramme auf Sieger an gymnischen und hippischen Agonen* (*ASAW*, Phil.-hist. Kl. 63.2; Berlin).

EFFENTERRE, H. VAN (1989), *Les Béotiens: Aux frontières de l'Athènes antique* (Paris).

EGGER, E. (1865), 'Papyrus n° 71: Fragment inédit du poëte Alcman', in *Notices et extraits des manuscripts de la Bibliothèque Nationale et autres bibliothèques* (Paris), xviii/2. 416–20, with pl. L in the separate volume of plates (*Notices . . . xviii/2. Papyrus grecs du Louvre et de la Bibliothèque Impériale: Planches*).

EISENBERGER, H. (1956), *Der Mythos in der äolischen Lyrik* (diss. Frankfurt).

—— (1959), 'Ein Beitrag zur Interpretation von Sapphos Fragment 16 LP', *Philologus,* 103: 130–5.

—— (1991), 'Zu Alkmans Partheneion fr. 3 Calame', *Philologus,* 135: 274–89.

EKSCHMITT, W. (1993), *Die Kykladen: Bronzezeit, Geometrische und Archaische Zeit* (Mainz am Rhein).

ELLIOTT, A. (1969), *Euripides,* Medea (Oxford).

ELMSLEY, P. (1828), *Euripidis Heraclidae et Medea* (Oxford).

EMLEY, M. L. B. (1971), 'A Note on Anacreon, *P.M.G.* 347 fr. 1', *CR* 21: 169.

ERBSE, H. (1974), 'Zur Exodos der *Sieben*: Aisch. *Sept.* 1005–78', in J. L. Heller (ed.), *Serta Turyniana* (Urbana, Chicago, and London), 169–98.

478   Bibliography

—— (1997), 'Sapphos Sperlinge', *Hermes*, 125: 232–4.
ERP TAALMAN KIP, A. M. VAN (1984), 'Some Remarks on Alcaeus fr. 298 (Voigt)', *Mnemosyne*, 37: 1–13.
—— (1987), 'Alcaeus: "Aias and Kassandra"', in J. M. Bremer, A. Maria van Erp Taalman Kip, and S. R. Slings, *Some Recently Found Greek Poems: Text and Commentary* (*Mnemosyne*, suppl. 99; Leiden etc.), 95–127.
ERVIN, M. (1963), 'A Relief Pithos from Mykonos', *Archaiologikon Deltion*, 18: 37–75.
EVANS, J. A. S. (1963), 'A Fragment of Anacreon (P. Oxy. 2322)', *SO* 38: 22–4.
FALKNER, T. M. (1995), *The Poetics of Old Age in Greek Epic, Lyric, and Tragedy* (Norman).
FARNELL, L. R. (1932), *The Works of Pindar, Translated, with Literary and Critical Commentaries* (3 vols.; London).
FATOUROS, G. (1997), 'Der Vergleich mit dem Mond in Sapphos Arigno-talied (Fr. 98 D., 96 L.–P.)', *Gymnasium*, 104: 193–201.
FEHLING, D. (1969), *Die Wiederholungsfiguren und ihr Gebrauch bei den Griechen vor Gorgias* (Berlin).
—— (1985), *Die sieben Weisen und die frühgriechische Chronologie: Eine traditionsgeschichtliche Studie* (Bern).
FENNELL, C. A. M. (1893–9), *Pindar* (2 vols.; Cambridge).
FERGUSON, W. S. (1938), 'The Salaminioi of Heptaphylai and Sounion', *Hesperia*, 7: 1–74.
FERNÁNDEZ GALIANO, M. (1948), 'Los papiros pindáricos', *Emerita*, 16: 165–200.
FINKELBERG, M. (1986), 'Is κλέος ἄφθιτον a Homeric Formula?', *CQ*, NS 36: 1–5.
FINLEY, M. I. (1968), *A History of Sicily: Ancient Sicily to the Arab Conquest* (London).
—— and PLEKET, H. W. (1976), *The Olympic Games: The First Thousand Years* (London).
FISKER, D. (1989), *Pindars erste olympische Ode* (Odense).
FITZHARDINGE, L. F. (1980), *The Spartans* (London).
FORDYCE, C. J. (1977), *P. Vergili Maronis Aeneidos Libri VII–VIII: With a Commentary* (Oxford).
FORREST, W. G. (1969), 'Two Chronographic Notes', *CQ*, NS 19: 95–110.
—— (1980), *A History of Sparta 950–192 B.C.*[2] (London).
FORSSMAN, B. (1966), *Untersuchungen zur Sprache Pindars* (Wiesbaden).
—— (1975), 'Zur Lautform der lesbischen Lyrik', *Münchener Studien zur Sprachwissenschaft* 33: 15–37.
FOWLER, R. L. (1979), 'Reconstructing the Cologne Alcaeus', *ZPE* 33: 17–30.

—— (1987*a*), *The Nature of Early Greek Lyric: Three Preliminary Studies* (*Phoenix*, suppl. 21; Toronto).

—— (1987*b*), 'Sappho fr. 31. 9', *GRBS* 28: 433–9.

FRAENKEL, ED. (1950), *Aeschylus, Agamemnon: Edited with a Commentary* (3 vols.; Oxford).

FRÄNKEL, H. (1960*a* [orig. 1924]), 'Eine Stileigenheit der frühgriechischen Literatur', in id., *Wege und Formen frühgriechischen Denkens* (Munich), 40–96.

—— (1960*b* [orig. 1946]), 'ἐφήμεροϲ als Kennwort für die menschliche Natur', in id., *Wege und Formen frühgriechischen Denkens* (Munich), 23–39.

—— (1962 [orig. 1951]), *Dichtung und Philosophie des frühen Griechentums*[2] (Munich).

FRENCH, E. B. (1992), 'Archaeology in Greece 1991–92', *AR* 1991–2: 4–70.

FRIEDRICH, R. (1993), 'Medea Apolis: On Euripides' Dramatization of the Crisis of the Polis', in A. H. Sommerstein *et al.* (eds.), *Tragedy, Comedy and the Polis* (Bari), 219–39.

FRIIS JOHANSEN, H. (1973), 'Agesias, Hieron, and Pindar's Sixth Olympian Ode', in O. S. Due *et al.* (eds.), *Classica et Mediaevalia Francisco Blatt Septuagenario Dedicata* (Copenhagen), 1–9.

—— and WHITTLE, E. W. (1980), *Aeschylus: The Suppliants* (3 vols.; Copenhagen).

FROIDEFOND, CHR. (1989), *Lire Pindare* (Namur).

FÜHRER, R. (1967), *Formproblem-Untersuchungen zu den Reden in der frühgriechischen Lyrik* (Zetemata, 44; Munich).

—— (1976), *Beiträge zur Metrik und Textkritik der griechischen Lyriker* (*NGAW* 4–6; Göttingen).

FURTWÄNGLER, A., and KIENAST, H. J. (1989), *Samos*, iii. *Der Nordbau im Heraion von Samos* (Bonn).

GABBA, E., and VALLET, G. (eds.) (1980), *La Sicilia antica* (3 vols.; Naples).

GAISFORD, T. (1848), *Etymologicon Magnum* (Oxford).

GALLAVOTTI, C. (1942), 'Studi sulla lirica greca, 5: Nuovi carmi di Alceo da Ossirinco', *RIFC* 20: 161–81.

—— (1948), *Storia e poesia di Lesbo nel VII–VI secolo a.C.* (Bari).

—— (1955), 'Anacreonte e la chioma recisa', *PP* 10: 41–7.

—— (1969), 'Alcaei carmen de Aiace', *ZPE* 4: 174.

GALLO, I. (1968), *Una nuova biografia di Pindaro (POxy. 2438): Introduzione, testo critico e commentario* (Salerno).

GARDINER, C. P. (1987), *The Sophoclean Chorus: A Study of Character and Function* (Iowa City).

GARNER, R. (1992), 'Mules, Mysteries, and Song in Pindar's *Olympian 6*', *CA* 11: 45–67.

GARROD, H. W. (1907), 'On Four Passages of Pindar', *CQ* 1: 143–7.

GARVIE, A. F. (1965), 'A Note on the Deity of Alcman's *Partheneion*', *CQ*, NS 15, 185–7.

—— (1994), *Homer, Odyssey, Books VI–VIII* (Cambridge).

—— (1998), *Sophocles, Ajax: Edited with Introduction, Translation and Commentary* (Warminster).

GARZYA, A. (1954), *Alcmane, I frammenti: Testo critico, traduzione, commentario* (Naples).

GENTILI, B. (1958a), *Anacreonte: Introduzione, testo critico, traduzione, studio sui frammenti papiracei* (Rome).

—— (1958b), *Bacchilide. Studi²* (Urbino).

—— (1964), 'Studi su Simonide II: Simonide e Platone', *Maia*, 16: 278–306.

—— (1972), 'Il "letto insaziato" di Medea e il tema dell'adikia a livello amoroso nei lirici (Saffo, Teognide), e nella *Medea* di Euripide', *Studi classici e orientali*, 21: 60–72.

—— (1973), 'La ragazza di Lesbo', *QUCC* 16: 124–8.

—— *et al.* (1995), *Pindaro, Le Pitiche* (Milan).

—— (1999), 'Polemichetta metrica: "*Anceps-biceps*" nella *Tebaide* di Stesicoro?', *QUCC* 61: 89–91.

GERBER, D. E. (1962), 'What Time Can Do (Pindar, *Nemean* 1. 46–47)', *TAPA* 93: 30–3.

—— (1982), *Pindar's* Olympian One: *A Commentary* (*Phoenix*, suppl. 25; Toronto etc.).

—— (1993), 'Greek Lyric Poetry since 1920, Part I: General, Lesbian Poets', *Lustrum*, 35: 7–179.

—— (1994), 'Greek Lyric Poetry since 1920, Part II: From Alcman to Adespota', *Lustrum*, 36: 1–188.

—— (ed.) (1997), *A Companion to the Greek Lyric Poets* (*Mnemosyne*, suppl. 173; Leiden, etc.).

—— (1999), 'Pindar, *Nemean* Six: A Commentary', *HSCP* 99: 33–91.

GIANGRANDE, G. (1967), 'Sympotic Literature and Epigram', in *L'Épigramme grecque* (Entretiens Hardt, 14; Geneva), 91–177.

—— (1973), 'Anacreon and the Lesbian Girl', *QUCC* 16: 129–33.

—— (1976), 'On Anacreon's Poetry', *QUCC* 21: 43–6.

—— (1977), 'On Alcman's Partheneion', *Museum Philologum Londiniense*, 2: 151–64.

GIANNINI, A. (1959), 'Alcmane POx. 2387', *Istituto Lombardo, Rend. Lett.* 93: 183–202.

GIANOTTI, G. F. (1973), 'Mito ed encomio: Il carme di Ibico in onore di Policrate', *RIFC* 101: 401–10.

GILDERSLEEVE, B. (1885), *Pindar: The Olympian and Pythian Odes* (London).

GIULIANO, F. M. (1991), 'Esegesi letteraria in Platone: La discussione sul carme simonideo nel *Protagora*', *Studi classici e orientali*, 41: 105–90.

GÖBEL, M. (1915), *Ethnica*, i. *De Graecarum civitatum proprietatibus proverbio notatis* (Breslau).

GOINS, S. E. (1997), 'The Date of Aeschylus' Perseus Tetralogy', *RhM* 140: 193–210.

GOLDHILL, S. (1987), 'The Dance of the Veils: Reading Five Fragments of Anacreon', *Eranos*, 85: 9–18.

——(1996), 'Collectivity and Otherness: The Authority of the Tragic Chorus. Response to Gould', in M. S. Silk (ed.), *Tragedy and the Tragic: Greek Theatre and Beyond* (Oxford), 244–56.

GOODWIN, W. W. (1889), *Syntax of the Moods and Tenses of the Greek Verb* (London etc.).

GOODYEAR, F. R. D. (1965), *Incerti Auctoris Aetna: Edited with an Introduction and Commentary* (Cambridge).

GOOSSENS, R. (1944), 'Notes sur quelques papyrus littéraires, cinquième série', *Chronique d'Égypte*, 38: 265–70.

GOSTOLI, A. (1978), 'Some Aspects of the Theban Myth in the Lille Stesichorus', *GRBS* 19: 23–7.

——(1979), 'Osservazioni metriche sull'encomio a Policrate di Ibico', *QUCC* 2: 93–9.

GOULD, J. (1996), 'Tragedy and Collective Experience', in M. S. Silk (ed.), *Tragedy and the Tragic: Greek Theatre and Beyond* (Oxford), 217–43.

——(1999), 'Myth, Memory, and the Chorus: "Tragic Rationality"', in R. G. A. Buxton (ed.), *From Myth to Reason? Studies in the Development of Greek Thought* (Oxford), 107–16.

GOW, A. S. F. (1952), *Theocritus: Edited with a Translation and Commentary* (2 vols.; Cambridge).

——and PAGE, D. L. (1965), *The Greek Anthology: Hellenistic Epigrams* (2 vols.; Cambridge).

GRAHAM, A. J. (1991), 'A Passage in the New Inscription of Public Imprecations from Teos', *JHS* 111: 176–8.

——(1992), 'Abdera and Teos', *JHS* 112: 44–73.

GRAYSON, A. K. (1975), *Assyrian and Babylonian Chronicles* (New York).

GREENE, E. (ed.) (1996), *Reading Sappho* (Berkeley, Los Angeles, and London).

GREENE, W. C. (1938), *Scholia Platonica* (Haverford).

GREENEWALT, C. H., Jr., and RAUTMAN, M. L. (1998), 'The Sardis Campaigns of 1994 and 1995', *AJA* 102: 469–505.

GREENGARD, C. (1980), *The Structure of Pindar's Epinician Odes* (Amsterdam).

GREIFENHAGEN, A. (1957), *Griechische Eroten* (Berlin).

482 Bibliography

GRENFELL, B. P., and HUNT, A. S. (1919), The Oxyrhynchus Papyri, xiii (London).
——— (1922), The Oxyrhynchus Papyri, xv (London).
GRIMM, J., and HOOG, I. (1968), in J. Latacz, J. Grimm, and I. Hoog, 'ἀνήρ', Lexikon des frühgriechischen Epos (Göttingen 1955–), i. 824–68.
GRONEWALD, M. (1974), 'Fragmente aus einem Sapphokommentar: Pap. Colon. inv. 5860', ZPE 14: 114–18.
GRONINGEN, B. A. VAN (1960), Pindare au banquet: Les Fragments des scolies édités avec un commentaire critique et explicatif (Leiden).
GROSS, N. P. (1985), Amatory Persuasion in Antiquity: Studies in Theory and Practice (Newark etc.).
GSCHITZNER, F. (1978), Ein neuer spartanischer Staatsvertrag und die Verfassung des Peloponnesischen Bundes (Beiträge zur klassischen Philologie, 93; Frankfurt am Main).
GUERRINI, L. (1991), 'Un balsamo ciprio in Alcmane (fr. 26, 71–72 Calame)', Prometheus, 17: 204–12.
GUNDERT, H. (1977 [orig. 1952]), 'Die Simonides-Interpretation in Platons Protagoras', Platonstudien (Amsterdam), 23–45.
GÜNTHER, H.-C. (1998), Ein neuer metrischer Traktat und das Studium der pindarischen Metrik in der Philologie der Paläologenzeit (Mnemosyne, suppl. 180; Leiden etc.).
GUSMANI, R. (1964), Lydisches Wörterbuch, mit grammatischer Skizze und Inschriftensammlung, with (1980–6) Ergänzungsband, pts. 1–3 (Heidelberg).
HAGUE, R. (1984), 'Sappho's Consolation for Atthis, fr. 96 LP', AJP 105: 29–36.
HAJDÚ, I. (1989), Über die Stellung der Enklitika und Quasi-Enklitika bei Pindar und Bakchylides (Lund).
HALL, E. (1989), Inventing the Barbarian: Greek Self-definition through Tragedy (Oxford).
HALLIDAY, W. R. (1913), Greek Divination (London).
HALLIWELL, S. (1980), 'Aristophanes' Apprenticeship', CQ, NS 30: 33–45.
HALPORN, J. W. (1972), 'Agido, Hagesichora and the Chorus (Alcman 1. 37 ff. PMG)', in R. Hanslik et al. (eds.), Antidosis: Festschrift für Walther Kraus zum 70. Geburtstag (Vienna), 124–38.
HAMBURGER, K. (1980), Die Logik der Dichtung³ (Frankfurt am Main etc.).
HAMILTON, R. (1974), Epinikion: General Form in the Odes of Pindar (The Hague and Paris).
HAMM, E.-M. (1958), Grammatik zu Sappho und Alkaios² (Berlin).
HAMMOND, N. G. L., GRIFFITH, G. T., and WALBANK, F. W. (1972–88), A History of Macedonia (3 vols.; Oxford).
HANFMANN, G. M. A. (1983), Sardis from Prehistoric to Roman Times: Re-

sults of the Archaeological Exploration of Sardis 1958–1975 (Cambridge, Mass., and London).

—— and RAMAGE, N. H. (1978), *Sculpture from Sardis: The Finds through 1975* (Cambridge, Mass., and London).

HANSEN, P. A. (1983–9), *Carmina Epigraphica Graeca* (Texte und Kommentare, 12, 15; Berlin and New York).

HARTUNG, J. A. (1855–6), *Pindar's Werke* (4 vols.; Leipzig).

HARVEY, A. E. (1957), 'Homeric Epithets in Greek Lyric Poetry', *CQ*, NS 7: 206–23.

—— (1967), 'Oxyrhynchus Papyrus 2390 and Early Spartan History', *JHS* 87: 62–73.

HASLAM, M. W. (1974), 'Stesichorean Metre', *QUCC* 17: 7–57.

—— (1978), 'The Versification of the New Stesichorus (*P. Lille* 76abc)', *GRBS* 19: 29–57.

—— (1986), *The Oxyrhynchus Papyri*, liii (London).

—— EL-MAGHRABI, H., and THOMAS, J. D. (1990), *The Oxyrhynchus Papyri*, lvii (London).

HAUPT, M., and EHWALD, R. (1966 [⁹1915]), with additions by M. von Albrecht, *P. Ovidius Naso: Metamorphosen* (2 vols.; Zurich).

HEADLAM, C. E. S. (1897), *The Medea of Euripides: Edited with Introduction and Notes* (Cambridge).

HEADLAM, W. G. (1922), ed. A. D. Knox, *Herodas: The Mimes and Fragments* (Cambridge).

HEATH, M. (1988), 'Receiving the κῶμος: The Context and Performance of Epinician', *AJP* 109: 180–95.

—— and LEFKOWITZ, M. R. (1991), 'Epinician Performance', *CP* 85: 173–91.

HEIMBERG, U. (1973), 'Boiotische Reliefs im Museum von Theben', *Antike Plastik* (Berlin), xii. 15–36.

HELLY, B. (1995), *L'État thessalien: Aleuas le Roux, les tétrades et les tagoi* (Lyons).

HENDERSON, J. (1987), *Aristophanes, Lysistrata: Edited with an Introduction and Commentary* (Oxford).

—— (1991), *The Maculate Muse: Obscene Language in Attic Comedy*² (New York and Oxford).

HENDERSON, W. J. (1998), 'Received Responses: Ancient Testimony on Greek Lyric Imagery', *Acta Classica*, 41: 5–27.

HENRICHS, A. (1978), 'Greek Maenadism from Olympias to Messalina', *HSCP* 82: 121–60.

—— (1981), 'Human Sacrifice in Greek Religion: Three Case Studies', in *Le Sacrifice dans l'antiquité* (Entretiens Hardt, 27; Geneva), 195–242.

—— (1993), 'The Tomb of Aias and the Prospect of Hero Cult in Sophocles', *CA* 12: 165–80.

484   *Bibliography*

—— (1994–5), ' "Why Should I Dance?" ': Choral Self-referentiality in Greek Tragedy', *Arion*, 3.1: 56–111.

HENRY, W. B. (1998), 'Simonides, *PMG* 541', *ZPE* 121: 303–4.

—— (1999), 'Simonides, *PMG* 542. 1–3', *CQ*, NS 49: 621.

HEPDING, H. (1914), 'Iamos', *RE* ix. 685–9.

HERINGTON, J. (1985), *Poetry into Drama: Early Tragedy and the Greek Poetic Tradition* (Berkeley etc.).

HERMANN, G. (1817), 'Dissertationes Pindaricae', in Chr. G. Heyne, *Pindari Carmina* . . . (Leipzig), iii. 179–410.

—— (1828 [orig. 1819]), 'Adnotationes ad Medeam ab Elmsleio editam', in id., *Opuscula*, iii (Leipzig), 143–261.

—— and ERFURDT, CHR. G. A. (1848), *Sophoclis Aiax*³ (Leipzig).

HERMARY, A., CASSIMATIS, H., and VOLLKOMMER, R. (1986), 'Eros', *LIMC* iii/1. 850–942.

HERRMANN, H.-V. (1972), *Olympia: Heiligtum und Wettkampfstätte* (Munich).

HERRMANN, P. (1981), 'Teos und Abdera im 5. Jahrhundert v. Chr.', *Chiron*, 11: 1–30.

HEYNE, CHR. G. (1817), *Pindari Carmina cum Lectionis Varietate et Adnotationibus*² (Leipzig).

HIGGINS, R. A. (1967), *Greek Terracottas* (London).

HILLER VON GÄRTRINGEN, F. (1913), *Inscriptiones Graecae*, v/2 (Berlin).

HINGE, G. (1997), 'Kritische Beiträge zum alkmanischen Digamma', *C&M* 48: 37–51.

HINZ, V. (1993), 'Zum Louvre-Partheneion Alkmans (PGMF 1)', *ZPE* 99: 15–16.

HODOT, R. (1990), *Le Dialecte éolien d'Asie: La Langue des inscriptions VIIᵉ s. a.C.–IVᵉ s. p.C.* (Paris).

HÖLLEIN, H. (1991), 'Wer, Sappho, fügt dir ein Leid zu?', *Gymnasium*, 98: 255–63.

HOLLEY, N. M. (1949), 'The Floating Chest', *JHS* 69: 39–47.

HOLLOWAY, R. R. (1991), *The Archaeology of Ancient Sicily* (London and New York).

HOLMES, N. (1998), 'Lucan 7, 425: Planets or Stars?', *Mnemosyne*, 51: 446–8.

HOMOLLE, TH. (1897), 'Ex-voto trouvés à Delphes', *BCH* 21: 585–90.

—— (1898), 'Les offrandes delphiques des fils de Deinoménès et l'épigramme de Simonide', in *Mélanges Henri Weil* (Paris), 207–24.

HOOKER, J. T. (1977), *The Language and Text of the Lesbian Poets* (Innsbruck).

—— (1979), 'The Unity of Alcman's Partheneion', *RhM* 122: 211–21.

—— (1980), *The Ancient Spartans* (London etc.).

Bibliography

485

HOPE, C. A., and WORP, K. A. (1998), 'A New Fragment of Homer', *Mnemosyne*, 51: 206–9.

HORNBLOWER, S. (1991–), *A Commentary on Thucydides* (2 vols. to date; Oxford).

HOSE, M. (1990–1), *Studien zum Chor bei Euripides* (Beiträge zur Altertumskunde, 10, 20; Stuttgart).

HOUSMAN, A. E. (1972 [orig. 1898]), 'Notes on Bacchylides', *Classical Papers* (3 vols.; Cambridge), ii. 442–54.

HOWGEGO, C. (1995), *Ancient History from Coins* (London and New York).

HUBBARD, T. (1985), *The Pindaric Mind: A Study of Logical Structure in Early Greek Poetry* (*Mnemosyne*, suppl. 85; Leiden).

HUMMEL, P. (1993), *La Syntaxe de Pindare* (Paris).

—— (1997), 'Connivence binaire et créativité sérielle: Les composés à premier terme superlatif chez Pindare et Bacchylide', *QUCC* 56: 61–6.

HUNTER, R. L. (1993), 'One Party or Two? Simonides 22 West²', *ZPE* 99: 11–14.

HUTCHINSON, G. O. (1985), *Aeschylus, Septem contra Thebas: Edited with an Introduction and Commentary* (Oxford).

—— (1999), 'Sophocles and Time', in J. Griffin (ed.), *Sophocles Revisited: Essays Presented to Sir Hugh Lloyd-Jones* (Oxford), 47–72.

HUXLEY, G. L. (1969), 'Aigai in Alkaios', *GRBS* 10: 5–11.

—— (1987), 'Onomakles and the Alopekonnesians', *JHS* 107: 187–8.

IERANÒ, G. (1997), *Il ditirambo di Dioniso* (Pisa and Rome).

INSTONE, S. (1996), *Pindar, Selected Odes: Olympian One, Pythian Nine, Nemeans Two and Three, Isthmian One* (Warminster).

IRIGOIN, J. (1974), *Pindare: Olympiques. Reproduction du Vaticanus graecus 1312 (fol. 1–95)* (Vatican).

—— DUCHEMIN, J., and BARDOLLET, L. (1993), *Bacchylide: Dithyrambes—Épinicies—Fragments* (Paris).

IRWIN, M. E. (1994), 'Roses and the Bodies of Beautiful Women in Greek Poetry', *EMC* 13: 1–13.

ISAAC, B. (1986), *The Greek Settlements in Thrace until the Macedonian Conquest* (Leiden).

ITSUMI, K. (1982), 'The "Choriambic Dimeter" of Euripides', *CQ*, NS 32: 59–74.

—— (1984), 'The Glyconic in Tragedy', *CQ*, NS 34: 66–82.

—— (1991–3), 'Enoplian in Tragedy', *BICS* 38: 243–61.

JACOBSTAHL, P. (1931), *Die melischen Reliefs* (Berlin).

JACOBY, F. [and now others] (1923–), *Fragmente der griechischen Historiker* (Berlin etc.).

JAHN, O., and VAHLEN, J. (1967 [⁴1910]), with additions by H.-D. Blume, *Dionysii vel Longini de sublimitate libellus* (Stuttgart).

JAKOB, D. J. (1988), 'Zum Lille-Stesichoros 225–31', *ZPE* 73: 13–14.

JANKO, R. (1982), 'Sappho fr. 96,8 L-P: A Textual Note', *Mnemosyne*, 35: 322-4.

JANNI, P. (1964), 'Agido e Agesicora', *RFIC* 92: 59-65.

JEBB, R. C. (1905), *Bacchylides: The Poems and Fragments* (Cambridge).

JEFFERY, L. H., rev. A. W. Johnston (1990), *The Local Scripts of Archaic Greece*² (Oxford).

JENKINS, G. K. (1970), *The Coinage of Gela* (Berlin).

JENKYNS, R. (1982), *Three Classical Poets: Sappho, Catullus and Juvenal* (London).

JENNER, E. A. B. (1986), 'Further Speculations on Ibycus and the Epinician Ode: S220, S176, and the "Bellerophon" Ode', *BICS* 33: 59-66.

——(1998), 'Troilus and Polyxena in Archaic Greek Lyric: Ibycus fr. S224 Dav.', *Prudentia*, 30: 1-15.

JOHNSTONE, H. (1997), 'A Fragment of Simonides', *CQ*, NS 47: 293-5.

JOST, M. (1985), *Sanctuaires et cultes d'Arcadie* (Paris).

JUDET DE LA COMBE, P. (1996), 'Abstraction et récit dans le poème thébain de Stésichore', in L. Dubois (ed.), *Poésie et lyrique antiques* (Lille), 11-27.

KAIMIO, M. (1970), *The Chorus of Greek Drama within the Light of the Person and Number Used* (Commentationes Humanarum Litterarum, 46; Helsinki).

KAKRIDIS, J. TH. (1970 [orig. 1928]), 'Des Pelops und Iamos Gebet bei Pindar', in W. M. Calder III and J. Stern (eds.), *Pindaros und Bakchylides* (Wege der Forschung, 134; Darmstadt), 159-74.

KAMERBEEK, J. C. (1963), *The Plays of Sophocles: Commentaries*, i. *The Ajax*² (Leiden).

KANNICHT, R. (1997), 'Griechische Metrik', in H.-G. Nesselrath (ed.), *Einleitung in die griechische Philologie* (Stuttgart and Leipzig), 343-62.

KAZIK-ZAWADZKA, I. (1958), *De Sapphicae Alcaicaeque elocutionis colore epico* (Wrocław).

KENYON, F. G. (1897), *The Poems of Bacchylides: From a Papyrus in the British Museum* (London).

KIDD, D. A. (1997), *Aratus: Phaenomena* (Cambridge).

KIENAST, H. J. (1978), *Samos*, xv. *Die Stadtmauer von Samos* (Bonn).

——(1992), 'Topographische Studien im Heraion von Samos', *Arch. Anz.* 1992: 171-213.

——(1995), *Samos*, xix. *Die Wasserleitung des Eupalinos auf Samos* (Bonn).

KIRKWOOD, G. (1982), *Selections from Pindar: Edited with an Introduction and Commentary* (APA Textbook Series 7; Chico).

KISSEL, W. (1990), *Aules Persius Flaccus, Satiren: Herausgegeben, übersetzt und kommentiert* (Heidelberg).

KLEINGÜNTHER, A. (1933), Πρῶτος Εὑρετής: *Untersuchungen zur Geschichte einer Fragestellung* (*Philologus*, suppl. 26.1; Leipzig).

KNOX, B. M. W. (1979 [orig. 1977]), 'The "Medea" of Euripides', in id., *Word and Action: Essays on the Ancient Theater* (Baltimore and London), 295–322.

KOENEN, L. (1981), 'Alkaios: P. Köln II 59 and P. Oxy. XXI 2303', *ZPE* 44: 183–4.

KÖHNKEN, A. (1971), *Die Funktion des Mythos bei Pindar: Interpretationen zu sechs Pindargedichten* (Untersuchungen zur antiken Literatur und Geschichte, 12; Berlin and New York).

KONIARIS, G. (1967), 'On Sappho, Fr. 16 (L.P.)', *Hermes*, 95: 257–68.

KOSSATZ-DEISSMANN, A. (1981), 'Achilleus', *LIMC* i/1. 37–200.

KOSTER, W. J. W. (1968), 'Ad Sapph. 1, 18–19', *Mnemosyne*, 21: 415–17.

KOVACS, D. (1994), *Euripides, Cyclops, Alcestis, Medea: Edited and Translated* (Harvard).

KRAAY, C. M. (1976), *Archaic and Classical Greek Coins* (London).

—— (1984), *The Archaic Coinage of Himera* (Naples).

KRANZ, W. (1910), *De forma stasimi* (Berlin).

—— (1933), *Stasimon: Untersuchungen zu Form und Gehalt der griechischen Tragödie* (Berlin).

KRAUSE, J. H. (1838), *Olympia oder Darstellung der großen olympischen Spiele und der damit verbundenen Festlichkeiten* (Ἑλληνικά, 2.1; Vienna).

KRAUSKOPF, I. (1974), *Der thebanische Sagenkreis und andere griechische Sagen in der etruskischen Kunst* (Mainz am Rhein).

—— (1981), 'Amphiaraos', *LIMC* i/1. 690–713.

—— (1990), 'Iokaste', *LIMC* v/1. 682–6.

KRISCHER, T. (1968), 'Sapphos Ode an Aphrodite (Typologische Bemerkungen)', *Hermes*, 96: 1–14.

KRUMMEN, E. (1990), *Pyrsos hymnon: Festliche Gegenwart und mythisch-rituelle Tradition als Voraussetzung einer Pindarinterpretation* (*Isthmie 4, Pythie 5, Olympie 1 und 3*) (Untersuchungen zur antiken Literatur und Geschichte, 35; Berlin and New York).

KUGELMEIER, CHR. (1996), *Reflexe früher und zeitgenössischer Lyrik in der alten attischen Komödie* (Beiträge zur Altertumskunde, 80; Stuttgart).

KÜHNER, R., and GERTH, B. (1898–1904), *Ausführliche Grammatik der griechischen Sprache*, ii. *Satzlehre*³ (2 vols.; Hanover and Leipzig).

KUHRT, A. (1995), *The Ancient Near East: c. 3000–330 B.C.* (2 vols.; London).

KUNZE, E. (1950), *Archaische Schildbänder: Olympische Forschungen*, ii (Berlin).

—— (1967), *VIII. Bericht über die Ausgrabungen in Olympia* (Berlin).

KURKE, L. (1991), *The Traffic in Praise: Pindar and the Poetics of Social Economy* (Ithaca and London).

KURTZ, D. C., and BOARDMAN, J. (1986), 'Booners', in *Greek Vases in the J. Paul Getty Museum* (Malibu), ii. 35–70.

KYRIELEIS, H. (1996), *Samos*, x. *Der große Kuros von Samos* (Bonn).

LAHR, S. VON DER (1992), *Dichter und Tyrannen im archaischen Griechenland: Das Corpus Theognideum als zeitgenössische Quelle politischer Wertvorstellungen archaisch-griechischer Aristokraten* (Munich).

LAMBERT, S. D. (1999), '*IG* II² 2345, Thiasoi of Herakles and the Salaminioi Again', *ZPE* 125: 93–130.

LANE, E. A. (1933–4), "Lakonian Vase-painting', *BSA* 34: 99–198.

LAPINI, W. (1996), *Il POxy. 664 di Eraclide Pontico e la cronologia dei Cipselidi* (Florence).

LATACZ, J. (1985), 'Realität und Imagination: Eine neue Lyrik-Theorie und Sappho κῆνος-Lied', *MH* 42: 67–94.

LATTE, K. (1955), review of *The Oxyrhynchus Papyri*, xxii, in *Gnomon*, 27: 491–9.

——(1968 [orig. 1947]), 'Zu den neuen Alkaiosbruchstücken (P. Ox. 18, 2165)', in id., *Kleine Schriften* (Munich), 485–91.

LAVECCHIA, S., and MARTINELLI, M. C. (1999), 'P. Oxy. XXXV 2736: Quattro *Fragmenta Dubia* di Pindaro', *ZPE* 125: 1–24.

LEE, H. M. (1986), 'Pindar, *Olympian* 3. 33–34: "The Twelve-turned *terma*" and the Length of the Four-horse Chariot Race', *AJP* 107: 162–74.

LEFKOWITZ, M. R. (1973), 'Critical Stereotypes and the Poetry of Sappho', *GRBS* 14: 113–23.

——(1976), *The Victory Ode: An Introduction* (Park Ridge).

——(1991), *First-person Fictions: Pindar's Poetic 'I'* (Oxford).

——(1995), 'The First Person in Pindar Reconsidered—Again', *BICS* 40: 139–95.

——and LLOYD-JONES, H. (1990 [orig. 1987]), 'Λυκαιχμίαις', in H. Lloyd-Jones, *Greek Epic, Lyric, and Tragedy: The Academic Papers of Sir Hugh Lloyd-Jones* (Oxford), 53–4.

LEHNUS, L. (1979), *L'inno a Pan di Pindaro* (Milan).

LEO, FR. (1912), *Plautinische Forschungen: Zur Kritik und Geschichte der Komödie*² (Berlin).

LESSING, E., and OBERLEITNER, W. (1978), *Ephesos: Weltstadt der Antike* (Vienna and Heidelberg).

LEUMANN, M. (1959 [orig. 1947]), 'Die lateinische Dichtersprache', in id., *Kleine Schriften* (Zurich), 131–56.

LEWIS, D. M. (1988), 'The Tyranny of the Pisistratids', in *CAH* iv². 287–302.

——(1992), 'Mainland Greece, 479–451 B.C.', *CAH* v². 96–120.

——(1997a [orig. 1973]), 'The Athenian *Rationes Centesimarum*', in id., *Selected Papers in Greek and Near Eastern History* (Cambridge), 263–93.

——(1997b [orig. 1981]), 'The Origins of the First Peloponnesian War', in id., *Selected Papers in Greek and Near Eastern History* (Cambridge), 9–21.

—— (1997c [orig. 1982]), 'On the New Text of Teos', in id., *Selected Papers in Greek and Near Eastern History* (Cambridge), 7–8.

LIBERMAN, G. (1989), 'Quelques remarques sur la jonction de P. Köln Inv. 2021 11 ss à P. Oxy. XXI 2303 fr. 1 a+b 25 ss=Alcée 298 Voigt', *ZPE* 77: 27–9.

—— (1999), *Alcée, Fragments: Texte établi, traduit et annoté* (2 vols.; Paris).

LIEBERMANN, W.-L. (1980), 'Überlegungen zu Sapphos "Höchstwert"', *A. u. A.* 26: 51–74.

LIGHTFOOT, J. L. (1999), *Parthenius of Nicaea: The Poetical Fragments and the Ἐρωτικὰ Παθήματα* (Oxford).

LLOYD, A. B. (1988), *Herodotus, Book II: Commentary 99–182* (Leiden etc.).

LLOYD, M. (1999), 'The Tragic Aorist', *CQ*, NS 49: 24–45.

LLOYD-JONES, H. (1958), review of *The Oxyrhynchus Papyri*, xxiii, in *CR*, NS 8: 16–22.

—— (1965), review of *The Oxyrhynchus Papyri*, xxix, in *CR*, NS 15: 70–2.

—— (1985), review of *Greek Poetry and Philosophy: Studies in Honour of Leonard Woodbury*, in *Phoenix*, 39: 275–80.

—— (1990a [orig. 1966]), 'Problems of Early Greek Tragedy: Pratinas and Phrynichus', in id., *Greek Epic, Lyric, and Tragedy: The Academic Papers of Sir Hugh Lloyd-Jones* (Oxford), 225–37.

—— (1990b [orig. 1968]), 'The Cologne Fragment of Alcaeus [=Page, *SLG* S 262]', in id., *Greek Epic, Lyric, and Tragedy: The Academic Papers of Sir Hugh Lloyd-Jones* (Oxford), 38–52.

—— and WILSON, N. G. (1990a), *Sophoclis Fabulae* (Oxford).

—— —— (1990b), *Sophoclea: Studies on the Text of Sophocles* (Oxford).

LOBECK, CHR. A. (1837), *Paralipomena Grammaticae Graecae* (Leipzig).

—— (1866), *Sophoclis Aiax³* (Berlin).

LOBEL, E. (1925), Cαπφοῦς Μέλη (Oxford).

—— (1927), Ἀλκαίου Μέλη (Oxford).

—— (1951), *The Oxyrhynchus Papyri*, xxi (London).

—— (1956), *The Oxyrhynchus Papyri*, xxiii (London).

—— (1968), *The Oxyrhynchus Papyri*, xxxv (London).

—— and ROBERTS, C. H. (1954), *The Oxyrhynchus Papyri*, xxii (London).

—— and TURNER, E. G. (1959), *The Oxyrhynchus Papyri*, xxv (London).

—— *et al.* (1957), *The Oxyrhynchus Papyri*, xxiv (London).

LÖFFLER, I. (1963), *Die Melampodie: Versuch einer Rekonstruktion des Inhalts* (Beiträge zur klassischen Philologie, 7; Meisenheim am Glan).

LOOY, H. VAN (1992), *Euripides*, Medea (Stuttgart and Leipzig).

LÜBBERT, ED. (1883), *In Pindari Locum de Aegidis et Sacris Carneis* [preceding *Natalicia Regis Augustissimi Guilelmi . . .*] (Bonn).

490   Bibliography

LUPPE, W. (1979), 'ἀνάγκα im Kölner Alkaios', *ZPE* 33: 29–30.
—— (1987), review of *The Oxyrhynchus Papyri*, liii, in *CR*, NS 37: 279–83.
LUPPINO, A. (1950), 'Per l'interpretazione del nuovo Alceo', *PP* 5: 206–14.
LURAGHI, N. (1994), *Tirannidi archaiche in Sicilia e Magna Grecia da Panezio di Leontini alla caduta dei Dinomenidi* (Florence).
MAAS, P. (1916), 'Ibykos', *RE* ix. 815–18.
—— (1922), review of *The Oxyrhynchus Papyri*, xv, in *Berliner Philologische Wochenschrift*, 42, 578–83.
MAASS, M. (1993), *Das antike Delphi: Orakel, Schätze und Monumente* (Darmstadt).
MCCABE, D. F., and PLUNKETT, M. A. (1985), *Teos: Inscriptions. Texts and Lists* (Princeton).
MCDIARMID, J. B. (1987), 'Pindar *Olympian* 6. 82–83: The *doxa*, the Whetstone, and the Tongue', *AJP* 108: 369–76.
MACDOWELL, D. (1982), 'Aristophanes and Kallistratos', *CQ*, NS 32: 21–6.
—— (1990), *Demosthenes against Meidias (Oration 21): Edited with Introduction, Translation, and Commentary* (Oxford).
MCGLEW, J. F. (1993), *Tyranny and Political Culture in Ancient Greece* (Ithaca and London).
MACLACHLAN, B. (1997), 'Personal Poetry', in D. E. Gerber (ed.), *A Companion to the Greek Lyric Poets* (*Mnemosyne*, suppl. 173; Leiden, etc.), 133–220.
MACLEOD, C. (1983 [orig. 1974]), 'Two Comparisons in Sappho', in id., *Collected Essays* (Oxford), 16–19.
MAEHLER, H. (1963), *Die Auffassung des Dichterberufs im frühen Griechentum bis zur Zeit Pindars* (Hypomnemata, 3; Göttingen).
—— (1976), 'Der Metiochos-Parthenope-Roman', *ZPE* 23: 1–20.
—— (1982–97), *Die Lieder des Bakchylides* (3 vols.; *Mnemosyne*, suppl. 62, 167; Leiden).
—— (1985), 'Bemerkungen zu Pindar', *Hermes*, 113: 392–403.
MAFFRE, J.-J. (1975), 'Collection Paul Canellopoulos (VIII): Vases béotiens', *BCH* 99: 409–520.
—— (1981), 'Akrisios', *LIMC* i/1. 449–52.
—— (1986), 'Danae', *LIMC* iii/1. 325–37.
MAINGON, A. D. (1989), 'Form and Content in the Lille Stesichorus', *QUCC* 31: 31–56.
MALKIN, I. (1994), *Myth and Territory in the Spartan Mediterranean* (Cambridge).
MALTOMINI, F. (1985), 'Stesicoro, P. Lille 76,220', *ZPE* 58: 9–10.
MANFREDI, M. (1965), '2. Sull'ode 31 L.-P. di Saffo', in *Dai Papiri della Società Italiana: Omaggio all'XI Congresso Internazionale di Papirologia* (Florence), 16–17.

MANNI PIRAINO, M. T. (1974), 'Alcune iscrizioni inedite dall'area sacra e dall'abitato di Himera', *Kokalos*, 20: 265–71.

—— (1976), 'Le iscrizioni', in A. Adriani *et al.* (eds.), *Himera*, i–iii (Rome), ii/2, 665–701.

MANTHOS, K., ed. L. G. Mendoni (1991), *Ἀρχαιολογία καὶ Ἱστορία τῆς νήσου Κέας* (Athens).

MANUWALD, B. (1999), *Platon: Protagoras. Übersetzung und Kommentar* (Göttingen).

MARCH, J. (1987), *The Creative Poet: Studies on the Treatment of Myths in Greek Poetry* (*BICS* suppl. 49; London).

—— (1991–3), 'Sophocles' *Ajax*: The Death and Burial of a Hero', *BICS* 38: 1–36.

MARCOVICH, M. (1991*a* [orig. 1972]), 'Sappho fr. 31: Anxiety Attack or Love Declaration?', in id., *Studies in Greek Poetry* (*ICS* suppl. 1; Atlanta), 29–46.

—— (1991*b* [orig. 1983]), 'Anacreon, 358 *PMG* (ap. Athen. XIII. 599C)', in id., *Studies in Greek Poetry* (*ICS* suppl. 1; Atlanta), 47–57.

MARCOVIGI, G. (1970), *Le citazioni dei lirici corali presso l'Etymologicum Genuinum: Edizione comparata* (Trieste).

MARIOTTI, I. (1997), 'Alcmane 1, 93', in U. Criscuolo and R. Maisano (eds.), *Synodia: Studia Humanitatis Antonio Garzya Septuagenario . . . Dicata* (Naples), 635–7.

MARTIN, A., and PRIMAVESI, O. (1998), *L'Empédocle de Strasbourg* (P. Strasb. gr. *Inv. 1665–1666): Introduction, édition et commentaire* (Berlin and New York).

MARTIN, R. P. (1993), 'The Seven Sages as Performers of Wisdom', in C. Dougherty and L. Kurke (eds.), *Cultural Poetics in Archaic Greece: Cult, Performance, Poetics* (Cambridge), 108–28.

MARTIN, W. KEBLE (1965), *The Concise British Flora in Colour* (London).

MARTINELLI TEMPESTA, S. (1999), 'Nota a Saffo, fr. 16, 12–13 V. (*P. Oxy.* 1231)', *QUCC* 62: 7–14.

MARZULLO, B. (1964), 'Il primo Partenio di Alcmane', *Philologus*, 108: 174–210.

—— (1996), 'Sappho fr. 31, 7–9 V.', *Philologus*, 140: 39–47.

—— (1997), 'Nuovamente Sapph. fr. 31, 7–9 V.', *QUCC* 56: 91–4.

MASON, H. J. (1993), 'Mytilene and Methymna: Quarrels, Borders and Topography', *EMC* 12: 225–50.

MASSIMILLA, G. (1988), 'Lo Stesicoro di Lille: Nuove letture e integrazioni', *SIFC* 6: 25–9.

MASTRONARDE, D. J. (1994), *Euripides, Phoenissae: Edited with Introduction and Commentary* (Cambridge).

—— (1998), 'Il coro euripideo: Autorità e integrazione', *QUCC* 60: 55–80.

MATTHIAE, A. (1813–37), *Euripides, Tragoediae* (10 vols.; Leipzig).

MAY, J. M. F. (1966), ed. C. M. Kraay and G. K. Jenkins, *The Coinage of Abdera (540–345 B.C.)* (London).

MAYSER, E., and SCHMOLL, H. (1970), *Grammatik der griechischen Papyri aus der Ptolemäerzeit*[2], i/1. *Einleitung und Lautlehre* (Berlin).

MAZZARINO, S. (1943), 'Per la storia di Lesbo nel VI° secolo a.c. (A proposito dei nuovi frammenti di Saffo e Alceo)', *Athenaeum*, 21: 38–78.

MAZZOLDI, S. (1997), 'Cassandra, Aiace e lo ξόανον di Aiace', *QUCC* 55: 7–22.

MAZZUCCHI, C. M. (1992), *Dionisio Longino: Del sublime. Introduzione, testo critico, traduzione e commentario* (Milan).

MEIGGS, R., and LEWIS, D. M. (1988), *A Selection of Greek Historical Inscriptions: To the End of the Fifth Century B.C.*[2] (Oxford)

MEILLIER, CL. (1977), 'P. Lille 73 (et P. Lille 76 a et c) recto: Stésichore', *ZPE* 26: 1–5.

—— (1978), 'La succession d'Œdipe d'après le P. Lille 76a+73, poème lyrique probablement de Stésichore', *RÉG* 91: 12–43.

——, ANCHER, G. P., and AUGER, D. (1976), 'Callimaque (P.L. 76 d, 78 abc, 82, 84, 111 c). Stésichore (?) (P.L. 76 abc)', *Cahiers de recherches de l'Institut de Papyrologie et d'Égyptologie de Lille*, 4 (*Études sur l'Égypte et le Soudan anciens*), 255–360.

MELLINK, M. J. (1967), 'Archaeology in Asia Minor', *AJA* 71: 155–74.

—— (1991), 'The Native Kingdoms of Anatolia', in *CAH*[2] iii/2. 619–65.

MERIDOR, R. (1986), 'Euripides, *Medea* 639', *CQ*, NS 36: 95–100.

MERKELBACH, R. (1957), 'Sappho und ihr Kreis', *Philologus*, 101: 1–29.

—— (1967), 'Ein Alkaios-Papyrus', *ZPE* 1: 81–95.

—— (1968), 'Nachträge zu Band I (Alkaios, Aristophanes, Menander)', *ZPE* 2: 154.

METZGER, F. (1880), *Pindars Siegeslieder* (Leipzig).

MEYERHOFF, D. (1984), *Traditioneller Stoff und individuelle Gestaltung: Untersuchungen zu Alkaios und Sappho* (Beiträge zur Altertumswissenschaft, 3; Hildesheim etc.).

MITCHELL, B. M. (1975), 'Herodotus and Samos', *JHS* 95: 75–91.

MITCHELL, T. C. (1991), 'Judah until the Fall of Jerusalem (c. 700–586 B.C.)', *CAH*[2] iii/2. 371–409.

MOLYNEUX, J. H. (1992), *Simonides: A Historical Study* (Wauconda).

MOMMSEN, K. J. T. (1864a), *Pindari Carmina* (Berlin).

—— (1864b), *Annotationis Criticae Supplementum ad Pindari Olympias* (Berlin).

MONTEFIORE, J. (1987), *Feminism and Poetry: Language, Experience, Identity in Women's Writing* (London and New York).

MORET, J.-M. (1992), appendix in B. K. Braswell, *A Commentary on Pindar, Nemean One* (Fribourg), 83–90.

MORPURGO DAVIES, A. (1976), 'The -εσσι Datives, Aeolic -σσ-, and the

Lesbian Poets', in A. Morpurgo Davies and W. Meid (eds.), *Studies in Greek, Italic, and Indo-European Linguistics, Offered to Leonard R. Palmer* . . . (Innsbruck), 181–97.

MOSSHAMMER, A. A. (1979), *The Chronicle of Eusebius and Greek Chronographic Tradition* (Lewisburg and London).

MOST, G. W. (1981), 'Sappho Fr. 16. 6–7 L–P', *CQ*, NS 31: 11–17.

——(1985), *The Measures of Praise: Structure and Function in Pindar's Second Pythian and Seventh Nemean Odes* (Hypomnemata, 83; Göttingen).

——(1987), 'Alcman's "Cosmogonic" Fragment (fr. 5 Page, 81 Calame)', *CQ*, NS 37: 1–19.

——(1994), 'Simonides' Ode to Scopas in Contexts', in I. J. F. De Jong and J. P. Sullivan (eds.), *Modern Critical Theory and Classical Literature* (*Mnemosyne*, suppl. 130; Leiden etc.), 127–52.

MÜHLL, P. VON DER (1976*a* [orig. 1958]), 'Alkman, fr. 1, 97', in id., *Ausgewählte kleine Schriften* (Basle), 260.

——(1976*b* [orig. 1963]), 'Weitere pindarische Notizen. 1', in id., *Ausgewählte kleine Schriften* (Basle), 203–5.

MURGATROYD, P. (1980), *Tibullus I: A Commentary on the First Book of the Elegies of Albius Tibullus* (Pietermaritzburg).

——(1986), 'Ring-structure in Bacchylides *Epinikion* 3', *LCM* 11: 138.

——(1988), 'Sappho 31. 7–16 V.', *Hermes*, 116: 477–8.

MUSGRAVE, S. (1778), *Euripidis Quæ Extant Omnia* (4 vols.; Oxford).

NASH, L. L. (1975), '*Olympian* 6: ἀλίβατον and Iamos' Emergence into Light', *AJP* 96: 110–16.

NEBLUNG, D. (1997), *Die Gestalt der Kassandra in der antiken Literatur* (Beiträge zur Altertumskunde, 97; Stuttgart and Leipzig).

NENCI, G., and VALLET, G. (1977–), *Bibliografia topografica della colonizzazione greca in Italia e nelle isole tirreniche* (14 vols. to date; Pisa and Rome).

NESSELRATH, H.-G. (1992), *Ungeschehenes Geschehen: 'Beinahe-Episoden' im griechischen und römischen Epos von Homer bis zur Spätantike* (Beiträge zur Altertumskunde, 27; Stuttgart).

NEUMANN, G. (1965), *Gesten und Gebärden in der griechischen Kunst* (Berlin).

NICASTRI, L. (1962–3), 'Riflessioni critiche sul partenio I di Alcmane', *AFLN* 10: 7–17.

NICKAU, KL. (1977), *Untersuchungen zur textkritischen Methode des Zenodotos von Ephesos* (Untersuchungen zur antiken Literatur und Geschichte, 16; Berlin and New York).

NISBET, R. G. M., and HUBBARD, M. (1970), *A Commentary on Horace: Odes, Book I* (Oxford).

——(1978), *A Commentary on Horace: Odes, Book II* (Oxford).

NORDEN, ED. (1916), *P. Vergilius Maro: Aeneis, Buch VI*[2] (Stuttgart).

NORTH, H. (1966), *Sophrosyne: Self-knowledge and Self-restraint in Greek Literature* (Ithaca and New York).

NORWOOD, G. (1941), 'Pindar *Olympian* vi. 82–88', *CP* 36: 394–6.

NÖTHIGER, M. (1971), *Die Sprache des Stesichorus und des Ibycus* (diss. Zurich).

NÜNLIST, R. (1998), *Poetologische Bildersprache in der frühgriechischen Dichtung* (Beiträge zur Altertumskunde, 101; Stuttgart and Leipzig).

OSBORNE, R. G. (1994), 'The Politics of Sacred Space in Attica', in S. E. Aldcock and R. G. Osborne (ed.), *Placing the Gods: Sanctuaries and Sacred Space in Ancient Greece* (Oxford), 143–60.

—— (1996), *Greece in the Making, 1200–479 BC* (London).

—— (1998), *Archaic and Classical Greek Art* (Oxford).

OSTWALD, M. (1969), *Nomos and the Beginnings of the Athenian Democracy* (Oxford).

PAGE, D. L. (1938), *Euripides, Medea: The Text Edited with Introduction and Commentary* (Oxford).

—— (1951*a*), *Alcman: The Partheneion* (Oxford).

—— (1951*b*), 'Ibycus' Poem in Honour of Polycrates', *Aegyptus*, 31: 158–72.

—— (1951*c*), 'Simonidea', *JHS* 71: 133–42.

—— (1955), *Sappho and Alcaeus: An Introduction to the Study of Ancient Lesbian Poetry* (Oxford).

—— (1959), review of *The Oxyrhynchus Papyri*, xxiv (1957), in *CR* 9: 15–23.

—— (1962), *Poetae Melici Graeci* (Oxford).

—— (1966), 'Anacreon and Megistes', *WS* 79: 27–32.

—— (1981), *Further Greek Epigrams* (Cambridge).

PALEY, F. A. (1872–80), *Euripides, with an English Commentary*[2] (London).

PANVINI, R. (1996), Γέλας: *Storia e archeologia dell'antica Gela* (Turin).

PARCA, M. (1982), 'Sappho 1. 18–19', *ZPE* 46: 47–50.

PARKE, H. W. (1967), *The Oracles of Zeus: Dodona, Olympia, Ammon* (Oxford).

—— and WORMELL, D. E. W. (1956), *The Delphic Oracle* (2 vols.; Oxford).

PARKER, H. N. (1993), 'Sappho Schoolmistress', *TAPA* 123: 309–51.

PARKER, L. P. E. (1966), 'Porson's Law Extended', *CQ*, NS 16: 1–26.

—— (1970), 'Greek Metric 1957–1970', *Lustrum*, 15:37–98.

—— (1976), 'Catalexis', *CQ*, NS 26: 14–28.

—— (1997), *The Songs of Aristophanes* (Oxford).

PARKER, R. C. T. (1983), *Miasma: Pollution and Purification in Early Greek Religion* (Oxford).

—— (1989), 'Spartan Religion', in A. Powell (ed.), *Classical Sparta: Techniques behind her Success* (London), 142–72.

—— (1996), *Athenian Religion: A History* (Oxford).

PARRY, H. (1965), 'An Interpretation of Simonides 4 (Diehl)', *TAPA* 96: 297–320.

PARSONS, P. J. (1977), 'The Lille Stesichorus', *ZPE* 26: 7–36.

—— (1984), 'Recent Papyrus Finds: Greek Poetry', in J. Harmatta (ed.), *Actes du VIIe Congrès de la Fédération Internationale des Associations d'Études Classiques* (2 vols.; Budapest), ii. 517–31.

—— (1996a), 'Stesichorus', in *OCD³*. 1442–3.

—— (1996b), 'Simonides', in *OCD³*. 1409.

PATTERSON, C. (1985), '"Not Worth the Rearing": The Causes of Infant Exposure in Ancient Greece', *TAPA* 115: 103–23.

PAVESE, C. O. (1964), 'Pindarica', *Maia*, 16: 307–12.

—— (1967), 'Alcmane, il *Partenio* del Louvre', *QUCC* 4: 113–33.

—— (1992), *Il grande Partenio di Alcmane* (*Lexis* suppl. 1; Amsterdam).

—— (1997), 'Sulla "Thebais" di Stesicoro', *Hermes*, 125: 259–68.

PAYNE, H. (1931), *Necrocorinthia: A Study of Corinthian Art in the Archaic Period* (Oxford).

PEARSON, A. C. (1917), *The Fragments of Sophocles* (3 vols.; Cambridge).

—— (1931), 'Pindar, *Ol.* 6. 82', *CR* 45: 210.

PEDLEY, J. G. (1972), *Ancient Literary Sources on Sardis* (Cambridge, Mass., and London).

PEEK, W. (1955–6), 'Neue Bruchstücke frühgriechischer Dichtung', *Wissenschaftliche Zeitschrift der Martin-Luther-Universität Halle-Wittenberg*, 5: 189–207.

—— (1958), 'Pindar, Ol. VI 42', *Philologus*, 102: 319–20.

—— (1960), 'Das neue Alkman-Partheneion', *Philologus*, 104: 163–80.

—— (1974), *Ein neuer spartanischer Staatsvertrag* (*ASAW*, Phil.-hist. Kl. 65.3; Berlin).

PELLICCIA, H. (1991), 'Anacreon 13 (358 *PMG*)', *CP* 86: 30–6.

—— (1995), 'Ambiguity against Ambiguity: Anacreon 13 Again', *ICS* 20: 23–4.

PÉRON, J. (1974), *Les Images maritimes de Pindare* (Études et Commentaires, 87; Paris).

—— (1982), 'Le poème à Polycrate: une "Palinodie" d'Ibycus?', *RPh* 56: 33–56.

PETRAKOS, V. CH. (1968), Ὁ Ὠρωπὸς καὶ τὸ Ἱερὸν τοῦ Ἀμφιαράου (Athens).

PETROPOULOS, J. C. B. (1993), 'Sappho the Sorceress: Another Look at Fr. 1 (LP)', *ZPE* 97: 43–56.

PFEIFFER, R. (1949–53), *Callimachus* (2 vols.; Oxford).

—— (1968–76), *A History of Classical Scholarship* (2 vols.; Oxford).

PFEIJFFER, I. L. (1999), *Three Aeginetan Odes of Pindar: Nemean 5, Nemean 3, Pythian 8* (*Mnemosyne*, suppl. 197; Leiden etc.).

PFLUGK, A. J. E., and KLOTZ, R. (1867), *Euripidis Tragoediae*, i³ (Leipzig).

PICARD, CH. (1948), 'Sur trois exégèses', *RÉG* 61: 337–57.

—— (1962), 'Où fut à Lesbos, au VIIe siècle, l'asyle temporaire du poète Alcée?', *Revue archéologique* 1962/2: 43–69.

PICCOLOMINI, A. (1892), 'Ad Sapphus Carmen in Venerem Apparatus Criticus Auctus', *Hermes*, 27: 1–10.

PIERACCIONI, D. (1948), 'Un nuovo papiro pindarico della raccolta fiorentina', *Maia*, 1: 287–8.

PINGIATOGLOU, S. (1994), 'Rituelle Frauengelage auf schwarzfigurigen attischen Vasen', *MDAI Ath.* 109: 39–51.

POE, J. P. (1987), *Genre and Meaning in Sophocles'* Ajax (Beiträge zur klassischen Philologie, 172; Frankfurt am Main).

POHLSANDER, H. A. (1964), *Metrical Studies in the Lyrics of Sophocles* (Leiden).

POLTERA, O. (1997), *Le Langage de Simonide: Étude sur la tradition poétique et son renouvellement* (Sapheneia, 1; (Bern).

PORSON, R. (1826), ed. J. Scholefield, *Euripidis Tragoediae Priores Quatuor* (Cambridge).

PRICE, S. D. (1990), 'Anacreontic Vases Reconsidered', *GRBS* 31: 133–75.

PRIVITERA, G. A. (1965), *Laso di Ermione nella cultura ateniese e nella tradizione storiografica* (Rome).

—— (1969), 'Saffo fr. 31, 13 LP', *Hermes*, 97: 267–72.

—— (1974), *La rete di Afrodite: Studi su Saffo* (Palermo).

—— (1982), *Pindaro: Le Isthmiche* (Milan).

PUCCI, P. (1980), *The Violence of Pity in Euripides'* Medea (Ithaca and London).

PUELMA, M. (1977), 'Die Selbstbeschreibung des Chores in Alkmans großem Partheneion-Fragment', *MH* 34: 1–55.

PULLEYN, S. (1997), *Prayer in Greek Religion* (Oxford).

QUINN, J. D. (1961), 'Cape Phokas, Lesbos: Site of an Archaic Sanctuary for Zeus, Hera and Dionysus?', *AJA* 65: 391–3.

RACE, W. H. (1982), *The Classical Priamel from Homer to Boethius* (Mnemosyne, suppl. 74; Leiden).

—— (1983), '"That Man" in Sappho fr. 31 L–P', *CA* 2: 92–101.

—— (1990), *Style and Rhetoric in Pindar's Odes* (Atlanta).

—— (1992), 'How Greek Poems Begin', *YCS* 29: 13–38.

RADT, S. L. (1958), *Pindars zweiter und sechster Paian: Text, Scholien und Kommentar* (Amsterdam).

RAMAGE, A. (1978), *Lydian Houses and Architectural Terracottas* (Cambridge, Mass., and London).

REGEL, W. (1982 [orig. 1892–1917]), *Fontes Rerum Byzantinarum: Rhetorum Saeculi xii Orationes Politicae*, i/1–2 (Leipzig).

REITZENSTEIN, R. (1890–1), 'Inedita Poetarum Graecorum Fragmenta', *Index Lectionum Hibernarum Rostochii* (Rostock).

RENEHAN, R. (1972), 'διαιπετής in Alcman', *RhM* 115: 93–6.

—— (1983), 'The Early Greek Poets: Some Interpretations', *HSCP* 87: 1–29.

—— (1984), 'Anacreon Fragment 13 Page', *CP* 79: 28–32.

—— (1993), 'On the Interpretation of a Poem of Anacreon', *ICS* 18: 39–47.

RHODES, P. J. (1976), 'Pisistratid Chronology Again', *Phoenix*, 30: 219–33.

—— (1981), *A Commentary on the Aristotelian Athenaion Politeia* (Oxford).

RICHARDSON, N. J. (1993), *The Iliad: A Commentary*, vi. *Books 21–24* (Cambridge).

RICHTER, G. M. A. (1965), *The Portraits of the Greeks* (3 vols.; London).

—— (1968), *Korai: Archaic Greek Maidens* (London and New York).

—— (1970), *Kouroi: Archaic Greek Youths*[3] (London and New York).

RIHLL, T. E., and TUCKER, J. V. (1995), 'Greek Engineering: The Case of Eupalinos' Tunnel', in A. Powell (ed.), *The Greek World* (London), 403–31.

RISCH, E. (1954), 'Die Sprache Alkmans', *MH* 11: 20–37.

—— (1974), *Wortbildung der homerischen Sprache*[2] (Berlin and New York).

RISSMAN, L. (1983), *Love as War: Homeric Allusion in the Poetry of Sappho* (Beiträge zur klassischen Philologie, 157; Königstein).

ROBBINS, E. (1980), ' "Every Time I Look at You . . ." ': Sappho Thirty-One', *TAPA* 110: 255–61.

—— (1994), 'Alcman's *Partheneion*: Legend and Choral Ceremony', *CQ*, NS 44: 7–16.

ROBERT, L. (1969 [orig. 1960]), 'Recherches épigraphiques IV–IX', in id., *Opera Minora Selecta* (7 vols. to date; Amsterdam), ii. 792–877.

ROBERTS, D. H. (1997), 'Ending and Aftermath', in D. H. Roberts, F. M. Dunn, and D. Fowler (eds), *Classical Closure: Reading the End in Greek and Latin Literature* (Princeton), 251–73.

ROBERTSON, M. (1970), 'Ibycus: Polycrates, Troilus, Polyxena', *BICS* 17: 11–15.

ROBINSON, D. M., and GRAHAM, W. J. (1938), *Excavations at Olynthus*, viii. *The Hellenic House* (Baltimore etc.).

ROBINSON, E. G. (1946), 'Rhegion, Zankle-Messana and the Samians', *JHS* 66: 13–20.

ROBINSON, E. W. (1997), *The First Democracies: Early Popular Government outside Athens* (*Hermes* Einzelschriften, 107; Stuttgart).

RODRÍGUEZ ADRADOS, F. (1973), 'Alcmán, el partenio del Louvre: Estructura e interpretación', *Emerita*, 41: 323–44.

RONNET, G. (1969), *Sophocle: Poète tragique* (Paris).

ROSENMEYER, P. A. (1991), 'Simonides' Danae Fragment Reconsidered', *Arethusa*, 24: 5–29.

—— (1997a), *The Poetics of Imitation: Anacreon and the Anacreontic Tradition* (Cambridge).

—— (1997b), 'Her Master's Voice: Sappho's Dialogue with Homer', *MD* 39: 123–49.

RÖSLER, W. (1980), *Dichter und Gruppe: Eine Untersuchung zu den Bedingungen und zur historischen Funktion früher griechischer Lyrik am Beispiel Alkaios* (Munich).

—— (1987), 'Der Frevel des Aias in der "Iliupersis"', *ZPE* 69: 1–8.

—— (1988), 'Formes narratives d'un mythe dans la poésie lyrique et les arts plastiques: Ajax de Locres et les Achéens', in C. Calame (ed.), *Métamorphoses du mythe en Grèce antique* (Geneva), 201–9.

—— (1990), 'Realitätsbezug und Imagination in Sapphos Gedicht Φαίνεταί μοι κῆνος', in W. Kullmann and M. Reichel (eds.), *Der Übergang von der Mündlichkeit zur Literatur bei den Griechen* (Tübingen), 271–87.

ROUSSEL, D. (1976), *Tribu et cité: Études sur les groupes sociaux dans les cités grecques aux époques archaïque et classique* (Paris).

RUBIN, N. F. (1980–1), 'Pindar's Creation of Epinician Symbols: *Olympians* 7 and 6', *CW* 74: 67–87.

RUCK, C. A. P. (1975–6), 'On the Sacred Names of Iamos and Ion: Ethnobotanical Referents in the Hero's Parentage', *CJ* 71: 235–52.

RUMPF, A. (1927), *Chalkidische Vasen* (3 vols.; Berlin and Leipzig).

RUSSELL, D. A. (1964), *'Longinus' On the Sublime: Edited with Introduction and Commentary* (Oxford).

RUTHERFORD, I. (1997a), 'Odes and Ends: Closure in Greek Lyric', in D. H. Roberts, F. M. Dunn, and D. Fowler (eds.), *Classical Closure: Reading the End in Greek and Latin Literature* (Princeton), 43–61.

—— (1997b), 'For the Aeginetans to Aiakos a Prosodion: An Unnoticed Title at Pindar, *Paean* 6, 123, and its Significance for the Poem', *ZPE* 118: 1–21.

—— (2000), *Pindar's Paeans: A Reading of the Fragments, with a Survey of the Genre* (Oxford).

RUTHERFORD, R. B. (1992), 'Unifying the Protagoras', *Apeiron*, 25: 133–56.

SAAKE, H. (1972), *Sapphostudien: Forschungsgeschichtliche, biographische und literarästhetische Forschungen* (Munich etc.).

SALLARES, J. R. (1991), *The Ecology of the Ancient Greek World* (London).

SALVADOR, J. A. (1997), 'Iamos and ἴα in Pindar (*O*. 6. 53–57)', *QUCC* 56: 37–59.

SANCASSANO, M. (1996–7), "Ο δράκων ποικίλος: Beobachtungen zum Schlangenmotiv in der ältesten griechischen Dichtung', *Würzb. Jahrb.* 21: 79–92.

SCHACHTER, A. (1981–), *Cults of Boiotia* (4 vols. to date; London).

SCHADEWALDT, W. (1928), *Der Aufbau des pindarischen Epinikion* (Schrif-

Bibliography   499

ten der Königsberger gelehrten Gesellschaft, Geisteswiss. Kl. 5. 3; Halle (Saale)).

SCHAEFER, W. (1901), *De Tertio Bacchylidis Carmine* (diss. Erlangen).

SCHAUS, G. P. (1992), 'Archaic Imported Fine Wares from the Acropolis, Mytilene', *Hesperia*, 61: 355–74.

—— (1996), 'An Archaeological Field Survey at Eresos, Lesbos', *EMC* 15: 27–74.

SCHEFOLD, K. (1993), *Götter- und Heldensagen der Griechen in der früh- und hocharchaischen Kunst* (Munich).

—— (1997), *Die Bildnisse der antiken Dichter, Redner und Denker* (Basle).

SCHILD-XENIDOU, W. (1972), *Boiotische Grab- und Weihreliefs archaischer und klassischer Zeit* (diss. Munich).

SCHLEIF, H. (1934), 'Der Zeusaltar in Olympia', *JDAI* 49: 139–56.

SCHMALTZ, B. (1980), *Das Kabirenheiligtum bei Theben*, vi. *Metallfiguren aus dem Kabirenheiligtum bei Theben* (Berlin).

SCHMID, E. (1616), Πινδάρου Περίοδος . . . (Wittenberg).

SCHMIDT, D. (1999), 'An Unusual Victory List from Keos: *IG* XII, 5, 608 and the Dating of Bakchylides', *JHS* 119: 67–85.

SCHMITT, R. (1975), 'Bakchylides' ἀβροβάτας und die Iranier-Namen mit Anlaut ABRA/O', *Glotta*, 53: 207–17.

—— (1977), *Einführung in die griechischen Dialekte* (Darmstadt).

SCHNEIDER, J. (1985), 'La chronologie d'Alcman', *RÉG* 98: 1–64.

SCHNEIDEWIN, F. W. (1833), *Ibyci Rhegini Carminum Reliquiae* (Göttingen).

—— (1835), *Simonidis Cei Carminum Reliquiae* (Brunswick).

—— and NAUCK, A. (1882), *Sophokles*, i. *Allgemeine Einleitung. Aias*⁸ (Berlin).

—— —— and RADERMACHER, L. (1913), *Sophokles* . . . *Aias*¹⁰ (Berlin).

SCHRECKENBERG, H. (1964), *Ananke: Untersuchungen zur Geschichte des Wortgebrauchs* (Zetemata, 36; Munich).

SCHRÖDER, ST. (1999), *Geschichte und Theorie der Gattung Paian* (Beiträge zur Altertumskunde, 121; Stuttgart and Leipzig).

SCHROEDER, O. (1900), *Pindari Carmina* (Leipzig).

—— (1922), *Pindars Pythien* (Leipzig and Berlin).

SCHUBART, W. (1902), 'Neue Bruchstücke der Sappho und des Alkaios', *SBAW* 10 (Berlin).

—— and WILAMOWITZ-MOELLENDORFF, U. VON (1907), *Griechische Dichterfragmente* (Berliner Klassikertexte, 5; Berlin).

SCHULLER, M. (1985), 'Die dorische Architektur der Kykladen in spätarchaischer Zeit', *JDAI* 100: 319–98.

SCHULZE, W. (1892), *Quaestiones Epicae* (Gütersloh).

SCHÜTRUMPF, E. (1987), 'Simonides an Skopas (542 PMG)', *Würzb. Jahrb.* 13: 11–23.

500   Bibliography

SCHWARTZ, ED. (1887–91), *Scholia in Euripidem* (2 vols.; Berlin).
SCHWENN, F. (1937), 'Zu Alkmans großem Partheneion-Fragment', *RhM* 86: 289–315.
SCHWYZER, ED. (1953–71), *Griechische Grammatik* (4 vols.; Munich).
SCOTT, E. J. L. (preface) (1897), *The Poems of Bacchylides: Facsimile of Papyrus DCCXXXIII in the British Museum* (London).
SEGAL, C. (1981), *Tragedy and Civilization: An Interpretation of Sophocles* (Cambridge, Mass., and London).
——(1986), *Pindar's Mythmaking: The Fourth Pythian Ode* (Princeton).
——(1995), *Sophocles' Tragic World: Divinity, Nature, Society* (Cambridge, Mass., and London).
——(1998*a* [orig. 1971]), 'Croesus on the Pyre: Herodotus and Bacchylides', in id., *Aglaia: The Poetry of Alcman, Sappho, Pindar, Bacchylides, and Corinna* (Lanham etc.), 281–93.
——(1998*b* [orig. 1976]), 'Bacchylides Reconsidered: Epithets and the Dynamics of Lyric Narrative', ibid. 251–79.
——(1998*c* [orig. 1983]), 'Sirius and the Pleiades in Alcman's Louvre Partheneion', ibid. 25–41.
SEIBERT, J. (1979), *Die politischen Flüchtlinge und Verbannten in der griechischen Geschichte* (2 vols.; Impulse der Forschung, 30; Darmstadt).
SERVAIS, J. (1969), 'Hérodote et la chronologie des Cypsélides', *AC* 38: 28–81.
SHIPLEY, G. (1987), *A History of Samos, 800–188 BC* (Oxford).
SIHLER, A. L. (1995), *New Comparative Grammar of Greek and Latin* (New York and Oxford).
SILK, M. S. (1974), *Interaction in Poetic Imagery: With Special Reference to Early Greek Poetry* (Cambridge).
SIMON, E. (1982), *The Ancient Theatre* (London and New York).
——(1985), *Die Götter der Griechen*³ (Munich).
SIMONINI, L. (1979), 'Il fr. 282 P. di Ibico', *Acme*, 32: 285–98.
SISTI, F. (1966), 'Ibico e Policrate', *QUCC* 2: 91–102.
——(1967), 'L'ode a Policrate: Un caso di *recusatio* in Ibico', *QUCC* 4: 59–79.
——(1971–2), 'Alcmane fr. 3, 63 Page', *Helikon*, 11–12: 431–2.
SLATER, W. J. (1969), 'Futures in Pindar', *CQ*, NS 19: 86–94.
SLINGS, S. R. (1979), 'Ἀπαππένα γενήω: Some Problems in Lesbian Grammar', *Mnemosyne*, 32: 243–67.
——(1991), 'Sappho Fr. 1, 8 V.: Golden House or Golden Chariot?', *Mnemosyne*, 44: 404–10.
SMITH, K. F. (1913), *The Elegies of Albius Tibullus* (New York etc.).
SMITH, S. (1924), *Babylonian Historical Texts relating to the Capture and Downfall of Babylon* (London).

SNELL, B. (1973), 'Gyges und Kroisos als Tragödien-Figuren', *ZPE* 12: 197–205.

—— and MAEHLER, H. (1987–9), *Pindari Carmina cum Fragmentis* (2 vols.; Leipzig).

SNODGRASS, A. (1998), *Homer and the Artists: Text and Picture in Early Greek Art* (Cambridge).

SNYDER, J. McI. (1997), *Lesbian Desire in the Lyrics of Sappho* (New York and Chichester).

SOTIRIOU, M. (1998), *Pindarus Homericus: Homer-Rezeption in Pindars Epinikien* (Hypomnemata, 119; Göttingen).

SPENCER, N. (1995a), *A Gazetteer of Archaeological Sites in Lesbos* (Oxford).

—— (1995b), 'Respecting your Elders and Betters: Ancestor Worship at Antissa, Lesbos', *EMC* 14: 45–60.

SPRANGER, J. A. (1920), *Euripidis Quae Inveniuntur in Codice Laurentiano Pl. xxxii. 2 Phototypice Expressa* (2 vols.; Florence).

—— (1938), *Euripidis Quae in Cod. Par. gr. 2713 Servantur Phototypice Expressa* (2 vols.; Florence).

—— (1939–46), *Euripidis Quae in Codicibus Palatino Graeco inter Vaticanos et Laurentiano conv. soppr. 172 Inveniuntur Phototypice Expressa* (2 vols.; Florence).

STANFORD, W. B. (1963), *Sophocles, Ajax: Edited with Introduction, etc.* (London).

STANLEY, K. (1976), 'The Role of Aphrodite in Sappho Fr. 1', *GRBS* 17: 305–21.

STEHLE, E. (1981), 'Sappho's Private World', in H. P. Foley (ed.), *Reflections of Women in Antiquity* (New York etc.), 45–61.

—— (1997), *Performance and Gender in Ancient Greece: Nondramatic Poetry in its Setting* (Princeton).

STEINER, D. (1986), *The Crown of Song: Metaphor in Pindar* (London).

STEINHAUSEN, J. (1910), Κωμῳδούμενοι: *De Grammaticorum Veterum Studiis ad Homines in Comoedia Attica Irrisos Pertinentibus* (diss. Bonn).

STEINRÜCK, M. (1999), 'Homer bei Sappho?', *Mnemosyne*, 52: 139–49.

STELLA, L. A. (1946), 'Studi simonidei, I: Per la cronologia di Simonide', *RIFC* 24: 1–24.

STENGEL, P. (1910), *Opferbräuche der Griechen* (Leipzig and Berlin).

STERN, J. (1970), 'The Myth of Pindar's *Olympian* 6', *AJP* 91: 331–40.

STEWART, A. F. (1990), *Greek Sculpture: An Exploration* (2 vols.; New Haven and London).

STIBBE, C. M. (1972), *Lakonische Vasenmaler des sechsten Jahrhunderts v. Chr.* (2 vols.; Amsterdam and London).

—— (1989), *Laconian Mixing Bowls: A History of the krater Lakonikos from the Seventh to the Fifth Century B.C.* (Amsterdam).

502 Bibliography

—— (1996), *Das andere Sparta* (Mainz am Rhein).
STRUNK, KL. (1957), *Die sogennanten Äolismen der homerischen Sprache* (diss. Cologne).
SVENBRO, J. (1975), 'Sappho and Diomedes: Some Notes on Sappho 1 LP and the Epic', *Mus. Philol. Lond.* 1: 37–49.
SYMEONOGLOU, S. (1985), *The Topography of Thebes from the Bronze Age to Modern Times* (Princeton).
TAILLARDAT, J. (1953), 'Une prétendue forme laconienne chez Alcman: *ἰανογλέφαρος* (*Parthénée*, 69)', *RPh* 27: 131–4.
TAPLIN, O. (1996), 'Comedy and the Tragic', in M. S. Silk (ed.), *Tragedy and the Tragic: Greek Theatre and Beyond* (Oxford), 188–202.
TARÁN, L. (1965), *Parmenides: A Text with Translation, Commentary, and Critical Essays* (Princeton).
TATAKI, A. B. (1978), *Sounion: The Temple of Poseidon* (Athens).
TAYLOR, C. C. W. (1975), *Plato, Protagoras: Translated with Notes* (Oxford).
TESSIER, A. (1995), *Tradizione metrica di Pindaro* (Padua).
THALMANN, W. G. (1982), 'The Lille Stesichorus and the "Seven against Thebes"', *Hermes*, 110: 385–91.
THEANDER, C. (1934), 'Studia Sapphica', *Eranos*, 32: 57–85.
THESLEFF, H. (1965), *The Pythagorean Texts of the Hellenistic Period* (Åbo).
THOMMEN, L. (1999), 'Spartanische Frauen', *MH* 56: 129–49.
THOMPSON, E. M., and JEBB, R. C. (1885), *Facsimile of the Laurentian Manuscript of Sophocles* (London).
THUMB, A., KIECKERS, E., and SCHERER, A. (1932–59), *Handbuch der griechischen Dialekte*[2] (2 vols.; Heidelberg).
THUMMER, E. (1968–9), *Pindar: Die isthmischen Gedichte* (2 vols.; Heidelberg).
TOD, M. N., and WACE, A. J. B. (1906), *A Catalogue of the Sparta Museum* (Oxford).
TOMLINSON, R. A. (1995), 'Archaeology in Greece 1994–5', *AR* 1994–5: 1–74.
TOO, Y. L. (1991), '"Ἥρα Παρθενία and Poetic Self-reference in Pindar 'Olympian' 6. 87–90', *Hermes*, 119: 257–64.
—— (1997), 'Alcman's *Partheneion*: The Maidens Dance the City', *QUCC* 56: 7–29.
TOSI, R. (1978–9), 'Note al nuovo Stesicoro', *Mus. Crit.* 13–14: 125–42.
TOUCHEFEU, O. (1981), 'Aias II', *LIMC* i/1. 336–51.
TRAVLOS, J. (1988), *Bildlexikon zur Topographie des antiken Attika* (Tübingen).
TREU, M. (1965), 'Von der Weisheit der Dichter', *Gymnasium*, 72: 433–9.
—— (1968–9), 'Sizilische Mythologie bei Simonides (P. Ox. 2637)', *Kokalos*, 14–15: 428–38.

TRUMPF, J. (1958), *Studien zur griechischen Lyrik* (diss. Cologne).

—— (1973), 'Über das Trinken in der Poesie des Alkaios', *ZPE* 12: 139–60.

TSERETELI, G. F. (1896), *Sokraščenija v' grečeskikh' rukopisjakh' preimuš-čestvenno po datirovannym' rukopisjam' S.-Peterburga i Moskvy* (St Petersburg).

TÜMPEL, K. (1891), 'Lesbiaka, 5: Pylaïdes', *Philologus*, 4: 566–8.

TURNER, E. G. (1973), *The Papyrologist at Work* (*GRBS* Monograph 6; Durham, NC).

—— (1977), *The Typology of the Early Codex* (Pennsylvania).

—— (1980), 'Ptolemaic Bookhands and the Lille Stesichorus', *Scrittura e civiltà*, 4: 19–40.

—— (1987), *Greek Manuscripts of the Ancient World*[2], ed. P. J. Parsons (*BICS* suppl. 4; London).

TURYN, A. (1929), *Studia Sapphica* (*Eos* suppl. 6; Lvov).

—— (1948), *Pindari carmina cum Fragmentis* (Kraków).

TZAMALI, E. (1996), *Syntax und Stil bei Sappho* (*Münchener Studien zur Sprachwissenschaft*, suppl. 16; Dettelbach).

URE, P. N. (1927), *Sixth and Fifth Century Pottery from Excavations Made at Rhitsona . . .* (Oxford).

URIOS-APARISI , E. (1993), 'Anacreon: Love and Poetry (On 358 *PMG*, 13 Gent.)', *QUCC* 44: 51–70.

USENER, H., and RADERMACHER, L. (1904–29), *Dionysii Halicarnasei Opuscula*, ii/1–2 (Leipzig).

VALLET, G. (1958), *Rhégion et Zancle: Histoire, commerce et civilisation des cités chalcidiennes du détroit de Messine* (Paris).

—— (1996a [orig. 1977]), 'Rhégion et Zancle, vingt ans après', in id., *Le Monde grec colonial d'Italie du sud et de Sicile* (Coll. Éc. fr. 218; Rome), 389–403.

—— (1996b [orig. 1993]), 'Après le XXVIe Convegno di studi sulla Magna Grecia: Quelques réflexions sur le Détroit de Messine', in id., *Le Monde grec colonial d'Italie du sud et de Sicile* (Coll. Éc. fr. 218; Rome), 421–33.

VASSALLO, S. (1993–4), 'Ricerche nella necropoli orientale di Himera in località Pestavecchia (1990–1993)', *Kokalos*, 39–40, 1243–55.

—— (1996), 'Il territorio di Himera in età arcaica', *Kokalos*, 42: 199–223.

—— et al. (1991), 'Himera: Necropoli di Pestavecchia', in C. A. Di Stefano (ed.), *Di terra in terra: Nuove scoperte archeologiche nella provinzia di Palermo* (Palermo), 89–112.

VERDENIUS, W. J. (1987–8), *Commentaries on Pindar* (2 vols.; *Mnemosyne*, suppl. 97, 101; Leiden).

VERDIER, CHR. (1972), *Les Éolismes non-épiques de la langue de Pindare* (Innsbrucker Beiträge zur Sprachwissenschaft, 7; Innsbruck).

VERRALL, A. W. (1881), *The 'Medea' of Euripides: With an Introduction and Commentary* (London).

504   Bibliography

VISSER, E. (1997), *Homers Katalog der Schiffe* (Stuttgart and Leipzig).
VIVIERS, D. (1987), 'La conquête de Sigée par Pisistrate', *AC* 56: 7–25.
VOGLIANO, A. (1942), 'Una strofe della II delle odi berlinesi di Saffo', *Athenaeum*, 20: 114–18.
—— (1943), 'Per il nuovissimo Alceo', *Athenaeum*, 21: 125–6.
VOIGT, E.-M. (1971), *Sappho et Alcaeus: Fragmenta* (Amsterdam).
VOX, O. (1990), *Studi anacreonti* (Bari).
VOZA, G. (1980), 'Cultura artistica fino al V secolo a.C.', in E. Gabba and G. Vallet (eds.), *La Sicilia antica*, ii/1. *La Sicilia greca dal VI secolo a.C. alle guerre puniche* (Naples), 103–28.
VULIĆ, N. (1933), 'Neue Gräber bei Trebenischte', *Arch. Anz.* 459–82.
WADE-GERY, H. (1933), 'Classical Epigrams and Epitaphs', *JHS* 53: 71–104, 460.
WÆRN, I. (1960), 'Greek Lullabies', *Eranos*, 58: 1–8.
WAIBLINGER, A. (1974), *Corpus Vasorum Antiquorum Louvre N° 17 (France N° 26)* (Paris).
WALDBAUM, J. C. (1983), *Metalwork from Sardis: The Finds through 1974* (Cambridge, Mass., and London).
WALTER, H. (1976), *Das Heraion von Samos: Ursprung und Wandel eines griechischen Heiligtums* (Munich).
WALTER-KARYDI, E. (1973), *Samos*, vi/1. *Samische Gefäße des 6. Jahrhunderts v. Chr.* (Bonn).
WALTON, K. L. (1990), *Mimesis as Make-believe: On the Foundations of the Representational Arts* (Cambridge, Mass., and London).
WARING, P. (1984), 'A Textual and Linguistic Commentary on Five Nemean Odes of Pindar' (diss. Cambridge, unpublished).
WECKLEIN, N. (1909), *Ausgewählte Tragödien des Euripides für den Schulgebrauch erklärt*, i. *Medea*[4] (Leipzig and Berlin).
WEGNER, M. (1973), *Brygosmaler* (Berlin).
WEHRLI, FR. (1969), *Die Schule des Aristoteles: Texte und Kommentar*[2] (10 vols.; Basle and Stuttgart).
WEIDEN, M. J. H. VAN DER (1991), *The Dithyrambs of Pindar: Introduction, Text, and Commentary* (Amsterdam).
WEIL, H. (1879), *Sept tragédies d'Euripide* (Paris).
WELCKER, F. G. (1865–82), *Der epische Cyclus oder die homerischen Dichter*[2] (Bonn).
WELLMANN, M. (1886), *De Istro Callimachio* (diss. Greifswald).
WENIGER, L. (1913), 'Der Hochaltar des Zeus in Olympia', *Neue Jahrbücher für das klassische Altertum* 31: 241–60.
—— (1915), 'Die Seher von Olympia', *Archiv für Religionswissenschaft*, 18: 53–115.
WENTZEL, G. (1894), 'Aipytos 2', in *RE* i. 1045.

WESCOAT, B. D. (ed.) (1989), *Syracuse, the Fairest Greek City: Ancient Art from the Museo Archeologico Regionale 'Paolo Orsi'* (Atlanta).

WEST, M. L. (1965), 'Alcmanica', *CQ*, NS 15: 188–202.

——(1996a), *Hesiod,* Theogony: *Edited with Prolegomena and Commentary* (Oxford).

——(1966b), 'Conjectures on 46 Greek Poets', *Philologus*, 110: 147–68.

——(1967), 'Alcman and Pythagoras', *CQ*, NS 17: 1–15.

——(1969), 'Stesichorus Redivivus', *ZPE* 4: 135–49.

——(1970a), 'Burning Sappho', *Maia*, 22: 307–30.

——(1970b), 'Melica', *CQ*, NS 20: 205–15.

——(1971), 'Stesichorus', *CQ*, NS 21: 302–14.

——(1974), *Studies in Greek Elegy and Iambus* (Berlin and New York).

——(1975), 'Some Lyric Fragments Reconsidered', *CQ*, NS 25: 307–9.

——(1978a), *Hesiod,* Works and Days: *Edited with Prolegomena and Commentary* (Oxford).

——(1978b), 'Stesichorus at Lille', *ZPE* 29: 1–4.

——(1980), 'Iambics in Simonides, Bacchylides and Pindar', *ZPE* 37: 137–55.

——(1981), 'Simonides' Danae Fragment: A Metrical Analysis', *BICS* 28: 30–8.

——(1982), *Greek Metre.*

——(1985), *The Hesiodic Catalogue of Women* (Oxford).

——(1990a), 'Notes on Sappho and Alcaeus', *ZPE* 80: 1–8.

——(1990b), *Aeschyli Tragoediae, cum Incerti Poetae Prometheo* (Stuttgart).

——(1992), *Ancient Greek Music* (Oxford).

——(1993), 'Simonides Redivivus', *ZPE* 98: 1–14.

——(1995), 'The Date of the *Iliad*', *MH* 52: 203–19.

——(1996), *Die griechische Dichterin: Bild und Rolle* (Stuttgart and Leipzig).

——(1997), *The East Face of Helicon: West Asiatic Elements in Early Greek Poetry and Myth* (Oxford).

——(1998–), *Homeri Ilias* (1 vol. to date; Stuttgart and Leipzig).

WIDE, S. (1893), *Lakonische Kulte* (Leipzig).

WIGODSKY, M. (1962), 'Anacreon and the Girl from Lesbos', *CPh* 57: 109.

WILAMOWITZ-MOELLENDORFF, U. VON (1886), *Isyllos von Epidauros* (Berlin).

——(1901), 'Hieron und Pindaros', *SBBA* 53: 1273–318.

——(1913), *Sappho und Simonides: Untersuchungen über griechische Lyriker* (Berlin).

——(1921), *Griechische Verskunst* (Berlin).

——(1922), *Pindaros* (Berlin).

——(1935 [orig. 1897]), 'Der Chor der Hagesichora', in id., *Kleine Schriften* (6 vols.; Berlin), i. 209–20.

——(1970 [orig. 1898]), review of F. Kenyon, *The Poems of Bacchylides* (1897), in W. M. Calder III and J. Stern (eds.), *Pindar und Bakchylides* (Wege der Forschung, 134; Darmstadt), 322–63.

WILL, ED. (1955), *Korinthiaka: Recherches sur l'histoire et la civilisation de Corinthe des origines aux guerres médiques* (Paris).

WILLCOCK, M. M. (1995), *Pindar, Victory Odes:* Olympians *2, 7, 11;* Nemean *4* (Cambridge).

WILLIAMS, C., and WILLIAMS, H. (1985), 'Excavations on the Acropolis of Mytilene, 1984', *EMC* 4: 225–33.

————(1988), 'Excavations at Mytilene (Lesbos), 1987' *EMC* 7: 135–49.

————(1989), 'Excavations at Mytilene, 1988' *EMC* 8: 167–81.

————(1990), 'Excavations at Mytilene, 1989' *EMC* 9: 181–93.

————(1991), 'Excavations at Mytilene, 1990' *EMC* 10: 175–92.

WILLIAMS, H. (1993), 'Archaic Architectural Fragments from Ancient Mytilene', in J. des Courtils and J.-C. Moretti (eds.), *Les Grands Atéliers d'architecture dans le monde égéen du VIe siècle av. J.-C.* (Paris), 83–7.

——(1995), 'Investigations at Mytilene, 1994', *EMC* 14: 95–100.

——*et al.* (1997), 'Excavations at Ancient Stymphalos, 1996', *ECM* 16: 23–73.

WILLIAMSON, M. (1990), 'A Woman's Place in Euripides' *Medea*', in A. Powell (ed.), *Euripides, Women, and Sexuality* (London and New York), 16–31.

——(1995), *Sappho's Immortal Daughters* (Cambridge, Mass., and London).

——(1998), 'Eros the Blacksmith: Performing Masculinity in Anakreon's Love Lyrics', in L. Foxhall and J. Salmon (eds.), *Thinking Men: Masculinity and Self-representation in the Classical Tradition* (London and New York), 71–82.

WILLIGER, ED. (1928), *Sprachliche Untersuchungen zu den Komposita der griechischen Dichter des 5. Jahrhunderts* (Göttingen).

WILLINK, C. (1986), *Euripides, Orestes: With Introduction and Commentary* (Oxford).

WILLS, G. (1967), 'Sappho 31 and Catullus 51', *GRBS* 8: 167–97.

WILSON, L. H. (1996), *Sappho's Sweetbitter Songs: Configurations of Female and Male in Ancient Greek Lyric* (London).

WILSON, P., and TAPLIN, O. (1993), 'The "Aetiology" of Tragedy in the *Oresteia*', *PCPS* 39: 169–80.

WILSON, R. J. A. (1996), 'Archaeology in Sicily: 1988–95', *AR* 1995–6: 59–123.

WINKLER, J. J. (1996 [orig. 1981]), 'Gardens of Nymphs: Public and Private in Sappho's Lyrics', in E. Greene (ed.), *Reading Sappho: Contemporary Approaches* (Berkeley, Los Angeles, and London), 89–109.

WINTER, N. (1993), 'Kroisos' Role in the Diffusion of Greek Mainland Architectural Terracottas to Ionia', in J. des Courtils and J.-C. Moretti (eds.), *Les Grands Atéliers d'architecture dans le monde égéen du VIe siècle av. J.-C.* (Paris), 29–33.

WOLTERS, R., BRUNS, G., *et al.* (1940–), *Das Kabirenheiligtum bei Theben* (6 vols. to date; Berlin).

WOODBURY, L. E. (1991*a* [orig. 1953]), 'Simonides on ἀρετή', in id., *Collected Writings* (Atlanta), 46–71.

—— (1991*b* [orig. 1955]), 'The Tongue and the Whetstone: Pindar, *Ol.* 6. 82–83', in id., *Collected Writings* (Atlanta), 72–9.

—— (1991*c* [orig. 1963]), review of Bowra, *Greek Lyric Poetry from Alcman to Simonides*, in id., *Collected Writings* (Atlanta), 583–92.

—— (1991*d* [orig. 1985]), 'Ibycus and Polycrates', in id., *Collected Writings* (Atlanta), 410–38.

—— (1991*e* [orig.] 1979), 'Gold Hair and Grey, or The Game of Love: Anacreon fr. 13: 358 *PMG*, 13 Gentili', in id., *Collected Writings* (Atlanta), 325–34.

WROTH, W. (1894), *A Catalogue of the Greek Coins in the British Museum: Catalogue of the Greek Coins of Troas, Aeolis, and Lesbos* (London).

WUNDER, ED. (1856), *Sophoclis Tragoediae*, i/2, *continens Oedipum Regem*⁴ (Göttingen and Erfurdt).

—— (1857), *Sophoclis Tragoediae*, ii/2, *continens Aiacem*³ (Göttingen and Erfurdt).

YATROMANOLAKIS, D. (1993), 'The Song of Polycrates (P. Oxy. 1790): A Commentary' (Oxford M.St. thesis, unpublished).

YAVIS, C. G. (1949), *Greek Altars: Origin and Typology* (Saint Louis).

YOUNG, D. C. (1968), *Three Odes of Pindar: A Literary Study of* Pythian *11,* Pythian *3, and* Olympian *7* (*Mnemosyne*, suppl. 11; Leiden).

YOUNG, DOUGLAS (1970 [orig. 1965]), 'Some Types of Scribal Error in Manuscripts of Pindar', in W. M. Calder III and J. Stern (eds.), *Pindaros und Bakchylides* (Wege der Forschung, 134; Darmstadt), 96–126.

ZIEHEN, L. (1929), 'Sparta (Kulte)', in *RE* iiiA. 1453–525.

ZIMMERMANN, B. (1992), *Dithyrambos: Geschichte einer Gattung* (Hypomnemata, 98; Göttingen).

ZUNTZ, G. (1939), 'De Sapphus Carminibus ε 3, ε 4, ε 5', *Mnemosyne*, 7: 81–114.

—— (1971), *Persephone: Three Essays on Religion and Thought in Magna Graecia* (Oxford).

Index of Passages Discussed

Greek Index

See also General Index under 'dialect'

518 Greek Index

General Index